Complete Letters of Mark Twain

By Mark Twain

MARK TWAIN--A BIOGRAPHICAL SUMMARY

SAMUEL LANGHORNE CLEMENS, for nearly half a century known and celebrated as "Mark Twain," was born in Florida, Missouri, on November 30, 1835. He was one of the foremost American philosophers of his day; he was the world's most famous humorist of any day. During the later years of his life he ranked not only as America's chief man of letters, but likewise as her best known and best loved citizen.

The beginnings of that life were sufficiently unpromising. The family was a good one, of old Virginia and Kentucky stock, but its circumstances were reduced, its environment meager and disheartening. The father, John Marshall Clemens--a lawyer by profession, a merchant by vocation--had brought his household to Florida from Jamestown, Tennessee, somewhat after the manner of judge Hawkins as pictured in The Gilded Age. Florida was a small town then, a mere village of twenty-one houses located on Salt River, but judge Clemens, as he was usually called, optimistic and speculative in his temperament, believed in its future. Salt River would be made navigable; Florida would become a metropolis. He established a small business there, and located his family in the humble frame cottage where, five months later, was born a baby boy to whom they gave the name of Samuel--a family name--and added Langhorne, after an old Virginia friend of his father.

The child was puny, and did not make a very sturdy fight for life. Still he weathered along, season after season, and survived two stronger children, Margaret and Benjamin. By 1839 Judge Clemens had lost faith in Florida. He removed his family to Hannibal, and in this Mississippi River town the little lad whom the world was to know as Mark Twain spent his early life. In Tom Sawyer we have a picture of the Hannibal of those days and the atmosphere of his boyhood there.

His schooling was brief and of a desultory kind. It ended one day in 1847, when his father died and it became necessary that each one should help somewhat in the domestic crisis. His brother Orion, ten years his senior, was already a printer by trade. Pamela, his sister; also considerably older, had acquired music, and now took a few pupils. The little boy Sam, at twelve, was apprenticed to a printer named Ament. His wages consisted of his board and clothes--"more board than clothes," as he once remarked to the writer.

He remained with Ament until his brother Orion bought out a small paper in Hannibal in 1850. The paper, in time, was moved into a part of the Clemens home, and the two brothers ran it, the younger setting most of the type. A still younger brother, Henry, entered the office as an apprentice. The Hannibal journal was no great paper from the beginning, and it did not improve with time. Still, it managed to survive--country papers nearly always manage to survive--year after year, bringing in some sort of return. It was on this paper that young Sam Clemens began his writings--burlesque, as a rule, of local characters and conditions-- usually published in his brother's absence; generally resulting in trouble on his return. Yet they made the paper sell, and if Orion had but realized his brother's talent he might have turned it into capital even then.

In 1853 (he was not yet eighteen) Sam Clemens grew tired of his limitations and pined for the wider horizon of the world. He gave out to his family that he was going to St. Louis, but he kept on to New York, where a World's Fair was then going on. In New York he found employment at his trade, and during the hot months of 1853 worked in a printing- office in Cliff Street. By and by he went to Philadelphia, where he worked a brief time; made a trip to Washington, and presently set out for the West again, after an absence of more than a year.

Onion, meanwhile, had established himself at Muscatine, Iowa, but soon after removed to Keokuk, where the brothers were once more together, till following their trade. Young Sam Clemens remained in Keokuk until the winter of 1856-57, when he caught a touch of the South-American fever then prevalent; and decided to go to Brazil. He left Keokuk for Cincinnati, worked that winter in a printing-office there, and in April took the little steamer, Paul Jones, for New Orleans, where he expected to find a South-American vessel. In Life on the Mississippi we have his story of how he met Horace Bixby and decided to become a pilot instead of a South American adventurer--jauntily setting himself the stupendous task of learning the twelve hundred miles of the Mississippi River between St. Louis and New Orleans--of knowing it as exactly and as unfailingly, even in the dark, as one knows the way to his own features. It seems incredible to those who knew Mark Twain in his later years--dreamy, unpractical, and indifferent to details-- that he could have acquired so vast a store of minute facts as were required by that task. Yet within eighteen months he had become not only a pilot, but one of the best and most careful pilots on the river, intrusted with some of the largest and most valuable steamers. He continued in that profession for two and a half years longer, and during that time met with no disaster that cost his owners a single dollar for damage.

Then the war broke out. South Carolina seceded in December, 1860 and other States followed. Clemens was in New Orleans in January, 1861, when Louisiana seceded, and his boat was put into the Confederate service and sent up the Red River. His occupation gone, he took steamer for the North--the last one before the blockade closed. A blank cartridge was fired at them from Jefferson Barracks when they reached St. Louis, but they did not understand the signal, and kept on. Presently a shell carried away part of the pilot-house and considerably disturbed its inmates. They realized, then, that war had really begun.

In those days Clemens's sympathies were with the South. He hurried up to Hannibal and enlisted with a company of young fellows who were recruiting with the avowed purpose of "throwing off the yoke of the invader." They were ready for the field, presently, and set out in good order, a sort of nondescript cavalry detachment, mounted on animals more picturesque than beautiful. Still, it was a resolute band, and might have done very well, only it rained a good deal, which made soldiering disagreeable and hard. Lieutenant Clemens resigned at the end of two weeks, and decided to go to Nevada with Orion, who was a Union abolitionist and had received an appointment from Lincoln as Secretary of the new Territory.

In 'Roughing It' Mark Twain gives us the story of the overland journey made by the two brothers, and a picture of experiences at the other end --true in aspect, even if here and there elaborated in detail. He was Orion's private secretary, but there was no private-secretary work to do, and no salary attached to the position. The incumbent presently went to mining, adding that to his other trades.

He became a professional miner, but not a rich one. He was at Aurora, California, in the Esmeralda district, skimping along, with not much to eat and less to wear, when he was summoned by Joe Goodman, owner and editor of the Virginia City Enterprise, to come up and take the local editorship of that paper. He had been contributing sketches to it now and then, under the pen, name of "Josh," and Goodman, a man of fine literary instincts, recognized a talent full of possibilities. This was in the late summer of 1862. Clemens walked one hundred and thirty miles over very bad roads to take the job, and arrived way-worn and travel- stained. He began on a salary of twenty-five dollars a week, picking up news items here and there, and contributing occasional sketches, burlesques, hoaxes, and the like. When the Legislature convened at Carson City he was sent down to report it, and then, for the first time, began signing his articles "Mark Twain," a river term, used in making soundings, recalled from his piloting days. The name presently became known up and down the Pacific coast. His articles were, copied and commented upon. He was recognized as one of the foremost among a little coterie of overland writers, two of whom, Mark Twain and Bret Harte, were soon to acquire a world-wide fame.

He left Carson City one day, after becoming involved in a duel, the result of an editorial squib written in Goodman's absence, and went across the Sierras to San Francisco. The duel turned out farcically enough, but the Nevada law, which regarded even a challenge or its acceptance as a felony, was an inducement to his departure. Furthermore, he had already aspired to a wider field of literary effort. He attached himself to the Morning Call, and wrote occasionally for one or two literary papers--the Golden Era and the Californian---prospering well enough during the better part of the year. Bret Harte and the rest of the little Pacific-slope group were also on the staff of these papers, and for a time, at least, the new school of American humor mustered in San Francisco.

The connection with the Call was not congenial. In due course it came to a natural end, and Mark Twain arranged to do a daily San Francisco letter for his old paper, the Enterprise. The Enterprise letters stirred up trouble. They criticized the police of San Francisco so severely that the officials found means of making the writer's life there difficult and comfortless. With Jim Gillis, brother of a printer of whom he was fond, and who had been the indirect cause of his troubles, he went up into Calaveras County, to a cabin on jackass Hill. Jim Gillis, a lovable, picturesque character (the Truthful James of Bret Harte), owned mining claims. Mark Twain decided to spend his vacation in pocket-mining, and soon added that science to his store of knowledge. It was a halcyon, happy three months that he lingered there, but did not make his fortune; he only laid the corner-stone.

They tried their fortune at Angel's Camp, a place well known to readers of Bret Harte. But it rained pretty steadily, and they put in most of their time huddled around the single stove of the dingy hotel of Angel's, telling yarns. Among the stories was one told by a dreary narrator named Ben Coon. It was about a frog that had been trained to jump, but failed to win a wager because the owner of a rival frog had surreptitiously loaded him with shot. The story had been circulated among the camps, but Mark Twain had never heard it until then. The tale and the tiresome fashion of its telling amused him. He made notes to remember it.

Their stay in Angel's Camp came presently to an end. One day, when the mining partners were following the specks of gold that led to a pocket somewhere up the hill, a chill, dreary rain set in. Jim, as usual was washing, and Clemens was carrying water. The "color" became better and better as they ascended, and Gillis, possessed with the mining passion, would have gone on, regardless of the rain. Clemens, however, protested, and declared that each pail of water was his last. Finally he said, in his deliberate drawl:

"Jim, I won't carry any more water. This work is too disagreeable. Let's go to the house and wait till it clears up."

Gillis had just taken out a pan of earth. "Bring one more pail, Sam," he pleaded.

"I won't do it, Jim! Not a drop! Not if I knew there was a million dollars in that pan!"

They left the pan standing there and went back to Angel's Camp. The rain continued and they returned to jackass Hill without visiting their claim again. Meantime the rain had washed away the top of the pan of earth left standing on the slope above Angel's, and exposed a handful of nuggets--pure gold. Two strangers came along and, observing it, had sat down to wait until the thirty-day claim-notice posted by Jim Gillis should expire. They did not mind the rain--not with that gold in sight-- and the minute the thirty days were up they followed the lead a few pans further, and took out--some say ten, some say twenty, thousand dollars. It was a good pocket. Mark Twain missed it by one pail of water. Still, it is just as well, perhaps, when one remembers The Jumping Frog.

Matters having quieted down in San Francisco, he returned and took up his work again. Artemus Ward, whom he had met in Virginia City, wrote him for something to use in his (Ward's) new book. Clemens sent the frog story, but he had been dilatory in preparing it, and when it reached New York, Carleton, the publisher, had Ward's book about ready for the press. It did not seem worth while to Carleton to include the frog story, and handed it over to Henry Clapp, editor of the Saturday Press--a perishing sheet-saying:

"Here, Clapp, here's something you can use."

The story appeared in the Saturday Press of November 18, 1865. According to the accounts of that time it set all New York in a roar, which annoyed, rather than gratified, its author. He had thought very little of it, indeed, yet had been wondering why some of his more highly regarded work had not found fuller recognition.

But The Jumping Frog did not die. Papers printed it and reprinted it, and it was translated into foreign tongues. The name of "Mark Twain" became known as the author of that sketch, and the two were permanently associated from the day of its publication.

Such fame as it brought did not yield heavy financial return. Its author continued to win a more or less precarious livelihood doing miscellaneous work, until March, 1866, when he was employed by the Sacramento Union to contribute a series of letters from the Sandwich Islands.

They were notable letters, widely read and freely copied, and the sojourn there was a generally fortunate one. It was during his stay in the islands that the survivors of the wrecked vessel, the Hornet, came in, after long privation at sea. Clemens was sick at the time, but Anson Burlingame, who was in Honolulu, on the way to China, had him carried in a cot to the hospital, where he could interview the surviving sailors and take down their story. It proved a great "beat" for the Union, and added considerably to its author's prestige. On his return to San Francisco he contributed an article on the Hornet disaster to Harper's Magazine, and looked forward to its publication as a beginning of a real career. But, alas! when it appeared the printer and the proof-reader had somehow converted "Mark Twain" into "Mark Swain," and his dreams perished.

Undecided as to his plans, he was one day advised by a friend to deliver a lecture. He was already known as an entertaining talker, and his adviser judged his possibilities well. In Roughing It we find the story of that first lecture and its success. He followed it with other lectures up and down the Coast. He had added one more profession to his intellectual stock in trade.

Mark Twain, now provided with money, decided to pay a visit to his people. He set out for the East in December, 1866, via Panama, arriving in New York in January. A few days later he was with his mother, then living with his sister, in St. Louis. A little later he lectured in Keokuk, and in Hannibal, his old home.

It was about this time that the first great Mediterranean steamship excursion began to be exploited. No such ocean picnic had ever been planned before, and it created a good deal of interest East and West. Mark Twain heard of it and wanted to go. He wrote to friends on the 'Alta California,' of San Francisco, and the publishers of that paper had sufficient faith to advance the money for his passage, on the understanding that he was to contribute frequent letters, at twenty dollars apiece. It was a liberal offer, as rates went in those days, and a godsend in the fullest sense of the word to Mark Twain.

Clemens now hurried to New York in order to be there in good season for the sailing date, which was in June. In New York he met Frank Fuller, whom he had known as territorial Governor of Utah, an energetic and enthusiastic admirer of the Western humorist. Fuller immediately proposed that Clemens give a lecture in order to establish his reputation on the Atlantic coast. Clemens demurred, but Fuller insisted, and engaged Cooper Union for the occasion. Not many tickets were sold. Fuller, however, always ready for an emergency, sent out a flood of complimentaries to the school-teachers of New York and adjacent territory, and the house was crammed. It turned out to be a notable event. Mark Twain was at his best that night; the audience laughed until, as some of them declared when the lecture was over, they were too weak to leave their seats. His success as a lecturer was assured.

The Quaker City was the steamer selected for the great oriental tour. It sailed as advertised, June 8, 1867, and was absent five months, during which Mark Twain contributed regularly to the 'Alta-California', and wrote several letters for the New York Tribune. They were read and copied everywhere. They preached a new gospel in travel literature-- a gospel of seeing with an overflowing honesty; a gospel of sincerity in according praise to whatever he considered genuine, and ridicule to the things believed to be shams. It was a gospel that Mark Twain continued to preach during his whole career. It became, in fact, his chief literary message to the world, a world ready for that message.

He returned to find himself famous. Publishers were ready with plans for collecting the letters in book form. The American Publishing Company, of Hartford, proposed a volume, elaborately illustrated, to be sold by subscription. He agreed with them as to terms, and went to Washington' to prepare copy. But he could not work quietly there, and presently was back in San Francisco, putting his book together, lecturing occasionally, always to crowded houses. He returned in August, 1868, with the manuscript of the Innocents Abroad, and that winter, while his book was being manufactured, lectured throughout the East and Middle West, making his headquarters in Hartford, and in Elmira, New York.

He had an especial reason for going to Elmira. On the Quaker City he had met a young man by the name of Charles Langdon, and one day, in the Bay of Smyrna, had seen a miniature of the boy's sister, Olivia Langdon, then a girl of about twenty-two. He fell in love with that picture, and still more deeply in love with the original when he met her in New York on his return. The Langdon home was in Elmira, and it was for this reason that as time passed he frequently sojourned there. When the proofs of the Innocents Abroad were sent him he took them along, and he and sweet "Livy" Langdon read them together. What he lacked in those days in literary delicacy she detected, and together they pruned it away. She became his editor that winter--a position which she held until her death.

The book was published in July, 1869, and its success was immediate and abundant. On his wedding-day, February 2, 1870, Clemens received a check from his publishers for more than four thousand dollars, royalty accumulated during the three months preceding. The sales soon amounted to more than fifty thousand copies, and had increased to very nearly one hundred thousand at the end of the first three years. It was a book of travel, its lowest price three dollars and fifty cents. Even with our increased reading population no such sale is found for a book of that description to-day. And the Innocents Abroad holds its place--still outsells every other book in its particular field. [This in 1917. D.W.]

Mark Twain now decided to settle down. He had bought an interest in the Express, of Buffalo, New York, and took up his residence in that city in a house presented to the young couple by Mr. Langdon. It did not prove a fortunate beginning. Sickness, death, and trouble of many kinds put a blight on the happiness of their first married year and gave, them a distaste for the home in which they had made such a promising start. A baby boy, Langdon Clemens, came along in November, but he was never a strong child. By the end of the following year the Clemenses had arranged for a residence in Hartford, temporary at first, later made permanent. It was in Hartford that little Langdon died, in 1872.

Clemens, meanwhile, had sold out his interest in the Express, severed his connection with the Galaxy, a magazine for which he was doing a department each month, and had written a second book for the American Publishing Company, Roughing It, published in 1872. In August of the same year he made a trip to London, to get material for a book on England, but was too much sought after, too continuously feted, to do any work. He went alone, but in November returned with the purpose of taking Mrs. Clemens and the new baby, Susy, to England the following spring. They sailed in April, 1873, and spent a good portion of the year in England and Scotland. They returned to America in November, and Clemens hurried back to London alone to deliver a notable series of lectures under the management of George Dolby, formerly managing agent for Charles Dickens. For two months Mark Twain lectured steadily to London audiences--the big Hanover Square rooms always filled. He returned to his family in January, 1874.

Meantime, a home was being built for them in Hartford, and in the autumn of 1874 they took up residence in ita happy residence, continued through seventeen years--well-nigh perfect years. Their summers they spent in Elmira, on Quarry Farm--a beautiful hilltop, the home of Mrs. Clemens's sister. It was in Elmira that much of Mark Twain's literary work was done. He had a special study there, some distance from the house, where he loved to work out his fancies and put them into visible form.

It was not so easy to work at Hartford; there was too much going on. The Clemens home was a sort of general headquarters for literary folk, near and far, and for distinguished foreign visitors of every sort. Howells and Aldrich used it as their half-way station between Boston and New York, and every foreign notable who visited America made a pilgrimage to Hartford to see Mark Twain. Some even went as far as Elmira, among them Rudyard Kipling, who recorded his visit in a chapter of his American Notes. Kipling declared he had come all the way from India to see Mark Twain.

Hartford had its own literary group. Mrs. Harriet Beecher Stowe lived near the Clemens home; also Charles Dudley Warner. The Clemens and Warner families were constantly associated, and The Gilded Age, published in 1873, resulted from the friendship of Warner and Mark Twain. The character of Colonel Sellers in that book has become immortal, and it is a character that only Mark Twain could create, for, though drawn from his mother's cousin, James Lampton, it embodies--and in no very exaggerated degree--characteristics that were his own. The tendency to make millions was always imminent; temptation was always hard to resist. Money-making schemes are continually being placed before men of means and prominence, and Mark Twain, to the day of his death, found such schemes fatally attractive.

It was because of the Sellers characteristics in him that he invested in a typesetting-machine which cost him nearly two hundred thousand dollars and helped to wreck his fortunes by and by. It was because of this characteristic that he invested in numberless schemes of lesser importance, but no less disastrous in the end. His one successful commercial venture was his association with Charles L. Webster in the publication of the Grant Memoirs, of which enough copies were sold to pay a royalty of more than four hundred thousand dollars to Grant's widow-- the largest royalty ever paid from any single publication. It saved the Grant family from poverty. Yet even this triumph was a misfortune to Mark Twain, for it led to scores of less profitable book ventures and eventual disaster.

Meanwhile he had written and published a number of books. Tom Sawyer, The Prince and the Pauper, Life on the Mississippi, Huckleberry Finn, and A Connecticut Yankee in King Arthur's Court were among the volumes that had entertained the world and inspired it with admiration and love for their author. In 1878-79 he had taken his family to Europe, where they spent their time in traveling over the Continent. It was during this period that he was joined by his intimate friend, the Rev. Joseph H. Twichell, of Hartford, and the two made a journey, the story of which is told in A Tramp Abroad.

In 1891 the Hartford house was again closed, this time indefinitely, and the family, now five in number, took up residence in Berlin. The typesetting-machine and the unfortunate publishing venture were drawing heavily on the family finances at this period, and the cost of the Hartford establishment was too great to be maintained. During the next three years he was distracted by the financial struggle which ended in April, 1894, with the failure of Charles L. Webster & Co. Mark Twain now found himself bankrupt, and nearly one hundred thousand dollars in debt. It had been a losing fight, with this bitter ending always in view; yet during this period of hard, hopeless effort he had written a large portion of the book which of all his works will perhaps survive the longest-- his tender and beautiful story of Joan of Arc. All his life Joan had been his favorite character in the world's history, and during those trying months and years of the early nineties--in Berlin, in Florence, in Paris--he was conceiving and putting his picture of that gentle girl-warrior into perfect literary form. It was published in Harper's Magazine--anonymously, because, as he said, it would not have been received seriously had it appeared over his own name. The authorship was presently recognized. Exquisitely, reverently, as the story was told, it had in it the, touch of quaint and gentle humor which could only have been given to it by Mark Twain.

It was only now and then that Mark Twain lectured during these years. He had made a reading tour with George W. Cable during the winter of 1884-85, but he abominated the platform, and often vowed he would never appear before an audience again. Yet, in 1895, when he was sixty years old, he decided to rebuild his fortunes by making a reading tour around the world. It was not required of him to pay his debts in full. The creditors were willing to accept fifty per cent. of the liabilities, and had agreed to a settlement on that basis. But this did not satisfy Mrs. Clemens, and it did not satisfy him. They decided to pay dollar for dollar. They sailed for America, and in July, 1895, set out from Elmira on the long trail across land and sea. Mrs. Clemens, and Clara Clemens, joined this pilgrimage, Susy and Jean Clemens remaining at Elmira with their aunt. Looking out of the car windows, the travelers saw Susy waving them an adieu. It was a picture they would long remember.

The reading tour was one of triumph. High prices and crowded houses prevailed everywhere. The author-reader visited Australia, New Zealand, India, Ceylon, South Africa, arriving in England, at last, with the money and material which would pay off the heavy burden of debt and make him once more free before the world. And in that hour of triumph came the heavy blow. Susy Clemens, never very strong, had been struck down. The first cable announced her illness. The mother and Clara sailed at once. Before they were half-way across the ocean a second cable announced that Susy was dead. The father had to meet and endure the heartbreak alone; he could not reach America, in time for the burial. He remained in England, and was joined there by the sorrowing family.

They passed that winter in London, where he worked at the story of his travels, Following the Equator, the proofs of which he read the next summer in Switzerland. The returns from it, and from his reading venture, wiped away Mark Twain's indebtedness and made him free. He could go back to America; as he said, able to look any man in the face again.

Yet he did not go immediately. He could live more economically abroad, and economy was still necessary. The family spent two winters in Vienna, and their apartments there constituted a veritable court where the world's notables gathered. Another winter in England followed, and then, in the latter part of 1900, they went home--that is, to America. Mrs. Clemens never could bring herself to return to Hartford, and never saw their home there again.

Mark Twain's return to America, was in the nature of a national event. Wherever he appeared throngs turned out to bid him welcome. Mighty banquets were planned in his honor.

In a house at 14 West Tenth Street, and in a beautiful place at Riverdale, on the Hudson, most of the next three years were passed. Then Mrs. Clemens's health failed, and in the autumn of 1903 the family went to Florence for her benefit. There, on the 5th of June, 1904, she died. They brought her back and laid her beside Susy, at Elmira. That winter the family took up residence at 21 Fifth Avenue, New York, and remained there until the completion of Stormfield, at Redding, Connecticut, in 1908.

In his later life Mark Twain was accorded high academic honors. Already, in 1888, he had received from Yale College the degree of Master of Arts, and the same college made him a Doctor of Literature in 1901. A year later the university of his own State, at Columbia, Missouri, conferred the same degree, and then, in 1907, came the crowning honor, when venerable Oxford tendered him the doctor's robe.

"I don't know why they should give me a degree like that," he said, quaintly. "I never doctored any literature--I wouldn't know how."

He had thought never to cross the ocean again, but he declared he would travel to Mars and back, if necessary, to get that Oxford degree. He appreciated its full meaning-recognition by the world's foremost institution of learning of the achievements of one who had no learning of the institutionary kind. He sailed in June, and his sojourn in England was marked by a continuous ovation. His hotel was besieged by callers. Two secretaries were busy nearly twenty hours a day attending to visitors and mail. When he appeared on the street his name went echoing in every direction and the multitudes gathered. On the day when he rose, in his scarlet robe and black mortar-board, to receive his degree (he must have made a splendid picture in that dress, with his crown of silver hair), the vast assembly went wild. What a triumph, indeed, for the little Missouri printer-boy! It was the climax of a great career.

Mark Twain's work was always of a kind to make people talk, always important, even when it was mere humor. Yet it was seldom that; there was always wisdom under it, and purpose, and these things gave it dynamic force and enduring life. Some of his aphorisms--so quaint in form as to invite laughter--are yet fairly startling in their purport. His paraphrase, "When in doubt, tell the truth," is of this sort. "Frankness is a jewel; only the young can afford it," he once said to the writer, apropos of a little girl's remark. His daily speech was full of such things. The secret of his great charm was his great humanity and the gentle quaintness and sincerity of his utterance.

His work did not cease when the pressing need of money came to an end. He was full of ideas, and likely to begin a new article or story at any time. He wrote and published a number of notable sketches, articles, stories, even books, during these later years, among them that marvelous short story--"The Man That Corrupted Hadleyburg." In that story, as in most of his later work, he proved to the world that he was much more than a humorist--that he was, in fact, a great teacher, moralist, philosopher- -the greatest, perhaps, of his age.

His life at Stormfield--he had never seen the place until the day of his arrival, June 18, 1908--was a peaceful and serene old age. Not that he was really old; he never was that. His step, his manner, his point of view, were all and always young. He was fond of children and frequently had them about him. He delighted in games--especially in billiards--and in building the house at Stormfield the billiard-room was first considered. He had a genuine passion for the sport; without it his afternoon was not complete. His mornings he was likely to pass in bed, smoking--he was always smoking--and attending to his correspondence and reading. History and the sciences interested him, and his bed was strewn with biographies and stories of astronomical and geological research. The vastness of distances and periods always impressed him. He had no head for figures, but he would labor for hours over scientific calculations, trying to compass them and to grasp their gigantic import. I remember once finding him highly elated over the fact that he had figured out for himself the length in hours and minutes of a "light year." He showed me the pages covered with figures, and was more proud of them than if they had been the pages of an immortal story. Then we played billiards, but even his favorite game could not make him altogether forget his splendid achievement.

It was on the day before Christmas, 1909, that heavy bereavement once more came into the life of Mark Twain. His daughter Jean, long subject to epileptic attacks, was seized with a convulsion while in her bath and died before assistance reached her. He was dazed by the suddenness of the blow. His philosophy sustained him. He was glad, deeply glad for the beautiful girl that had been released.

"I never greatly envied anybody but the dead," he said, when he had looked at her. "I always envy the dead."

The coveted estate of silence, time's only absolute gift, it was the one benefaction he had ever considered worth while.

Yet the years were not unkindly to Mark Twain. They brought him sorrow, but they brought him likewise the capacity and opportunity for large enjoyment, and at the last they laid upon him a kind of benediction. Naturally impatient, he grew always more gentle, more generous, more tractable and considerate as the seasons passed. His final days may be said to have been spent in the tranquil light of a summer afternoon.

His own end followed by a few months that of his daughter. There were already indications that his heart was seriously affected, and soon after Jean's death he sought the warm climate of Bermuda. But his malady made rapid progress, and in April he returned to Stormfield. He died there just a week later, April 21, 1910.

Any attempt to designate Mark Twain's place in the world's literary history would be presumptuous now. Yet I cannot help thinking that he will maintain his supremacy in the century that produced him. I think so because, of all the writers of that hundred years, his work was the most human his utterances went most surely to the mark. In the long analysis of the ages it is the truth that counts, and he never approximated, never compromised, but pronounced those absolute verities to which every human being of whatever rank must instantly respond.

His understanding of subjective human nature--the vast, unwritten life within--was simply amazing. Such knowledge he acquired at the fountainhead--that is, from himself. He recognized in himself an extreme example of the human being with all the attributes of power and of weakness, and he made his exposition complete.

The world will long miss Mark Twain; his example and his teaching will be neither ignored nor forgotten. Genius defies the laws of perspective and looms larger as it recedes. The memory of Mark Twain remains to us a living and intimate presence that today, even more than in life, constitutes a stately moral bulwark reared against hypocrisy and superstition--a mighty national menace to sham.

MARK TWAIN'S LETTERS

I

EARLY LETTERS, 1853. NEW YORK AND PHILADELPHIA

We have no record of Mark Twain's earliest letters. Very likely they were soiled pencil notes, written to some school sweetheart-- to "Becky Thatcher," perhaps--and tossed across at lucky moments, or otherwise, with happy or disastrous results. One of those smudgy, much-folded school notes of the Tom Sawyer period would be priceless to-day, and somewhere among forgotten keepsakes it may exist, but we shall not be likely to find it. No letter of his boyhood, no scrap of his earlier writing, has come to light except his penciled name, SAM CLEMENS, laboriously inscribed on the inside of a small worn purse that once held his meager, almost non-existent wealth. He became a printer's apprentice at twelve, but as he received no salary, the need of a purse could not have been urgent. He must have carried it pretty steadily, however, from its appearance--as a kind of symbol of hope, maybe--a token of that Sellers-optimism which dominated his early life, and was never entirely subdued.

No other writing of any kind has been preserved from Sam Clemens's boyhood, none from that period of his youth when he had served his apprenticeship and was a capable printer on his brother's paper, a contributor to it when occasion served. Letters and manuscripts of those days have vanished--even his contributions in printed form are unobtainable. It is not believed that a single number of Orion Clemens's paper, the Hannibal Journal, exists to-day.

It was not until he was seventeen years old that Sam Clemens wrote a letter any portion of which has survived. He was no longer in Hannibal. Orion's unprosperous enterprise did not satisfy him. His wish to earn money and to see the world had carried him first to St. Louis, where his sister Pamela was living, then to New York City, where a World's Fair in a Crystal Palace was in progress. The letter tells of a visit to this great exhibition. It is not complete, and the fragment bears no date, but it was written during the summer of 1853.

Fragment of a letter from Sam L. Clemens to his sister Pamela Moffett, in St. Louis, summer of 1853:

. . . From the gallery (second floor) you have a glorious sight--the flags of the different countries represented, the lofty dome, glittering jewelry, gaudy tapestry, &c., with the busy crowd passing to and fro--tis a perfect fairy palace--beautiful beyond description.

The Machinery department is on the main floor, but I cannot enumerate any of it on account of the lateness of the hour (past 8 o'clock.) It would take more than a week to examine everything on exhibition; and as I was only in a little over two hours tonight, I only glanced at about one- third of the articles; and having a poor memory; I have enumerated scarcely any of even the principal objects. The visitors to the Palace average 6,000 daily--double the population of Hannibal. The price of admission being 50 cents, they take in about $3,000.

The Latting Observatory (height about 280 feet) is near the Palace--from it you can obtain a grand view of the city and the country round. The Croton Aqueduct, to supply the city with water, is the greatest wonder yet. Immense sewers are laid across the bed of the Hudson River, and pass through the country to Westchester county, where a whole river is turned from its course, and brought to New York. From the reservoir in the city to the Westchester county reservoir, the distance is thirty- eight miles! and if necessary, they could supply every family in New York with one hundred barrels of water per day!

I am very sorry to learn that Henry has been sick. He ought to go to the country and take exercise; for he is not half so healthy as Ma thinks he is. If he had my walking to do, he would be another boy entirely. Four times every day I walk a little over one mile; and working hard all day, and walking four miles, is exercise--I am used to it, now, though, and it is no trouble. Where is it Orion's going to? Tell Ma my promises are faithfully kept, and if I have my health I will take her to Ky. in the spring--I shall save money for this. Tell Jim and all the rest of them to write, and give me all the news. I am sorry to hear such bad news from Will and Captain Bowen. I shall write to Will soon. The Chatham-square Post Office and the Broadway office too, are out of my way, and I always go to the General Post Office; so you must write the direction of my letters plain, "New York City, N. Y.," without giving the street or anything of the kind, or they may go to some of the other offices. (It has just struck 2 A.M. and I always get up at 6, and am at work at 7.) You ask me where I spend my evenings. Where would you suppose, with a free printers' library containing more than 4,000 volumes within a quarter of a mile of me, and nobody at home to talk to? I shall write to Ella soon. Write soon Truly your Brother SAM.

P. S. I have written this by a light so dim that you nor Ma could not read by it.

He was lodging in a mechanics' cheap boarding-house in Duane Street, and we may imagine the bareness of his room, the feeble poverty of his lamp.

"Tell Ma my promises are faithfully kept." It was the day when he had left Hannibal. His mother, Jane Clemens, a resolute, wiry woman of forty-nine, had put together his few belongings. Then, holding up a little Testament:

"I want you to take hold of the end of this, Sam," she said, "and make me a promise. I want you to repeat after me these words: 'I do solemnly swear that I will not throw a card, or drink a drop of liquor while I am gone.'"

It was this oath, repeated after her, that he was keeping faithfully. The Will Bowen mentioned is a former playmate, one of Tom Sawyer's outlaw band. He had gone on the river to learn piloting with an elder brother, the "Captain." What the bad news was is no longer remembered, but it could not have been very serious, for the Bowen boys remained on the river for many years. "Ella" was Samuel Clemens's cousin and one-time sweetheart, Ella Creel. "Jim" was Jim Wolfe, an apprentice in Orion's office, and the hero of an adventure which long after Mark Twain wrote under the title of, "Jim Wolfe and the Cats."

There is scarcely a hint of the future Mark Twain in this early letter. It is the letter of a boy of seventeen who is beginning to take himself rather seriously--who, finding himself for the first time far from home and equal to his own responsibilities, is willing to carry the responsibility of others. Henry, his brother, three years younger, had been left in the printing-office with Orion, who, after a long, profitless fight, is planning to remove from Hannibal. The young traveler is concerned as to the family outlook, and will furnish advice if invited. He feels the approach of prosperity, and will take his mother on a long-coveted trip to her old home in the spring. His evenings? Where should he spend them, with a free library of four thousand volumes close by? It is distinctly a youthful letter, a bit pretentious, and wanting in the spontaneity and humor of a later time. It invites comment, now, chiefly because it is the first surviving document in the long human story.

He was working in the printing-office of John A. Gray and Green, on Cliff Street, and remained there through the summer. He must have written more than once during this period, but the next existing letter--also to Sister Pamela--was written in October. It is perhaps a shade more natural in tone than the earlier example, and there is a hint of Mark Twain in the first paragraph.

To Mrs. Moffett, in St. Louis:

NEW YORK . . . , Oct. Saturday '53. MY DEAR SISTER,--I have not written to any of the family for some time, from the fact, firstly, that I didn't know where they were, and secondly, because I have been fooling myself with the idea that I was going to leave New York every day for the last two weeks. I have taken a liking to the abominable place, and every time I get ready to leave, I put it off a day or so, from some unaccountable cause. It is as hard on my conscience to leave New York, as it was easy to leave Hannibal. I think I shall get off Tuesday, though.

Edwin Forrest has been playing, for the last sixteen days, at the Broadway Theatre, but I never went to see him till last night. The play was the "Gladiator." I did not like parts of it much, but other portions were really splendid. In the latter part of the last act, where the "Gladiator" (Forrest) dies at his brother's feet, (in all the fierce pleasure of gratified revenge,) the man's whole soul seems absorbed in the part he is playing; and it is really startling to see him. I am sorry I did not see him play "Damon and Pythias" the former character being his greatest. He appears in Philadelphia on Monday night.

I have not received a letter from home lately, but got a "'Journal'" the other day, in which I see the office has been sold. I suppose Ma, Orion and Henry are in St. Louis now. If Orion has no other project in his head, he ought to take the contract for getting out some weekly paper, if he cannot get a foremanship. Now, for such a paper as the "Presbyterian" (containing about 60,000,--[Sixty thousand ems, type measurement.]) he could get $20 or $25 per week, and he and Henry could easily do the work; nothing to do but set the type and make up the forms....

If my letters do not come often, you need not bother yourself about me; for if you have a brother nearly eighteen years of age, who is not able to take care of himself a few miles from home, such a brother is not worth one's thoughts: and if I don't manage to take care of No. 1, be assured you will never know it. I am not afraid, however; I shall ask favors from no one, and endeavor to be (and shall be) as "independent as a wood-sawyer's clerk."

I never saw such a place for military companies as New York. Go on the street when you will, you are sure to meet a company in full uniform, with all the usual appendages of drums, fifes, &c. I saw a large company of soldiers of 1812 the other day, with a '76 veteran scattered here and there in the ranks. And as I passed through one of the parks lately, I came upon a company of boys on parade. Their uniforms were neat, and their muskets about half the common size. Some of them were not more than seven or eight years of age; but had evidently been well-drilled.

Passage to Albany (160 miles) on the finest steamers that ply' the Hudson, is now 25 cents--cheap enough, but is generally cheaper than that in the summer.

I want you to write as soon as I tell you where to direct your letter. I would let you know now, if I knew myself. I may perhaps be here a week longer; but I cannot tell. When you write tell me the whereabouts of the family. My love to Mr. Moffett and Ella. Tell Ella I intend to write to her soon, whether she wants me to nor not. Truly your Brother, SAML L. CLEMENS.

He was in Philadelphia when he wrote the nest letter that has come down to us, and apparently satisfied with the change. It is a letter to Orion Clemens, who had disposed of his paper, but evidently was still in Hannibal. An extended description of a trip to Fairmount Park is omitted because of its length, its chief interest being the tendency it shows to descriptive writing--the field in which he would make his first great fame. There is, however, no hint of humor, and only a mild suggestion of the author of the Innocents Abroad in this early attempt. The letter as here given is otherwise complete, the omissions being indicated.

To Orion Clemens, in Hannibal:

PHILADELPHIA, PA. Oct. 26,1853. MY DEAR BROTHER,--It was at least two weeks before I left New York, that I received my last letter from home: and since then, not a word have I heard from any of you. And now, since I think of it, it wasn't a letter, either, but the last number of the "Daily Journal," saying that that paper was sold, and I very naturally supposed from that, that the family had disbanded, and taken up winter quarters in St. Louis. Therefore, I have been writing to Pamela, till I've tired of it, and have received no answer. I have been writing for the last two or three weeks, to send Ma some money, but devil take me if I knew where she was, and so the money has slipped out of my pocket somehow or other, but I have a dollar left, and a good deal owing to me, which will be paid next Monday. I shall enclose the dollar in this letter, and you can hand it to her. I know it's a small amount, but then it will buy her a handkerchief, and at the same time serve as a specimen of the kind of stuff we are paid with in Philadelphia, for you see it's against the law, in Pennsylvania, to keep or pass a bill of less denomination than $5. I have only seen two or three bank bills since I have been in the State. On Monday the hands are paid off in sparkling gold, fresh from the Mint; so your dreams are not troubled with the fear of having doubtful money in your pocket.

I am subbing at the Inquirer office. One man has engaged me to work for him every Sunday till the first of next April, (when I shall return home to take Ma to Ky;) and another has engaged my services for the 24th of next month; and if I want it, I can get subbing every night of the week. I go to work at 7 o'clock in the evening, and work till 3 o'clock the next morning. I can go to the theatre and stay till 12 o'clock and then go to the office, and get work from that till 3 the next morning; when I go to bed, and sleep till 11 o'clock, then get up and loaf the rest of the day. The type is mostly agate and minion, with some bourgeois; and when one gets a good agate take,--["Agate," "minion," etc., sizes of type; "take," a piece of work. Type measurement is by ems, meaning the width of the letter 'm'.]--he is sure to make money. I made $2.50 last Sunday, and was laughed at by all the hands, the poorest of whom sets 11,000 on Sunday; and if I don't set 10,000, at least, next Sunday, I'll give them leave to laugh as much as they want to. Out of the 22 compositors in this office, 12 at least, set 15,000 on Sunday.

Unlike New York, I like this Philadelphia amazingly, and the people in it. There is only one thing that gets my "dander" up--and that is the hands are always encouraging me: telling me--"it's no use to get discouraged--no use to be down-hearted, for there is more work here than you can do!" "Down-hearted," the devil! I have not had a particle of such a feeling since I left Hannibal, more than four months ago. I fancy they'll have to wait some time till they see me down-hearted or afraid of starving while I have strength to work and am in a city of 400,000 inhabitants. When I was in Hannibal, before I had scarcely stepped out of the town limits, nothing could have convinced me that I would starve as soon as I got a little way from home....

The grave of Franklin is in Christ Church-yard, corner of Fifth and Arch streets. They keep the gates locked, and one can only see the flat slab that lies over his remains and that of his wife; but you cannot see the inscription distinctly enough to read it. The inscription, I believe, reads thus:

"Benjamin | and | Franklin" Deborah |

I counted 27 cannons (6 pounders) planted in the edge of the sidewalk in Water St. the other day. They are driven into the ground, about a foot, with the mouth end upwards. A ball is driven fast into the mouth of each, to exclude the water; they look like so many posts. They were put there during the war. I have also seen them planted in this manner, round the old churches, in N. Y.....

There is one fine custom observed in Phila. A gentleman is always expected to hand up a lady's money for her. Yesterday, I sat in the front end of the 'bus, directly under the driver's box--a lady sat opposite me. She handed me her money, which was right. But, Lord! a St. Louis lady would think herself ruined, if she should be so familiar with a stranger. In St. Louis a man will sit in the front end of the stage, and see a lady stagger from the far end, to pay her fare. The Phila. 'bus drivers cannot cheat. In the front of the stage is a thing like an office clock, with figures from 0 to 40, marked on its face. When the stage starts, the hand of the clock is turned toward the 0. When you get in and pay your fare, the driver strikes a bell, and the hand moves to the figure 1--that is, "one fare, and paid for," and there is your receipt, as good as if you had it in your pocket. When a passenger pays his fare and the driver does not strike the bell immediately, he is greeted "Strike that bell! will you?"

I must close now. I intend visiting the Navy Yard, Mint, etc., before I write again. You must write often. You see I have nothing to write interesting to you, while you can write nothing that will not interest me. Don't say my letters are not long enough. Tell Jim Wolfe to write. Tell all the boys where I am, and to write. Jim Robinson, particularly. I wrote to him from N. Y. Tell me all that is going on in H--l. Truly your brother SAM.

Those were primitive times. Imagine a passenger in these easy-going days calling to a driver or conductor to "Strike that bell!"

"H--l" is his abbreviation for Hannibal. He had first used it in a title of a poem which a few years before, during one of Orion's absences, he had published in the paper. "To Mary in Hannibal" was too long to set as a display head in single column. The poem had no great merit, but under the abbreviated title it could hardly fail to invite notice. It was one of several things he did to liven up the circulation during a brief period of his authority.

The doubtful money he mentions was the paper issued by private banks, "wild cat," as it was called. He had been paid with it in New York, and found it usually at a discount--sometimes even worthless. Wages and money were both better in Philadelphia, but the fund for his mother's trip to Kentucky apparently did not grow very rapidly.

The next letter, written a month later, is also to Orion Clemens, who had now moved to Muscatine, Iowa, and established there a new paper with an old title, 'The Journal'.

To Orion Clemens, in Muscatine, Iowa:

PHILADELPHIA, Nov. 28th, 1853. MY DEAR BROTHER,--I received your letter today. I think Ma ought to spend the winter in St. Louis. I don't believe in that climate--it's too cold for her.

The printers' annual ball and supper came off the other night. The proceeds amounted to about $1,000. The printers, as well as other people, are endeavoring to raise money to erect a monument to Franklin, but there are so many abominable foreigners here (and among printers, too,) who hate everything American, that I am very certain as much money for such a purpose could be raised in St. Louis, as in Philadelphia. I was in Franklin's old office this morning--the "North American" (formerly "Philadelphia Gazette") and there was at least one foreigner for every American at work there.

How many subscribers has the Journal got? What does the job-work pay? and what does the whole concern pay?.....

I will try to write for the paper occasionally, but I fear my letters will be very uninteresting, for this incessant night-work dulls one's ideas amazingly.

From some cause, I cannot set type nearly so fast as when I was at home. Sunday is a long day, and while others set 12 and 15,000, yesterday, I only set 10,000. However, I will shake this laziness off, soon, I reckon ....

How do you like "free-soil?"--I would like amazingly to see a good old- fashioned negro. My love to all Truly your brother SAM.

We may believe that it never occurred to the young printer, looking up landmarks of Ben Franklin, that time would show points of resemblance between the great Franklin's career and his own. Yet these seem now rather striking. Like Franklin, he had been taken out of school very young and put at the printer's trade; like Franklin, he had worked in his brother's office, and had written for the paper. Like him, too, he had left quietly for New York and Philadelphia to work at the trade of printing, and in time Samuel Clemens, like Benjamin Franklin, would become a world-figure, many- sided, human, and of incredible popularity. The boy Sam Clemens may have had such dreams, but we find no trace of them.

There is but one more letter of this early period. Young Clemens spent some time in Washington, but if he wrote from there his letters have disappeared. The last letter is from Philadelphia and seems to reflect homesickness. The novelty of absence and travel was wearing thin.

To Mrs. Moffett, in St. Louis:

PHILADELPHIA, Dec. 5, '53. MY DEAR SISTER,--I have already written two letters within the last two hours, and you will excuse me if this is not lengthy. If I had the money, I would come to St. Louis now, while the river is open; but within the last two or three weeks I have spent about thirty dollars for clothing, so I suppose I shall remain where I am. I only want to return to avoid night-work, which is injuring my eyes. I have received one or two letters from home, but they are not written as they should be, and I know no more about what is going on there than the man in the moon. One only has to leave home to learn how to write an interesting letter to an absent friend when he gets back. I suppose you board at Mrs. Hunter's yet--and that, I think, is somewhere in Olive street above Fifth. Philadelphia is one of the healthiest places in the Union. I wanted to spend this winter in a warm climate, but it is too late now. I don't like our present prospect for cold weather at all. Truly your brother SAM.

But he did not return to the West for another half year. The letters he wrote during that period have not survived. It was late in the summer of 1854 when he finally started for St. Louis. He sat up for three days and nights in a smoking-car to make the journey, and arrived exhausted. The river packet was leaving in a few hours for Muscatine, Iowa, where his mother and his two brothers were now located. He paid his sister a brief visit, and caught the boat. Worn-out, he dropped into his berth and slept the thirty-six hours of the journey.

It was early when-he arrived--too early to arouse the family. In the office of the little hotel where he waited for daylight he found a small book. It contained portraits of the English rulers, with the brief facts of their reigns. Young Clemens entertained himself by learning this information by heart. He had a fine memory for such things, and in an hour or two had the printed data perfectly and permanently committed. This incidentally acquired knowledge proved of immense value to him. It was his groundwork for all English history.

II

LETTERS 1856-61. KEOKUK, AND THE RIVER. END OF PILOTING

There comes a period now of nearly four years, when Samuel Clemens was either a poor correspondent or his letters have not been preserved. Only two from this time have survived--happily of intimate biographical importance.

Young Clemens had not remained in Muscatine. His brother had no inducements to offer, and he presently returned to St. Louis, where he worked as a compositor on the Evening News until the following spring, rooming with a young man named Burrough, a journeyman chair-maker with a taste for the English classics. Orion Clemens, meantime, on a trip to Keokuk, had casually married there, and a little later removed his office to that city. He did not move the paper; perhaps it did not seem worth while, and in Keokuk he confined himself to commercial printing. The Ben Franklin Book and Job Office started with fair prospects. Henry Clemens and a boy named Dick Hingham were the assistants, and somewhat later, when brother Sam came up from St. Louis on a visit, an offer of five dollars a week and board induced him to remain. Later, when it became increasingly difficult to pay the five dollars, Orion took his brother into partnership, which perhaps relieved the financial stress, though the office methods would seem to have left something to be desired. It is about at this point that the first of the two letters mentioned was written. The writer addressed it to his mother and sister--Jane Clemens having by this time taken up her home with her daughter, Mrs. Moffett.

To Mrs. Clemens and Mrs. Moffett, in St. Louis:

KEOKUK, Iowa, June 10th, 1856. MY DEAR MOTHER & SISTER,--I have nothing to write. Everything is going on well. The Directory is coming on finely. I have to work on it occasionally, which I don't like a particle I don't like to work at too many things at once. They take Henry and Dick away from me too. Before we commenced the Directory, I could tell before breakfast just how much work could be done during the day, and manage accordingly--but now, they throw all my plans into disorder by taking my hands away from their work. I have nothing to do with the book--if I did I would have the two book hands do more work than they do, or else I would drop it. It is not a mere supposition that they do not work fast enough--I know it; for yesterday the two book hands were at work all day, Henry and Dick all the afternoon, on the advertisements, and they set up five pages and a half- and I set up two pages and a quarter of the same matter after supper, night before last, and I don't work fast on such things. They are either excessively slow motioned or very lazy. I am not getting along well with the job work. I can't work blindly--without system. I gave Dick a job yesterday, which I calculated he would set in two hours and I could work off in three, and therefore just finish it by supper time, but he was transferred to the Directory, and the job, promised this morning, remains untouched. Through all the great pressure of job work lately, I never before failed in a promise of the kind. Your Son SAM Excuse brevity this is my 3rd letter to-night.

Samuel Clemens was never celebrated for his patience; we may imagine that the disorder of the office tried his nerves. He seems, on the whole, however, to have been rather happy in Keokuk. There were plenty of young people there, and he was a favorite among them. But he had grown dissatisfied, and when one day some weeks later there fell into His hands an account of the riches of the newly explored regions of the upper Amazon, he promptly decided to find his fortune at the headwaters of the great South-American river. The second letter reports this momentous decision. It was written to Henry Clemens, who was temporarily absent-probably in Hannibal.

To Henry Clemens:

KEOKUK, August 5th, '56. MY DEAR BROTHER,--..... Ward and I held a long consultation,

Sunday morning, and the result was that we two have determined to start to Brazil, if possible, in six weeks from now, in order to look carefully into matters there and report to Dr. Martin in time for him to follow on the first of March. We propose going via New York. Now, between you and I and the fence you must say nothing about this to Orion, for he thinks that Ward is to go clear through alone, and that I am to stop at New York or New Orleans until he reports. But that don't suit me. My confidence in human nature does not extend quite that far. I won't depend upon Ward's judgment, or anybody's else--I want to see with my own eyes, and form my own opinion. But you know what Orion is. When he gets a notion into his head, and more especially if it is an erroneous one, the Devil can't get it out again. So I know better than to combat his arguments long, but apparently yielded, inwardly determined to go clear through. Ma knows my determination, but even she counsels me to keep it from Orion. She says I can treat him as I did her when I started to St. Louis and went to New York--I can start to New York and go to South America! Although Orion talks grandly about furnishing me with fifty or a hundred dollars in six weeks, I could not depend upon him for ten dollars, so I have "feelers" out in several directions, and have already asked for a hundred dollars from one source (keep it to yourself.) I will lay on my oars for awhile, and see how the wind sets, when I may probably try to get more. Mrs. Creel is a great friend of mine, and has some influence with Ma and Orion, though I reckon they would not acknowledge it. I am going up there tomorrow, to press her into my service. I shall take care that Ma and Orion are plentifully supplied with South American books. They have Herndon's Report now. Ward and the Dr. and myself will hold a grand consultation tonight at the office. We have agreed that no more shall be admitted into our company.

I believe the Guards went down to Quincy today to escort our first locomotive home. Write soon. Your Brother, SAM.

Readers familiar with the life of Mark Twain know that none of the would-be adventurers found their way to the Amazon: His two associates gave up the plan, probably for lack of means. Young Clemens himself found a fifty-dollar bill one bleak November day blowing along the streets of Keokuk, and after duly advertising his find without result, set out for the Amazon, by way of Cincinnati and New Orleans.

"I advertised the find and left for the Amazon the same day," he once declared, a statement which we may take with a literary discount.

He remained in Cincinnati that winter (1856-57) working at his trade. No letters have been preserved from that time, except two that were sent to a Keokuk weekly, the Saturday Post, and as these were written for publication, and are rather a poor attempt at burlesque humor--their chief feature being a pretended illiteracy-- they would seem to bear no relation to this collection. He roomed that winter with a rugged, self-educated Scotchman--a mechanic, but a man of books and philosophies, who left an impress on Mark Twain's mental life.

In April he took up once more the journey toward South America, but presently forgot the Amazon altogether in the new career that opened to him. All through his boyhood and youth Samuel Clemens had wanted to be a pilot. Now came the long-deferred opportunity. On the little

Cincinnati steamer, the Paul Jones, there was a pilot named Horace Bixby. Young Clemens idling in the pilot-house was one morning seized with the old ambition, and laid siege to Bixby to teach him the river. The terms finally agreed upon specified a fee to Bixby of five hundred dollars, one hundred down, the balance when the pupil had completed the course and was earning money. But all this has been told in full elsewhere, and is only summarized here because the letters fail to complete the story.

Bixby soon made some trips up the Missouri River, and in his absence turned his apprentice, or "cub," over to other pilots, such being the river custom. Young Clemens, in love with the life, and a favorite with his superiors, had a happy time until he came under a pilot named Brown. Brown was illiterate and tyrannical, and from the beginning of their association pilot and apprentice disliked each other cordially.

It is at this point that the letters begin once more--the first having been written when young Clemens, now twenty-two years old, had been on the river nearly a year. Life with Brown, of course, was not all sorrow, and in this letter we find some of the fierce joy of adventure which in those days Samuel Clemens loved.

To Onion Clemens and Wife, in Keokuk, Iowa:

SAINT LOUIS, March 9th, 1858. DEAR BROTHER AND SISTER,--I must take advantage of the opportunity now presented to write you, but I shall necessarily be dull, as I feel uncommonly stupid. We have had a hard trip this time. Left Saint Louis three weeks ago on the Pennsylvania. The weather was very cold, and the ice running densely. We got 15 miles below town, landed the boat, and then one pilot. Second Mate and four deck hands took the sounding boat and shoved out in the ice to hunt the channel. They failed to find it, and the ice drifted them ashore. The pilot left the men with the boat and walked back to us, a mile and a half. Then the other pilot and myself, with a larger crew of men started out and met with the same fate. We drifted ashore just below the other boat. Then the fun commenced. We made fast a line 20 fathoms long, to the bow of the yawl, and put the men (both crews) to it like horses, on the shore. Brown, the pilot, stood in the bow, with an oar, to keep her head out, and I took the tiller. We would start the men, and all would go well till the yawl would bring up on a heavy cake of ice, and then the men would drop like so many ten-pins, while Brown assumed the horizontal in the bottom of the boat. After an hour's hard work we got back, with ice half an inch thick on the oars. Sent back and warped up the other yawl, and then George (the first mentioned pilot,) and myself, took a double crew of fresh men and tried it again. This time we found the channel in less than half an hour, and landed on an island till the Pennsylvania came along and took us off. The next day was colder still. I was out in the yawl twice, and then we got through, but the infernal steamboat came near running over us. We went ten miles further, landed, and George and I cleared out again--found the channel first trial, but got caught in the gorge and drifted helplessly down the river. The Ocean Spray came along and started into the ice after us, but although she didn't succeed in her kind intention of taking us aboard, her waves washed us out, and that was all we wanted. We landed on an island, built a big fire and waited for the boat. She started, and ran aground! It commenced raining and sleeting, and a very interesting time we had on that barren sandbar for the next four hours, when the boat got off and took us aboard. The next day was terribly cold. We sounded Hat Island, warped up around a bar and sounded again-- but in order to understand our situation you will have to read Dr. Kane. It would have been impossible to get back to the boat. But the Maria Denning was aground at the head of the island--they hailed us--we ran alongside and they hoisted us in and thawed us out. We had then been out in the yawl from 4 o'clock in the morning till half past 9 without being near a fire. There was a thick coating of ice over men, yawl, ropes and everything else, and we looked like rock-candy statuary. We got to Saint Louis this morning, after an absence of 3 weeks--that boat generally makes the trip in 2.

Henry was doing little or nothing here, and I sent him to our clerk to work his way for a trip, by measuring wood piles, counting coal boxes, and other clerkly duties, which he performed satisfactorily. He may go down with us again, for I expect he likes our bill of fare better than that of his boarding house.

I got your letter at Memphis as I went down. That is the best place to write me at. The post office here is always out of my route, somehow or other. Remember the direction: "S.L.C., Steamer Pennsylvania Care Duval & Algeo, Wharfboat, Memphis." I cannot correspond with a paper, because when one is learning the river, he is not allowed to do or think about anything else.

I am glad to see you in such high spirits about the land, and I hope you will remain so, if you never get richer. I seldom venture to think about our landed wealth, for "hope deferred maketh the heart sick."

I did intend to answer your letter, but I am too lazy and too sleepy now. We have had a rough time during the last 24 hours working through the ice between Cairo and Saint Louis, and I have had but little rest.

I got here too late to see the funeral of the 10 victims by the burning of the Pacific hotel in 7th street. Ma says there were 10 hearses, with the fire companies (their engines in mourning--firemen in uniform,) the various benevolent societies in uniform and mourning, and a multitude of citizens and strangers, forming, altogether, a procession of 30,000 persons! One steam fire engine was drawn by four white horses, with crape festoons on their heads. Well I am--just--about--asleep-- Your brother SAM.

Among other things, we gather from this letter that Orion Clemens had faith in his brother as a newspaper correspondent, though the two contributions from Cincinnati, already mentioned, were not promising. Furthermore, we get an intimation of Orion's unfailing confidence in the future of the "land"--that is to say, the great tract of land in Eastern Tennessee which, in an earlier day, his father had bought as a heritage for his children. It is the same Tennessee land that had "millions in it" for Colonel Sellers--the land that would become, as Orion Clemens long afterward phrased it, "the worry of three generations."

The Doctor Kane of this letter is, of course, Dr. Elisha Kent Kane, the American Arctic explorer. Any book of exploration always appealed to Mark Twain, and in those days Kane was a favorite.

The paragraph concerning Henry, and his employment on the Pennsylvania, begins the story of a tragedy. The story has been fully told elsewhere,--[Mark Twain: A Biography, by same author.]-- and need only be sketched briefly here. Henry, a gentle, faithful boy, shared with his brother the enmity of the pilot Brown. Some two months following the date of the foregoing letter, on a down trip of the Pennsylvania, an unprovoked attack made by Brown upon the boy brought his brother Sam to the rescue. Brown received a good pummeling at the hands of the future humorist, who, though upheld by the captain, decided to quit the Pennsylvania at New Orleans and to come up the river by another boat. The Brown episode has no special bearing on the main tragedy, though now in retrospect it seems closely related to it. Samuel Clemens, coming up the river on the A. T. Lacey, two days behind the Pennsylvania, heard a voice shout as they approached the Greenville, Mississippi, landing:

"The Pennsylvania is blown up just below Memphis, at Ship Island! One hundred and fifty lives lost!"

It was a true report. At six o'clock of a warm, mid-June morning, while loading wood, sixty miles below Memphis, the Pennsylvania's boilers had exploded with fearful results. Henry Clemens was among the injured. He was still alive when his brother reached Memphis on the Lacey, but died a few days later. Samuel Clemens had idolized the boy, and regarded himself responsible for his death. The letter that follows shows that he was overwrought by the scenes about him and the strain of watching, yet the anguish of it is none the less real.

To Mrs. Onion Clemens:

MEMPHIS, TENN., Friday, June 18th, 1858. DEAR SISTER MOLLIE,--Long before this reaches you, my poor Henry my darling, my pride, my glory, my all, will have finished his blameless career, and the light of my life will have gone out in utter darkness. (O, God! this is hard to bear.) Hardened, hopeless,--aye, lost--lost-- lost and ruined sinner as I am--I, even I, have humbled myself to the ground and prayed as never man prayed before, that the great God might let this cup pass from me--that he would strike me to the earth, but spare my brother--that he would pour out the fulness of his just wrath upon my wicked head, but have mercy, mercy, mercy upon that unoffending boy. The horrors of three days have swept over me--they have blasted my youth and left me an old man before my time. Mollie, there are gray hairs in my head tonight. For forty-eight hours I labored at the bedside of my poor burned and bruised, but uncomplaining brother, and then the star of my hope went out and left me in the gloom of despair. Men take me by the hand and congratulate me, and call me "lucky" because I was not on the Pennsylvania when she blew up! May God forgive them, for they know not what they say.

Mollie you do not understand why I was not on that boat--I will tell you. I left Saint Louis on her, but on the way down, Mr. Brown, the pilot that was killed by the explosion (poor fellow,) quarreled with Henry without cause, while I was steering. Henry started out of the pilot-house-- Brown jumped up and collared him--turned him half way around and struck him in the face!--and him nearly six feet high--struck my little brother. I was wild from that moment. I left the boat to steer herself, and avenged the insult--and the Captain said I was right--that he would discharge Brown in N. Orleans if he could get another pilot, and would do it in St. Louis, anyhow. Of course both of us could not return to St. Louis on the same boat--no pilot could be found, and the Captain sent me to the A. T. Lacey, with orders to her Captain to bring me to Saint Louis. Had another pilot been found, poor Brown would have been the "lucky" man.

I was on the Pennsylvania five minutes before she left N. Orleans, and I must tell you the truth, Mollie--three hundred human beings perished by that fearful disaster. Henry was asleep--was blown up--then fell back on the hot boilers, and I suppose that rubbish fell on him, for he is injured internally. He got into the water and swam to shore, and got into the flatboat with the other survivors.--[Henry had returned once to the Pennsylvania to render assistance to the passengers. Later he had somehow made his way to the flatboat.]--He had nothing on but his wet shirt, and he lay there burning up with a southern sun and freezing in the wind till the Kate Frisbee came along. His wounds were not dressed till he got to Memphis, 15 hours after the explosion. He was senseless and motionless for 12 hours after that. But may God bless Memphis, the noblest city on the face of the earth. She has done her duty by these poor afflicted creatures--especially Henry, for he has had five--aye, ten, fifteen, twenty times the care and attention that any one else has had. Dr. Peyton, the best physician in Memphis (he is exactly like the portraits of Webster) sat by him for 36 hours. There are 32 scalded men in that room, and you would know Dr. Peyton better than I can describe him, if you could follow him around and hear each man murmur as he passes, "May the God of Heaven bless you, Doctor!" The ladies have done well, too. Our second Mate, a handsome, noble hearted young fellow, will die. Yesterday a beautiful girl of 15 stooped timidly down by his side and handed him a pretty bouquet. The poor suffering boy's eyes kindled, his lips quivered out a gentle "God bless you, Miss," and he burst into tears. He made them write her name on a card for him, that he might not forget it.

Pray for me, Mollie, and pray for my poor sinless brother. Your unfortunate Brother, SAML. L. CLEMENS.

P. S. I got here two days after Henry.

It is said that Mark Twain never really recovered from the tragedy of his brother's death--that it was responsible for the serious, pathetic look that the face of the world's greatest laugh-maker always wore in repose.

He went back to the river, and in September of the same year, after an apprenticeship of less than eighteen months, received his license as a St. Louis and New Orleans pilot, and was accepted by his old chief, Bixby, as full partner on an important boat. In Life on the Mississippi Mark Twain makes the period of his study from two to two and a half years, but this is merely an attempt to magnify his dullness. He was, in fact, an apt pupil and a pilot of very high class.

Clemens was now suddenly lifted to a position of importance. The Mississippi River pilot of those days was a person of distinction, earning a salary then regarded as princely. Certainly two hundred and fifty dollars a month was large for a boy of twenty-three. At once, of course, he became the head of the Clemens family. His brother Orion was ten years older, but he had not the gift of success. By common consent the younger brother assumed permanently the position of family counselor and financier. We expect him to feel the importance of his new position, and he is too human to disappoint us. Incidentally, we notice an improvement in his English. He no longer writes "between you and I"

Fragment of a letter to Orion Clemens. Written at St. Louis in 1859:

.....I am not talking nonsense, now--I am in earnest, I want you to keep your troubles and your plans out of the reach of meddlers, until the latter are consummated, so that in case you fail, no one will know it but yourself.

Above all things (between you and me) never tell Ma any of your troubles; she never slept a wink the night your last letter came, and she looks distressed yet. Write only cheerful news to her. You know that she will not be satisfied so long as she thinks anything is going on that she is ignorant of--and she makes a little fuss about it when her suspicions are awakened; but that makes no difference--. I know that it is better that she be kept in the dark concerning all things of an unpleasant nature. She upbraids me occasionally for giving her only the bright side of my affairs (but unfortunately for her she has to put up with it, for I know that troubles that I curse awhile and forget, would disturb her slumbers for some time.) (Parenthesis No. 2--Possibly because she is deprived of the soothing consolation of swearing.) Tell her the good news and me the bad.

Putting all things together, I begin to think I am rather lucky than otherwise--a notion which I was slow to take up. The other night I was about to round to for a storm--but concluded that I could find a smoother bank somewhere. I landed 5 miles below. The storm came--passed away and did not injure us. Coming up, day before yesterday, I looked at the spot I first chose, and half the trees on the bank were torn to shreds. We couldn't have lived 5 minutes in such a tornado. And I am also lucky in having a berth, while all the young pilots are idle. This is the luckiest circumstance that ever befell me. Not on account of the wages-- for that is a secondary consideration--but from the fact that the City of Memphis is the largest boat in the trade and the hardest to pilot, and consequently I can get a reputation on her, which is a thing I never could accomplish on a transient boat. I can "bank" in the neighborhood of $100 a month on her, and that will satisfy me for the present (principally because the other youngsters are sucking their fingers.) Bless me! what a pleasure there is in revenge! and what vast respect Prosperity commands! Why, six months ago, I could enter the "Rooms," and receive only a customary fraternal greeting--but now they say, "Why, how are you, old fellow--when did you get in?"

And the young pilots who used to tell me, patronizingly, that I could never learn the river cannot keep from showing a little of their chagrin at seeing me so far ahead of them. Permit me to "blow my horn," for I derive a living pleasure from these things, and I must confess that when I go to pay my dues, I rather like to let the d---d rascals get a glimpse of a hundred dollar bill peeping out from amongst notes of smaller dimensions, whose face I do not exhibit! You will despise this egotism, but I tell you there is a "stern joy" in it.....

Pilots did not remain long on one boat, as a rule; just why it is not so easy to understand. Perhaps they liked the experience of change; perhaps both captain and pilot liked the pursuit of the ideal. In the light-hearted letter that follows--written to a friend of the family, formerly of Hannibal--we get something of the uncertainty of the pilot's engagements.

To Mrs. Elizabeth W. Smith, in Jackson, Cape Girardeau County, Mo.:

ST. Louis, Oct. 31 [probably 1859]. DEAR AUNT BETSEY,--Ma has not written you, because she did not know when I would get started down the river again.....

You see, Aunt Betsey, I made but one trip on the packet after you left, and then concluded to remain at home awhile. I have just discovered this morning that I am to go to New Orleans on the "Col. Chambers"--fine, light-draught, swift-running passenger steamer--all modern accommodations and improvements--through with dispatch--for freight or passage apply on board, or to--but--I have forgotten the agent's name--however, it makes no difference--and as I was saying, or had intended to say, Aunt Betsey, probably, if you are ready to come up, you had better take the "Ben Lewis," the best boat in the packet line. She will be at Cape Girardeau at noon on Saturday (day after tomorrow,) and will reach here at breakfast time, Sunday. If Mr. Hamilton is chief clerk,--very well, I am slightly acquainted with him. And if Messrs. Carter Gray and Dean Somebody (I have forgotten his other name,) are in the pilot-house--very well again-I am acquainted with them. Just tell Mr. Gray, Aunt Betsey-- that I wish him to place himself at your command.

All the family are well--except myself--I am in a bad way again--disease, Love, in its most malignant form. Hopes are entertained of my recovery, however. At the dinner table--excellent symptom--I am still as "terrible as an army with banners."

Aunt Betsey--the wickedness of this world--but I haven't time to moralize this morning. Goodbye
SAM CLEMENS.

As we do not hear of this "attack" again, the recovery was probably prompt. His letters are not frequent enough for us to keep track of his boats, but we know that he was associated with Bixby from time to time, and now and again with one of the Bowen boys, his old Hannibal schoolmates. He was reveling in the river life, the ease and distinction and romance of it. No other life would ever suit him as well. He was at the age to enjoy just what it brought him --at the airy, golden, overweening age of youth.

To Orion Clemens, in Keokuk, Iowa:

ST. LOUIS, Mch. 1860. MY DEAR BRO.,--Your last has just come to hand. It reminds me strongly of Tom Hood's letters to his family, (which I have been reading lately). But yours only remind me of his, for although there is a striking likeness, your humour is much finer than his, and far better expressed. Tom Hood's wit, (in his letters) has a savor of labor about it which is very disagreeable. Your letter is good. That portion of it wherein the old sow figures is the very best thing I have seen lately. Its quiet style resembles Goldsmith's "Citizen of the World," and "Don Quixote,"-- which are my beau ideals of fine writing.

You have paid the preacher! Well, that is good, also. What a man wants with religion in these breadless times, surpasses my comprehension.

Pamela and I have just returned from a visit to the most wonderfully beautiful painting which this city has ever seen--Church's "Heart of the Andes"--which represents a lovely valley with its rich vegetation in all the bloom and glory of a tropical summer--dotted with birds and flowers of all colors and shades of color, and sunny slopes, and shady corners, and twilight groves, and cool cascades--all grandly set off with a majestic mountain in the background with its gleaming summit clothed in everlasting ice and snow! I have seen it several times, but it is always a new picture--totally new--you seem to see nothing the second time which you saw the first. We took the opera glass, and examined its beauties minutely, for the naked eye cannot discern the little wayside flowers, and soft shadows and patches of sunshine, and half-hidden bunches of grass and jets of water which form some of its most enchanting features. There is no slurring of perspective effect about it--the most distant-- the minutest object in it has a marked and distinct personality--so that you may count the very leaves on the trees. When you first see the tame, ordinary-looking picture, your first impulse is to turn your back upon it, and say "Humbug"--but your third visit will find your brain gasping and straining with futile efforts to take all the wonder in--and appreciate it in its fulness--and understand how such a miracle could have been conceived and executed by human brain and human hands. You will never get tired of looking at the picture, but your reflections--your efforts to grasp an intelligible Something--you hardly know what --will grow so painful that you will have to go away from the thing, in order to obtain relief. You may find relief, but you cannot banish the picture--It remains with you still. It is in my mind now--and the smallest feature could not be removed without my detecting it. So much for the "Heart of the Andes."

Ma was delighted with her trip, but she was disgusted with the girls for allowing me to embrace and kiss them--and she was horrified at the Schottische as performed by Miss Castle and myself. She was perfectly willing for me to dance until 12 o'clock at the imminent peril of my going to sleep on the after watch--but then she would top off with a very inconsistent sermon on dancing in general; ending with a terrific broadside aimed at that heresy of heresies, the Schottische.

I took Ma and the girls in a carriage, round that portion of New Orleans where the finest gardens and residences are to be seen, and although it was a blazing hot dusty day, they seemed hugely delighted. To use an expression which is commonly ignored in polite society, they were "hell-bent" on stealing some of the luscious-looking oranges from branches which overhung the fences, but I restrained them. They were not aware before that shrubbery could be made to take any queer shape which a skilful gardener might choose to twist it into, so they found not only beauty but novelty in their visit. We went out to Lake Pontchartrain in the cars. Your Brother SAM CLEMENS

We have not before heard of Miss Castle, who appears to have been one of the girls who accompanied Jane Clemens on the trip which her son gave her to New Orleans, but we may guess that the other was his cousin and good comrade, Ella Creel. One wishes that he might have left us a more extended account of that long-ago river journey, a fuller glimpse of a golden age that has vanished as completely as the days of Washington.

We may smile at the natural youthful desire to air his reading, and his art appreciation, and we may find his opinions not without interest. We may even commend them--in part. Perhaps we no longer count the leaves on Church's trees, but Goldsmith and Cervantes still deserve the place assigned them.

He does not tell us what boat he was on at this time, but later in the year he was with Bixby again, on the Alonzo Child. We get a bit of the pilot in port in his next.

To Orion Clemens, in Keokuk, Iowa:

"ALONZO CHILD," N. ORLEANS, Sep. 28th 1860. DEAR BROTHER,--I just received yours and Mollies letter yesterday--they had been here two weeks--forwarded from St. Louis. We got here yesterday--will leave at noon to-day. Of course I have had no time, in 24 hours, to do anything. Therefore I'll answer after we are under way again. Yesterday, I had many things to do, but Bixby and I got with the pilots of two other boats and went off dissipating on a ten dollar dinner at a French restaurant breathe it not unto Ma!--where we ate sheep-head, fish with mushrooms, shrimps and oysters--birds--coffee with brandy burnt in it, &c &c,-ate, drank and smoked, from 2 p.m. until 5 o'clock, and then--then the day was too far gone to do any thing.

Please find enclosed and acknowledge receipt of--$20.00 In haste SAM L. CLEMENS

It should be said, perhaps, that when he became pilot Jane Clemens had released her son from his pledge in the matter of cards and liquor. This license did not upset him, however. He cared very little for either of these dissipations. His one great indulgence was tobacco, a matter upon which he was presently to receive some grave counsel. He reports it in his next letter, a sufficiently interesting document. The clairvoyant of this visit was Madame Caprell, famous in her day. Clemens had been urged to consult her, and one idle afternoon concluded to make the experiment. The letter reporting the matter to his brother is fragmentary, and is the last remaining to us of the piloting period.

Fragment of a letter to Orion Clemens, in Keokuk, Iowa:

NEW ORLEANS February 6, 1862. .....She's a very pleasant little lady--rather pretty--about 28,--say 5 feet 2 and one quarter--would weigh 116--has black eyes and hair--is polite and intelligent--used good language, and talks much faster than I do.

She invited me into the little back parlor, closed the door; and we were alone. We sat down facing each other. Then she asked my age. Then she put her hands before her eyes a moment, and commenced talking as if she had a good deal to say and not much time to say it in. Something after this style:

MADAME. Yours is a watery planet; you gain your livelihood on the water; but you should have been a lawyer--there is where your talents lie: you might have distinguished yourself as an orator, or as an editor; you have written a great deal; you write well--but you are rather out of practice; no matter--you will be in practice some day; you have a superb constitution, and as excellent health as any man in the world; you have great powers of endurance; in your profession your strength holds out against the longest sieges, without flagging; still, the upper part of your lungs, the top of them is slightly affected--you must take care of yourself; you do not drink, but you use entirely too much tobacco; and you must stop it; mind, not moderate, but stop the use of it totally; then I can almost promise you 86 when you will surely die; otherwise look out for 28, 31, 34, 47, and 65; be careful--for you are not of a long- lived race, that is on your father's side; you are the only healthy member of your family, and the only one in it who has anything like the certainty of attaining to a great age--so, stop using tobacco, and be careful of yourself..... In some respects you take after your father, but you are much more like your mother, who belongs to the long-lived, energetic side of the house.... You never brought all your energies to bear upon any subject but what you accomplished it--for instance, you are self-made, self-educated.

S. L. C. Which proves nothing.

MADAME. Don't interrupt. When you sought your present occupation you found a thousand obstacles in the way--obstacles unknown--not even suspected by any save you and me, since you keep such matters to yourself--but you fought your way, and hid the long struggle under a mask of cheerfulness, which saved your friends anxiety on your account. To do all this requires all the qualities I have named.

S. L. C. You flatter well, Madame.

MADAME. Don't interrupt: Up to within a short time you had always lived from hand to mouth--now you are in easy circumstances--for which you need give credit to no one but yourself. The turning point in your life occurred in 1840-7-8.

S. L. C. Which was?

MADAME. A death perhaps, and this threw you upon the world and made you what you are; it was always intended that you should make yourself; therefore, it was well that this calamity occurred as early as it did. You will never die of water, although your career upon it in the future seems well sprinkled with misfortune. You will continue upon the water for some time yet; you will not retire finally until ten years from now .... What is your brother's age? 35--and a lawyer? and in pursuit of an office? Well, he stands a better chance than the other two, and he may get it; he is too visionary--is always flying off on a new hobby; this will never do--tell him I said so. He is a good lawyer--a, very good lawyer--and a fine speaker--is very popular and much respected, and makes many friends; but although he retains their friendship, he loses their confidence by displaying his instability of character..... The land he has now will be very valuable after a while--

S. L. C. Say a 50 years hence, or thereabouts. Madame--

MADAME. No--less time-but never mind the land, that is a secondary consideration--let him drop that for the present, and devote himself to his business and politics with all his might, for he must hold offices under the Government.....

After a while you will possess a good deal of property--retire at the end of ten years--after which your pursuits will be literary--try the law-- you will certainly succeed. I am done now. If you have any questions to ask--ask them freely--and if it be in my power, I will answer without reserve-- without reserve.

I asked a few questions of minor importance--paid her $2--and left, under the decided impression that going to the fortune teller's was just as good as going to the opera, and the cost scarcely a trifle more--ergo, I will disguise myself and go again, one of these days, when other amusements fail. Now isn't she the devil? That is to say, isn't she a right smart little woman?

When you want money, let Ma know, and she will send it. She and Pamela are always fussing about change, so I sent them a hundred and twenty quarters yesterday--fiddler's change enough to last till I get back, I reckon. SAM.

It is not so difficult to credit Madame Caprell with clairvoyant powers when one has read the letters of Samuel Clemens up to this point. If we may judge by those that have survived, her prophecy of literary distinction for him was hardly warranted by anything she could have known of his past performance. These letters of his youth have a value to-day only because they were written by the man who later was to become Mark Twain. The squibs and skits which he sometimes contributed to the New Orleans papers were bright, perhaps, and pleasing to his pilot associates, but they were without literary value. He was twenty-five years old. More than one author has achieved reputation at that age. Mark Twain was of slower growth; at that age he had not even developed a definite literary ambition: Whatever the basis of Madame Caprell's prophecy, we must admit that she was a good guesser on several matters, "a right smart little woman," as Clemens himself phrased it.

She overlooked one item, however: the proximity of the Civil War. Perhaps it was too close at hand for second sight. A little more than two months after the Caprell letter was written Fort Sumter was fired upon. Mask Twain had made his last trip as a pilot up the river to St. Louis--the nation was plunged into a four years' conflict.

There are no letters of this immediate period. Young Clemens went to Hannibal, and enlisting in a private company, composed mainly of old schoolmates, went soldiering for two rainy, inglorious weeks, by the end of which he had had enough of war, and furthermore had discovered that he was more of a Union abolitionist than a slave- holding secessionist, as he had at first supposed. Convictions were likely to be rather infirm during those early days of the war, and subject to change without notice. Especially was this so in a border State.

III

LETTERS 1861-62. ON THE FRONTIER. MINING ADVENTURES. JOURNALISTIC BEGINNINGS

Clemens went from the battle-front to Keokuk, where Orion was preparing to accept the appointment prophesied by Madame Caprell. Orion was a stanch Unionist, and a member of Lincoln's Cabinet had offered him the secretaryship of the new Territory of Nevada. Orion had accepted, and only needed funds to carry him to his destination. His pilot brother had the funds, and upon being appointed "private" secretary, agreed to pay both passages on the overland stage, which would bear them across the great plains from St. Jo to Carson City. Mark Twain, in Roughing It, has described that glorious journey and the frontier life that followed it. His letters form a supplement of realism to a tale that is more or less fictitious, though marvelously true in color and background. The first bears no date, but it was written not long after their arrival, August 14, 1861. It is not complete, but there is enough of it to give us a very fair picture of Carson City, "a wooden town; its population two thousand souls."

Part of a letter to Mrs. Jane Clemens, in St. Louis:

(Date not given, but Sept, or Oct., 1861.) MY DEAR MOTHER,--I hope you will all come out here someday. But I shan't consent to invite you, until we can receive you in style. But I guess we shall be able to do that, one of these days. I intend that Pamela shall live on Lake Bigler until she can knock a bull down with her fist--say, about three months.

"Tell everything as it is--no better, and no worse."

Well, "Gold Hill" sells at $5,000 per foot, cash down; "Wild cat" isn't worth ten cents. The country is fabulously rich in gold, silver, copper, lead, coal, iron, quick silver, marble, granite, chalk, plaster of Paris, (gypsum,) thieves, murderers, desperadoes, ladies, children, lawyers, Christians, Indians, Chinamen, Spaniards, gamblers, sharpers, coyotes (pronounced Ki-yo-ties,) poets, preachers, and jackass rabbits. I overheard a gentleman say, the other day, that it was "the d---dest country under the sun."--and that comprehensive conception I fully subscribe to. It never rains here, and the dew never falls. No flowers grow here, and no green thing gladdens the eye. The birds that fly over the land carry their provisions with them. Only the crow and the raven tarry with us. Our city lies in the midst of a desert of the purest-- most unadulterated, and compromising sand--in which infernal soil nothing but that fag-end of vegetable creation, "sage-brush," ventures to grow. If you will take a Lilliputian cedar tree for a model, and build a dozen imitations of it with the stiffest article of telegraph wire--set them one foot apart and then try to walk through them, you'll understand (provided the floor is covered 12 inches deep with sand,) what it is to wander through a sage-brush desert. When crushed, sage brush emits an odor which isn't exactly magnolia and equally isn't exactly polecat but is a sort of compromise between the two. It looks a good deal like grease-wood, and is the ugliest plant that was ever conceived of. It is gray in color.

On the plains, sage-brush and grease-wood grow about twice as large as the common geranium--and in my opinion they are a very good substitute for that useless vegetable. Grease-wood is a perfect- most perfect imitation in miniature of a live oak tree-barring the color of it. As to the other fruits and flowers of the country, there ain't any, except "Pulu" or "Tuler," or what ever they call it,--a species of unpoetical willow that grows on the banks of the Carson--a RIVER, 20 yards wide, knee deep, and so villainously rapid and crooked, that it looks like it had wandered into the country without intending it, and had run about in a bewildered way and got lost, in its hurry to get out again before some thirsty man came along and drank it up. I said we are situated in a flat, sandy desert--true. And surrounded on all sides by such prodigious mountains, that when you gaze at them awhile,--and begin to conceive of their grandeur--and next to feel their vastness expanding your soul--and ultimately find yourself growing and swelling and spreading into a giant--I say when this point is reached, you look disdainfully down upon the insignificant village of Carson, and in that instant you are seized with a burning desire to stretch forth your hand, put the city in your pocket, and walk off with it.

As to churches, I believe they have got a Catholic one here, but like that one the New York fireman spoke of, I believe "they don't run her now:" Now, although we are surrounded by sand, the greatest part of the town is built upon what was once a very pretty grassy spot; and the streams of pure water that used to poke about it in rural sloth and solitude, now pass through on dusty streets and gladden the hearts of men by reminding them that there is at least something here that hath its prototype among the homes they left behind them. And up "King's Canon," (please pronounce canyon, after the manner of the natives,) there are "ranches," or farms, where they say hay grows, and grass, and beets and onions, and turnips, and other "truck" which is suitable for cows--yes, and even Irish potatoes; also, cabbage, peas and beans.

The houses are mostly frame, unplastered, but "papered" inside with flour-sacks sewed together, and the handsomer the "brand" upon the sacks is, the neater the house looks. Occasionally, you stumble on a stone house. On account of the dryness of the country, the shingles on the houses warp till they look like short joints of stove pipe split lengthwise.

(Remainder missing.)

In this letter is something of the "wild freedom of the West," which later would contribute to his fame. The spirit of the frontier--of Mark Twain--was beginning to stir him.

There had been no secretary work for him to do, and no provision for payment. He found his profit in studying human nature and in prospecting native resources. He was not interested in mining not yet. With a boy named John Kinney he made an excursion to Lake Bigler--now Tahoe--and located a timber claim, really of great value. They were supposed to build a fence around it, but they were too full of the enjoyment of camp-life to complete it. They put in most of their time wandering through the stately forest or drifting over the transparent lake in a boat left there by lumbermen. They built themselves a brush house, but they did not sleep in it. In 'Roughing It' he writes, "It never occurred to us, for one thing; and, besides, it was built to hold the ground, and that was enough. We did not wish to strain it."

They were having a glorious time, when their camp-fire got away from them and burned up their claim. His next letter, of which the beginning is missing, describes the fire.

Fragment of a letter to Mrs. Jane Clemens and Mrs. Moffett, in St. Louis:

.....The level ranks of flame were relieved at intervals by the standard- bearers, as we called the tall dead trees, wrapped in fire, and waving their blazing banners a hundred feet in the air. Then we could turn from this scene to the Lake, and see every branch, and leaf, and cataract of flame upon its bank perfectly reflected as in a gleaming, fiery mirror. The mighty roaring of the conflagration, together with our solitary and somewhat unsafe position (for there was no one within six miles of us,) rendered the scene very impressive. Occasionally, one of us would remove his pipe from his mouth and say, "Superb! magnificent! Beautiful! but- by the Lord God Almighty, if we attempt to sleep in this little patch tonight, we'll never live till morning! for if we don't burn up, we'll certainly suffocate." But he was persuaded to sit up until we felt pretty safe as far as the fire was concerned, and then we turned in, with many misgivings. When we got up in the morning, we found that the fire had burned small pieces of drift wood within six feet of our boat, and had made its way to within 4 or 5 steps of us on the South side. We looked like lava men, covered as we were with ashes, and begrimed with smoke. We were very black in the face, but we soon washed ourselves white again.

John D. Kinney, a Cincinnati boy, and a first-rate fellow, too, who came out with judge Turner, was my comrade. We staid at the Lake four days-- I had plenty of fun, for John constantly reminded me of Sam Bowen when we were on our campaign in Missouri. But first and foremost, for Annie's, Mollies, and Pamela's comfort, be it known that I have never been guilty of profane language since I have been in this Territory, and Kinney hardly ever swears.--But sometimes human nature gets the better of him. On the second day we started to go by land to the lower camp, a distance of three miles, over the mountains, each carrying an axe. I don't think we got lost exactly, but we wandered four hours over the steepest, rockiest and most dangerous piece of country in the world. I couldn't keep from laughing at Kinney's distress, so I kept behind, so that he could not see me. After he would get over a dangerous place, with infinite labor and constant apprehension, he would stop, lean on his axe, and look around, then behind, then ahead, and then drop his head and ruminate awhile.--Then he would draw a long sigh, and say: "Well--could any Billygoat have scaled that place without breaking his --- ------ neck?" And I would reply, "No,--I don't think he could." "No--you don't think he could--" (mimicking me,) "Why don't you curse the infernal place? You know you want to.--I do, and will curse the --- ------ thieving country as long as I live." Then we would toil on in silence for awhile. Finally I told him--"Well, John, what if we don't find our way out of this today--we'll know all about the country when we do get out." "Oh stuff--I know enough--and too much about the d---d villainous locality already." Finally, we reached the camp. But as we brought no provisions with us, the first subject that presented itself to us was, how to get back. John swore he wouldn't walk back, so we rolled a drift log apiece into the Lake, and set about making paddles, intending to straddle the logs and paddle ourselves back home sometime or other. But the Lake objected--got stormy, and we had to give it up. So we set out for the only house on this side of the Lake--three miles from there, down the shore. We found the way without any trouble, reached there before sundown, played three games of cribbage, borrowed a dug-out and pulled back six miles to the upper camp. As we had eaten nothing since sunrise, we did not waste time in cooking our supper or in eating it, either. After supper we got out our pipes--built a rousing camp fire in the open air-established a faro bank (an institution of this country,) on our huge flat granite dining table, and bet white beans till one o'clock, when John went to bed. We were up before the sun the next morning, went out on the Lake and caught a fine trout for breakfast. But unfortunately, I spoilt part of the breakfast. We had coffee and tea boiling on the fire, in coffee-pots and fearing they might not be strong enough, I added more ground coffee, and more tea, but--you know mistakes will happen.--I put the tea in the coffee-pot, and the coffee in the teapot--and if you imagine that they were not villainous mixtures, just try the effect once.

And so Bella is to be married on the 1st of Oct. Well, I send her and her husband my very best wishes, and--I may not be here--but wherever I am on that night, we'll have a rousing camp-fire and a jollification in honor of the event.

In a day or two we shall probably go to the Lake and build another cabin and fence, and get everything into satisfactory trim before our trip to Esmeralda about the first of November.

What has become of Sam Bowen? I would give my last shirt to have him out here. I will make no promises, but I believe if John would give him a thousand dollars and send him out here he would not regret it. He might possibly do very well here, but he could do little without capital.

Remember me to all my St. Louis and Keokuk friends, and tell Challie and Hallie Renson that I heard a military band play "What are the Wild Waves Saying?" the other night, and it reminded me very forcibly of them. It brought Ella Creel and Belle across the Desert too in an instant, for they sang the song in Orion's yard the first time I ever heard it. It was like meeting an old friend. I tell you I could have swallowed that whole band, trombone and all, if such a compliment would have been any gratification to them. Love to the young folks, SAM.

The reference in the foregoing letter to Esmeralda has to do with mining plans. He was beginning to be mildly interested, and, with his brother Orion, had acquired "feet" in an Esmeralda camp, probably at a very small price--so small as to hold out no exciting prospect of riches. In his next letter he gives us the size of this claim, which he has visited. His interest, however, still appears to be chiefly in his timber claim on Lake Bigler (Tahoe), though we are never to hear of it again after this letter.

To Mrs. Moffett, in St. Louis:

CARSON CITY, Oct. 25, 1861. MY DEAR SISTER,--I have just finished reading your letter and Ma's of Sept. 8th. How in the world could they have been so long coming? You ask me if I have for gotten my promise to lay a claim for Mr. Moffett. By no means. I have already laid a timber claim on the borders of a lake (Bigler) which throws Como in the shade--and if we succeed in getting one Mr. Jones, to move his saw-mill up there, Mr. Moffett can just consider that claim better than bank stock. Jones says he will move his mill up next spring. In that claim I took up about two miles in length by one in width--and the names in it are as follows: "Sam. L Clemens, Wm. A. Moffett, Thos. Nye" and three others. It is situated on "Sam Clemens Bay"--so named by Capt. Nye--and it goes by that name among the inhabitants of that region. I had better stop about "the Lake," though, --for whenever I think of it I want to go there and die, the place is so beautiful. I'll build a country seat there one of these days that will make the Devil's mouth water if he ever visits the earth. Jim Lampton will never know whether I laid a claim there for him or not until he comes here himself. We have now got about 1,650 feet of mining ground-- and if it proves good, Mr. Moffett's name will go in--if not, I can get "feet" for him in the Spring which will be good. You see, Pamela, the trouble does not consist in getting mining ground--for that is plenty enough-- but the money to work it with after you get it is the mischief. When I was in Esmeralda, a young fellow gave me fifty feet in the "Black Warrior"--an unprospected claim. The other day he wrote me that he had gone down eight feet on the ledge, and found it eight feet thick--and pretty good rock, too. He said he could take out rock now if there were a mill to crush it--but the mills are all engaged (there are only four of them) so, if I were willing, he would suspend work until Spring. I wrote him to let it alone at present--because, you see, in the Spring I can go down myself and help him look after it. There will then be twenty mills there. Orion and I have confidence enough in this country to think that if the war will let us alone we can make Mr. Moffett rich without its ever costing him a cent of money or particle of trouble. We shall lay plenty of claims for him, but if they never pay him anything, they will never cost him anything, Orion and I are not financiers. Therefore, you must persuade Uncle Jim to come out here and help us in that line. I have written to him twice to come. I wrote him today. In both letters I told him not to let you or Ma know that we dealt in such romantic nonsense as "brilliant prospects," because I always did hate for anyone to know what my plans or hopes or prospects were--for, if I kept people in ignorance in these matters, no one could be disappointed but myself, if they were not realized. You know I never told you that I went on the river under a promise to pay Bixby $500, until I had paid the money and cleared my skirts of the possibility of having my judgment criticised. I would not say anything about our prospects now, if we were nearer home. But I suppose at this distance you are more anxious than you would be if you saw us every month-and therefore it is hardly fair to keep you in the dark. However, keep these matters to yourselves, and then if we fail, we'll keep the laugh in the family.

What we want now is something that will commence paying immediately. We have got a chance to get into a claim where they say a tunnel has been run 150 feet, and the ledge struck. I got a horse yesterday, and went out with the Attorney-General and the claim-owner--and we tried to go to the claim by a new route, and got lost in the mountains--sunset overtook us before we found the claim--my horse got too lame to carry me, and I got down and drove him ahead of me till within four miles of town--then we sent Rice on ahead. Bunker, (whose horse was in good condition,) undertook, to lead mine, and I followed after him. Darkness shut him out from my view in less than a minute, and within the next minute I lost the road and got to wandering in the sage brush. I would find the road occasionally and then lose it again in a minute or so. I got to Carson about nine o'clock, at night, but not by the road I traveled when I left it. The General says my horse did very well for awhile, but soon refused to lead. Then he dismounted, and had a jolly time driving both horses ahead of him and chasing them here and there through the sage brush (it does my soul good when I think of it) until he got to town, when both animals deserted him, and he cursed them handsomely and came home alone. Of course the horses went to their stables.

Tell Sammy I will lay a claim for him, and he must come out and attend to it. He must get rid of that propensity for tumbling down, though, for when we get fairly started here, I don't think we shall have time to pick up those who fall.....

That is Stoughter's house, I expect, that Cousin Jim has moved into. This is just the country for Cousin Jim to live in. I don't believe it would take him six months to make $100,000 here, if he had 3,000 dollars to commence with. I suppose he can't leave his family though.

Tell Mrs. Benson I never intend to be a lawyer. I have been a slave several times in my life, but I'll never be one again. I always intend to be so situated (unless I marry,) that I can "pull up stakes" and clear out whenever I feel like it.

We are very thankful to you, Pamela, for the papers you send. We have received half a dozen or more, and, next to letters, they are the most welcome visitors we have. Write oftener, Pamela. Yr. Brother SAM.

The "Cousin Jim" mentioned in this letter is the original of the character of Colonel Sellers. Whatever Mark Twain's later opinion of Cousin Jim Lampton's financial genius may have been, he seems to have respected it at this time.

More than three months pass until we have another letter, and in that time the mining fever had become well seated. Mark Twain himself was full of the Sellers optimism, and it was bound to overflow, fortify as he would against it.

He met with little enough encouragement. With three companions, in midwinter, he made a mining excursion to the much exploited Humboldt region, returning empty-handed after a month or two of hard experience. This is the trip picturesquely described in

Chapters

XXVII to XXXIII of Roughing It.--[It is set down historically in Mark Twain 'A Biography.' Harper & brothers.]--He, mentions the Humboldt in his next letter, but does not confess his failure.

To Mrs. Jane Clemens and Mrs. Moffett, in St. Louis:

CARSON CITY, Feb. 8, 1862. MY DEAR MOTHER AND SISTER,--By George Pamela, I begin to fear that I have invoked a Spirit of some kind or other which I will find some difficulty in laying. I wasn't much terrified by your growing inclinations, but when you begin to call presentiments to your aid, I confess that I "weaken." Mr. Moffett is right, as I said before--and I am not much afraid of his going wrong. Men are easily dealt with--but when you get the women started, you are in for it, you know. But I have decided on two things, viz: Any of you, or all of you, may live in California, for that is the Garden of Eden reproduced--but you shall never live in Nevada; and secondly, none of you, save Mr. Moffett, shall ever cross the Plains. If you were only going to Pike's Peak, a little matter of 700 miles from St. Jo, you might take the coach, and I wouldn't say a word. But I consider it over 2,000 miles from St. Jo to Carson, and the first 6 or 800 miles is mere Fourth of July, compared to the balance of the route. But Lord bless you, a man enjoys every foot of it. If you ever come here or to California, it must be by sea. Mr. Moffett must come by overland coach, though, by all means. He would consider it the jolliest little trip he ever took in his life. Either June, July, or August are the proper months to make the journey in. He could not suffer from heat, and three or four heavy army blankets would make the cold nights comfortable. If the coach were full of passengers, two good blankets would probably be sufficient. If he comes, and brings plenty of money, and fails to invest it to his entire satisfaction; I will prophesy no more.

But I will tell you a few things which you wouldn't have found out if I hadn't got myself into this scrape. I expect to return to St. Louis in July--per steamer. I don't say that I will return then, or that I shall be able to do it--but I expect to--you bet. I came down here from Humboldt, in order to look after our Esmeralda interests, and my sore- backed horse and the bad roads have prevented me from making the journey. Yesterday one of my old Esmeralda friends, Bob Howland, arrived here, and I have had a talk with him. He owns with me in the "Horatio and Derby" ledge. He says our tunnel is in 52 feet, and a small stream of water has been struck, which bids fair to become a "big thing" by the time the ledge is reached--sufficient to supply a mill. Now, if you knew anything of the value of water, here; you would perceive, at a glance that if the water should amount to 50 or 100 inches, we wouldn't care whether school kept or not. If the ledge should prove to be worthless, we'd sell the water for money enough to give us quite a lift. But you see, the ledge will not prove to be worthless. We have located, near by, a fine site for a mill; and when we strike the ledge, you know, we'll have a mill- site, water power, and pay-rock, all handy. Then we shan't care whether we have capital or not. Mill-folks will build us a mill, and wait for their pay. If nothing goes wrong, we'll strike the ledge in June--and if we do, I'll be home in July, you know.

Pamela, don't you know that undemonstrated human calculations won't do to bet on? Don't you know that I have only talked, as yet, but proved nothing? Don't you know that I have expended money in this country but have made none myself? Don't you know that I have never held in my hands a gold or silver bar that belonged to me? Don't you know that it's all talk and no cider so far? Don't you know that people who always feel jolly, no matter where they are or what happens to them--who have the organ of hope preposterously developed--who are endowed with an uncongealable sanguine temperament--who never feel concerned about the price of corn--and who cannot, by any possibility, discover any but the bright side of a picture--are very apt to go to extremes, and exaggerate with 40-horse microscopic power? Of course I never tried to raise these suspicions in your mind, but then your knowledge of the fact that some people's poor frail human nature is a sort of crazy institution anyhow, ought to have suggested them to you. Now, if I hadn't thoughtlessly got you into the notion of coming out here, and thereby got myself into a scrape, I wouldn't have given you that highly-colored paragraph about the mill, etc., because, you know, if that pretty little picture should fail, and wash out, and go the Devil generally, it wouldn't cost me the loss of an hour's sleep, but you fellows would be so much distressed on my account as I could possibly be if "circumstances beyond my control" were to prevent my being present at my own funeral. But--but--

"In the bright lexicon of youth, There's no such word as Fail--" and I'll prove it!

And look here. I came near forgetting it. Don't you say a word to me about "trains" across the plains. Because I am down on that arrangement. That sort of thing is "played out," you know. The Overland Coach or the Mail Steamer is the thing.

You want to know something about the route between California and Nevada Territory? Suppose you take my word for it, that it is exceedingly jolly. Or take, for a winter view, J. Ross Brown's picture, in Harper's Monthly, of pack mules tumbling fifteen hundred feet down the side of a mountain. Why bless you, there's scenery on that route. You can stand on some of those noble peaks and see Jerusalem and the Holy Land. And you can start a boulder, and send it tearing up the earth and crashing over trees-down-down-down-to the very devil, Madam. And you would probably stand up there and look, and stare and wonder at the magnificence spread out before you till you starved to death, if let alone. But you should take someone along to keep you moving.

Since you want to know, I will inform you that an eight-stamp water mill, put up and ready for business would cost about $10,000 to $12,000. Then, the water to run it with would cost from $1,000 to $30,000--and even more, according to the location. What I mean by that, is, that water powers in THIS vicinity, are immensely valuable. So, also, in Esmeralda. But Humboldt is a new country, and things don't cost so much there yet. I saw a good water power sold there for $750.00. But here is the way the thing is managed. A man with a good water power on Carson river will lean his axe up against a tree (provided you find him chopping cord-wood at $4 a day,) and taking his chalk pipe out of his mouth to afford him an opportunity to answer your questions, will look you coolly in the face and tell you his little property is worth forty or fifty thousand dollars! But you can easily fix him. You tell him that you'll build a quartz mill on his property, and make him a fourth or a third, or half owner in said mill in consideration of the privilege of using said property--and that will bring him to his milk in a jiffy. So he spits on his hands, and goes in again with his axe, until the mill is finished, when lo! out pops the quondam wood-chopper, arrayed in purple and fine linen, and prepared to deal in bank-stock, or bet on the races, or take government loans, with an air, as to the amount, of the most don't care- a-d---dest unconcern that you can conceive of. By George, if I just had a thousand dollars--I'd be all right! Now there's the "Horatio," for instance. There are five or six shareholders in it, and I know I could buy half of their interests at, say $20 per foot, now that flour is worth $50 per barrel and they are pressed for money. But I am hard up myself, and can't buy--and in June they'll strike the ledge and then "good-bye canary." I can't get it for love or money. Twenty dollars a foot! Think of it. For ground that is proven to be rich. Twenty dollars, Madam--and we wouldn't part with a foot of our 75 for five times the sum. So it will be in Humboldt next summer. The boys will get pushed and sell ground for a song that is worth a fortune. But I am at the helm, now. I have convinced Orion that he hasn't business talent enough to carry on a peanut stand, and he has solemnly promised me that he will meddle no more with mining, or other matters not connected with the Secretary's office. So, you see, if mines are to be bought or sold, or tunnels run, or shafts sunk, parties have to come to me--and me only. I'm the "firm," you know.

"How long does it take one of those infernal trains to go through?" Well, anywhere between three and five months.

Tell Margaret that if you ever come to live in California, that you can promise her a home for a hundred years, and a bully one--but she wouldn't like the country. Some people are malicious enough to think that if the devil were set at liberty and told to confine himself to Nevada Territory, that he would come here--and look sadly around, awhile, and then get homesick and go back to hell again. But I hardly believe it, you know. I am saying, mind you, that Margaret wouldn't like the country, perhaps--nor the devil either, for that matter, or any other man but I like it. When it rains here, it never lets up till it has done all the raining it has got to do--and after that, there's a dry spell, you bet. Why, I have had my whiskers and moustaches so full of alkali dust that you'd have thought I worked in a starch factory and boarded in a flour barrel.

Since we have been here there has not been a fire--although the houses are built of wood. They "holler" fire sometimes, though, but I am always too late to see the smoke before the fire is out, if they ever have any. Now they raised a yell here in front of the office a moment ago. I put away my papers, and locked up everything of value, and changed my boots, and pulled off my coat, and went and got a bucket of water, and came back to see what the matter was, remarking to myself, "I guess I'll be on hand this time, any way." But I met a friend on the pavement, and he said, "Where you been? Fire's out half an hour ago."

Ma says Axtele was above "suspition"--but I have searched through Webster's Unabridged, and can't find the word. However, it's of no consequence--I hope he got down safely. I knew Axtele and his wife as well as I know Dan Haines. Mrs. A. once tried to embarrass me in the presence of company by asking me to name her baby, when she was well aware that I didn't know the sex of that Phenomenon. But I told her to call it Frances, and spell it to suit herself. That was about nine years ago, and Axtele had no property, and could hardly support his family by his earnings. He was a pious cuss, though. Member of Margaret Sexton's Church.

And Ma says "it looks like a man can't hold public office and be honest." Why, certainly not, Madam. A man can't hold public office and be honest. Lord bless you, it is a common practice with Orion to go about town stealing little things that happen to be lying around loose. And I don't remember having heard him speak the truth since we have been in Nevada. He even tries to prevail upon me to do these things, Ma, but I wasn't brought up in that way, you know. You showed the public what you could do in that line when you raised me, Madam. But then you ought to have raised me first, so that Orion could have had the benefit of my example. Do you know that he stole all the stamps out of an 8 stamp quartz mill one night, and brought them home under his over-coat and hid them in the back room? Yrs. etc., SAM

A little later he had headed for the Esmeralda Hills. Some time in February he was established there in a camp with a young man by the name of Horatio Phillips (Raish). Later he camped with Bob Howland, who, as City Marshal of Aurora, became known as the most fearless man in the Territory, and, still later, with Calvin H. Higbie (Cal), to whom 'Roughing It' would one day be dedicated. His own funds were exhausted by this time, and Orion, with his rather slender salary, became the financial partner of the firm.

It was a comfortless life there in the Esmeralda camp. Snow covered everything. There was nothing to do, and apparently nothing to report; for there are no letters until April. Then the first one is dated Carson City, where he seems to be making a brief sojourn. It is a rather heavy attempt to be light-hearted; its playfulness suggests that of a dancing bear.

To Mrs. Jane Clemens, in St. Louis:

CARSON CITY, April 2, 1862. MY DEAR MOTHER,--Yours of March 2nd has just been received. I see I am in for it again--with Annie. But she ought to know that I was always stupid. She used to try to teach me lessons from the Bible, but I never could understand them. Doesn't she remember telling me the story of Moses, one Sunday, last Spring, and how hard she tried to explain it and simplify it so that I could understand it--but I couldn't? And how she said it was strange that while her ma and her grandma and her uncle Orion could understand anything in the world, I was so dull that I couldn't understand the "ea-siest thing?" And doesn't she remember that finally a light broke in upon me and I said it was all right--that I knew old Moses himself--and that he kept a clothing store in Market Street? And then she went to her ma and said she didn't know what would become of her uncle Sam he was too dull to learn anything--ever! And I'm just as dull yet. Now I have no doubt her letter was spelled right, and was correct in all particulars--but then I had to read it according to my lights; and they being inferior, she ought to overlook the mistakes I make specially, as it is not my fault that I wasn't born with good sense. I am sure she will detect an encouraging ray of intelligence in that last argument.....

I am waiting here, trying to rent a better office for Orion. I have got the refusal after next week of a room on first floor of a fire-proof brick-rent, eighteen hundred dollars a year. Don't know yet whether we can get it or not. If it is not rented before the week is up, we can.

I was sorry to hear that Dick was killed. I gave him his first lesson in the musket drill. We had half a dozen muskets in our office when it was over Isbell's Music Rooms.

I hope I am wearing the last white shirt that will embellish my person for many a day--for I do hope that I shall be out of Carson long before this reaches you. Love to all. Very Respectfully SAM.

The "Annie" in this letter was his sister Pamela's little daughter; long years after, she would be the wife of Charles L. Webster, Mark Twain's publishing partner. "Dick" the reader may remember as Dick Hingham, of the Keokuk printing-office; he was killed in charging the works at

Fort Donelson.

Clemens was back in Esmeralda when the next letter was written, and we begin now to get pictures of that cheerless mining-camp, and to know something of the alternate hopes and discouragements of the hunt for gold--the miner one day soaring on wings of hope, on the next becoming excited, irritable, profane. The names of new mines appear constantly and vanish almost at a touch, suggesting the fairy-like evanescence of their riches.

But a few of the letters here will best speak for themselves; not all of them are needed. It is perhaps unnecessary to say that there is no intentional humor in these documents.

To Orion Clemens, in Carson City:

ESMERALDA, 13th April, 1862. MY DEAR BROTHER,--Wasson got here night before last "from the wars." Tell Lockhart he is not wounded and not killed--is altogether unhurt. He says the whites left their stone fort before he and Lieut. Noble got there. A large amount of provisions and ammunition, which they left behind them, fell into the hands of the Indians. They had a pitched battle with the savages some fifty miles from the fort, in which Scott (sheriff) and another man was killed. This was the day before the soldiers came up with them. I mean Noble's men, and those under Cols. Evans and Mayfield, from Los Angeles. Evans assumed the chief command-- and next morning the forces were divided into three parties, and marched against the enemy. Col. Mayfield was killed, and Sergeant Gillespie, also Noble's colonel was wounded. The California troops went back home, and Noble remained, to help drive the stock over here. And, as Cousin Sally Dillard says, this is all I know about the fight.

Work not yet begun on the H. and Derby--haven't seen it yet. It is still in the snow. Shall begin on it within 3 or 4 weeks--strike the ledge in July. Guess it is good--worth from $30 to $50 a foot in California.

Why didn't you send the "Live Yankee" deed-the very one I wanted? Have made no inquiries about it, much. Don't intend to until I get the deed. Send it along--by mail--d---n the Express--have to pay three times for all express matter; once in Carson and twice here. I don't expect to take the saddle-bags out of the express office. I paid twenty-five cts. for the Express deeds.

Man named Gebhart shot here yesterday while trying to defend a claim on Last Chance Hill. Expect he will die.

These mills here are not worth a d---n--except Clayton's--and it is not in full working trim yet.

Send me $40 or $50--by mail--immediately.

The Red Bird is probably good--can't work on the tunnel on account of snow. The "Pugh" I have thrown away--shan't re-locate it. It is nothing but bed-rock croppings--too much work to find the ledge, if there is one. Shan't record the "Farnum" until I know more about it--perhaps not at all.

"Governor" under the snow.

"Douglas" and "Red Bird" are both recorded.

I have had opportunities to get into several ledges, but refused all but three--expect to back out of two of them.

Stir yourself as much as possible, and lay up $100 or $15,000, subject to my call. I go to work to-morrow, with pick and shovel. Something's got to come, by G--, before I let go, here.

Col. Youngs says you must rent Kinkead's room by all means--Government would rather pay $150 a month for your office than $75 for Gen. North's. Says you are playing your hand very badly, for either the Government's good opinion or anybody's else, in keeping your office in a shanty. Says put Gov. Nye in your place and he would have a stylish office, and no objections would ever be made, either. When old Col. Youngs talks this way, I think it time to get a fine office. I wish you would take that office, and fit it up handsomely, so that I can omit telling people that by this time you are handsomely located, when I know it is no such thing.

I am living with "Ratio Phillips." Send him one of those black portfolios--by the stage, and put a couple of pen-holders and a dozen steel pens in it.

If you should have occasion to dispose of the long desk before I return, don't forget to break open the middle drawer and take out my things. Envelop my black cloth coat in a newspaper and hang it in the back room.

Don't buy anything while I am here--but save up some money for me. Don't send any money home. I shall have your next quarter's salary spent before you get it, I think. I mean to make or break here within the next two or three months. Yrs. SAM

The "wars" mentioned in the opening paragraph of this letter were incident to the trouble concerning the boundary line between California and Nevada. The trouble continued for some time, with occasional bloodshed. The next letter is an exultant one. There were few enough of this sort. We cannot pretend to keep track of the multiplicity of mines and shares which lure the gold-hunters, pecking away at the flinty ledges, usually in the snow. It has been necessary to abbreviate this letter, for much of it has lost all importance with the years, and is merely confusing. Hope is still high in the writer's heart, and confidence in his associates still unshaken. Later he was to lose faith in "Raish," whether with justice or not we cannot know now.

To Orion Clowns, in Carson City:

ESMERALDA, May 11, 1862. MY DEAR BRO.,--TO use a French expression I have "got my d--d satisfy" at last. Two years' time will make us capitalists, in spite of anything. Therefore, we need fret and fume, and worry and doubt no more, but just lie still and put up with privations for six months. Perhaps three months will "let us out." Then, if Government refuses to pay the rent on your new office we can do it ourselves. We have got to wait six weeks, anyhow, for a dividend, maybe longer--but that it will come there is no shadow of a doubt, I have got the thing sifted down to a dead moral certainty. I own one-eighth of the new "Monitor Ledge, Clemens Company," and money can't buy a foot of it; because I know it to contain our fortune. The ledge is six feet wide, and one needs no glass to see gold and silver in it. Phillips and I own one half of a segregated claim in the "Flyaway" discovery, and good interests in two extensions on it. We put men to work on our part of the discovery yesterday, and last night they brought us some fine specimens. Rock taken from ten feet below the surface on the other part of the discovery, has yielded $150.00 to the ton in the mill and we are at work 300 feet from their shaft.

May 12--Yours by the mail received last night. "Eighteen hundred feet in the C. T. Rice's Company!" Well, I am glad you did not accept of the 200 feet. Tell Rice to give it to some poor man.

But hereafter, when anybody holds up a glittering prospect before you, just argue in this wise, viz: That, if all spare change be devoted to working the "Monitor" and "Flyaway," 12 months, or 24 at furthest, will find all our earthly wishes satisfied, so far as money is concerned--and the more "feet" we have, the more anxiety we must bear--therefore, why not say "No--d---n your 'prospects,' I wait on a sure thing--and a man is less than a man, if he can't wait 2 years for a fortune?" When you and I came out here, we did not expect '63 or '64 to find us rich men-- and if that proposition had been made, we would have accepted it gladly. Now, it is made.

Well, I am willing, now, that "Neary's tunnel," or anybody else's tunnel shall succeed. Some of them may beat us a few months, but we shall be on hand in the fullness of time, as sure as fate. I would hate to swap chances with any member of the "tribe"--in fact, I am so lost to all sense and reason as to be capable of refusing to trade "Flyaway" (with but 200 feet in the Company of four,) foot for foot for that splendid "Lady Washington," with its lists of capitalist proprietors, and its 35,000 feet of Priceless ground.

I wouldn't mind being in some of those Clear Creek claims, if I lived in Carson and we could spare the money. But I have struck my tent in Esmeralda, and I care for no mines but those which I can superintend myself. I am a citizen here now, and I am satisfied--although R. and I are strapped and we haven't three days' rations in the house.

Raish is looking anxiously for money and so am I. Send me whatever you can spare conveniently--I want it to work the Flyaway with. My fourth of that claim only cost me $50, (which isn't paid yet, though,) and I suppose I could sell it here in town for ten times that amount today, but I shall probably hold onto it till the cows come home. I shall work the "Monitor" and the other claims with my own hands. I prospected of a pound of "M," yesterday, and Raish reduced it with the blow-pipe, and got about ten or twelve cents in gold and silver, besides the other half of it which we spilt on the floor and didn't get. The specimen came from the croppings, but was a choice one, and showed much free gold to the naked eye.

Well, I like the corner up-stairs office amazingly--provided, it has one fine, large front room superbly carpeted, for the safe and a $150 desk, or such a matter--one handsome room amidships, less handsomely gotten up, perhaps, for records and consultations, and one good-sized bedroom and adjoining it a kitchen, neither of which latter can be entered by anybody but yourself--and finally, when one of the ledges begins to pay, the whole to be kept in parlor order by two likely contrabands at big wages, the same to be free of expense to the Government. You want the entire second story--no less room than you would have had in Harris and Co's. Make them fix for you before the 1st of July-for maybe you might want to "come out strong" on the 4th, you know.

No, the Post Office is all right and kept by a gentleman but W. F. Express isn't. They charge 25 cts to express a letter from here, but I believe they have quit charging twice for letters that arrive prepaid.

The "Flyaway" specimen I sent you, (taken by myself from DeKay's shaft, 300 feet from where we are going to sink) cannot be called "choice," exactly--say something above medium, to be on the safe side. But I have seen exceedingly choice chunks from that shaft. My intention at first in sending the Antelope specimen was that you might see that it resembles the Monitor--but, come to think, a man can tell absolutely nothing about that without seeing both ledges themselves. I tried to break a handsome chunk from a huge piece of my darling Monitor which we brought from the croppings yesterday, but it all splintered up, and I send you the scraps. I call that "choice"--any d---d fool would. Don't ask if it has been assayed, for it hasn't. It don't need it. It is amply able to speak for itself. It is six feet wide on top, and traversed through and through with veins whose color proclaims their worth. What the devil does a man want with any more feet when he owns in the Flyaway and the invincible bomb-proof Monitor?

If I had anything more to say I have forgotten what it was, unless, perhaps, that I want a sum of money--anywhere from $20 to $150, as soon as possible.

Raish sends regards. He or I, one will drop a line to the "Age" occasionally. I suppose you saw my letters in the "Enterprise." Yr. BRO, SAM

P. S. I suppose Pamela never will regain her health, but she could improve it by coming to California--provided the trip didn't kill her.

You see Bixby is on the flag-ship. He always was the best pilot on the Mississippi, and deserves his "posish." They have done a reckless thing, though, in putting Sam Bowen on the "Swan"--for if a bomb-shell happens to come his way, he will infallibly jump overboard.

Send me another package of those envelopes, per Bagley's coat pocket.

We see how anxious he was for his brother to make a good official showing. If a niggardly Government refused to provide decent quarters--no matter; the miners, with gold pouring in, would themselves pay for a suite "superbly carpeted," and all kept in order by "two likely contrabands"--that is to say, negroes. Samuel Clemens in those days believed in expansion and impressive surroundings. His brother, though also mining mad, was rather inclined to be penny wise in the matter of office luxury--not a bad idea, as it turned out.

Orion, by the way, was acquiring "feet" on his own account, and in one instance, at least, seems to have won his brother's commendation.

The 'Enterprise' letters mentioned we shall presently hear of again.

To Orion Clemens, in Carson City:

ESMERALDA, Sunday, May--, 1862. MY DEAR BROTHER,--Well, if you haven't "struck it rich--"that is, if the piece of rock you sent me came from a bona fide ledge--and it looks as if it did. If that is a ledge, and you own 200 feet in it, why, it's a big thing--and I have nothing more to say. If you have actually made something by helping to pay somebody's prospecting expenses it is a wonder of the first magnitude, and deserves to rank as such.

If that rock came from a well-defined ledge, that particular vein must be at least an inch wide, judging from this specimen, which is fully that thick.

When I came in the other evening, hungry and tired and ill-natured, and threw down my pick and shovel, Raish gave me your specimen--said Bagley brought it, and asked me if it were cinnabar. I examined it by the waning daylight, and took the specks of fine gold for sulphurets--wrote you I did not think much of it--and posted the letter immediately.

But as soon as I looked at it in the broad light of day, I saw my mistake. During the week, we have made three horns, got a blow-pipe, &c, and yesterday, all prepared, we prospected the "Mountain House." I broke the specimen in two, and found it full of fine gold inside. Then we washed out one-fourth of it, and got a noble prospect. This we reduced with the blow-pipe, and got about two cents (herewith enclosed) in pure gold.

As the fragment prospected weighed rather less than an ounce, this would give about $500 to the ton. We were eminently well satisfied. Therefore, hold on to the "Mountain House," for it is a "big thing." Touch it lightly, as far as money is concerned, though, for it is well to reserve the code of justice in the matter of quartz ledges--that is, consider them all (and their owners) guilty (of "shenanigan") until they are proved innocent.

P. S.--Monday--Ratio and I have bought one-half of a segregated claim in the original "Flyaway," for $100--$50 down. We haven't a cent in the house. We two will work the ledge, and have full control, and pay all expenses. If you can spare $100 conveniently, let me have it--or $50, anyhow, considering that I own one fourth of this, it is of course more valuable than one 1/7 of the "Mountain House," although not so rich ....

There is too much of a sameness in the letters of this period to use all of them. There are always new claims, and work done, apparently without system or continuance, hoping to uncover sudden boundless affluence.

In the next letter and the one following it we get a hint of an episode, or rather of two incidents which he combined into an episode in Roughing It. The story as told in that book is an account of what might have happened, rather than history. There was never really any money in the "blind lead" of the Wide West claim, except that which was sunk in it by unfortunate investors. Only extracts from these letters are given. The other portions are irrelevant and of slight value.

Extract from a letter to Orion Clemens, in Carson City:

1862. Two or three of the old "Salina" company entered our hole on the Monitor yesterday morning, before our men got there, and took possession, armed with revolvers. And according to the d---d laws of this forever d---d country, nothing but the District Court (and there ain't any) can touch the matter, unless it assumes the shape of an infernal humbug which they call "forcible entry and detainer," and in order to bring that about, you must compel the jumpers to use personal violence toward you! We went up and demanded possession, and they refused. Said they were in the hole, armed and meant to die for it, if necessary.

I got in with them, and again demanded possession. They said I might stay in it as long as I pleased, and work but they would do the same. I asked one of our company to take my place in the hole, while I went to consult a lawyer. He did so. The lawyer said it was no go. They must offer some "force."

Our boys will try to be there first in the morning--in which case they may get possession and keep it. Now you understand the shooting scrape in which Gebhart was killed the other day. The Clemens Company--all of us--hate to resort to arms in this matter, and it will not be done until it becomes a forced hand--but I think that will be the end of it, never- the-less.

The mine relocated in this letter was not the "Wide West," but it furnished the proper incident. The only mention of the "Wide West" is found in a letter written in July.

Extract from a letter to Orion Clemens, in Carson City: 1862 If I do not forget it, I will send you, per next mail, a pinch of decom. (decomposed rock) which I pinched with thumb and finger from "Wide West" ledge awhile ago. Raish and I have secured 200 out of a 400 ft. in it, which perhaps (the ledge, I mean) is a spur from the W. W.--our shaft is about 100 ft. from the W. W. shaft. In order to get in, we agreed to sink 30 ft. We have sub-let to another man for 50 ft., and we pay for powder and sharpening tools.

The "Wide West" claim was forfeited, but there is no evidence to show that Clemens and his partners were ever, except in fiction, "millionaires for ten days." The background, the local color, and the possibilities are all real enough, but Mark Twain's aim in this, as in most of his other reminiscent writing, was to arrange and adapt his facts to the needs of a good story.

The letters of this summer (1862) most of them bear evidence of waning confidence in mining as a source of fortune--the miner has now little faith in his own judgment, and none at all in that of his brother, who was without practical experience.

Letter to Orion Clemens, in Carson City:

ESMERALDA, Thursday. MY DEAR BRO.,--Yours of the 17th, per express, just received. Part of it pleased me exceedingly, and part of it didn't. Concerning the letter, for instance: You have PROMISED me that you would leave all mining matters, and everything involving an outlay of money, in my hands.

Sending a man fooling around the country after ledges, for God's sake! when there are hundreds of feet of them under my nose here, begging for owners, free of charge. I don't want any more feet, and I won't touch another foot--so you see, Orion, as far as any ledges of Perry's are concerned, (or any other except what I examine first with my own eyes,) I freely yield my right to share ownership with you.

The balance of your letter, I say, pleases me exceedingly. Especially that about the H. and D. being worth from $30 to $50 in Cal. It pleases me because, if the ledges prove to be worthless, it will be a pleasant reflection to know that others were beaten worse than ourselves. Raish sold a man 30 feet, yesterday, at $20 a foot, although I was present at the sale, and told the man the ground wasn't worth a d---n. He said he had been hankering after a few feet in the H. and D. for a long time, and he had got them at last, and he couldn't help thinking he had secured a good thing. We went and looked at the ledges, and both of them acknowledged that there was nothing in them but good "indications." Yet the owners in the H. and D. will part with anything else sooner than with feet in these ledges. Well, the work goes slowly--very slowly on, in the tunnel, and we'll strike it some day. But--if we "strike it rich,"--I've lost my guess, that's all. I expect that the way it got so high in Cal. was, that Raish's brother, over there was offered $750.00 for 20 feet of it, and he refused .....

Couldn't go on the hill today. It snowed. It always snows here, I expect.

Don't you suppose they have pretty much quit writing, at home?

When you receive your next 1/4 yr's salary, don't send any of it here until after you have told me you have got it. Remember this. I am afraid of that H. and D.

They have struck the ledge in the Live Yankee tunnel, and I told the President, Mr. Allen, that it wasn't as good as the croppings. He said that was true enough, but they would hang to it until it did prove rich. He is much of a gentleman, that man Allen.

And ask Gaslerie why the devil he don't send along my commission as Deputy Sheriff. The fact of my being in California, and out of his country, wouldn't amount to a d---n with me, in the performance of my official duties.

I have nothing to report, at present, except that I shall find out all I want to know about this locality before I leave it.

How do the Records pay? Yr. Bro. SAM.

In one of the foregoing letters--the one dated May 11 there is a reference to the writer's "Enterprise Letters." Sometimes, during idle days in the camp, the miner had followed old literary impulses and written an occasional burlesque sketch, which he had signed "Josh," and sent to the Territorial Enterprise, at Virginia City.-- [One contribution was sent to a Keokuk paper, The Gate City, and a letter written by Mrs. Jane Clemens at the time would indicate that Mark Twain's mother did not always approve of her son's literary efforts. She hopes that he will do better, and some time write something "that his kin will be proud of."]--The rough, vigorous humor of these had attracted some attention, and Orion, pleased with any measure of success that might come to his brother, had allowed the authorship of them to become known. When, in July, the financial situation became desperate, the Esmeralda miner was moved to turn to literature for relief. But we will let him present the situation himself.

To Orion Clemens, in Carson City:

ESMERALDA, July 23d, 1862. MY DEAR BRO.,--No, I don't own a foot in the "Johnson" ledge--I will tell the story some day in a more intelligible manner than Tom has told it. You needn't take the trouble to deny Tom's version, though. I own 25 feet (1-16) of the 1st east ex. on it--and Johnson himself has contracted to find the ledge for 100 feet. Contract signed yesterday. But as the ledge will be difficult to find he is allowed six months to find it in. An eighteenth of the Ophir was a fortune to John D. Winters--and the Ophir can't beat the Johnson any.....

My debts are greater than I thought for; I bought $25 worth of clothing, and sent $25 to Higbie, in the cement diggings. I owe about $45 or $50, and have got about $45 in my pocket. But how in the h--l I am going to live on something over $100 until October or November, is singular. The fact is, I must have something to do, and that shortly, too.....

Now write to the Sacramento Union folks, or to Marsh, and tell them I'll write as many letters a week as they want, for $10 a week--my board must be paid. Tell them I have corresponded with the N. Orleans Crescent, and other papers--and the Enterprise. California is full of people who have interests here, and it's d---d seldom they hear from this country. I can't write a specimen letter--now, at any rate--I'd rather undertake to write a Greek poem. Tell 'em the mail and express leave three times a week, and it costs from 25 to 50 cents to send letters by the blasted express. If they want letters from here, who'll run from morning till night collecting materials cheaper. I'll write a short letter twice a week, for the present, for the "Age," for $5 per week. Now it has been a long time since I couldn't make my own living, and it shall be a long time before I loaf another year.....

If I get the other 25 feet in the Johnson ex., I shan't care a d---n. I'll be willing to curse awhile and wait. And if I can't move the bowels of those hills this fall, I will come up and clerk for you until I get money enough to go over the mountains for the winter. Yr. Bro. SAM.

The Territorial Enterprise at Virginia City was at this time owned by Joseph T. Goodman, who had bought it on the eve of the great Comstock silver-mining boom, and from a struggling, starving sheet had converted it into one of the most important--certainly the most picturesque--papers on the coast. The sketches which the Esmeralda miner had written over the name of "Josh" fitted into it exactly, and when a young man named Barstow, in the business office, urged Goodman to invite "Josh" to join their staff, the Enterprise owner readily fell in with the idea. Among a lot of mining matters of no special interest, Clemens, July 3oth, wrote his brother: "Barstow has offered me the post as local reporter for the Enterprise at $25 a week, and I have written him that I will let him know next mail, if possible."

In Roughing It we are told that the miner eagerly accepted the proposition to come to Virginia City, but the letters tell a different story. Mark Twain was never one to abandon any undertaking easily. His unwillingness to surrender in a lost cause would cost him more than one fortune in the years to come. A week following the date of the foregoing he was still undecided.

To Orion Clemens, in Carson City:

ESMERALDA, Aug. 7, 1862. MY DEAR BRO,--Barstow wrote that if I wanted the place I could have it. I wrote him that I guessed I would take it, and asked him how long before I must come up there. I have not heard from him since.

Now, I shall leave at mid-night tonight, alone and on foot for a walk of 60 or 70 miles through a totally uninhabited country, and it is barely possible that mail facilities may prove infernally "slow" during the few weeks I expect to spend out there. But do you write Barstow that I have left here for a week or so, and in case he should want me he must write me here, or let me know through you.

The Contractors say they will strike the Fresno next week. After fooling with those assayers a week, they concluded not to buy "Mr. Flower" at $50, although they would have given five times the sum for it four months ago. So I have made out a deed for one half of all Johnny's ground and acknowledged and left in judge F. K. Becktel's hands, and if judge Turner wants it he must write to Becktel and pay him his Notary fee of $1.50. I would have paid that fee myself, but I want money now as I leave town tonight. However, if you think it isn't right, you can pay the fee to judge Turner yourself.

Hang to your money now. I may want some when I get back.....

See that you keep out of debt-to anybody. Bully for B.! Write him that I would write him myself, but I am to take a walk tonight and haven't time. Tell him to bring his family out with him. He can rely upon what I say--and I say the land has lost its ancient desolate appearance; the rose and the oleander have taken the place of the departed sage-bush; a rich black loam, garnished with moss, and flowers, and the greenest of grass, smiles to Heaven from the vanished sand-plains; the "endless snows" have all disappeared, and in their stead, or to repay us for their loss, the mountains rear their billowy heads aloft, crowned with a fadeless and eternal verdure; birds, and fountains, and trees-tropical bees--everywhere!--and the poet dreamt of Nevada when he wrote:

"and Sharon waves, in solemn praise, Her silent groves of palm."

and today the royal Raven listens in a dreamy stupor to the songs of the thrush and the nightingale and the canary--and shudders when the gaudy-- plumaged birds of the distant South sweep by him to the orange groves of Carson. Tell him he wouldn't recognize the d--d country. He should bring his family by all means.

I intended to write home, but I haven't done it. Yr. Bro. SAM.

In this letter we realize that he had gone into the wilderness to reflect--to get a perspective on the situation. He was a great walker in those days, and sometimes with Higbie, sometimes alone, made long excursions. One such is recorded in Roughing It, the trip to Mono Lake. We have no means of knowing where his seventy-mile tour led him now, but it is clear that he still had not reached a decision on his return. Indeed, we gather that he is inclined to keep up the battle among the barren Esmeralda hills.

Last mining letter; written to Mrs. Moffett, in St. Louis:

ESMERALDA, CAL., Aug. 15, 1862. MY DEAR SISTER,-I mailed a letter to you and Ma this morning, but since then I have received yours to Orion and me. Therefore, I must answer right away, else I may leave town without doing it at all. What in thunder are pilot's wages to me? which question, I beg humbly to observe, is of a general nature, and not discharged particularly at you. But it is singular, isn't it, that such a matter should interest Orion, when it is of no earthly consequence to me? I never have once thought of returning home to go on the river again, and I never expect to do any more piloting at any price. My livelihood must be made in this country--and if I have to wait longer than I expected, let it be so--I have no fear of failure. You know I have extravagant hopes, for Orion tells you everything which he ought to keep to himself--but it's his nature to do that sort of thing, and I let him alone. I did think for awhile of going home this fall--but when I found that that was and had been the cherished intention and the darling aspiration every year, of these old care-worn Californians for twelve weary years--I felt a little uncomfortable, but I stole a march on Disappointment and said I would not go home this fall. I will spend the winter in San Francisco, if possible. Do not tell any one that I had any idea of piloting again at present--for it is all a mistake. This country suits me, and--it shall suit me, whether or no....

Dan Twing and I and Dan's dog, "cabin" together--and will continue to do so for awhile--until I leave for--

The mansion is 10x12, with a "domestic" roof. Yesterday it rained--the first shower for five months. "Domestic," it appears to me, is not water-proof. We went outside to keep from getting wet. Dan makes the bed when it is his turn to do it--and when it is my turn, I don't, you know. The dog is not a good hunter, and he isn't worth shucks to watch-- but he scratches up the dirt floor of the cabin, and catches flies, and makes himself generally useful in the way of washing dishes. Dan gets up first in the morning and makes a fire--and I get up last and sit by it, while he cooks breakfast. We have a cold lunch at noon, and I cook supper--very much against my will. However, one must have one good meal a day, and if I were to live on Dan's abominable cookery, I should lose my appetite, you know. Dan attended Dr. Chorpenning's funeral yesterday, and he felt as though he ought to wear a white shirt--and we had a jolly good time finding such an article. We turned over all our traps, and he found one at last--but I shall always think it was suffering from yellow fever. He also found an old black coat, greasy, and wrinkled to that degree that it appeared to have been quilted at some time or other. In this gorgeous costume he attended the funeral. And when he returned, his own dog drove him away from the cabin, not recognizing him. This is true.

You would not like to live in a country where flour was $40 a barrel? Very well; then, I suppose you would not like to live here, where flour was $100 a barrel when I first came here. And shortly afterwards, it couldn't be had at any price--and for one month the people lived on barley, beans and beef--and nothing beside. Oh, no--we didn't luxuriate then! Perhaps not. But we said wise and severe things about the vanity and wickedness of high living. We preached our doctrine and practised it. Which course I respectfully recommend to the clergymen of St. Louis.

Where is Beack Jolly?--[a pilot]--and Bixby? Your Brother SAM.

IV

LETTERS 1863-64. "MARK TWAIN." COMSTOCK JOURNALISM. ARTEMUS WARD

There is a long hiatus in the correspondence here. For a space of many months there is but one letter to continue the story. Others were written, of course, but for some reason they have not survived. It was about the end of August (1862) when the miner finally abandoned the struggle, and with his pack on his shoulders walked the one and thirty miles over the mountains to Virginia City, arriving dusty, lame, and travel-stained to claim at last his rightful inheritance. At the Enterprise office he was welcomed, and in a brief time entered into his own. Goodman, the proprietor, himself a man of great ability, had surrounded himself with a group of gay-hearted fellows, whose fresh, wild way of writing delighted the Comstock pioneers far more than any sober presentation of mere news. Samuel Clemens fitted exactly into this group. By the end of the year he had become a leader of it. When he asked to be allowed to report the coming Carson legislature, Goodman consented, realizing that while Clemens knew nothing of parliamentary procedure, he would at least make the letters picturesque.

It was in the midst of this work that he adopted the name which he was to make famous throughout the world. The story of its adoption has been fully told elsewhere and need not be repeated here.--[See Mark Twain: A Biography, by the same author;

Chapter XL

.]

"Mark Twain" was first signed to a Carson letter, February 2, 1863, and from that time was attached to all of Samuel Clemens's work. The letters had already been widely copied, and the name now which gave them personality quickly obtained vogue. It was attached to himself as well as to the letters; heretofore he had been called Sam or Clemens, now he became almost universally Mark Twain and Mark.

This early period of Mark Twain's journalism is full of delicious history, but we are permitted here to retell only such of it as will supply connection to the infrequent letters. He wrote home briefly in February, but the letter contained nothing worth preserving. Then two months later he gives us at least a hint of his employment.

To Mrs. Jane Clemens and Mrs. Moffett, in St. Louis:

VIRGINIA, April 11, 1863. MY DEAR MOTHER AND SISTER,--It is very late at night, and I am writing in my room, which is not quite as large or as nice as the one I had at home. My board, washing and lodging cost me seventy-five dollars a month.

I have just received your letter, Ma, from Carson--the one in which you doubt my veracity about the statements I made in a letter to you. That's right. I don't recollect what the statements were, but I suppose they were mining statistics. I have just finished writing up my report for the morning paper, and giving the Unreliable a column of advice about how to conduct himself in church, and now I will tell you a few more lies, while my hand is in. For instance, some of the boys made me a present of fifty feet in the East India G. and S. M. Company ten days ago. I was offered ninety-five dollars a foot for it, yesterday, in gold. I refused it--not because I think the claim is worth a cent for I don't but because I had a curiosity to see how high it would go, before people find out how worthless it is. Besides, what if one mining claim does fool me? I have got plenty more. I am not in a particular hurry to get rich. I suppose I couldn't well help getting rich here some time or other, whether I wanted to or not. You folks do not believe in Nevada, and I am glad you don't. Just keep on thinking so.

I was at the Gould and Curry mine, the other day, and they had two or three tons of choice rock piled up, which was valued at $20,000 a ton. I gathered up a hat-full of chunks, on account of their beauty as specimens--they don't let everybody supply themselves so liberally. I send Mr. Moffett a little specimen of it for his cabinet. If you don't know what the white stuff on it is, I must inform you that it is purer silver than the minted coin. There is about as much gold in it as there is silver, but it is not visible. I will explain to you some day how to detect it.

Pamela, you wouldn't do for a local reporter--because you don't appreciate the interest that attaches to names. An item is of no use unless it speaks of some person, and not then, unless that person's name is distinctly mentioned. The most interesting letter one can write, to an absent friend, is one that treats of persons he has been acquainted with rather than the public events of the day. Now you speak of a young lady who wrote to Hollie Benson that she had seen me; and you didn't mention her name. It was just a mere chance that I ever guessed who she was--but I did, finally, though I don't remember her name, now. I was introduced to her in San Francisco by Hon. A. B. Paul, and saw her afterwards in Gold Hill. They were a very pleasant lot of girls--she and her sisters.

P. S. I have just heard five pistol shots down street--as such things are in my line, I will go and see about it.

P. S. No 2--5 A.M.--The pistol did its work well--one man--a Jackson County Missourian, shot two of my friends, (police officers,) through the heart--both died within three minutes. Murderer's name is John Campbell.

The "Unreliable" of this letter was a rival reporter on whom Mark Twain had conferred this name during the legislative session. His real name was Rice, and he had undertaken to criticize Clemens's reports. The brisk reply that Rice's letters concealed with a show of parliamentary knowledge a "festering mass of misstatements the author of whom should be properly termed the 'Unreliable," fixed that name upon him for life. This burlesque warfare delighted the frontier and it did not interfere with friendship. Clemens and Rice were constant associates, though continually firing squibs at each other in their respective papers--a form of personal journalism much in vogue on the Comstock.

In the next letter we find these two journalistic "blades" enjoying themselves together in the coast metropolis. This letter is labeled "No. 2," meaning, probably, the second from San Francisco, but No. 1 has disappeared, and even No, 2 is incomplete.

To Mrs. Jane Clemens and Mrs. Moffett, in St. Louis:

No. 2--($20.00 Enclosed) LICK HOUSE, S. F., June 1, '63. MY DEAR MOTHER AND SISTER,--The Unreliable and myself are still here, and still enjoying ourselves. I suppose I know at least a thousand people here--a, great many of them citizens of San Francisco, but the majority belonging in Washoe--and when I go down Montgomery street, shaking hands with Tom, Dick and Harry, it is just like being in Main street in Hannibal and meeting the old familiar faces. I do hate to go back to Washoe. We fag ourselves completely out every day, and go to sleep without rocking, every night. We dine out and we lunch out, and we eat, drink and are happy--as it were. After breakfast, I don't often see the hotel again until midnight--or after. I am going to the Dickens mighty fast. I know a regular village of families here in the house, but I never have time to call on them. Thunder! we'll know a little more about this town, before we leave, than some of the people who live in it. We take trips across the Bay to Oakland, and down to San Leandro, and Alameda, and those places; and we go out to the Willows, and Hayes Park, and Fort Point, and up to Benicia; and yesterday we were invited out on a yachting excursion, and had a sail in the fastest yacht on the Pacific Coast. Rice says: "Oh, no--we are not having any fun, Mark--Oh, no, I reckon not--it's somebody else--it's probably the 'gentleman in the wagon'!" (popular slang phrase.) When I invite Rice to the Lick House to dinner, the proprietors send us champagne and claret, and then we do put on the most disgusting airs. Rice says our calibre is too light--we can't stand it to be noticed!

I rode down with a gentleman to the Ocean House, the other day, to see the sea horses, and also to listen to the roar of the surf, and watch the ships drifting about, here, and there, and far away at sea. When I stood on the beach and let the surf wet my feet, I recollected doing the same thing on the shores of the Atlantic--and then I had a proper appreciation of the vastness of this country--for I had traveled from ocean to ocean across it. (Remainder missing.)

Not far from Virginia City there are some warm springs that constantly send up jets of steam through fissures in the mountainside. The place was a health resort, and Clemens, always subject to bronchial colds, now and again retired there for a cure.

A letter written in the late summer--a gay, youthful document-- belongs to one of these periods of convalescence.

To Mrs. Jane Clemens and Mrs. Moffett, in St. Louis:

No. 12--$20 enclosed. STEAMBOAT SPRINGS, August 19, '63. MY DEAR MOTHER AND SISTER,--Ma, you have given my vanity a deadly thrust. Behold, I am prone to boast of having the widest reputation, as a local editor, of any man on the Pacific coast, and you gravely come forward and tell me "if I work hard and attend closely to my business, I may aspire to a place on a big San Francisco daily, some day." There's a comment on human vanity for you! Why, blast it, I was under the impression that I could get such a situation as that any time I asked for it. But I don't want it. No paper in the United States can afford to pay me what my place on the "Enterprise" is worth. If I were not naturally a lazy, idle, good-for-nothing vagabond, I could make it pay me $20,000 a year. But I don't suppose I shall ever be any account. I lead an easy life, though, and I don't care a cent whether school keeps or not. Everybody knows me, and I fare like a prince wherever I go, be it on this side of the mountains or the other. And I am proud to say I am the most conceited ass in the Territory.

You think that picture looks old? Well, I can't help it--in reality I am not as old as I was when I was eighteen.

I took a desperate cold more than a week ago, and I seduced Wilson (a Missouri boy, reporter of the Daily Union,) from his labors, and we went over to Lake Bigler. But I failed to cure my cold. I found the "Lake House" crowded with the wealth and fashion of Virginia, and I could not resist the temptation to take a hand in all the fun going. Those Virginians--men and women both--are a stirring set, and I found if I went with them on all their eternal excursions, I should bring the consumption home with me--so I left, day before yesterday, and came back into the Territory again. A lot of them had purchased a site for a town on the Lake shore, and they gave me a lot. When you come out, I'll build you a house on it. The Lake seems more supernaturally beautiful now, than ever. It is the masterpiece of the Creation.

The hotel here at the Springs is not so much crowded as usual, and I am having a very comfortable time of it. The hot, white steam puffs up out of fissures in the earth like the jets that come from a steam-boat's 'scape pipes, and it makes a boiling, surging noise like a steam-boat, too--hence the name. We put eggs in a handkerchief and dip them in the springs--they "soft boil" in 2 Minutes, and boil as hard as a rock in 4 minutes. These fissures extend more than a quarter of a mile, and the long line of steam columns looks very pretty. A large bath house is built over one of the springs, and we go in it and steam ourselves as long as we can stand it, and then come out and take a cold shower bath. You get baths, board and lodging, all for $25 a week--cheaper than living in Virginia without baths..... Yrs aft MARK.

It was now the autumn of 1863. Mark Twain was twenty-eight years old. On the Coast he had established a reputation as a gaily original newspaper writer. Thus far, however, he had absolutely no literary standing, nor is there any evidence that he had literary ambitions; his work was unformed, uncultivated--all of which seems strange, now, when we realize that somewhere behind lay the substance of immortality. Rudyard Kipling at twenty-eight had done his greatest work.

Even Joseph Goodman, who had a fine literary perception and a deep knowledge of men, intimately associated with Mark Twain as he was, received at this time no hint of his greater powers. Another man on the staff of the Enterprise, William Wright, who called himself "Dan de Quille," a graceful humorist, gave far more promise, Goodman thought, of future distinction.

It was Artemus Ward who first suspected the value of Mark Twain's gifts, and urged him to some more important use of them. Artemus in the course of a transcontinental lecture tour, stopped in Virginia City, and naturally found congenial society on the Enterprise staff. He had intended remaining but a few days, but lingered three weeks, a period of continuous celebration, closing only with the holiday season. During one night of final festivities, Ward slipped away and gave a performance on his own account. His letter to Mark Twain, from Austin, Nevada, written a day or two later, is most characteristic.

Artemus Ward's letter to Mark Twain:

AUSTIN, Jan. 1, '64. MY DEAREST LOVE,--I arrived here yesterday a.m. at 2 o'clock. It is a wild, untamable place, full of lionhearted boys. I speak tonight. See small bills.

Why did you not go with me and save me that night?--I mean the night I left you after that dinner party. I went and got drunker, beating, I may say, Alexander the Great, in his most drinkinist days, and I blackened my face at the Melodeon, and made a gibbering, idiotic speech. God-dam it! I suppose the Union will have it. But let it go. I shall always remember Virginia as a bright spot in my existence, as all others must or rather cannot be, as it were.

Love to Jo. Goodman and Dan. I shall write soon, a powerfully convincing note to my friends of "The Mercury." Your notice, by the way, did much good here, as it doubtlessly will elsewhere. The miscreants of the Union will be batted in the snout if they ever dare pollute this rapidly rising city with their loathsome presence.

Some of the finest intellects in the world have been blunted by liquor.

Do not, sir--do not flatter yourself that you are the only chastely- humorous writer onto the Pacific slopes.

Good-bye, old boy--and God bless you! The matter of which I spoke to you so earnestly shall be just as earnestly attended to--and again with very many warm regards for Jo. and Dan., and regards to many of the good friends we met. I am Faithfully, gratefully yours, ARTEMUS WARD.

The Union which Ward mentions was the rival Virginia. City paper; the Mercury was the New York Sunday Mercury, to which he had urged Mark Twain to contribute. Ward wrote a second letter, after a siege of illness at Salt Lake City. He was a frail creature, and three years later, in London, died of consumption. His genius and encouragement undoubtedly exerted an influence upon Mark Twain. Ward's second letter here follows.

Artemus Ward to S. L. Clemens:

SALT LAKE CITY, Jan. 21, '64. MY DEAR MARK,--I have been dangerously ill for the past two weeks here, of congestive fever. Very grave fears were for a time entertained of my recovery, but happily the malady is gone, though leaving me very, very weak. I hope to be able to resume my journey in a week or so. I think I shall speak in the Theater here, which is one of the finest establishments of the kind in America.

The Saints have been wonderfully kind to me, I could not have been better or more tenderly nursed at home--God bless them!

I am still exceedingly weak--can't write any more. Love to Jo and Dan, and all the rest. Write me at St. Louis. Always yours, ARTEMUS WARD.

If one could only have Mark Twain's letters in reply to these! but they have vanished and are probably long since dust. A letter which he wrote to his mother assures us that he undertook to follow Ward's advice. He was not ready, however, for serious literary effort. The article, sent to the Mercury, was distinctly of the Comstock variety; it was accepted, but it apparently made no impression, and he did not follow it up.

For one thing, he was just then too busy reporting the Legislature at Carson City and responding to social demands. From having been a scarcely considered unit during the early days of his arrival in Carson Mark Twain had attained a high degree of importance in the little Nevada capital.

In the Legislature he was a power; as correspondent for the Enterprise he was feared and respected as well as admired. His humor, his satire, and his fearlessness were dreaded weapons.

Also, he was of extraordinary popularity. Orion's wife, with her little daughter, Jennie, had come out from the States. The Governor of Nevada had no household in Carson City, and was generally absent. Orion Clemens reigned in his stead, and indeed was usually addressed as "Governor" Clemens. His home became the social center of the capital, and his brilliant brother its chief ornament. From the roughest of miners of a year before he had become, once more, almost a dandy in dress, and no occasion was complete without him. When the two Houses of the Legislature assembled, in January, 1864, a burlesque Third House was organized and proposed to hold a session, as a church benefit. After very brief consideration it was decided to select Mark Twain to preside at this Third House assembly under the title of "Governor," and a letter of invitation was addressed to him. His reply to it follows:

To S. Pixley and G. A. Sears, Trustees:

CARSON CITY, January 23, 1864. GENTLEMEN, Certainly. If the public can find anything in a grave state paper worth paying a dollar for, I am willing that they should pay that amount, or any other; and although I am not a very dusty Christian myself, I take an absorbing interest in religious affairs, and would willingly inflict my annual message upon the Church itself if it might derive benefit thereby. You can charge what you please; I promise the public no amusement, but I do promise a reasonable amount of instruction. I am responsible to the Third House only, and I hope to be permitted to make it exceedingly warm for that body, without caring whether the sympathies of the public and the Church be enlisted in their favor, and against myself, or not. Respectfully, MARK TWAIN.

There is a quality in this letter more suggestive of the later Mark Twain than anything that has preceded it. His Third House address, unfortunately, has not been preserved, but those who heard it regarded it as a classic. It probably abounded in humor of the frontier sort-unsparing ridicule of the Governor, the Legislature, and individual citizens. It was all taken in good part, of course, and as a recognition of his success he received a gold watch, with the case properly inscribed to "The Governor of the Third House." This was really his first public appearance in a field in which he was destined to achieve very great fame.

V

LETTERS 1864-66. SAN FRANCISCO AND HAWAII

Life on the Comstock came to an end for Mark Twain in May, 1864. It was the time of The Flour Sack Sanitary Fund, the story of which he has told in Roughing It. He does not, however, refer to the troubles which this special fund brought upon himself. Coming into the Enterprise office one night, after a gay day of "Fund" celebration, Clemens wrote, for next day's paper, a paragraph intended to be merely playful, but which proved highly offending to certain ladies concerned with the flour-sack enterprise. No files of the paper exist today, so we cannot judge of the quality of humor that stirred up trouble.

The trouble, however, was genuine enough. Virginia's rival paper seized upon the chance to humiliate its enemy, and presently words were passed back and forth until nothing was left to write but a challenge. The story of this duel, which did not come off, has been quite fully told elsewhere, both by Mark Twain and the present writer; but the following letter--a revelation of his inner feelings in the matter of his offense--has never before been published.

To Mrs. Cutler, in Carson City:

VIRGINIA, May 23rd, 1864. MRS. W. K. CUTLER:

MADAM,--I address a lady in every sense of the term. Mrs. Clemens has informed me of everything that has occurred in Carson in connection with that unfortunate item of mine about the Sanitary Funds accruing from the ball, and from what I can understand, you are almost the only lady in your city who has understood the circumstances under which my fault was committed, or who has shown any disposition to be lenient with me. Had the note of the ladies been properly worded, I would have published an ample apology instantly--and possibly I might even have done so anyhow, had that note arrived at any other time--but it came at a moment when I was in the midst of what ought to have been a deadly quarrel with the publishers of the Union, and I could not come out and make public apologies to any one at such a time. It is bad policy to do it even now (as challenges have already passed between myself and a proprietor of the Union, and the matter is still in abeyance,) but I suppose I had better say a word or two to show the ladies that I did not wilfully and maliciously do them a wrong.

But my chief object, Mrs. Cutler, in writing you this note (and you will pardon the liberty I have taken,) was to thank you very kindly and sincerely for the consideration you have shown me in this matter, and for your continued friendship for Mollie while others are disposed to withdraw theirs on account of a fault for which I alone am responsible. Very truly yours, SAM. L. CLEMENS.

The matter did not end with the failure of the duel. A very strict law had just been passed, making it a felony even to send or accept a challenge. Clemens, on the whole, rather tired of Virginia City and Carson, thought it a good time to go across the mountains to San Francisco. With Steve Gillis, a printer, of whom he was very fond-- an inveterate joker, who had been more than half responsible for the proposed duel, and was to have served as his second--he took the stage one morning, and in due time was in the California metropolis, at work on the Morning Call.

Clemens had been several times in San Francisco, and loved the place. We have no letter of that summer, the first being dated several months after his arrival. He was still working on the Call when it was written, and contributing literary articles to the Californian, of which Bret Harte, unknown to fame, was editor. Harte had his office just above the rooms of the Call, and he and

Clemens were good friends. San Francisco had a real literary group that, for a time at least, centered around the offices of the Golden Era. In a letter that follows Clemens would seem to have scorned this publication, but he was a frequent contributor to it at one period. Joaquin Miller was of this band of literary pioneers; also Prentice Mulford, Charles Warren Stoddard, Fitzhugh Ludlow, and Orpheus C. Kerr.

To Mrs. Jane Clemens and Mrs. Moffett, in St. Louis:

Sept. 25, 1864. MY DEAR MOTHER AND SISTER,--You can see by my picture that this superb climate agrees with me. And it ought, after living where I was never out of sight of snow peaks twenty-four hours during three years. Here we have neither snow nor cold weather; fires are never lighted, and yet summer clothes are never worn--you wear spring clothing the year round.

Steve Gillis, who has been my comrade for two years, and who came down here with me, is to be married, in a week or two, to a very pretty girl worth $130,000 in her own right--and then I shall be alone again, until they build a house, which they will do shortly.

We have been here only four months, yet we have changed our lodgings five times, and our hotel twice. We are very comfortably fixed where we are, now, and have no fault to find with the rooms or with the people--we are the only lodgers in a well-to-do private family, with one grown daughter and a piano in the parlor adjoining our room. But I need a change, and must move again. I have taken rooms further down the street. I shall stay in this little quiet street, because it is full of gardens and shrubbery, and there are none but dwelling houses in it.

I am taking life easy, now, and I mean to keep it up for awhile. I don't work at night any more. I told the "Call" folks to pay me $25 a week and let me work only in daylight. So I get up at ten every morning, and quit work at five or six in the afternoon. You ask if I work for greenbacks? Hardly. What do you suppose I could do with greenbacks here?

I have engaged to write for the new literary paper--the "Californian"-- same pay I used to receive on the "Golden Era"--one article a week, fifty dollars a month. I quit the "Era," long ago. It wasn't high-toned enough. The "Californian" circulates among the highest class of the community, and is the best weekly literary paper in the United States --and I suppose I ought to know.

I work as I always did--by fits and starts. I wrote two articles last night for the Californian, so that lets me out for two weeks. That would be about seventy-five dollars, in greenbacks, wouldn't it?

Been down to San Jose (generally pronounced Sannozay--emphasis on last syllable)--today fifty miles from here, by railroad. Town of 6,000 inhabitants, buried in flowers and shrubbery. The climate is finer than ours here, because it is not so close to the ocean, and is protected from the winds by the coast range.

I had an invitation today, to go down on an excursion to San Luis Obispo, and from thence to the city of Mexico, to be gone six or eight weeks, or possibly longer, but I could not accept, on account of my contract to act as chief mourner or groomsman at Steve's wedding.

I have triumphed. They refused me and other reporters some information at a branch of the Coroner's office--Massey's undertaker establishment, a few weeks ago. I published the wickedest article on them I ever wrote in my life, and you can rest assured we got all the information we wanted after that.

By the new census, San Francisco has a population of 130,000. They don't count the hordes of Chinamen. Yrs aftly, SAM.

I send a picture for Annie, and one for Aunt Ella--that is, if she will have it.

Relations with the Call ceased before the end of the year, though not in the manner described in Roughing It. Mark Twain loved to make fiction of his mishaps, and to show himself always in a bad light. As a matter of fact, he left the Call with great willingness, and began immediately contributing a daily letter to the Enterprise, which brought him a satisfactory financial return.

In the biographical sketch with which this volume opens, and more extendedly elsewhere, has been told the story of the trouble growing out of the Enterprise letters, and of Mark Twain's sojourn with James Gillis in the Tuolumne Hills. Also how, in the frowsy hotel at Angel's Camp, he heard the frog anecdote that would become the corner-stone of his fame. There are no letters of this period--only some note-book entries. It is probable that he did not write home, believing, no doubt, that he had very little to say.

For more than a year there is not a line that has survived. Yet it had been an important year; the jumping frog story, published in New York, had been reprinted East and West, and laughed over in at least a million homes. Fame had not come to him, but it was on the way.

Yet his outlook seems not to have been a hopeful one.

To Mrs. Jane Clemens and Mrs. Moffett, in St. Louis:

SAN FRANCISCO, Jan. 20, 1866. MY DEAR MOTHER AND SISTER,--I do not know what to write; my life is so uneventful. I wish I was back there piloting up and down the river again. Verily, all is vanity and little worth--save piloting.

To think that, after writing many an article a man might be excused for thinking tolerably good, those New York people should single out a villainous backwoods sketch to compliment me on! "Jim Smiley and His Jumping Frog"--a squib which would never have been written but to please Artemus Ward, and then it reached New York too late to appear in his book.

But no matter. His book was a wretchedly poor one, generally speaking, and it could be no credit to either of us to appear between its covers.

This paragraph is from the New York correspondence of the San Francisco Alta:

(Clipping pasted in.)

"Mark Twain's story in the Saturday Press of November 18th, called 'Jim Smiley and His Jumping Frog,' has set all New York in a roar, and he may be said to have made his mark. I have been asked fifty times about it and its author, and the papers are copying it far and near. It is voted the best thing of the day. Cannot the Californian afford to keep Mark all to itself? It should not let him scintillate so widely without first being filtered through the California press."

The New York publishing house of Carleton & Co. gave the sketch to the Saturday Press when they found it was too late for the book.

Though I am generally placed at the head of my breed of scribblers in this part of the country, the place properly belongs to Bret Harte, I think, though he denies it, along with the rest. He wants me to club a lot of old sketches together with a lot of his, and publish a book. I wouldn't do it, only he agrees to take all the trouble. But I want to know whether we are going to make anything out of it, first. However, he has written to a New York publisher, and if we are offered a bargain that will pay for a month's labor we will go to work and prepare the volume for the press. Yours affy, SAM.

Bret Harte and Clemens had by this time quit the Californian, expecting to contribute to Eastern periodicals. Clemens, however, was not yet through with Coast journalism. There was much interest just at this time in the Sandwich Islands, and he was selected by the foremost Sacramento paper to spy out the islands and report aspects and conditions there. His letters home were still infrequent, but this was something worth writing.

To Mrs. Jane Clemens and Mrs. Moffett, in St. Louis:

SAN FRANCISCO, March 5th, 1866. MY DEAR MOTHER AND SISTER,--I start to do Sandwich Islands day after tomorrow, (I suppose Annie is geographer enough by this time to find them on the map), in the steamer "Ajax." We shall arrive there in about twelve days. My friends seem determined that I shall not lack acquaintances, for I only decided today to go, and they have already sent me letters of introduction to everybody down there worth knowing. I am to remain there a month and ransack the islands, the great cataracts and the volcanoes completely, and write twenty or thirty letters to the Sacramento Union--for which they pay me as much money as I would get if I staid at home.

If I come back here I expect to start straight across the continent by way of the Columbia river, the Pend d'Oreille Lakes, through Montana and down the Missouri river,--only 200 miles of land travel from San Francisco to New Orleans. Goodbye for the present. Yours, SAM.

His home letters from the islands are numerous enough; everything there being so new and so delightful that he found joy in telling of it; also, he was still young enough to air his triumphs a little, especially when he has dined with the Grand Chamberlain and is going to visit the King!

The languorous life of the islands exactly suited Mask Twain. All his life he remembered them--always planning to return, some day, to stay there until he died. In one of his note-books he wrote: "Went with Mr. Dam to his cool, vine-shaded home; no care-worn or eager, anxious faces in this land of happy contentment. God, what a contrast with California and the Washoe!"

And again:

"Oh, Islands there are on the face of the deep Where the leaves never fade and the skies never weep."

The letters tell the story of his sojourn, which stretched itself into nearly five months.

To Mrs. Jane Clemens and Mrs. Moffett, in St. Louis:

HONOLULU, SANDWICH ISLANDS, April 3, 1866. MY DEAR MOTHER AND SISTER,--I have been here two or three weeks, and like the beautiful tropical climate better and better. I have ridden on horseback all over this island (Oahu) in the meantime, and have visited all the ancient battle-fields and other places of interest. I have got a lot of human bones which I took from one of these battle-fields--I guess I will bring you some of them. I went with the American Minister and took dinner this evening with the King's Grand Chamberlain, who is related to the royal family, and although darker than a mulatto, he has an excellent English education and in manners is an accomplished gentleman. The dinner was as ceremonious as any I ever attended in California--five regular courses, and five kinds of wine and one of brandy. He is to call for me in the morning with his carriage, and we will visit the King at the palace--both are good Masons--the King is a Royal Arch Mason. After dinner tonight they called in the "singing girls," and we had some beautiful music; sung in the native tongue.

The steamer I came here in sails tomorrow, and as soon as she is gone I shall sail for the other islands of the group and visit the great volcano--the grand wonder of the world. Be gone two months. Yrs. SAM.

To Mrs. Jane Clemens and Mrs. Moffett, in St. Louis:

WAILUKU SUGAR PLANTATION, ISLAND OF MAUI, H. I., May 4,1866. MY DEAR MOTHER AND SISTER,--11 O'clock at night.--This is the infernalist darkest country, when the moon don't shine; I stumbled and fell over my horse's lariat a minute ago and hurt my leg, so I must stay here tonight.

I got the same leg hurt last week; I said I hadn't got hold of a spirited horse since I had been on the island, and one of the proprietors loaned me a big vicious colt; he was altogether too spirited; I went to tighten the cinch before mounting him, when he let out with his left leg (?) and kicked me across a ten-acre lot. A native rubbed and doctored me so well that I was able to stand on my feet in half an hour. It was then half after four and I had an appointment to go seven miles and get a girl and take her to a card party at five.

I have been clattering around among the plantations for three weeks, now, and next week I am going to visit the extinct crater of Mount Haleakala-- the largest in the world; it is ten miles to the foot of the mountain; it rises 10,000 feet above the valley; the crater is 29 miles in circumference and 1,000 feet deep. Seen from the summit, the city of St. Louis would look like a picture in the bottom of it.

As soon as I get back from Haleakala (pronounced Hally-ekka-lah) I will sail for Honolulu again and thence to the Island of Hawaii (pronounced Hah-wy-ye,) to see the greatest active volcano in the world--that of Kilauea (pronounced Kee-low-way-ah)--and from thence back to San Francisco--and then, doubtless, to the States. I have been on this trip two months, and it will probably be two more before I get back to California. Yrs affy SAM.

He was having a glorious time--one of the most happy, carefree adventures of his career. No form of travel or undertaking could discountenance Mark Twain at thirty.

To Mrs. Orion Clemens, in Carson City:

HONOLULU, May 22, 1866. MY DEAR SISTER,--I have just got back from a sea voyage-- from the beautiful island of Maui, I have spent five weeks there, riding backwards and forwards among the sugar plantations--looking up the splendid scenery and visiting the lofty crater of Haleakala. It has been a perfect jubilee to me in the way of pleasure.

I have not written a single line, and have not once thought of business, or care or human toil or trouble or sorrow or weariness. Few such months come in a lifetime.

I set sail again, a week hence, for the island of Hawaii, to see the great active volcano of Kilauea. I shall not get back here for four or five weeks, and shall not reach San Francisco before the latter part of July.

So it is no use to wait for me to go home. Go on yourselves.

If I were in the east now, I could stop the publication of a piratical book which has stolen some of my sketches.

It is late-good-bye, Mollie, Yr Bro SAM.

To Mrs. Jane Clemens and Mrs. Moffett, in St. Louis:

HONOLULU, SANDWICH ISLANDS, June 21,1866. MY DEAR MOTHER AND SISTER,--I have just got back from a hard trip through the Island of Hawaii, begun on the 26th of May and finished on the 18th of June--only six or seven days at sea--all the balance horse-back, and the hardest mountain road in the world. I staid at the volcano about a week and witnessed the greatest eruption that has occurred for years. I lived well there. They charge $4 a day for board, and a dollar or two extra for guides and horses. I had a pretty good time. They didn't charge me anything. I have got back sick--went to bed as soon as I arrived here--shall not be strong again for several days yet. I rushed too fast. I ought to have taken five or six weeks on that trip.

A week hence I start for the Island of Kauai, to be gone three weeks and then I go back to California.

The Crown Princess is dead and thousands of natives cry and wail and dance and dance for the dead, around the King's Palace all night and every night. They will keep it up for a month and then she will be buried.

Hon. Anson Burlingame, U. S. Minister to China, and Gen. Van Valkenburgh, Minister to Japan, with their families and suites, have just arrived here en route. They were going to do me the honor to call on me this morning, and that accounts for my being out of bed now. You know what condition my room is always in when you are not around--so I climbed out of bed and dressed and shaved pretty quick and went up to the residence of the American Minister and called on them. Mr. Burlingame told me a good deal about Hon. Jere Clemens and that Virginia Clemens who was wounded in a duel. He was in Congress years with both of them. Mr. B. sent for his son, to introduce him--said he could tell that frog story of mine as well as anybody. I told him I was glad to hear it for I never tried to tell it myself without making a botch of it. At his request I have loaned Mr. Burlingame pretty much everything I ever wrote. I guess he will be an almighty wise man by the time he wades through that lot.

If the New United States Minister to the Sandwich Islands (Hon. Edwin McCook,) were only here now, so that I could get his views on this new condition of Sandwich Island politics, I would sail for California at once. But he will not arrive for two weeks yet and so I am going to spend that interval on the island of Kauai.

I stopped three days with Hon. Mr. Cony, Deputy Marshal of the Kingdom, at Hilo, Hawaii, last week and by a funny circumstance he knew everybody that I ever knew in Hannibal and Palmyra. We used to sit up all night talking and then sleep all day. He lives like a Prince. Confound that Island! I had a streak of fat and a streak of lean all over it--got lost several times and had to sleep in huts with the natives and live like a dog.

Of course I couldn't speak fifty words of the language. Take it altogether, though, it was a mighty hard trip. Yours Affect. SAM.

Burlingame and Van Valkenburgh were on their way to their posts, and their coming to the islands just at this time proved a most important circumstance to Mark Twain. We shall come to this presently, in a summary of the newspaper letters written to the Union. June 27th he wrote to his mother and sister a letter, only a fragment of which survives, in which he tells of the arrival in Honolulu of the survivors of the ship Hornet, burned on the line, and of his securing the first news report of the lost vessel.

Part of a letter to Mrs. Jane Clemens and Mrs. Moffett, in St. Louis:

HONOLULU, June 27, 1866 . . . . with a gill of water a day to each man. I got the whole story from the third mate and two of the sailors. If my account gets to the Sacramento Union first, it will be published first all over the United States, France, England, Russia and Germany--all over the world; I may say. You will see it. Mr. Burlingame went with me all the time, and helped me question the men--throwing away invitations to dinner with the princes and foreign dignitaries, and neglecting all sorts of things to accommodate me. You know how I appreciate that kind of thing--especially from such a man, who is acknowledged to have no superior in the diplomatic circles of the world, and obtained from China concessions in favor of America which were refused to Sir Frederick Bruce and Envoys of France and Russia until procured for them by Burlingame himself--which service was duly acknowledged by those dignitaries. He hunted me up as soon as he came here, and has done me a hundred favors since, and says if I will come to China in the first trip of the great mail steamer next January and make his house in Pekin my home, he will afford me facilities that few men can have there for seeing and learning. He will give me letters to the chiefs of the great Mail Steamship Company which will be of service to me in this matter. I expect to do all this, but I expect to go to the States first--and from China to the Paris World's Fair.

Don't show this letter. Yours affly SAM.

P. S. The crown Princess of this Kingdom will be buried tomorrow with great ceremony--after that I sail in two weeks for California.

This concludes Mark Twain's personal letters from the islands. Of his descriptive news letters there were about twenty, and they were regarded by the readers of the Union as distinctly notable. Re-reading those old letters to-day it is not altogether easy to understand why. They were set in fine nonpareil type, for one thing, which present-day eyes simply refuse at any price, and the reward, by present-day standards, is not especially tempting.

The letters began in the Union with the issue of April the 16th, 1866. The first--of date March 18th--tells of the writer's arrival at Honolulu. The humor in it is not always of a high order; it would hardly pass for humor today at all. That the same man who wrote the Hawaiian letters in 1866 (he was then over thirty years old) could, two years later, have written that marvelous book, the Innocents Abroad, is a phenomenon in literary development.

The Hawaiian letters, however, do show the transition stage between the rough elemental humor of the Comstock and the refined and subtle style which flowered in the Innocents Abroad. Certainly Mark Twain's genius was finding itself, and his association with the refined and cultured personality of Anson Burlingame undoubtedly aided in that discovery. Burlingame pointed out his faults to him, and directed him to a better way. No more than that was needed at such a time to bring about a transformation.

The Sandwich Islands letters, however, must have been precisely adapted to their audience--a little more refined than the log Comstock, a little less subtle than the Atlantic public--and they added materially to his Coast prestige. But let us consider a sample extract from the first Sandwich Islands letter:

Our little band of passengers were as well and thoughtfully cared for by the friends they left weeping upon the wharf, as ever were any similar body of pilgrims. The traveling outfit conferred upon me began with a naval uniform, continued with a case of wine, a small assortment of medicinal liquors and brandy, several boxes of cigars, a bunch of matches, a fine-toothed comb, and a cake of soap, and ended with a pair of socks. (N. B. I gave the soap to Brown, who bit into it, and then. shook his head and said that, as a general thing, he liked to prospect curious, foreign dishes, and find out what they were made of, but he couldn't go that, and threw it overboard.)

It is nearly impossible to imagine humor in this extract, yet it is a fair sample of the entire letter.

He improves in his next, at least, in description, and gives us a picture of the crater. In this letter, also, he writes well and seriously, in a prophetic strain, of the great trade that is to be established between San Francisco and Hawaii, and argues for a line of steamers between the ports, in order that the islands might be populated by Americans, by which course European trade in that direction could be superseded. But the humor in this letter, such as it is, would scarcely provoke a smile to-day.

As the letters continue, he still urges the fostering of the island trade by the United States, finds himself impressed by the work of the missionaries, who have converted cannibals to Christians, and gives picturesque bits of the life and scenery.

Hawaii was then dominated chiefly by French and English; though the American interests were by no means small.

Extract from letter No. 4:

Cap. Fitch said "There's the king. That's him in the buggy. I know him as far as I can see him."

I had never seen a king, and I naturally took out a note-book and put him down: "Tall, slender, dark, full-bearded; green frock-coat, with lapels and collar bordered with gold band an inch wide; plug hat, broad gold band around it; royal costume looks too much like livery; this man is not as fleshy as I thought he was."

I had just got these notes when Cap. Fitch discovered that he'd got hold of the wrong king, or rather, that he'd got hold of the king's driver, or a carriage driver of one of the nobility. The king wasn't present at all. It was a great disappointment to me. I heard afterwards that the comfortable, easy-going king, Kamehameha V., had been seen sitting on a barrel on the wharf, the day before, fishing. But there was no consolation in that. That did not restore me my lost king.

This has something of the flavor of the man we were to know later; the quaint, gentle resignation to disappointment which is one of the finest touches in his humor.

Further on he says: "I had not shaved since I left San Francisco. As soon as I got ashore I hunted up a striped pole, and shortly found one. I always had a yearning to be a king. This may never be, I suppose, but, at any rate, it will always be a satisfaction to me to know that, if I am not a king, I am the next thing to it. I have been shaved by the king's barber."

Honolulu was a place of cats. He saw cats of every shade and variety. He says: "I saw cats--tomcats, Mary-Ann cats, bobtailed cats, blind cats, one-eyed cats, wall-eyed cats, cross-eyed cats, gray cats, black cats, white cats, yellow cats, striped cats, spotted cats, tame cats, wild cats, singed cats, individual cats, groups of cats, platoons of cats, companies of cats, armies of cats, multitudes of cats, millions of cats, and all of them sleek, fat, and lazy, and sound asleep." Which illustrates another characteristic of the humor we were to know later--the humor of grotesque exaggeration, in which he was always strong.

He found the islands during his periods of inaction conducive to indolence. "If I were not so fond of looking into the rich mass of green leaves," he says, "that swathe the stately tamarind right before my door, I would idle less, and write more, I think."

The Union made good use of his letters. Sometimes it printed them on the front page. Evidently they were popular from the beginning. The Union was a fine, handsome paper--beautiful in its minute typography, and in its press-work; more beautiful than most papers of to-day, with their machine-set type, their vulgar illustrations, and their chain-lightning presses. A few more extracts:

"The only cigars here are those trifling, insipid, tasteless, flavorless things they call Manilas--ten for twenty-five cents--and it would take a thousand of them to be worth half the money. After you have smoked about thirty-five dollars' worth of them in the forenoon, you feel nothing but a desperate yearning to go out somewhere and take a smoke."

"Captains and ministers form about half the population. The third fourth is composed of Kanakas and mercantile foreigners and their families. The final fourth is made up of high officers of the Hawaiian government, and there are just about enough cats to go round."

In No. 6, April the 2d, he says: "An excursion to Diamond Head, and the king's cocoanut grove, was planned to-day, at 4.30 P. M., the party to consist of half a dozen gentlemen and three ladies. They all started at the appointed hour except myself. Somebody remarked that it was twenty minutes past five o'clock, and that woke me up. It was a fortunate circumstance that Cap. Phillips was there with his 'turn-out,' as he calls his top buggy that Cap. Cook brought here in 1778, and a horse that was here when Cap. Cook came."

This bit has something the savor of his subsequent work, but, as a rule, the humor compares poorly with that which was to come later.

In No. 7 he speaks of the natives singing American songs--not always to his comfort. "Marching Through Georgia" was one of their favorite airs. He says: "If it had been all the same to Gen. Sherman, I wish he had gone around by the way of the Gulf of Mexico, instead of marching through Georgia."

Letters Nos. 8, 9, and 10 were not of special importance. In No. 10 he gives some advice to San Francisco as to the treatment of whalers. He says:

"If I were going to advise San Francisco as to the best strategy to employ in order to secure the whaling trade, I should say, 'Cripple your facilities for "pulling" sea captains on any pretence that sailors can trump up, and show the whaler a little more consideration when he is in port.'"

In No. 11, May 24th, he tells of a trip to the Kalehi Valley, and through historic points. At one place he looked from a precipice over which old Kamehameha I. drove the army of Oahu, three-quarters of a century before.

The vegetation and glory of the tropics attracted him. "In one open spot a vine of a species unknown had taken possession of two tall dead stumps, and wound around and about them, and swung out from their tops, and twined their meeting tendrils together into a faultless arch. Man, with all his art, could not improve upon its symmetry."

He saw Sam Brannan's palace, "The Bungalow," built by one Shillaber of San Francisco at a cost of from thirty to forty thousand dollars. In its day it had outshone its regal neighbor, the palace of the king, but had fallen to decay after passing into Brannan's hands, and had become a picturesque Theban ruin by the time of Mark Twain's visit.

In No. 12, June 20th (written May 23d), he tells of the Hawaiian Legislature, and of his trip to the island of Maui, where, as he says, he never spent so pleasant a month before, or bade any place good-by so regretfully.

In No. 13 he continues the Legislature, and gives this picture of Minister Harris: "He is six feet high, bony and rather slender; long, ungainly arms; stands so straight he leans back a little; has small side whiskers; his head long, up and down; he has no command of language or ideas; oratory all show and pretence; a big washing and a small hang-out; weak, insipid, and a damn fool in general."

In No. 14, June 22d, published July 16th, he tells of the death and burial ceremonies of the Princess Victoria K. K., and, what was to be of more importance to him, of the arrival of Anson Burlingame, U. S. Minister to China, and Gen. Van Valkenburgh, U. S. Minister to Japan. They were to stay ten or fourteen days, he said, but an effort would be made to have them stay over July 4th.

Speaking of Burlingame: "Burlingame is a man who could be esteemed, respected, and popular anywhere, no matter whether he was among Christians or cannibals." Then, in the same letter, comes the great incident. "A letter arrived here yesterday, giving a meagre account of the arrival, on the Island of Hawaii, of nineteen poor, starving wretches, who had been buffeting a stormy sea, in an open boat, for forty-three days. Their ship, the Hornet, from New York, with a quantity of kerosene on board had taken fire and burned in Lat. 2d. north, and Long. 35d. west. When they had been entirely out of provisions for a day or two, and the cravings of hunger become insufferable, they yielded to the ship-wrecked mariner's fearful and awful alternative, and solemnly drew lots to determine who of their number should die, to furnish food for his comrades; and then the morning mists lifted, and they saw land. They are being cared for at Sanpahoe (Not yet corroborated)."

The Hornet disaster was fully told in his letter of June 27th. The survivors were brought to Honolulu, and with the assistance of the Burlingame party, Clemens, laid up with saddle boils, was carried on a stretcher to the hospital, where, aided by Burlingame, he interviewed the shipwrecked men, securing material for the most important piece of serious writing he had thus far performed. Letter No. 15 to the Union--of date June 25th--occupied the most of the first page in the issue of July 19. It was a detailed account of the sufferings of officers and crew, as given by the third officer and members of the crew.

From letter No. 15:

In the postscript of a letter which I wrote two or three days ago, and sent by the ship "Live Yankee," I gave you the substance of a letter received here from Hilo, by Walker Allen and Co., informing them that a boat, containing fifteen men in a helpless and starving condition, had drifted ashore at Sanpahoe, Island of Hawaii, and that they had belonged to the clipper ship "Hornet"-- Cap. Mitchell, master--had been afloat since the burning of that vessel, about one hundred miles north of the equator, on the third of May--forty-three days.

The Third Mate, and ten of the seamen have arrived here, and are now in the hospital. Cap. Mitchell, one seaman named Antonio Passene, and two passengers, Samuel and Henry Ferguson, of New York City, eighteen and twenty-eight years, are still at Hilo, but are expected here within the week. In the Captain's modest epitome of the terrible romance you detect the fine old hero through it. It reads like Grant.

Here follows the whole terrible narrative, which has since been published in more substantial form, and has been recognized as literature. It occupied three and a half columns on the front page of the Union, and, of course, constituted a great beat for that paper--a fact which they appreciated to the extent of one hundred dollars the column upon the writer's return from the islands.

In letters Nos. 14. and 15. he gives further particulars of the month of mourning for the princess, and funeral ceremonials. He refers to Burlingame, who was still in the islands. The remaining letters are unimportant.

The Hawaiian episode in Mark Twain's life was one of those spots that seemed to him always filled with sunlight. From beginning to end it had been a long luminous dream; in the next letter, written on the homeward-bound ship, becalmed under a cloudless sky, we realize the fitting end of the experience.

To Mrs. Jane Clemens and Mrs. Moffett, in St. Louis:

ON BOARD SHIP Smyrniote, AT SEA, July 30, 1866. DEAR MOTHER AND SISTER,--I write, now, because I must go hard at work as soon as I get to San Francisco, and then I shall have no time for other things--though truth to say I have nothing now to write which will be calculated to interest you much. We left the, Sandwich Islands eight or ten days--or twelve days ago--I don't know which, I have been so hard at work until today (at least part of each day,) that the time has slipped away almost unnoticed. The first few days we came at a whooping gait being in the latitude of the "North-east trades," but we soon ran out of them. We used them as long as they lasted-hundred of miles--and came dead straight north until exactly abreast of San Francisco precisely straight west of the city in a bee-line--but a long bee-line, as we were about two thousand miles at sea-consequently, we are not a hundred yards nearer San Francisco than you are. And here we lie becalmed on a glassy sea--we do not move an inch-we throw banana and orange peel overboard and it lies still on the water by the vessel's side. Sometimes the ocean is as dead level as the Mississippi river, and glitters glassily as if polished--but usually, of course, no matter how calm the weather is, we roll and surge over the grand ground-swell. We amuse ourselves tying pieces of tin to the ship's log and sinking them to see how far we can distinguish them under water--86 feet was the deepest we could see a small piece of tin, but a white plate would show about as far down as the steeple of Dr. Bullard's church would reach, I guess. The sea is very dark and blue here.

Ever since we got becalmed--five days--I have been copying the diary of one of the young Fergusons (the two boys who starved and suffered, with thirteen others, in an open boat at sea for forty-three days, lately, after their ship, the "Hornet," was burned on the equator.) Both these boys, and Captain Mitchell, are passengers with us. I am copying the diary to publish in Harper's Magazine, if I have time to fix it up properly when I get to San Francisco.

I suppose, from present appearances,--light winds and calms,--that we shall be two or three weeks at sea, yet--and I hope so--I am in no hurry to go to work.

Sunday Morning, Aug. 6. This is rather slow. We still drift, drift, drift along--at intervals a spanking breeze and then--drift again--hardly move for half a day. But I enjoy it. We have such snowy moonlight, and such gorgeous sunsets. And the ship is so easy--even in a gale she rolls very little, compared to other vessels--and in this calm we could dance on deck, if we chose. You can walk a crack, so steady is she. Very different from the Ajax. My trunk used to get loose in the stateroom and rip and tear around the place as if it had life in it, and I always had to take my clothes off in bed because I could not stand up and do it.

There is a ship in sight--the first object we have seen since we left Honolulu. We are still 1300 or 1400 miles from land and so anything like this that varies the vast solitude of the ocean makes all hands light- hearted and cheerful. We think the ship is the "Comet," which left Honolulu several hours before we did. She is about twelve miles away, and so we cannot see her hull, but the sailors think it is the Comet because of some peculiarity about her fore-top-gallant sails. We have watched her all the forenoon.

Afternoon We had preaching on the quarter-deck by Rev. Mr. Rising, of Virginia City, old friend of mine. Spread a flag on the booby-hatch, which made a very good pulpit, and then ranged the chairs on either side against the bulwarks; last Sunday we had the shadow of the mainsail, but today we were on the opposite tack, close hauled, and had the sun. I am leader of the choir on this ship, and a sorry lead it is. I hope they will have a better opinion of our music in Heaven than I have down here. If they don't a thunderbolt will come down and knock the vessel endways.

The other ship is the Comet--she is right abreast three miles away, sailing on our course--both of us in a dead calm. With the glasses we can see what we take to be men and women on her decks. I am well acquainted with nearly all her passengers, and being so close seems right sociable.

Monday 7--I had just gone to bed a little after midnight when the 2d mate came and roused up the captain and said "The Comet has come round and is standing away on the other tack." I went up immediately, and so did all our passengers, without waiting to dress-men, women and children. There was a perceptible breeze. Pretty soon the other ship swept down upon us with all her sails set, and made a fine show in the luminous starlight. She passed within a hundred yards of us, so we could faintly see persons on her decks. We had two minutes' chat with each other, through the medium of hoarse shouting, and then she bore away to windward.

In the morning she was only a little black peg standing out of the glassy sea in the distant horizon--an almost invisible mark in the bright sky. Dead calm. So the ships have stood, all day long--have not moved 100 yards.

Aug. 8--The calm continues. Magnificent weather. The gentlemen have all turned boys. They play boyish games on the poop and quarter-deck. For instance: They lay a knife on the fife-rail of the mainmast--stand off three steps, shut one eye, walk up and strike at it with the fore-finger; (seldom hit it;) also they lay a knife on the deck and walk seven or eight steps with eyes close shut, and try to find it. They kneel--place elbows against knees--extend hands in front along the deck--place knife against end of fingers--then clasp hands behind back and bend forward and try to pick up the knife with their teeth and rise up from knees without rolling over or losing their balance. They tie a string to the shrouds-- stand with back against it walk three steps (eyes shut)--turn around three times and go and put finger on the string; only a military man can do it. If you want to know how perfectly ridiculous a grown man looks performing such absurdities in the presence of ladies, get one to try it.

Afternoon--The calm is no more. There are three vessels in sight. It is so sociable to have them hovering about us on this broad waste of water. It is sunny and pleasant, but blowing hard. Every rag about the ship is spread to the breeze and she is speeding over the sea like a bird. There is a large brig right astern of us with all her canvas set and chasing us at her best. She came up fast while the winds were light, but now it is hard to tell whether she gains or not. We can see the people on the forecastle with the glass. The race is exciting. I am sorry to know that we shall soon have to quit the vessel and go ashore if she keeps up this speed.

Friday, Aug. 10--We have breezes and calms alternately. The brig is two miles to three astern, and just stays there. We sail directly east--this brings the brig, with all her canvas set, almost in the eye of the sun, when it sets--beautiful. She looks sharply cut and black as a coal, against a background of fire and in the midst of a sea of blood.

San Francisco, Aug. 20.--We never saw the Comet again till the 13th, in the morning, three miles away. At three o'clock that afternoon, 25 days out from Honolulu, both ships entered the Golden Gate of San Francisco side by side, and 300 yards apart. There was a gale blowing, and both vessels clapped on every stitch of canvas and swept up through the channel and past the fortresses at a magnificent gait.

I have been up to Sacramento and squared accounts with the Union. They paid me a great deal more than they promised me. Yrs aff SAM.

VI.

LETTERS 1866-67. THE LECTURER. SUCCESS ON THE COAST. IN NEW YORK. THE GREAT OCEAN EXCURSION

It was August 13th when he reached San Francisco and wrote in his note-book, "Home again. No--not home again--in prison again, and all the wild sense of freedom gone. City seems so cramped and so dreary with toil and care and business anxieties. God help me, I wish I were at sea again!"

The transition from the dreamland of a becalmed sailing-vessel to the dull, cheerless realities of his old life, and the uncertainties of his future, depressed him--filled him with forebodings. At one moment he felt himself on the verge of suicide--the world seemed so little worth while.

He wished to make a trip around the world, a project that required money. He contemplated making a book of his island letters and experiences, and the acceptance by Harper's Magazine of the revised version of the Hornet Shipwreck story encouraged this thought.

Friends urged him to embody in a lecture the picturesque aspect of Hawaiian life. The thought frightened him, but it also appealed to him strongly. He believed he could entertain an audience, once he got started on the right track. As Governor of the Third House at Carson City he had kept the audience in hand. Men in whom he had the utmost confidence insisted that he follow up the lecture idea and engage the largest house in the city for his purpose. The possibility of failure appalled him, but he finally agreed to the plan.

In Roughing It, and elsewhere, has been told the story of this venture--the tale of its splendid success. He was no longer concerned, now, as to his immediate future. The lecture field was profitable. His audience laughed and shouted. He was learning the flavor of real success and exulting in it. With Dennis McCarthy, formerly one of the partners in the Enterprise, as manager, he made a tour of California and Nevada.

To Mrs. Jane Clemens and others, in St. Louis:

VIRGINIA CITY, Nov. 1, 1866. ALL THE FOLKS, AFFECTIONATE GREETING,--You know the flush time's are past, and it has long been impossible to more than half fill the Theatre here, with any sort of attraction, but they filled it for me, night before last--full--dollar all over the house.

I was mighty dubious about Carson, but the enclosed call and some telegrams set that all right--I lecture there tomorrow night.

They offer a full house and no expense in Dayton--go there next. Sandy Baldwin says I have made the most sweeping success of any man he knows of.

I have lectured in San Francisco, Sacramento, Marysville, Grass Valley, Nevada, You Bet, Red Dog and Virginia. I am going to talk in Carson, Gold Hill, Silver City, Dayton, Washoe, San Francisco again, and again here if I have time to re-hash the lecture.

Then I am bound for New York--lecture on the Steamer, maybe.

I'll leave toward 1st December--but I'll telegraph you. Love to all. Yrs. MARK.

His lecture tour continued from October until December, a period of picturesque incident, the story of which has been recorded elsewhere. --[See Mark Twain: A Biography, by the same author]--It paid him well; he could go home now, without shame. Indeed, from his next letter, full of the boyish elation which always to his last years was the complement of his success, we gather that he is going home with special honors-- introductions from ministers and the like to distinguished personages of the East.

To Mrs. Jane Clemens and family, in St. Louis:

SAN F., Dec. 4, 1866. MY DEAR FOLKS,--I have written to Annie and Sammy and Katie some time ago--also, to the balance of you.

I called on Rev. Dr. Wadsworth last night with the City College man, but he wasn't at home. I was sorry, because I wanted to make his acquaintance. I am thick as thieves with the Rev. Stebbings, and I am laying for the Rev. Scudder and the Rev. Dr. Stone. I am running on preachers, now, altogether. I find them gay. Stebbings is a regular brick. I am taking letters of introduction to Henry Ward Beecher, Rev. Dr. Tyng, and other eminent parsons in the east.

Whenever anybody offers me a letter to a preacher, now I snaffle it on the spot. I shall make Rev. Dr. Bellows trot out the fast nags of the cloth for me when I get to New York. Bellows is an able, upright and eloquent man--a man of imperial intellect and matchless power--he is Christian in the truest sense of the term and is unquestionably a brick....

Gen. Drum has arrived in Philadelphia and established his head-quarters there, as Adjutant Genl. to Maj. Gen. Meade. Col. Leonard has received a letter from him in which he offers me a complimentary benefit if I will come there. I am much obliged, really, but I am afraid I shan't lecture much in the States.

The China Mail Steamer is getting ready and everybody says I am throwing away a fortune in not going in her. I firmly believe it myself.

I sail for the States in the Opposition steamer of the 5th inst., positively and without reserve. My room is already secured for me, and is the choicest in the ship. I know all the officers.

Yrs. Affy MARK.

We get no hint of his plans, and perhaps he had none. If his purpose was to lecture in the East, he was in no hurry to begin. Arriving in New York, after an adventurous voyage, he met a number of old Californians--men who believed in him--and urged him to lecture. He also received offers of newspaper engagements, and from Charles Henry Webb, who had published the Californian, which Bret Harte had edited, came the proposal to collect his published sketches, including the jumping Frog story, in book form. Webb himself was in New York, and offered the sketches to several publishers, including Canton, who had once refused the Frog story by omitting it from Artemus Ward's book. It seems curious that Canton should make a second mistake and refuse it again, but publishers were wary in those days, and even the newspaper success of the Frog story did not tempt him to venture it as the title tale of a book. Webb finally declared he would publish the book himself, and Clemens, after a few weeks of New York, joined his mother and family in St. Louis and gave himself up to a considerable period of visiting, lecturing meantime in both Hannibal and Keokuk.

Fate had great matters in preparation for him. The Quaker City Mediterranean excursion, the first great ocean picnic, was announced that spring, and Mark Twain realized that it offered a possible opportunity for him to see something of the world. He wrote at once to the proprietors of the Alta-California and proposed that they send him as their correspondent. To his delight his proposition was accepted, the Alta agreeing to the twelve hundred dollars passage money, and twenty dollars each for letters.

The Quaker City was not to sail until the 8th of June, but the Alta wished some preliminary letters from New York. Furthermore, Webb had the Frog book in press, and would issue it May 1st. Clemens, therefore, returned to New York in April, and now once more being urged by the Californians to lecture, he did not refuse. Frank Fuller, formerly Governor of Utah, took the matter in hand and engaged Cooper Union for the venture. He timed it for May 6th, which would be a few days after the appearance of Webb's book. Clemens was even more frightened at the prospect of this lecture than he had been in San Francisco, and with more reason, for in New York his friends were not many, and competition for public favor was very great. There are two letters written May 1st, one to his people, and one to Bret Harte, in San Francisco; that give us the situation.

End of this Project Gutenberg Etext of Letters Vol. 1, by Mark Twain

MARK TWAIN'S LETTERS 1867-1875

ARRANGED WITH COMMENT BY ALBERT BIGELOW PAINE

VOLUME II.

To Bret Harte, in San Francisco:

WESTMINSTER HOTEL, May 1, 1867. DEAR BRET,--I take my pen in hand to inform you that I am well and hope these few lines will find you enjoying the same God's blessing.

The book is out, and is handsome. It is full of damnable errors of grammar and deadly inconsistencies of spelling in the Frog sketch because I was away and did not read the proofs; but be a friend and say nothing about these things. When my hurry is over, I will send you an autograph copy to pisen the children with.

I am to lecture in Cooper Institute next Monday night. Pray for me.

We sail for the Holy Land June 8. Try to write me (to this hotel,) and it will be forwarded to Paris, where we remain 10 or 15 days.

Regards and best wishes to Mrs. Bret and the family. Truly Yr Friend MARK.

To Mrs. Jane Clemens and family, in St. Louis:

WESTMINSTER HOTEL, May 1, 1867. DEAR FOLKS,--Don't expect me to write for a while. My hands are full of business on account of my lecture for the 6th inst., and everything looks shady, at least, if not dark. I have got a good agent--but now after we have hired Cooper Institute and gone to an expense in one way or another of $500, it comes out that I have got to play against Speaker Colfax at Irving Hall, Ristori, and also the double troupe of Japanese jugglers, the latter opening at the great Academy of Music--and with all this against me I have taken the largest house in New York and cannot back water. Let her slide! If nobody else cares I don't.

I'll send the book soon. I am awfully hurried now, but not worried. Yrs. SAM.

The Cooper Union lecture proved a failure, and a success. When it became evident to Fuller that the venture was not going to pay, he sent out a flood of complimentaries to the school-teachers of New York City and the surrounding districts. No one seems to have declined them. Clemens lectured to a jammed house and acquired much reputation. Lecture proposals came from several directions, but he could not accept them now. He wrote home that he was eighteen Alta letters behind and had refused everything. Thos. Nast, the cartoonist, then in his first fame, propped a joint tour, Clemens to lecture while he, Nast, would illustrate with "lightning" sketches; but even this could not be considered now. In a little while he would sail, and the days were overfull. A letter written a week before he sailed is full of the hurry and strain of these last days.

To Mrs. Jane Clemens and family, in St. Louis:

WESTMINSTER HOTEL, NEW YORK, June 1, 1867. DEAR FOLKS,--I know I ought to write oftener (just got your last,) and more fully, but I cannot overcome my repugnance to telling what I am doing or what I expect to do or propose to do. Then, what have I left to write about? Manifestly nothing.

It isn't any use for me to talk about the voyage, because I can have no faith in that voyage till the ship is under way. How do I know she will ever sail? My passage is paid, and if the ship sails, I sail in her--but I make no calculations, have bought no cigars, no sea-going clothing --have made no preparation whatever--shall not pack my trunk till the morning we sail. Yet my hands are full of what I am going to do the day before we sail--and what isn't done that day will go undone.

All I do know or feel, is, that I am wild with impatience to move--move --move! Half a dozen times I have wished I had sailed long ago in some ship that wasn't going to keep me chained here to chafe for lagging ages while she got ready to go. Curse the endless delays! They always kill me--they make me neglect every duty and then I have a conscience that tears me like a wild beast. I wish I never had to stop anywhere a month. I do more mean things, the moment I get a chance to fold my hands and sit down than ever I can get forgiveness for.

Yes, we are to meet at Mr. Beach's next Thursday night, and I suppose we shall have to be gotten up regardless of expense, in swallow-tails, white kids and everything en regle.

I am resigned to Rev. Mr. Hutchinson's or anybody else's supervision. I don't mind it. I am fixed. I have got a splendid, immoral, tobacco- smoking, wine-drinking, godless room-mate who is as good and true and right-minded a man as ever lived--a man whose blameless conduct and example will always be an eloquent sermon to all who shall come within their influence. But send on the professional preachers--there are none I like better to converse with. If they're not narrow minded and bigoted they make good companions.

I asked them to send the N. Y. Weekly to you--no charge. I am not going to write for it. Like all other, papers that pay one splendidly it circulates among stupid people and the 'canaille.' I have made no arrangement with any New York paper--I will see about that Monday or Tuesday. Love to all Good bye, Yrs affy SAM.

The "immoral" room-mate whose conduct was to be an "eloquent example" was Dan Slote, immortalized in the Innocents as "Dan" --a favorite on the ship, and later beloved by countless readers.

There is one more letter, written the night before the Quaker City sailed-a letter which in a sense marks the close of the first great period of his life--the period of aimless wandering--adventure -- youth.

Perhaps a paragraph of explanation should precede this letter. Political changes had eliminated Orion in Nevada, and he was now undertaking the practice of law. "Bill Stewart" was Senator Stewart, of Nevada, of whom we shall hear again. The "Sandwich Island book," as may be imagined, was made up of his letters to the Sacramento Union. Nothing came of the venture, except some chapters in 'Roughing It', rewritten from the material. "Zeb and John Leavenworth" were pilots whom he had known on the river.

To Mrs. Jane Clemens and family in St. Louis:

NEW YORK, June 7th, 1867. DEAR FOLKS, I suppose we shall be many a league at sea tomorrow night, and goodness knows I shall be unspeakably glad of it.

I haven't got anything to write, else I would write it. I have just written myself clear out in letters to the Alta, and I think they are the stupidest letters that were ever written from New York. Corresponding has been a perfect drag ever since I got to the states. If it continues abroad, I don't know what the Tribune and Alta folks will think. I have withdrawn the Sandwich Island book--it would be useless to publish it in these dull publishing times. As for the Frog book, I don't believe that will ever pay anything worth a cent. I published it simply to advertise myself--not with the hope of making anything out of it.

Well, I haven't anything to write, except that I am tired of staying in one place--that I am in a fever to get away. Read my Alta letters--they contain everything I could possibly write to you. Tell Zeb and John Leavenworth to write me. They can get plenty of gossip from the pilots.

An importing house sent two cases of exquisite champagne aboard the ship for me today--Veuve Clicquot and Lac d'Or. I and my room-mate have set apart every Saturday as a solemn fast day, wherein we will entertain no light matters of frivolous conversation, but only get drunk. (That is a joke.) His mother and sisters are the best and most homelike people I have yet found in a brown stone front. There is no style about them, except in house and furniture.

I wish Orion were going on this voyage, for I believe he could not help but be cheerful and jolly. I often wonder if his law business is going satisfactorily to him, but knowing that the dull season is setting in now (it looked like it had already set in before) I have felt as if I could almost answer the question myself--which is to say in plain words, I was afraid to ask. I wish I had gone to Washington in the winter instead of going West. I could have gouged an office out of Bill Stewart for him, and that would atone for the loss of my home visit. But I am so worthless that it seems to me I never do anything or accomplish anything that lingers in my mind as a pleasant memory. My mind is stored full of unworthy conduct toward Orion and towards you all, and an accusing conscience gives me peace only in excitement and restless moving from place to place. If I could say I had done one thing for any of you that entitled me to your good opinion, (I say nothing of your love, for I am sure of that, no matter how unworthy of it I may make myself, from Orion down you have always given me that, all the days of my life, when God Almighty knows I seldom deserve it,) I believe I could go home and stay there and I know I would care little for the world's praise or blame. There is no satisfaction in the world's praise anyhow, and it has no worth to me save in the way of business. I tried to gather up its compliments to send to you, but the work was distasteful and I dropped it.

You observe that under a cheerful exterior I have got a spirit that is angry with me and gives me freely its contempt. I can get away from that at sea, and be tranquil and satisfied-and so, with my parting love and benediction for Orion and all of you, I say goodbye and God bless you all--and welcome the wind that wafts a weary soul to the sunny lands of the Mediterranean! Yrs. Forever, SAM.

VII.

LETTERS 1867. THE TRAVELER. THE VOYAGE OF THE "QUAKER CITY"

Mark Twain, now at sea, was writing many letters; not personal letters, but those unique descriptive relations of travel which would make him his first great fame--those fresh first impressions preserved to us now as chapters of The Innocents Abroad. Yet here and there in the midst of sight-seeing and reporting he found time to send a brief line to those at home, merely that they might have a word from his own hand, for he had ordered the papers to which he was to contribute--the Alta and the New York Tribune--sent to them, and these would give the story of his travels. The home letters read like notebook entries.

Letters to Mrs. Jane Clemens and family, in St. Louis:

FAYAL (Azores,) June 20th, 1867. DEAR FOLKS,--We are having a lively time here, after a stormy trip. We meant to go to San Miguel, but were driven here by stress of weather. Beautiful climate. Yrs. Affect. SAM.

GIBRALTAR, June 30th, 1867. DEAR FOLKS,--Arrived here this morning, and am clear worn out with riding and climbing in and over and around this monstrous rock and its fortifications. Summer climate and very pleasant. Yrs. SAM.

TANGIER, MOROCCO, (AFRICA), July 1, 1867. DEAR FOLKS, Half a dozen of us came here yesterday from Gibraltar and some of the company took the other direction; went up through Spain, to Paris by rail. We decided that Gibraltar and San Roque were all of Spain that we wanted to see at present and are glad we came here among the Africans, Moors, Arabs and Bedouins of the desert. I would not give this experience for all the balance of the trip combined. This is the infernalest hive of infernally costumed barbarians I have ever come across yet. Yrs. SAM.

AT SEA, July 2, 1867. DR. FOLKS,--We are far up the intensely blue and ravishingly beautiful Mediterranean. And now we are just passing the island of Minorca. The climate is perfectly lovely and it is hard to drive anybody to bed, day or night. We remain up the whole night through occasionally, and by this means enjoy the rare sensation of seeing the sun rise. But the sunsets are soft, rich, warm and superb!

We had a ball last night under the awnings of the quarter deck, and the share of it of three of us was masquerade. We had full, flowing, picturesque Moorish costumes which we purchased in the bazaars of Tangier. Yrs. SAM.

MARSEILLES, FRANCE, July 5, 1867. We are here. Start for Paris tomorrow. All well. Had gorgeous 4th of July jollification yesterday at sea. Yrs. SAM.

The reader may expand these sketchy outlines to his heart's content by following the chapters in The Innocents Abroad, which is very good history, less elaborated than might be supposed. But on the other hand, the next letter adds something of interest to the book- circumstances which a modest author would necessarily omit.

To Mrs. Jane Clemens and family, in St. Louis:

YALTA, RUSSIA, Aug. 25, 1867. DEAR FOLKS,--We have been representing the United States all we knew how today. We went to Sebastopol, after we got tired of Constantinople (got your letter there, and one at Naples,) and there the Commandant and the whole town came aboard and were as jolly and sociable as old friends. They said the Emperor of Russia was at Yalta, 30 miles or 40 away, and urged us to go there with the ship and visit him--promised us a cordial welcome. They insisted on sending a telegram to the Emperor, and also a courier overland to announce our coming. But we knew that a great English Excursion party, and also the Viceroy of Egypt, in his splendid yacht, had been refused an audience within the last fortnight, so we thought it not safe to try it. They said, no difference--the Emperor would hardly visit our ship, because that would be a most extraordinary favor, and one which he uniformly refuses to accord under any circumstances, but he would certainly receive us at his palace. We still declined. But we had to go to Odessa, 250 miles away, and there the Governor General urged us, and sent a telegram to the

Emperor, which we hardly expected to be answered, but it was, and promptly. So we sailed back to Yalta.

We all went to the palace at noon, today, (3 miles) in carriages and on horses sent by the Emperor, and we had a jolly time. Instead of the usual formal audience of 15 minutes, we staid 4 hours and were made a good deal more at home than we could have been in a New York drawing-room. The whole tribe turned out to receive our party-Emperor, Empress, the oldest daughter (Grand-Duchess Marie, a pretty girl of 14,) a little Grand Duke, her brother, and a platoon of Admirals, Princes, Peers of the Empire, etc., and in a little while an aid-de-camp arrived with a request from the Grand Duke Michael, the Emperor's brother, that we would visit his palace and breakfast with him. The Emperor also invited us, on behalf of his absent eldest son and heir (aged 22,) to visit his palace and consider it a visit to him. They all talk English and they were all very neatly but very plainly dressed. You all dress a good deal finer than they were dressed. The Emperor and his family threw off all reserve and showed us all over the palace themselves. It is very rich and very elegant, but in no way gaudy.

I had been appointed chairman of a committee to draught an address to the Emperor in behalf of the passengers, and as I fully expected, and as they fully intended, I had to write the address myself. I didn't mind it, because I have no modesty and would as soon write to an Emperor as to anybody else--but considering that there were 5 on the committee I thought they might have contributed one paragraph among them, anyway. They wanted me to read it to him, too, but I declined that honor--not because I hadn't cheek enough (and some to spare,) but because our Consul at Odessa was along, and also the Secretary of our Legation at St. Petersburgh, and of course one of those ought to read it. The Emperor accepted the address--it was his business to do it--and so many others have praised it warmly that I begin to imagine it must be a wonderful sort of document and herewith send you the original draught of it to be put into alcohol and preserved forever like a curious reptile.

They live right well at the Grand Duke Michael's their breakfasts are not gorgeous but very excellent--and if Mike were to say the word I would go there and breakfast with him tomorrow. Yrs aff SAM.

P. S. [Written across the face of the last page.] They had told us it would be polite to invite the Emperor to visit the ship, though he would not be likely to do it. But he didn't give us a chance--he has requested permission to come on board with his family and all his relations tomorrow and take a sail, in case it is calm weather. I can, entertain them. My hand is in, now, and if you want any more Emperors feted in style, trot them out.

The next letter is of interest in that it gives us the program and volume of his work. With all the sight seeing he was averaging a full four letters a week--long letters, requiring careful observation and inquiry. How fresh and impressionable and full of vigor he was, even in that fierce southern heat! No one makes the Mediterranean trip in summer to-day, and the thought of adding constant letter-writing to steady travel through southern France, Italy, Greece, and Turkey in blazing midsummer is stupefying. And Syria and Egypt in September!

To Mrs. Jane Clemens and family, in St. Louis:

CONSTANTINOPLE, Sept. 1, '67.

DEAR FOLKS,--All well. Do the Alta's come regularly? I wish I knew whether my letters reach them or not. Look over the back papers and see. I wrote them as follows: 1 Letter from Fayal, in the Azores Islands. 1 from Gibraltar, in Spain. 1 from Tangier, in Africa. 2 from Paris and Marseilles, in France. 1 from Genoa, in Italy. 1 from Milan. 1 from Lake Como. 1 from some little place in Switzerland--have forgotten the name. 4 concerning Lecce, Bergamo, Padua, Verona, Battlefield of Marengo, Pestachio, and some other cities in Northern Italy. 2 from Venice. 1 about Bologna. 1 from Florence. 1 from Pisa. 1 from Leghorn. 1 from Rome and Civita Vecchia. 2 from Naples. 1 about Pazzuoli, where St. Paul landed, the Baths of Nero, and the ruins of Baia, Virgil's tomb, the Elysian Fields, the Sunken Cities and the spot where Ulysses landed. 1 from Herculaneum and Vesuvius. 1 from Pompeii. 1 from the Island of Ischia. 1 concerning the Volcano of Stromboli, the city and Straits of Messina, the land of Sicily, Scylla and Charybdis etc. 1 about the Grecian Archipelago. 1 about a midnight visit to Athens, the Piraeus and the ruins of the Acropolis. 1 about the Hellespont, the site of ancient Troy, the Sea of Marmara, etc. 2 about Constantinople, the Golden Horn and the beauties of the Bosphorus. 1 from Odessa and Sebastopol in Russia, the Black Sea, etc. 2 from Yalta, Russia, concerning a visit to the Czar. And yesterday I wrote another letter from Constantinople and 1 today about its neighbor in Asia, Scatter. I am not done with Turkey yet. Shall write 2 or 3 more.

I have written to the New York Herald 2 letters from Naples, (no name signed,) and 1 from Constantinople.

To the New York Tribune I have written 1 from Fayal. 1 from Civita Vecchia in the Roman States. 2 from Yalta, Russia. And 1 from Constantinople.

I have never seen any of these letters in print except the one to the Tribune from Fayal and that was not worth printing.

We sail hence tomorrow, perhaps, and my next letters will be mailed at Smyrna, in Syria. I hope to write from the Sea of Tiberius, Damascus, Jerusalem, Joppa, and possibly other points in the Holy Land. The letters from Egypt, the Nile and Algiers I will look out for, myself. I will bring them in my pocket.

They take the finest photographs in the world here. I have ordered some. They will be sent to Alexandria, Egypt.

You cannot conceive of anything so beautiful as Constantinople, viewed from the Golden Horn or the Bosphorus. I think it must be the handsomest city in the world. I will go on deck and look at it for you, directly. I am staying in the ship, tonight. I generally stay on shore when we are in port. But yesterday I just ran myself down. Dan Slote, my room-mate, is on shore. He remained here while we went up the Black Sea, but it seems he has not got enough of it yet. I thought Dan had got the state- room pretty full of rubbish at last, but a while ago his dragoman arrived with a bran new, ghastly tomb-stone of the Oriental pattern, with his name handsomely carved and gilded on it, in Turkish characters. That fellow will buy a Circassian slave, next.

I am tired. We are going on a trip, tomorrow. I must to bed. Love to all. Yrs SAM.

U. S. CONSUL'S OFFICE, BEIRUT, SYRIA, Sept. 11. (1867) DEAR FOLKS,--We are here, eight of us, making a contract with a dragoman to take us to Baalbek, then to Damascus, Nazareth, &c. then to Lake Genassareth (Sea of Tiberias,) then South through all the celebrated Scriptural localities to Jerusalem--then to the Dead Sea, the Cave of Macpelah and up to Joppa where the ship will be. We shall be in the saddle three weeks--we have horses, tents, provisions, arms, a dragoman and two other servants, and we pay five dollars a day apiece, in gold. Love to all, yrs. SAM.

We leave tonight, at two o'clock in the morning.

There appear to be no further home letters written from Syria--and none from Egypt. Perhaps with the desert and the delta the heat at last became too fearful for anything beyond the actual requirements of the day. When he began his next it was October, and the fiercer travel was behind him.

To Mrs. Jane Clemens and family, in St. Louis:

CAGHARI, SARDINIA, Oct, 12, 1867. DEAR FOLKS,--We have just dropped anchor before this handsome city and--

ALGIERS, AFRICA, Oct. 15. They would not let us land at Caghari on account of cholera. Nothing to write.

MALAGA, SPAIN, Oct. 17. The Captain and I are ashore here under guard, waiting to know whether they will let the ship anchor or not. Quarantine regulations are very strict here on all vessels coming from Egypt. I am a little anxious because I want to go inland to Granada and see the Alhambra. I can go on down by Seville and Cordova, and be picked up at Cadiz.

Later: We cannot anchor--must go on. We shall be at Gibraltar before midnight and I think I will go horseback (a long days) and thence by rail and diligence to Cadiz. I will not mail this till I see the Gibraltar lights--I begin to think they won't let us in anywhere.

11.30 P. M.--Gibraltar. At anchor and all right, but they won't let us land till morning--it is a waste of valuable time. We shall reach New York middle of November. Yours, SAM.

CADIZ, Oct 24, 1867. DEAR FOLKS,--We left Gibraltar at noon and rode to Algeciras, (4 hours) thus dodging the quarantine, took dinner and then rode horseback all night in a swinging trot and at daylight took a caleche (a wheeled vehicle) and rode 5 hours--then took cars and traveled till twelve at night. That landed us at Seville and we were over the hard part of our trip, and somewhat tired. Since then we have taken things comparatively easy, drifting around from one town to another and attracting a good deal of attention, for I guess strangers do not wander through Andalusia and the other Southern provinces of Spain often. The country is precisely as it was when Don Quixote and Sancho Panza were possible characters.

But I see now what the glory of Spain must have been when it was under Moorish domination. No, I will not say that, but then when one is carried away, infatuated, entranced, with the wonders of the Alhambra and the supernatural beauty of the Alcazar, he is apt to overflow with admiration for the splendid intellects that created them.

I cannot write now. I am only dropping a line to let you know I am well. The ship will call for us here tomorrow. We may stop at Lisbon, and shall at the Bermudas, and will arrive in New York ten days after this letter gets there. SAM.

This is the last personal letter written during that famous first sea-gipsying, and reading it our regret grows that he did not put something of his Spanish excursion into his book. He never returned to Spain, and he never wrote of it. Only the barest mention of "seven beautiful days" is found in The Innocents Abroad.

VIII.

LETTERS 1867-68. WASHINGTON AND SAN FRANCISCO. THE PROPOSED BOOK OF TRAVEL. A NEW LECTURE

From Mark Twain's home letters we get several important side-lights on this first famous book. We learn, for in stance, that it was he who drafted the ship address to the Emperor--the opening lines of which became so wearisome when repeated by the sailors. Furthermore, we learn something of the scope and extent of his newspaper correspondence, which must have kept him furiously busy, done as it was in the midst of super-heated and continuous sight-seeing. He wrote fifty three letters to the Alta-California, six to the New York Tribune, and at least two to the New York Herald more than sixty, all told, of an average, length of three to four thousand words each. Mark Twain always claimed to be a lazy man, and certainly he was likely to avoid an undertaking not suited to his gifts, but he had energy in abundance for work in his chosen field. To have piled up a correspondence of that size in the time, and under the circumstances already noted, quality considered, may be counted a record in the history of travel letters.

They made him famous. Arriving in New York, November 19, 1867, Mark Twain found himself no longer unknown to the metropolis, or to any portion of America. Papers East and West had copied his Alta and Tribune letters and carried his name into every corner of the States and Territories. He had preached a new gospel in travel literature, the gospel of frankness and sincerity that Americans could understand. Also his literary powers had awakened at last. His work was no longer trivial, crude, and showy; it was full of dignity, beauty, and power; his humor was finer, worthier. The difference in quality between the Quaker City letters and those written from the Sandwich Islands only a year before can scarcely be measured.

He did not remain in New York, but went down to Washington, where he had arranged for a private secretaryship with Senator William M. Stewart,--[The "Bill" Stewart mentioned in the preceding chapter.] whom he had known in Nevada. Such a position he believed would make but little demand upon his time, and would afford him an insight into Washington life, which he could make valuable in the shape of newspaper correspondence.

But fate had other plans for him. He presently received the following letter:

From Elisha Bliss, Jr., in Hartford OFFICE OF THE AMERICAN PUBLISHING COMPANY.

HARTFORD, CONN, Nov 21, 1867. SAMUEL L. CLEMENS Esq. Tribune Office, New York.

DR. SIR,--We take the liberty to address you this, in place of a letter which we had recently written and was about to forward to you, not knowing your arrival home was expected so soon. We are desirous of obtaining from you a work of some kind, perhaps compiled from your letters from the East, &c., with such interesting additions as may be proper. We are the publishers of A. D. Richardson's works, and flatter ourselves that we can give an author as favorable terms and do as full justice to his productions as any other house in the country. We are perhaps the oldest subscription house in the country, and have never failed to give a book an immense circulation. We sold about 100,000 copies of Richardson's F. D. & E. (Field, Dungeon and Escape) and are now printing 41,000, of "Beyond the Mississippi," and large orders ahead. If you have any thought of writing a book, or could be induced to do so, we should be pleased to see you; and will do so. Will you do us the favor to reply at once, at your earliest convenience. Very truly, &c., E. BLISS, Jr. Secty.

Clemens had already the idea of a book in mind and. welcomed this proposition.

To Elisha Bliss, Jr., in Hartford:

WASHINGTON, Dec. 2, 1867. E. BLISS, Jr. Esq. Sec'y American Publishing Co.--

DEAR SIR,--I only received your favor of Nov. 21st last night, at the rooms of the Tribune Bureau here. It was forwarded from the Tribune office, New York, where it had lain eight or ten days. This will be a sufficient apology for the seeming discourtesy of my silence.

I wrote fifty-two (three) letters for the San Francisco "Alta California" during the Quaker City excursion, about half of which number have been printed, thus far. The "Alta" has few exchanges in the East, and I suppose scarcely any of these letters have been copied on this side of the Rocky Mountains. I could weed them of their chief faults of construction and inelegancies of expression and make a volume that would be more acceptable in many respects than any I could now write. When those letters were written my impressions were fresh, but now they have lost that freshness; they were warm then--they are cold, now. I could strike out certain letters, and write new ones wherewith to supply their places. If you think such a book would suit your purpose, please drop me a line, specifying the size and general style of the volume; when the matter ought to be ready; whether it should have pictures in it or not; and particularly what your terms with me would be, and what amount of money I might possibly make out of it. The latter clause has a degree of importance for me which is almost beyond my own comprehension. But you understand that, of course.

I have other propositions for a book, but have doubted the propriety of interfering with good newspaper engagements, except my way as an author could be demonstrated to be plain before me. But I know Richardson, and learned from him some months ago, something of an idea of the subscription plan of publishing. If that is your plan invariably, it looks safe.

I am on the N. Y. Tribune staff here as an "occasional,", among other things, and a note from you addressed to Very truly &c. SAM L. CLEMENS,

New York Tribune Bureau, Washington, will find me, without fail.

The exchange of these two letters marked the beginning of one of the most notable publishing connections in American literary history. The book, however, was not begun immediately. Bliss was in poor health and final arrangements were delayed; it was not until late in January that Clemens went to Hartford and concluded the arrangement.

Meantime, fate had disclosed another matter of even greater importance; we get the first hint of it in the following letter, though to him its beginning had been earlier--on a day in the blue harbor of Smyrna, when young Charles Langdon, a fellow-passenger on the Quaker City, had shown to Mark Twain a miniature of young Langdon's sister at home:

To Mrs. Jane Clemens and Mrs. Moffett, in St. Louis:

224 F. STREET, WASH, Jan. 8, 1868. MY DEAR MOTHER AND SISTER,--And so the old Major has been there, has he? I would like mighty well to see him. I was a sort of benefactor to him once. I helped to snatch him out when he was about to ride into a Mohammedan Mosque in that queer old Moorish town of Tangier, in Africa. If he had got in, the Moors would have knocked his venerable old head off, for his temerity.

I have just arrived from New York-been there ever since Christmas staying at the house of Dan Slote my Quaker City room-mate, and having a splendid time. Charley Langdon, Jack Van Nostrand, Dan and I, (all Quaker City night-hawks,) had a blow-out at Dan's' house and a lively talk over old times. We went through the Holy Land together, and I just laughed till my sides ached, at some of our reminiscences. It was the unholiest gang that ever cavorted through Palestine, but those are the best boys in the world. We needed Moulton badly. I started to make calls, New Year's Day, but I anchored for the day at the first house I came to--Charlie Langdon's sister was there (beautiful girl,) and Miss Alice Hooker, another beautiful girl, a niece of Henry Ward Beecher's. We sent the old folks home early, with instructions not to send the carriage till midnight, and then I just staid there and worried the life out of those girls. I am going to spend a few days with the Langdon's in Elmira, New York, as soon as I get time, and a few days at Mrs. Hooker's in Hartford, Conn., shortly.

Henry Ward Beecher sent for me last Sunday to come over and dine (he lives in Brooklyn, you know,) and I went. Harriet Beecher Stowe was there, and Mrs. and Miss Beecher, Mrs. Hooker and my old Quaker City favorite, Emma Beach.

We had a very gay time, if it was Sunday. I expect I told more lies than I have told before in a month.

I went back by invitation, after the evening service, and finished the blow-out, and then staid all night at Mr. Beach's. Henry Ward is a brick.

I found out at 10 o'clock, last night, that I was to lecture tomorrow evening and so you must be aware that I have been working like sin all night to get a lecture written. I have finished it, I call it "Frozen Truth." It is a little top-heavy, though, because there is more truth in the title than there is in the lecture.

But thunder, I mustn't sit here writing all day, with so much business before me.

Good by, and kind regards to all. Yrs affy SAM L. CLEMENS.

Jack Van Nostrand of this letter is "Jack" of the Innocents. Emma Beach was the daughter of Moses S. Beach, of the 'New York Sun.' Later she became the wife of the well-known painter, Abbot H. Thayer.

We do not hear of Miss Langdon again in the letters of that time, but it was not because she was absent from his thoughts. He had first seen her with her father and brother at the old St. Nicholas Hotel, on lower Broadway, where, soon after the arrival of the Quaker City in New York, he had been invited to dine. Long afterward he said: "It is forty years ago; from that day to this she has never been out of my mind."

From his next letter we learn of the lecture which apparently was delivered in Washington.

To Mrs. Jane Clemens and Mrs. Moffett, in St. Louis:

WASH. Jan. 9, 1868. MY DEAR MOTHER AND SISTER,--That infernal lecture is over, thank Heaven! It came near being a villainous failure. It was not advertised at all. The manager was taken sick yesterday, and the man who was sent to tell me, never got to me till afternoon today. There was the dickens to pay. It was too late to do anything--too late to stop the lecture. I scared up a door-keeper, and was ready at the proper time, and by pure good luck a tolerably good house assembled and I was saved! I hardly knew what I was going to talk about, but it went off in splendid style. I was to have preached again Saturday night, but I won't--I can't get along without a manager.

I have been in New York ever since Christmas, you know, and now I shall have to work like sin to catch up my correspondence.

And I have got to get up that book, too. Cut my letters out of the Alta's and send them to me in an envelop. Some, here, that are not mailed yet, I shall have to copy, I suppose.

I have got a thousand things to do, and am not doing any of them. I feel perfectly savage. Good bye Yrs aff SAM.

On the whole, matters were going well with him. His next letter is full of his success--overflowing with the boyish radiance which he never quite outgrew.

To Mrs. Jane Clemens and Mrs. Moffett, in St. Louis:

HARTFORD, CONN. Jan. 24-68. DEAR MOTHER AND SISTER,--This is a good week for me. I stopped in the Herald office as I came through New York, to see the boys on the staff, and young James Gordon Bennett asked me to write twice a week, impersonally, for the Herald, and said if I would I might have full swing, and (write) about anybody and everybody I wanted to. I said I must have the very fullest possible swing, and he said "all right." I said "It's a contract--" and that settled that matter.

I'll make it a point to write one letter a week, any-how.

But the best thing that has happened was here. This great American Publishing Company kept on trying to bargain with me for a book till I thought I would cut the matter short by coming up for a talk. I met Rev. Henry Ward Beecher in Brooklyn, and with his usual whole-souled way of dropping his own work to give other people a lift when he gets a chance, he said, "Now, here, you are one of the talented men of the age--nobody is going to deny that---but in matters of business, I don't suppose you know more than enough to came in when it rains. I'll tell you what to do, and how to do it." And he did.

And I listened well, and then came up here and made a splendid contract for a Quaker City book of 5 or 600 large pages, with illustrations, the manuscript to be placed in the publishers' hands by the middle of July. My percentage is to be a fifth more than they have ever paid any author, except Horace Greeley. Beecher will be surprised, I guess, when he hears this.

But I had my mind made up to one thing--I wasn't going to touch a book unless there was money in it, and a good deal of it. I told them so. I had the misfortune to "bust out" one author of standing. They had his manuscript, with the understanding that they would publish his book if they could not get a book from me, (they only publish two books at a time, and so my book and Richardson's Life of Grant will fill the bill for next fall and winter)--so that manuscript was sent back to its author today.

These publishers get off the most tremendous editions of their books you can imagine. I shall write to the Enterprise and Alta every week, as usual, I guess, and to the Herald twice a week--occasionally to the Tribune and the Magazines (I have a stupid article in the Galaxy, just issued) but I am not going to write to this, that and the other paper any more.

The Chicago Tribune wants letters, but I hope and pray I have charged them so much that they will not close the contract. I am gradually getting out of debt, but these trips to New York do cost like sin. I hope you have cut out and forwarded my printed letters to Washington --please continue to do so as they arrive.

I have had a tip-top time, here, for a few days (guest of Mr. Jno. Hooker's family--Beecher's relatives-in a general way of Mr. Bliss, also, who is head of the publishing firm.) Puritans are mighty straight-laced and they won't let me smoke in the parlor, but the Almighty don't make any better people.

Love to all-good-bye. I shall be in New York 3 days--then go on to the Capital. Yrs affly, especially Ma., Yr SAM.

I have to make a speech at the annual Herald dinner on the 6th of May.

No formal contract for the book had been made when this letter was written. A verbal agreement between Bliss and Clemens had been reached, to be ratified by an exchange of letters in the near future. Bliss had made two propositions, viz., ten thousand dollars, cash in hand, or a 5-per-cent. royalty on the selling price of the book. The cash sum offered looked very large to Mark Twain, and he was sorely tempted to accept it. He had faith, however, in the book, and in Bliss's ability to sell it. He agreed, therefore, to the royalty proposition; "The best business judgment I ever displayed" he often declared in after years. Five per cent. royalty sounds rather small in these days of more liberal contracts. But the American Publishing Company sold its books only by subscription, and the agents' commissions and delivery expenses ate heavily into the profits. Clemens was probably correct in saying that his percentage was larger than had been paid to any previous author except Horace Greeley. The John Hooker mentioned was the husband of Henry Ward Beecher's sister, Isabel. It was easy to understand the Beecher family's robust appreciation of Mark Twain.

From the office of Dan Slote, his room-mate of the Quaker City-- "Dan" of the Innocents-- Clemens wrote his letter that closed the agreement with Bliss.

To Elisha Bliss, Jr., in Hartford:

Office of SLOTE & WOODMAN, Blank Book Manufacturers, Nos. 119-121 William St. NEW

YORK, January 27, 1868. Mr. E. Bliss, Jr. Sec'y American Publishing Co. Hartford Conn.

DEAR SIR, Your favor of Jan. 25th is received, and in reply, I will say that I accede to your several propositions, viz: That I furnish to the American Publishing Company, through you, with MSS sufficient for a volume of 500 to 600 pages, the subject to be the Quaker City, the voyage, description of places, &c., and also embodying the substance of the letters written by me during that trip, said MSS to be ready about the first of August, next, I to give all the usual and necessary attention in preparing said MSS for the press, and in preparation of illustrations, in correction of proofs--no use to be made by me of the material for this work in any way which will conflict with its interest --the book to be sold by the American Publishing Co., by subscription-- and for said MS and labor on my part said Company to pay me a copyright of 5 percent, upon the subscription price of the book for all copies sold.

As further proposed by you, this understanding, herein set forth shall be considered a binding contract upon all parties concerned, all minor details to be arranged between us hereafter. Very truly yours, SAM. L. CLEMENS.

(Private and General.)

I was to have gone to Washington tonight, but have held over a day, to attend a dinner given by a lot of newspaper Editors and literary scalliwags, at the Westminster Hotel. Shall go down tomorrow, if I survive the banquet. Yrs truly SAM. CLEMENS.

Mark Twain, in Washington, was in line for political preferment: His wide acquaintance on the Pacific slope, his new fame and growing popularity, his powerful and dreaded pen, all gave him special distinction at the capital. From time to time the offer of one office or another tempted him, but he wisely, or luckily, resisted. In his letters home are presented some of his problems.

To Mrs. Jane Clemens and Mrs. Moffett, in St. Louis:

224 F. STREET WASHINGTON Feb. 6, 1868. MY DEAR MOTHER AND SISTER,--For two months there have been some fifty applications before the government for the postmastership of San Francisco, which is the heaviest concentration of political power on the coast and consequently is a post which is much coveted.,

When I found that a personal friend of mine, the Chief Editor of the Alta was an applicant I said I didn't want it--I would not take $10,000 a year out of a friend's pocket.

The two months have passed, I heard day before yesterday that a new and almost unknown candidate had suddenly turned up on the inside track, and was to be appointed at once. I didn't like that, and went after his case in a fine passion. I hunted up all our Senators and representatives and found that his name was actually to come from the President early in the morning.

Then Judge Field said if I wanted the place he could pledge me the President's appointment--and

Senator Conness said he would guarantee me the Senate's confirmation. It was a great temptation, but it would render it impossible to fill my book contract, and I had to drop the idea.

I have to spend August and September in Hartford which isn't San Francisco. Mr. Conness offers me any choice out of five influential California offices. Now, some day or other I shall want an office and then, just my luck, I can't get it, I suppose.

They want to send me abroad, as a Consul or a Minister. I said I didn't want any of the pie. God knows I am mean enough and lazy enough, now, without being a foreign consul.

Sometime in the course of the present century I think they will create a Commissioner of Patents, and then I hope to get a berth for Orion.

I published 6 or 7 letters in the Tribune while I was gone, now I cannot get them. I suppose I must have them copied. Love to all SAM.

Orion Clemens was once more a candidate for office: Nevada had become a State; with regularly elected officials, and Orion had somehow missed being chosen. His day of authority had passed, and the law having failed to support him, he was again back at his old occupation, setting type in St. Louis. He was, as ever, full of dreams and inventions that would some day lead to fortune. With the gift of the Sellers imagination, inherited by all the family, he lacked the driving power which means achievement. More and more as the years went by he would lean upon his brother for moral and physical support. The chances for him in Washington do not appear to have been bright. The political situation under Andrew Johnson was not a happy one.

To Orion Clemens, in St. Louis:

224 F. STREET, WASH., Feb. 21. (1868) MY DEAR BRO.,--I am glad you do not want the clerkship, for that Patent Office is in such a muddle that there would be no security for the permanency of a place in it. The same remark will apply to all offices here, now, and no doubt will, till the close of the present administration.

Any man who holds a place here, now, stands prepared at all times to vacate it. You are doing, now, exactly what I wanted you to do a year ago.

We chase phantoms half the days of our lives.

It is well if we learn wisdom even then, and save the other half.

I am in for it. I must go on chasing them until I marry--then I am done with literature and all other bosh,--that is, literature wherewith to please the general public.

I shall write to please myself, then. I hope you will set type till you complete that invention, for surely government pap must be nauseating food for a man--a man whom God has enabled to saw wood and be independent. It really seemed to me a falling from grace, the idea of going back to San Francisco nothing better than a mere postmaster, albeit the public would have thought I came with gilded honors, and in great glory.

I only retain correspondence enough, now, to make a living for myself, and have discarded all else, so that I may have time to spare for the book. Drat the thing, I wish it were done, or that I had no other writing to do.

This is the place to get a poor opinion of everybody in. There isn't one man in Washington, in civil office, who has the brains of Anson Burlingame--and I suppose if China had not seized and saved his great talents to the world, this government would have discarded him when his time was up.

There are more pitiful intellects in this Congress! Oh, geeminy! There are few of them that I find pleasant enough company to visit.

I am most infernally tired of Wash. and its "attractions." To be busy is a man's only happiness--and I am--otherwise I should die Yrs. aff SAM.

The secretarial position with Senator Stewart was short-lived. One cannot imagine Mark Twain as anybody's secretary, and doubtless there was little to be gained on either side by the arrangement. They parted without friction, though in later years, when Stewart had become old and irascible, he used to recount a list of grievances and declare that he had been obliged to threaten violence in order to bring Mark to terms; but this was because the author of Roughing It had in that book taken liberties with the Senator, to the extent of an anecdote and portrait which, though certainly harmless enough, had for some reason given deep offense.

Mark Twain really had no time for secretary work. For one thing he was associated with John Swinton in supplying a Washington letter to a list of newspapers, and then he was busy collecting his Quaker City letters, and preparing the copy for his book. Matters were going well enough, when trouble developed from an unexpected quarter. The Alta-California had copyrighted the letters and proposed to issue them in book form. There had been no contract which would prevent this, and the correspondence which Clemens undertook with the Alta management led to nothing. He knew that he had powerful friends among the owners, if he could reach them personally, and he presently concluded to return to San Francisco, make what arrangement he could, and finish his book there. It was his fashion to be prompt; in his next letter we find him already on the way.

To Mrs. Jane Clemens and family, in St. Louis:

AT SEA, Sunday, March 15, Lat. 25. (1868) DEAR FOLKS,--I have nothing to write, except that I am well--that the weather is fearfully hot-that the Henry Chauncey is a magnificent ship--that we have twelve hundred, passengers on board-that I have two staterooms, and so am not crowded--that I have many pleasant friends here, and the people are not so stupid as on the Quaker City--that we had Divine Service in the main saloon at 10.30 this morning--that we expect to meet the upward bound vessel in Latitude 23, and this is why I am writing now.

We shall reach Aspinwall Thursday morning at 6 o'clock, and San Francisco less than two weeks later. I worry a great deal about being obliged to go without seeing you all, but it could not be helped.

Dan Slote, my splendid room-mate in the Quaker City and the noblest man on earth, will call to see you within a month. Make him dine with you and spend the evening. His house is my home always in. New York. Yrs affy, SAM.

The San Francisco trip proved successful. Once on the ground Clemens had little difficulty in convincing the Alta publishers that they had received full value in the newspaper use of the letters, and that the book rights remained with the author. A letter to Bliss conveys the situation.

To Elisha Bliss, Jr., in Hartford:

SAN FRANCISCO, May 5, '68.

E. BLISS, Jr. Esq.

Dr. SIR,--The Alta people, after some hesitation, have given me permission to use my printed letters, and have ceased to think of publishing them themselves in book form. I am steadily at work, and shall start East with the completed Manuscript, about the middle of June.

I lectured here, on the trip, the other night-over sixteen hundred dollars in gold in the house--every seat taken and paid for before night. Yrs truly, MARK TWAIN.

But he did not sail in June. His friends persuaded him to cover his lecture circuit of two years before, telling the story of his travels. This he did with considerable profit, being everywhere received with great honors. He ended this tour with a second lecture in San Francisco, announced in a droll and characteristic fashion which delighted his Pacific admirers, and insured him a crowded house.--[See Mark Twain: A Biography, chap xlvi, and Appendix H.]

His agreement had been to deliver his MS. about August 1st. Returning by the Chauncey, July 28th, he was two days later in Hartford, and had placid the copy for the new book in Bliss's hands. It was by no means a compilation of his newspaper letters. His literary vision was steadily broadening. All of the letters had been radically edited, some had been rewritten, some entirely eliminated. He probably thought very well of the book, an opinion shared by Bliss, but it is unlikely that either of them realized that it was to become a permanent classic, and the best selling book of travel for at least fifty years.

IX.

LETTERS 1868-70. COURTSHIP, AND "THE INNOCENTS ABROAD"

The story of Mark Twain's courtship has been fully told in the completer story of his life; it need only be briefly sketched here as a setting for the letters of this period. In his letter of January 8th we note that he expects to go to Elmira for a few days as soon as he has time.

But he did not have time, or perhaps did not receive a pressing invitation until he had returned with his MS. from California. Then, through young Charles Langdon, his Quaker City shipmate, he was invited to Elmira. The invitation was given for a week, but through a subterfuge-- unpremeditated, and certainly fair enough in a matter of love-he was enabled to considerably prolong his visit. By the end of his stay he had become really "like one of the family," though certainly not yet accepted as such. The fragmentary letter that follows reflects something of his pleasant situation. The Mrs. Fairbanks mentioned in this letter had been something more than a "shipmother" to Mark Twain. She was a woman of fine literary taste, and Quaker City correspondent for her husband's paper, the Cleveland Herald. She had given Mark Twain sound advice as to his letters, which he had usually read to her, and had in no small degree modified his early natural tendency to exaggeration and outlandish humor. He owed her much, and never failed to pay her tribute.

Part of a letter to Mrs. Jane Clemens and family, in St. Louis:

ELMIRA, N.Y. Aug. 26, 1868. DEAR FOLKS,--You see I am progressing--though slowly. I shall be here a week yet maybe two--for Charlie Langdon cannot get away until his father's chief business man returns from a journey--and a visit to Mrs. Fairbanks, at Cleveland, would lose half its pleasure if Charlie were not along. Moulton of St. Louis ought to be there too. We three were Mrs. F's "cubs," in the Quaker City. She took good care that we were at church regularly on Sundays; at the 8-bells prayer meeting every night; and she kept our buttons sewed on and our clothing in order--and in a word was as busy and considerate, and as watchful over her family of uncouth and unruly cubs, and as patient and as long-suffering, withal, as a natural mother. So we expect.....

Aug. 25th. Didn't finish yesterday. Something called me away. I am most comfortably situated here. This is the pleasantest family I ever knew. I only have one trouble, and that is they give me too much thought and too much time and invention to the object of making my visit pass delightfully. It needs----

Just how and when he left the Langdon home the letters do not record. Early that fall he began a lecture engagement with James Redpath, proprietor of the Boston Lyceum Bureau, and his engagements were often within reach of Elmira. He had a standing invitation now to the Langdon home, and the end of the week often found him there. Yet when at last he proposed for the hand of Livy Langdon the acceptance was by no means prompt. He was a favorite in the Langdon household, but his suitability as a husband for the frail and gentle daughter was questioned.

However, he was carrying everything, just then, by storm. The largest houses everywhere were crowded to hear him. Papers spoke of him as the coming man of the age, people came to their doors to see him pass. There is but one letter of this period, but it gives us the picture.

To Mrs. Jane Clemens and family, in St. Louis:

CLEVELAND, Nov. 20, 1868. DEAR FOLKS,--I played against the Eastern favorite, Fanny Kemble, in Pittsburgh, last night. She had 200 in her house, and I had upwards of 1,500. All the seats were sold (in a driving rain storm, 3 days ago,) as reserved seats at 25 cents extra, even those in the second and third tiers--and when the last seat was gone the box office had not been open more than 2 hours. When I reached the theatre they were turning people away and the house was crammed, 150 or 200 stood up, all the evening.

I go to Elmira tonight. I am simply lecturing for societies, at $100 a pop. Yrs SAM.

It would be difficult for any family to refuse relationship with one whose star was so clearly ascending, especially when every inclination was in his favor, and the young lady herself encouraged his suit. A provisional engagement was presently made, but it was not finally ratified until February of the following year. Then in a letter from one of his lecture points he tells his people something of his happiness.

To Mrs. Jane Clemens and family, in St. Louis:

LOCKPORT, N. Y. Feb. 27, 1868. DEAR FOLKS,--I enclose $20 for Ma. I thought I was getting ahead of her little assessments of $35 a month, but find I am falling behind with her instead, and have let her go without money. Well, I did not mean to do it. But you see when people have been getting ready for months in a quiet way to get married, they are bound to grow stingy, and go to saving up money against that awful day when it is sure to be needed. I am particularly anxious to place myself in a position where I can carry on my married life in good shape on my own hook, because I have paddled my own canoe so long that I could not be satisfied now to let anybody help me--and my proposed father-in-law is naturally so liberal that it would be just like him to want to give us a start in life. But I don't want it that way. I can start myself. I don't want any help. I can run this institution without any outside assistance, and I shall have a wife who will stand by me like a soldier through thick and thin, and never complain. She is only a little body, but she hasn't her peer in Christendom. I gave her only a plain gold engagement ring, when fashion imperatively demands a two-hundred dollar diamond one, and told her it was typical of her future lot--namely, that she would have to flourish on substantials rather than luxuries. (But you see I know the girl--she don't care anything about luxuries.) She is a splendid girl. She spends no money but her usual year's allowance, and she spends nearly every cent of that on other people. She will be a good sensible little wife, without any airs about her. I don't make intercession for her beforehand and ask you to love her, for there isn't any use in that--you couldn't help it if you were to try.

I warn you that whoever comes within the fatal influence of her beautiful nature is her willing slave for evermore. I take my affidavit on that statement. Her father and mother and brother embrace and pet her constantly, precisely as if she were a sweetheart, instead of a blood relation. She has unlimited power over her father, and yet she never uses it except to make him help people who stand in need of help....

But if I get fairly started on the subject of my bride, I never shall get through--and so I will quit right here. I went to Elmira a little over a week ago, and staid four days and then had to go to New York on business.

....

No further letters have been preserved until June, when he is in Elmira and with his fiancee reading final proofs on the new book. They were having an idyllic good time, of course, but it was a useful time, too, for Olivia Langdon had a keen and refined literary instinct, and the Innocents Abroad, as well as Mark Twain's other books, are better to-day for her influence.

It has been stated that Mark Twain loved the lecture platform, but from his letters we see that even at this early date, when he was at the height of his first great vogue as a public entertainer, he had no love for platform life. Undoubtedly he rejoiced in the brief periods when he was actually before his audience and could play upon it with his master touch, but the dreary intermissions of travel and broken sleep were too heavy a price to pay.

To Mrs. Jane Clemens and family, in St. Louis

ELMIRA, June 4. (1868) DEAR FOLKS,--Livy sends you her love and loving good wishes, and I send you mine. The last 3 chapters of the book came tonight--we shall read it in the morning and then thank goodness, we are done.

In twelve months (or rather I believe it is fourteen,) I have earned just eighty dollars by my pen-- two little magazine squibs and one newspaper letter--altogether the idlest, laziest 14 months I ever spent in my life. And in that time my absolute and necessary expenses have been scorchingly heavy--for I have now less than three thousand six hundred dollars in bank out of the eight or nine thousand I have made during those months, lecturing. My expenses were something frightful during the winter. I feel ashamed of my idleness, and yet I have had really no inclination to do anything but court Livy. I haven't any other inclination yet. I have determined not to work as hard traveling, any more, as I did last winter, and so I have resolved not to lecture outside of the 6 New England States next winter. My Western course would easily amount to $10,000, but I would rather make 2 or 3 thousand in New England than submit again to so much wearing travel. (I have promised to talk ten nights for a thousand dollars in the State of New York, provided the places are close together.) But after all if I get located in a newspaper in a way to suit me, in the meantime, I don't want to lecture at all next winter, and probably shan't. I most cordially hate the lecture field. And after all, I shudder to think that I may never get out of it.

In all conversations with Gough, and Anna Dickinson, Nasby, Oliver Wendell Holmes, Wendell

Phillips and the other old stagers, I could not observe that they ever expected or hoped to get out of the business. I don't want to get wedded to it as they are. Livy thinks we can live on a very moderate sum and that we'll not need to lecture. I know very well that she can live on a small allowance, but I am not so sure about myself. I can't scare her by reminding her that her father's family expenses are forty thousand dollars a year, because she produces the documents at once to show that precious little of this outlay is on her account. But I must not commence writing about Livy, else I shall never stop. There isn't such another little piece of perfection in the world as she is.

My time is become so short, now, that I doubt if I get to California this summer. If I manage to buy into a paper, I think I will visit you a while and not go to Cal. at all. I shall know something about it after my next trip to Hartford. We all go there on the l0th--the whole family --to attend a wedding, on the 17th. I am offered an interest in a Cleveland paper which would pay me $2,300 to $2,500 a year, and a salary added of $3,000. The salary is fair enough, but the interest is not large enough, and so I must look a little further. The Cleveland folks say they can be induced to do a little better by me, and urge me to come out and talk business. But it don't strike me--I feel little or no inclination to go.

I believe I haven't anything else to write, and it is bed-time. I want to write to Orion, but I keep putting it off--I keep putting everything off. Day after day Livy and I are together all day long and until 10 at night, and then I feel dreadfully sleepy. If Orion will bear with me and forgive me I will square up with him yet. I will even let him kiss Livy.

My love to Mollie and Annie and Sammie and all. Good-bye. Affectionately, SAM.

It is curious, with his tendency to optimism and general expansion of futures, that he says nothing of the possible sales of the new book, or of his expectations in that line. It was issued in July, and by June the publishers must have had promising advance orders from their canvassers; but apparently he includes none of these chickens in his financial forecast. Even when the book had been out a full month, and was being shipped at the rate of several hundreds a day, he makes no reference to it in a letter to his sister, other than to ask if she has not received a copy. This, however, was a Mark Twain peculiarity. Writing was his trade; the returns from it seldom excited him. It was only when he drifted into strange and untried fields that he began to chase rainbows, to blow iridescent bubbles, and count unmined gold.

To Mrs. Moffett, in St. Louis:

BUFFALO, Aug. 20, 1869. MY DEAR SISTER,--I have only time to write a line. I got your letter this morning and mailed it to Livy. She will be expecting me tonight and I am sorry to disappoint her so, but then I couldn't well get away. I will go next Saturday.

I have bundled up Livy's picture and will try and recollect to mail it tomorrow. It is a porcelaintype and I think you will like it.

I am sorry I never got to St. Louis, because I may be too busy to go, for a long time. But I have been busy all the time and St. Louis is clear out of the way, and remote from the world and all ordinary routes of travel. You must not place too much weight upon this idea of moving the capital from Washington. St. Louis is in some respects a better place for it than Washington, though there isn't more than a toss-up between the two after all. One is dead and the other in a trance. Washington is in the centre of population and business, while St. Louis is far removed from both. And you know there is no geographical centre any more. The railroads and telegraph have done away with all that. It is no longer a matter of sufficient importance to be gravely considered by thinking men. The only centres, now, are narrowed down to those of intelligence, capital and population. As I said before Washington is the nearest to those and you don't have to paddle across a river on ferry boats of a pattern popular in the dark ages to get to it, nor have to clamber up vilely paved hills in rascally omnibuses along with a herd of all sorts of people after you are there. Secondly, the removal of the capital is one of those old, regular, reliable dodges that are the bread-and meat of back country congressmen. It is agitated every year. It always has been, it always will be; It is not new in any respect. Thirdly. The Capitol has cost $40,000,000 already and lacks a good deal of being finished, yet. There are single stones in the Treasury building (and a good many of them) that cost twenty-seven thousand dollars apiece--and millions were spent in the construction of that and the Patent Office and the other great government buildings. To move to St. Louis, the country must throw away a hundred millions of capital invested in those buildings, and go right to work to spend a hundred millions on new buildings in St. Louis. Shall we ever have a Congress, a majority of whose members are hopelessly insane? Probably not. But it is possible- unquestionably such a thing is possible. Only I don't believe it will happen in our time; and I am satisfied the capital will not be moved until it does happen. But if St. Louis would donate the ground and the buildings, it would be a different matter. No, Pamela, I don't see any good reason to believe you or I will ever see the capital moved.

I have twice instructed the publishers to send you a book--it was the first thing I did--long before the proofs were finished. Write me if it is not yet done.

Livy says we must have you all at our marriage, and I say we can't. It will be at Christmas or New Years, when such a trip across the country would be equivalent to murder & arson & everything else.--And it would cost five hundred dollars--an amount of money she don't know the value of now, but will before a year is gone. She grieves over it, poor little rascal, but it can't be helped. She must wait awhile, till I am firmly on my legs, & then she shall see you. She says her father and mother will invite you just as soon as the wedding date is definitely fixed, anyway--& she thinks that's bound to settle it. But the ice & snow, & the long hard journey, & the injudiciousness of laying out any money except what we are obliged to part with while we are so much in debt, settles the case differently. For it is a debt.

.....Mr. Langdon is just as good as bound for $25,000 for me, and has already advanced half of it in cash. I wrote and asked whether I had better send him my note, or a due-bill, or how he would prefer to have the indebtedness made of record and he answered every other topic in the letter pleasantly but never replied to that at all. Still, I shall give my note into the hands of his business agent here, and pay him the interest as it falls due. We must "go slow." We are not in the

Cleveland Herald. We are a hundred thousand times better off, but there isn't so much money in it.

(Remainder missing.)

In spite of the immediate success of his book--a success the like of which had scarcely been known in America-Mark Twain held himself to be, not a literary man, but a journalist: He had no plans for another book; as a newspaper owner and editor he expected, with his marriage, to settle down and devote the rest of his life to journalism. The paper was the Buffalo Express; his interest in it was one-third--the purchase price, twenty-five thousand dollars, of which he had paid a part, Jervis Langdon, his future father-in-law, having furnished cash and security for the remainder. He was already in possession in August, but he was not regularly in Buffalo that autumn, for he had agreed with Redpath to deliver his Quaker City lecture, and the tour would not end until a short time before his wedding-day, February 2, 1870.

Our next letter hardly belongs in this collection; as it was doubtless written with at least the possibility of publication in view. But it is too amusing, too characteristic of Mark Twain, to be omitted. It was sent in response to an invitation from the New York Society of California Pioneers to attend a banquet given in New York City, October 13, 1869, and was, of course, read to the assembled diners.

To the New York Society of California Pioneers, in New York City:

ELMIRA, October 11, 1869. GENTLEMEN,--Circumstances render it out of my power to take advantage of the invitation extended to me through Mr. Simonton, and be present at your dinner at New York. I regret this very much, for there are several among you whom I would have a right to join hands with on the score of old friendship, and I suppose I would have a sublime general right to shake hands with the rest of you on the score of kinship in California ups and downs in search of fortune.

If I were to tell some of my experience, you would recognize California blood in me; I fancy the old, old story would sound familiar, no doubt. I have the usual stock of reminiscences. For instance: I went to Esmeralda early. I purchased largely in the "Wide West," "Winnemucca," and other fine claims, and was very wealthy. I fared sumptuously on bread when flour was $200 a barrel and had beans for dinner every Sunday, when none but bloated aristocrats could afford such grandeur. But I finished by feeding batteries in a quartz mill at $15 a week, and wishing I was a battery myself and had somebody to feed me. My claims in Esmeralda are there yet. I suppose I could be persuaded to sell.

I went to Humboldt District when it was new; I became largely interested in the "Alba Nueva" and other claims with gorgeous names, and was rich again--in prospect. I owned a vast mining property there. I would not have sold out for less than $400,000 at that time. But I will now. Finally I walked home--200 miles partly for exercise, and partly because stage fare was expensive. Next I entered upon an affluent career in Virginia City, and by a judicious investment of labor and the capital of friends, became the owner of about all the worthless wild cat mines there were in that part of the country. Assessments did the business for me there. There were a hundred and seventeen assessments to one dividend, and the proportion of income to outlay was a little against me. My financial barometer went down to 32 Fahrenheit, and the subscriber was frozen out.

I took up extensions on the main lead-extensions that reached to British America, in one direction, and to the Isthmus of Panama in the other--and I verily believe I would have been a rich man if I had ever found those infernal extensions. But I didn't. I ran tunnels till I tapped the Arctic Ocean, and I sunk shafts till I broke through the roof of perdition; but those extensions turned up missing every time. I am willing to sell all that property and throw in the improvements.

Perhaps you remember that celebrated "North Ophir?" I bought that mine. It was very rich in pure silver. You could take it out in lumps as large as a filbert. But when it was discovered that those lumps were melted half dollars, and hardly melted at that, a painful case of "salting" was apparent, and the undersigned adjourned to the poorhouse again.

I paid assessments on "Hale and Norcross" until they sold me out, and I had to take in washing for a living--and the next month that infamous stock went up to $7,000 a foot.

I own millions and millions of feet of affluent silver leads in Nevada-- in fact the entire undercrust of that country nearly, and if Congress would move that State off my property so that I could get at it, I would be wealthy yet. But no, there she squats--and here am I. Failing health persuades me to sell. If you know of any one desiring a permanent investment, I can furnish one that will have the virtue of being eternal.

I have been through the California mill, with all its "dips, spurs and angles, variations and sinuosities." I have worked there at all the different trades and professions known to the catalogues. I have been everything, from a newspaper editor down to a cow-catcher on a locomotive, and I am encouraged to believe that if there had been a few more occupations to experiment on, I might have made a dazzling success at last, and found out what mysterious designs Providence had in creating me.

But you perceive that although I am not a Pioneer, I have had a sufficiently variegated time of it to enable me to talk Pioneer like a native, and feel like a Forty-Niner. Therefore, I cordially welcome you to your old-remembered homes and your long deserted firesides, and close this screed with the sincere hope that your visit here will be a happy one, and not embittered by the sorrowful surprises that absence and lapse of years are wont to prepare for wanderers; surprises which come in the form of old friends missed from their places; silence where familiar voices should be; the young grown old; change and decay everywhere; home a delusion and a disappointment; strangers at hearthstone; sorrow where gladness was; tears for laughter; the melancholy-pomp of death where the grace of life has been!

With all good wishes for the Returned Prodigals, and regrets that I cannot partake of a small piece of the fatted calf (rare and no gravy,) I am yours, cordially, MARK TWAIN.

In the next letter we find him in the midst of a sort of confusion of affairs, which, in one form or another, would follow him throughout the rest of his life. It was the price of his success and popularity, combined with his general gift for being concerned with a number of things, and a natural tendency for getting into hot water, which becomes more evident as the years and letters pass in review. Orion Clemens, in his attempt to save money for the government, had employed methods and agents which the officials at Washington did not understand, and refused to recognize. Instead of winning the credit and commendation he had expected, he now found himself pursued by claims of considerable proportions. The "land" referred to is the Tennessee tract, the heritage which John Clemens had provided for his children. Mark Twain had long since lost faith in it, and was not only willing, but eager to renounce his rights.

"Nasby" is, of course, David R. Locke, of the Toledo Blade, whose popularity at this time both as a lecturer and writer was very great. Clemens had met him here and there on their platform tour, and they had become good friends. Clemens, in fact, had once proposed to Nasby a joint trip to the Pacific coast.

The California idea had been given up, but both Mark Twain and Nasby found engagements enough, and sufficient profit east of the Mississippi. Boston was often their headquarters that winter ('69 and '70), and they were much together. "Josh Billings," another of Redpath's lecturers, was likewise often to be found in the Lyceum offices. There is a photograph of Mark Twain, Nasby, and Josh Billings together.

Clemens also, that winter, met William Dean Howells, then in the early days of his association with the Atlantic Monthly. The two men, so widely different, became firm friends at sight, and it was to Howells in the years to come that Mark Twain would write more letters, and more characteristic letters, than to any other living man. Howells had favorably reviewed 'The Innocents Abroad,' and after the first moment of their introduction had passed Clemens said: "When I read that review of yours I felt like the woman who said that she was so glad that her baby had come white." It was not the sort of thing that Howells would have said, but it was the sort of thing that he could understand and appreciate from Mark Twain.

In company with Nasby Clemens, that season, also met Oliver Wendell Holmes. Later he had sent Holmes a copy of his book and received a pleasantly appreciative reply. "I always like," wrote Holmes, "to hear what one of my fellow countrymen, who is not a Hebrew scholar, or a reader of hiero-glyphics, but a good-humored traveler with a pair of sharp, twinkling Yankee (in the broader sense) eyes in his head, has to say about the things that learned travelers often make unintelligible, and sentimental ones ridiculous or absurd .... I hope your booksellers will sell a hundred thousand copies of your travels." A wish that was realized in due time, though it is doubtful if Doctor Holmes or any one else at the moment believed that a book of that nature and price (it was $3.50 a copy) would ever reach such a sale.

To Mrs. Moffett, in St. Louis:

BOSTON, Nov. 9, 1869. MY DEAR SISTER,--Three or four letters just received from home. My first impulse was to send Orion a check on my publisher for the money he wants, but a sober second thought suggested that if he has not defrauded the government out of money, why pay, simply because the government chooses to consider him in its debt? No: Right is right. The idea don't suit me. Let him write the Treasury the state of the case, and tell them he has no money. If they make his sureties pay, then I will make the sureties whole, but I won't pay a cent of an unjust claim. You talk of disgrace. To my mind it would be just as disgraceful to allow one's self to be bullied into paying that which is unjust.

Ma thinks it is hard that Orion's share of the land should be swept away just as it is right on the point (as it always has been) of becoming valuable. Let her rest easy on that point. This letter is his ample authority to sell my share of the land immediately and appropriate the proceeds--giving no account to me, but repaying the amount to Ma first, or in case of her death, to you or your heirs, whenever in the future he shall be able to do it. Now, I want no hesitation in this matter. I renounce my ownership from this date, for this purpose, provided it is sold just as suddenly as he can sell it.

In the next place--Mr. Langdon is old, and is trying hard to withdraw from business and seek repose. I will not burden him with a purchase-- but I will ask him to take full possession of a coal tract of the land without paying a cent, simply conditioning that he shall mine and throw the coal into market at his own cost, and pay to you and all of you what he thinks is a fair portion of the profits accruing--you can do as you please with the rest of the land. Therefore, send me (to Elmira,) information about the coal deposits so framed that he can comprehend the matter and can intelligently instruct an agent how to find it and go to work.

Tomorrow night I appear for the first time before a Boston audience-- 4,000 critics--and on the success of this matter depends my future success in New England. But I am not distressed. Nasby is in the same boat. Tonight decides the fate of his brand-new lecture. He has just left my room-- been reading his lecture to me--was greatly depressed. I have convinced him that he has little to fear.

I get just about five hundred more applications to lecture than I can possibly fill--and in the West they say "Charge all you please, but come." I shan't go West at all. I stop lecturing the 22d of January, sure. But I shall talk every night up to that time. They flood me with high-priced invitations to write for magazines and papers, and publishers besiege me to write books. Can't do any of these things.

I am twenty-two thousand dollars in debt, and shall earn the money and pay it within two years-- and therefore I am not spending any money except when it is necessary.

I had my life insured for $10,000 yesterday (what ever became of Mr. Moffett's life insurance?) "for the benefit of my natural heirs"--the same being my mother, for Livy wouldn't claim it, you may be sure of that. This has taken $200 out of my pocket which I was going to send to Ma. But I will send her some, soon. Tell Orion to keep a stiff upper lip--when the worst comes to the worst I will come forward. Must talk in Providence, R. I., tonight. Must leave now. I thank Mollie and Orion and the rest for your letters, but you see how I am pushed--ought to have 6 clerks. Affectionately, SAM.

By the end of January, 1870 more than thirty thousand copies of the Innocents had been sold, and in a letter to his publisher the author expressed his satisfaction.

To Elisha Bliss, in Hartford:

ELMIRA, Jan. 28 '70. FRIEND BLISS,--..... Yes, I am satisfied with the way you are running the book. You are running it in staving, tip-top, first-class style. I never wander into any corner of the country but I find that an agent has been there before me, and many of that community have read the book. And on an average about ten people a day come and hunt me up to thank me and tell me I'm a benefactor! I guess this is a part of the programme we didn't expect in the first place.

I think you are rushing this book in a manner to be proud of; and you will make the finest success of it that has ever been made with a subscription book, I believe. What with advertising, establishing agencies, &c., you have got an enormous lot of machinery under way and hard at work in a wonderfully short space of time. It is easy to see, when one travels around, that one must be endowed with a deal of genuine generalship in order to maneuvre a publication whose line of battle stretches from end to end of a great continent, and whose foragers and skirmishers invest every hamlet and besiege every village hidden away in all the vast space between.

I'll back you against any publisher in America, Bliss--or elsewhere. Yrs as ever CLEMENS.

There is another letter written just at this time which of all letters must not be omitted here. Only five years earlier Mark Twain, poor, and comparatively unknown, had been carrying water while Jim Gillis and Dick Stoker washed out the pans of dirt in search of the gold pocket which they did not find. Clemens must have received a letter from Gillis referring to some particular occasion, but it has disappeared; the reply, however, always remained one of James Gillis's treasured possessions.

To James Gillis, in his cabin on Jackass Hill, Tuolumne Co., California:

ELMIRA, N.Y. Jan. 26, '70. DEAR JIM,--I remember that old night just as well! And somewhere among my relics I have your remembrance stored away. It makes my heart ache yet to call to mind some of those days. Still, it shouldn't--for right in the depths of their poverty and their pocket-hunting vagabondage lay the germ of my coming good fortune. You remember the one gleam of jollity that shot across our dismal sojourn in the rain and mud of Angels' Camp I mean that day we sat around the tavern stove and heard that chap tell about the frog and how they filled him with shot. And you remember how we quoted from the yarn and laughed over it, out there on the hillside while you and dear old Stoker panned and washed. I jotted the story down in my notebook that day, and would have been glad to get ten or fifteen dollars for it--I was just that blind.

But then we were so hard up! I published that story, and it became widely known in America, India, China, England--and the reputation it made for me has paid me thousands and thousands of dollars since. Four or five months ago I bought into the Express (I have ordered it sent to you as long as you live--and if the book keeper sends you any bills, you let me hear of it.) I went heavily in debt never could have dared to do that, Jim, if we hadn't heard the jumping Frog story that day.

And wouldn't I love to take old Stoker by the hand, and wouldn't I love to see him in his great specialty, his wonderful rendition of "Rinalds" in the" Burning Shame!" Where is Dick and what is he doing? Give him my fervent love and warm old remembrances.

A week from today I shall be married to a girl even better, and lovelier than the peerless "Chapparal Quails." You can't come so far, Jim, but still I cordially invite you to come, anyhow-- and I invite Dick, too. And if you two boys were to land here on that pleasant occasion, we would make you right royally welcome. Truly your friend, SAML L. CLEMENS.

P. S. "California plums are good, Jim--particularly when they are stewed."

Steve Gillis, who sent a copy of his letter to the writer, added: "Dick Stoker--dear, gentle unselfish old Dick-died over three years ago, aged 78. I am sure it will be a melancholy pleasure to Mark to know that Dick lived in comfort all his later life, sincerely loved and respected by all who knew him. He never left Jackass Hill. He struck a pocket years ago containing enough not only to build himself a comfortable house near his old cabin, but to last him, without work, to his painless end. He was a Mason, and was buried by the Order in Sonora.

"The 'Quails'--the beautiful, the innocent, the wild little Quails-- lived way out in the Chapparal; on a little ranch near the Stanislaus River, with their father and mother. They were famous for their beauty and had many suitors."

The mention of "California plums" refers to some inedible fruit which Gillis once, out of pure goodness of heart, bought of a poor wandering squaw, and then, to conceal his motive, declared that they were something rare and fine, and persisted in eating them, though even when stewed they nearly choked him.

X.

LETTERS 1870-71. MARK TWAIN IN BUFFALO. MARRIAGE. THE BUFFALO EXPRESS. "MEMORANDA." LECTURES. A NEW BOOK

Samuel L. Clemens and Olivia Langdon were married in the Langdon home at Elmira, February 2, 1870, and took up their residence in Buffalo in a beautiful home, a wedding present from the bride's father. The story of their wedding, and the amusing circumstances connected with their establishment in Buffalo, have been told elsewhere.--[Mark Twain: A Biography, chap. lxxiv.]

Mark Twain now believed that he was through with lecturing. Two letters to Redpath, his agent, express his comfortable condition.

To James Redpath, in Boston:

BUFFALO, March 22, 1890. DEAR RED,--I am not going to lecture any more forever. I have got things ciphered down to a fraction now. I know just about what it will cost us to live and I can make the money without lecturing. Therefore old man, count me out. Your friend, S. L. CLEMENS.

To James Redpath, in Boston:

ELMIRA, N. Y. May 10, 1870. FRIEND REDPATH,--I guess I am out of the field permanently.

Have got a lovely wife; a lovely house, bewitchingly furnished; a lovely carriage, and a coachman whose style and dignity are simply awe- inspiring--nothing less--and I am making more money than necessary--by considerable, and therefore why crucify myself nightly on the platform. The subscriber will have to be excused from the present season at least.

Remember me to Nasby, Billings and Fall.--[Redpath's partner in the lecture lyceum.]--Luck to you! I am going to print your menagerie, Parton and all, and make comments.

In next Galaxy I give Nasby's friend and mine from Philadelphia (John Quill, a literary thief) a "hyste." Yours always and after. MARK.

The reference to the Galaxy in the foregoing letter has to do with a department called Memoranda, which he had undertaken to conduct for the new magazine. This work added substantially to his income, and he believed it would be congenial. He was allowed free hand to write and print what he chose, and some of his best work at this time was published in the new department, which he continued for a year.

Mark Twain now seemed to have his affairs well regulated. His mother and sister were no longer far away in St. Louis. Soon after his marriage they had, by his advice, taken up residence at Fredonia, New York, where they could be easily visited from Buffalo.

Altogether, the outlook seemed bright to Mark Twain and his wife, during the first months of their marriage. Then there came a change. In a letter which Clemens wrote to his mother and sister we get the first chapter of disaster.

To Mrs. Jane Clemens, and Mrs. Moffett, in Fredonia, N. Y.:

ELMIRA, N. Y. June 25, 1870. MY DEAR MOTHER AND SISTER,--We were called here suddenly by telegram, 3 days ago. Mr. Langdon is very low. We have well-nigh lost hope--all of us except Livy.

Mr. Langdon, whose hope is one of his most prominent characteristics, says himself, this morning, that his recovery is only a possibility, not a probability. He made his will this morning--that is, appointed executors--nothing else was necessary. The household is sad enough Charley is in Bavaria. We telegraphed Munroe & Co. Paris, to notify Charley to come home--they sent the message to Munich. Our message left here at 8 in the morning and Charley's answer arrived less than eight hours afterward. He sailed immediately.

He will reach home two weeks from now. The whole city is troubled. As I write (at the office,) a dispatch arrives from Charley who has reached London, and will sail thence on 28th. He wants news. We cannot send him any. Affectionately SAM.

P. S. I sent $300 to Fredonia Bank for Ma--It is in her name.

Mrs. Clemens, herself, was not in the best of health at this time, but devotion to her father took her to his bedside, where she insisted upon standing long, hard watches, the strain of which told upon her severely. Meantime, work must go on; the daily demand of the newspaper and the monthly call of the Memoranda could not go unheeded. Also, Bliss wanted a new book, and met Mark Twain at Elmira to arrange for it. In a letter to Orion we learn of this project.

To Orion Clemens, in St. Louis:

ELMIRA, July 15, 1870 MY DEAR BRO.,--Per contract I must have another 600-page book ready for my publisher Jan. z, and I only began it today. The subject of it is a secret, because I may possibly change it. But as it stands, I propose to do up Nevada and Cal., beginning with the trip across the country in the stage. Have you a memorandum of the route we took--or the names of any of the Stations we stopped at? Do you remember any of the scenes, names, incidents or adventures of the coach trip?--for I remember next to nothing about the matter. Jot down a foolscap page of items for me. I wish I could have two days' talk with you.

I suppose I am to get the biggest copyright, this time, ever paid on a subscription book in this country.

Give our love to Mollie.--Mr. Langdon is very low. Yr Bro SAM.

The "biggest copyright," mentioned in this letter, was a royalty of 7 1/2 per cent., which Bliss had agreed to pay, on the retail price of the book. The book was Roughing It, though this title was not decided upon until considerably later. Orion Clemens eagerly furnished a detailed memorandum of the route of their overland journey, which brought this enthusiastic acknowledgment:

To Orion Clemens, in St. Louis:

BUF., 1870. DEAR BRO.,--I find that your little memorandum book is going to be ever so much use to me, and will enable me to make quite a coherent narrative of the Plains journey instead of slurring it over and jumping 2,000 miles at a stride. The book I am writing will sell. In return for the use of the little memorandum book I shall take the greatest pleasure in forwarding to you the third $1,000 which the publisher of the forthcoming work sends me or the first $1,000, I am not particular--they will both be in the first quarterly statement of account from the publisher. In great haste, Yr Obliged Bro. SAM.

Love to Mollie. We are all getting along tolerably well.

Mr. Langdon died early in August, and Mrs. Clemens returned to Buffalo, exhausted in mind and body. If she hoped for rest now, in the quiet of her own home, she was disappointed, as the two brief letters that follow clearly show.

To Mrs. Moffett, in Fredonia, N. Y.:

BUFFALO, Aug. 31, 70. MY DEAR SISTER,--I know I ought to be thrashed for not writing you, but I have kept putting it off. We get heaps of letters every day; it is a comfort to have somebody like you that will let us shirk and be patient over it. We got the book and I did think I wrote a line thanking you for it-but I suppose I neglected it.

We are getting along tolerably well. Mother [Mrs. Langdon] is here, and Miss Emma Nye. Livy cannot sleep since her father's death--but I give her a narcotic every night and make her. I am just as busy as I can be-- am still writing for the Galaxy and also writing a book like the "Innocents" in size and style. I have got my work ciphered down to days, and I haven't a single day to spare between this and the date which, by written contract I am to deliver the M.S. of the book to the publisher. ----In a hurry Affectionately SAM

To Orion Clemens, in St, Louis:

BUF. Sept. 9th, 1870. MY DEAR BRO,--O here! I don't want to be consulted at all about Tenn. I don't want it even mentioned to me. When I make a suggestion it is for you to act upon it or throw it aside, but I beseech you never to ask my advice, opinion or consent about that hated property. If it was because I felt the slightest personal interest in the infernal land that I ever made a suggestion, the suggestion would never be made.

Do exactly as you please with the land--always remember this--that so trivial a percentage as ten per cent will never sell it.

It is only a bid for a somnambulist.

I have no time to turn round, a young lady visitor (schoolmate of Livy's) is dying in the house of typhoid fever (parents are in South Carolina) and the premises are full of nurses and doctors and we are all fagged out. Yrs. SAM.

Miss Nye, who had come to cheer her old schoolmate, had been prostrated with the deadly fever soon after her arrival. Another period of anxiety and nursing followed. Mrs. Clemens, in spite of her frail health, devoted much time to her dying friend, until by the time the end came she was herself in a precarious condition. This was at the end of September. A little more than a month later, November 7th, her first child, Langdon Clemens, was prematurely born. To the Rev. Joseph H. Twichell and wife, of Hartford, Mark Twain characteristically announced the new arrival.

To Rev. Joseph H. Twichell and wife, in Hartford, Conn.:

BUFFALO, Nov 12, '70. DEAR UNCLE AND AUNT,--I came into the world on the 7th inst., and consequently am about five days old, now. I have had wretched health ever since I made my appearance. First one thing and then another has kept me under the weather, and as a general thing I have been chilly and uncomfortable.

I am not corpulent, nor am I robust in any way. At birth I only weighed 4 1/2 pounds with my clothes on--and the clothes were the chief feature of the weight, too, I am obliged to confess. But I am doing finely, all things considered. I was at a standstill for 3 days and a half, but during the last 24 hours I have gained nearly an ounce, avoirdupois.

They all say I look very old and venerable-and I am aware, myself, that I never smile. Life seems a serious thing, what I have seen of it--and my observation teaches me that it is made up mainly of hiccups, unnecessary washings, and colic. But no doubt you, who are old, have long since grown accustomed and reconciled to what seems to me such a disagreeable novelty.

My father said, this morning, when my face was in repose and thoughtful, that I looked precisely as young Edward Twichell of Hartford used to look some is months ago--chin, mouth, forehead, expression--everything.

My little mother is very bright and cheery, and I guess she is pretty happy, but I don't know what about. She laughs a great deal, notwithstanding she is sick abed. And she eats a great deal, though she says that is because the nurse desires it. And when she has had all the nurse desires her to have, she asks for more. She is getting along very well indeed.

My aunt Susie Crane has been here some ten days or two weeks, but goes home today, and Granny Fairbanks of Cleveland arrives to take her place. --[Mrs. Fairbanks, of the Quaker City excursion.] Very lovingly, LANGDON CLEMENS.

P. S. Father said I had better write because you would be more interested in me, just now, than in the rest of the family.

Clemens had made the acquaintance of the Rev. Joseph Hopkins Twichell and his wife during his several sojourns in Hartford, in connection with his book publication, and the two men had immediately become firm friends. Twichell had come to Elmira in February to the wedding to assist Rev. Thos. K. Beecher in the marriage ceremony. Joseph Twichell was a devout Christian, while Mark Twain was a doubter, even a scoffer, where orthodoxy was concerned, yet the sincerity and humanity of the two men drew them together; their friendship was lifelong.

A second letter to Twichell, something more than a month later, shows a somewhat improved condition in the Clemens household.

To Rev. Twichell, in Hartford:

BUF. Dec. 19th, 1870. DEAR J. H.,--All is well with us, I believe--though for some days the baby was quite ill. We consider him nearly restored to health now, however. Ask my brother about us--you will find him at Bliss's publishing office, where he is gone to edit Bliss's new paper--left here last Monday. Make his and his wife's acquaintance. Take Mrs. T. to see them as soon as they are fixed.

Livy is up, and the prince keeps her busy and anxious these latter days and nights, but I am a bachelor up stairs and don't have to jump up and get the soothing syrup--though I would as soon do it as not, I assure you. (Livy will be certain to read this letter.)

Tell Harmony (Mrs. T.) that I do hold the baby, and do it pretty handily, too, although with occasional apprehensions that his loose head will fall off. I don't have to quiet him--he hardly ever utters a cry. He is always thinking about something. He is a patient, good little baby.

Smoke? I always smoke from 3 till 5 Sunday afternoons--and in New York the other day I smoked a week, day and night. But when Livy is well I smoke only those two hours on Sunday. I'm "boss" of the habit, now, and shall never let it boss me any more. Originally, I quit solely on Livy's account, (not that I believed there was the faintest reason in the matter, but just as I would deprive myself of sugar in my coffee if she wished it, or quit wearing socks if she thought them immoral,) and I stick to it yet on Livy's account, and shall always continue to do so, without a pang. But somehow it seems a pity that you quit, for Mrs. T. didn't mind it if I remember rightly. Ah, it is turning one's back upon a kindly Providence to spurn away from us the good creature he sent to make the breath of life a luxury as well as a necessity, enjoyable as well as useful, to go and quit smoking when then ain't any sufficient excuse for it! Why, my old boy, when they use to tell me I would shorten my life ten years by smoking, they little knew the devotee they were wasting their puerile word upon--they little knew how trivial and valueless I would regard a decade that had no smoking in it! But I won't persuade you, Twichell--I won't until I see you again--but then we'll smoke for a week together, and then shut off again.

I would have gone to Hartford from New York last Saturday, but I got so homesick I couldn't. But maybe I'll come soon.

No, Sir, catch me in the metropolis again, to get homesick.

I didn't know Warner had a book out.

We send oceans and continents of love--I have worked myself down, today. Yrs always MARK.

With his establishment in Buffalo, Clemens, as already noted, had persuaded his sister, now a widow, and his mother, to settle in Fredonia, not far away. Later, he had found a position for Orion, as editor of a small paper which Bliss had established. What with these several diversions and the sorrows and sicknesses of his own household, we can readily imagine that literary work had been performed under difficulties. Certainly, humorous writing under such disturbing conditions could not have been easy, nor could we expect him to accept an invitation to be present and make a comic speech at an agricultural dinner, even though Horace Greeley would preside. However, he sent to the secretary of the association a letter which might be read at the gathering:

To A. B. Crandall, in Woodberry Falls, N. Y., to be read at an agricultural dinner:

BUFFALO, Dec. 26, 1870. GENTLEMEN,--I thank you very much for your invitation to the Agricultural dinner, and would promptly accept it and as promptly be there but for the fact that Mr. Greeley is very busy this month and has requested me to clandestinely continue for him in The Tribune the articles "What I Know about Farming." Consequently the necessity of explaining to the readers of that journal why buttermilk cannot be manufactured profitably at 8 cents a quart out of butter that costs 60 cents a pound compels my stay at home until the article is written. With reiterated thanks, I am Yours truly, MARK TWAIN.

In this letter Mark Twain made the usual mistake as to the title of the Greeley farming series, "What I Know of Farming" being the correct form.

The Buffalo Express, under Mark Twain's management, had become a sort of repository for humorous efforts, often of an indifferent order. Some of these things, signed by nom de plumes, were charged to Mark Twain. When Bret Harte's "Heathen Chinee" devastated the country, and was so widely parodied, an imitation of it entitled, "Three Aces," and signed "Carl Byng," was printed in the Express. Thomas Bailey Aldrich, then editor of Every Saturday, had not met Mark Twain, and, noticing the verses printed in the exchanges over his signature, was one of those who accepted them as Mark Twain's work. He wrote rather an uncomplimentary note in Every Saturday concerning the poem and its authorship, characterizing it as a feeble imitation of Bret Harte's "Heathen Chinee." Clemens promptly protested to Aldrich, then as promptly regretted having done so, feeling that he was making too much of a small matter. Hurriedly he sent a second brief note.

To Thomas Bailey Aldrich, editor of "Every Saturday," Boston, Massachusetts:

BUFFALO, Jan. 22, 1870. DEAR SIR,--Please do not publish the note I sent you the other day about "Hy. Slocum's" plagiarism entitled "Three Aces"--it is not important enough for such a long paragraph. Webb writes me that he has put in a paragraph about it, too--and I have requested him to suppress it. If you would simply state, in a line and a half under "Literary Notes," that you mistook one "Hy. Slocum" (no, it was one "Carl Byng," I perceive) "Carl Byng" for Mark Twain, and that it was the former who wrote the plagiarism entitled "Three Aces," I think that would do a fair justice without any unseemly display. But it is hard to be accused of plagiarism--a crime I never have committed in my life. Yrs. Truly MARK TWAIN.

But this came too late. Aldrich replied that he could not be prevented from doing him justice, as forty-two thousand copies of the first note, with the editor's apology duly appended, were already in press. He would withdraw his apology in the next number of Every Saturday, if Mark Twain said so. Mark Twain's response this time assumed the proportions of a letter.

To Thomas Bailey Aldrich, in Boston:

472 DELAWARE ST., BUFFALO, Jan. 28. DEAR MR. ALDRICH,--No indeed, don't take back the apology! Hang it, I don't want to abuse a man's civility merely because he gives me the chance.

I hear a good deal about doing things on the "spur of the moment"-- I invariably regret the things I do on the spur of the moment. That disclaimer of mine was a case in point. I am ashamed every time I think of my bursting out before an unconcerned public with that bombastic pow- wow about burning publishers' letters, and all that sort of imbecility, and about my not being an imitator, etc. Who would find out that I am a natural fool if I kept always cool and never let nature come to the surface? Nobody.

But I did hate to be accused of plagiarizing Bret Harte, who trimmed and trained and schooled me patiently until he changed me from an awkward utterer of coarse grotesquenesses to a writer of paragraphs and chapters that have found a certain favor in the eyes of even some of the very decentest people in the land--and this grateful remembrance of mine ought to be worth its face, seeing that Bret broke our long friendship a year ago without any cause or provocation that I am aware of.

Well, it is funny, the reminiscences that glare out from murky corners of one's memory, now and then, without warning. Just at this moment a picture flits before me: Scene--private room in Barnum's Restaurant, Virginia, Nevada; present, Artemus Ward, Joseph T. Goodman, (editor and proprietor Daily "Enterprise"), and "Dan de Quille" and myself, reporters for same; remnants of the feast thin and scattering, but such tautology and repetition of empty bottles everywhere visible as to be offensive to the sensitive eye; time, 2.30 A.M.; Artemus thickly reciting a poem about a certain infant you wot of, and interrupting himself and being interrupted every few lines by poundings of the table and shouts of "Splendid, by Shorzhe!" Finally, a long, vociferous, poundiferous and vitreous jingling of applause announces the conclusion, and then Artemus: "Let every man 'at loves his fellow man and 'preciates a poet 'at loves his fellow man, stan' up!--Stan' up and drink health and long life to Thomas Bailey Aldrich!--and drink it stanning!" (On all hands fervent, enthusiastic, and sincerely honest attempts to comply.) Then Artemus: "Well--consider it stanning, and drink it just as ye are!" Which was done.

You must excuse all this stuff from a stranger, for the present, and when I see you I will apologize in full.

Do you know the prettiest fancy and the neatest that ever shot through Harte's brain? It was this: When they were trying to decide upon a vignette for the cover of the Overland, a grizzly bear (of the arms of the State of California) was chosen. Nahl Bras. carved him and the page was printed, with him in it, looking thus: [Rude sketch of a grizzly bear.]

As a bear, he was a success--he was a good bear--. But then, it was objected, that he was an objectless bear--a bear that meant nothing in particular, signified nothing,--simply stood there snarling over his shoulder at nothing--and was painfully and manifestly a boorish and ill- natured intruder upon the fair page. All hands said that--none were satisfied. They hated badly to give him up, and yet they hated as much to have him there when there was no paint to him. But presently Harte took a pencil and drew these two simple lines under his feet and behold he was a magnificent success!--the ancient symbol of California savagery snarling at the approaching type of high and progressive Civilization, the first Overland locomotive!: [Sketch of a small section of railway track.]

I just think that was nothing less than inspiration itself.

Once more I apologize, and this time I do it "stanning!" Yrs. Truly SAML. L. CLEMENS.

The "two simple lines," of course, were the train rails under the bear's feet, and completed the striking cover design of the Overland monthly.

The brief controversy over the "Three Aces" was the beginning of along and happy friendship between Aldrich and Mark Twain. Howells, Aldrich, Twichell, and Charles Dudley Warner--these were Mark Twain's intimates, men that he loved, each for his own special charm and worth.

Aldrich he considered the most brilliant of living men.

In his reply to Clemens's letter, Aldrich declared that he was glad now that, for the sake of such a letter, he had accused him falsely, and added:

"Mem. Always abuse people.

"When you come to Boston, if you do not make your presence manifest to me, I'll put in a !! in 'Every Saturday' to the effect that though you are generally known as Mark Twain your favorite nom de plume is 'Barry Gray.'"

Clemens did not fail to let Aldrich know when he was in Boston again, and the little coterie of younger writers forgathered to give him welcome.

Buffalo agreed with neither Mrs. Clemens nor the baby. What with nursing and anguish of mind, Mark Twain found that he could do nothing on the new book, and that he must give up his magazine department. He had lost interest in his paper and his surroundings in general. Journalism and authorship are poor yoke-mates. To Onion Clemens, at this time editing Bliss's paper at Hartford, he explained the situation.

To Onion Clemens, in Hartford:

BUFFALO, 4th 1871. MY DEAR BRO,--What I wanted of the "Liar" Sketch, was to work it into the California book--which I shall do. But day before yesterday I concluded to go out of the Galaxy on the strength of it, so I have turned it into the last Memoranda I shall ever write, and published it as a "specimen chapter" of my forthcoming book.

I have written the Galaxy people that I will never furnish them another article long or short, for any price but $500.00 cash--and have requested them not to ask me for contributions any more, even at that price.

I hope that lets them out, for I will stick to that. Now do try and leave me clear out of the 'Publisher' for the present, for I am endangering my reputation by writing too much--I want to get out of the public view for awhile.

I am still nursing Livy night and day and cannot write anything. I am nearly worn out. We shall go to Elmira ten days hence (if Livy can travel on a mattress then,) and stay there till I have finished the California book--say three months. But I can't begin work right away when I get there--must have a week's rest, for I have been through 30 days' terrific siege.

That makes it after the middle of March before I can go fairly to work-- and then I'll have to hump myself and not lose a moment. You and Bliss just put yourselves in my place and you will see that my hands are full and more than full.

When I told Bliss in N. Y. that I would write something for the Publisher I could not know that I was just about to lose fifty days. Do you see the difference it makes? Just as soon as ever I can, I will send some of the book M.S. but right in the first chapter I have got to alter the whole style of one of my characters and re-write him clear through to where I am now. It is no fool of a job, I can tell you, but the book will be greatly bettered by it. Hold on a few days--four or five--and I will see if I can get a few chapters fixed to send to Bliss.

I have offered this dwelling house and the Express for sale, and when we go to Elmira we leave here for good. I shall not select a new home till the book is finished, but we have little doubt that Hartford will be the place.

We are almost certain of that. Ask Bliss how it would be to ship our furniture to Hartford, rent an upper room in a building and unbox it and store it there where somebody can frequently look after it. Is not the idea good? The furniture is worth $10,000 or $12,000 and must not be jammed into any kind of a place and left unattended to for a year.

The first man that offers $25,000 for our house can take it--it cost that. What are taxes there?

Here, all bunched together--of all kinds, they are 7 per cent--simply ruin.

The things you have written in the Publisher are tip-top. In haste, Yr Bro SAM

There are no further letters until the end of April, by which time the situation had improved. Clemens had sold his interest in the Express (though at a loss), had severed his magazine connection, and was located at Quarry Farm, on a beautiful hilltop above Elmira, the home of Mrs. Clemens's sister, Mrs. Theodore Crane. The pure air and rest of that happy place, where they were to spend so many idyllic summers, had proved beneficial to the sick ones, and work on the new book progressed in consequence. Then Mark Twain's old editor, "Joe" Goodman, came from Virginia City for a visit, and his advice and encouragement were of the greatest value. Clemens even offered to engage Goodman on a salary, to remain until he had finished his book. Goodman declined the salary, but extended his visit, and Mark Twain at last seems to have found himself working under ideal conditions. He jubilantly reports his progress.

To Elisha Bliss, in Hartford:

ELMIRA, Monday. May 15th 1871 FRIEND BLISS,--Yrs rec'd enclosing check for $703.35 The old "Innocents" holds out handsomely.

I have MS. enough on hand now, to make (allowing for engravings) about 400 pages of the book--consequently am two-thirds done. I intended to run up to Hartford about the middle of the week and take it along; because it has chapters in it that ought by all means to be in the prospectus; but I find myself so thoroughly interested in my work, now (a thing I have not experienced for months) that I can't bear to lose a single moment of the inspiration. So I will stay here and peg away as long as it lasts. My present idea is to write as much more as I have already written, and then cull from the mass the very best chapters and discard the rest. I am not half as well satisfied with the first part of the book as I am with what I am writing now. When I get it done I want to see the man who will begin to read it and not finish it. If it falls short of the "Innocents" in any respect I shall lose my guess.

When I was writing the "Innocents" my daily stunt was 30 pages of MS and I hardly ever got beyond it; but I have gone over that nearly every day for the last ten. That shows that I am writing with a red-hot interest. Nothing grieves me now--nothing troubles me, nothing bothers me or gets my attention--I don't think of anything but the book, and I don't have an hour's unhappiness about anything and don't care two cents whether school keeps or not. It will be a bully book. If I keep up my present lick three weeks more I shall be able and willing to scratch out half of the chapters of the Overland narrative--and shall do it.

You do not mention having received my second batch of MS, sent a week or two ago--about 100 pages.

If you want to issue a prospectus and go right to canvassing, say the word and I will forward some more MS--or send it by hand--special messenger. Whatever chapters you think are unquestionably good, we will retain of course, so they can go into a prospectus as well one time as another. The book will be done soon, now. I have 1200 pages of MS already written and am now writing 200 a week--more than that, in fact; during the past week wrote 23 one day, then 30, 33, 35, 52, and 65. --How's that?

It will be a starchy book, and should be full of snappy pictures-- especially pictures worked in with the letterpress. The dedication will be worth the price of the volume--thus:

To the Late Cain. This Book is Dedicated:

Not on account of respect for his memory, for it merits little respect; not on account of sympathy with him, for his bloody deed placed him without the pale of sympathy, strictly speaking: but out of a mere human commiseration for him that it was his misfortune to live in a dark age that knew not the beneficent Insanity Plea.

I think it will do. Yrs. CLEMENS.

P. S.--The reaction is beginning and my stock is looking up. I am getting the bulliest offers for books and almanacs; am flooded with lecture invitations, and one periodical offers me $6,000 cash for 12 articles, of any length and on any subject, treated humorously or otherwise.

The suggested dedication "to the late Cain" may have been the humoristic impulse of the moment. At all events, it did not materialize.

Clemens's enthusiasm for work was now such that he agreed with Redpath to return to the platform that autumn, and he began at once writing lectures. His disposal of the Buffalo paper had left him considerably in debt, and platforming was a sure and quick method of retrenchment. More than once in the years ahead Mark Twain would return to travel and one-night stands to lift a burden of debt. Brief letters to Redpath of this time have an interest and even a humor of their own.

Letters to James Redpath, in Boston:

ELMIRA, June 27, 1871. DEAR RED,--Wrote another lecture--a third one-today. It is the one I am going to deliver. I think I shall call it "Reminiscences of Some Pleasant Characters Whom I Have Met," (or should the "whom" be left out?) It covers my whole acquaintance--kings, lunatics, idiots and all. Suppose you give the item a start in the Boston papers. If I write fifty lectures I shall only choose one and talk that one only.

No sir: Don't you put that scarecrow (portrait) from the Galaxy in, I won't stand that nightmare. Yours, MARK.

ELMIRA, July 10, 1871. DEAR REDPATH,--I never made a success of a lecture delivered in a church yet. People are afraid to laugh in a church. They can't be made to do it in any possible way.

Success to Fall's carbuncle and many happy returns. Yours, MARK.

To Mr. Fall, in Boston:

ELMIRA, N. Y. July 20, 1871. FRIEND FALL,--Redpath tells me to blow up. Here goes! I wanted you to scare Rondout off with a big price. $125 ain't big. I got $100 the first time I ever talked there and now they have a much larger hall. It is a hard town to get to--I run a chance of getting caught by the ice and missing next engagement. Make the price $150 and let them draw out. Yours MARK

Letters to James Redpath, in Boston:

HARTFORD, Tuesday Aug. 8, 1871. DEAR RED,--I am different from other women; my mind changes oftener. People who have no mind can easily be steadfast and firm, but when a man is loaded down to the guards with it, as I am, every heavy sea of foreboding or inclination, maybe of indolence, shifts the cargo. See? Therefore, if you will notice, one week I am likely to give rigid instructions to confine me to New England; next week, send me to Arizona; the next week withdraw my name; the next week give you full untrammelled swing; and the week following modify it. You must try to keep the run of my mind, Redpath, it is your business being the agent, and it always was too many for me. It appears to me to be one of the finest pieces of mechanism I have ever met with. Now about the West, this week, I am willing that you shall retain all the Western engagements. But what I shall want next week is still with God.

Let us not profane the mysteries with soiled hands and prying eyes of sin. Yours, MARK.

P. S. Shall be here 2 weeks, will run up there when Nasby comes.

ELMIRA, N. Y. Sept. 15, 1871. DEAR REDPATH,--I wish you would get me released from the lecture at Buffalo. I mortally hate that society there, and I don't doubt they hired me. I once gave them a packed house free of charge, and they never even had the common politeness to thank me. They left me to shift for myself, too, a la Bret Harte at Harvard. Get me rid of Buffalo! Otherwise I'll have no recourse left but to get sick the day I lecture there. I can get sick easy enough, by the simple process of saying the word--well never mind what word--I am not going to lecture there. Yours, MARK.

BUFFALO, Sept. 26, 1871. DEAR REDPATH,--We have thought it all over and decided that we can't possibly talk after Feb. 2.

We shall take up our residence in Hartford 6 days from now Yours MARK.

XI.

LETTERS 1871-72. REMOVAL TO HARTFORD. A LECTURE TOUR. "ROUGHING IT." FIRST LETTER TO HOWELLS

The house they had taken in Hartford was the Hooker property on Forest Street, a handsome place in a distinctly literary neighborhood. Harriet Beecher Stowe, Charles Dudley Warner, and other well-known writers were within easy walking distance; Twichell was perhaps half a mile away.

It was the proper environment for Mark Twain. He settled his little family there, and was presently at Redpath's office in Boston, which was a congenial place, as we have seen before. He did not fail to return to the company of Nasby, Josh Billings, and those others of Redpath's "attractions" as long and as often as distance would permit. Bret Harte, who by this time had won fame, was also in Boston now, and frequently, with Howells, Aldrich, and Mark Twain, gathered in some quiet restaurant corner for a luncheon that lasted through a dim winter afternoon--a period of anecdote, reminiscence, and mirth. They were all young then, and laughed easily. Howells, has written of one such luncheon given by Ralph Keeler, a young Californian--a gathering at which James T. Fields was present "Nothing remains to me of the happy time but a sense of idle and aimless and joyful talk-play, beginning and ending nowhere, of eager laughter, of countless good stories from Fields, of a heat-lightning shimmer of wit from Aldrich, of an occasional concentration of our joint mockeries upon our host, who took it gladly."

But a lecture circuit cannot be restricted to the radius of Boston. Clemens was presently writing to Redpath from Washington and points farther west.

To James Redpath, in Boston:

WASHINGTON, Tuesday, Oct. 28, 1871. DEAR RED,--I have come square out, thrown "Reminiscences" overboard, and taken "Artemus Ward, Humorist," for my subject. Wrote it here on Friday and Saturday, and read it from MS last night to an enormous house. It suits me and I'll never deliver the nasty, nauseous "Reminiscences" any more. Yours, MARK.

The Artemus Ward lecture lasted eleven days, then he wrote:

To Redpath and Fall, in Boston:

BUFFALO DEPOT, Dec. 8, 1871. REDPATH & FALL, BOSTON,--Notify all hands that from this time I shall talk nothing but selections from my forthcoming book "Roughing It." Tried it last night. Suits me tip-top. SAM'L L. CLEMENS.

The Roughing It chapters proved a success, and continued in high favor through the rest of the season.

To James Redpath, in Boston:

LOGANSPORT, IND. Jan. 2, 1872. FRIEND REDPATH,--Had a splendid time with a splendid audience in Indianapolis last night--a perfectly jammed house, just as I have had all the time out here. I like the new lecture but I hate the "Artemus Ward" talk and won't talk it any more. No man ever approved that choice of subject in my hearing, I think.

Give me some comfort. If I am to talk in New York am I going to have a good house? I don't care now to have any appointments cancelled. I'll even "fetch" those Dutch Pennsylvanians with this lecture.

Have paid up $4000 indebtedness. You are the, last on my list. Shall begin to pay you in a few days and then I shall be a free man again. Yours, MARK.

With his debts paid, Clemens was anxious to be getting home. Two weeks following the above he wrote Redpath that he would accept no more engagements at any price, outside of New England, and added, "The fewer engagements I have from this time forth the better I shall be pleased." By the end of February he was back in Hartford, refusing an engagement in Boston, and announcing to Redpath, "If I had another engagement I'd rot before I'd fill it." From which we gather that he was not entirely happy in the lecture field.

As a matter of fact, Mark Twain loathed the continuous travel and nightly drudgery of platform life. He was fond of entertaining, and there were moments of triumph that repaid him for a good deal, but the tyranny of a schedule and timetables was a constant exasperation.

Meantime, Roughing It had appeared and was selling abundantly. Mark Twain, free of debt, and in pleasant circumstances, felt that the outlook was bright. It became even more so when, in March, the second child, a little girl, Susy, was born, with no attending misfortunes. But, then, in the early summer little Langdon died. It was seldom, during all of Mark Twain's life, that he enjoyed more than a brief period of unmixed happiness.

It was in June of that year that Clemens wrote his first letter to William Dean Howells the first of several hundred that would follow in the years to come, and has in it something that is characteristic of nearly all the Clemens-Howells letters--a kind of tender playfulness that answered to something in Howells's make-up, his sense of humor, his wide knowledge of a humanity which he pictured so amusingly to the world.

To William Dean Howells, in Boston:

HARTFORD, June 15, 1872. FRIEND HOWELLS,--Could you tell me how I could get a copy of your portrait as published in Hearth and Home? I hear so much talk about it as being among the finest works of art which have yet appeared in that journal, that I feel a strong desire to see it. Is it suitable for framing? I have written the publishers of H & H time and again, but they say that the demand for the portrait immediately exhausted the edition and now a copy cannot be had, even for the European demand, which has now begun. Bret Harte has been here, and says his family would not be without that portrait for any consideration. He says his children get up in the night and yell for it. I would give anything for a copy of that portrait to put up in my parlor. I have Oliver Wendell Holmes and Bret Harte's, as published in Every Saturday, and of all the swarms that come every day to gaze upon them none go away that are not softened and humbled and made more resigned to the will of God. If I had yours to put up alongside of them, I believe the combination would bring more souls to earnest reflection and ultimate conviction of their lost condition, than any other kind of warning would. Where in the nation can I get that portrait? Here are heaps of people that want it,--that need it. There is my uncle. He wants a copy. He is lying at the point of death. He has been lying at the point of death for two years. He wants a copy--and I want him to have a copy. And I want you to send a copy to the man that shot my dog. I want to see if he is dead to every human instinct.

Now you send me that portrait. I am sending you mine, in this letter; and am glad to do it, for it has been greatly admired. People who are judges of art, find in the execution a grandeur which has not been equalled in this country, and an expression which has not been approached in any. Yrs truly, S. L. CLEMENS.

P. S. 62,000 copies of "Roughing It" sold and delivered in 4 months.

The Clemens family did not spend the summer at Quarry Farm that year. The sea air was prescribed for Mrs. Clemens and the baby, and they went to Saybrook, Connecticut, to Fenwick Hall. Clemens wrote very little, though he seems to have planned Tom Sawyer, and perhaps made its earliest beginning, which was in dramatic form.

His mind, however, was otherwise active. He was always more or less given to inventions, and in his next letter we find a description of one which he brought to comparative perfection.

He had also conceived the idea of another book of travel, and this was his purpose of a projected trip to England.

To Orion Clemens, in Hartford:

FENWICK HALL, SAYBROOK, CONN. Aug. 11, 1872. MY DEAR BRO.--I shall sail for England in the Scotia, Aug. 21.

But what I wish to put on record now, is my new invention--hence this note, which you will preserve. It is this--a self-pasting scrap-book --good enough idea if some juggling tailor does not come along and ante- date me a couple of months, as in the case of the elastic veststrap.

The nuisance of keeping a scrap-book is: 1. One never has paste or gum tragacanth handy; 2. Mucilage won't stick, or stay, 4 weeks; 3. Mucilage sucks out the ink and makes the scraps unreadable; 4. To daub and paste 3 or 4 pages of scraps is tedious, slow, nasty and tiresome. My idea is this: Make a scrap-book with leaves veneered or coated with gum-stickum of some kind; wet the page with sponge, brush, rag or tongue, and dab on your scraps like postage stamps.

Lay on the gum in columns of stripes.

Each stripe of gum the length of say 20 ems, small pica, and as broad as your finger; a blank about as broad as your finger between each 2 stripes--so in wetting the paper you need not wet any more of the gum than your scrap or scraps will cover--then you may shut up the book and the leaves won't stick together.

Preserve, also, the envelope of this letter--postmark ought to be good evidence of the date of this great humanizing and civilizing invention.

I'll put it into Dan Slote's hands and tell him he must send you all over America, to urge its use upon stationers and booksellers--so don't buy into a newspaper. The name of this thing is "Mark Twain's Self-Pasting Scrapbook."

All well here. Shall be up a P. M. Tuesday. Send the carriage. Yr Bro. S. L. CLEMENS.

The Dan Slote of this letter is, of course, his old Quaker City shipmate, who was engaged in the blank-book business, the firm being Slote & Woodman, located at 119 and 121 William Street, New York.

XII.

LETTERS 1872-73. MARK TWAIN IN ENGLAND. LONDON HONORS. ACQUAINTANCE WITH DR. JOHN BROWN. A LECTURE TRIUMPH. "THE GILDED AGE"

Clemens did, in fact, sail for England on the given date, and was lavishly received there. All literary London joined in giving him a good time. He had not as yet been received seriously by the older American men of letters, but England made no question as to his title to first rank. Already, too, they classified him as of the human type of Lincoln, and reveled in him without stint. Howells writes: "In England, rank, fashion, and culture rejoiced in him. Lord Mayors, Lord Chief justices, and magnates of many kinds were his hosts."

He was treated so well and enjoyed it all so much that he could not write a book--the kind of book he had planned. One could not poke fun at a country or a people that had welcomed him with open arms. He made plenty of notes, at first, but presently gave up the book idea and devoted himself altogether to having a good time.

He had one grievance--a publisher by the name of Hotten, a sort of literary harpy, of which there were a great number in those days of defective copyright, not merely content with pilfering his early work, had reprinted, under the name of Mark Twain, the work of a mixed assortment of other humorists, an offensive volume bearing the title, Screamers and Eye-openers, by Mark Twain.

They besieged him to lecture in London, and promised him overflowing houses. Artemus Ward, during his last days, had earned London by storm with his platform humor, and they promised Mark Twain even greater success. For some reason, however, he did not welcome the idea; perhaps there was too much gaiety. To Mrs. Clemens he wrote:

To Mrs. Clemens, in Hartford:

LONDON, Sep. 15, 1872. Livy, darling, everybody says lecture-lecture-lecture--but I have not the least idea of doing it--certainly not at present. Mr. Dolby, who took Dickens to America, is coming to talk business to me tomorrow, though I have sent him word once before, that I can't be hired to talk here, because I have no time to spare.

There is too much sociability--I do not get along fast enough with work. Tomorrow I lunch with Mr. Toole and a Member of Parliament--Toole is the most able Comedian of the day. And then I am done for a while. On Tuesday I mean to hang a card to my keybox, inscribed--"Gone out of the City for a week"--and then I shall go to work and work hard. One can't be caught in a hive of 4,000,000 people, like this.

I have got such a perfectly delightful razor. I have a notion to buy some for Charley, Theodore and Slee--for I know they have no such razors there. I have got a neat little watch-chain for Annie--$20.

I love you my darling. My love to all of you. SAML.

That Mark Twain should feel and privately report something of his triumphs we need not wonder at. Certainly he was never one to give himself airs, but to have the world's great literary center paying court to him, who only ten years before had been penniless and unknown, and who once had been a barefoot Tom Sawyer in Hannibal, was quite startling. It is gratifying to find evidence of human weakness in the following heart-to-heart letter to his publisher, especially in view of the relating circumstances.

To Elisha Bliss, in Hartford:

LONDON, Sept. 28, 1872. FRIEND BLISS,--I have been received in a sort of tremendous way, tonight, by the brains of London, assembled at the annual dinner of the Sheriffs of London--mine being (between you and me) a name which was received with a flattering outburst of spontaneous applause when the long list of guests was called.

I might have perished on the spot but for the friendly support and assistance of my excellent friend Sir John Bennett--and I want you to paste the enclosed in a couple of the handsomest copies of the "Innocents" and "Roughing It," and send them to him. His address is

"Sir John Bennett, Cheapside, London." Yrs Truly S. L. CLEMENS.

The "relating circumstances" were these: At the abovementioned dinner there had been a roll-call of the distinguished guests present, and each name had been duly applauded. Clemens, conversing in a whisper with his neighbor, Sir John Bennett, did not give very close attention to the names, applauding mechanically with the others.

Finally, a name was read that brought out a vehement hand-clapping. Mark Twain, not to be outdone in cordiality, joined vigorously, and kept his hands going even after the others finished. Then, remarking the general laughter, he whispered to Sir John: "Whose name was that we were just applauding?"

"Mark Twain's."

We may believe that the "friendly support" of Sir John Bennett was welcome for the moment. But the incident could do him no harm; the diners regarded it as one of his jokes, and enjoyed him all the more for it.

He was ready to go home by November, but by no means had he had enough of England. He really had some thought of returning there permanently. In a letter to Mrs. Crane, at Quarry Farm, he wrote:

"If you and Theodore will come over in the Spring with Livy and me, and spend the summer you will see a country that is so beautiful that you will be obliged to believe in Fairyland..... and Theodore can browse with me among dusty old dens that look now as they looked five hundred years ago; and puzzle over books in the British Museum that were made before Christ was born; and in the customs of their public dinners, and the ceremonies of every official act, and the dresses of a thousand dignitaries, trace the speech and manners of all the centuries that have dragged their lagging decades over England since the Heptarchy fell asunder. I would a good deal rather live here if I could get the rest of you over."

In a letter home, to his mother and sister, we get a further picture of his enjoyment.

To Mrs. Jane Clemens and Mrs. Moffett:

LONDON, Nov. 6, 1872. MY DEAR MOTHER AND SISTER,--I have been so everlasting busy that I couldn't write--and moreover I have been so unceasingly lazy that I couldn't have written anyhow. I came here to take notes for a book, but I haven't done much but attend dinners and make speeches. But have had a jolly good time and I do hate to go away from these English folks; they make a stranger feel entirely at home--and they laugh so easily that it is a comfort to make after-dinner speeches here. I have made hundreds of friends; and last night in the crush of the opening of the New Guild-hall Library and Museum, I was surprised to meet a familiar face every few steps. Nearly 4,000 people, of both sexes, came and went during the evening, so I had a good opportunity to make a great many new acquaintances.

Livy is willing to come here with me next April and stay several months --so I am going home next Tuesday. I would sail on Saturday, but that is the day of the Lord Mayor's annual grand state dinner, when they say 900 of the great men of the city sit down to table, a great many of them in their fine official and court paraphernalia, so I must not miss it. However, I may yet change my mind and sail Saturday. I am looking at a fine Magic lantern which will cost a deal of money, and if I buy it Sammy may come and learn to make the gas and work the machinery, and paint pictures for it on glass. I mean to give exhibitions for charitable purposes in Hartford, and charge a dollar a head. In a hurry, Ys affly SAM.

He sailed November 12th on the Batavia, arriving in New York two weeks later. There had been a presidential election in his absence. General Grant had defeated Horace Greeley, a result, in some measure at least, attributed to the amusing and powerful pictures of the cartoonist, Thomas Nast. Mark Twain admired Greeley's talents, but he regarded him as poorly qualified for the nation's chief executive. He wrote:

To Th. Nast, in Morristown, N. J.:

HARTFORD, Nov. 1872. Nast, you more than any other man have won a prodigious victory for Grant--I mean, rather, for civilization and progress. Those pictures were simply marvelous, and if any man in the land has a right to hold his head up and be honestly proud of his share in this year's vast events that man is unquestionably yourself. We all do sincerely honor you, and are proud of you. MARK TWAIN.

Perhaps Mark Twain was too busy at this time to write letters. His success in England had made him more than ever popular in America, and he could by no means keep up with the demands on him. In January he contributed to the New York Tribune some letters on the Sandwich Islands, but as these were more properly articles they do not seem to belong here.

He refused to go on the lecture circuit, though he permitted Redpath to book him for any occasional appearance, and it is due to one of these special engagements that we have the only letter preserved from this time. It is to Howells, and written with that exaggeration with which he was likely to embellish his difficulties. We are not called upon to believe that there were really any such demonstrations as those ascribed to Warner and himself.

To W. D. Howells, in Boston:

FARMINGTON AVE, Hartford Feb. 27. MY DEAR HOWELLS,--I am in a sweat and Warner is in another. I told Redpath some time ago I would lecture in Boston any two days he might choose provided they were consecutive days--

I never dreamed of his choosing days during Lent since that was his special horror--but all at once he telegraphs me, and hollers at me in ail manner of ways that I am booked for Boston March 5 of all days in the year--and to make matters just as mixed and uncertain as possible, I can't find out to save my life whether he means to lecture me on the 6th or not.

Warner's been in here swearing like a lunatic, and saying he had written you to come on the 4th,--and I said, "You leather-head, if I talk in Boston both afternoon and evening March 5, I'll have to go to Boston the 4th,"--and then he just kicked up his heels and went off cursing after a fashion I never heard of before.

Now let's just leave this thing to Providence for 24 hours--you bet it will come out all right. Yours ever MARK.

He was writing a book with Warner at this time--The Gilded Age-- the two authors having been challenged by their wives one night at dinner to write a better book than the current novels they had been discussing with some severity. Clemens already had a story in his mind, and Warner agreed to collaborate in the writing. It was begun without delay. Clemens wrote the first three hundred and ninety- nine pages, and read there aloud to Warner, who took up the story at this point and continued it through twelve chapters, after which they worked alternately, and with great enjoyment. They also worked rapidly, and in April the story was completed. For a collaboration by two men so different in temperament and literary method it was a remarkable performance.

Another thing Mark Twain did that winter was to buy some land on Farmington Avenue and begin the building of a home. He had by no means given up returning to England, and made his plans to sail with Mrs. Clemens and Susy in May. Miss Clara Spaulding, of Elmira-- [Later Mrs. John B. Stanchfield, of New York.]--a girlhood friend of Mrs. Clemens--was to accompany them.

The Daily Graphic heard of the proposed journey, and wrote, asking for a farewell word. His characteristic reply is the only letter of any kind that has survived from that spring.

To the Editor of "The Daily Graphic," in New York City:

HARTFORD, Apl. 17, 1873. ED. GRAPHIC,--Your note is received. If the following two lines which I have cut from it are your natural handwriting, then I understand you to ask me "for a farewell letter in the name of the American people." Bless you, the joy of the American people is just a little premature; I haven't gone yet. And what is more, I am not going to stay, when I do go.

Yes, it is true. I am only going to remain beyond the sea, six months, that is all. I love stir and excitement; and so the moment the spring birds begin to sing, and the lagging weariness of summer to threaten, I grow restless, I get the fidgets; I want to pack off somewhere where there's something going on. But you know how that is--you must have felt that way. This very day I saw the signs in the air of the coming dullness, and I said to myself, "How glad I am that I have already chartered a steamship!" There was absolutely nothing in the morning papers. You can see for yourself what the telegraphic headings were:

BY TELEGRAPH

A Father Killed by His Son

A Bloody Fight in Kentucky

A Court House Fired, and Negroes Therein Shot while Escaping

A Louisiana Massacre

An Eight-year-old murderer Two to Three Hundred Men Roasted Alive!

A Town in a State of General Riot

A Lively Skirmish in Indiana (and thirty other similar headings.)

The items under those headings all bear date yesterday, Apl. 16 (refer to your own paper)--and I give you my word of honor that that string of commonplace stuff was everything there was in the telegraphic columns that a body could call news. Well, said I to myself this is getting pretty dull; this is getting pretty dry; there don't appear to be anything going on anywhere; has this progressive nation gone to sleep? Have I got to stand another month of this torpidity before I can begin to browse among the lively capitals of Europe?

But never mind-things may revive while I am away. During the last two months my next-door neighbor, Chas. Dudley Warner, has dropped his "Back- Log Studies," and he and I have written a bulky novel in partnership. He has worked up the fiction and I have hurled in the facts. I consider it one of the most astonishing novels that ever was written. Night after night I sit up reading it over and over again and crying. It will be published early in the Fall, with plenty of pictures. Do you consider this an advertisement?--and if so, do you charge for such things when a man is your friend? Yours truly, SAML. L. CLEMENS, "MARK TWAIN,"

An amusing, even if annoying, incident happened about the time of Mark Twain's departure. A man named Chew related to Twichell a most entertaining occurrence. Twichell saw great possibilities in it, and suggested that Mark Twain be allowed to make a story of it, sharing the profits with Chew. Chew agreed, and promised to send the facts, carefully set down. Twichell, in the mean time, told the story to Clemens, who was delighted with it and strongly tempted to write it at once, while he was in the spirit, without waiting on Chew. Fortunately, he did not do so, for when Chew's material came it was in the form of a clipping, the story having been already printed in some newspaper. Chew's knowledge of literary ethics would seem to have been slight. He thought himself entitled to something under the agreement with Twichell. Mark Twain, by this time in London, naturally had a different opinion.

To Rev. J. H. Twichell, in Hartford:

LONDON, June 9, '73. DEAR OLD JOE,--I consider myself wholly at liberty to decline to pay Chew anything, and at the same time strongly tempted to sue him into the bargain for coming so near ruining me. If he hadn't happened to send me that thing in print, I would have used the story (like an innocent fool) and would straightway have been hounded to death as a plagiarist. It would have absolutely destroyed me. I cannot conceive of a man being such a hopeless ass (after serving as a legislative reporter, too) as to imagine that I or any other literary man in his senses would consent to chew over old stuff that had already been in print. If that man wern't an infant in swaddling clothes, his only reply to our petition would have been, "It has been in print." It makes me as mad as the very Old Harry every time I think of Mr. Chew and the frightfully narrow escape I have had at his hands. Confound Mr. Chew, with all my heart! I'm willing that he should have ten dollars for his trouble of warming over his cold victuals--cheerfully willing to that--but no more. If I had had him near when his letter came, I would have got out my tomahawk and gone for him. He didn't tell the story half as well as you did, anyhow.

I wish to goodness you were here this moment--nobody in our parlor but Livy and me,--and a very good view of London to the fore. We have a luxuriously ample suite of apartments in the Langham Hotel, 3rd floor, our bedroom looking straight up Portland Place and our parlor having a noble array of great windows looking out upon both streets (Portland Place and the crook that joins it to Regent Street.)

9 P.M. Full twilight--rich sunset tints lingering in the west.

I am not going to write anything--rather tell it when I get back. I love you and Harmony, and that is all the fresh news I've got, anyway. And I mean to keep that fresh all the time. Lovingly MARK.

P. S.--Am luxuriating in glorious old Pepy's Diary, and smoking.

Letters are exceedingly scarce through all this period. Mark Twain, now on his second visit to London, was literally overwhelmed with honors and entertainment; his rooms at the Langham were like a court. Such men as Robert Browning, Turgenieff, Sir John Millais, and Charles Kingsley hastened to call. Kingsley and others gave him dinners. Mrs. Clemens to her sister wrote: "It is perfectly discouraging to try to write you."

The continuous excitement presently told on her. In July all further engagements were canceled, and Clemens took his little family to Scotland, for quiet and rest. They broke the journey at York, and it was there that Mark Twain wrote the only letter remaining from this time.

Part of a letter to Mrs. Jervis Langdon, of Elmira, N. Y.:

For the present we shall remain in this queer old walled town, with its crooked, narrow lanes, that tell us of their old day that knew no wheeled vehicles; its plaster-and-timber dwellings, with upper stories far overhanging the street, and thus marking their date, say three hundred years ago; the stately city walls, the castellated gates, the ivy-grown, foliage-sheltered, most noble and picturesque ruin of St. Mary's Abbey, suggesting their date, say five hundred years ago, in the heart of Crusading times and the glory of English chivalry and romance; the vast Cathedral of York, with its worn carvings and quaintly pictured windows, preaching of still remoter days; the outlandish names of streets and courts and byways that stand as a record and a memorial, all these centuries, of Danish dominion here in still earlier times; the hint here and there of King Arthur and his knights and their bloody fights with Saxon oppressors round about this old city more than thirteen hundred years gone by; and, last of all, the melancholy old stone coffins and sculptured inscriptions, a venerable arch and a hoary tower of stone that still remain and are kissed by the sun and caressed by the shadows every day, just as the sun and the shadows have kissed and caressed them every lagging day since the Roman Emperor's soldiers placed them here in the times when Jesus the Son of Mary walked the streets of Nazareth a youth, with no more name or fame than the Yorkshire boy who is loitering down this street this moment.

Their destination was Edinburgh, where they remained a month. Mrs. Clemens's health gave way on their arrival there, and her husband, knowing the name of no other physician in the place, looked up Dr. John Brown, author of Rab and His Friends, and found in him not only a skilful practitioner, but a lovable companion, to whom they all became deeply attached. Little Susy, now seventeen months old, became his special favorite. He named her Megalops, because of her great eyes.

Mrs. Clemens regained her strength and they returned to London. Clemens, still urged to lecture, finally agreed with George Dolby to a week's engagement, and added a promise that after taking his wife and daughter back to America he would return immediately for a more extended course. Dolby announced him to appear at the Queen's Concert Rooms, Hanover Square, for the week of October 13-18, his lecture to be the old Sandwich Islands talk that seven years before had brought him his first success. The great hall, the largest in London, was thronged at each appearance, and the papers declared that Mark Twain had no more than "whetted the public appetite" for his humor. Three days later, October 1873, Clemens, with his little party, sailed for home. Half-way across the ocean he wrote the friend they had left in Scotland:

To Dr. John Brown, in Edinburgh:

MID-ATLANTIC, Oct. 30, 1873. OUR DEAR FRIEND THE DOCTOR,--We have plowed a long way over the sea, and there's twenty-two hundred miles of restless water between us, now, besides the railway stretch. And yet you are so present with us, so close to us that a span and a whisper would bridge the distance.

The first three days were stormy, and wife, child, maid, and Miss Spaulding were all sea-sick 25 hours out of the 24, and I was sorry I ever started. However, it has been smooth, and balmy, and sunny and altogether lovely for a day or two now, and at night there is a broad luminous highway stretching over the sea to the moon, over which the spirits of the sea are traveling up and down all through the secret night and having a genuine good time, I make no doubt.

Today they discovered a "collie" on board! I find (as per advertisement which I sent you) that they won't carry dogs in these ships at any price. This one has been concealed up to this time. Now his owner has to pay L10 or heave him overboard. Fortunately the doggie is a performing doggie and the money will be paid. So after all it was just as well you didn't intrust your collie to us.

A poor little child died at midnight and was buried at dawn this morning --sheeted and shotted, and sunk in the middle of the lonely ocean in water three thousand fathoms deep. Pity the poor mother. With our love. S. L. CLEMENS.

Mark Twain was back in London, lecturing again at the Queen's Concert Rooms, after barely a month's absence. Charles Warren Stoddard, whom he had known in California, shared his apartment at the Langham, and acted as his secretary--a very necessary office, for he was besieged by callers and bombarded with letters.

He remained in London two months, lecturing steadily at Hanover Square to full houses. It is unlikely that there is any other platform record to match it. One letter of this period has been preserved. It is written to Twichell, near the end of his engagement.

To Rev. J. H. Twichell, in Hartford:

LONDON, Jan. 5 1874. MY DEAR OLD JOE,--I knew you would be likely to graduate into an ass if I came away; and so you have--if you have stopped smoking. However, I have a strong faith that it is not too late, yet, and that the judiciously managed influence of a bad example will fetch you back again.

I wish you had written me some news--Livy tells me precious little. She mainly writes to hurry me home and to tell me how much she respects me: but she's generally pretty slow on news. I had a letter from her along with yours, today, but she didn't tell me the book is out. However, it's all right. I hope to be home 20 days from today, and then I'll see her, and that will make up for a whole year's dearth of news. I am right down grateful that she is looking strong and "lovelier than ever." I only wish I could see her look her level best, once--I think it would be a vision.

I have just spent a good part of this day browsing through the Royal Academy Exhibition of Landseer's paintings. They fill four or five great salons, and must number a good many hundreds. This is the only opportunity ever to see them, because the finest of them belong to the queen and she keeps them in her private apartments. Ah, they're wonderfully beautiful! There are such rich moonlights and dusks in "The Challenge" and "The Combat;" and in that long flight of birds across a lake in the subdued flush of sunset (or sunrise--for no man can ever tell tother from which in a picture, except it has the filmy morning mist breathing itself up from the water). And there is such a grave analytical profundity in the faces of "The Connoisseurs;" and such pathos in the picture of the fawn suckling its dead mother, on a snowy waste, with only the blood in the footprints to hint that she is not asleep. And the way he makes animals absolute flesh and blood-- insomuch that if the room were darkened ever so little and a motionless living animal placed beside a painted one, no man could tell which was which.

I interrupted myself here, to drop a line to Shirley Brooks and suggest a cartoon for Punch. It was this. In one of the Academy salons (in the suite where these pictures are), a fine bust of Landseer stands on a pedestal in the centre of the room. I suggest that some of Landseer's best known animals be represented as having come down out of their frames in the moonlight and grouped themselves about the bust in mourning attitudes.

Well, old man, I am powerful glad to hear from you and shall be powerful glad to see you and Harmony. I am not going to the provinces because I cannot get halls that are large enough. I always felt cramped in Hanover Square Rooms, but I find that everybody here speaks with awe and respect of that prodigious place, and wonder that I could fill it so long.

I am hoping to be back in 20 days, but I have so much to go home to and enjoy with a jubilant joy, that it seems hardly possible that it can ever come to pass in so uncertain a world as this.

I have read the novel--[The Gilded Age, published during his absence, December, 1873.]--here, and I like it. I have made no inquiries about it, though. My interest in a book ceases with the printing of it. With a world of love, SAML.

XIII.

LETTERS 1874. HARTFORD AND ELMIRA. A NEW STUDY. BEGINNING "TOM SAWYER." THE SELLERS PLAY.

Naturally Redpath would not give him any peace now. His London success must not be wasted. At first his victim refused point-blank, and with great brevity. But he was overborne and persuaded, and made occasional appearances, wiring at last this final defiant word:

Telegram to James Redpath, in Boston:

HARTFORD, March 3, 1874. JAMES REDPATH,--Why don't you congratulate me?

I never expect to stand on a lecture platform again after Thursday night. MARK.

That he was glad to be home again we may gather from a letter sent at this time to Doctor Brown, of Edinburgh.

To Dr. John Brown, in Edinburgh:

FARMINGTON AVENUE, HARTFORD Feby. 28, 1874. MY DEAR FRIEND,--We are all delighted with your commendations of the Gilded Age-and the more so because some of our newspapers have set forth the opinion that Warner really wrote the book and I only added my name to the title page in order to give it a larger sale. I wrote the first eleven chapters, every word. and every line. I also wrote chapters 24, 25, 27, 28, 30, 32, 33, 34, 36, 37, 21, 42, 43, 45, 51, 52. 53, 57, 59, 60, 61, 62, and portions of 35, 49 and 56. So I wrote 32 of the 63 chapters entirely and part of 3 others beside.

The fearful financial panic hit the book heavily, for we published it in the midst of it. But nevertheless in the 8 weeks that have now elapsed since the day we published, we have sold 40,000 copies; which gives L3,000 royalty to be divided between the authors. This is really the largest two-months' sale which any American book has ever achieved (unless one excepts the cheaper editions of Uncle Tom's Cabin). The average price of our book is 16 shillings a copy-- Uncle Tom was 2 shillings a copy. But for the panic our sale would have been doubled, I verily believe. I do not believe the sale will ultimately go over 100,000 copies.

I shipped to you, from Liverpool, Barley's Illustrations of Judd's "Margaret" (the waiter at the Adelphi Hotel agreeing to ship it securely per parcel delivery,) and I do hope it did not miscarry, for we in America think a deal of Barley's--[Felix Octavius Carr barley, 1822-1888, illustrator of the works of Irving, Cooper, etc. Probably the most distinguished American illustrator of his time.]--work. I shipped the novel (" Margaret") to you from here a week ago.

Indeed I am thankful for the wife and the child--and if there is one individual creature on all this footstool who is more thoroughly and uniformly and unceasingly happy than I am I defy the world to produce him and prove him. In my opinion, he doesn't exist. I was a mighty rough, coarse, unpromising subject when Livy took charge of me 4 years ago, and I may still be, to the rest of the world, but not to her. She has made a very creditable job of me.

Success to the Mark Twain Club!-and the novel shibboleth of the Whistle. Of course any member rising to speak would be required to preface his remark with a keen respectful whistle at the chair-the chair recognizing the speaker with an answering shriek, and then as the speech proceeded its gravity and force would be emphasized and its impressiveness augmented by the continual interjection of whistles in place of punctuation-pauses; and the applause of the audience would be manifested in the same way ....

They've gone to luncheon, and I must follow. With strong love from us both. Your friend, SAML. L. CLEMENS.

These were the days when the Howells and Clemens families began visiting back and forth between Boston and Hartford, and sometimes Aldrich came, though less frequently, and the gatherings at the homes of Warner and Clemens were full of never-to-be-forgotten happiness. Of one such visit Howells wrote:

"In the good-fellowship of that cordial neighborhood we had two such days as the aging sun no longer shines on in his round. There was constant running in and out of friendly houses, where the lively hosts and guests called one another by their christian names or nicknames, and no such vain ceremony as knocking or ringing at doors. Clemens was then building the stately mansion in which he satisfied his love of magnificence as if it had been another sealskin coat, and he was at the crest of the prosperity which enabled him to humor every whim or extravagance."

It was the delight of such a visit that kept Clemens constantly urging its repetition. One cannot but feel the genuine affection of these letters.

To W. D. Howells, in Boston:

Mch. 1, 1876. MY DEAR HOWELLS,--Now you will find us the most reasonable people in the world. We had thought of precipitating upon you George Warner and wife one day; Twichell and his jewel of a wife another day, and Chas. Perkins and wife another. Only those--simply members of our family, they are. But I'll close the door against them all--which will "fix" all of the lot except Twichell, who will no more hesitate to climb in at the back window than nothing.

And you shall go to bed when you please, get up when you please, talk when you please, read when you please. Mrs. Howells may even go to New York Saturday if she feels that she must, but if some gentle, unannoying coaxing can beguile her into putting that off a few days, we shall be more than glad, for I do wish she and Mrs. Clemens could have a good square chance to get acquainted with each other. But first and last and all the time, we want you to feel untrammeled and wholly free from restraint, here.

The date suits--all dates suit. Yrs ever MARK.

To W. D. Howells, in Boston:

FARMINGTON AVENUE, HARTFORD, Mch. 20, 1876. DEAR HOWELLS,--You or Aldrich or both of you must come to Hartford to live. Mr. Hall, who lives in the house next to Mrs. Stowe's (just where we drive in to go to our new house) will sell for $16,000 or $17,000. The lot is 85 feet front and 150 deep--long time and easy payments on the purchase? You can do your work just as well here as in Cambridge, can't you? Come, will one of you boys buy that house? Now say yes.

Mrs. Clemens is an invalid yet, but is getting along pretty fairly.

We send best regards. MARK.

April found the Clemens family in Elmira. Mrs. Clemens was not over-strong, and the cares of house-building were many. They went early, therefore, remaining at the Langdon home in the city until Quarry Farm should feel a touch of warmer sun, Clemens wrote the news to Doctor Brown.

To Dr. John Brown, in Edinburgh:

ELMIRA, N. Y., April 27, '86. DEAR DOCTOR,--This town is in the interior of the State of New York-- and was my wife's birth-place. We are here to spend the whole summer. Although it is so near summer, we had a great snow-storm yesterday, and one the day before. This is rather breaking in upon our plans, as it may keep us down here in the valley a trifle longer than we desired. It gets fearfully hot here in the summer, so we spend our summers on top of a hill 6 or 700 feet high, about two or three miles from here--it never gets hot up there.

Mrs. Clemens is pretty strong, and so is the "little wifie" barring a desperate cold in the head the child grows in grace and beauty marvellously. I wish the nations of the earth would combine in a baby show and give us a chance to compete. I must try to find one of her latest photographs to enclose in this. And this reminds me that Mrs. Clemens keeps urging me to ask you for your photograph and last night she said, "and be sure to ask him for a photograph of his sister, and Jock- but say Master Jock--do not be headless and forget that courtesy; he is Jock in our memories and our talk, but he has a right to his title when a body uses his name in a letter." Now I have got it all in--I can't have made any mistake this time. Miss Clara Spaulding looked in, a moment, yesterday morning, as bright and good as ever. She would like to lay her love at your feet if she knew I was writing--as would also fifty friends of ours whom you have never seen, and whose homage is as fervent as if the cold and clouds and darkness of a mighty sea did not lie between their hearts and you. Poor old Rab had not many "friends" at first, but if all his friends of today could gather to his grave from the four corners of the earth what a procession there would be! And Rab's friends are your friends.

I am going to work when we get on the hill-till then I've got to lie fallow, albeit against my will. We join in love to you and yours. Your friend ever, SAML. L. CLEMENS.

P. S. I enclose a specimen of villainy. A man pretends to be my brother and my lecture agent--gathers a great audience together in a city more than a thousand miles from here, and then pockets the money and elopes, leaving the audience to wait for the imaginary lecturer! I am after him with the law.

It was a historic summer at the Farm. A new baby arrived in June; a new study was built for Mark Twain by Mrs. Crane, on the hillside near the old quarry; a new book was begun in it--The Adventures of Tom Sawyer--and a play, the first that Mark Twain had really attempted, was completed--the dramatization of The Gilded Age.

An early word went to Hartford of conditions at the Farm.

To Rev. and Mrs. Twichell, in Hartford:

ELMIRA, June 11, 1874.

MY DEAR OLD JOE AND HARMONY,--The baby is here and is the great American Giantess--weighing 7 3/4 pounds. We had to wait a good long time for her, but she was full compensation when she did come.

The Modoc was delighted with it, and gave it her doll at once. There is nothing selfish about the Modoc. She is fascinated with the new baby. The Modoc rips and tears around out doors, most of the time, and consequently is as hard as a pine knot and as brown as an Indian. She is bosom friend to all the ducks, chickens, turkeys and guinea hens on the place. Yesterday as she marched along the winding path that leads up the hill through the red clover beds to the summer-house, there was a long procession of these fowls stringing contentedly after her, led by a stately rooster who can look over the Modoc's head. The devotion of these vassals has been purchased with daily largess of Indian meal, and so the Modoc, attended by her bodyguard, moves in state wherever she goes.

Susie Crane has built the loveliest study for me, you ever saw. It is octagonal, with a peaked roof, each octagon filled with a spacious window, and it sits perched in complete isolation on top of an elevation that commands leagues of valley and city and retreating ranges of distant blue hills. It is a cosy nest, with just room in it for a sofa and a table and three or four chairs--and when the storms sweep down the remote valley and the lightning flashes above the hills beyond, and the rain beats upon the roof over my head, imagine the luxury of it! It stands 500 feet above the valley and 2 1/2 miles from it.

However one must not write all day. We send continents of love to you and yours. Affectionately MARK.

We have mentioned before that Clemens had settled his mother and sister at Fredonia, New York, and when Mrs. Clemens was in condition to travel he concluded to pay them a visit.

It proved an unfortunate journey; the hot weather was hard on Mrs. Clemens, and harder still, perhaps, on Mark Twain's temper. At any period of his life a bore exasperated him, and in these earlier days he was far more likely to explode than in his mellower age. Remorse always followed--the price he paid was always costly. We cannot know now who was the unfortunate that invited the storm, but in the next letter we get the echoes of it and realize something of its damage.

To Mrs. Jane Clemens and Mrs. Moffett, in Fredonia:

ELMIRA, Aug. 15. MX DEAR MOTHER AND SISTER,--I came away from Fredonia ashamed of myself; --almost too much humiliated to hold up my head and say good-bye. For I began to comprehend how much harm my conduct might do you socially in your village. I would have gone to that detestable oyster-brained bore and apologized for my inexcusable rudeness to him, but that I was satisfied he was of too small a calibre to know how to receive an apology with magnanimity.

Pamela appalled me by saying people had hinted that they wished to visit Livy when she came, but that she had given them no encouragement. I feared that those people would merely comprehend that their courtesies were not wanted, and yet not know exactly why they were not wanted.

I came away feeling that in return for your constant and tireless efforts to secure our bodily comfort and make our visit enjoyable, I had basely repaid you by making you sad and sore-hearted and leaving you so. And the natural result has fallen to me likewise--for a guilty conscience has harassed me ever since, and I have not had one short quarter of an hour of peace to this moment.

You spoke of Middletown. Why not go there and live? Mr. Crane says it is only about a hundred miles this side of New York on the Erie road. The fact that one or two of you might prefer to live somewhere else is not a valid objection--there are no 4 people who would all choose the same place--so it will be vain to wait for the day when your tastes shall be a unit. I seriously fear that our visit has damaged you in Fredonia, and so I wish you were out of it.

The baby is fat and strong, and Susie the same. Susie was charmed with the donkey and the doll. Ys affectionately SAML.

P. S.--DEAR MA AND PAMELA--I am mainly grieved because I have been rude to a man who has been kind to you--and if you ever feel a desire to apologize to him for me, you may be sure that I will endorse the apology, no matter how strong it may be. I went to his bank to apologize to him, but my conviction was strong that he was not man enough to know how to take an apology and so I did not make it.

William Dean Howells was in those days writing those vividly realistic, indeed photographic stories which fixed his place among American men of letters. He had already written 'Their Wedding Journey' and 'A Chance Acquaintance' when 'A Foregone Conclusion' appeared. For the reason that his own work was so different, and perhaps because of his fondness for the author, Clemens always greatly admired the books of Howells. Howells's exact observation and his gift for human detail seemed marvelous to Mark Twain, who with a bigger brush was inclined to record the larger rather than the minute aspects of life. The sincerity of his appreciation of Howells, however, need not be questioned, nor, for that matter, his detestation of Scott.

To W. D. Howells, in Boston:

ELMIRA, Aug. 22, 1874. DEAR HOWELLS,--I have just finished reading the 'Foregone Conclusion' to Mrs. Clemens and we think you have even outdone yourself. I should think that this must be the daintiest, truest, most admirable workmanship that was ever put on a story. The creatures of God do not act out their natures more unerringly than yours do. If your genuine stories can die, I wonder by what right old Walter Scott's artificialities shall continue to live.

I brought Mrs. Clemens back from her trip in a dreadfully broken-down condition--so by the doctor's orders we unpacked the trunks sorrowfully to lie idle here another month instead of going at once to Hartford and proceeding to furnish the new house which is now finished. We hate to have it go longer desolate and tenantless, but cannot help it.

By and by, if the madam gets strong again, we are hoping to have the Grays there, and you and the Aldrich households, and Osgood, down to engage in an orgy with them. Ys Ever MARK

Howells was editor of the Atlantic by this time, and had been urging Clemens to write something suitable for that magazine. He had done nothing, however, until this summer at Quarry Farm. There, one night in the moonlight, Mrs. Crane's colored cook, who had been a slave, was induced to tell him her story. It was exactly the story to appeal to Mark Twain, and the kind of thing he could write. He set it down next morning, as nearly in her own words and manner as possible, without departing too far from literary requirements.

He decided to send this to Howells. He did not regard it very highly, but he would take the chance. An earlier offering to the magazine had been returned. He sent the "True Story," with a brief note:

To W. D. Howells, in Boston:

ELMIRA, Sept. 2, '74. MY DEAR HOWELLS,--.....I enclose also a "True Story" which has no humor in it. You can pay as lightly as you choose for that, if you want it, for it is rather out of my line. I have not altered the old colored woman's story except to begin at the beginning, instead of the middle, as she did--and traveled both ways..... Yrs Ever MARK.

But Howells was delighted with it. He referred to its "realest kind of black talk," and in another place added, "This little story delights me more and more. I wish you had about forty of them."

Along with the "True Story" Mark Twain had sent the "Fable for Good Old Boys and Girls"; but this Howells returned, not, as he said, because he didn't like it, but because the Atlantic on matters of religion was just in that "Good Lord, Good Devil condition when a little fable like yours wouldn't leave it a single Presbyterian, Baptist, Unitarian, Episcopalian, Methodist, or Millerite paying subscriber, while all the deadheads would stick to it and abuse it in the denominational newspapers!"

But the shorter MS. had been only a brief diversion. Mark Twain was bowling along at a book and a play. The book was Tom Sawyer, as already mentioned, and the play a dramatization from The Gilded Age. Clemens had all along intended to dramatize the story of Colonel Sellers, and was one day thunderstruck to receive word from California that a San Francisco dramatist had appropriated his character in a play written for John T. Raymond. Clemens had taken out dramatic copyright on the book, and immediately stopped the performance by telegraph. A correspondence between the author and the dramatist followed, leading to a friendly arrangement by which the latter agreed to dispose of his version to Mark Twain. A good deal of discussion from time to time having arisen over the authorship of the Sellers play, as presented by Raymond, certain among the letters that follow may be found of special interest. Meanwhile we find Clemens writing to Dr. John Brown, of Edinburgh, on these matters and events in general. The book MS., which he mentions as having put aside, was not touched again for nearly a year.

To Dr. John Brown, in Edinburgh:

QUARRY FARM, NEAR ELMIRA, N. Y. Sept. 4, 1874. DEAR FRIEND,--I have been writing fifty pages of manuscript a day, on an average, for sometime now, on a book (a story) and consequently have been so wrapped up in it and so dead to anything else, that I have fallen mighty short in letter-writing. But night before last I discovered that that day's chapter was a failure, in conception, moral truth to nature, and execution--enough blemish to impair the excellence of almost any chapter--and so I must burn up the day's work and do it all over again. It was plain that

I had worked myself out, pumped myself dry. So I knocked off, and went to playing billiards for a change. I haven't had an idea or a fancy for two days, now--an excellent time to write to friends who have plenty of ideas and fancies of their own, and so will prefer the offerings of the heart before those of the head. Day after to-morrow I go to a neighboring city to see a five-act-drama of mine brought out, and suggest amendments in it, and would about as soon spend a night in the Spanish Inquisition as sit there and be tortured with all the adverse criticisms I can contrive to imagine the audience is indulging in. But whether the play be successful or not, I hope I shall never feel obliged to see it performed a second time. My interest in my work dies a sudden and violent death when the work is done.

I have invented and patented a pretty good sort of scrap-book (I think) but I have backed down from letting it be known as mine just at present --for I can't stand being under discussion on a play and a scrap-book at the same time!

I shall be away two days, and then return to take our tribe to New York, where we shall remain five days buying furniture for the new house, and then go to Hartford and settle solidly down for the winter. After all that fallow time I ought to be able to go to work again on the book. We shall reach Hartford about the middle of September, I judge.

We have spent the past four months up here on top of a breezy hill, six hundred feet high, some few miles from Elmira, N. Y., and overlooking that town; (Elmira is my wife's birthplace and that of Susie and the new baby). This little summer house on the hill-top (named Quarry Farm because there's a quarry on it,) belongs to my wife's sister, Mrs. Crane.

A photographer came up the other day and wanted to make some views, and I shall send you the result per this mail.

My study is a snug little octagonal den, with a coal-grate, 6 big windows, one little one, and a wide doorway (the latter opening upon the distant town.) On hot days I spread the study wide open, anchor my papers down with brickbats and write in the midst of the hurricanes, clothed in the same thin linen we make shirts of. The study is nearly on the peak of the hill; it is right in front of the little perpendicular wall of rock left where they used to quarry stones. On the peak of the hill is an old arbor roofed with bark and covered with the vine you call the "American Creeper"--its green is almost bloodied with red. The Study is 30 yards below the old arbor and 200 yards above the dwelling-house-it is remote from all noises.....

Now isn't the whole thing pleasantly situated?

In the picture of me in the study you glimpse (through the left-hand window) the little rock bluff that rises behind the pond, and the bases of the little trees on top of it. The small square window is over the fireplace; the chimney divides to make room for it. Without the stereoscope it looks like a framed picture. All the study windows have Venetian blinds; they long ago went out of fashion in America but they have not been replaced with anything half as good yet.

The study is built on top of a tumbled rock-heap that has morning-glories climbing about it and a stone stairway leading down through and dividing it.

There now--if you have not time to read all this, turn it over to "Jock" and drag in the judge to help.

Mrs. Clemens must put in a late picture of Susie--a picture which she maintains is good, but which I think is slander on the child.

We revisit the Rutland Street home many a time in fancy, for we hold every individual in it in happy and grateful memory. Goodbye, Your friend, SAML. L. CLEMENS.

P. S.--I gave the P. O. Department a blast in the papers about sending misdirected letters of mine back to the writers for reshipment, and got a blast in return, through a New York daily, from the New York postmaster. But I notice that misdirected letters find me, now, without any unnecessary fooling around.

The new house in Hartford was now ready to be occupied, and in a letter to Howells, written a little more than a fortnight after the foregoing, we find them located in "part" of it. But what seems more interesting is that paragraph of the letter which speaks of close friendly relations still existing with the Warners, in that it refutes a report current at this time that there was a break between Clemens and Warner over the rights in the Sellers play. There was, in fact, no such rupture. Warner, realizing that he had no hand in the character of Sellers, and no share in the work of dramatization, generously yielded all claim to any part of the returns.

To W. D. Howells, in Boston:

FARMINGTON AVENUE, HARTFORD, Sept. 20, 1876. MY DEAR HOWELLS,--All right, my boy, send proof sheets here. I amend dialect stuff by talking and talking and talking it till it sounds right- and I had difficulty with this negro talk because a negro sometimes (rarely) says "goin" and sometimes "gwyne," and they make just such discrepancies in other words--and when you come to reproduce them on paper they look as if the variation resulted from the writer's carelessness. But I want to work at the proofs and get the dialect as nearly right as possible.

We are in part of the new house. Goodness knows when we'll get in the rest of it--full of workmen yet.

I worked a month at my play, and launched it in New York last Wednesday. I believe it will go. The newspapers have been complimentary. It is simply a setting for the one character, Col. Sellers--as a play I guess it will not bear a critical assault in force.

The Warners are as charming as ever. They go shortly to the devil for a year--(which is but a poetical way of saying they are going to afflict themselves with the unsurpassable--(bad word) of travel for a spell.) I believe they mean to go and see you, first-so they mean to start from heaven to the other place; not from earth. How is that?

I think that is no slouch of a compliment--kind of a dim religious light about it. I enjoy that sort of thing. Yrs ever MARK.

Raymond, in a letter to the Sun, stated that not "one line" of the California dramatization had been used by Mark Twain, "except that which was taken bodily from The Gilded Age." Clemens himself, in a statement that he wrote for the Hartford Post, but suppressed, probably at the request of his wife, gave a full history of the play's origin, a matter of slight interest to-day.

Sellers on the stage proved a great success. The play had no special merit as a literary composition, but the character of Sellers delighted the public, and both author and actor were richly repaid for their entertainment.

XIV.

LETTERS 1874. MISSISSIPPI

CHAPTERS

. VISITS TO BOSTON. A JOKE ON ALDRICH

"Couldn't you send me some such story as that colored one for our January number--that is, within a month?" wrote Howells, at the end of September, and during the week following Mark Twain struggled hard to comply, but without result. When the month was nearly up he wrote:

To W. D. Howells, in Boston:

HARTFORD, Oct. 23, 1874. MY DEAR HOWELLS,--I have delayed thus long, hoping I might do something for the January number and Mrs. Clemens has diligently persecuted me day by day with urgings to go to work and do that something, but it's no use --I find I can't. We are in such a state of weary and endless confusion that my head won't go. So I give it up..... Yrs ever, MARK.

But two hours later, when he had returned from one of the long walks which he and Twichell so frequently took together, he told a different story.

Later, P.M. HOME, 24th '74.

MY DEAR HOWELLS,--I take back the remark that I can't write for the Jan. number. For Twichell and I have had a long walk in the woods and I got to telling him about old Mississippi days of steam-boating glory and grandeur as I saw them (during 5 years) from the pilothouse. He said "What a virgin subject to hurl into a magazine!" I hadn't thought of that before. Would you like a series of papers to run through 3 months or 6 or 9?--or about 4 months, say? Yrs ever, MARK.

Howells himself had come from a family of pilots, and rejoiced in the idea. A few days later Mark Twain forwarded the first instalment of the new series--those wonderful chapters that begin, now, with chapter four in the Mississippi book. Apparently he was not without doubt concerning the manuscript, and accompanied it with a brief line.

To W. D. Howells, in Boston:

DEAR HOWELLS,--Cut it, scarify it, reject it handle it with entire freedom. Yrs ever, MARK.

But Howells had no doubts as to the quality of the new find. He declared that the "piece" about the Mississippi was capital, that it almost made the water in their ice-pitcher turn muddy as he read it. "The sketch of the low-lived little town was so good that I could have wished that there was more of it. I want the sketches, if you can make them, every month."

The "low-lived little town" was Hannibal, and the reader can turn to the vivid description of it in the chapter already mentioned.

In the same letter Howells refers to a "letter from Limerick," which he declares he shall keep until he has shown it around--especially to Aldrich and Osgood.

The "letter from Limerick" has to do with a special episode. Mention has just been made of Mark Twain's walk with Twichell. Frequently their walks were extended tramps, and once in a daring moment one or the other of them proposed to walk to Boston. The time was November, and the bracing air made the proposition seem attractive. They were off one morning early, Twichell carrying a little bag, and Clemens a basket of luncheon. A few days before, Clemens had written Redpath that the Rev. J. H. Twichell and he expected to start at eight o'clock Thursday morning "to walk to Boston in twenty-four hours--or more. We shall telegraph Young's Hotel for rooms Saturday night, in order to allow for a low average of pedestrianism."

They did not get quite to Boston. In fact, they got only a little farther than the twenty-eight miles they made the first day. Clemens could hardly walk next morning, but they managed to get to North Ashford, where they took a carriage for the nearest railway station. There they telegraphed to Redpath and Howells that they would be in Boston that evening. Howells, of course, had a good supper and good company awaiting them at his home, and the pedestrians spent two happy days visiting and recounting their adventures.

It was one morning, at his hotel, that Mark Twain wrote the Limerick letter. It was addressed to

Mrs. Clemens, but was really intended for Howells and Twichell and the others whom it mentions. It was an amusing fancy, rather than a letter, but it deserves place here.

To Mrs. Clemens---intended for Howells, Aldrich, etc.

BOSTON, Nov. 16, 1935. [1874] DEAR LIVY, You observe I still call this beloved old place by the name it had when I was young. Limerick! It is enough to make a body sick.

The gentlemen-in-waiting stare to see me sit here telegraphing this letter to you, and no doubt they are smiling in their sleeves. But let them! The slow old fashions are good enough for me, thank God, and I will none other. When I see one of these modern fools sit absorbed, holding the end of a telegraph wire in his hand, and reflect that a thousand miles away there is another fool hitched to the other end of it, it makes me frantic with rage; and then am I more implacably fixed and resolved than ever, to continue taking twenty minutes to telegraph you what I communicate in ten sends by the new way if I would so debase myself. And when I see a whole silent, solemn drawing-room full of idiots sitting with their hands on each other's foreheads "communing," I tug the white hairs from my head and curse till my asthma brings me the blessed relief of suffocation. In our old day such a gathering talked pure drivel and "rot," mostly, but better that, a thousand times, than these dreary conversational funerals that oppress our spirits in this mad generation.

It is sixty years since I was here before. I walked hither, then, with my precious old friend. It seems incredible, now, that we did it in two days, but such is my recollection. I no longer mention that we walked back in a single day, it makes me so furious to see doubt in the face of the hearer. Men were men in those old times. Think of one of the puerile organisms in this effeminate age attempting such a feat.

My air-ship was delayed by a collision with a fellow from China loaded with the usual cargo of jabbering, copper-colored missionaries, and so I was nearly an hour on my journey. But by the goodness of God thirteen of the missionaries were crippled and several killed, so I was content to lose the time. I love to lose time, anyway, because it brings soothing reminiscences of the creeping railroad days of old, now lost to us forever.

Our game was neatly played, and successfully.--None expected us, of course. You should have seen the guards at the ducal palace stare when I said, "Announce his grace the Archbishop of Dublin and the Rt. Hon. the Earl of Hartford." Arrived within, we were all eyes to see the Duke of Cambridge and his Duchess, wondering if we might remember their faces, and they ours. In a moment, they came tottering in; he, bent and withered and bald; she blooming with wholesome old age. He peered through his glasses a moment, then screeched in a reedy voice: "Come to my arms! Away with titles--I'll know ye by no names but Twain and Twichell! Then fell he on our necks and jammed his trumpet in his ear, the which we filled with shoutings to this effect: God bless you, old Howells what is left of you!"

We talked late that night--none of your silent idiot "communings" for us --of the olden time. We rolled a stream of ancient anecdotes over our tongues and drank till the lord Archbishop grew so mellow in the mellow past that Dublin ceased to be Dublin to him and resumed its sweeter forgotten name of New York. In truth he almost got back into his ancient religion, too, good Jesuit, as he has always been since O'Mulligan the First established that faith in the Empire.

And we canvassed everybody. Bailey Aldrich, Marquis of Ponkapog, came in, got nobly drunk, and told us all about how poor Osgood lost his earldom and was hanged for conspiring against the second Emperor--but he didn't mention how near he himself came to being hanged, too, for engaging in the same enterprise. He was as chaffy as he was sixty years ago, too, and swore the Archbishop and I never walked to Boston--but there was never a day that Ponkapog wouldn't lie, so be it by the grace of God he got the opportunity.

The Lord High Admiral came in, a hale gentleman close upon seventy and bronzed by the suns and storms of many climes and scarred with the wounds got in many battles, and I told him how I had seen him sit in a high chair and eat fruit and cakes and answer to the name of Johnny. His granddaughter (the eldest) is but lately warned to the youngest of the Grand Dukes, and so who knows but a day may come when the blood of the Howells's may reign in the land? I must not forget to say, while I think of it, that your new false teeth are done, my dear, and your wig. Keep your head well bundled with a shawl till the latter comes, and so cheat your persecuting neuralgias and rheumatisms. Would you believe it?--the Duchess of Cambridge is deafer than you--deafer than her husband. They call her to breakfast with a salvo of artillery; and usually when it thunders she looks up expectantly and says "come in....."

The monument to the author of "Gloverson and His Silent partners" is finished. It is the stateliest and the costliest ever erected to the memory of any man. This noble classic has now been translated into all the languages of the earth and is adored by all nations and known to all creatures. Yet I have conversed as familiarly with the author of it as I do with my own great-grandchildren.

I wish you could see old Cambridge and Ponkapog. I love them as dearly as ever, but privately, my dear, they are not much improvement on idiots. It is melancholy to hear them jabber over the same pointless anecdotes three and four times of an evening, forgetting that they had jabbered them over three or four times the evening before. Ponkapog still writes poetry, but the old-time fire has mostly gone out of it. Perhaps his best effort of late years is this:

"O soul, soul, soul of mine: Soul, soul, soul of thine! Thy soul, my soul, two souls entwine, And sing thy lauds in crystal wine!"

This he goes about repeating to everybody, daily and nightly, insomuch that he is become a sore affliction to all that know him.

But I must desist. There are drafts here, everywhere and my gout is something frightful. My left foot hath resemblance to a snuff-bladder. God be with you. HARTFORD.

These to Lady Hartford, in the earldom of Hartford, in the upper portion of the city of Dublin.

One may imagine the joy of Howells and the others in this ludicrous extravaganza, which could have been written by no one but Mark Twain. It will hardly take rank as prophecy, though certainly true forecast in it is not wholly lacking.

Clemens was now pretty well satisfied with his piloting story, but he began to have doubts as to its title, "Old Times on the Mississippi." It seemed to commit him to too large an undertaking.

To W. D. Howells, in Boston:

Dec. 3, 1874. MY DEAR HOWELLS,--Let us change the heading to "Piloting on the Miss in the Old Times"--or to "Steamboating on the M. in Old Times"--or to "Personal Old Times on the Miss."--We could change it for Feb. if now too late for Jan.--I suggest it because the present heading is too pretentious, too broad and general. It seems to command me to deliver a Second Book of Revelation to the world, and cover all the Old Times the Mississippi (dang that word, it is worse than "type" or "Egypt ") ever saw--whereas here I have finished Article No. III and am about to start on No. 4. and yet I have spoken of nothing but of Piloting as a science so far; and I doubt if I ever get beyond that portion of my subject. And I don't care to. Any muggins can write about Old Times on the Miss. of 500 different kinds, but I am the only man alive that can scribble about the piloting of that day--and no man ever has tried to scribble about it yet. Its newness pleases me all the time--and it is about the only new subject I know of. If I were to write fifty articles they would all be about pilots and piloting--therefore let's get the word Piloting into the heading. There's a sort of freshness about that, too. Ys ever, MARK.

But Howells thought the title satisfactory, and indeed it was the best that could have been selected for the series. He wrote every few days of his delight in the papers, and cautioned the author not to make an attempt to please any "supposed Atlantic audience," adding, "Yarn it off into my sympathetic ear." Clemens replied:

To W. D. Howells, in Boston:

H't'f'd. Dec. 8, 1874. MY DEAR HOWELLS,--It isn't the Atlantic audience that distresses me; for it is the only audience that I sit down before in perfect serenity (for the simple reason that it doesn't require a "humorist" to paint himself striped and stand on his head every fifteen minutes.) The trouble was, that I was only bent on "working up an atmosphere" and that is to me a most fidgety and irksome thing, sometimes. I avoid it, usually, but in this case it was absolutely necessary, else every reader would be applying the atmosphere of his own or sea experiences, and that shirt wouldn't fit, you know.

I could have sent this Article II a week ago, or more, but I couldn't bring myself to the drudgery of revising and correcting it. I have been at that tedious work 3 hours, now, and by George but I am glad it is over.

Say--I am as prompt as a clock, if I only know the day a thing is wanted --otherwise I am a natural procrastinaturalist. Tell me what day and date you want Nos. 3 and 4, and I will tackle and revise them and they'll be there to the minute.

I could wind up with No. 4., but there are some things more which I am powerfully moved to write. Which is natural enough, since I am a person who would quit authorizing in a minute to go to piloting, if the madam would stand it. I would rather sink a steamboat than eat, any time.

My wife was afraid to write you--so I said with simplicity, "I will give you the language--and ideas." Through the infinite grace of God there has not been such another insurrection in the family before as followed this. However, the letter was written, and promptly, too--whereas, heretofore she has remained afraid to do such things.

With kind regards to Mrs. Howells, Yrs ever, MARK.

The "Old Times" papers appeared each month in the Atlantic until July, 1875, and take rank to-day with Mark Twain's best work. When the first number appeared, John Hay wrote: "It is perfect; no more nor less. I don't see how you do it." Which was reported to Howells, who said: "What business has Hay, I should like to know, praising a favorite of mine? It's interfering."

These were the days when the typewriter was new. Clemens and Twichell, during their stay in Boston, had seen the marvel in operation, and Clemens had been unable to resist owning one. It was far from being the perfect machine of to-day; the letters were all capitals, and one was never quite certain, even of those. Mark Twain, however, began with enthusiasm and practised faithfully. On the day of its arrival he wrote two letters that have survived, the first to his brother, the other to Howells.

Typewritten letter to W. D. Howells, in Boston:

HARTFORD, Dec. 9, 1874. MY DEAR HOWELLS,--I want to add a short paragraph to article No. 1, when the proof comes. Merely a line or two, however.

I don't know whether I am going to make this typewriting machine go or nto: that last word was intended for n-not; but I guess I shall make some sort of a succss of it before I run it very long. I am so thick-fingered that I miss the keys.

You needn't a swer this; I am only practicing to get three; another slip- up there; only practici?ng to get the hang of the thing. I notice I miss fire & get in a good many unnecessary letters and punctuation marks. I am simply using you for a target to bang at. Blame my cats but this thing requires genius in order to work it just right. Yours ever, (M)ARK.

Knowing Mark Twain, Howells wrote: "When you get tired of the machine send it to me." Clemens naturally did get tired of the machine; it was ruining his morals, he said. He presently offered it to Howells, who by this time hesitated, but eventually yielded and accepted it. If he was blasted by its influence the fact has not been recorded.

One of the famous Atlantic dinners came along in December. "Don't you dare to refuse that invitation," wrote Howells, "to meet Emerson, Aldrich, and all those boys at the Parker House, at six o'clock, Tuesday, December 15th. Come!"

Clemens had no desire to refuse; he sent word that he would come, and followed it with a characteristic line.

To W. D. Howells, in Boston:

HARTFORD, Sunday. MY DEAR HOWELLS,--I want you to ask Mrs. Howells to let you stay all night at the Parker House and tell lies and have an improving time, and take breakfast with me in the morning. I will have a good room for you, and a fire. Can't you tell her it always makes you sick to go home late at night, or something like that? That sort of thing rouses Mrs. Clemens's sympathies, easily; the only trouble is to keep them up. Twichell and I talked till 2 or 3 in the morning, the night we supped at your house and it restored his health, on account of his being drooping for some time and made him much more robuster than what he was before. Will Mrs. Howells let you? Yrs ever, S. L. C.

Aldrich had issued that year a volume of poems, and he presented Clemens with a copy of it during this Boston visit. The letter of appreciation which follows contains also reference to an amusing incident; but we shall come to that presently.

To T. B. Aldrich, in Ponkapog, Mass.

FARMINGTON AVENUE, HARTFORD. Dec. 18, 1874. MY DEAR ALDRICH,--I read the "Cloth of Gold" through, coming down in the cars, and it is just lightning poetry--a thing which it gravels me to say because my own efforts in that line have remained so persistently unrecognized, in consequence of the envy and jealousy of this generation. "Baby Bell" always seemed perfection, before, but now that I have children it has got even beyond that. About the hour that I was reading it in the cars, Twichell was reading it at home and forthwith fell upon me with a burst of enthusiasm about it when I saw him. This was pleasant, because he has long been a lover of it.

"Thos. Bailey Aldrich responded" etc., "in one of the brightest speeches of the evening."

That is what the Tribune correspondent says. And that is what everybody that heard it said. Therefore, you keep still. Don't ever be so unwise as to go on trying to unconvince those people.

I've been skating around the place all day with some girls, with Mrs. Clemens in the window to do the applause. There would be a power of fun in skating if you could do it with somebody else's muscles.--There are about twenty boys booming by the house, now, and it is mighty good to look at.

I'm keeping you in mind, you see, in the matter of photographs. I have a couple to enclose in this letter and I want you to say you got them, and then I shall know I have been a good truthful child.

I am going to send more as I ferret them out, about the place.--And I won't forget that you are a "subscriber."

The wife and I unite in warm regards to you and Mrs. Aldrich. Yrs ever, S. L. CLEMENS.

A letter bearing the same date as the above went back to Howells, we find, in reference to still another incident, which perhaps should come first.

Mark Twain up to this time had worn the black "string" necktie of the West--a decoration which disturbed Mrs. Clemens, and invited remarks from his friends. He had persisted in it, however, up to the date of the Atlantic dinner, when Howells and Aldrich decided that something must be done about it.

To W. D. Howells, in Boston:

HARTFORD, Dec. 18, 1874. MY DEAR HOWELLS,--I left No. 3, (Miss. chapter) in my eldest's reach, and it may have gone to the postman and it likewise may have gone into the fire. I confess to a dread that the latter is the case and that that stack of MS will have to be written over again. If so, O for the return of the lamented Herod!

You and Aldrich have made one woman deeply and sincerely grateful--Mrs. Clemens. For months--I may even say years--she had shown unaccountable animosity toward my neck-tie, even getting up in the night to take it with the tongs and blackguard it--sometimes also going so far as to threaten it.

When I said you and Aldrich had given me two new neck-ties, and that they were in a paper in my overcoat pocket, she was in a fever of happiness until she found I was going to frame them; then all the venom in her nature gathered itself together,--insomuch that I, being near to a door, went without, perceiving danger.

Now I wear one of the new neck-ties, nothing being sacred in Mrs. Clemens's eyes that can be perverted to a gaud that shall make the person of her husband more alluring than it was aforetime.

Jo Twichell was the delightedest old boy I ever saw, when he read the words you had written in that book. He and I went to the Concert of the Yale students last night and had a good time.

Mrs. Clemens dreads our going to New Orleans, but I tell her she'll have to give her consent this time.

With kindest regards unto ye both. Yrs ever, S. L. CLEMENS.

The reference to New Orleans at the end of this letter grew naturally out of the enthusiasm aroused by the Mississippi papers. The more Clemens wrote about the river the more he wished to revisit it and take Howells with him. Howells was willing enough to go and they eventually arranged to take their wives on the excursion. This seemed all very well and possible, so long as the time was set for some date in the future still unfixed. But Howells was a busy editor, and it was much more easy for him to promise good-naturedly than to agree on a definite time of departure. He explained at length why he could not make the journey, and added: "Forgive me having led you on to fix a time; I never thought it would come to that; I supposed you would die, or something. I am really more sorry and ashamed than I can make it appear." So the beautiful plan was put aside, though it was not entirely abandoned for a long time.

We now come to the incident mentioned in Mark Twain's letter to Aldrich, of December the 18th. It had its beginning at the Atlantic dinner, where Aldrich had abused Clemens for never sending him any photographs of himself. It was suggested by one or the other that his name be put down as a "regular subscriber" for all Mark Twain photographs as they "came out." Clemens returned home and hunted up fifty-two different specimens, put each into an envelope, and began mailing them to him, one each morning. When a few of them had arrived Aldrich wrote, protesting.

"The police," he said, "have a way of swooping down on that kind of publication. The other day they gobbled up an entire edition of 'The Life in New York.'"

Whereupon Clemens bundled up the remaining collection--forty-five envelopes of photographs and prints-and mailed them together.

Aldrich wrote, now, violently declaring the perpetrator of the outrage to be known to the police; that a sprawling yellow figure against a green background had been recognized as an admirable likeness of Mark Twain, alias the jumping Frog, a well-known Californian desperado, formerly the chief of Henry Plummer's band of road agents in Montana. The letter was signed, "T. Bayleigh, Chief of Police." On the back of the envelope "T. Bayleigh" had also written that it was "no use for the person to send any more letters, as the post-office at that point was to be blown up. Forty-eight hogs-head of nitroglycerine had been syrupticiously introduced into the cellar of the building, and more was expected. R.W.E. H.W.L. O.W.H., and other conspirators in masks have been seen flitting about the town for some days past. The greatest excitement combined with the most intense quietness reigns at Ponkapog."

XV.

LETTERS FROM HARTFORD, 1875. MUCH CORRESPONDENCE WITH HOWELLS

Orion Clemens had kept his job with Bliss only a short time. His mental make-up was such that it was difficult for him to hold any position long. He meant to do well, but he was unfortunate in his efforts. His ideas were seldom practical, his nature was yielding and fickle. He had returned to

Keokuk presently, and being convinced there was a fortune in chickens, had prevailed upon his brother to purchase for him a little farm not far from the town. But the chicken business was not lively and Orion kept the mail hot with manuscripts and propositions of every sort, which he wanted his brother to take under advisement.

Certainly, to Mark Twain Orion Clemens was a trial. The letters of the latter show that scarcely one of them but contains the outline of some rainbow-chasing scheme, full of wild optimism, and the certainty that somewhere just ahead lies the pot of gold. Only, now and then, there is a letter of abject humiliation and complete surrender, when some golden vision, some iridescent soap-bubble, had vanished at his touch. Such depression did not last; by sunrise he was ready with a new dream, new enthusiasm, and with a new letter inviting his "brother Sam's" interest and investment. Yet, his fear of incurring his brother's displeasure was pitiful, regardless of the fact that he constantly employed the very means to insure that result. At one time Clemens made him sign a sworn agreement that he would not suggest any plan or scheme of investment for the period of twelve months. Orion must have kept this agreement. He would have gone to the stake before he would have violated an oath, but the stake would have probably been no greater punishment than his sufferings that year.

On the whole, Samuel Clemens was surprisingly patient and considerate with Orion, and there was never a time that he was not willing to help. Yet there were bound to be moments of exasperation; and once, when his mother, or sister, had written, suggesting that he encourage his brother's efforts, he felt moved to write at considerable freedom.

To Mrs. Jane Clemens and Mrs. Moffett, in Fredonia, N. Y.:

HARTFORD, Sunday, 1875. MY DEAR MOTHER AND SISTER,--I Saw Gov. Newell today and he said he was still moving in the matter of Sammy's appointment--[As a West Point cadet.]-- and would stick to it till he got a result of a positive nature one way or the other, but thus far he did not know whether to expect success or defeat.

Ma, whenever you need money I hope you won't be backward about saying so --you can always have it. We stint ourselves in some ways, but we have no desire to stint you. And we don't intend to, either.

I can't "encourage" Orion. Nobody can do that, conscientiously, for the reason that before one's letter has time to reach him he is off on some new wild-goose chase. Would you encourage in literature a man who, the older he grows the worse he writes? Would you encourage Orion in the glaring insanity of studying law? If he were packed and crammed full of law, it would be worthless lumber to him, for his is such a capricious and ill-regulated mind that he would apply the principles of the law with no more judgment than a child of ten years. I know what I am saying. I laid one of the plainest and simplest of legal questions before Orion once, and the helpless and hopeless mess he made of it was absolutely astonishing. Nothing aggravates me so much as to have Orion mention law or literature to me.

Well, I cannot encourage him to try the ministry, because he would change his religion so fast that he would have to keep a traveling agent under wages to go ahead of him to engage pulpits and board for him.

I cannot conscientiously encourage him to do anything but potter around his little farm and put in his odd hours contriving new and impossible projects at the rate of 365 a year--which is his customary average. He says he did well in Hannibal! Now there is a man who ought to be entirely satisfied with the grandeurs, emoluments and activities of a hen farm--

If you ask me to pity Orion, I can do that. I can do it every day and all day long. But one can't "encourage" quick-silver, because the instant you put your finger on it it isn't there. No, I am saying too much--he does stick to his literary and legal aspirations; and he naturally would select the very two things which he is wholly and preposterously unfitted for. If I ever become able, I mean to put Orion on a regular pension without revealing the fact that it is a pension. That is best for him. Let him consider it a periodical loan, and pay interest out of the principal. Within a year's time he would be looking upon himself as a benefactor of mine, in the way of furnishing me a good permanent investment for money, and that would make him happy and satisfied with himself. If he had money he would share with me in a moment and I have no disposition to be stingy with him. Affly SAM. Livy sends love.

The New Orleans plan was not wholly dead at this time. Howells wrote near the end of January that the matter was still being debated, now and then, but was far from being decided upon. He hoped to go somewhere with Mrs. Howells for a brief time in March, he said. Clemens, in haste, replied:

To W. D. Howells, in Boston:

HARTFORD, Jan. 26, 1875. MY DEAR HOWELLS,--When Mrs. Clemens read your letter she said: "Well, then, wherever they go, in March, the direction will be southward and so they must give us a visit on the way." I do not know what sort of control you may be under, but when my wife speaks as positively as that, I am not in the habit of talking back and getting into trouble. Situated as I am, I would not be able to understand, now, how you could pass by this town without feeling that you were running a wanton risk and doing a daredevil thing. I consider it settled that you are to come in March, and I would be sincerely sorry to learn that you and Mrs. Howells feel differently about it.

The piloting material has been uncovering itself by degrees, until it has exposed such a huge hoard to my view that a whole book will be required to contain it if I use it. So I have agreed to write the book for Bliss. --[The book idea was later given up for the time being.]--I won't be able to run the articles in the Atlantic later than the September number, for the reason that a subscription book issued in the fall has a much larger sale than if issued at any other season of the year. It is funny when I reflect that when I originally wrote you and proposed to do from 6 to 9 articles for the magazine, the vague thought in my mind was that 6 might exhaust the material and 9 would be pretty sure to do it. Or rather it seems to me that that was my thought--can't tell at this distance. But in truth 9 chapters don't now seem to more than open up the subject fairly and start the yarn to wagging.

I have been sick a-bed several days, for the first time in 21 years. How little confirmed invalids appreciate their advantages. I was able to read the English edition of the Greville Memoirs through without interruption, take my meals in bed, neglect all business without a pang, and smoke 18 cigars a day. I try not to look back upon these 21 years with a feeling of resentment, and yet the partialities of Providence do seem to me to be slathered around (as one may say) without that gravity and attention to detail which the real importance of the matter would seem to suggest. Yrs ever MARK.

The New Orleans idea continued to haunt the letters. The thought of drifting down the Mississippi so attracted both Clemens and Howells, that they talked of it when they met, and wrote of it when they were separated. Howells, beset by uncertainties, playfully tried to put the responsibility upon his wife. Once he wrote: "She says in the noblest way, 'Well, go to New Orleans, if you want to so much' (you know the tone). I suppose it will do if I let you know about the middle of February?"

But they had to give it up in the end. Howells wrote that he had been under the weather, and on half work the whole winter. He did not feel that he had earned his salary, he said, or that he was warranted in taking a three weeks' pleasure trip. Clemens offered to pay all the expenses of the trip, but only indefinite postponement followed. It would be seven years more before Mark Twain would return to the river, and then not with Howells.

In a former chapter mention has been made of Charles Warren Stoddard, whom Mark Twain had known in his California days. He was fond of Stoddard, who was a facile and pleasing writer of poems and descriptive articles. During the period that he had been acting as Mark Twain's secretary in London, he had taken pleasure in collecting for him the news reports of the celebrated Tichborn Claimant case, then in the English courts. Clemens thought of founding a story on it, and did, in fact, use the idea, though 'The American Claimant,' which he wrote years later, had little or no connection with the Tichborn episode.

To C. W. Stoddard:

HARTFORD, Feb. 1, 1875. DEAR CHARLEY,--All right about the Tichborn scrapbooks; send them along when convenient. I mean to have the Beecher-Tilton trial scrap-book as a companion.....

I am writing a series of 7-page articles for the Atlantic at $20 a page; but as they do not pay anybody else as much as that, I do not complain (though at the same time I do swear that I am not content.) However the awful respectability of the magazine makes up.

I have cut your articles about San Marco out of a New York paper (Joe Twichell saw it and brought it home to me with loud admiration,) and sent it to Howells. It is too bad to fool away such good literature in a perishable daily journal.

Do remember us kindly to Lady Hardy and all that rare family--my wife and I so often have pleasant talks about them. Ever your friend, SAML. L. CLEMENS.

The price received by Mark Twain for the Mississippi papers, as quoted in this letter, furnishes us with a realizing sense of the improvement in the literary market, with the advent of a flood of cheap magazines and the Sunday newspaper. The Atlantic page probably contained about a thousand words, which would make his price average, say, two cents per word. Thirty years later, when his fame was not much more extended, his pay for the same matter would have been fifteen times as great, that is to say, at the rate of thirty cents per word. But in that early time there were no Sunday magazines--no literary magazines at all except the Atlantic, and Harpers, and a few fashion periodicals. Probably there were news-stands, but it is hard to imagine what they must have looked like without the gay pictorial cover-femininity that to-day pleases and elevates the public and makes author and artist affluent.

Clemens worked steadily on the river chapters, and Howells was always praising him and urging him to go on. At the end of January he wrote: "You're doing the science of piloting splendidly. Every word's interesting. And don't you drop the series 'til you've got every bit of anecdote and reminiscence into it."

To W. D. Howells, in Boston:

HARTFORD, Feb. 10, 1875. MY DEAR HOWELLS,--Your praises of my literature gave me the solidest gratification; but I never did have the fullest confidence in my critical penetration, and now your verdict on S-----has knocked what little I did have gully-west! I didn't enjoy his gush, but I thought a lot of his similes were ever so vivid and good. But it's just my luck; every time I go into convulsions of admiration over a picture and want to buy it right away before I've lost the chance, some wretch who really understands art comes along and damns it. But I don't mind. I would rather have my ignorance than another man's knowledge, because I have got so much more of it.

I send you No. 5 today. I have written and re-written the first half of it three different times, yesterday and today, and at last Mrs. Clemens says it will do. I never saw a woman so hard to please about things she doesn't know anything about. Yours ever, MARK.

Of course, the reference to his wife's criticism in this is tenderly playful, as always--of a pattern with the severity which he pretends for her in the next.

To Mrs. W. D. Howells, in Boston:

1875 DEAR MRS. HOWELLS,--Mrs. Clemens is delighted to get the pictures, and so am I. I can perceive in the group, that Mr. Howells is feeling as I so often feel, viz: "Well, no doubt I am in the wrong, though I do not know how or where or why--but anyway it will be safest to look meek, and walk circumspectly for a while, and not discuss the thing." And you look exactly as Mrs. Clemens does after she has said, "Indeed I do not wonder that you can frame no reply: for you know only too well, that your conduct admits of no excuse, palliation or argument--none!"

I shall just delight in that group on account of the good old human domestic spirit that pervades it--bother these family groups that put on a state aspect to get their pictures taken in.

We want a heliotype made of our eldest daughter. How soft and rich and lovely the picture is. Mr. Howells must tell me how to proceed in the matter. Truly Yours SAM. L. CLEMENS.

In the next letter we have a picture of Susy--[This spelling of the name was adopted somewhat later and much preferred. It appears as "Susie" in most of the earlier letters.]--Clemens's third birthday, certainly a pretty picture, and as sweet and luminous and tender today as it was forty years ago-as it will be a hundred years hence, if these lines should survive that long. The letter is to her uncle Charles Langdon, the "Charlie" of the Quaker City. "Atwater" was associated with the Langdon coal interests in Elmira. "The play" is, of course, "The Gilded Age."

To Charles Langdon, in Elmira:

Mch. 19, 1875. DEAR CHARLIE,--Livy, after reading your letter, used her severest form of expression about Mr. Atwater--to wit: She did not "approve" of his conduct. This made me shudder; for it was equivalent to Allie Spaulding's saying "Mr. Atwater is a mean thing;" or Rev. Thomas Beecher's saying "Damn that Atwater," or my saying "I wish Atwater was three hundred million miles in----!"

However, Livy does not often get into one of these furies, God be thanked.

In Brooklyn, Baltimore, Washington, Cincinnati, St. Louis and Chicago, the play paid me an average of nine hundred dollars a week. In smaller towns the average is $400 to $500.

This is Susie's birth-day. Lizzie brought her in at 8.30 this morning (before we were up) hooded with a blanket, red curl-papers in her hair, a great red japonica, in one hand (for Livy) and a yellow rose-bud nestled in violets (for my buttonhole) in the other--and she looked wonderfully pretty. She delivered her memorials and received her birth-day kisses. Livy laid her japonica, down to get a better "holt" for kissing-which Susie presently perceived, and became thoughtful: then said sorrowfully, turning the great deeps of her eyes upon her mother: "Don't you care for you wow?"

Right after breakfast we got up a rousing wood fire in the main hall (it is a cold morning) illuminated the place with a rich glow from all the globes of the newell chandelier, spread a bright rug before the fire, set a circling row of chairs (pink ones and dove-colored) and in the midst a low invalid-table covered with a fanciful cloth and laden with the presents--a pink azalia in lavish bloom from Rosa; a gold inscribed Russia-leather bible from Patrick and Mary; a gold ring (inscribed) from "Maggy Cook;" a silver thimble (inscribed with motto and initials) from Lizzie; a rattling mob of Sunday clad dolls from Livy and Annie, and a Noah's Ark from me, containing 200 wooden animals such as only a human being could create and only God call by name without referring to the passenger list. Then the family and the seven servants assembled there, and Susie and the "Bay" arrived in state from above, the Bay's head being fearfully and wonderfully decorated with a profusion of blazing red flowers and overflowing cataracts of lycopodium. Wee congratulatory notes accompanied the presents of the servants. I tell you it was a great occasion and a striking and cheery group, taking all the surroundings into account and the wintry aspect outside.

(Remainder missing.)

There was to be a centennial celebration that year of the battles of Lexington and Concord, and Howells wrote, urging Clemens and his wife to visit them and attend it. Mrs. Clemens did not go, and Clemens and Howells did not go, either--to the celebration. They had their own ideas about getting there, but found themselves unable to board the thronged train at Concord, and went tramping about in the cold and mud, hunting a conveyance, only to return at length to the cheer of the home, defeated and rather low in spirits.

Twichell, who went on his own hook, had no such difficulties. To Howells, Mark Twain wrote the adventures of this athletic and strenuous exponent of the gospel.

The "Winnie" mentioned in this letter was Howells's daughter Winifred. She had unusual gifts, but did not live to develop them.

To W. D. Howells, in Boston:

FARMINGTON AVENUE, HARTFORD. Apl. 23, 1875. MY DEAR HOWELLS,--I've got Mrs. Clemens's picture before me, and hope I shall not forget to send it with this.

Joe Twichell preached morning and evening here last Sunday; took midnight train for Boston; got an early breakfast and started by rail at 7.30 A. M. for Concord; swelled around there until 1 P. M., seeing everything; then traveled on top of a train to Lexington; saw everything there; traveled on top of a train to Boston, (with hundreds in company) deluged with dust, smoke and cinders; yelled and hurrahed all the way like a schoolboy; lay flat down to dodge numerous bridges, and sailed into the depot, howling with excitement and as black as a chimney-sweep; got to Young's Hotel at 7 P. M.; sat down in reading-room and immediately fell asleep; was promptly awakened by a porter who supposed he was drunk; wandered around an hour and a half; then took 9 P. M. train, sat down in smoking car and remembered nothing more until awakened by conductor as the train came into Hartford at 1.30 A. M. Thinks he had simply a glorious time--and wouldn't have missed the Centennial for the world. He would have run out to see us a moment at Cambridge, but was too dirty. I wouldn't have wanted him there--his appalling energy would have been an insufferable reproach to mild adventurers like you and me.

Well, he is welcome to the good time he had--I had a deal better one. My narrative has made Mrs.

Clemens wish she could have been there.--When I think over what a splendid good sociable time I had in your house I feel ever so thankful to the wise providence that thwarted our several ably-planned and ingenious attempts to get to Lexington. I am coming again before long, and then she shall be of the party.

Now you said that you and Mrs. Howells could run down here nearly any Saturday. Very well then, let us call it next Saturday, for a "starter." Can you do that? By that time it will really be spring and you won't freeze. The birds are already out; a small one paid us a visit yesterday. We entertained it and let it go again, Susie protesting.

The spring laziness is already upon me--insomuch that the spirit begins to move me to cease from Mississippi articles and everything else and give myself over to idleness until we go to New Orleans. I have one article already finished, but somehow it doesn't seem as proper a chapter to close with as the one already in your hands. I hope to get in a mood and rattle off a good one to finish with--but just now all my moods are lazy ones.

Winnie's literature sings through me yet! Surely that child has one of these "futures" before her.

Now try to come--will you?

With the warmest regards of the two of us-- Yrs ever, S. L. CLEMENS.

Mrs. Clemens sent a note to Mrs. Howells, which will serve as a pendant to the foregoing.

From Mrs. Clemens to Mrs. Howells, in Boston:

MY DEAR MRS. HOWELLS,--Don't dream for one instant that my not getting a letter from you kept me from Boston. I am too anxious to go to let such a thing as that keep me.

Mr. Clemens did have such a good time with you and Mr. Howells. He evidently has no regret that he did not get to the Centennial. I was driven nearly distracted by his long account of Mr. Howells and his wanderings. I would keep asking if they ever got there, he would never answer but made me listen to a very minute account of everything that they did. At last I found them back where they started from.

If you find misspelled words in this note, you will remember my infirmity and not hold me responsible. Affectionately yours, LIVY L. CLEMENS.

In spite of his success with the Sellers play and his itch to follow it up, Mark Twain realized what he believed to be his literary limitations. All his life he was inclined to consider himself wanting in the finer gifts of character-shading and delicate portrayal. Remembering Huck Finn, and the rare presentation of Joan of Arc, we may not altogether agree with him. Certainly, he was never qualified to delineate those fine artificialities of life which we are likely to associate with culture, and perhaps it was something of this sort that caused the hesitation confessed in the letter that follows. Whether the plan suggested interested Howells or not we do not know. In later years Howells wrote a novel called The Story of a Play; this may have been its beginning.

To W. D. Howells, in Boston:

FARMINGTON AVENUE, HARTFORD, Apl. 26, 1875. MY DEAR HOWELLS,--An actor named D. H. Harkins has been here to ask me to put upon paper a 5-act play which he has been mapping out in his mind for 3 or 4 years. He sat down and told me his plot all through, in a clear, bright way, and I was a deal taken with it; but it is a line of characters whose fine shading and artistic development requires an abler hand than mine; so I easily perceived that I must not make the attempt. But I liked the man, and thought there was a good deal of stuff in him; and therefore I wanted his play to be written, and by a capable hand, too. So I suggested you, and said I would write and see if you would be willing to undertake it. If you like the idea, he will call upon you in the course of two or three weeks and describe his plot and his characters. Then if it doesn't strike you favorably, of course you can simply decline; but it seems to me well worth while that you should hear what he has to say. You could also "average" him while he talks, and judge whether he could play your priest--though I doubt if any man can do that justice.

Shan't I write him and say he may call? If you wish to communicate directly with him instead, his address is "Larchmont Manor, Westchester Co., N. Y."

Do you know, the chill of that 19th of April seems to be in my bones yet? I am inert and drowsy all the time. That was villainous weather for a couple of wandering children to be out in. Ys ever MARK.

The sinister typewriter did not find its way to Howells for nearly a year. Meantime, Mark Twain had refused to allow the manufacturers to advertise his ownership. He wrote to them:

HARTFORD, March 19, 1875. Please do not use my name in any way. Please do not even divulge the fact that I own a machine. I have entirely stopped using the typewriter, for the reason that I never could write a letter with it to anybody without receiving a request by return mail that I would not only describe the machine, but state what progress I had made in the use of it, etc., etc. I don't like to write letters, and so I don't want people to know I own this curiosity-breeding little joker.

Three months later the machine was still in his possession. Bliss had traded a twelve-dollar saddle for it, but apparently showed little enthusiasm in his new possession.

To W. D. Howells, in Boston:

June 25, 1875. MY DEAR HOWELLS,--I told Patrick to get some carpenters and box the machine and send it to you--and found that Bliss had sent for the machine and earned it off.

I have been talking to you and writing to you as if you were present when I traded the machine to

Bliss for a twelve-dollar saddle worth $25 (cheating him outrageously, of course--but conscience got the upper hand again and I told him before I left the premises that I'd pay for the saddle if he didn't like the machine--on condition that he donate said machine to a charity)

This was a little over five weeks ago--so I had long ago concluded that Bliss didn't want the machine and did want the saddle--wherefore I jumped at the chance of shoving the machine off onto you, saddle or no saddle so I got the blamed thing out of my sight.

The saddle hangs on Tara's walls down below in the stable, and the machine is at Bliss's grimly pursuing its appointed mission, slowly and implacably rotting away another man's chances for salvation.

I have sent Bliss word not to donate it to a charity (though it is a pity to fool away a chance to do a charity an ill turn,) but to let me know when he has got his dose, because I've got another candidate for damnation. You just wait a couple of weeks and if you don't see the Type-Writer come tilting along toward Cambridge with an unsatisfied appetite in its eye, I lose my guess.

Don't you be mad about this blunder, Howells--it only comes of a bad memory, and the stupidity which is inseparable from true genius. Nothing intentionally criminal in it. Yrs ever MARK.

It was November when Howells finally fell under the baleful influence of the machine. He wrote:

"The typewriter came Wednesday night, and is already beginning to have its effect on me. Of course, it doesn't work: if I can persuade some of the letters to get up against the ribbon they won't get down again without digital assistance. The treadle refuses to have any part or parcel in the performance; and I don't know how to get the roller to turn with the paper. Nevertheless I have begun several letters to My d-a-r lemans, as it prefers to spell your respected name, and I don't despair yet of sending you something in its beautiful handwriting--after I've had a man out from the agent's to put it in order. It's fascinating in the meantime, and it wastes my time like an old friend."

The Clemens family remained in Hartford that summer, with the exception of a brief season at Bateman's Point, R. I., near Newport. By this time Mark Twain had taken up and finished the Tom Sawyer story begun two years before. Naturally he wished Howells to consider the MS.

To W. D. Howells, in Boston:

HARTFORD, July 5th, 1875. MY DEAR HOWELLS,--I have finished the story and didn't take the chap beyond boyhood. I believe it would be fatal to do it in any shape but autobiographically--like Gil Blas. I perhaps made a mistake in not writing it in the first person. If I went on, now, and took him into manhood, he would just like like all the one-horse men in literature and the reader would conceive a hearty contempt for him. It is not a boy's book, at all. It will only be read by adults. It is only written for adults.

Moreover the book is plenty long enough as it stands. It is about 900 pages of MS, and may be 1000 when I shall have finished "working up" vague places; so it would make from 130 to 150 pages of the Atlantic-- about what the Foregone Conclusion made, isn't it?

I would dearly like to see it in the Atlantic, but I doubt if it would pay the publishers to buy the privilege, or me to sell it. Bret Harte has sold his novel (same size as mine, I should say) to Scribner's Monthly for $6,500 (publication to begin in September, I think,) and he gets a royalty of 7 1/2 per cent from Bliss in book form afterwards. He gets a royalty of ten per cent on it in England (issued in serial numbers) and the same royalty on it in book form afterwards, and is to receive an advance payment of five hundred pounds the day the first No. of the serial appears. If I could do as well, here, and there, with mine, it might possibly pay me, but I seriously doubt it though it is likely I could do better in England than Bret, who is not widely known there.

You see I take a vile, mercenary view of things--but then my household expenses are something almost ghastly.

By and by I shall take a boy of twelve and run him on through life (in the first person) but not Tom Sawyer--he would not be a good character for it.

I wish you would promise to read the MS of Tom Sawyer some time, and see if you don't really decide that I am right in closing with him as a boy- and point out the most glaring defects for me. It is a tremendous favor to ask, and I expect you to refuse and would be ashamed to expect you to do otherwise. But the thing has been so many months in my mind that it seems a relief to snake it out. I don't know any other person whose judgment I could venture to take fully and entirely. Don't hesitate about saying no, for I know how your time is taxed, and I would have honest need to blush if you said yes.

Osgood and I are "going for" the puppy G---- on infringement of trademark. To win one or two suits of this kind will set literary folks on a firmer bottom. I wish Osgood would sue for stealing Holmes's poem. Wouldn't it be gorgeous to sue R---- for petty larceny? I will promise to go into court and swear I think him capable of stealing pea-nuts from a blind pedlar. Yrs ever, CLEMENS.

Of course Howells promptly replied that he would read the story, adding: "You've no idea what I may ask you to do for me, some day. I'm sorry that you can't do it for the Atlantic, but I succumb. Perhaps you will do Boy No. 2 for us." Clemens, conscience- stricken, meantime, hastily put the MS. out of reach of temptation.

To W. D. Howells, in Boston:

July 13, 1875 MY DEAR HOWELLS,--Just as soon as you consented I realized all the atrocity of my request, and straightway blushed and weakened. I telegraphed my theatrical agent to come here and carry off the MS and copy it.

But I will gladly send it to you if you will do as follows: dramatize it, if you perceive that you can, and take, for your remuneration, half of the first $6000 which I receive for its representation on the stage. You could alter the plot entirely, if you chose. I could help in the work, most cheerfully, after you had arranged the plot. I have my eye upon two young girls who can play "Tom" and "Huck." I believe a good deal of a drama can be made of it. Come--can't you tackle this in the odd hours of your vacation? or later, if you prefer?

I do wish you could come down once more before your holiday. I'd give anything! Yrs ever, MARK.

Howells wrote that he had no time for the dramatization and urged Clemens to undertake it himself. He was ready to read the story, whenever it should arrive. Clemens did not hurry, however, The publication of Tom Sawyer could wait. He already had a book in press--the volume of Sketches New and Old, which he had prepared for Bliss several years before.

Sketches was issued that autumn, and Howells gave it a good notice-- possibly better than it deserved.

Considered among Mark Twain's books to-day, the collection of sketches does not seem especially important. With the exception of the frog story and the "True Story" most of those included--might be spared. Clemens himself confessed to Howells that He wished, when it was too late, that he had destroyed a number of them. The book, however, was distinguished in a special way: it contains Mark Twain's first utterance in print on the subject of copyright, a matter in which he never again lost interest. The absurdity and injustice of the copyright laws both amused and irritated him, and in the course of time he would be largely instrumental in their improvement. In the book his open petition to Congress that all property rights, as well as literary ownership, should be put on the copyright basis and limited to a "beneficent term of forty-two years," was more or less of a joke, but, like so many of Mark Twain's jokes, it was founded on reason and justice.

He had another idea, that was not a joke: an early plan in the direction of international copyright. It was to be a petition signed by the leading American authors, asking the United States to declare itself to be the first to stand for right and justice by enacting laws against the piracy of foreign books. It was a rather utopian scheme, as most schemes for moral progress are, in their beginning. It would not be likely ever to reach Congress, but it would appeal to Howells and his Cambridge friends. Clemens wrote, outlining his plan of action.

To W. D. Howells, in Boston:

HARTFORD, Sept. 18, 1875. MY DEAR HOWELLS,--My plan is this--you are to get Mr. Lowell and Mr. Longfellow to be the first signers of my copyright petition; you must sign it yourself and get Mr. Whittier to do likewise. Then Holmes will sign--he said he would if he didn't have to stand at the head. Then I'm fixed. I will then put a gentlemanly chap under wages and send him personally to every author of distinction in the country, and corral the rest of the signatures. Then I'll have the whole thing lithographed (about a thousand copies) and move upon the

President and Congress in person, but in the subordinate capacity of a party who is merely the agent of better and wiser men--men whom the country cannot venture to laugh at.

I will ask the President to recommend the thing in his message (and if he should ask me to sit down and frame the paragraph for him I should blush --but still I would frame it.)

Next I would get a prime leader in Congress: I would also see that votes enough to carry the measure were privately secured before the bill was offered. This I would try through my leader and my friends there.

And then if Europe chose to go on stealing from us, we would say with noble enthusiasm, "American lawmakers do steal but not from foreign authors--Not from foreign authors!"

You see, what I want to drive into the Congressional mind is the simple fact that the moral law is "Thou shalt not steal"--no matter what Europe may do.

I swear I can't see any use in robbing European authors for the benefit of American booksellers, anyway.

If we can ever get this thing through Congress, we can try making copyright perpetual, some day. There would be no sort of use in it, since only one book in a hundred millions outlives the present copyright term--no sort of use except that the writer of that one book have his rights--which is something.

If we only had some God in the country's laws, instead of being in such a sweat to get Him into the Constitution, it would be better all around.

The only man who ever signed my petition with alacrity, and said that the fact that a thing was right was all-sufficient, was Rev. Dr. Bushnell.

I have lost my old petition, (which was brief) but will draft and enclose another--not in the words it ought to be, but in the substance. I want Mr. Lowell to furnish the words (and the ideas too,) if he will do it.

Say--Redpath beseeches me to lecture in Boston in November--telegraphs that Beecher's and Nast's withdrawal has put him in the tightest kind of a place. So I guess I'll do that old "Roughing It" lecture over again in November and repeat it 2 or 3 times in New York while I am at it.

Can I take a carriage after the lecture and go out and stay with you that night, provided you find at that distant time that it will not inconvenience you? Is Aldrich home yet? With love to you all Yrs ever, S. L. C.

Of course the petition never reached Congress. Holmes's comment that governments were not in the habit of setting themselves up as high moral examples, except for revenue, was shared by too many others. The petition was tabled, but Clemens never abandoned his purpose and lived to see most of his dream fulfilled. Meantime, Howells's notice of the Sketches appeared in the Atlantic, and brought grateful acknowledgment from the author.

To W. D. Howells, in Boston:

HARTFORD, Oct. 19, 1875. MY DEAR HOWELLS,--That is a perfectly superb notice. You can easily believe that nothing ever gratified me so much before. The newspaper praises bestowed upon the "Innocents Abroad" were large and generous, but somehow I hadn't confidence in the critical judgement of the parties who furnished them. You know how that is, yourself, from reading the newspaper notices of your own books. They gratify a body, but they always leave a small pang behind in the shape of a fear that the critic's good words could not safely be depended upon as authority. Yours is the recognized critical Court of Last Resort in this country; from its decision there is no appeal; and so, to have gained this decree of yours before I am forty years old, I regard as a thing to be right down proud of. Mrs. Clemens says, "Tell him I am just as grateful to him as I can be." (It sounds as if she were grateful to you for heroically trampling the truth under foot in order to praise me but in reality it means that she is grateful to you for being bold enough to utter a truth which she fully believes all competent people know, but which none has heretofore been brave enough to utter.) You see, the thing that gravels her is that I am so persistently glorified as a mere buffoon, as if that entirely covered my case--which she denies with venom.

The other day Mrs. Clemens was planning a visit to you, and so I am waiting with a pleasurable hope for the result of her deliberations. We are expecting visitors every day, now, from New York; and afterward some are to come from Elmira. I judge that we shall then be free to go Bostonward. I should be just delighted; because we could visit in comfort, since we shouldn't have to do any shopping--did it all in New York last week, and a tremendous pull it was too.

Mrs. C. said the other day, "We will go to Cambridge if we have to walk; for I don't believe we can ever get the Howellses to come here again until we have been there." I was gratified to see that there was one string, anyway, that could take her to Cambridge. But I will do her the justice to say that she is always wanting to go to Cambridge, independent of the selfish desire to get a visit out of you by it. I want her to get started, now, before children's diseases are fashionable again, because they always play such hob with visiting arrangements. With love to you all Yrs Ever S. L. CLEMENS.

Mark Twain's trips to Boston were usually made alone. Women require more preparation to go visiting, and Mrs. Clemens and Mrs. Howells seem to have exchanged visits infrequently. For Mark Twain, perhaps, it was just as well that his wife did not always go with him; his absent-mindedness and boyish ingenuousness often led him into difficulties which Mrs. Clemens sometimes found embarrassing. In the foregoing letter they were planning a visit to Cambridge. In the one that follows they seem to have made it--with certain results, perhaps not altogether amusing at the moment.

To W. D. Howells, in Boston:

Oct. 4, '75. MY DEAR HOWELLS,--We had a royal good time at your house, and have had a royal good time ever since, talking about it, both privately and with the neighbors.

Mrs. Clemens's bodily strength came up handsomely under that cheery respite from household and nursery cares. I do hope that Mrs. Howells's didn't go correspondingly down, under the added burden to her cares and responsibilities. Of course I didn't expect to get through without committing some crimes and hearing of them afterwards, so I have taken the inevitable lashings and been able to hum a tune while the punishment went on. I "caught it" for letting Mrs. Howells bother and bother about her coffee when it was "a good deal better than we get at home." I "caught it" for interrupting Mrs. C. at the last moment and losing her the opportunity to urge you not to forget to send her that MS when the printers are done with it. I "caught it" once more for personating that drunken Col. James. I "caught it" for mentioning that Mr. Longfellow's picture was slightly damaged; and when, after a lull in the storm, I confessed, shame-facedly, that I had privately suggested to you that we hadn't any frames, and that if you wouldn't mind hinting to Mr. Houghton, &c., &c., &c., the Madam was simply speechless for the space of a minute. Then she said:

"How could you, Youth! The idea of sending Mr. Howells, with his sensitive nature, upon such a repulsive er--"

"Oh, Howells won't mind it! You don't know Howells. Howells is a man who--" She was gone. But George was the first person she stumbled on in the hall, so she took it out of George. I was glad of that, because it saved the babies.

I've got another rattling good character for my novel! That great work is mulling itself into shape gradually.

Mrs. Clemens sends love to Mrs. Howells--meantime she is diligently laying up material for a letter to her. Yrs ever MARK.

The "George" of this letter was Mark Twain's colored butler, a valued and even beloved member of the household--a most picturesque character, who "one day came to wash windows," as Clemens used to say, "and remained eighteen years." The fiction of Mrs. Clemens's severity he always found amusing, because of its entire contrast with the reality of her gentle heart.

Clemens carried the Tom Sawyer MS. to Boston himself and placed it in Howells's hands. Howells had begged to be allowed to see the story, and Mrs. Clemens was especially anxious that he should do so. She had doubts as to certain portions of it, and had the fullest faith in Howells's opinion.

It was a gratifying one when it came. Howells wrote: "I finished reading Tom Sawyer a week ago, sitting up till one A.M. to get to the end, simply because it was impossible to leave off. It's altogether the best boy's story I ever read. It will be an immense success. But I think you ought to treat it explicitly as a boy's story. Grown-ups will enjoy it just as much if you do; and if you should put it forth as a study of boy character from the grown-up point of view, you give the wrong key to it.... The adventures are enchanting. I wish I had been on that island. The treasure-hunting, the loss in the cave--it's all exciting and splendid. I shouldn't think of publishing this story serially. Give me a hint when it's to be out, and I'll start the sheep to jumping in the right places"--meaning that he would have an advance review ready for publication in the Atlantic, which was a leader of criticism in America.

Mark Twain was writing a great deal at this time. Howells was always urging him to send something to the Atlantic, declaring a willingness to have his name appear every month in their pages, and Clemens was generally contributing some story or sketch. The "proof" referred to in the next letter was of one of these articles.

To W. D. Howells, in Boston:

HARTFORD, Nov. 23, '75. MY DEAR HOWELLS,--Herewith is the proof. In spite of myself, how awkwardly I do jumble words together; and how often I do use three words where one would answer--a thing I am always trying to guard against. I shall become as slovenly a writer as Charles Francis Adams, if I don't look out. (That is said in jest; because of course I do not seriously fear getting so bad as that. I never shall drop so far toward his and Bret Harte's level as to catch myself saying "It must have been wiser to have believed that he might have accomplished it if he could have felt that he would have been supported by those who should have &c. &c. &c.") The reference to Bret Harte reminds me that I often accuse him of being a deliberate imitator of Dickens; and this in turn reminds me that I have charged unconscious plagiarism upon Charley Warner; and this in turn reminds me that I have been delighting my soul for two weeks over a bran new and ingenious way of beginning a novel--and behold, all at once it flashes upon me that Charley Warner originated the idea 3 years ago and told me about it! Aha! So much for self-righteousness! I am well repaid. Here are 108 pages of MS, new and clean, lying disgraced in the waste paper basket, and I am beginning the novel over again in an unstolen way. I would not wonder if I am the worst literary thief in the world, without knowing it.

It is glorious news that you like Tom Sawyer so well. I mean to see to it that your review of it shall have plenty of time to appear before the other notices. Mrs. Clemens decides with you that the book should issue as a book for boys, pure and simple--and so do I. It is surely the correct idea. As to that last chapter, I think of just leaving it off and adding nothing in its place. Something told me that the book was done when I got to that point--and so the strong temptation to put Huck's life at the Widow's into detail, instead of generalizing it in a paragraph was resisted. Just send Sawyer to me by express--I enclose money for it. If it should get lost it will be no great matter.

Company interfered last night, and so "Private Theatricals" goes over till this evening, to be read aloud. Mrs. Clemens is mad, but the story will take that all out. This is going to be a splendid winter night for fireside reading, anyway.

I am almost at a dead stand-still with my new story, on account of the misery of having to do it all over again. We--all send love to you--all. Yrs ever MARK.

The "story" referred to may have been any one of several begun by him at this time. His head was full of ideas for literature of every sort. Many of his beginnings came to nothing, for the reason that he started wrong, or with no definitely formed plan. Others of his literary enterprises were condemned by his wife for their grotesqueness or for the offense they might give in one way or another, however worthy the intention behind them. Once he wrote a burlesque on family history "The Autobiography of a Damned Fool." "Livy wouldn't have it," he said later, "so I gave it up." The world is indebted to Mark Twain's wife for the check she put upon his fantastic or violent impulses. She was his public, his best public--clearheaded and wise. That he realized this, and was willing to yield, was by no means the least of his good fortunes. We may believe that he did not always yield easily, and perhaps sometimes only out of love for her. In the letter which he wrote her on her thirtieth birthday we realize something of what she had come to mean in his life.

To Mrs. Clemens on her Thirtieth Birthday:

HARTFORD, November 27, 1875. Livy darling, six years have gone by since I made my first great success in life and won you, and thirty years have passed since Providence made preparation for that happy success by sending you into the world. Every day we live together adds to the security of my confidence, that we can never any more wish to be separated than that we can ever imagine a regret that we were ever joined. You are dearer to me to-day, my child, than you were upon the last anniversary of this birth-day; you were dearer then than you were a year before--you have grown more and more dear from the first of those anniversaries, and I do not doubt that this precious progression will continue on to the end.

Let us look forward to the coming anniversaries, with their age and their gray hairs without fear and without depression, trusting and believing that the love we bear each other will be sufficient to make them blessed.

So, with abounding affection for you and our babies, I hail this day that brings you the matronly grace and dignity of three decades!

Always Yours S. L. C.

End of this Project Gutenberg Etext of Letters Vol. 2, by Mark Twain

MARK TWAIN'S LETTERS 1876-1885

ARRANGED WITH COMMENT BY ALBERT BIGELOW PAINE

VOLUME III.

XVI.

LETTERS, 1876, CHIEFLY TO W. D. HOWELLS. LITERATURE AND POLITICS. PLANNING A PLAY WITH BRET HARTE

The Monday Evening Club of Hartford was an association of most of the literary talent of that city, and it included a number of very distinguished members. The writers, the editors, the lawyers, and the ministers of the gospel who composed it were more often than not men of national or international distinction. There was but one paper at each meeting, and it was likely to be a paper that would later find its way into some magazine.

Naturally Mark Twain was one of its favorite members, and his contributions never failed to arouse interest and discussion. A "Mark Twain night" brought out every member. In the next letter we find the first mention of one of his most memorable contributions--a story of one of life's moral aspects. The tale, now included in his collected works, is, for some reason, little read to-day; yet the curious allegory, so vivid in its seeming reality, is well worth consideration.

To W. D. Howells, in Boston:

HARTFORD, Jan. 11, '76. MY DEAR HOWELLS,--Indeed we haven't forgotten the Howellses, nor scored up a grudge of any kind against them; but the fact is I was under the doctor's hands for four weeks on a stretch and have been disabled from working for a week or so beside. I thought I was well, about ten days ago, so I sent for a short-hand writer and dictated answers to a bushel or so of letters that had been accumulating during my illness. Getting everything shipshape and cleared up, I went to work next day upon an Atlantic article, which ought to be worth $20 per page (which is the price they usually pay for my work, I believe) for although it is only 70 pages MS (less than two days work, counting by bulk,) I have spent 3 more days trimming, altering and working at it. I shall put in one more day's polishing on it, and then read it before our Club, which is to meet at our house Monday evening, the 24th inst. I think it will bring out considerable discussion among the gentlemen of the Club--though the title of the article will not give them much notion of what is to follow,--this title being "The Facts Concerning the Recent Carnival of Crime in Connecticut"--which reminds me that today's Tribune says there will be a startling article in the current Atlantic, in which a being which is tangible bud invisible will figure-exactly the case with the sketch of mine which I am talking about! However, mine can lie unpublished a year or two as well as not--though I wish that contributor of yours had not interfered with his coincidence of heroes.

But what I am coming at, is this: won't you and Mrs. Howells come down Saturday the 22nd and remain to the Club on Monday night? We always have a rattling good time at the Club and we do want you to come, ever so much. Will you? Now say you will. Mrs. Clemens and I are persuading ourselves that you twain will come.

My volume of sketches is doing very well, considering the times; received my quarterly statement today from Bliss, by which I perceive that 20,000 copies have been sold--or rather, 20,000 had been sold 3 weeks ago; a lot more, by this time, no doubt.

I am on the sick list again--and was, day before yesterday--but on the whole I am getting along. Yrs ever MARK

Howells wrote that he could not come down to the club meeting, adding that sickness was "quite out of character" for Mark Twain, and hardly fair on a man who had made so many other people feel well. He closed by urging that Bliss "hurry out" 'Tom Sawyer.' "That boy is going to make a prodigious hit." Clemens answered:

To W. D. Howells, in Boston.

HARTFORD, Jan. 18, '76. MY DEAR HOWELLS,--Thanks, and ever so many, for the good opinion of 'Tom Sawyer.' Williams has made about 300 rattling pictures for it--some of them very dainty. Poor devil, what a genius he has and how he does murder it with rum. He takes a book of mine, and without suggestion from anybody builds no end of pictures just from his reading of it.

There was never a man in the world so grateful to another as I was to you day before yesterday, when I sat down (in still rather wretched health) to set myself to the dreary and hateful task of making final revision of Tom Sawyer, and discovered, upon opening the package of MS that your pencil marks were scattered all along. This was splendid, and swept away all labor. Instead of reading the MS, I simply hunted out the pencil marks and made the emendations which they suggested. I reduced the boy battle to a curt paragraph; I finally concluded to cut the Sunday school speech down to the first two sentences, leaving no suggestion of satire, since the book is to be for boys and girls; I tamed the various obscenities until I judged that they no longer carried offense. So, at a single sitting I began and finished a revision which I had supposed would occupy 3 or 4. days and leave me mentally and physically fagged out at the end. I was careful not to inflict the MS upon you until I had thoroughly and painstakingly revised it. Therefore, the only faults left were those that would discover themselves to others, not me--and these you had pointed out.

There was one expression which perhaps you overlooked. When Huck is complaining to Tom of the rigorous system in vogue at the widow's, he says the servants harass him with all manner of compulsory decencies, and he winds up by saying: "and they comb me all to hell." (No exclamation point.) Long ago, when I read that to Mrs. Clemens, she made no comment; another time I created occasion to read that chapter to her aunt and her mother (both sensitive and loyal subjects of the kingdom of heaven, so to speak) and they let it pass. I was glad, for it was the most natural remark in the world for that boy to make (and he had been allowed few privileges of speech in the book;) when I saw that you, too, had let it go without protest, I was glad, and afraid; too--afraid you hadn't observed it. Did you? And did you question the propriety of it? Since the book is now professedly and confessedly a boy's and girl's hook, that darn word bothers me some, nights, but it never did until I had ceased to regard the volume as being for adults.

Don't bother to answer now, (for you've writing enough to do without allowing me to add to the burden,) but tell me when you see me again!

Which we do hope will be next Saturday or Sunday or Monday. Couldn't you come now and mull over the alterations which you are going to make in your MS, and make them after you go back? Wouldn't it assist the work if you dropped out of harness and routine for a day or two and have that sort of revivification which comes of a holiday-forgetfulness of the work-shop? I can always work after I've been to your house; and if you will come to mine, now, and hear the club toot their various horns over the exasperating metaphysical question which I mean to lay before them in the disguise of a literary extravaganza, it would just brace you up like a cordial.

(I feel sort of mean trying to persuade a man to put down a critical piece of work at a critical time, but yet I am honest in thinking it would not hurt the work nor impair your interest in it to come under the circumstances.) Mrs. Clemens says, "Maybe the Howellses could come Monday if they cannot come Saturday; ask them; it is worth trying." Well, how's that? Could you? It would be splendid if you could. Drop me a postal card--I should have a twinge of conscience if I forced you to write a letter, (I am honest about that,)--and if you find you can't make out to come, tell me that you bodies will come the next Saturday if the thing is possible, and stay over Sunday. Yrs ever MARK.

Howells, however, did not come to the club meeting, but promised to come soon when they could have a quiet time to themselves together. As to Huck's language, he declared:

"I'd have that swearing out in an instant. I suppose I didn't notice it because the locution was so familiar to my Western sense, and so exactly the thing that Huck would say." Clemens changed the phrase to, "They comb me all to thunder," and so it stands to-day.

The "Carnival of Crime," having served its purpose at the club, found quick acceptance by Howells for the Atlantic. He was so pleased with it, in fact, that somewhat later he wrote, urging that its author allow it to be printed in a dainty book, by Osgood, who made a specialty of fine publishing. Meantime Howells had written his Atlantic notice of Tom Sawyer, and now inclosed Clemens a proof of it. We may judge from the reply that it was satisfactory.

To W. D. Howells, in Boston:

Apl 3, '76. MY DEAR HOWELLS,--It is a splendid notice and will embolden weak-kneed journalistic admirers to speak out, and will modify or shut up the unfriendly. To "fear God and dread the Sunday school" exactly described that old feeling which I used to have, but I couldn't have formulated it. I want to enclose one of the illustrations in this letter, if I do not forget it. Of course the book is to be elaborately illustrated, and I think that many of the pictures are considerably above the American average, in conception if not in execution.

I do not re-enclose your review to you, for you have evidently read and corrected it, and so I judge you do not need it. About two days after the Atlantic issues I mean to begin to send books to principal journals and magazines.

I read the "Carnival of Crime" proof in New York when worn and witless and so left some things unamended which I might possibly have altered had I been at home. For instance, "I shall always address you in your own S-n-i-v-e-l-i-n-g d-r-a-w-l, baby." I saw that you objected to something there, but I did not understand what! Was it that it was too personal? Should the language be altered?--or the hyphens taken out? Won't you please fix it the way it ought to be, altering the language as you choose, only making it bitter and contemptuous?

"Deuced" was not strong enough; so I met you halfway with "devilish."

Mrs. Clemens has returned from New York with dreadful sore throat, and bones racked with rheumatism. She keeps her bed. "Aloha nui!" as the Kanakas say. MARK.

Henry Irving once said to Mark Twain: "You made a mistake by not adopting the stage as a profession. You would have made even a greater actor than a writer."

Mark Twain would have made an actor, certainly, but not a very tractable one. His appearance in Hartford in "The Loan of a Lover" was a distinguished event, and his success complete, though he made so many extemporaneous improvements on the lines of thick-headed Peter Spuyk, that he kept the other actors guessing as to their cues, and nearly broke up the performance. It was, of course, an amateur benefit, though Augustin Daly promptly wrote, offering to put it on for a long run.

The "skeleton novelette" mentioned in the next letter refers to a plan concocted by Howells and Clemens, by which each of twelve authors was to write a story, using the same plot, "blindfolded" as to what the others had written. It was a regular "Mark Twain" notion, and it is hard to-day to imagine Howells's continued enthusiasm in it. Neither he nor Clemens gave up the idea for a long time. It appears in their letters again and again, though perhaps it was just as well for literature that it was never carried out.

To W. D. Howells, in Boston:

Apl. 22, 1876. MY DEAR HOWELLS, You'll see per enclosed slip that I appear for the first time on the stage next Wednesday. You and Mrs. H. come down and you shall skip in free.

I wrote my skeleton novelette yesterday and today. It will make a little under 12 pages.

Please tell Aldrich I've got a photographer engaged, and tri-weekly issue is about to begin. Show him the canvassing specimens and beseech him to subscribe. Ever yours, S. L. C.

In his next letter Mark Twain explains why Tom Sawyer is not to appear as soon as planned. The reference to "The Literary Nightmare" refers to the "Punch, Conductor, Punch with Care" sketch, which had recently appeared in the Atlantic. Many other versifiers had had their turn at horse-car poetry, and now a publisher was anxious to collect it in a book, provided he could use the Atlantic sketch. Clemens does not tell us here the nature of Carlton's insult, forgiveness of which he was not yet qualified to grant, but there are at least two stories about it, or two halves of the same incident, as related afterward by Clemens and Canton. Clemens said that when he took the Jumping Frog book to Carlton, in 1867, the latter, pointing to his stock, said, rather scornfully: "Books? I don't want your book; my shelves are full of books now," though the reader may remember that it was Carlton himself who had given the frog story to the Saturday Press and had seen it become famous. Carlton's half of the story was that he did not accept Mark Twain's book because the author looked so disreputable. Long afterward, when the two men met in Europe, the publisher said to the now rich and famous author: "Mr. Clemens, my one claim on immortality is that I declined your first book."

To W. D. Howells, in Boston:

HARTFORD, Apl. 25, 1876 MY DEAR HOWELLS,--Thanks for giving me the place of honor.

Bliss made a failure in the matter of getting Tom Sawyer ready on time-- the engravers assisting, as usual. I went down to see how much of a delay there was going to be, and found that the man had not even put a canvasser on, or issued an advertisement yet--in fact, that the electrotypes would not all be done for a month! But of course the main fact was that no canvassing had been done--because a subscription harvest is before publication, (not after, when people have discovered how bad one's book is.)

Well, yesterday I put in the Courant an editorial paragraph stating that Tam Sawyer is "ready to issue, but publication is put off in order to secure English copyright by simultaneous publication there and here. The English edition is unavoidably delayed."

You see, part of that is true. Very well. When I observed that my "Sketches" had dropped from a sale of 6 or 7000 a month down to 1200 a month, I said "this ain't no time to be publishing books; therefore, let Tom lie still till Autumn, Mr. Bliss, and make a holiday book of him to beguile the young people withal."

I shall print items occasionally, still further delaying Tom, till I ease him down to Autumn without shock to the waiting world.

As to that "Literary Nightmare" proposition. I'm obliged to withhold consent, for what seems a good reason--to wit: A single page of horse-car poetry is all that the average reader can stand, without nausea; now, to stack together all of it that has been written, and then add it to my article would be to enrage and disgust each and every reader and win the deathless enmity of the lot.

Even if that reason were insufficient, there would still be a sufficient reason left, in the fact that Mr. Carlton seems to be the publisher of the magazine in which it is proposed to publish this horse-car matter. Carlton insulted me in Feb. 1867, and so when the day arrives that sees me doing him a civility I shall feel that I am ready for Paradise, since my list of possible and impossible forgivenesses will then be complete.

Mrs. Clemens says my version of the blindfold novelette "A Murder and A Marriage" is "good." Pretty strong language--for her.

The Fieldses are coming down to the play tomorrow, and they promise to get you and Mrs. Howells to come too, but I hope you'll do nothing of the kind if it will inconvenience you, for I'm not going to play either strikingly bad enough or well enough to make the journey pay you.

My wife and I think of going to Boston May 7th to see Anna Dickinson's debut on the 8th. If I find we can go, I'll try to get a stage box and then you and Mrs. Howells must come to Parker's and go with us to the crucifixion.

(Is that spelt right?--somehow it doesn't look right.)

With our very kindest regards to the whole family. Yrs ever, MARK.

The mention of Anna Dickinson, at the end of this letter, recalls a prominent reformer and lecturer of the Civil War period. She had begun her crusades against temperance and slavery in 1857, when she was but fifteen years old, when her success as a speaker had been immediate and extraordinary. Now, in this later period, at the age of thirty-four, she aspired to the stage-- unfortunately for her, as her gifts lay elsewhere. Clemens and Howells knew Miss Dickinson, and were anxious for the success which they hardly dared hope for. Clemens arranged a box party.

To W. D. Howells, in Boston:

May 4, '76. MY DEAR HOWELLS,--I shall reach Boston on Monday the 8th, either at 4:30 p.m. or 6 p.m. (Which is best?) and go straight to Parker's. If you and Mrs. Howells cannot be there by half past 4, I'll not plan to arrive till the later train-time (6,) because I don't want to be there alone-- even a minute. Still, Joe Twichell will doubtless go with me (forgot that,) he is going to try hard to. Mrs. Clemens has given up going, because Susy is just recovering from about the savagest assault of diphtheria a child ever did recover from, and therefore will not be entirely her healthy self again by the 8th.

Would you and Mrs. Howells like to invite Mr. and Mrs. Aldrich? I have a large proscenium box--plenty of room. Use your own pleasure about it --I mainly (that is honest,) suggest it because I am seeking to make matters pleasant for you and Mrs. Howells. I invited Twichell because I thought I knew you'd like that. I want you to fix it so that you and the Madam can remain in Boston all night; for I leave next day and we can't have a talk, otherwise. I am going to get two rooms and a parlor; and would like to know what you decide about the Aldriches, so as to know whether to apply for an additional bedroom or not.

Don't dine that evening, for I shall arrive dinnerless and need your help.

I'll bring my Blindfold Novelette, but shan't exhibit it unless you exhibit yours. You would simply go to work and write a novelette that would make mine sick. Because you would know all about where my weak points lay. No, Sir, I'm one of these old wary birds!

Don't bother to write a letter--3 lines on a postal card is all that I can permit from a busy man. Yrs ever MARK.

P. S. Good! You'll not have to feel any call to mention that debut in the Atlantic--they've made me pay the grand cash for my box!--a thing which most managers would be too worldly-wise to do, with journalistic folks. But I'm most honestly glad, for I'd rather pay three prices, any time, than to have my tongue half paralyzed with a dead-head ticket.

Hang that Anna Dickinson, a body can never depend upon her debuts! She has made five or six false starts already. If she fails to debut this time, I will never bet on her again.

In his book, My Mark Twain, Howells refers to the "tragedy" of Miss Dickinson's appearance. She was the author of numerous plays, some of which were successful, but her career as an actress was never brilliant.

At Elmira that summer the Clemenses heard from their good friend Doctor Brown, of Edinburgh, and sent eager replies.

To Dr. John Brown, in Edinburgh:

ELMIRA, NEW YORK, U. S. June 22, 1876. DEAR FRIEND THE DOCTOR,--It was a perfect delight to see the well-known handwriting again! But we so grieve to know that you are feeling miserable. It must not last--it cannot last. The regal summer is come and it will smile you into high good cheer; it will charm away your pains, it will banish your distresses. I wish you were here, to spend the summer with us. We are perched on a hill-top that overlooks a little world of green valleys, shining rivers, sumptuous forests and billowy uplands veiled in the haze of distance. We have no neighbors. It is the quietest of all quiet places, and we are hermits that eschew caves and live in the sun. Doctor, if you'd only come!

I will carry your letter to Mrs. C. now, and there will be a glad woman, I tell you! And she shall find one of those pictures to put in this for Mrs. Barclays and if there isn't one here we'll send right away to Hartford and get one. Come over, Doctor John, and bring the Barclays, the Nicolsons and the Browns, one and all! Affectionately, SAML. L. CLEMENS.

From May until August no letters appear to have passed between Clemens and Howells; the latter finally wrote, complaining of the lack of news. He was in the midst of campaign activities, he said, writing a life of Hayes, and gaily added: "You know I wrote the life of Lincoln, which elected him." He further reported a comedy he had completed, and gave Clemens a general stirring up as to his own work.

Mark Twain, in his hillside study, was busy enough. Summer was his time for work, and he had tried his hand in various directions. His mention of Huck Finn in his reply to Howells is interesting, in that it shows the measure of his enthusiasm, or lack of it, as a gauge of his ultimate achievement

To W. D. Howells, in Boston:

ELMIRA, Aug. 9, 1876. MY DEAR HOWELLS,--I was just about to write you when your letter came-- and not one of those obscene postal cards, either, but reverently, upon paper.

I shall read that biography, though the letter of acceptance was amply sufficient to corral my vote without any further knowledge of the man. Which reminds me that a campaign club in Jersey City wrote a few days ago and invited me to be present at the raising of a Tilden and Hendricks flag there, and to take the stand and give them some "counsel." Well, I could not go, but gave them counsel and advice by letter, and in the kindliest terms as to the raising of the flag--advised them "not to raise it."

Get your book out quick, for this is a momentous time. If Tilden is elected I think the entire country will go pretty straight to--Mrs. Howells's bad place.

I am infringing on your patent--I started a record of our children's sayings, last night. Which reminds me that last week I sent down and got Susie a vast pair of shoes of a most villainous pattern, for I discovered that her feet were being twisted and cramped out of shape by a smaller and prettier article. She did not complain, but looked degraded and injured. At night her mamma gave her the usual admonition when she was about to say her prayers--to wit:

"Now, Susie--think about God."

"Mamma, I can't, with those shoes."

The farm is perfectly delightful this season. It is as quiet and peaceful as a South Sea Island. Some of the sunsets which we have witnessed from this commanding eminence were marvelous. One evening a rainbow spanned an entire range of hills with its mighty arch, and from a black hub resting upon the hill-top in the exact centre, black rays diverged upward in perfect regularity to the rainbow's arch and created a very strongly defined and altogether the most majestic, magnificent and startling half-sunk wagon wheel you can imagine. After that, a world of tumbling and prodigious clouds came drifting up out of the West and took to themselves a wonderfully rich and brilliant green color--the decided green of new spring foliage. Close by them we saw the intense blue of the skies, through rents in the cloud-rack, and away off in another quarter were drifting clouds of a delicate pink color. In one place hung a pall of dense black clouds, like compacted pitch-smoke. And the stupendous wagon wheel was still in the supremacy of its unspeakable grandeur. So you see, the colors present in the sky at once and the same time were blue, green, pink, black, and the vari-colored splendors of the rainbow. All strong and decided colors, too. I don't know whether this weird and astounding spectacle most suggested heaven, or hell. The wonder, with its constant, stately, and always surprising changes, lasted upwards of two hours, and we all stood on the top of the hill by my study till the final miracle was complete and the greatest day ended that we ever saw.

Our farmer, who is a grave man, watched that spectacle to the end, and then observed that it was "dam funny."

The double-barreled novel lies torpid. I found I could not go on with it. The chapters I had written were still too new and familiar to me. I may take it up next winter, but cannot tell yet; I waited and waited to see if my interest in it would not revive, but gave it up a month ago and began another boys' book--more to be at work than anything else. I have written 400 pages on it-- therefore it is very nearly half done. It is Huck Finn's Autobiography. I like it only tolerably well, as far as I have got, and may possibly pigeonhole or burn the MS when it is done.

So the comedy is done, and with a "fair degree of satisfaction." That rejoices me, and makes me mad, too--for I can't plan a comedy, and what have you done that God should be so good to you? I have racked myself baldheaded trying to plan a comedy harness for some promising characters of mine to work in, and had to give it up. It is a noble lot of blooded stock and worth no end of money, but they must stand in the stable and be profitless. I want to be present when the comedy is produced and help enjoy the success.

Warner's book is mighty readable, I think. Love to yez. Yrs ever MARK

Howells promptly wrote again, urging him to enter the campaign for Hayes. "There is not another man in this country," he said, "who could help him so much as you." The "farce" which Clemens refers to in his reply, was "The Parlor Car," which seems to have been about the first venture of Howells in that field.

To W. D. Howells, in Boston:

ELMIRA, August 23, 1876. MY DEAR HOWELLS,--I am glad you think I could do Hayes any good, for I have been wanting to write a letter or make a speech to that end. I'll be careful not to do either, however, until the opportunity comes in a natural, justifiable and unlugged way; and shall not then do anything unless I've got it all digested and worded just right. In which case I might do some good--in any other I should do harm. When a humorist ventures upon the grave concerns of life he must do his job better than another man or he works harm to his cause.

The farce is wonderfully bright and delicious, and must make a hit. You read it to me, and it was mighty good; I read it last night and it was better; I read it aloud to the household this morning and it was better than ever. So it would be worth going a long way to see it well played; for without any question an actor of genius always adds a subtle something to any man's work that none but the writer knew was there before. Even if he knew it. I have heard of readers convulsing audiences with my "Aurelia's Unfortunate Young Man." If there is anything really funny in the piece, the author is not aware of it.

All right--advertise me for the new volume. I send you herewith a sketch which will make 3 pages of the Atlantic. If you like it and accept it, you should get it into the December No. because I shall read it in public in Boston the 13th and 14th of Nov. If it went in a month earlier it would be too old for me to read except as old matter; and if it went in a month later it would be too old for the Atlantic--do you see? And if you wish to use it, will you set it up now, and send me three proofs?--one to correct for Atlantic, one to send to Temple Bar (shall I tell them to use it not earlier than their November No. and one to use in practising for my Boston readings.

We must get up a less elaborate and a much better skeleton-plan for the Blindfold Novels and make a success of that idea. David Gray spent Sunday here and said we could but little comprehend what a rattling stir that thing would make in the country. He thought it would make a mighty strike. So do I. But with only 8 pages to tell the tale in, the plot must be less elaborate, doubtless. What do you think?

When we exchange visits I'll show you an unfinished sketch of Elizabeth's time which shook David Gray's system up pretty exhaustively. Yrs ever, MARK.

The MS. sketch mentioned in the foregoing letter was "The Canvasser's Tale," later included in the volume, Tom Sawyer Abroad, and Other Stories. It is far from being Mark Twain's best work, but was accepted and printed in the Atlantic. David Gray was an able journalist and editor whom Mark Twain had known in Buffalo.

The "sketch of Elizabeth's time" is a brilliant piece of writing --an imaginary record of conversation and court manners in the good old days of free speech and performance, phrased in the language of the period. Gray, John Hay, Twichell, and others who had a chance to see it thought highly of it, and Hay had it set in type and a few proofs taken for private circulation. Some years afterward a West Point officer had a special font of antique type made for it, and printed a hundred copies. But the present-day reader would hardly be willing to include "Fireside Conversation in the Time of Queen Elizabeth" in Mark Twain's collected works.

Clemens was a strong Republican in those days, as his letters of this period show. His mention of the "caves" in the next is another reference to "The Canvasser's Tale."

To W. D. Howells, in Boston:

Sept. 14, 1876. MY DEAR HOWELLS,--Yes, the collection of caves was the origin of it. I changed it to echoes because these being invisible and intangible, constituted a still more absurd species of property, and yet a man could really own an echo, and sell it, too, for a high figure-- such an echo as that at the Villa Siminetti, two miles from Milan, for instance. My first purpose was to have the man make a collection of caves and afterwards of echoes; but perceived that the element of absurdity and impracticability was so nearly identical as to amount to a repetition of an idea.....

I will not, and do not, believe that there is a possibility of Hayes's defeat, but I want the victory to be sweeping.....

It seems odd to find myself interested in an election. I never was before. And I can't seem to get over my repugnance to reading or thinking about politics, yet. But in truth I care little about any party's politics--the man behind it is the important thing.

You may well know that Mrs. Clemens liked the Parlor Car--enjoyed it ever so much, and was indignant at you all through, and kept exploding into rages at you for pretending that such a woman ever existed--closing each and every explosion with "But it is just what such a woman would do."-- "It is just what such a woman would say." They all voted the Parlor Car perfection--except me. I said they wouldn't have been allowed to court and quarrel there so long, uninterrupted; but at each critical moment the odious train-boy would come in and pile foul literature all over them four or five inches deep, and the lover would turn his head aside and curse--and presently that train-boy would be back again (as on all those Western roads) to take up the literature and leave prize candy.

Of course the thing is perfect, in the magazine, without the train-boy; but I was thinking of the stage and the groundlings. If the dainty touches went over their heads, the train-boy and other possible interruptions would fetch them every time. Would it mar the flow of the thing too much to insert that devil? I thought it over a couple of hours and concluded it wouldn't, and that he ought to be in for the sake of the groundlings (and to get new copyright on the piece.)

And it seemed to me that now that the fourth act is so successfully written, why not go ahead and write the 3 preceding acts? And then after it is finished, let me put into it a low-comedy character (the girl's or the lover's father or uncle) and gobble a big pecuniary interest in your work for myself. Do not let this generous proposition disturb your rest --but do write the other 3 acts, and then it will be valuable to managers. And don't go and sell it to anybody, like Harte, but keep it for yourself.

Harte's play can be doctored till it will be entirely acceptable and then it will clear a great sum every year. I am out of all patience with Harte for selling it. The play entertained me hugely, even in its present crude state. Love to you all. Yrs ever, MARK

Following the Sellers success, Clemens had made many attempts at dramatic writing. Such undertakings had uniformly failed, but he had always been willing to try again. In the next letter we get the beginning of what proved his first and last direct literary association, that is to say, collaboration, with Bret Harte. Clemens had great admiration for Harte's ability and believed that between them they could turn out a successful play. Whether or not this belief was justified will appear later. Howells's biography of Hayes, meanwhile, had not gone well. He reported that only two thousand copies had been sold in what was now the height of the campaign. "There's success for you," he said; "it makes me despair of the Republic."

Clemens, on his part, had made a speech for Hayes that Howells declared had put civil-service reform in a nutshell; he added: "You are the only Republican orator, quoted without distinction of party by all the newspapers."

To W. D. Howells, in Boston:

HARTFORD, Oct. 11, 1876. MY DEAR HOWELLS, This is a secret, to be known to nobody but you (of course I comprehend that Mrs. Howells is part of you) that Bret Harte came up here the other day and asked me to help him write a play and divide the swag, and I agreed. I am to put in Scotty Briggs (See Buck Fanshaw's Funeral, in "Roughing It.") and he is to put in a Chinaman (a, wonderfully funny creature, as Bret presents him--for 5 minutes--in his Sandy Bar play.) This Chinaman is to be the character of the play, and both of us will work on him and develop him. Bret is to draw a plot, and I am to do the same; we shall use the best of the two, or gouge from both and build a third. My plot is built--finished it yesterday--six days' work, 8 or 9 hours a day, and has nearly killed me.

Now the favor I ask of you is that you will have the words "Ah Sin, a Drama," printed in the middle of a note-paper page and send the same to me, with Bill. We don't want anybody to know that we are building this play. I can't get this title page printed here without having to lie so much that the thought of it is disagreeable to one reared as I have been. And yet the title of the play must be printed--the rest of the application for copyright is allowable in penmanship.

We have got the very best gang of servants in America, now. When George first came he was one of the most religious of men. He had but one fault--young George Washington's. But I have trained him; and now it fairly breaks Mrs. Clemens's heart to hear George stand at that front door and lie to the unwelcome visitor. But your time is valuable; I must not dwell upon these things.....I'll ask Warner and Harte if they'll do Blindfold Novelettes. Some time I'll simplify that plot. All it needs is that the hanging and the marriage shall not be appointed for the same day. I got over that difficulty, but it required too much MS to reconcile the thing--so the movement of the story was clogged.

I came near agreeing to make political speeches with our candidate for Governor the 16th and 23 inst., but I had to give up the idea, for Harte and I will be here at work then. Yrs ever, MARK

Mark Twain was writing few letters these days to any one but Howells, yet in November he sent one to an old friend of his youth, Burrough, the literary chair-maker who had roomed with him in the days when he had been setting type for the St. Louis Evening News.

To Mr. Burrough, of St. Louis:

HARTFORD, Nov. 1, 1876. MY DEAR BURROUGHS,--As you describe me I can picture myself as I was 20 years ago. The portrait is correct. You think I have grown some; upon my word there was room for it. You have described a callow fool, a self- sufficient ass, a mere human tumble-bug.... imagining that he is remodeling the world and is entirely capable of doing it right. Ignorance, intolerance, egotism, self-assertion, opaque perception, dense and pitiful chuckle-headedness--and an almost pathetic unconsciousness of it all. That is what I was at 19 and 20; and that is what the average Southerner is at 60 today. Northerners, too, of a certain grade. It is of children like this that voters are made. And such is the primal source of our government! A man hardly knows whether to swear or cry over it.

I think I comprehend the position there--perfect freedom to vote just as you choose, provided you choose to vote as other people think--social ostracism, otherwise. The same thing exists here, among the Irish. An Irish Republican is a pariah among his people. Yet that race find fault with the same spirit in Know-Nothingism.

Fortunately a good deal of experience of men enabled me to choose my residence wisely. I live in the freest corner of the country. There are no social disabilities between me and my Democratic personal friends. We break the bread and eat the salt of hospitality freely together and never dream of such a thing as offering impertinent interference in each other's political opinions.

Don't you ever come to New York again and not run up here to see me. I Suppose we were away for the summer when you were East; but no matter, you could have telegraphed and found out. We were at Elmira N. Y. and right on your road, and could have given you a good time if you had allowed us the chance.

Yes, Will Bowen and I have exchanged letters now and then for several years, but I suspect that I made him mad with my last--shortly after you saw him in St. Louis, I judge. There is one thing which I can't stand and won't stand, from many people. That is sham sentimentality--the kind a school-girl puts into her graduating composition; the sort that makes up the Original Poetry column of a country newspaper; the rot that deals in the "happy days of yore," the "sweet yet melancholy past," with its "blighted hopes" and its "vanished dreams" and all that sort of drivel. Will's were always of this stamp. I stood it years. When I get a letter like that from a grown man and he a widower with a family, it gives me the stomach ache. And I just told Will Bowen so, last summer. I told him to stop being 16 at 40; told him to stop drooling about the sweet yet melancholy past, and take a pill. I said there was but one solitary thing about the past worth remembering, and that was the fact that it is the past--can't be restored. Well, I exaggerated some of these truths a little--but only a little--but my idea was to kill his sham sentimentality once and forever, and so make a good fellow of him again. I went to the unheard-of trouble of re-writing the letter and saying the same harsh things softly, so as to sugarcoat the anguish and make it a little more endurable and I asked him to write and thank me honestly for doing him the best and kindliest favor that any friend ever had done him --but he hasn't done it yet. Maybe he will, sometime. I am grateful to God that I got that letter off before he was married (I get that news from you) else he would just have slobbered all over me and drowned me when that event happened.

I enclose photograph for the young ladies. I will remark that I do not wear seal-skin for grandeur, but because I found, when I used to lecture in the winter, that nothing else was able to keep a man warm sometimes, in these high latitudes. I wish you had sent pictures of yourself and family--I'll trade picture for picture with you, straight through, if you are commercially inclined. Your old friend, SAML L. CLEMENS.

XVII.

LETTERS, 1877. TO BERMUDA WITH TWICHELL. PROPOSITION TO TH. NAST. THE WHITTIER DINNER

Mark Twain must have been too busy to write letters that winter. Those that have survived are few and unimportant. As a matter of fact, he was writing the play, "Ah Sin," with Bret Harte, and getting it ready for production. Harte was a guest in the Clemens home while the play was being written, and not always a pleasant one. He was full of requirements, critical as to the 'menage,' to the point of sarcasm. The long friendship between Clemens and Harte weakened under the strain of collaboration and intimate daily intercourse, never to renew its old fiber. It was an unhappy outcome of an enterprise which in itself was to prove of little profit. The play, "Ah Sin," had many good features, and with Charles T. Parsloe in an amusing Chinese part might have been made a success, if the two authors could have harmoniously undertaken the needed repairs. It opened in Washington in May, and a letter from Parsloe, written at the moment, gives a hint of the situation.

From Charles T. Parsloe to S. L. Clemens:

WASHINGTON, D. C. May 11th, 1877. MR. CLEMENS,--I forgot whether I acknowledged receipt of check by telegram. Harte has been here since Monday last and done little or nothing yet, but promises to have something fixed by tomorrow morning. We have been making some improvements among ourselves. The last act is weak at the end, and I do hope Mr. Harte will have something for a good finish to the piece. The other acts I think are all right, now.

Hope you have entirely recovered. I am not very well myself, the excitement of a first night is bad enough, but to have the annoyance with Harte that I have is too much for a beginner. I ain't used to it. The houses have been picking up since Tuesday Mr. Ford has worked well and hard for us. Yours in, haste, CHAS. THOS. PARSLOE.

The play drew some good houses in Washington, but it could not hold them for a run. Never mind what was the matter with it; perhaps a very small change at the right point would have turned it into a fine success. We have seen in a former letter the obligation which Mark Twain confessed to Harte--a debt he had tried in many ways to repay--obtaining for him a liberal book contract with Bliss; advancing him frequent and large sums of money which Harte could not, or did not, repay; seeking to advance his fortunes in many directions. The mistake came when he introduced another genius into the intracacies of his daily life. Clemens went down to Washington during the early rehearsals of "Ah Sin."

Meantime, Rutherford B. Hayes had been elected President, and Clemens one day called with a letter of introduction from Howells, thinking to meet the Chief Executive. His own letter to Howells, later, probably does not give the real reason of his failure, but it will be amusing to those who recall the erratic personality of George Francis Train. Train and Twain were sometimes confused by the very unlettered; or pretendedly, by Mark Twain's friends.

To W. D. Howells, in Boston:

BALTIMORE, May 1, '77. MY DEAR HOWELLS,--Found I was not absolutely needed in Washington so I only staid 24 hours, and am on my way home, now. I called at the White House, and got admission to Col. Rodgers, because I wanted to inquire what was the right hour to go and infest the, President. It was my luck to strike the place in the dead waste and middle of the day, the very busiest time. I perceived that Mr. Rodgers took me for George Francis Train and had made up his mind not to let me get at the President; so at the end of half an hour I took my letter of introduction from the table and went away. It was a great pity all round, and a great loss to the nation, for I was brim full of the Eastern question. I didn't get to see the President or the Chief Magistrate either, though I had sort of a glimpse of a lady at a window who resembled her portraits. Yrs ever, MARK.

Howells condoled with him on his failure to see the President, "but," he added, "if you and I had both been there, our combined skill would have no doubt procured us to be expelled from the White House by Fred Douglass. But the thing seems to be a complete failure as it was." Douglass at this time being the Marshal of Columbia, gives special point to Howells's suggestion.

Later, in May, Clemens took Twichell for an excursion to Bermuda. He had begged Howells to go with them, but Howells, as usual, was full of literary affairs. Twichell and Clemens spent four glorious days tramping the length and breadth of the beautiful island, and remembered it always as one of their happiest adventures. "Put it down as an Oasis!" wrote Twichell on his return, "I'm afraid I shall not see as green a spot again soon. And it was your invention and your gift. And your company was the best of it. Indeed, I never took more comfort in being with you than on this journey, which, my boy, is saying a great deal."

To Howells, Clemens triumphantly reported the success of the excursion.

To W. D. Howells, in Boston:

FARMINGTON AVENUE, HARTFORD, May 29, 1877. Confound you, Joe Twichell and I roamed about Bermuda day and night and never ceased to gabble and enjoy. About half the talk was--"It is a burning shame that Howells isn't here." "Nobody could get at the very meat and marrow of this pervading charm and deliciousness like Howells;" "How Howells would revel in the quaintness, and the simplicity of this people and the Sabbath repose of this land." "What an imperishable sketch Howells would make of Capt. West the whaler, and Capt. Hope with the patient, pathetic face, wanderer in all the oceans for 42 years, lucky in none; coming home defeated once more, now, minus his ship-- resigned, uncomplaining, being used to this." "What a rattling chapter Howells would make out of the small boy Alfred, with his alert eye and military brevity and exactness of speech; and out of the old landlady; and her sacred onions; and her daughter; and the visiting clergyman; and the ancient pianos of Hamilton and the venerable music in vogue there-- and forty other things which we shall leave untouched or touched but lightly upon, we not being worthy." "Dam Howells for not being here!" (this usually from me, not Twichell.)

O, your insufferable pride, which will have a fall some day! If you had gone with us and let me pay the $50 which the trip and the board and the various nicknacks and mementoes would cost, I would have picked up enough droppings from your conversation to pay me 500 per cent profit in the way of the several magazine articles which I could have written, whereas I can now write only one or two and am therefore largely out of pocket by your proud ways. Ponder these things. Lord, what a perfectly bewitching excursion it was! I traveled under an assumed name and was never molested with a polite attention from anybody. Love to you all. Yrs ever MARK

Aldrich, meantime, had invited the Clemenses to Ponkapog during the Bermuda absence, and Clemens hastened to send him a line expressing regrets. At the close he said:

To T. B. Aldrich, in Ponkapog, Mass.:

FARMINGTON AVENUE, HARTFORD, June 3, 1877. Day after tomorrow we leave for the hills beyond Elmira, N. Y. for the summer, when I shall hope to write a book of some sort or other to beat the people with. A work similar to your new one in the Atlantic is what I mean, though I have not heard what the nature of that one is. Immoral, I suppose. Well, you are right. Such books sell best, Howells says. Howells says he is going to make his next book indelicate. He says he thinks there is money in it. He says there is a large class of the young, in schools and seminaries who--But you let him tell you. He has ciphered it all down to a demonstration.

With the warmest remembrances to the pair of you Ever Yours SAMUEL L. CLEMENS.

Clemens would naturally write something about Bermuda, and began at once, "Random Notes of an Idle Excursion," and presently completed four papers, which Howells eagerly accepted for the Atlantic. Then we find him plunging into another play, this time alone.

To W. D. Howells, in Boston:

ELMIRA, June 27, 1877. MY DEAR HOWELLS,--If you should not like the first 2 chapters, send them to me and begin with

Chapter 3

--or Part 3, I believe you call these things in the magazine. I have finished No. 4., which closes the series, and will mail it tomorrow if I think of it. I like this one, I liked the preceding one (already mailed to you some time ago) but I had my doubts about 1 and 2. Do not hesitate to squelch them, even with derision and insult.

Today I am deep in a comedy which I began this morning--principal character, that old detective--I skeletoned the first act and wrote the second, today; and am dog-tired, now. Fifty-four close pages of MS in 7 hours. Once I wrote 55 pages at a sitting--that was on the opening chapters of the "Gilded Age" novel. When I cool down, an hour from now, I shall go to zero, I judge. Yrs ever, MARK.

Clemens had doubts as to the quality of the Bermuda papers, and with some reason. They did not represent him at his best. Nevertheless, they were pleasantly entertaining, and Howells expressed full approval of them for Atlantic use. The author remained troubled.

To W. D. Howells, in Boston:

ELMIRA, July 4,1877. MY DEAR HOWELLS,--It is splendid of you to say those pleasant things. But I am still plagued with doubts about Parts 1 and 2. If you have any, don't print. If otherwise, please make some cold villain like Lathrop read and pass sentence on them. Mind, I thought they were good, at first--it was the second reading that accomplished its hellish purpose on me. Put them up for a new verdict. Part 4 has lain in my pigeon-hole a good while, and when I put it there I had a Christian's confidence in 4 aces in it; and you can be sure it will skip toward Connecticut tomorrow before any fatal fresh reading makes me draw my bet.

I've piled up 151 MS pages on my comedy. The first, second and fourth acts are done, and done to my satisfaction, too. Tomorrow and next day will finish the 3rd act and the play. I have not written less than 30 pages any day since I began. Never had so much fun over anything in my life-never such consuming interest and delight. (But Lord bless you the second reading will fetch it!) And just think!--I had Sol Smith Russell in my mind's eye for the old detective's part, and hang it he has gone off pottering with Oliver Optic, or else the papers lie.

I read everything about the President's doings there with exultation.

I wish that old ass of a private secretary hadn't taken me for George Francis Train. If ignorance were a means of grace I wouldn't trade that gorilla's chances for the Archbishop of Canterbury's.

I shall call on the President again, by and by. I shall go in my war paint; and if I am obstructed the nation will have the unusual spectacle of a private secretary with a pen over one ear a tomahawk over the other.

I read the entire Atlantic this time. Wonderful number. Mrs. Rose Terry Cooke's story was a ten-strike. I wish she would write 12 old-time New England tales a year.

Good times to you all! Mind if you don't run here for a few days you will go to hence without having had a fore-glimpse of heaven.

MARK.

The play, "Ah Sin," that had done little enough in Washington, was that summer given another trial by Augustin Daly, at the Fifth Avenue Theater, New York, with a fine company. Clemens had undertaken to doctor the play, and it would seem to have had an enthusiastic reception on the opening night. But it was a summer audience, unspoiled by many attractions. "Ah Sin" was never a success in the New York season--never a money-maker on the road.

The reference in the first paragraph of the letter that follows is to the Bermuda chapters which Mark Twain was publishing simultaneously in England and America.

ELMIRA, Aug 3,1877. MY DEAR HOWELLS,--I have mailed one set of the slips to London, and told Bentley you would print Sept. 15, in October Atlantic, and he must not print earlier in Temple Bar. Have I got the dates and things right?

I am powerful glad to see that No. 1 reads a nation sight better in print than it did in MS. I told Bentley we'd send him the slips, each time, 6 weeks before day of publication. We can do that can't we? Two months ahead would be still better I suppose, but I don't know.

"Ah Sin" went a-booming at the Fifth Avenue. The reception of Col. Sellers was calm compared to it.

*The criticisms were just; the criticisms of the great New York dailies are always just, intelligent, and square and honest--notwithstanding, by a blunder which nobody was seriously to blame for, I was made to say exactly the opposite of this in a newspaper some time ago. Never said it at all, and moreover I never thought it. I could not publicly correct it before the play appeared in New York, because that would look as if I had really said that thing and then was moved by fears for my pocket and my reputation to take it back. But I can correct it now, and shall do it; for now my motives cannot be impugned. When I began this letter, it had not occurred to me to use you in this connection, but it occurs to me now. Your opinion and mine, uttered a year ago, and repeated more than once since, that the candor and ability of the New York critics were beyond question, is a matter which makes it proper enough that I should speak through you at this time. Therefore if you will print this paragraph somewhere, it may remove the impression that I say unjust things which I do not think, merely for the pleasure of talking.

There, now, Can't you say--

"In a letter to Mr. Howells of the Atlantic Monthly, Mark Twain describes the reception of the new comedy 'Ali Sin,' and then goes on to say:" etc.

Beginning at the star with the words, "The criticisms were just." Mrs. Clemens says, "Don't ask that of Mr. Howells--it will be disagreeable to him." I hadn't thought of it, but I will bet two to one on the correctness of her instinct. We shall see.

Will you cut that paragraph out of this letter and precede it with the remarks suggested (or with better ones,) and send it to the Globe or some other paper? You can't do me a bigger favor; and yet if it is in the least disagreeable, you mustn't think of it. But let me know, right away, for I want to correct this thing before it grows stale again. I explained myself to only one critic (the World)--the consequence was a noble notice of the play. This one called on me, else I shouldn't have explained myself to him.

I have been putting in a deal of hard work on that play in New York, but it is full of incurable defects.

My old Plunkett family seemed wonderfully coarse and vulgar on the stage, but it was because they were played in such an outrageously and inexcusably coarse way. The Chinaman is killingly funny. I don't know when I have enjoyed anything as much as I did him. The people say there isn't enough of him in the piece. That's a triumph--there'll never be any more of him in it.

John Brougham said, "Read the list of things which the critics have condemned in the piece, and you have unassailable proofs that the play contains all the requirements of success and a long life."

That is true. Nearly every time the audience roared I knew it was over something that would be condemned in the morning (justly, too) but must be left in--for low comedies are written for the drawing-room, the kitchen and the stable, and if you cut out the kitchen and the stable the drawing-room can't support the play by itself.

There was as much money in the house the first two nights as in the first ten of Sellers. Haven't heard from the third--I came away. Yrs ever, MARK.

In a former letter we have seen how Mark Twain, working on a story that was to stand as an example of his best work, and become one of his surest claims to immortality (The Adventures of Huckleberry Finn), displayed little enthusiasm in his undertaking. In the following letter, which relates the conclusion of his detective comedy, we find him at the other extreme, on very tiptoe with enthusiasm over something wholly without literary value or dramatic possibility. One of the hall-marks of genius is the inability to discriminate as to the value of its output. "Simon Wheeler, Amateur Detective" was a dreary, absurd, impossible performance, as wild and unconvincing in incident and dialogue as anything out of an asylum could well be. The title which he first chose for it, "Balaam's Ass," was properly in keeping with the general scheme. Yet Mark Twain, still warm with the creative fever, had the fullest faith in it as a work of art and a winner of fortune. It would never see the light of production, of course. We shall see presently that the distinguished playwright, Dion Boucicault, good-naturedly complimented it as being better than "Ahi Sin." One must wonder what that skilled artist really thought, and how he could do even this violence to his conscience.

To W. D. Howells, in Boston:

ELMIRA, Wednesday P.M. (1877) MY DEAR HOWELLS,--It's finished. I was misled by hurried mis-paging. There were ten pages of notes, and over 300 pages of MS when the play was done. Did it in 42 hours, by the clock; 40 pages of the Atlantic--but then of course it's very "fat." Those are the figures, but I don't believe them myself, because the thing's impossible.

But let that pass. All day long, and every day, since I finished (in the rough) I have been diligently altering, amending, re-writing, cutting down. I finished finally today. Can't think of anything else in the way of an improvement. I thought I would stick to it while the interest was hot--and I am mighty glad I did. A week from now it will be frozen--then revising would be drudgery. (You see I learned something from the fatal blunder of putting "Ah Sin" aside before it was finished.)

She's all right, now. She reads in two hours and 20 minutes and will play not longer than 2 3/4 hours. Nineteen characters; 3 acts; (I bunched 2 into 1.)

Tomorrow I will draw up an exhaustive synopsis to insert in the printed title-page for copyrighting, and then on Friday or Saturday I go to New York to remain a week or ten days and lay for an actor. Wish you could run down there and have a holiday. 'Twould be fun.

My wife won't have "Balaam's Ass"; therefore I call the piece "Cap'n Simon Wheeler, The Amateur Detective." Yrs MARK.

To W. D. Howells, in Boston:

ELMIRA, Aug. 29, 1877. MY DEAR HOWELLS,--Just got your letter last night. No, dern that article,--[One of the Bermuda chapters.]--it made me cry when I read it in proof, it was so oppressively and ostentatiously poor. Skim your eye over it again and you will think as I do. If Isaac and the prophets of Baal can be doctored gently and made permissible, it will redeem the thing: but if it can't, let's burn all of the articles except the tail- end of it and use that as an introduction to the next article--as I suggested in my letter to you of day before yesterday. (I had this proof from Cambridge before yours came.)

Boucicault says my new play is ever so much better than "Ah Sin;" says the Amateur detective is a bully character, too. An actor is chawing over the play in New York, to see if the old Detective is suited to his abilities. Haven't heard from him yet.

If you've got that paragraph by you yet, and if in your judgment it would be good to publish it, and if you absolutely would not mind doing it, then I think I'd like to have you do it--or else put some other words in my mouth that will be properer, and publish them. But mind, don't think of it for a moment if it is distasteful--and doubtless it is. I value your judgment more than my own, as to the wisdom of saying anything at all in this matter. To say nothing leaves me in an injurious position-- and yet maybe I might do better to speak to the men themselves when I go to New York.

This was my latest idea, and it looked wise.

We expect to leave here for home Sept. 4, reaching there the 8th--but we may be delayed a week.

Curious thing. I read passages from my play, and a full synopsis, to Boucicault, who was re-writing a play, which he wrote and laid aside 3 or 4 years ago. (My detective is about that age, you know.) Then he read a passage from his play, where a real detective does some things that are as idiotic as some of my old Wheeler's performances. Showed me the passages, and behold, his man's name is Wheeler! However, his Wheeler is not a prominent character, so we'll not alter the names. My Wheeler's name is taken from the old jumping Frog sketch.

I am re-reading Ticknor's diary, and am charmed with it, though I still say he refers to too many good things when he could just as well have told them. Think of the man traveling 8 days in convoy and familiar intercourse with a band of outlaws through the mountain fastnesses of Spain--he the fourth stranger they had encountered in thirty years--and compressing this priceless experience into a single colorless paragraph of his diary! They spun yarns to this unworthy devil, too.

I wrote you a very long letter a day or two ago, but Susy Crane wanted to make a copy of it to keep, so it has not gone yet. It may go today, possibly.

We unite in warm regards to you and yours. Yrs ever, MARK.

The Ticknor referred to in a former letter was Professor George Ticknor, of Harvard College, a history-writer of distinction. On the margin of the "Diary" Mark Twain once wrote, "Ticknor is a Millet, who makes all men fall in love with him." And adds: "Millet was the cause of lovable qualities in people, and then he admired and loved those persons for the very qualities which he (without knowing it) had created in them. Perhaps it would be strictly truer of these two men to say that they bore within them the divine something in whose presence the evil in people fled away and hid itself, while all that was good in them came spontaneously forward out of the forgotten walls and corners in their systems where it was accustomed to hide."

It is Frank Millet, the artist, he is speaking of--a knightly soul whom all the Clemens household loved, and who would one day meet his knightly end with those other brave men that found death together when the Titanic went down.

The Clemens family was still at Quarry Farm at the end of August, and one afternoon there occurred a startling incident which Mark Twain thought worth setting down in practically duplicate letters to Howells and to Dr. John Brown. It may be of interest to the reader to know that John T. Lewis, the colored man mentioned, lived to a good old age--a pensioner of the Clemens family and, in the course of time, of H. H. Rogers. Howells's letter follows. It is the "very long letter" referred to in the foregoing.

To W. D. Howells and wife, in Boston:

ELMIRA, Aug. 25 '77. MY DEAR HOWELLSES,--I thought I ought to make a sort of record of it for further reference; the pleasantest way to do that would be to write it to somebody; but that somebody would let it leak into print and that we wish to avoid. The Howellses would be safe--so let us tell the Howellses about it.

Day before yesterday was a fine summer day away up here on the summit. Aunt Marsh and Cousin May Marsh were here visiting Susie Crane and Livy at our farmhouse. By and by mother Langdon came up the hill in the "high carriage" with Nora the nurse and little Jervis (Charley Langdon's little boy)--Timothy the coachman driving. Behind these came Charley's wife and little girl in the buggy, with the new, young, spry, gray horse--a high- stepper. Theodore Crane arrived a little later.

The Bay and Susy were on hand with their nurse, Rosa. I was on hand, too. Susy Crane's trio of colored servants ditto--these being Josie, house-maid; Aunty Cord, cook, aged 62, turbaned, very tall, very broad, very fine every way (see her portrait in "A True Story just as I Heard It" in my Sketches;) Chocklate (the laundress) (as the Bay calls her--she can't say Charlotte,) still taller, still more majestic of proportions, turbaned, very black, straight as an Indian--age 24. Then there was the farmer's wife (colored) and her little girl, Susy.

Wasn't it a good audience to get up an excitement before? Good excitable, inflammable material?

Lewis was still down town, three miles away, with his two-horse wagon, to get a load of manure. Lewis is the farmer (colored). He is of mighty frame and muscle, stocky, stooping, ungainly, has a good manly face and a clear eye. Age about 45--and the most picturesque of men, when he sits in his fluttering work-day rags, humped forward into a bunch, with his aged slouch hat mashed down over his ears and neck. It is a spectacle to make the broken-hearted smile. Lewis has worked mighty hard and remained mighty poor. At the end of each whole year's toil he can't show a gain of fifty dollars. He had borrowed money of the Cranes till he owed them $700 and he being conscientious and honest, imagine what it was to him to have to carry this stubborn, helpless load year in and year out.

Well, sunset came, and Ida the young and comely (Charley Langdon's wife) and her little Julia and the nurse Nora, drove out at the gate behind the new gray horse and started down the long hill--the high carriage receiving its load under the porte cochere. Ida was seen to turn her face toward us across the fence and intervening lawn--Theodore waved good-bye to her, for he did not know that her sign was a speechless appeal for help.

The next moment Livy said, "Ida's driving too fast down hill!" She followed it with a sort of scream, "Her horse is running away!"

We could see two hundred yards down that descent. The buggy seemed to fly. It would strike obstructions and apparently spring the height of a man from the ground.

Theodore and I left the shrieking crowd behind and ran down the hill bare-headed and shouting. A neighbor appeared at his gate--a tenth of a second too late! the buggy vanished past him like a thought. My last glimpse showed it for one instant, far down the descent, springing high in the air out of a cloud of dust, and then it disappeared. As I flew down the road my impulse was to shut my eyes as I turned them to the right or left, and so delay for a moment the ghastly spectacle of mutilation and death I was expecting.

I ran on and on, still spared this spectacle, but saying to myself: "I shall see it at the turn of the road; they never can pass that turn alive." When I came in sight of that turn I saw two wagons there bunched together--one of them full of people. I said, "Just so--they are staring petrified at the remains."

But when I got amongst that bunch, there sat Ida in her buggy and nobody hurt, not even the horse or the vehicle. Ida was pale but serene. As I came tearing down, she smiled back over her shoulder at me and said, "Well, we're alive yet, aren't we?" A miracle had been performed--nothing else.

You see Lewis, the prodigious, humped upon his front seat, had been toiling up, on his load of manure; he saw the frantic horse plunging down the hill toward him, on a full gallop, throwing his heels as high as a man's head at every jump. So Lewis turned his team diagonally across the road just at the "turn," thus making a V with the fence--the running horse could not escape that, but must enter it. Then Lewis sprang to the ground and stood in this V. He gathered his vast strength, and with a perfect Creedmoor aim he seized the gray horse's bit as he plunged by and fetched him up standing!

It was down hill, mind you. Ten feet further down hill neither Lewis nor any other man could have saved them, for they would have been on the abrupt "turn," then. But how this miracle was ever accomplished at all, by human strength, generalship and accuracy, is clean beyond my comprehension--and grows more so the more I go and examine the ground and try to believe it was actually done. I know one thing, well; if Lewis had missed his aim he would have been killed on the spot in the trap he had made for himself, and we should have found the rest of the remains away down at the bottom of the steep ravine.

Ten minutes later Theodore and I arrived opposite the house, with the servants straggling after us, and shouted to the distracted group on the porch, "Everybody safe!"

Believe it? Why how could they? They knew the road perfectly. We might as well have said it to people who had seen their friends go over Niagara.

However, we convinced them; and then, instead of saying something, or going on crying, they grew very still--words could not express it, I suppose.

Nobody could do anything that night, or sleep, either; but there was a deal of moving talk, with long pauses between pictures of that flying carriage, these pauses represented--this picture intruded itself all the time and disjointed the talk.

But yesterday evening late, when Lewis arrived from down town he found his supper spread, and some presents of books there, with very complimentary writings on the fly-leaves, and certain very complimentary letters, and more or less greenbacks of dignified denomination pinned to these letters and fly-leaves,--and one said, among other things, (signed by the Cranes) "We cancel $400 of your indebtedness to us," &c. &c.

(The end thereof is not yet, of course, for Charley Langdon is West and will arrive ignorant of all these things, today.)

The supper-room had been kept locked and imposingly secret and mysterious until Lewis should arrive; but around that part of the house were gathered Lewis's wife and child, Chocklate, Josie, Aunty Cord and our Rosa, canvassing things and waiting impatiently. They were all on hand when the curtain rose.

Now, Aunty Cord is a violent Methodist and Lewis an implacable Dunker-- Baptist. Those two are inveterate religious disputants. The revealments having been made Aunty Cord said with effusion--

"Now, let folks go on saying there ain't no God! Lewis, the Lord sent you there to stop that horse."

Says Lewis:

"Then who sent the horse there in sich a shape?"

But I want to call your attention to one thing. When Lewis arrived the other evening, after saving those lives by a feat which I think is the most marvelous of any I can call to mind--when he arrived, hunched up on his manure wagon and as grotesquely picturesque as usual, everybody wanted to go and see how he looked. They came back and said he was beautiful. It was so, too-- and yet he would have photographed exactly as he would have done any day these past 7 years that he has occupied this farm.

Aug. 27. P. S. Our little romance in real life is happily and satisfactorily completed. Charley has come, listened, acted--and now John T. Lewis has ceased to consider himself as belonging to that class called "the poor."

It has been known, during some years, that it was Lewis's purpose to buy a thirty dollar silver watch some day, if he ever got where he could afford it. Today Ida has given him a new, sumptuous gold Swiss stem- winding stop-watch; and if any scoffer shall say, "Behold this thing is out of character," there is an inscription within, which will silence him; for it will teach him that this wearer aggrandizes the watch, not the watch the wearer.

I was asked beforehand, if this would be a wise gift, and I said "Yes, the very wisest of all;" I know the colored race, and I know that in Lewis's eyes this fine toy will throw the other more valuable testimonials far away into the shade. If he lived in England the Humane Society would give him a gold medal as costly as this watch, and nobody would say: "It is out of character." If Lewis chose to wear a town clock, who would become it better?

Lewis has sound common sense, and is not going to be spoiled. The instant he found himself possessed of money, he forgot himself in a plan to make his old father comfortable, who is wretchedly poor and lives down in Maryland. His next act, on the spot, was the proffer to the Cranes of the $300 of his remaining indebtedness to them. This was put off by them to the indefinite future, for he is not going to be allowed to pay that at all, though he doesn't know it.

A letter of acknowledgment from Lewis contains a sentence which raises it to the dignity of literature:

"But I beg to say, humbly, that inasmuch as divine providence saw fit to use me as a instrument for the saving of those presshious lives, the honner conferd upon me was greater than the feat performed."

That is well said. Yrs ever MARK.

Howells was moved to use the story in the. "Contributors' Club," and warned Clemens against letting it get into the newspapers. He declared he thought it one of the most impressive things he had ever read. But Clemens seems never to have allowed it to be used in any form. In its entirety, therefore, it is quite new matter.

To W. D. Howells, in Boston:

HARTFORD, Sept. 19, 1877. MY DEAR HOWELLS,--I don't really see how the story of the runaway horse could read well with the little details of names and places and things left out. They are the true life of all narrative. It wouldn't quite do to print them at this time. We'll talk about it when you come. Delicacy--a sad, sad false delicacy--robs literature of the best two things among its belongings. Family-circle narrative and obscene stories. But no matter; in that better world which I trust we are all going to I have the hope and belief that they will not be denied us.

Say--Twichell and I had an adventure at sea, 4 months ago, which I did not put in my Bermuda articles, because there was not enough to it. But the press dispatches bring the sequel today, and now there's plenty to it. A sailless, wasteless, chartless, compassless, grubless old condemned tub that has been drifting helpless about the ocean for 4 months and a half, begging bread and water like any other tramp, flying a signal of distress permanently, and with 13 innocent, marveling chuckleheaded Bermuda niggers on board, taking a Pleasure Excursion! Our ship fed the poor devils on the 25th of last May, far out at sea and left them to bullyrag their way to New York--and now they ain't as near New York as they were then by 250 miles! They have drifted 750 miles and are still drifting in the relentless Gulf Stream! What a delicious magazine chapter it would make--

but I had to deny myself. I had to come right out in the papers at once, with my details, so as to try to raise the government's sympathy sufficiently to have better succor sent them than the cutter Colfax, which went a little way in search of them the other day and then struck a fog and gave it up.

If the President were in Washington I would telegraph him.

When I hear that the "Jonas Smith" has been found again, I mean to send for one of those darkies, to come to Hartford and give me his adventures for an Atlantic article.

Likely you will see my today's article in the newspapers. Yrs ever, MARK.

The revenue cutter Colfax went after the Jonas Smith, thinking there was mutiny or other crime on board. It occurs to me now that, since there is only mere suffering and misery and nobody to punish, it ceases to be a matter which (a republican form of) government will feel authorized to interfere in further. Dam a republican form of government.

Clemens thought he had given up lecturing for good; he was prosperous and he had no love for the platform. But one day an idea popped into his head: Thomas Nast, the "father of the American cartoon," had delivered a successful series of illustrated lectures- talks for which he made the drawings as he went along. Mark Twain's idea was to make a combination with Nast. His letter gives us the plan in full.

To Thomas Nast, Morristown, N. J.:

HARTFORD, CONN. 1877. MY DEAR NAST,--I did not think I should ever stand on a platform again until the time was come for me to say "I die innocent." But the same old offers keep arriving. I have declined them all, just as usual, though sorely tempted, as usual.

Now, I do not decline because I mind talking to an audience, but because (1) traveling alone is so heartbreakingly dreary, and (2) shouldering the whole show is such a cheer-killing responsibility.

Therefore, I now propose to you what you proposed to me in 1867, ten years ago (when I was unknown) viz., that you stand on the platform and make pictures, and I stand by you and blackguard the audience. I should enormously enjoy meandering around (to big towns--don't want to go to the little ones) with you for company.

My idea is not to fatten the lecture agents and lyceums on the spoils, but put all the ducats religiously into two equal piles, and say to the artist and lecturer, "Absorb these."

For instance--[Here follows a plan and a possible list of cities to be visited. The letter continues]

Call the gross receipts $100,000 for four months and a half, and the profit from $60,000 to $75,000 (I try to make the figures large enough, and leave it to the public to reduce them.)

I did not put in Philadelphia because Pugh owns that town, and last winter when I made a little reading-trip he only paid me $300 and pretended his concert (I read fifteen minutes in the midst of a concert) cost him a vast sum, and so he couldn't afford any more. I could get up a better concert with a barrel of cats.

I have imagined two or three pictures and concocted the accompanying remarks to see how the thing would go. I was charmed.

Well, you think it over, Nast, and drop me a line. We should have some fun. Yours truly, SAMUEL L. CLEMENS.

The plan came to nothing. Nast, like Clemens, had no special taste for platforming, and while undoubtedly there would have been large profits in the combination, the promise of the venture did not compel his acceptance.

In spite of his distaste for the platform Mark Twain was always giving readings and lectures, without charge, for some worthy Hartford cause. He was ready to do what he could to help an entertainment along, if he could do it in his own way--an original way, sometimes, and not always gratifying to the committee, whose plans were likely to be prearranged.

For one thing, Clemens, supersensitive in the matter of putting himself forward in his own town, often objected to any special exploitation of his name. This always distressed the committee, who saw a large profit to their venture in the prestige of his fame. The following characteristic letter was written in self-defense when, on one such occasion, a committee had become sufficiently peevish to abandon a worthy enterprise.

To an Entertainment Committee, in Hartford:

Nov. 9. E. S. SYKES, Esq:

Dr. SIR,--Mr. Burton's note puts upon me all the blame of the destruction of an enterprise which had for its object the succor of the Hartford poor. That is to say, this enterprise has been dropped because of the "dissatisfaction with Mr. Clemens's stipulations." Therefore I must be allowed to say a word in my defense.

There were two "stipulations"--exactly two. I made one of them; if the other was made at all, it was a joint one, from the choir and me.

My individual stipulation was, that my name should be kept out of the newspapers. The joint one was that sufficient tickets to insure a good sum should be sold before the date of the performance should be set. (Understand, we wanted a good sum--I do not think any of us bothered about a good house; it was money we were after)

Now you perceive that my concern is simply with my individual stipulation. Did that break up the enterprise?

Eugene Burton said he would sell $300 worth of the tickets himself.--Mr. Smith said he would sell $200 or $300 worth himself. My plan for Asylum Hill Church would have ensured $150 from that quarter.--All this in the face of my "Stipulation." It was proposed to raise $1000; did my stipulation render the raising of $400 or $500 in a dozen churches impossible?

My stipulation is easily defensible. When a mere reader or lecturer has appeared 3 or 4 times in a town of Hartford's size, he is a good deal more than likely to get a very unpleasant snub if he shoves himself forward about once or twice more. Therefore I long ago made up my mind that whenever I again appeared here, it should be only in a minor capacity and not as a chief attraction.

Now, I placed that harmless and very justifiable stipulation before the committee the other day; they carried it to headquarters and it was accepted there. I am not informed that any objection was made to it, or that it was regarded as an offense. It seems late in the day, now, after a good deal of trouble has been taken and a good deal of thankless work done by the committees, to, suddenly tear up the contract and then turn and bowl me down from long range as being the destroyer of it.

If the enterprise has failed because of my individual stipulation, here you have my proper and reasonable reasons for making that stipulation.

If it has failed because of the joint stipulation, put the blame there, and let us share it collectively.

I think our plan was a good one. I do not doubt that Mr. Burton still approves of it, too. I believe the objections come from other quarters, and not from him. Mr. Twichell used the following words in last Sunday's sermon, (if I remember correctly):

"My hearers, the prophet Deuteronomy says this wise thing: 'Though ye plan a goodly house for the poor, and plan it with wisdom, and do take off your coats and set to to build it, with high courage, yet shall the croaker presently come, and lift up his voice, (having his coat on,) and say, Verily this plan is not well planned--and he will go his way; and the obstructionist will come, and lift up his voice, (having his coat on,) and say, Behold, this is but a sick plan--and he will go his way; and the man that knows it all will come, and lift up his voice, (having his coat on,) and say, Lo, call they this a plan? then will he go his way; and the places which knew him once shall know him no more forever, because he was not, for God took him. Now therefore I say unto you, Verily that house will not be budded. And I say this also: He that waiteth for all men to be satisfied with his plan, let him seek eternal life, for he shall need it.'"

This portion of Mr. Twichell's sermon made a great impression upon me, and I was grieved that some one had not wakened me earlier so that I might have heard what went before.

S. L. CLEMENS.

Mr. Sykes (of the firm of Sykes & Newton, the Allen House Pharmacy) replied that he had read the letter to the committee and that it had set those gentlemen right who had not before understood the situation. "If others were as ready to do their part as yourself our poor would not want assistance," he said, in closing.

We come now to an incident which assumes the proportions of an episode-even of a catastrophe--in Mark Twain's career. The disaster was due to a condition noted a few pages earlier--the inability of genius to judge its own efforts. The story has now become history-- printed history--it having been sympathetically told by Howells in My Mark Twain, and more exhaustively, with a report of the speech that invited the lightning, in a former work by the present writer.

The speech was made at John Greenleaf Whittier's seventieth birthday dinner, given by the Atlantic staff on the evening of December 17, 1877. It was intended as a huge joke--a joke that would shake the sides of these venerable Boston deities, Longfellow, Emerson, Holmes, and the rest of that venerated group. Clemens had been a favorite at the Atlantic lunches and dinners--a speech by him always an event. This time he decided to outdo himself.

He did that, but not in the way he had intended. To use one of his own metaphors, he stepped out to meet the rainbow and got struck by lightning. His joke was not of the Boston kind or size. When its full nature burst upon the company--when the ears of the assembled diners heard the sacred names of Longfellow, Emerson, and Holmes lightly associated with human aspects removed--oh, very far removed --from Cambridge and Concord, a chill fell upon the diners that presently became amazement, and then creeping paralysis. Nobody knew afterward whether the great speech that he had so gaily planned ever came to a natural end or not. Somebody--the next on the program--attempted to follow him, but presently the company melted out of the doors and crept away into the night.

It seemed to Mark Twain that his career had come to an end. Back in Hartford, sweating and suffering through sleepless nights, he wrote Howells his anguish.

To W. D. Howells, in Boston:

Sunday Night. 1877. MY DEAR HOWELLS,--My sense of disgrace does not abate. It grows. I see that it is going to add itself to my list of permanencies--a list of humiliations that extends back to when I was seven years old, and which keep on persecuting me regardless of my repentancies.

I feel that my misfortune has injured me all over the country; therefore it will be best that I retire from before the public at present. It will hurt the Atlantic for me to appear in its pages, now. So it is my opinion and my wife's that the telephone story had better be suppressed. Will you return those proofs or revises to me, so that I can use the same on some future occasion?

It seems as if I must have been insane when I wrote that speech and saw no harm in it, no disrespect toward those men whom I reverenced so much. And what shame I brought upon you, after what you said in introducing me! It burns me like fire to think of it.

The whole matter is a dreadful subject--let me drop it here--at least on paper. Penitently yrs, MARK.

Howells sent back a comforting letter. "I have no idea of dropping you out of the Atlantic," he wrote; "and Mr. Houghton has still less, if possible. You are going to help and not hurt us many a year yet, if you will.... You are not going to be floored by it; there is more justice than that, even in this world."

Howells added that Charles Elliot Norton had expressed just the right feeling concerning the whole affair, and that many who had not heard the speech, but read the newspaper reports of it, had found it without offense.

Clemens wrote contrite letters to Holmes, Emerson, and Longfellow, and received most gracious acknowledgments. Emerson, indeed, had not heard the speech: His faculties were already blurred by the mental mists that would eventually shut him in. Clemens wrote again to Howells, this time with less anguish.

To W. D. Howells, in Boston:

HARTFORD, Friday, 1877. MY DEAR HOWELLS,--Your letter was a godsend; and perhaps the welcomest part of it was your consent that I write to those gentlemen; for you discouraged my hints in that direction that morning in Boston--rightly, too, for my offense was yet too new, then. Warner has tried to hold up our hands like the good fellow he is, but poor Twichell could not say a word, and confessed that he would rather take nearly any punishment than face Livy and me. He hasn't been here since.

It is curious, but I pitched early upon Mr. Norton as the very man who would think some generous thing about that matter, whether he said it or not. It is splendid to be a man like that--but it is given to few to be.

I wrote a letter yesterday, and sent a copy to each of the three. I wanted to send a copy to Mr. Whittier also, since the offense was done also against him, being committed in his presence and he the guest of the occasion, besides holding the well-nigh sacred place he does in his people's estimation; but I didn't know whether to venture or not, and so ended by doing nothing. It seemed an intrusion to approach him, and even Livy seemed to have her doubts as to the best and properest way to do in the case. I do not reverence Mr. Emerson less, but somehow I could approach him easier.

Send me those proofs, if you have got them handy; I want to submit them to Wylie; he won't show them to anybody.

Had a very pleasant and considerate letter from Mr. Houghton, today, and was very glad to receive it.

You can't imagine how brilliant and beautiful that new brass fender is, and how perfectly naturally it takes its place under the carved oak. How they did scour it up before they sent it! I lied a good deal about it when I came home--so for once I kept a secret and surprised Livy on a Christmas morning!

I haven't done a stroke of work since the Atlantic dinner; have only moped around. But I'm going to try tomorrow. How could I ever have.

Ah, well, I am a great and sublime fool. But then I am God's fool, and all His works must be contemplated with respect.

Livy and I join in the warmest regards to you and yours, Yrs ever, MARK.

Longfellow, in his reply, said: "I do not believe anybody was much hurt. Certainly I was not, and Holmes tells me he was not. So I think you may dismiss the matter from your mind without further remorse."

Holmes wrote: "It never occurred to me for a moment to take offense, or feel wounded by your playful use of my name."

Miss Ellen Emerson replied for her father (in a letter to Mrs. Clemens) that the speech had made no impression upon him, giving at considerable length the impression it had made on herself and other members of the family.

Clearly, it was not the principals who were hurt, but only those who held them in awe, though one can realize that this would not make it much easier for Mark Twain.

XVIII.

LETTERS FROM EUROPE, 1878-79. TRAMPING WITH TWICHELL. WRITING A NEW TRAVEL BOOK. LIFE IN MUNICH

Whether the unhappy occurrence at the Whittier dinner had anything to do with Mark Twain's resolve to spend a year or two in Europe cannot be known now. There were other good reasons for going, one in particular being a demand for another book of travel. It was also true, as he explains in a letter to his mother, that his days were full of annoyances, making it difficult for him to work. He had a tendency to invest money in almost any glittering enterprise that came along, and at this time he was involved in the promotion of a variety of patent rights that brought him no return other than assessment and vexation.

Clemens's mother was by this time living with her son Onion and his wife, in Iowa.

To Mrs. Jane Clemens, in Keokuk, Iowa:

HARTFORD, Feb. 17, 1878 MY DEAR MOTHER,--I suppose I am the worst correspondent in the whole world; and yet I grow worse and worse all the time. My conscience blisters me for not writing you, but it has ceased to abuse me for not writing other folks.

Life has come to be a very serious matter with me. I have a badgered, harassed feeling, a good part of my time. It comes mainly of business responsibilities and annoyances, and the persecution of kindly letters from well meaning strangers--to whom I must be rudely silent or else put in the biggest half of my time bothering over answers. There are other things also that help to consume my time and defeat my projects. Well, the consequence is, I cannot write a book at home. This cuts my income down. Therefore, I have about made up my mind to take my tribe and fly to some little corner of Europe and budge no more until I shall have completed one of the half dozen books that lie begun, up stairs. Please say nothing about this at present.

We propose to sail the 11th of April. I shall go to Fredonia to meet you, but it will not be well for Livy to make that trip I am afraid. However, we shall see. I will hope she can go.

Mr. Twichell has just come in, so I must go to him. We are all well, and send love to you all. Affly, SAM.

He was writing few letters at this time, and doing but little work. There were always many social events during the winter, and what with his European plans and a diligent study of the German language, which the entire family undertook, his days and evenings were full enough. Howells wrote protesting against the European travel and berating him for his silence:

"I never was in Berlin and don't know any family hotel there. I should be glad I didn't, if it would keep you from going. You deserve to put up at the Sign of the Savage in Vienna. Really, it's a great blow to me to hear of that prospected sojourn. It's a shame. I must see you, somehow, before you go. I'm in dreadfully low spirits about it.

"I was afraid your silence meant something wicked."

Clemens replied promptly, urging a visit to Hartford, adding a postscript for Mrs. Howells, characteristic enough to warrant preservation.

P. S. to Mrs. Howells, in Boston:

Feb. '78. DEAR MRS. HOWELLS. Mrs. Clemens wrote you a letter, and handed it to me half an hour ago, while I was folding mine to Mr. Howells. I laid that letter on this table before me while I added the paragraph about R,'s application. Since then I have been hunting and swearing, and swearing and hunting, but I can't find a sign of that letter. It is the most astonishing disappearance I ever heard of. Mrs. Clemens has gone off driving--so I will have to try and give you an idea of her communication from memory. Mainly it consisted of an urgent desire that you come to see us next week, if you can possibly manage it, for that will be a reposeful time, the turmoil of breaking up beginning the week after. She wants you to tell her about Italy, and advise her in that connection, if you will. Then she spoke of her plans--hers, mind you, for I never have anything quite so definite as a plan. She proposes to stop a fortnight in (confound the place, I've forgotten what it was,) then go and live in Dresden till sometime in the summer; then retire to Switzerland for the hottest season, then stay a while in Venice and put in the winter in Munich. This program subject to modifications according to circumstances. She said something about some little by-trips here and there, but they didn't stick in my memory because the idea didn't charm me.

(They have just telephoned me from the Courant office that Bayard Taylor and family have taken rooms in our ship, the Holsatia, for the 11th April.)

Do come, if you possibly can!--and remember and don't forget to avoid letting Mrs. Clemens find out I lost her letter. Just answer her the same as if you had got it. Sincerely yours S. L. CLEMENS.

The Howellses came, as invited, for a final reunion before the breaking up. This was in the early half of March; the Clemenses were to sail on the 11th of the following month.

Orion Clemens, meantime, had conceived a new literary idea and was piling in his MS. as fast as possible to get his brother's judgment on it before the sailing-date. It was not a very good time to send MS., but Mark Twain seems to have read it and given it some consideration. "The Journey in Heaven," of his own, which he mentions, was the story published so many years later under the title of "Captain Stormfield's Visit to Heaven." He had began it in 1868, on his voyage to San Francisco, it having been suggested by conversations with Capt. Ned Wakeman, of one of the Pacific steamers. Wakeman also appears in 'Roughing It,' Chap. L, as Capt. Ned Blakely, and again in one of the "Rambling Notes of an Idle Excursion," as "Captain Hurricane Jones."

To Orion Clemens, in Keokuk:

HARTFORD, Mch. 23, 1878. MY DEAR BRO.,--Every man must learn his trade--not pick it up. God requires that he learn it by slow and painful processes. The apprentice- hand, in black-smithing, in medicine, in literature, in everything, is a thing that can't be hidden. It always shows.

But happily there is a market for apprentice work, else the "Innocents Abroad" would have had no sale. Happily, too, there's a wider market for some sorts of apprentice literature than there is for the very best of journey-work. This work of yours is exceedingly crude, but I am free to say it is less crude than I expected it to be, and considerably better work than I believed you could do, it is too crude to offer to any prominent periodical, so I shall speak to the N. Y. Weekly people. To publish it there will be to bury it. Why could not same good genius have sent me to the N. Y. Weekly with my apprentice sketches?

You should not publish it in book form at all--for this reason: it is only an imitation of Verne--it is not a burlesque. But I think it may be regarded as proof that Verne cannot be burlesqued.

In accompanying notes I have suggested that you vastly modify the first visit to hell, and leave out the second visit altogether. Nobody would, or ought to print those things. You are not advanced enough in literature to venture upon a matter requiring so much practice. Let me show you what a man has got to go through:

Nine years ago I mapped out my "Journey in Heaven." I discussed it with literary friends whom I could trust to keep it to themselves.

I gave it a deal of thought, from time to time. After a year or more I wrote it up. It was not a success. Five years ago I wrote it again, altering the plan. That MS is at my elbow now. It was a considerable improvement on the first attempt, but still it wouldn't do--last year and year before I talked frequently with Howells about the subject, and he kept urging me to do it again.

So I thought and thought, at odd moments and at last I struck what I considered to be the right plan! Mind I have never altered the ideas, from the first--the plan was the difficulty. When Howells was here last, I laid before him the whole story without referring to my MS and he said: "You have got it sure this time. But drop the idea of making mere magazine stuff of it. Don't waste it. Print it by itself--publish it first in England--ask Dean Stanley to endorse it, which will draw some of the teeth of the religious press, and then reprint in America." I doubt my ability to get Dean Stanley to do anything of the sort, but I shall do the rest--and this is all a secret which you must not divulge.

Now look here--I have tried, all these years, to think of some way of "doing" hell too--and have always had to give it up. Hell, in my book, will not occupy five pages of MS I judge--it will be only covert hints, I suppose, and quickly dropped, I may end by not even referring to it.

And mind you, in my opinion you will find that you can't write up hell so it will stand printing. Neither Howells nor I believe in hell or the divinity of the Savior, but no matter, the Savior is none the less a sacred Personage, and a man should have no desire or disposition to refer to him lightly, profanely, or otherwise than with the profoundest reverence.

The only safe thing is not to introduce him, or refer to him at all, I suspect. I have entirely rewritten one book 3 (perhaps 4.) times, changing the plan every time--1200 pages of MS. wasted and burned--and shall tackle it again, one of these years and maybe succeed at last. Therefore you need not expect to get your book right the first time. Go to work and revamp or rewrite it. God only exhibits his thunder and lightning at intervals, and so they always command attention. These are God's adjectives. You thunder and lightning too much; the reader ceases to get under the bed, by and by.

Mr. Perkins will send you and Ma your checks when we are gone. But don't write him, ever, except a single line in case he forgets the checks--for the man is driven to death with work.

I see you are half promising yourself a monthly return for your book. In my experience, previously counted chickens never do hatch. How many of mine I have counted! and never a one of them but failed! It is much better to hedge disappointment by not counting.--Unexpected money is a delight. The same sum is a bitterness when you expected more.

My time in America is growing mighty short. Perhaps we can manage in this way: Imprimis, if the N. Y. Weekly people know that you are my brother, they will turn that fact into an advertisement--a thing of value to them, but not to you and me. This must be prevented. I will write them a note to say you have a friend near Keokuk, Charles S. Miller, who has a MS for sale which you think is a pretty clever travesty on Verne; and if they want it they might write to him in your care. Then if any correspondence ensues between you and them, let Mollie write for you and sign your name--your own hand writing representing Miller's. Keep yourself out of sight till you make a strike on your own merits there is no other way to get a fair verdict upon your merits.

Later-I've written the note to Smith, and with nothing in it which he can use as an advertisement. I'm called--Good bye-love to you both.

We leave here next Wednesday for Elmira: we leave there Apl. 9 or 10--and sail 11th Yr Bro. SAM.

In the letter that follows the mention of Annie and Sam refers, of course, to the children of Mrs. Moffett, who had been, Pamela Clemens. They were grown now, and Annie Moffett was married to Charles L. Webster, who later was to become Mark Twain's business partner. The Moffetts and Websters were living in Fredonia at this time, and Clemens had been to pay them a good-by visit. The Taylor dinner mentioned was a farewell banquet given to Bayard Taylor, who had been appointed Minister to Germany, and was to sail on the ship with Mark Twain. Mark Twain's mother was visiting in Fredonia when this letter was written.

To Mrs. Jane Clemens, in Fredonia:

Apr. 7, '78. MY DEAR MOTHER,--I have told Livy all about Annie's beautiful house, and about Sam and Charley, and about Charley's ingenious manufactures and his strong manhood and good promise, and how glad I am that he and Annie married. And I have told her about Annie's excellent house-keeping, also about the great Bacon conflict; (I told you it was a hundred to one that neither Livy nor the European powers had heard of that desolating struggle.)

And I have told her how beautiful you are in your age and how bright your mind is with its old-time brightness, and how she and the children would enjoy you. And I have told her how singularly young Pamela is looking, and what a fine large fellow Sam is, and how ill the lingering syllable "my" to his name fits his port and figure.

Well, Pamela, after thinking it over for a day or so, I came near inquiring about a state-room in our ship for Sam, to please you, but my wiser former resolution came back to me. It is not for his good that he have friends in the ship. His conduct in the Bacon business shows that he will develop rapidly into a manly man as soon as he is cast loose from your apron strings.

You don't teach him to push ahead and do and dare things for himself, but you do just the reverse. You are assisted in your damaging work by the tyrannous ways of a village--villagers watch each other and so make cowards of each other. After Sam shall have voyaged to Europe by himself, and rubbed against the world and taken and returned its cuffs, do you think he will hesitate to escort a guest into any whisky-mill in Fredonia when he himself has no sinful business to transact there? No, he will smile at the idea. If he avoids this courtesy now from principle, of course I find no fault with it at all--only if he thinks it is principle he may be mistaken; a close examination may show it is only a bowing to the tyranny of public opinion.

I only say it may--I cannot venture to say it will. Hartford is not a large place, but it is broader than to have ways of that sort. Three or four weeks ago, at a Moody and Sankey meeting, the preacher read a letter from somebody "exposing" the fact that a prominent clergyman had gone from one of those meetings, bought a bottle of lager beer and drank it on the premises (a drug store.)

A tempest of indignation swept the town. Our clergymen and everybody else said the "culprit" had not only done an innocent thing, but had done it in an open, manly way, and it was nobody's right or business to find fault with it. Perhaps this dangerous latitude comes of the fact that we never have any temperance "rot" going on in Hartford.

I find here a letter from Orion, submitting some new matter in his story for criticism. When you write him, please tell him to do the best he can and bang away. I can do nothing further in this matter, for I have but 3 days left in which to settle a deal of important business and answer a bushel and a half of letters. I am very nearly tired to death.

I was so jaded and worn, at the Taylor dinner, that I found I could not remember 3 sentences of the speech I had memorized, and therefore got up and said so and excused myself from speaking. I arrived here at 3 o'clock this morning. I think the next 3 days will finish me. The idea of sitting down to a job of literary criticism is simply ludicrous.

A young lady passenger in our ship has been placed under Livy's charge. Livy couldn't easily get out of it, and did not want to, on her own account, but fully expected I would make trouble when I heard of it. But I didn't. A girl can't well travel alone, so I offered no objection. She leaves us at Hamburg. So I've got 6 people in my care, now--which is just 6 too many for a man of my unexecutive capacity. I expect nothing else but to lose some of them overboard.

We send our loving good-byes to all the household and hope to see you again after a spell. Affly Yrs. SAM.

There are no other American letters of this period. The Clemens party, which included Miss Clara Spaulding, of Elmira, sailed as planned, on the Holsatia, April 11, 1878. As before stated, Bayard Taylor was on the ship; also Murat Halstead and family. On the eve of departure, Clemens sent to Howells this farewell word:

"And that reminds me, ungrateful dog that I am, that I owe as much to your training as the rude country job-printer owes to the city boss who takes him in hand and teaches him the right way to handle his art. I was talking to Mrs. Clemens about this the other day, and grieving because I never mentioned it to you, thereby seeming to ignore it, or to be unaware of it. Nothing that has passed under your eye needs any revision before going into a volume, while all my other stuff does need so much."

A characteristic tribute, and from the heart.

The first European letter came from Frankfort, a rest on their way to Heidelberg.

To W. D. Howells, in Boston:

FRANKFORT ON THE MAIN, May 4, 1878. MY DEAR HOWELLS,--I only propose to write a single line to say we are still around. Ah, I have such a deep, grateful, unutterable sense of being "out of it all." I think I foretaste some of the advantages of being dead. Some of the joy of it. I don't read any newspapers or care for them. When people tell me England has declared war, I drop the subject, feeling that it is none of my business; when they tell me Mrs. Tilton has confessed and Mr. B. denied, I say both of them have done that before, therefore let the worn stub of the Plymouth white-wash brush be brought out once more, and let the faithful spit on their hands and get to work again regardless of me--for I am out of it all.

We had 2 almost devilish weeks at sea (and I tell you Bayard Taylor is a really lovable man--which you already knew) then we staid a week in the beautiful, the very beautiful city of Hamburg; and since then we have been fooling along, 4 hours per day by rail, with a courier, spending the other 20 in hotels whose enormous bedchambers and private parlors are an overpowering marvel to me: Day before yesterday, in Cassel, we had a love of a bedroom ,31 feet long, and a parlor with 2 sofas, 12 chairs, a writing desk and 4 tables scattered around, here and there in it. Made of red silk, too, by George.

The times and times I wish you were along! You could throw some fun into the journey; whereas I go on, day by day, in a smileless state of solemn admiration.

What a paradise this is! What clean clothes, what good faces, what tranquil contentment, what prosperity, what genuine freedom, what superb government. And I am so happy, for I am responsible for none of it. I am only here to enjoy. How charmed I am when I overhear a German word which I understand. With love from us 2 to you 2.

MARK.

P. S. We are not taking six days to go from Hamburg to Heidelberg because we prefer it. Quite on the contrary. Mrs. Clemens picked up a dreadful cold and sore throat on board ship and still keeps them in stock--so she could only travel 4 hours a day. She wanted to dive straight through, but I had different notions about the wisdom of it. I found that 4 hours a day was the best she could do. Before I forget it, our permanent address is Care Messrs. Koester & Co., Backers, Heidelberg. We go there tomorrow.

Poor Susy! From the day we reached German soil, we have required Rosa to speak German to the children--which they hate with all their souls. The other morning in Hanover, Susy came to us (from Rosa, in the nursery) and said, in halting syllables, "Papa, vie viel uhr ist es?"--then turned with pathos in her big eyes, and said, "Mamma, I wish Rosa was made in English."

(Unfinished)

Frankfort was a brief halting-place, their destination being Heidelberg. They were presently located there in the beautiful Schloss hotel, which overlooks the old castle with its forest setting, the flowing Neckar, and the distant valley of the Rhine. Clemens, who had discovered the location, and loved it, toward the end of May reported to Howells his felicities.

Part of letter to W. D. Howells, in Boston:

SCHLOSS-HOTEL HEIDELBERG, Sunday, a. m., May 26, 1878. MY DEAR HOWELLS,-- ....divinely located. From this airy porch among the shining groves we look down upon Heidelberg Castle, and upon the swift Neckar, and the town, and out over the wide green level of the Rhine valley--a marvelous prospect. We are in a Cul-de-sac formed of hill- ranges and river; we are on the side of a steep mountain; the river at our feet is walled, on its other side, (yes, on both sides,) by a steep and wooded mountain-range which rises abruptly aloft from the water's edge; portions of these mountains are densely wooded; the plain of the Rhine, seen through the mouth of this pocket, has many and peculiar charms for the eye.

Our bedroom has two great glass bird-cages (enclosed balconies) one looking toward the Rhine valley and sunset, the other looking up the Neckar cul-de-sac, and naturally we spend nearly all our time in these- when one is sunny the other is shady. We have tables and chairs in them; we do our reading, writing, studying, smoking and suppering in them.

The view from these bird-cages is my despair. The pictures change from one enchanting aspect to another in ceaseless procession, never keeping one form half an hour, and never taking on an unlovely one.

And then Heidelberg on a dark night! It is massed, away down there, almost right under us, you know, and stretches off toward the valley. Its curved and interlacing streets are a cobweb, beaded thick with lights--a wonderful thing to see; then the rows of lights on the arched bridges, and their glinting reflections in the water; and away at the far end, the Eisenbahnhof, with its twenty solid acres of glittering gas- jets, a huge garden, as one may say, whose every plant is a flame.

These balconies are the darlingest things. I have spent all the morning in this north one. Counting big and little, it has 256 panes of glass in it; so one is in effect right out in the free sunshine, and yet sheltered from wind and rain--and likewise doored and curtained from whatever may be going on in the bedroom. It must have been a noble genius who devised this hotel. Lord, how blessed is the repose, the tranquillity of this place! Only two sounds; the happy clamor of the birds in the groves, and the muffled music of the Neckar, tumbling over the opposing dykes. It is no hardship to lie awake awhile, nights, for this subdued roar has exactly the sound of a steady rain beating upon a roof. It is so healing to the spirit; and it bears up the thread of one's imaginings as the accompaniment bears up a song.

While Livy and Miss Spaulding have been writing at this table, I have sat tilted back, near by, with a pipe and the last Atlantic, and read Charley Warner's article with prodigious enjoyment. I think it is exquisite. I think it must be the roundest and broadest and completest short essay he has ever written. It is clear, and compact, and charmingly done.

The hotel grounds join and communicate with the Castle grounds; so we and the children loaf in the winding paths of those leafy vastnesses a great deal, and drink beer and listen to excellent music.

When we first came to this hotel, a couple of weeks ago, I pointed to a house across the river, and said I meant to rent the centre room on the 3d floor for a work-room. Jokingly we got to speaking of it as my office; and amused ourselves with watching "my people" daily in their small grounds and trying to make out what we could of their dress, &c., without a glass. Well, I loafed along there one day and found on that house the only sign of the kind on that side of the river: "Moblirte Wohnung zu Vermiethen!" I went in and rented that very room which I had long ago selected. There was only one other room in the whole double-house unrented.

(It occurs to me that I made a great mistake in not thinking to deliver a very bad German speech, every other sentence pieced out with English, at the Bayard Taylor banquet in New York. I think I could have made it one of the features of the occasion.)--[He used this plan at a gathering of the American students in Heidelberg, on July 4th, with great effect; so his idea was not wasted.]

We left Hartford before the end of March, and I have been idle ever since. I have waited for a call to go to work--I knew it would come. Well, it began to come a week ago; my note-book comes out more and more frequently every day since; 3 days ago I concluded to move my manuscript over to my den. Now the call is loud and decided at last. So tomorrow I shall begin regular, steady work, and stick to it till middle of July or 1st August, when I look for Twichell; we will then walk about Germany 2 or 3 weeks, and then I'll go to work again--(perhaps in Munich.)

We both send a power of love to the Howellses, and we do wish you were here. Are you in the new house? Tell us about it. Yrs Ever MARK.

There has been no former mention in the letters of the coming of Twichell; yet this had been a part of the European plan. Mark Twain had invited his walking companion to make a tramp with him through Europe, as his guest. Material for the new book would grow faster with Twichell as a companion; and these two in spite of their widely opposed views concerning Providence and the general scheme of creation, were wholly congenial comrades. Twichell, in Hartford, expecting to receive the final summons to start, wrote: "Oh, my! do you realize, Mark, what a symposium it is to be? I do. To begin with, I am thoroughly tired, and the rest will be worth everything. To walk with you and talk with you for weeks together--why, it's my dream of luxury."

August 1st brought Twichell, and the friends set out without delay on a tramp through the Black Forest, making short excursions at first, but presently extending them in the direction of Switzerland. Mrs. Clemens and the others remained in Heidelberg, to follow at their leisure. To Mrs. Clemens her husband sent frequent reports of their wanderings. It will be seen that their tramp did not confine itself to pedestrianism, though they did, in fact, walk a great deal, and Mark Twain in a note to his mother declared, "I loathe all travel, except on foot." The reports to Mrs. Clemens follow:

Letters to Mrs. Clemens, in Heidelberg:

ALLERHEILIGEN Aug. 5, 1878 8:30 p.m. Livy darling, we had a rattling good time to-day, but we came very near being left at Baden-Baden, for instead of waiting in the waiting-room, we sat down on the platform to wait where the trains come in from the other direction. We sat there full ten minutes--and then all of a sudden it occurred to me that that was not the right place.

On the train the principal of the big English school at Nauheim (of which Mr. Scheiding was a teacher), introduced himself to me, and then he mapped out our day for us (for today and tomorrow) and also drew a map and gave us directions how to proceed through Switzerland. He had his entire school with him, taking them on a prodigious trip through Switzerland--tickets for the round trip ten dollars apiece. He has done this annually for 10 years. We took a post carriage from Aachen to Otterhofen for 7 marks--stopped at the "Pflug" to drink beer, and saw that pretty girl again at a distance. Her father, mother, and two brothers received me like an ancient customer and sat down and talked as long as I had any German left. The big room was full of red-vested farmers (the Gemeindrath of the district, with the Burgermeister at the head,) drinking beer and talking public business. They had held an election and chosen a new member and had been drinking beer at his expense for several hours. (It was intensely Black-foresty.)

There was an Australian there (a student from Stuttgart or somewhere,) and Joe told him who I was and he laid himself out to make our course plain, for us--so I am certain we can't get lost between here and Heidelberg.

We walked the carriage road till we came to that place where one sees the foot path on the other side of the ravine, then we crossed over and took that. For a good while we were in a dense forest and judged we were lost, but met a native women who said we were all right. We fooled along and got there at 6 p.m.--ate supper, then followed down the ravine to the foot of the falls, then struck into a blind path to see where it would go, and just about dark we fetched up at the Devil's Pulpit on top of the hills. Then home. And now to bed, pretty sleepy. Joe sends love and I send a thousand times as much, my darling. S. L. C.

HOTEL GENNIN. Livy darling, we had a lovely day jogged right along, with a good horse and sensible driver--the last two hours right behind an open carriage filled with a pleasant German family--old gentleman and 3 pretty daughters. At table d'hote tonight, 3 dishes were enough for me, and then I bored along tediously through the bill of fare, with a back-ache, not daring to get up and bow to the German family and leave. I meant to sit it through and make them get up and do the bowing; but at last Joe took pity on me and said he would get up and drop them a curtsy and put me out of my misery. I was grateful. He got up and delivered a succession of frank and hearty bows, accompanying them with an atmosphere of good-fellowship which would have made even an English family surrender. Of course the Germans responded--then I got right up and they had to respond to my salaams, too. So "that was done."

We walked up a gorge and saw a tumbling waterfall which was nothing to Giessbach, but it made me resolve to drop you a line and urge you to go and see Giessbach illuminated. Don't fail--but take a long day's rest, first. I love you, sweetheart. SAML.

OVER THE GEMMI PASS. 4.30 p.m. Saturday, Aug. 24, 1878. Livy darling, Joe and I have had a most noble day. Started to climb (on foot) at 8.30 this morning among the grandest peaks! Every half hour carried us back a month in the season. We left them harvesting 2d crop of hay. At 9 we were in July and found ripe strawberries; at 9.30 we were in June and gathered flowers belonging to that month; at 10 we were in May and gathered a flower which appeared in Heidelberg the 17th of that month; also forget-me-nots, which disappeared from Heidelberg about mid-May; at 11.30 we were in April (by the flowers;) at noon we had rain and hail mixed, and wind and enveloping fogs, and considered it March; at 12.30 we had snowbanks above us and snowbanks below us, and considered it February. Not good February, though, because in the midst of the wild desolation the forget-me-not still bloomed, lovely as ever.

What a flower garden the Gemmi Pass is! After I had got my hands full Joe made me a paper bag, which I pinned to my lapel and filled with choice specimens. I gathered no flowers which I had ever gathered before except 4 or 5 kinds. We took it leisurely and I picked all I wanted to. I mailed my harvest to you a while ago. Don't send it to Mrs. Brooks until you have looked it over, flower by flower. It will pay.

Among the clouds and everlasting snows I found a brave and bright little forget-me-not growing in the very midst of a smashed and tumbled stone- debris, just as cheerful as if the barren and awful domes and ramparts that towered around were the blessed walls of heaven. I thought how Lilly Warner would be touched by such a gracious surprise, if she, instead of I, had seen it. So I plucked it, and have mailed it to her with a note.

Our walk was 7 hours--the last 2 down a path as steep as a ladder, almost, cut in the face of a mighty precipice. People are not allowed to ride down it. This part of the day's work taxed our knees, I tell you. We have been loafing about this village (Leukerbad) for an hour, now we stay here over Sunday. Not tired at all. (Joe's hat fell over the precipice--so he came here bareheaded.) I love you, my darling.

SAML.

ST. NICHOLAS, Aug. 26th, '78. Livy darling, we came through a-whooping today, 6 hours tramp up steep hills and down steep hills, in mud and water shoe-deep, and in a steady pouring rain which never moderated a moment. I was as chipper and fresh as a lark all the way and arrived without the slightest sense of fatigue. But we were soaked and my shoes full of water, so we ate at once, stripped and went to bed for 2 1/2 hours while our traps were thoroughly dried, and our boots greased in addition. Then we put our clothes on hot and went to table d'hote.

Made some nice English friends and shall see them at Zermatt tomorrow.

Gathered a small bouquet of new flowers, but they got spoiled. I sent you a safety-match box full of flowers last night from Leukerbad.

I have just telegraphed you to wire the family news to me at Riffel tomorrow. I do hope you are all well and having as jolly a time as we are, for I love you, sweetheart, and also, in a measure, the Bays.-- [Little Susy's word for "babies."]--Give my love to Clara Spaulding and also to the cubs.
SAML.

This, as far as it goes, is a truer and better account of the excursion than Mark Twain gave in the book that he wrote later. A Tramp Abroad has a quality of burlesque in it, which did not belong to the journey at all, but was invented to satisfy the craving for what the public conceived to be Mark Twain's humor. The serious portions of the book are much more pleasing--more like himself. The entire journey, as will be seen, lasted one week more than a month.

Twichell also made his reports home, some of which give us interesting pictures of his walking partner. In one place he wrote: "Mark is a queer fellow. There is nothing he so delights in as a swift, strong stream. You can hardly get him to leave one when once he is within the influence of its fascinations."

Twichell tells how at Kandersteg they were out together one evening where a brook comes plunging down from Gasternthal and how he pushed in a drift to see it go racing along the current. "When I got back to the path Mark was running down stream after it as hard as he could go, throwing up his hands and shouting in the wildest ecstasy, and when a piece went over a fall and emerged to view in the foam below he would jump up and down and yell. He said afterward that he had not been so excited in three months."

In other places Twichell refers to his companion's consideration for the feeling of others, and for animals. "When we are driving, his concern is all about the horse. He can't bear to see the whip used, or to see a horse pull hard."

After the walk over Gemmi Pass he wrote: "Mark to-day was immensely absorbed in flowers. He scrambled around and gathered a great variety, and manifested the intensest pleasure in them. He crowded a pocket of his note-book with his specimens, and wanted more room."

Whereupon Twichell got out his needle and thread and some stiff paper he had and contrived the little paper bag to hang to the front of his vest.

The tramp really ended at Lausanne, where Clemens joined his party, but a short excursion to Chillon and Chamonix followed, the travelers finally separating at Geneva, Twichell to set out for home by way of England, Clemens to remain and try to write the story of their travels. He hurried a good-by letter after his comrade:

To Rev. J. H. Twichell:

(No date) DEAR OLD JOE,--It is actually all over! I was so low-spirited at the station yesterday, and this morning, when I woke, I couldn't seem to accept the dismal truth that you were really gone, and the pleasant tramping and talking at an end. Ah, my boy! it has been such a rich holiday to me, and I feel under such deep and honest obligations to you for coming. I am putting out of my mind all memory of the times when I misbehaved toward you and hurt you: I am resolved to consider it forgiven, and to store up and remember only the charming hours of the journeys and the times when I was not unworthy to be with you and share a companionship which to me stands first after Livy's. It is justifiable to do this; for why should I let my small infirmities of disposition live and grovel among my mental pictures of the eternal sublimities of the Alps?

Livy can't accept or endure the fact that you are gone. But you are, and we cannot get around it. So take our love with you, and bear it also over the sea to Harmony, and God bless you both.

MARK.

From Switzerland the Clemens party worked down into Italy, sight-seeing, a diversion in which Mark Twain found little enough of interest. He had seen most of the sights ten years before, when his mind was fresh. He unburdened himself to Twichell and to Howells, after a period of suffering.

To J. H. Twichell, in Hartford:

ROME, Nov. 3, '78. DEAR JOE,--.....I have received your several letters, and we have prodigiously enjoyed them. How I do admire a man who can sit down and whale away with a pen just the same as if it was fishing--or something else as full of pleasure and as void of labor. I can't do it; else, in common decency, I would when I write to you. Joe, if I can make a book out of the matter gathered in your company over here, the book is safe; but I don't think I have gathered any matter before or since your visit worth writing up. I do wish you were in Rome to do my sightseeing for me. Rome interests me as much as East Hartford could, and no more. That is, the Rome which the average tourist feels an interest in; but there are other things here which stir me enough to make life worth living. Livy and Clara Spaulding are having a royal time worshiping the old Masters, and I as good a time gritting my ineffectual teeth over them.

A friend waits for me. A power of love to you all. Amen. MARK.

In his letter to Howells he said: "I wish I could give those sharp satires on European life which you mention, but of course a man can't write successful satire except he be in a calm, judicial good- humor; whereas I hate travel, and I hate hotels, and I hate the opera, and I hate the old masters. In truth, I don't ever seem to be in a good-enough humor with anything to satirize it. No, I want to stand up before it and curse it and foam at the mouth, or take a club and pound it to rags and pulp. I have got in two or three chapters about Wagner's operas, and managed to do it without showing temper, but the strain of another such effort would burst me!"

From Italy the Clemens party went to Munich, where they had arranged in advance for winter quarters. Clemens claims, in his report of the matter to Howells, that he took the party through without the aid of a courier, though thirty years later, in some comment which he set down on being shown the letter, he wrote concerning this paragraph: "Probably a lie." He wrote, also, that they acquired a great affection for Fraulein Dahlweiner: "Acquired it at once and it outlasted the winter we spent in her house."

To W. D. Howells, in Boston:

No 1a, Karlstrasse, 2e Stock. Care Fraulein Dahlweiner. MUNICH, Nov. 17, 1878. MY DEAR HOWELLS,--We arrived here night before last, pretty well fagged: an 8-hour pull from Rome to Florence; a rest there of a day and two nights; then 5 1/2 hours to Bologna; one night's rest; then from noon to 10:30 p.m. carried us to Trent, in the Austrian Tyrol, where the confounded hotel had not received our message, and so at that miserable hour, in that snowy region, the tribe had to shiver together in fireless rooms while beds were prepared and warmed, then up at 6 in the morning and a noble view of snow-peaks glittering in the rich light of a full moon while the hotel-devils lazily deranged a breakfast for us in the dreary gloom of blinking candles; then a solid 12 hours pull through the loveliest snow ranges and snow-draped forest--and at 7 p.m. we hauled up, in drizzle and fog, at the domicile which had been engaged for us ten months before. Munich did seem the horriblest place, the most desolate place, the most unendurable place!--and the rooms were so small, the conveniences so meagre, and the porcelain stoves so grim, ghastly, dismal, intolerable! So Livy and Clara (Spaulding) sat down forlorn, and cried, and I retired to a private, place to pray. By and by we all retired to our narrow German beds; and when Livy and I finished talking across the room, it was all decided that we would rest 24 hours then pay whatever damages were required, and straightway fly to the south of France.

But you see, that was simply fatigue. Next morning the tribe fell in love with the rooms, with the weather, with Munich, and head over heels in love with Fraulein Dahlweiner. We got a larger parlor--an ample one --threw two communicating bedrooms into one, for the children, and now we are entirely comfortable. The only apprehension, at present, is that the climate may not be just right for the children, in which case we shall have to go to France, but it will be with the sincerest regret.

Now I brought the tribe through from Rome, myself. We never had so little trouble before. The next time anybody has a courier to put out to nurse, I shall not be in the market.

Last night the forlornities had all disappeared; so we gathered around the lamp, after supper, with our beer and my pipe, and in a condition of grateful snugness tackled the new magazines. I read your new story aloud, amid thunders of applause, and we all agreed that Captain Jenness and the old man with the accordion-hat are lovely people and most skillfully drawn--and that cabin-boy, too, we like. Of course we are all glad the girl is gone to Venice--for there is no place like Venice. Now I easily understand that the old man couldn't go, because you have a purpose in sending Lyddy by herself: but you could send the old man over in another ship, and we particularly want him along. Suppose you don't need him there? What of that? Can't you let him feed the doves? Can't you let him fall in the canal occasionally? Can't you let his good-natured purse be a daily prey to guides and beggar-boys? Can't you let him find peace and rest and fellowship under Pere Jacopo's kindly wing? (However, you are writing the book, not I--still, I am one of the people you are writing it for, you understand.) I only want to insist, in a friendly way, that the old man shall shed his sweet influence frequently upon the page--that is all.

The first time we called at the convent, Pere Jacopo was absent; the next (Just at this moment Miss Spaulding spoke up and said something about Pere Jacopo--there is more in this acting of one mind upon another than people think) time, he was there, and gave us preserved rose-leaves to eat, and talked about you, and Mrs. Howells, and Winnie, and brought out his photographs, and showed us a picture of "the library of your new house," but not so--it was the study in your Cambridge house. He was very sweet and good. He called on us next day; the day after that we left Venice, after a pleasant sojourn Of 3 or 4 weeks. He expects to spend this winter in Munich and will see us often, he said.

Pretty soon, I am going to write something, and when I finish it I shall know whether to put it to itself or in the "Contributors' Club." That "Contributors' Club" was a most happy idea. By the way, I think that the man who wrote the paragraph beginning at the bottom of page 643 has said a mighty sound and sensible thing. I wish his suggestion could be adopted.

It is lovely of you to keep that old pipe in such a place of honor.

While it occurs to me, I must tell you Susie's last. She is sorely badgered with dreams; and her stock dream is that she is being eaten up by bears. She is a grave and thoughtful child, as you will remember. Last night she had the usual dream. This morning she stood apart (after telling it,) for some time, looking vacantly at the floor, and absorbed in meditation. At last she looked up, and with the pathos of one who feels he has not been dealt by with even-handed fairness, said "But Mamma, the trouble is, that I am never the bear, but always the person."

It would not have occurred to me that there might be an advantage, even in a dream, in occasionally being the eater, instead of always the party eaten, but I easily perceived that her point was well taken.

I'm sending to Heidelberg for your letter and Winnie's, and I do hope they haven't been lost.

My wife and I send love to you all. Yrs ever, MARK.

The Howells story, running at this time in the Atlantic, and so much enjoyed by the Clemens party, was "The Lady of the Aroostook." The suggestions made for enlarging the part of the "old man" are eminently characteristic.

Mark Twain's forty-third birthday came in Munich, and in his letter conveying this fact to his mother we get a brief added outline of the daily life in that old Bavarian city. Certainly, it would seem to have been a quieter and more profitable existence than he had known amid the confusion of things left behind in, America.

To Mrs. Jane Clemens and Mrs. Moffett, in America:

No. 1a Karlstrasse, Dec. 1, MUNICH. 1878. MY DEAR MOTHER AND SISTER,--I broke the back of life yesterday and started down-hill toward old age. This fact has not produced any effect upon me that I can detect.

I suppose we are located here for the winter. I have a pleasant work- room a mile from here where I do my writing. The walk to and from that place gives me what exercise I need, and all I take. We staid three weeks in Venice, a week in Florence, a fortnight in Rome, and arrived here a couple of weeks ago. Livy and Miss Spaulding are studying drawing and German, and the children have a German day-governess. I cannot see but that the children speak German as well as they do English.

Susie often translates Livy's orders to the servants. I cannot work and study German at the same time: so I have dropped the latter, and do not even read the language, except in the morning paper to get the news.

We have all pretty good health, latterly, and have seldom had to call the doctor. The children have been in the open air pretty constantly for months now. In Venice they were on the water in the gondola most of the time, and were great friends with our gondolier; and in Rome and Florence they had long daily tramps, for Rosa is a famous hand to smell out the sights of a strange place. Here they wander less extensively.

The family all join in love to you all and to Orion and Mollie. Affly Your son SAM.

XIX.

LETTERS 1879. RETURN TO AMERICA. THE GREAT GRANT REUNION

Life went on very well in Munich. Each day the family fell more in love with Fraulein Dahlweiner and her house.

Mark Twain, however, did not settle down to his work readily. His "pleasant work-room" provided exercise, but no inspiration. When he discovered he could not find his Swiss note-book he was ready to give up his travel-writing altogether. In the letter that follows we find him much less enthusiastic concerning his own performances than over the story by Howells, which he was following in the Atlantic.

The "detective" chapter mentioned in this letter was not included in 'A Tramp Abroad.' It was published separately, as 'The Stolen White Elephant' in a volume bearing that title. The play, which he had now found "dreadfully witless and flat," was no other than "Simon Wheeler, Detective," which he had once regarded so highly. The "Stewart" referred to was the millionaire merchant, A. T. Stewart, whose body was stolen in the expectation of reward.

To W. D. Howells, in Boston:

MUNICH, Jan. 21, (1879) MY DEAR HOWELLS,--It's no use, your letter miscarried in some way and is lost. The consul has made a thorough search and says he has not been able to trace it. It is unaccountable, for all the letters I did not want arrived without a single grateful failure. Well, I have read-up, now, as far as you have got, that is, to where there's a storm at sea approaching,--and we three think you are clear, out-Howellsing Howells. If your literature has not struck perfection now we are not able to see what is lacking. It is all such truth--truth to the life; every where your pen falls it leaves a photograph. I did imagine that everything had been said about life at sea that could be said, but no matter, it was all a failure and lies, nothing but lies with a thin varnish of fact,--only you have stated it as it absolutely is. And only you see people and their ways, and their insides and outsides as they are, and make them talk as they do talk. I think you are the very greatest artist in these tremendous mysteries that ever lived. There doesn't seem to be anything that can be concealed from your awful all-seeing eye. It must be a cheerful thing for one to live with you and be aware that you are going up and down in him like another conscience all the time. Possibly you will not be a fully accepted classic until you have been dead a hundred years,--it is the fate of the Shakespeares and of all genuine prophets, --but then your books will be as common as Bibles, I believe. You're not a weed, but an oak; not a summer-house, but a cathedral. In that day I shall still be in the Cyclopedias, too, thus: "Mark Twain; history and occupation unknown--but he was personally acquainted with Howells." There--I could sing your praises all day, and feel and believe every bit of it.

My book is half finished; I wish to heaven it was done. I have given up writing a detective novel--can't write a novel, for I lack the faculty; but when the detectives were nosing around after Stewart's loud remains, I threw a chapter into my present book in which I have very extravagantly burlesqued the detective business--if it is possible to burlesque that business extravagantly. You know I was going to send you that detective play, so that you could re-write it. Well I didn't do it because I couldn't find a single idea in it that could be useful to you. It was dreadfully witless and flat. I knew it would sadden you and unfit you for work.

I have always been sorry we threw up that play embodying Orion which you began. It was a mistake to do that. Do keep that MS and tackle it again. It will work out all right; you will see. I don't believe that that character exists in literature in so well-developed a condition as it exists in Orion's person. Now won't you put Orion in a story? Then he will go handsomely into a play afterwards. How deliciously you could paint him--it would make fascinating reading--the sort that makes a reader laugh and cry at the same time, for Orion is as good and ridiculous a soul as ever was.

Ah, to think of Bayard Taylor! It is too sad to talk about. I was so glad there was not a single sting and so many good praiseful words in the Atlantic's criticism of Deukalion. Love to you all
Yrs Ever MARK

We remain here till middle of March.

In 'A Tramp Abroad' there is an incident in which the author describes himself as hunting for a lost sock in the dark, in a vast hotel bedroom at Heilbronn. The account of the real incident, as written to Twichell, seems even more amusing.

The "Yarn About the Limburger Cheese and the Box of Guns," like "The Stolen White Elephant," did not find place in the travel-book, but was published in the same volume with the elephant story, added to the rambling notes of "An Idle Excursion."

With the discovery of the Swiss note-book, work with Mark Twain was going better. His letter reflects his enthusiasm.

To Rev. J. H. Twichell, in Hartford:

MUNICH, Jan 26 '79. DEAR OLD JOE,--Sunday. Your delicious letter arrived exactly at the right time. It was laid by my plate as I was finishing breakfast at 12 noon. Livy and Clara, (Spaulding) arrived from church 5 minutes later; I took a pipe and spread myself out on the sofa, and Livy sat by and read, and I warmed to that butcher the moment he began to swear. There is more than one way of praying, and I like the butcher's way because the petitioner is so apt to be in earnest. I was peculiarly alive to his performance just at this time, for another reason, to wit: Last night I awoke at 3 this morning, and after raging to my self for 2 interminable hours, I gave it up. I rose, assumed a catlike stealthiness, to keep from waking Livy, and proceeded to dress in the pitch dark. Slowly but surely I got on garment after garment--all down to one sock; I had one slipper on and the other in my hand. Well, on my hands and knees I crept softly around, pawing and feeling and scooping along the carpet, and among chair-legs for that missing sock; I kept that up; and still kept it up and kept it up. At first I only said to myself, "Blame that sock," but that soon ceased to answer; my expletives grew steadily stronger and stronger,--and at last, when I found I was lost, I had to sit flat down on the floor and take hold of something to keep from lifting the roof off with the profane explosion that was trying to get out of me. I could see the dim blur of the window, but of course it was in the wrong place and could give me no information as to where I was. But I had one comfort --I had not waked Livy; I believed I could find that sock in silence if the night lasted long enough. So I started again and softly pawed all over the place,--and sure enough at the end of half an hour I laid my hand on the missing article. I rose joyfully up and butted the wash-bowl and pitcher off the stand and simply raised----so to speak. Livy screamed, then said, "Who is that? what is the matter?" I said "There ain't anything the matter--I'm hunting for my sock." She said, "Are you hunting for it with a club?"

I went in the parlor and lit the lamp, and gradually the fury subsided and the ridiculous features of the thing began to suggest themselves. So I lay on the sofa, with note-book and pencil, and transferred the adventure to our big room in the hotel at Heilbronn, and got it on paper a good deal to my satisfaction.

I found the Swiss note-book, some time ago. When it was first lost I was glad of it, for I was getting an idea that I had lost my faculty of writing sketches of travel; therefore the loss of that note-book would render the writing of this one simply impossible, and let me gracefully out; I was about to write to Bliss and propose some other book, when the confounded thing turned up, and down went my heart into my boots. But there was now no excuse, so I went solidly to work--tore up a great part of the MS written in Heidelberg,--wrote and tore up,--continued to write and tear up,--and at last, reward of patient and noble persistence, my pen got the old swing again!

Since then I'm glad Providence knew better what to do with the Swiss note-book than I did, for I like my work, now, exceedingly, and often turn out over 30 MS pages a day and then quit sorry that Heaven makes the days so short.

One of my discouragements had been the belief that my interest in this tour had been so slender that I couldn't gouge matter enough out of it to make a book. What a mistake. I've got 900 pages written (not a word in it about the sea voyage) yet I stepped my foot out of Heidelberg for the first time yesterday,--and then only to take our party of four on our first pedestrian tour--to Heilbronn. I've got them dressed elaborately in walking costume--knapsacks, canteens, field-glasses, leather leggings, patent walking shoes, muslin folds around their hats, with long tails hanging down behind, sun umbrellas, and Alpenstocks. They go all the way to Wimpfen by rail-thence to Heilbronn in a chance vegetable cart drawn by a donkey and a cow; I shall fetch them home on a raft; and if other people shall perceive that that was no pedestrian excursion, they themselves shall not be conscious of it.--This trip will take 100 pages or more,--oh, goodness knows how many! for the mood is everything, not the material, and I already seem to see 300 pages rising before me on that trip. Then, I propose to leave Heidelberg for good. Don't you see, the book (1800 MS pages,) may really be finished before I ever get to Switzerland?

But there's one thing; I want to tell Frank Bliss and his father to be charitable toward me in,--that is, let me tear up all the MS I want to, and give me time to write more. I shan't waste the time--I haven't the slightest desire to loaf, but a consuming desire to work, ever since I got back my swing. And you see this book is either going to be compared with the Innocents Abroad, or contrasted with it, to my disadvantage. I think I can make a book that will be no dead corpse of a thing and I mean to do my level best to accomplish that.

My crude plans are crystalizing. As the thing stands now, I went to Europe for three purposes.

The first you know, and must keep secret, even from the Blisses; the second is to study Art; and the third to acquire a critical knowledge of the German language. My MS already shows that the two latter objects are accomplished. It shows that I am moving about as an Artist and a Philologist, and unaware that there is any immodesty in assuming these titles. Having three definite objects has had the effect of seeming to enlarge my domain and give me the freedom of a loose costume. It is three strings to my bow, too.

Well, your butcher is magnificent. He won't stay out of my mind.--I keep trying to think of some way of getting your account of him into my book without his being offended--and yet confound him there isn't anything you have said which he would see any offense in,--I'm only thinking of his friends--they are the parties who busy themselves with seeing things for people. But I'm bound to have him in. I'm putting in the yarn about the Limburger cheese and the box of guns, too--mighty glad Howells declined it. It seems to gather richness and flavor with age. I have very nearly killed several companies with that narrative,--the American Artists Club, here, for instance, and Smith and wife and Miss Griffith (they were here in this house a week or two.) I've got other chapters that pretty nearly destroyed the same parties, too.

O, Switzerland! the further it recedes into the enriching haze of time, the more intolerably delicious the charm of it and the cheer of it and the glory and majesty and solemnity and pathos of it grow. Those mountains had a soul; they thought; they spoke,--one couldn't hear it with the ears of the body, but what a voice it was!--and how real. Deep down in my memory it is sounding yet. Alp calleth unto Alp!--that stately old Scriptural wording is the right one for God's Alps and God's ocean. How puny we were in that awful presence--and how painless it was to be so; how fitting and right it seemed, and how stingless was the sense of our unspeakable insignificance. And Lord how pervading were the repose and peace and blessedness that poured out of the heart of the invisible Great Spirit of the Mountains.

Now what is it? There are mountains and mountains and mountains in this world--but only these take you by the heart-strings. I wonder what the secret of it is. Well, time and time again it has seemed to me that I must drop everything and flee to Switzerland once more. It is a longing --a deep, strong, tugging longing--that is the word. We must go again, Joe.--October days, let us get up at dawn and breakfast at the tower. I should like that first rate.

Livy and all of us send deluges of love to you and Harmony and all the children. I dreamed last night that I woke up in the library at home and your children were frolicing around me and Julia was sitting in my lap; you and Harmony and both families of Warners had finished their welcomes and were filing out through the conservatory door, wrecking Patrick's flower pots with their dress skirts as they went. Peace and plenty abide with you all! MARK.

I want the Blisses to know their part of this letter, if possible. They will see that my delay was not from choice.

Following the life of Mark Twain, whether through his letters or along the sequence of detailed occurrence, we are never more than a little while, or a little distance, from his brother Orion. In one form or another Orion is ever present, his inquiries, his proposals, his suggestions, his plans for improving his own fortunes, command our attention. He was one of the most human creatures that ever lived; indeed, his humanity excluded every form of artificiality-- everything that needs to be acquired. Talented, trusting, child- like, carried away by the impulse of the moment, despite a keen sense of humor he was never able to see that his latest plan or project was not bound to succeed. Mark Twain loved him, pitied him --also enjoyed him, especially with Howells. Orion's new plan to lecture in the interest of religion found its way to Munich, with the following result:

To W. D. Howells, in Boston:

MUNICH, Feb. 9. (1879) MY DEAR HOWELLS,--I have just received this letter from Orion-- take care of it, for it is worth preserving. I got as far as 9 pages in my answer to it, when Mrs. Clemens shut down on it, and said it was cruel, and made me send the money and simply wish his lecture success. I said I couldn't lose my 9 pages--so she said send them to you. But I will acknowledge that I thought I was writing a very kind letter.

Now just look at this letter of Orion's. Did you ever see the grotesquely absurd and the heart-breakingly pathetic more closely joined together? Mrs. Clemens said "Raise his monthly pension." So I wrote to Perkins to raise it a trifle.

Now only think of it! He still has 100 pages to write on his lecture, yet in one inking of his pen he has already swooped around the United States and invested the result!

You must put him in a book or a play right away. You are the only man capable of doing it. You might die at any moment, and your very greatest work would be lost to the world. I could write Orion's simple biography, and make it effective, too, by merely stating the bald facts--and this I will do if he dies before I do; but you must put him into romance. This was the understanding you and I had the day I sailed.

Observe Orion's career--that is, a little of it: (1) He has belonged to as many as five different religious denominations; last March he withdrew from the deaconship in a Congregational Church and the Superintendency of its Sunday School, in a speech in which he said that for many months (it runs in my mind that he said 13 years,) he had been a confirmed infidel, and so felt it to be his duty to retire from the flock.

2. After being a republican for years, he wanted me to buy him a democratic newspaper. A few days before the Presidential election, he came out in a speech and publicly went over to the democrats; he prudently "hedged" by voting for 6 state republicans, also.

The new convert was made one of the secretaries of the democratic meeting, and placed in the list of speakers. He wrote me jubilantly of what a ten-strike he was going to make with that speech. All right--but think of his innocent and pathetic candor in writing me something like this, a week later:

"I was more diffident than I had expected to be, and this was increased by the silence with which I was received when I came forward; so I seemed unable to get the fire into my speech which I had calculated upon, and presently they began to get up and go out; and in a few minutes they all rose up and went away."

How could a man uncover such a sore as that and show it to another? Not a word of complaint, you see--only a patient, sad surprise.

3. His next project was to write a burlesque upon Paradise Lost.

4. Then, learning that the Times was paying Harte $100 a column for stories, he concluded to write some for the same price. I read his first one and persuaded him not to write any more.

5. Then he read proof on the N. Y. Eve. Post at $10 a week and meekly observed that the foreman swore at him and ordered him around "like a steamboat mate."

6. Being discharged from that post, he wanted to try agriculture--was sure he could make a fortune out of a chicken farm. I gave him $900 and he went to a ten-house village a miles above Keokuk on the river bank-- this place was a railway station. He soon asked for money to buy a horse and light wagon,--because the trains did not run at church time on Sunday and his wife found it rather far to walk.

For a long time I answered demands for "loans" and by next mail always received his check for the interest due me to date. In the most guileless way he let it leak out that he did not underestimate the value of his custom to me, since it was not likely that any other customer of mine paid his interest quarterly, and this enabled me to use my capital twice in 6 months instead of only once. But alas, when the debt at last reached $1800 or $2500 (I have forgotten which) the interest ate too formidably into his borrowings, and so he quietly ceased to pay it or speak of it. At the end of two years I found that the chicken farm had long ago been abandoned, and he had moved into Keokuk. Later in one of his casual moments, he observed that there was no money in fattening a chicken on 65 cents worth of corn and then selling it for 50.

7. Finally, if I would lend him $500 a year for two years, (this was 4 or 5 years ago,) he knew he could make a success as a lawyer, and would prove it. This is the pension which we have just increased to $600. The first year his legal business brought him $5. It also brought him an unremunerative case where some villains were trying to chouse some negro orphans out of $700. He still has this case. He has waggled it around through various courts and made some booming speeches on it. The negro children have grown up and married off, now, I believe, and their litigated town-lot has been dug up and carted off by somebody--but Orion still infests the courts with his documents and makes the welkin ring with his venerable case. The second year, he didn't make anything. The third he made $6, and I made Bliss put a case in his hands--about half an hour's work. Orion charged $50 for it--Bliss paid him $15. Thus four or five years of laving has brought him $26, but this will doubtless be increased when he gets done lecturing and buys that "law library." Meantime his office rent has been $60 a year, and he has stuck to that lair day by

day as patiently as a spider.

8. Then he by and by conceived the idea of lecturing around America as "Mark Twain's Brother"--that to be on the bills. Subject of proposed lecture, "On the, Formation of Character."

9. I protested, and he got on his warpaint, couched his lance, and ran a bold tilt against total abstinence and the Red Ribbon fanatics. It raised a fine row among the virtuous Keokukians.

10. I wrote to encourage him in his good work, but I had let a mail intervene; so by the time my letter reached him he was already winning laurels as a Red Ribbon Howler.

11. Afterward he took a rabid part in a prayer-meeting epidemic; dropped that to travesty Jules Verne; dropped that, in the middle of the last chapter, last March, to digest the matter of an infidel book which he proposed to write; and now he comes to the surface to rescue our "noble and beautiful religion" from the sacrilegious talons of Bob Ingersoll.

Now come! Don't fool away this treasure which Providence has laid at your feet, but take it up and use it. One can let his imagination run riot in portraying Orion, for there is nothing so extravagant as to be out of character with him.

Well-good-bye, and a short life and a merry one be yours. Poor old Methusaleh, how did he manage to stand it so long? Yrs ever, MARK.

To Orion Clemens (Unsent and inclosed with the foregoing, to W. D. Howells):

MUNICH, Feb. 9, (1879) MY DEAR BRO.,--Yours has just arrived. I enclose a draft on Hartford for $25. You will have abandoned the project you wanted it for, by the time it arrives,-- but no matter, apply it to your newer and present project, whatever it is. You see I have an ineradicable faith in your unsteadfastness,--but mind you, I didn't invent that faith, you conferred it on me yourself. But fire away, fire away! I don't see why a changeable man shouldn't get as much enjoyment out of his changes, and transformations and transfigurations as a steadfast man gets out of standing still and pegging at the same old monotonous thing all the time. That is to say, I don't see why a kaleidoscope shouldn't enjoy itself as much as a telescope, nor a grindstone have as good a time as a whetstone, nor a barometer as good a time as a yardstick. I don't feel like girding at you any more about fickleness of purpose, because I recognize and realize at last that it is incurable; but before I learned to accept this truth, each new weekly project of yours possessed the power of throwing me into the most exhausting and helpless convulsions of profanity. But fire away, now! Your magic has lost its might. I am able to view your inspirations dispassionately and judicially, now, and say "This one or that one or the other one is not up to your average flight, or is above it, or below it."

And so, without passion, or prejudice, or bias of any kind, I sit in judgment upon your lecture project, and say it was up to your average, it was indeed above it, for it had possibilities in it, and even practical ones. While I was not sorry you abandoned it, I should not be sorry if you had stuck to it and given it a trial. But on the whole you did the wise thing to lay it aside, I think, because a lecture is a most easy thing to fail in; and at your time of life, and in your own town, such a failure would make a deep and cruel wound in your heart and in your pride. It was decidedly unwise in you to think for a moment of coming before a community who knew you, with such a course of lectures; because Keokuk is not unaware that you have been a Swedenborgian, a Presbyterian, a Congregationalist, and a Methodist (on probation), and that just a year ago you were an infidel. If Keokuk had gone to your lecture course, it would have gone to be amused, not instructed, for when a man is known to have no settled convictions of his own he can't convince other people. They would have gone to be amused and that would have been a deep humiliation to you. It could have been safe for you to appear only where you were unknown--then many of your hearers would think you were in earnest. And they would be right. You are in earnest while your convictions are new. But taking it by and large, you probably did best to discard that project altogether. But I leave you to judge of that, for you are the worst judge I know of.

(Unfinished.)

That Mark Twain in many ways was hardly less child-like than his brother is now and again revealed in his letters. He was of steadfast purpose, and he possessed the driving power which Orion Clemens lacked; but the importance to him of some of the smaller matters of life, as shown in a letter like the following, bespeaks a certain simplicity of nature which he never outgrew:

To Rev. J. H. Twichell, in Hartford:

MUNICH, Feb. 24. (1879) DEAR OLD JOE,--It was a mighty good letter, Joe--and that idea of yours is a rattling good one. But I have not sot down here to answer your letter,--for it is down at my study,--but only to impart some information.

For a months I had not shaved without crying. I'd spend 3/4 of an hour whetting away on my hand--no use, couldn't get an edge. Tried a razor strop-same result. So I sat down and put in an hour thinking out the mystery. Then it seemed plain--to wit: my hand can't give a razor an edge, it can only smooth and refine an edge that has already been given. I judge that a razor fresh from the hone is this shape V--the long point being the continuation of the edge--and that after much use the shape is this V--the attenuated edge all worn off and gone. By George I knew that was the explanation. And I knew that a freshly honed and freshly strapped razor won't cut, but after strapping on the hand as a final operation, it will cut.--So I sent out for an oil-stone; none to be had, but messenger brought back a little piece of rock the size of a Safety- match box--(it was bought in a shoemaker's shop) bad flaw in middle of it, too, but I put 4 drops of fine Olive oil on it, picked out the razor marked "Thursday" because it was never any account and would be no loss if I spoiled it--gave it a brisk and reckless honing for 10 minutes, then tried it on a hair--it wouldn't cut. Then I trotted it through a vigorous 20-minute course on a razor-strap and tried it on a hair-it wouldn't cut--tried it on my face--it made me cry--gave it a 5-minute stropping on my hand, and my land, what an edge she had! We thought we knew what sharp razors were when we were tramping in Switzerland, but it was a mistake--they were dull beside this old Thursday razor of mine-- which I mean to name Thursday October Christian, in gratitude. I took my whetstone, and in 20 minutes I put two more of my razors in splendid condition--but I leave them in the box--I never use any but Thursday O. C., and shan't till its edge is gone--and then I'll know how to restore it without any delay.

We all go to Paris next Thursday--address, Monroe & Co., Bankers. With love Ys Ever MARK.

In Paris they found pleasant quarters at the Hotel Normandy, but it was a chilly, rainy spring, and the travelers gained a rather poor impression of the French capital. Mark Twain's work did not go well, at first, because of the noises of the street. But then he found a quieter corner in the hotel and made better progress. In a brief note to Aldrich he said: "I sleep like a lamb and write like a lion--I mean the kind of a lion that writes--if any such." He expected to finish the book in six weeks; that is to say, before returning to America. He was looking after its illustrations himself, and a letter to Frank Bliss, of The American Publishing Company, refers to the frontpiece, which, from time to time, has caused question as to its origin. To Bliss he says: "It is a thing which I manufactured by pasting a popular comic picture into the middle of a celebrated Biblical one--shall attribute it to Titian. It needs to be engraved by a master."

The weather continued bad in France and they left there in July to find it little better in England. They had planned a journey to Scotland to visit Doctor Brown, whose health was not very good. In after years Mark Twain blamed himself harshly for not making the trip, which he declared would have meant so much to Mrs. Clemens. He had forgotten by that time the real reasons for not going--the continued storms and uncertainty of trains (which made it barely possible for them to reach Liverpool in time for their sailing- date), and with characteristic self-reproach vowed that only perversity and obstinacy on his part had prevented the journey to Scotland. From Liverpool, on the eve of sailing, he sent Doctor Brown a good-by word.

To Dr. John Brown, in Edinburgh:

WASHINGTON HOTEL, LIME STREET, LIVERPOOL. Aug. (1879) MY DEAR MR. BROWN,--During all the 15 months we have been spending on the continent, we have been promising ourselves a sight of you as our latest and most prized delight in a foreign land--but our hope has failed, our plan has miscarried. One obstruction after another intruded itself, and our short sojourn of three or four weeks on English soil was thus frittered gradually away, and we were at last obliged to give up the idea of seeing you at all. It is a great disappointment, for we wanted to show you how much "Megalopis" has grown (she is 7 now) and what a fine creature her sister is, and how prettily they both speak German. There are six persons in my party, and they are as difficult to cart around as nearly any other menagerie would be. My wife and Miss Spaulding are along, and you may imagine how they take to heart this failure of our long promised Edinburgh trip. We never even wrote you, because we were always so sure, from day to day, that our affairs would finally so shape themselves as to let us get to Scotland. But no,--everything went wrong we had only flying trips here and there in place of the leisurely ones which we had planned.

We arrived in Liverpool an hour ago very tired, and have halted at this hotel (by the advice of misguided friends)--and if my instinct and experience are worth anything, it is the very worst hotel on earth, without any exception. We shall move to another hotel early in the morning to spend tomorrow. We sail for America next day in the "Gallic."

We all join in the sincerest love to you, and in the kindest remembrance to "Jock"--[Son of Doctor Brown.]--and your sister. Truly yours, S. L. CLEMENS.

It was September 3, 1879, that Mark Twain returned to America by the steamer Gallic. In the seventeen months of his absence he had taken on a "traveled look" and had added gray hairs. A New York paper said of his arrival that he looked older than when he went to Germany, and that his hair had turned quite gray.

Mark Twain had not finished his book of travel in Paris--in fact, it seemed to him far from complete--and he settled down rather grimly to work on it at Quarry Farm. When, after a few days no word of greeting came from Howells, Clemens wrote to ask if he were dead or only sleeping. Howells hastily sent a line to say that he had been sleeping "The sleep of a torpid conscience. I will feign that I did not know where to write you; but I love you and all of yours, and I am tremendously glad that you are home again. When and where shall we meet? Have you come home with your pockets full of Atlantic papers?" Clemens, toiling away at his book, was, as usual, not without the prospect of other plans. Orion, as literary material, never failed to excite him.

To W. D. Howells, in Boston:

ELMIRA, Sept. 15, 1879. MY DEAR HOWELLS,--When and where? Here on the farm would be an elegant place to meet, but of course you cannot come so far. So we will say Hartford or Belmont, about the beginning of November. The date of our return to Hartford is uncertain, but will be three or four weeks hence, I judge. I hope to finish my book here before migrating.

I think maybe I've got some Atlantic stuff in my head, but there's none in MS, I believe.

Say--a friend of mine wants to write a play with me, I to furnish the broad-comedy cuss. I don't know anything about his ability, but his letter serves to remind me of our old projects. If you haven't used Orion or Old Wakeman, don't you think you and I can get together and grind out a play with one of those fellows in it? Orion is a field which grows richer and richer the more he mulches it with each new top-dressing of religion or other guano. Drop me an immediate line about this, won't you? I imagine I see Orion on the stage, always gentle, always melancholy, always changing his politics and religion, and trying to reform the world, always inventing something, and losing a limb by a new kind of explosion at the end of each of the four acts. Poor old chap, he is good material. I can imagine his wife or his sweetheart reluctantly adopting each of his new religious in turn, just in time to see him waltz into the next one and leave her isolated once more.

(Mem. Orion's wife has followed him into the outer darkness, after 30 years' rabid membership in the Presbyterian Church.)

Well, with the sincerest and most abounding love to you and yours, from all this family, I am, Yrs ever MARK.

The idea of the play interested Howells, but he had twinges of conscience in the matter of using Orion as material. He wrote: "More than once I have taken the skeleton of that comedy of ours and viewed it with tears..... I really have a compunction or two about helping to put your brother into drama. You can say that he is your brother, to do what you like with him, but the alien hand might inflict an incurable hurt on his tender heart."

As a matter of fact, Orion Clemens had a keen appreciation of his own shortcomings, and would have enjoyed himself in a play as much as any observer of it. Indeed, it is more than likely that he would have been pleased at the thought of such distinguished dramatization. From the next letter one might almost conclude that he had received a hint of this plan, and was bent upon supplying rich material.

To W. D. Howells, in Boston:

ELMIRA, Oct. 9 '79. MY DEAR HOWELLS,--Since my return, the mail facilities have enabled Orion to keep me informed as to his intentions. Twenty-eight days ago it was his purpose to complete a work aimed at religion, the preface to which he had already written. Afterward he began to sell off his furniture, with the idea of hurrying to Leadville and tackling silver-mining--threw up his law den and took in his sign. Then he wrote to Chicago and St. Louis newspapers asking for a situation as "paragrapher"--enclosing a taste of his quality in the shape of two stanzas of "humorous rhymes." By a later mail on the same day he applied to New York and Hartford insurance companies for copying to do.

However, it would take too long to detail all his projects. They comprise a removal to south-west Missouri; application for a reporter's berth on a Keokuk paper; application for a compositor's berth on a St. Louis paper; a re-hanging of his attorney's sign, "though it only creaks and catches no flies;" but last night's letter informs me that he has retackled the religious question, hired a distant den to write in, applied to my mother for $50 to re-buy his furniture, which has advanced in value since the sale--purposes buying $25 worth of books necessary to his labors which he had previously been borrowing, and his first chapter is already on its way to me for my decision as to whether it has enough ungodliness in it or not. Poor Orion!

Your letter struck me while I was meditating a project to beguile you, and John Hay and Joe Twichell, into a descent upon Chicago which I dream of making, to witness the re-union of the great Commanders of the Western Army Corps on the 9th of next month. My sluggish soul needs a fierce upstirring, and if it would not get it when Grant enters the meeting place I must doubtless "lay" for the final resurrection. Can you and Hay go? At the same time, confound it, I doubt if I can go myself, for this book isn't done yet. But I would give a heap to be there. I mean to heave some holiness into the Hartford primaries when I go back; and if there was a solitary office in the land which majestic ignorance and incapacity, coupled with purity of heart, could fill, I would run for it. This naturally reminds me of Bret Harte--but let him pass.

We propose to leave here for New York Oct. 21, reaching Hartford 24th or 25th. If, upon reflection, you Howellses find, you can stop over here on your way, I wish you would do it, and telegraph me. Getting pretty hungry to see you. I had an idea that this was your shortest way home, but like as not my geography is crippled again--it usually is. Yrs ever MARK.

The "Reunion of the Great Commanders," mentioned in the foregoing, was a welcome to General Grant after his journey around the world. Grant's trip had been one continuous ovation--a triumphal march. In '79 most of his old commanders were still alive, and they had planned to assemble in Chicago to do him honor. A Presidential year was coming on, but if there was anything political in the project there were no surface indications. Mark Twain, once a Confederate soldier, had long since been completely "desouthernized"--at least to the point where he felt that the sight of old comrades paying tribute to the Union commander would stir his blood as perhaps it had not been stirred, even in that earlier time, when that same commander had chased him through the Missouri swamps. Grant, indeed, had long since become a hero to Mark Twain, though it is highly unlikely that Clemens favored the idea of a third term. Some days following the preceding letter an invitation came for him to be present at the Chicago reunion; but by this time he had decided not to go. The letter he wrote has been preserved.

To Gen. William E. Strong, in Chicago:

FARMINGTON AVENUE, HARTFORD. Oct. 28, 1879. GEN. WM. E. STRONG, CH'M, AND GENTLEMEN OF THE COMMITTEE:

I have been hoping during several weeks that it might be my good fortune to receive an invitation to be present on that great occasion in Chicago; but now that my desire is accomplished my business matters have so shaped themselves as to bar me from being so far from home in the first half of November. It is with supreme regret that I lost this chance, for I have not had a thorough stirring up for some years, and I judged that if I could be in the banqueting hall and see and hear the veterans of the Army of the Tennessee at the moment that their old commander entered the room, or rose in his place to speak, my system would get the kind of upheaval it needs. General Grant's progress across the continent is of the marvelous nature of the returning Napoleon's progress from Grenoble to Paris; and as the crowning spectacle in the one case was the meeting with the Old Guard, so, likewise, the crowning spectacle in the other will be our great captain's meeting with his Old Guard--and that is the very climax which I wanted to witness.

Besides, I wanted to see the General again, any way, and renew the acquaintance. He would remember me, because I was the person who did not ask him for an office. However, I consume your time, and also wander from the point--which is, to thank you for the courtesy of your invitation, and yield up my seat at the table to some other guest who may possibly grace it better, but will certainly not appreciate its privileges more, than I should. With great respect, I am, Gentlemen, Very truly yours, S. L. CLEMENS.

Private:--I beg to apologize for my delay, gentlemen, but the card of invitation went to Elmira, N.

Y. and hence has only just now reached me.

This letter was not sent. He reconsidered and sent an acceptance, agreeing to speak, as the committee had requested. Certainly there was something picturesque in the idea of the Missouri private who had been chased for a rainy fortnight through the swamps of Ralls County being selected now to join in welcome to his ancient enemy.

The great reunion was to be something more than a mere banquet. It would continue for several days, with processions, great assemblages, and much oratory.

Mark Twain arrived in Chicago in good season to see it all. Three letters to Mrs. Clemens intimately present his experiences: his enthusiastic enjoyment and his own personal triumph.

The first was probably written after the morning of his arrival. The Doctor Jackson in it was Dr. A. Reeves Jackson, the guide- dismaying "Doctor" of Innocents Abroad.

To Mrs. Clemens, in Hartford:

PALMER HOUSE, CHICAGO, Nov. 11. Livy darling, I am getting a trifle leg-weary. Dr. Jackson called and dragged me out of bed at noon, yesterday, and then went off. I went down stairs and was introduced to some scores of people, and among them an elderly German gentleman named Raster, who said his wife owed her life to me--hurt in Chicago fire and lay menaced with death a long time, but the Innocents Abroad kept her mind in a cheerful attitude, and so, with the doctor's help for the body she pulled through.... They drove me to Dr. Jackson's and I had an hour's visit with Mrs. Jackson. Started to walk down Michigan Avenue, got a few steps on my way and met an erect, soldierly looking young gentleman who offered his hand; said, "Mr. Clemens, I believe--I wish to introduce myself--you were pointed out to me yesterday as I was driving down street--my name is Grant."

"Col. Fred Grant?"

"Yes. My house is not ten steps away, and I would like you to come and have a talk and a pipe, and let me introduce my wife."

So we turned back and entered the house next to Jackson's and talked something more than an hour and smoked many pipes and had a sociable good time. His wife is very gentle and intelligent and pretty, and they have a cunning little girl nearly as big as Bay but only three years old. They wanted me to come in and spend an evening, after the banquet, with them and Gen. Grant, after this grand pow-wow is over, but I said I was going home Friday. Then they asked me to come Friday afternoon, when they and the general will receive a few friends, and I said I would. Col. Grant said he and Gen. Sherman used the Innocents Abroad as their guide book when they were on their travels.

I stepped in next door and took Dr. Jackson to the hotel and we played billiards from 7 to 11.30

P.M. and then went to a beer-mill to meet some twenty Chicago journalists--talked, sang songs and made speeches till 6 o'clock this morning. Nobody got in the least degree "under the influence," and we had a pleasant time. Read awhile in bed, slept till 11, shaved, went to breakfast at noon, and by mistake got into the servants' hall. I remained there and breakfasted with twenty or thirty male and female servants, though I had a table to myself.

A temporary structure, clothed and canopied with flags, has been erected at the hotel front, and connected with the second-story windows of a drawing-room. It was for Gen. Grant to stand on and review the procession. Sixteen persons, besides reporters, had tickets for this place, and a seventeenth was issued for me. I was there, looking down on the packed and struggling crowd when Gen. Grant came forward and was saluted by the cheers of the multitude and the waving of ladies' handkerchiefs--for the windows and roofs of all neighboring buildings were massed full of life. Gen. Grant bowed to the people two or three times, then approached my side of the platform and the mayor pulled me forward and introduced me. It was dreadfully conspicuous. The General said a word or so--I replied, and then said, "But I'll step back, General, I don't want to interrupt your speech."

"But I'm not going to make any--stay where you are--I'll get you to make it for me."

General Sherman came on the platform wearing the uniform of a full General, and you should have heard the cheers. Gen. Logan was going to introduce me, but I didn't want any more conspicuousness.

When the head of the procession passed it was grand to see Sheridan, in his military cloak and his plumed chapeau, sitting as erect and rigid as a statue on his immense black horse--by far the most martial figure I ever saw. And the crowd roared again.

It was chilly, and Gen. Deems lent me his overcoat until night. He came a few minutes ago--5.45 P.M., and got it, but brought Gen. Willard, who lent me his for the rest of my stay, and will get another for himself when he goes home to dinner. Mine is much too heavy for this warm weather.

I have a seat on the stage at Haverley's Theatre, tonight, where the Army of the Tennessee will receive Gen. Grant, and where Gen. Sherman will make a speech. At midnight I am to attend a meeting of the Owl Club.

I love you ever so much, my darling, and am hoping to get a word from you yet. SAML.

Following the procession, which he describes, came the grand ceremonies of welcome at Haverley's Theatre. The next letter is written the following morning, or at least soiree time the following day, after a night of ratification.

To Mrs. Clemens, in Hartford:

CHICAGO, Nov. 12, '79. Livy darling, it was a great time. There were perhaps thirty people on the stage of the theatre, and I think I never sat elbow-to-elbow with so many historic names before. Grant, Sherman, Sheridan, Schofield, Pope, Logan, Augur, and so on. What an iron man Grant is! He sat facing the house, with his right leg crossed over his left and his right boot-sole tilted up at an angle, and his left hand and arm reposing on the arm of his chair--you note that position? Well, when glowing references were made to other grandees on the stage, those grandees always showed a trifle of nervous consciousness--and as these references came frequently, the nervous change of position and attitude were also frequent. But Grant!--he was under a tremendous and ceaseless bombardment of praise and gratulation, but as true as I'm sitting here he never moved a muscle of his body for a single instant, during 30 minutes! You could have played him on a stranger for an effigy. Perhaps he never would have moved, but at last a speaker made such a particularly ripping and blood-stirring remark about him that the audience rose and roared and yelled and stamped and clapped an entire minute--Grant sitting as serene as ever--when Gen. Sherman stepped to him, laid his hand affectionately on his shoulder, bent respectfully down and whispered in his ear. Gen. Grant got up and bowed, and the storm of applause swelled into a hurricane. He sat down, took about the same position and froze to it till by and by there was another of those deafening and protracted roars, when Sherman made him get up and bow again. He broke up his attitude once more--the extent of something more than a hair's breadth--to indicate me to Sherman when the house was keeping up a determined and persistent call for me, and poor bewildered Sherman, (who did not know me), was peering abroad over the packed audience for me, not knowing I was only three feet from him and most conspicuously located, (Gen. Sherman was Chairman.)

One of the most illustrious individuals on that stage was "Ole Abe," the historic war eagle. He stood on his perch--the old savage-eyed rascal-- three or four feet behind Gen. Sherman, and as he had been in nearly every battle that was mentioned by the orators his soul was probably stirred pretty often, though he was too proud to let on.

Read Logan's bosh, and try to imagine a burly and magnificent Indian, in General's uniform, striking a heroic attitude and getting that stuff off in the style of a declaiming school-boy.

Please put the enclosed scraps in the drawer and I will scrap-book them.

I only staid at the Owl Club till 3 this morning and drank little or nothing. Went to sleep without whisky. Ich liebe dish.

SAML.

But it is in the third letter that we get the climax. On the same day he wrote a letter to Howells, which, in part, is very similar in substance and need not be included here.

A paragraph, however, must not be omitted.

"Imagine what it was like to see a bullet-shredded old battle-flag reverently unfolded to the gaze of a thousand middle-aged soldiers, most of whom hadn't seen it since they saw it advancing over victorious fields, when they were in their prime. And imagine what it was like when Grant, their first commander, stepped into view while they were still going mad over the flag, and then right in the midst of it all somebody struck up, 'When we were marching through Georgia.' Well, you should have heard the thousand voices lift that chorus and seen the tears stream down. If I live a hundred years I shan't ever forget these things, nor be able to talk about them .... Grand times, my boy, grand times!"

At the great banquet Mark Twain's speech had been put last on the program, to hold the house. He had been invited to respond to the toast of "The Ladies," but had replied that he had already responded to that toast more than once. There was one class of the community, he said, commonly overlooked on these occasions--the babies--he would respond to that toast. In his letter to Howells he had not been willing to speak freely of his personal triumph, but to Mrs. Clemens he must tell it all, and with that child-like ingenuousness which never failed him to his last day.

To Mrs. Clemens, in Hartford:

CHICAGO, Nov. 14 '79. A little after 5 in the morning.

I've just come to my room, Livy darling, I guess this was the memorable night of my life. By George, I never was so stirred since I was born. I heard four speeches which I can never forget. One by Emory Storrs, one by Gen. Vilas (O, wasn't it wonderful!) one by Gen. Logan (mighty stirring), one by somebody whose name escapes me, and one by that splendid old soul, Col. Bob Ingersoll,--oh, it was just the supremest combination of English words that was ever put together since the world began. My soul, how handsome he looked, as he stood on that table, in the midst of those 500 shouting men, and poured the molten silver from his lips! Lord, what an organ is human speech when it is played by a master! All these speeches may look dull in print, but how the lightning glared around them when they were uttered, and how the crowd roared in response! It was a great night, a memorable night. I am so richly repaid for my journey--and how I did wish with all my whole heart that you were there to be lifted into the very seventh heaven of enthusiasm, as I was. The army songs, the military music, the crashing applause-- Lord bless me, it was unspeakable.

Out of compliment they placed me last in the list--No. 15--I was to "hold the crowd"--and bless my life I was in awful terror when No. 14. rose, at a o'clock this morning and killed all the enthusiasm by delivering the flattest, insipidest, silliest of all responses to "Woman" that ever a weary multitude listened to. Then Gen. Sherman (Chairman) announced my toast, and the crowd gave me a good round of applause as I mounted on top of the dinner table, but it was only on account of my name, nothing more --they were all tired and wretched. They let my first sentence go in. silence, till I paused and added "we stand on common ground"--then they burst forth like a hurricane and I saw that I had them! From that time on, I stopped at the end of each sentence, and let the tornado of applause and laughter sweep around me--and when I closed with "And if the child is but the prophecy of the man, there are mighty few who will doubt that he succeeded," I say it who oughtn't to say it, the house came down with a crash. For two hours and a half, now, I've been shaking hands and listening to congratulations. Gen. Sherman said, "Lord bless you, my boy, I don't know how you do it--it's a secret that's beyond me--but it was great--give me your hand again."

And do you know, Gen. Grant sat through fourteen speeches like a graven image, but I fetched him! I broke him up, utterly! He told me he laughed till the tears came and every bone in his body ached. (And do you know, the biggest part of the success of the speech lay in the fact that the audience saw that for once in his life he had been knocked out of his iron serenity.)

Bless your soul, 'twas immense. I never was so proud in my life. Lots and lots of people--hundreds I might say--told me my speech was the triumph of the evening--which was a lie. Ladies, Tom, Dick and Harry- even the policemen--captured me in the halls and shook hands, and scores of army officers said "We shall always be grateful to you for coming." General Pope came to bunt me up--I was afraid to speak to him on that theatre stage last night, thinking it might be presumptuous to tackle a man so high up in military history. Gen. Schofield, and other historic men, paid their compliments. Sheridan was ill and could not come, but I'm to go with a General of his staff and see him before I go to Col. Grant's. Gen. Augur--well, I've talked with them all, received invitations from them all--from people living everywhere--and as I said before, it's a memorable night. I wouldn't have missed it for anything in the world.

But my sakes, you should have heard Ingersoll's speech on that table! Half an hour ago he ran across me in the crowded halls and put his arms about me and said "Mark, if I live a hundred years, I'll always be grateful for your speech--Lord what a supreme thing it was." But I told him it wasn't any use to talk, he had walked off with the honors of that occasion by something of a majority. Bully boy is Ingersoll--traveled with him in the cars the other day, and you can make up your mind we had a good time.

Of course I forgot to go and pay for my hotel car and so secure it, but the army officers told me an hour ago to rest easy, they would go at once, at this unholy hour of the night and compel the railways to do their duty by me, and said "You don't need to request the Army of the Tennessee to do your desires--you can command its services."

Well, I bummed around that banquet hall from 8 in the evening till 2 in the morning, talking with people and listening to speeches, and I never ate a single bite or took a sup of anything but ice water, so if I seem excited now, it is the intoxication of supreme enthusiasm. By George, it was a grand night, a historical night.

And now it is a quarter past 6 A.M.--so good bye and God bless you and the Bays,--[Family word for babies]--my darlings

SAML.

Show it to Joe if you want to--I saw some of his friends here.

Mark Twain's admiration for Robert Ingersoll was very great, and we may believe that he was deeply impressed by the Chicago speech, when we find him, a few days later, writing to Ingersoll for a perfect copy to read to a young girls' club in Hartford. Ingersoll sent the speech, also some of his books, and the next letter is Mark Twain's acknowledgment.

To Col. Robert G. Ingersoll:

HARTFORD, Dec. 14. MY DEAR INGERSOLL,--Thank you most heartily for the books--I am devouring them--they have found a hungry place, and they content it and satisfy it to a miracle. I wish I could hear you speak these splendid chapters before a great audience--to read them by myself and hear the boom of the applause only in the ear of my imagination, leaves a something wanting-- and there is also a still greater lack, your manner, and voice, and presence.

The Chicago speech arrived an hour too late, but I was all right anyway, for I found that my memory had been able to correct all the errors. I read it to the Saturday Club (of young girls) and told them to remember that it was doubtful if its superior existed in our language. Truly Yours, S. L. CLEMENS.

The reader may remember Mark Twain's Whittier dinner speech of 1877, and its disastrous effects. Now, in 1879, there was to be another Atlantic gathering: a breakfast to Dr. Oliver Wendell Holmes, to which Clemens was invited. He was not eager to accept; it would naturally recall memories of two years before, but being urged by both Howells and Warner, he agreed to attend if they would permit him to speak. Mark Twain never lacked courage and he wanted to redeem himself. To Howells he wrote:

To W. D. Howells, in Boston:

HARTFORD, Nov. 28, 1879. MY DEAR HOWELLS,--If anybody talks, there, I shall claim the right to say a word myself, and be heard among the very earliest--else it would be confoundedly awkward for me--and for the rest, too. But you may read what I say, beforehand, and strike out whatever you choose.

Of course I thought it wisest not to be there at all; but Warner took the opposite view, and most strenuously.

Speaking of Johnny's conclusion to become an outlaw, reminds me of Susie's newest and very earnest longing--to have crooked teeth and glasses--"like Mamma."

I would like to look into a child's head, once, and see what its processes are. Yrs ever, S. L. CLEMENS.

The matter turned out well. Clemens, once more introduced by Howells--this time conservatively, it may be said--delivered a delicate and fitting tribute to Doctor Holmes, full of graceful humor and grateful acknowledgment, the kind of speech he should have given at the Whittier dinner of two years before. No reference was made to his former disaster, and this time he came away covered with glory, and fully restored in his self-respect.

XX.

LETTERS OF 1880, CHIEFLY TO HOWELLS. "THE PRINCE AND THE PAUPER." MARK TWAIN MUGWUMP SOCIETY

The book of travel,--[A Tramp Abroad.]--which Mark Twain had hoped to finish in Paris, and later in Elmira, for some reason would not come to an end. In December, in Hartford, he was still working on it, and he would seem to have finished it, at last, rather by a decree than by any natural process of authorship. This was early in January, 1880. To Howells he reports his difficulties, and his drastic method of ending them.

To W. D. Howells, in Boston:

HARTFORD, Jan. 8, '80. MY DEAR HOWELLS,--Am waiting for Patrick to come with the carriage. Mrs. Clemens and I are starting (without the children) to stay indefinitely in Elmira. The wear and tear of settling the house broke her down, and she has been growing weaker and weaker for a fortnight. All that time--in fact ever since I saw you--I have been fighting a life- and-death battle with this infernal book and hoping to get done some day. I required 300 pages of MS, and I have written near 600 since I saw you-- and tore it all up except 288. This I was about to tear up yesterday and begin again, when Mrs. Perkins came up to the billiard room and said, "You will never get any woman to do the thing necessary to save her life by mere persuasion; you see you have wasted your words for three weeks; it is time to use force; she must have a change; take her home and leave the children here."

I said, "If there is one death that is painfuller than another, may I get it if I don't do that thing."

So I took the 288 pages to Bliss and told him that was the very last line I should ever write on this book. (A book which required 2600 pages of MS, and I have written nearer four thousand, first and last.)

I am as soary (and flighty) as a rocket, to-day, with the unutterable joy of getting that Old Man of the Sea off my back, where he has been roosting for more than a year and a half. Next time I make a contract before writing the book, may I suffer the righteous penalty and be burnt, like the injudicious believer.

I am mighty glad you are done your book (this is from a man who, above all others, feels how much that sentence means) and am also mighty glad you have begun the next (this is also from a man who knows the felicity of that, and means straightway to enjoy it.) The Undiscovered starts off delightfully--I have read it aloud to Mrs. C. and we vastly enjoyed it.

Well, time's about up--must drop a line to Aldrich. Yrs ever, MARK.

In a letter which Mark Twain wrote to his brother Orion at this period we get the first hint of a venture which was to play an increasingly important part in the Hartford home and fortunes during the next ten or a dozen years. This was the type-setting machine investment, which, in the end, all but wrecked Mark Twain's finances. There is but a brief mention of it in the letter to Orion, and the letter itself is not worth preserving, but as references to the "machine" appear with increasing frequency, it seems proper to record here its first mention. In the same letter he suggests to his brother that he undertake an absolutely truthful autobiography, a confession in which nothing is to be withheld. He cites the value of Casanova's memories, and the confessions of Rousseau. Of course, any literary suggestion from "Brother Sam" was gospel to Orion, who began at once piling up manuscript at a great rate.

Meantime, Mark Twain himself, having got 'A Tramp Abroad' on the presses, was at work with enthusiasm on a story begun nearly three years before at Quarry Farm-a story for children-its name, as he called. it then, "The Little Prince and The Little Pauper." He was presently writing to Howells his delight in the new work.

To W. D. Howells, in Boston:

HARTFORD, Mch. 11, '80. MY DEAR HOWELLS,--.....I take so much pleasure in my story that I am loth to hurry, not wanting to get it done. Did I ever tell you the plot of it? It begins at 9 a.m., Jan. 27, 1547, seventeen and a half hours before Henry VIII's death, by the swapping of clothes and place, between the prince of Wales and a pauper boy of the same age and countenance (and half as much learning and still more genius and imagination) and after that, the rightful small King has a rough time among tramps and ruffians in the country parts of Kent, whilst the small bogus King has a gilded and worshipped and dreary and restrained and cussed time of it on the throne--and this all goes on for three weeks--till the midst of the coronation grandeurs in Westminster Abbey, Feb. 20, when the ragged true King forces his way in but cannot prove his genuineness--until the bogus King, by a remembered incident of the first day is able to prove it for him--whereupon clothes are changed and the coronation proceeds under the new and rightful conditions.

My idea is to afford a realizing sense of the exceeding severity of the laws of that day by inflicting some of their penalties upon the King himself and allowing him a chance to see the rest of them applied to others--all of which is to account for certain mildnesses which distinguished Edward VI's reign from those that preceded and followed it.

Imagine this fact--I have even fascinated Mrs. Clemens with this yarn for youth. My stuff generally gets considerable damning with faint praise out of her, but this time it is all the other way. She is become the horseleech's daughter and my mill doesn't grind fast enough to suit her. This is no mean triumph, my dear sir.

Last night, for the first time in ages, we went to the theatre--to see Yorick's Love. The magnificence of it is beyond praise. The language is so beautiful, the passion so fine, the plot so ingenious, the whole thing so stirring, so charming, so pathetic! But I will clip from the Courant -- it says it right.

And what a good company it is, and how like live people they all acted! The "thee's" and the "thou's" had a pleasant sound, since it is the language of the Prince and the Pauper. You've done the country a service in that admirable work.... Yrs Ever, MARK.

The play, "Yorick's Love," mentioned in this letter, was one which Howells had done for Lawrence Barrett.

Onion Clemens, meantime, was forwarding his manuscript, and for once seems to have won his brother's approval, so much so that Mark Twain was willing, indeed anxious, that Howells should run the "autobiography" in the Atlantic. We may imagine how Onion prized the words of commendation which follow:

To Orion Clemens:

May 6, '80. MY DEAR BROTHER,--It is a model autobiography.

Continue to develop your character in the same gradual inconspicuous and apparently unconscious way. The reader, up to this time, may have his doubts, perhaps, but he can't say decidedly, "This writer is not such a simpleton as he has been letting on to be." Keep him in that state of mind. If, when you shall have finished, the reader shall say, "The man is an ass, but I really don't know whether he knows it or not," your work will be a triumph.

Stop re-writing. I saw places in your last batch where re-writing had done formidable injury. Do not try to find those places, else you will mar them further by trying to better them. It is perilous to revise a book while it is under way. All of us have injured our books in that foolish way.

Keep in mind what I told you--when you recollect something which belonged in an earlier chapter, do not go back, but jam it in where you are. Discursiveness does not hurt an autobiography in the least.

I have penciled the MS here and there, but have not needed to make any criticisms or to knock out anything.

The elder Bliss has heart disease badly, and thenceforth his life hangs upon a thread. Yr Bro SAM.

But Howells could not bring himself to print so frank a confession as Orion had been willing to make. "It wrung my heart," he said, "and I felt haggard after I had finished it. The writer's soul is laid bare; it is shocking." Howells added that the best touches in it were those which made one acquainted with the writer's brother; that is to say, Mark Twain, and that these would prove valuable material hereafter--a true prophecy, for Mark Twain's early biography would have lacked most of its vital incident, and at least half of its background, without those faithful chapters, fortunately preserved. Had Onion continued, as he began, the work might have proved an important contribution to literature, but he went trailing off into by-paths of theology and discussion where the interest was lost. There were, perhaps, as many as two thousand pages of it, which few could undertake to read.

Mark Twain's mind was always busy with plans and inventions, many of them of serious intent, some semi-serious, others of a purely whimsical character. Once he proposed a "Modest Club," of which the first and main qualification for membership was modesty. "At present," he wrote, "I am the only member; and as the modesty required must be of a quite aggravated type, the enterprise did seem for a time doomed to stop dead still with myself, for lack of further material; but upon reflection I have come to the conclusion that you are eligible. Therefore, I have held a meeting and voted to offer you the distinction of membership. I do not know that we can find any others, though I have had some thought of Hay, Warner, Twichell, Aldrich, Osgood, Fields, Higginson, and a few more-- together with Mrs. Howells, Mrs. Clemens, and certain others of the sex."

Howells replied that the only reason he had for not joining the Modest Club was that he was too modest--too modest to confess his modesty. "If I could get over this difficulty I should like to join, for I approve highly of the Club and its object.... It ought to be given an annual dinner at the public expense. If you think I am not too modest you may put my name down and I will try to think the same of you. Mrs. Howells applauded the notion of the club from the very first. She said that she knew one thing: that she was modest enough, anyway. Her manner of saying it implied that the other persons you had named were not, and created a painful impression in my mind. I have sent your letter and the rules to Hay, but I doubt his modesty. He will think he has a right to belong to it as much as you or I; whereas, other people ought only to be admitted on sufferance."

Our next letter to Howells is, in the main, pure foolery, but we get in it a hint what was to become in time one of Mask Twain's strongest interests, the matter of copyright. He had both a personal and general interest in the subject. His own books were constantly pirated in Canada, and the rights of foreign authors were not respected in America. We have already seen how he had drawn a petition which Holmes, Lowell, Longfellow, and others were to sign, and while nothing had come of this plan he had never ceased to formulate others. Yet he hesitated when he found that the proposed protection was likely to work a hardship to readers of the poorer class. Once he wrote: "My notions have mightily changed lately.... I can buy a lot of the copyright classics, in paper, at from three to thirty cents apiece. These things must find their way into the very kitchens and hovels of the country..... And even if the treaty will kill Canadian piracy, and thus save me an average of $5,000 a year, I am down on it anyway, and I'd like cussed well to write an article opposing the treaty."

To W. D. Howells, in Belmont, Mass.:

Thursday, June 6th, 1880. MY DEAR HOWELLS,--There you stick, at Belmont, and now I'm going to Washington for a few days; and of course, between you and Providence that visit is going to get mixed, and you'll have been here and gone again just about the time I get back. Bother it all, I wanted to astonish you with a chapter or two from Orion's latest book--not the seventeen which he has begun in the last four months, but the one which he began last week.

Last night, when I went to bed, Mrs. Clemens said, "George didn't take the cat down to the cellar--Rosa says he has left it shut up in the conservatory." So I went down to attend to Abner (the cat.) About 3 in the morning Mrs. C. woke me and said, "I do believe I hear that cat in the drawing-room--what did you do with him?" I answered up with the confidence of a man who has managed to do the right thing for once, and said "I opened the conservatory doors, took the library off the alarm, and spread everything open, so that there wasn't any obstruction between him and the cellar." Language wasn't capable of conveying this woman's disgust. But the sense of what she said, was, "He couldn't have done any harm in the conservatory--so you must go and make the entire house free to him and the burglars, imagining that he will prefer the coal-bins to the drawing-room. If you had had Mr. Howells to help you, I should have admired but not been astonished, because I should know that together you would be equal to it; but how you managed to contrive such a stately blunder all by yourself, is what I cannot understand."

So, you see, even she knows how to appreciate our gifts.

Brisk times here.--Saturday, these things happened: Our neighbor Chas. Smith was stricken with heart disease, and came near joining the majority; my publisher, Bliss, ditto, ditto; a neighbor's child died; neighbor Whitmore's sixth child added to his five other cases of measles; neighbor Niles sent for, and responded; Susie Warner down, abed; Mrs. George Warner threatened with death during several hours; her son Frank, whilst imitating the marvels in Barnum's circus bills, thrown from his aged horse and brought home insensible: Warner's friend Max Yortzburgh, shot in the back by a locomotive and broken into 32 distinct pieces and his life threatened; and Mrs. Clemens, after writing all these cheerful things to Clara Spaulding, taken at midnight, and if the doctor had not been pretty prompt the contemplated Clemens would have called before his apartments were ready.

However, everybody is all right, now, except Yortzburg, and he is mending--that is, he is being mended. I knocked off, during these stirring times, and don't intend to go to work again till we go away for the Summer, 3 or 6 weeks hence. So I am writing to you not because I have anything to say, but because you don't have to answer and I need something to do this afternoon.....

I have a letter from a Congressman this morning, and he says Congress couldn't be persuaded to bother about Canadian pirates at a time like this when all legislation must have a political and Presidential bearing, else Congress won't look at it. So have changed my mind and my course; I go north, to kill a pirate. I must procure repose some way, else I cannot get down to work again.

Pray offer my most sincere and respectful approval to the President--is approval the proper word? I find it is the one I most value here in the household and seldomest get.

With our affection to you both. Yrs ever MARK.

It was always dangerous to send strangers with letters of introduction to Mark Twain. They were so apt to arrive at the wrong time, or to find him in the wrong mood. Howells was willing to risk it, and that the result was only amusing instead of tragic is the best proof of their friendship.

To W. D. Howells, in Belmont, Mass.:

June 9, '80. Well, old practical joker, the corpse of Mr. X----has been here, and I have bedded it and fed it, and put down my work during 24 hours and tried my level best to make it do something, or say something, or appreciate something--but no, it was worse than Lazarus. A kind-hearted, well- meaning corpse was the Boston young man, but lawsy bless me, horribly dull company. Now, old man, unless you have great confidence in Mr. X's judgment, you ought to make him submit his article to you before he prints it. For only think how true I was to you: Every hour that he was here I was saying, gloatingly, "O G-- d--- you, when you are in bed and your light out, I will fix you" (meaning to kill him)...., but then the thought would follow--" No, Howells sent him--he shall be spared, he shall be respected he shall travel hell-wards by his own route."

Breakfast is frozen by this time, and Mrs. Clemens correspondingly hot. Good bye. Yrs ever, MARK.

"I did not expect you to ask that man to live with you," Howells answered. "What I was afraid of was that you would turn him out of doors, on sight, and so I tried to put in a good word for him. After this when I want you to board people, I'll ask you. I am sorry for your suffering. I suppose I have mostly lost my smell for bores; but yours is preternaturally keen. I shall begin to be afraid I bore you. (How does that make you feel?)"

In a letter to Twichell--a remarkable letter--when baby Jean Clemens was about a month old, we get a happy hint of conditions at Quarry Farm, and in the background a glimpse of Mark Twain's unfailing tragic reflection.

To Rev. Twichell, in Hartford:

QUARRY FARM, Aug. 29 ['80]. DEAR OLD JOE,--Concerning Jean Clemens, if anybody said he "didn't see no pints about that frog that's any better'n any other frog," I should think he was convicting himself of being a pretty poor sort of observer.... I will not go into details; it is not necessary; you will soon be in Hartford, where I have already hired a hall; the admission fee will be but a trifle.

It is curious to note the change in the stock-quotation of the Affection Board brought about by throwing this new security on the market. Four weeks ago the children still put Mamma at the head of the list right along, where she had always been. But now:

Jean Mamma Motley [a cat] Fraulein [another] Papa

That is the way it stands, now Mamma is become No. 2; I have dropped from No. 4., and am become No. 5. Some time ago it used to be nip and tuck between me and the cats, but after the cats "developed" I didn't stand any more show.

I've got a swollen ear; so I take advantage of it to lie abed most of the day, and read and smoke and scribble and have a good time. Last evening Livy said with deep concern, "O dear, I believe an abscess is forming in your ear."

I responded as the poet would have done if he had had a cold in the head--

"Tis said that abscess conquers love, But O believe it not."

This made a coolness.

Been reading Daniel Webster's Private Correspondence. Have read a hundred of his diffuse, conceited, "eloquent," bathotic (or bathostic) letters written in that dim (no, vanished) Past when he was a student; and Lord, to think that this boy who is so real to me now, and so booming with fresh young blood and bountiful life, and sappy cynicisms about girls, has since climbed the Alps of fame and stood against the sun one brief tremendous moment with the world's eyes upon him, and then--f-z-t-! where is he? Why the only long thing, the only real thing about the whole shadowy business is the sense of the lagging dull and hoary lapse of time that has drifted by since then; a vast empty level, it seems, with a formless spectre glimpsed fitfully through the smoke and mist that lie along its remote verge.

Well, we are all getting along here first-rate; Livy gains strength daily, and sits up a deal; the baby is five weeks old and--but no more of this; somebody may be reading this letter 80 years hence. And so, my friend (you pitying snob, I mean, who are holding this yellow paper in your hand in 1960,) save yourself the trouble of looking further; I know how pathetically trivial our small concerns will seem to you, and I will not let your eye profane them. No, I keep my news; you keep your compassion. Suffice it you to know, scoffer and ribald, that the little child is old and blind, now, and once more toothless; and the rest of us are shadows, these many, many years. Yes, and your time cometh!

MARK.

At the Farm that year Mark Twain was working on The Prince and the Pauper, and, according to a letter to Aldrich, brought it to an end September 19th. It is a pleasant letter, worth preserving. The book by Aldrich here mentioned was 'The Stillwater Tragedy.'

To T. B. Aldrich, in Ponkapog, Mass.:

ELMIRA, Sept. 15, '80. MY DEAR ALDRICH,--Thank you ever so much for the book--I had already finished it, and prodigiously enjoyed it, in the periodical of the notorious Howells, but it hits Mrs. Clemens just right, for she is having a reading holiday, now, for the first time in same months; so between- times, when the new baby is asleep and strengthening up for another attempt to take possession of this place, she is going to read it. Her strong friendship for you makes her think she is going to like it.

I finished a story yesterday, myself. I counted up and found it between sixty and eighty thousand words--about the size of your book. It is for boys and girls--been at work at it several years, off and on.

I hope Howells is enjoying his journey to the Pacific. He wrote me that you and Osgood were going, also, but I doubted it, believing he was in liquor when he wrote it. In my opinion, this universal applause over his book is going to land that man in a Retreat inside of two months. I notice the papers say mighty fine things about your book, too. You ought to try to get into the same establishment with Howells. But applause does not affect me--I am always calm--this is because I am used to it.

Well, good-bye, my boy, and good luck to you. Mrs. Clemens asks me to send her warmest regards to you and Mrs. Aldrich--which I do, and add those of Yrs ever MARK.

While Mark Twain was a journalist in San Francisco, there was a middle-aged man named Soule, who had a desk near him on the Morning Call. Soule was in those days highly considered as a poet by his associates, most of whom were younger and less gracefully poetic. But Soule's gift had never been an important one. Now, in his old age, he found his fame still local, and he yearned for wider recognition. He wished to have a volume of poems issued by a publisher of recognized standing. Because Mark Twain had been one of Soule's admirers and a warm friend in the old days, it was natural that Soule should turn to him now, and equally natural that Clemens should turn to Howells.

To W. D. Howells, in Boston:

Sunday, Oct. 2 '80. MY DEAR HOWELLS,--Here's a letter which I wrote you to San Francisco the second time you didn't go there.... I told Soule he needn't write you, but simply send the MS. to you. O dear, dear, it is dreadful to be an unrecognized poet. How wise it was in Charles Warren Stoddard to take in his sign and go for some other calling while still young.

I'm laying for that Encyclopedical Scotchman--and he'll need to lock the door behind him, when he comes in; otherwise when he hears my proposed tariff his skin will probably crawl away with him. He is accustomed to seeing the publisher impoverish the author--that spectacle must be getting stale to him--if he contracts with the undersigned he will experience a change in that programme that will make the enamel peel off his teeth for very surprise--and joy. No, that last is what Mrs. Clemens thinks--but it's not so. The proposed work is growing, mightily, in my estimation, day by day; and I'm not going to throw it away for any mere trifle. If I make a contract with the canny Scot, I will then tell him the plan which you and I have devised (that of taking in the humor of all countries)--otherwise I'll keep it to myself, I think. Why should we assist our fellowman for mere love of God? Yrs ever MARK.

One wishes that Howells might have found value enough in the verses of Frank Soule to recommend them to Osgood. To Clemens he wrote: "You have touched me in regard to him, and I will deal gently with his poetry. Poor old fellow! I can imagine him, and how he must have to struggle not to be hard or sour."

The verdict, however, was inevitable. Soule's graceful verses proved to be not poetry at all. No publisher of standing could afford to give them his imprint.

The "Encyclopedical Scotchman" mentioned in the preceding letter was the publisher Gebbie, who had a plan to engage Howells and Clemens to prepare some sort of anthology of the world's literature. The idea came to nothing, though the other plan mentioned--for a library of humor--in time grew into a book.

Mark Twain's contracts with Bliss for the publication of his books on the subscription plan had been made on a royalty basis, beginning with 5 per cent. on 'The Innocents Abroad' increasing to 7 ?per cent. on 'Roughing It,' and to 10 per cent. on later books. Bliss had held that these later percentages fairly represented one half the profits. Clemens, however, had never been fully satisfied, and his brother Onion had more than once urged him to demand a specific contract on the half-profit basis. The agreement for the publication of 'A Tramp Abroad' was made on these terms. Bliss died before Clemens received his first statement of sales. Whatever may have been the facts under earlier conditions, the statement proved to Mark Twain's satisfaction; at least, that the half-profit arrangement was to his advantage. It produced another result; it gave Samuel Clemens an excuse to place his brother Onion in a position of independence.

To Onion Clemens, in Keokuk, Iowa:

Sunday, Oct 24 '80. MY DEAR BRO.,--Bliss is dead. The aspect of the balance-sheet is enlightening. It reveals the fact, through my present contract, (which is for half the profits on the book above actual cost of paper, printing and binding,) that I have lost considerably by all this nonsense--sixty thousand dollars, I should say--and if Bliss were alive I would stay with the concern and get it all back; for on each new book I would require a portion of that back pay; but as it is (this in the very strictest confidence,) I shall probably go to a new publisher 6 or 8 months hence, for I am afraid Frank, with his poor health, will lack push and drive.

Out of the suspicions you bred in me years ago, has grown this result, --to wit, that I shall within the twelvemonth get $40,000 out of this "Tramp" instead Of $20,000. Twenty thousand dollars, after taxes and other expenses are stripped away, is worth to the investor about $75 a month--so I shall tell Mr. Perkins to make your check that amount per month, hereafter, while our income is able to afford it. This ends the loan business; and hereafter you can reflect that you are living not on borrowed money but on money which you have squarely earned, and which has no taint or savor of charity about it--and you can also reflect that the money you have been receiving of me all these years is interest charged against the heavy bill which the next publisher will have to stand who gets a book of mine.

Jean got the stockings and is much obliged; Mollie wants to know whom she most resembles, but I can't tell; she has blue eyes and brown hair, and three chins, and is very fat and happy; and at one time or another she has resembled all the different Clemenses and Langdons, in turn, that have ever lived.

Livy is too much beaten out with the baby, nights, to write, these times; and I don't know of anything urgent to say, except that a basket full of letters has accumulated in the 7 days that I have been whooping and cursing over a cold in the head--and I must attack the pile this very minute. With love from us Y aff SAM $25 enclosed.

On the completion of The Prince and Pauper story, Clemens had naturally sent it to Howells for consideration. Howells wrote: "I have read the two P's and I like it immensely, it begins well and it ends well." He pointed out some things that might be changed or omitted, and added: "It is such a book as I would expect from you, knowing what a bottom of fury there is to your fun." Clemens had thought somewhat of publishing the story anonymously, in the fear that it would not be accepted seriously over his own signature.

The "bull story" referred to in the next letter is the one later used in the Joan of Arc book, the story told Joan by "Uncle Laxart," how he rode a bull to a funeral.

To W. D. Howells, in Boston:

Xmas Eve, 1880. MY DEAR HOWELLS,--I was prodigiously delighted with what you said about the book--so, on the whole, I've concluded to publish intrepidly, instead of concealing the authorship. I shall leave out that bull story.

I wish you had gone to New York. The company was small, and we had a first-rate time. Smith's an enjoyable fellow. I liked Barrett, too. And the oysters were as good as the rest of the company. It was worth going there to learn how to cook them.

Next day I attended to business--which was, to introduce Twichell to Gen. Grant and procure a private talk in the interest of the Chinese Educational Mission here in the U. S. Well, it was very funny. Joe had been sitting up nights building facts and arguments together into a mighty and unassailable array and had studied them out and got them by heart--all with the trembling half-hearted hope of getting Grant to add his signature to a sort of petition to the Viceroy of China; but Grant took in the whole situation in a jiffy, and before Joe had more than fairly got started, the old man said: "I'll write the Viceroy a Letter --a separate letter--and bring strong reasons to bear upon him; I know him well, and what I say will have weight with him; I will attend to it right away. No, no thanks--I shall be glad to do it--it will be a labor of love."

So all Joe's laborious hours were for naught! It was as if he had come to borrow a dollar, and been offered a thousand before he could unfold his case....

But it's getting dark. Merry Christmas to all of you. Yrs Ever, MARK.

The Chinese Educational Mission, mentioned in the foregoing, was a thriving Hartford institution, projected eight years before by a Yale graduate named Yung Wing. The mission was now threatened, and Yung Wing, knowing the high honor in which General Grant was held in China, believed that through him it might be saved. Twichell, of course, was deeply concerned and naturally overjoyed at Grant's interest. A day or two following the return to Hartford, Clemens received a letter from General Grant, in which he wrote: "Li Hung Chang is the most powerful and most influential Chinaman in his country. He professed great friendship for me when I was there, and I have had assurances of the same thing since. I hope, if he is strong enough with his government, that the decision to withdraw the Chinese students from this country may be changed."

But perhaps Li Hung Chang was experiencing one of his partial eclipses just then, or possibly he was not interested, for the Hartford Mission did not survive.

XXI.

LETTERS 1881, TO HOWELLS AND OTHERS. ASSISTING A YOUNG SCULPTOR. LITERARY PLANS

With all of Mark Twain's admiration for Grant, he had opposed him as a third-term President and approved of the nomination of Garfield. He had made speeches for Garfield during the campaign just ended, and had been otherwise active in his support. Upon Garfield's election, however, he felt himself entitled to no special favor, and the single request which he preferred at length could hardly be classed as, personal, though made for a "personal friend."

To President-elect James A. Garfield, in Washington:

HARTFORD, Jany. 12, '81. GEN. GARFIELD

DEAR SIR,--Several times since your election persons wanting office have asked me "to use my influence" with you in their behalf.

To word it in that way was such a pleasant compliment to me that I never complied. I could not without exposing the fact that I hadn't any influence with you and that was a thing I had no mind to do.

It seems to me that it is better to have a good man's flattering estimate of my influence--and to keep it--than to fool it away with trying to get him an office. But when my brother--on my wife's side--Mr. Charles J. Langdon--late of the Chicago Convention--desires me to speak a word for Mr. Fred Douglass, I am not asked "to use my influence" consequently I am not risking anything. So I am writing this as a simple citizen. I am not drawing on my fund of influence at all. A simple citizen may express a desire with all propriety, in the matter of a recommendation to office, and so I beg permission to hope that you will retain Mr. Douglass in his present office of Marshall of the District of Columbia, if such a course will not clash with your own preferences or with the expediencies and interest of your administration. I offer this petition with peculiar pleasure and strong desire, because I so honor this man's high and blemishless character and so admire his brave, long crusade for the liberties and elevation of his race.

He is a personal friend of mine, but that is nothing to the point, his history would move me to say these things without that, and I feel them too. With great respect I am, General, Yours truly, S. L. CLEMENS.

Clemens would go out of his way any time to grant favor to the colored race. His childhood associations were partly accountable for this, but he also felt that the white man owed the negro a debt for generations of enforced bondage. He would lecture any time in a colored church, when he would as likely as not refuse point-blank to speak for a white congregation. Once, in Elmira, he received a request, poorly and none too politely phrased, to speak for one of the churches. He was annoyed and about to send a brief refusal, when Mrs. Clemens, who was present, said:

"I think I know that church, and if so this preacher is a colored man; he does not know how to write a polished letter--how should he?" Her husband's manner changed so suddenly that she added: "I will give you a motto, and it will be useful to you if you will adopt it: Consider every man colored until he is proved white."

To W. D. Howells, in Boston:

HARTFORD, Feb. 27, 1881. MY DEAR HOWELLS,--I go to West Point with Twichell tomorrow, but shall be back Tuesday or Wednesday; and then just as soon thereafter as you and Mrs. Howells and Winny can come you will find us ready and most glad to see you--and the longer you can stay the gladder we shall be. I am not going to have a thing to do, but you shall work if you want to. On the evening of March 10th, I am going to read to the colored folk in the African Church here (no whites admitted except such as I bring with me), and a choir of colored folk will sing jubilee songs. I count on a good time, and shall hope to have you folks there, and Livy. I read in Twichell's chapel Friday night and had a most rattling high time--but the thing that went best of all was Uncle Remus's Tar Baby. I mean to try that on my dusky audience. They've all heard that tale from childhood-- at least the older members have.

I arrived home in time to make a most noble blunder--invited Charley Warner here (in Livy's name) to dinner with the Gerhardts, and told him Livy had invited his wife by letter and by word of mouth also. I don't know where I got these impressions, but I came home feeling as one does who realizes that he has done a neat thing for once and left no flaws or loop-holes. Well, Livy said she had never told me to invite Charley and she hadn't dreamed of inviting Susy, and moreover there wasn't any dinner, but just one lean duck. But Susy Warner's intuitions were correct--so she choked off Charley, and staid home herself--we waited dinner an hour and you ought to have seen that duck when he was done drying in the oven. MARK.

Clemens and his wife were always privately assisting worthy and ambitious young people along the way of achievement. Young actors were helped through dramatic schools; young men and women were assisted through college and to travel abroad. Among others Clemens paid the way of two colored students, one through a Southern institution and another through the Yale law school.

The mention of the name of Gerhardt in the preceding letter introduces the most important, or at least the most extensive, of these benefactions. The following letter gives the beginning of the story:

To W. D. Howells, in Boston:

Private and Confidential. HARTFORD, Feb. 21, 1881. MY DEAR HOWELLS,--Well, here is our romance.

It happened in this way. One morning, a month ago--no, three weeks-- Livy, and Clara Spaulding and I were at breakfast, at 10 A.M., and I was in an irritable mood, for the barber was up stairs waiting and his hot water getting cold, when the colored George returned from answering the bell and said: "There's a lady in the drawing-room wants to see you." "A book agent!" says I, with heat. "I won't see her; I will die in my tracks, first."

Then I got up with a soul full of rage, and went in there and bent scowling over that person, and began a succession of rude and raspy questions--and without even offering to sit down.

Not even the defendant's youth and beauty and (seeming) timidity were able to modify my savagery, for a time--and meantime question and answer were going on. She had risen to her feet with the first question; and there she stood, with her pretty face bent floorward whilst I inquired, but always with her honest eyes looking me in the face when it came her turn to answer.

And this was her tale, and her plea-diffidently stated, but straight- forwardly; and bravely, and most winningly simply and earnestly: I put it in my own fashion, for I do not remember her words:

Mr. Karl Gerhardt, who works in Pratt & Whitney's machine shops, has made a statue in clay, and would I be so kind as to come and look at it, and tell him if there is any promise in it? He has none to go to, and he would be so glad.

"O, dear me," I said, "I don't know anything about art--there's nothing I could tell him."

But she went on, just as earnestly and as simply as before, with her plea--and so she did after repeated rebuffs; and dull as I am, even I began by and by to admire this brave and gentle persistence, and to perceive how her heart of hearts was in this thing, and how she couldn't give it up, but must carry her point. So at last I wavered, and promised in general terms that I would come down the first day that fell idle--and as I conducted her to the door, I tamed more and more, and said I would come during the very next week--"We shall be so glad--but--but, would you please come early in the week?--the statue is just finished and we are so anxious--and--and--we did hope you could come this week--and"--well, I came down another peg, and said I would come Monday, as sure as death; and before I got to the dining room remorse was doing its work and I was saying to myself, "Damnation, how can a man be such a hound? why didn't I go with her now?" Yes, and how mean I should have felt if I had known that out of her poverty she had hired a hack and brought it along to convey me. But luckily for what was left of my peace of mind, I didn't know that.

Well, it appears that from here she went to Charley Warner's. There was a better light, there, and the eloquence of her face had a better chance to do its office. Warner fought, as I had done; and he was in the midst of an article and very busy; but no matter, she won him completely. He laid aside his MS and said, "Come, let us go and see your father's statue. That is--is he your father?" "No, he is my husband." So this child was married, you see.

This was a Saturday. Next day Warner came to dinner and said "Go!--go tomorrow--don't fail." He was in love with the girl, and with her husband too, and said he believed there was merit in the statue. Pretty crude work, maybe, but merit in it.

Patrick and I hunted up the place, next day; the girl saw us driving up, and flew down the stairs and received me. Her quarters were the second story of a little wooden house--another family on the ground floor. The husband was at the machine shop, the wife kept no servant, she was there alone. She had a little parlor, with a chair or two and a sofa; and the artist-husband's hand was visible in a couple of plaster busts, one of the wife, and another of a neighbor's child; visible also in a couple of water colors of flowers and birds; an ambitious unfinished portrait of his wife in oils: some paint decorations on the pine mantel; and an excellent human ear, done in some plastic material at 16.

Then we went into the kitchen, and the girl flew around, with enthusiasm, and snatched rag after rag from a tall something in the corner, and presently there stood the clay statue, life size--a graceful girlish creature, nude to the waist, and holding up a single garment with one hand the expression attempted being a modified scare--she was interrupted when about to enter the bath.

Then this young wife posed herself alongside the image and so remained --a thing I didn't understand. But presently I did--then I said:

"O, it's you!"

"Yes," she said, "I was the model. He has no model but me. I have stood for this many and many an hour--and you can't think how it does tire one! But I don't mind it. He works all day at the shop; and then, nights and Sundays he works on his statue as long as I can keep up."

She got a big chisel, to use as a lever, and between us we managed to twist the pedestal round and round, so as to afford a view of the statue from all points. Well, sir, it was perfectly charming, this girl's innocence and purity---exhibiting her naked self, as it were, to a stranger and alone, and never once dreaming that there was the slightest indelicacy about the matter. And so there wasn't; but it will be many along day before I run across another woman who can do the like and show no trace of self-consciousness.

Well, then we sat down, and I took a smoke, and she told me all about her people in Massachusetts--her father is a physician and it is an old and respectable family--(I am able to believe anything she says.) And she told me how "Karl" is 26 years old; and how he has had passionate longings all his life toward art, but has always been poor and obliged to struggle for his daily bread; and how he felt sure that if he could only have one or two lessons in--

"Lessons? Hasn't he had any lessons?"

No. He had never had a lesson.

And presently it was dinner time and "Karl" arrived--a slender young fellow with a marvelous head and a noble eye--and he was as simple and natural, and as beautiful in spirit as his wife was. But she had to do the talking--mainly--there was too much thought behind his cavernous eyes for glib speech.

I went home enchanted. Told Livy and Clara Spaulding all about the paradise down yonder where those two enthusiasts are happy with a yearly expense of $350. Livy and Clara went there next day and came away enchanted. A few nights later the Gerhardts kept their promise and came here for the evening. It was billiard night and I had company and so was not down; but Livy and Clara became more charmed with these children than ever.

Warner and I planned to get somebody to criticise the statue whose judgment would be worth something. So I laid for Champney, and after two failures I captured him and took him around, and he said "this statue is full of faults--but it has merits enough in it to make up for them"-- whereat the young wife danced around as delighted as a child. When we came away, Champney said, "I did not want to say too much there, but the truth is, it seems to me an extraordinary performance for an untrained hand. You ask if there is promise enough there to justify the Hartford folk in going to an expense of training this young man. I should say, yes, decidedly; but still, to make everything safe, you had better get the judgment of a sculptor."

Warner was in New York. I wrote him, and he said he would fetch up Ward --which he did. Yesterday they went to the Gerhardts and spent two hours, and Ward came away bewitched with those people and marveling at the winning innocence of the young wife, who dropped naturally into model-attitude beside the statue (which is stark naked from head to heel, now--G. had removed the drapery, fearing Ward would think he was afraid to try legs and hips) just as she has always done before.

Livy and I had two long talks with Ward yesterday evening. He spoke strongly. He said, "if any stranger had told me that this apprentice did not model that thing from plaster casts, I would not have believed it." He said "it is full of crudities, but it is full of genius, too. It is such a statue as the man of average talent would achieve after two years training in the schools. And the boldness of the fellow, in going straight to nature! He is an apprentice--his work shows that, all over; but the stuff is in him, sure. Hartford must send him to Paris--two years; then if the promise holds good, keep him there three more--and warn him to study, study, work, work, and keep his name out of the papers, and neither ask for orders nor accept them when offered."

Well, you see, that's all we wanted. After Ward was gone Livy came out with the thing that was in her mind. She said, "Go privately and start the Gerhardts off to Paris, and say nothing about it to any one else."

So I tramped down this morning in the snow-storm--and there was a stirring time. They will sail a week or ten days from now.

As I was starting out at the front door, with Gerhardt beside me and the young wife dancing and jubilating behind, this latter cried out impulsively, "Tell Mrs. Clemens I want to hug her--I want to hug you both!"

I gave them my old French book and they were going to tackle the language, straight off.

Now this letter is a secret--keep it quiet--I don't think Livy would mind my telling you these things, but then she might, you know, for she is a queer girl. Yrs ever, MARK.

Champney was J. Wells Champney, a portrait-painter of distinction; Ward was the sculptor, J. Q. A. Ward.

The Gerhardts were presently off to Paris, well provided with means to make their dreams reality; in due time the letters will report them again.

The Uncle Remus tales of Joel Chandler Harris gave Mark Twain great pleasure. He frequently read them aloud, not only at home but in public. Finally, he wrote Harris, expressing his warm appreciation, and mentioning one of the negro stories of his own childhood, "The Golden Arm," which he urged Harris to look up and add to his collection.

"You have pinned a proud feather in Uncle-Remus's cap," replied Harris. "I do not know what higher honor he could have than to appear before the Hartford public arm in arm with Mark Twain."

He disclaimed any originality for the stories, adding, "I understand that my relations toward Uncle Remus are similar to those that exist between an almanac maker and the calendar." He had not heard the "Golden Arm" story and asked for the outlines; also for some publishing advice, out of Mark Twain's long experience.

To Joel Chandler Harris, in Atlanta:

ELMIRA, N.Y., Aug. 10. MY DEAR MR. HARRIS,--You can argue yourself into the delusion that the principle of life is in the stories themselves and not in their setting; but you will save labor by stopping with that solitary convert, for he is the only intelligent one you will bag. In reality the stories are only alligator pears--one merely eats them for the sake of the salad-dressing. Uncle Remus is most deftly drawn, and is a lovable and delightful creation; he, and the little boy, and their relations with each other, are high and fine literature, and worthy to live, for their own sakes; and certainly the stories are not to be credited with them. But enough of this; I seem to be proving to the man that made the multiplication table that twice one are two.

I have been thinking, yesterday and to-day (plenty of chance to think, as I am abed with lumbago at our little summering farm among the solitudes of the Mountaintops,) and I have concluded that I can answer one of your questions with full confidence--thus: Make it a subscription book. Mighty few books that come strictly under the head of literature will sell by subscription; but if Uncle Remus won't, the gift of prophecy has departed out of me. When a book will sell by subscription, it will sell two or three times as many copies as it would in the trade; and the profit is bulkier because the retail price is greater.....

You didn't ask me for a subscription-publisher. If you had, I should have recommended Osgood to you. He inaugurates his subscription department with my new book in the fall.....

Now the doctor has been here and tried to interrupt my yarn about "The Golden Arm," but I've got through, anyway.

Of course I tell it in the negro dialect--that is necessary; but I have not written it so, for I can't spell it in your matchless way. It is marvelous the way you and Cable spell the negro and creole dialects.

Two grand features are lost in print: the weird wailing, the rising and falling cadences of the wind, so easily mimicked with one's mouth; and the impressive pauses and eloquent silences, and subdued utterances, toward the end of the yarn (which chain the attention of the children hand and foot, and they sit with parted lips and breathless, to be wrenched limb from limb with the sudden and appalling "You got it").

Old Uncle Dan'l, a slave of my uncle's' aged 60, used to tell us children yarns every night by the kitchen fire (no other light;) and the last yarn demanded, every night, was this one. By this time there was but a ghastly blaze or two flickering about the back-log. We would huddle close about the old man, and begin to shudder with the first familiar words; and under the spell of his impressive delivery we always fell a prey to that climax at the end when the rigid black shape in the twilight sprang at us with a shout.

When you come to glance at the tale you will recollect it--it is as common and familiar as the Tar Baby. Work up the atmosphere with your customary skill and it will "go" in print.

Lumbago seems to make a body garrulous--but you'll forgive it. Truly yours S. L. CLEMENS

The "Golden Arm" story was one that Clemens often used in his public readings, and was very effective as he gave it.

In his sketch, "How to Tell a Story," it appears about as he used to tell it. Harris, receiving the outlines of the old Missouri tale, presently announced that he had dug up its Georgia relative, an interesting variant, as we gather from Mark Twain's reply.

To Joel Chandler Harris, in Atlanta:

HARTFORD, '81. MY DEAR MR. HARRIS,--I was very sure you would run across that Story somewhere, and am glad you have. A Drummond light--no, I mean a Brush light--is thrown upon the negro estimate of values by his willingness to risk his soul and his mighty peace forever for the sake of a silver sev'm-punce. And this form of the story seems rather nearer the true field-hand standard than that achieved by my Florida, Mo., negroes with their sumptuous arm of solid gold.

I judge you haven't received my new book yet--however, you will in a day or two. Meantime you must not take it ill if I drop Osgood a hint about your proposed story of slave life.....

When you come north I wish you would drop me a line and then follow it in person and give me a day or two at our house in Hartford. If you will, I will snatch Osgood down from Boston, and you won't have to go there at all unless you want to. Please to bear this strictly in mind, and don't forget it. Sincerely yours S. L. CLEMENS.

Charles Warren Stoddard, to whom the next letter is written, was one of the old California literary crowd, a graceful writer of verse and prose, never quite arriving at the success believed by his friends to be his due. He was a gentle, irresponsible soul, well loved by all who knew him, and always, by one or another, provided against want. The reader may remember that during Mark Twain's great lecture engagement in London, winter of 1873-74, Stoddard lived with him, acting as his secretary. At a later period in his life he lived for several years with the great telephone magnate, Theodore N. Vail. At the time of this letter, Stoddard had decided that in the warm light and comfort of the Sandwich Islands he could survive on his literary earnings.

To Charles Warren Stoddard, in the Sandwich Islands:

HARTFORD, Oct. 26 '81. MY DEAR CHARLIE,--Now what have I ever done to you that you should not only slide off to Heaven before you have earned a right to go, but must add the gratuitous villainy of informing me of it?.....

The house is full of carpenters and decorators; whereas, what we really need here, is an incendiary. If the house would only burn down, we would pack up the cubs and fly to the isles of the blest, and shut ourselves up in the healing solitudes of the crater of Haleakala and get a good rest; for the mails do not intrude there, nor yet the telephone and the telegraph. And after resting, we would come down the mountain a piece and board with a godly, breech-clouted native, and eat poi and dirt and give thanks to whom all thanks belong, for these privileges, and never house-keep any more.

I think my wife would be twice as strong as she is, but for this wearing and wearying slavery of house-keeping. However, she thinks she must submit to it for the sake of the children; whereas, I have always had a tenderness for parents too, so, for her sake and mine, I sigh for the incendiary. When the evening comes and the gas is lit and the wear and tear of life ceases, we want to keep house always; but next morning we wish, once more, that we were free and irresponsible boarders.

Work?--one can't you know, to any purpose. I don't really get anything done worth speaking of, except during the three or four months that we are away in the Summer. I wish the Summer were seven years long. I keep three or four books on the stocks all the time, but I seldom add a satisfactory chapter to one of them at home. Yes, and it is all because my time is taken up with answering the letters of strangers. It can't be done through a short hand amanuensis--I've tried that--it wouldn't work --I couldn't learn to dictate. What does possess strangers to write so many letters? I never could find that out. However, I suppose I did it myself when I was a stranger. But I will never do it again.

Maybe you think I am not happy? the very thing that gravels me is that I am. I don't want to be happy when I can't work; I am resolved that hereafter I won't be. What I have always longed for, was the privilege of living forever away up on one of those mountains in the Sandwich Islands overlooking the sea. Yours ever MARK.

That magazine article of yours was mighty good: up to your very best I think. I enclose a book review written by Howells.

To W. D. Howells, in Boston:

HARTFORD, Oct. 26 '81. MY DEAR HOWELLS,--I am delighted with your review, and so is Mrs. Clemens. What you have said, there, will convince anybody that reads it; a body cannot help being convinced by it. That is the kind of a review to have; the doubtful man; even the prejudiced man, is persuaded and succumbs.

What a queer blunder that was, about the baronet. I can't quite see how I ever made it. There was an opulent abundance of things I didn't know; and consequently no need to trench upon the vest-pocketful of things I did know, to get material for a blunder.

Charley Warren Stoddard has gone to the Sandwich Islands permanently. Lucky devil. It is the only supremely delightful place on earth. It does seem that the more advantage a body doesn't earn, here, the more of them God throws at his head. This fellow's postal card has set the vision of those gracious islands before my mind, again, with not a leaf withered, nor a rainbow vanished, nor a sun-flash missing from the waves, and now it will be months, I reckon, before I can drive it away again. It is beautiful company, but it makes one restless and dissatisfied.

With love and thanks, Yrs ever, MARK.

The review mentioned in this letter was of The Prince and the Pauper. What the queer" blunder" about the baronet was, the present writer confesses he does not know; but perhaps a careful reader could find it, at least in the early edition; very likely it was corrected without loss of time.

Clemens now and then found it necessary to pay a visit to Canada in the effort to protect his copyright. He usually had a grand time on these trips, being lavishly entertained by the Canadian literary fraternity. In November, 1881, he made one of these journeys in the interest of The Prince and the Pauper, this time with Osgood, who was now his publisher. In letters written home we get a hint of his diversions. The Monsieur Frechette mentioned was a Canadian poet of considerable distinction. "Clara" was Miss Clara Spaulding, of Elmira, who had accompanied Mr. and Mrs. Clemens to Europe in 1873, and again in 1878. Later she became Mrs. John B. Staachfield, of New York City. Her name has already appeared in these letters many times.

To Mrs. Clemens, in Hartford:

MONTREAL, Nov. 28 '81. Livy darling, you and Clara ought to have been at breakfast in the great dining room this morning. English female faces, distinctive English costumes, strange and marvelous English gaits--and yet such honest, honorable, clean-souled countenances, just as these English women almost always have, you know. Right away--

But they've come to take me to the top of Mount Royal, it being a cold, dry, sunny, magnificent day. Going in a sleigh. Yours lovingly, SAML.

To Mrs. Clemens, in Hartford:

MONTREAL, Sunday, November 27, 1881. Livy dear, a mouse kept me awake last night till 3 or 4 o'clock--so I am lying abed this morning. I would not give sixpence to be out yonder in the storm, although it is only snow.

[The above paragraph is written in the form of a rebus illustrated with various sketches.]

There--that's for the children--was not sure that they could read writing; especially jean, who is strangely ignorant in some things.

I can not only look out upon the beautiful snow-storm, past the vigorous blaze of my fire; and upon the snow-veiled buildings which I have sketched; and upon the churchward drifting umbrellas; and upon the buffalo-clad cabmen stamping their feet and thrashing their arms on the corner yonder: but I also look out upon the spot where the first white men stood, in the neighborhood of four hundred years ago, admiring the mighty stretch of leafy solitudes, and being admired and marveled at by an eager multitude of naked savages. The discoverer of this region, and namer of it, Jacques Cartier, has a square named for him in the city. I wish you were here; you would enjoy your birthday, I think.

I hoped for a letter, and thought I had one when the mail was handed in, a minute ago, but it was only that note from Sylvester Baxter. You must write--do you hear?--or I will be remiss myself.

Give my love and a kiss to the children, and ask them to give you my love and a kiss from SAML.

To Mrs. Clemens, in Hartford:

QUEBEC, Sunday. '81. Livy darling, I received a letter from Monsieur Frechette this morning, in which certain citizens of Montreal tendered me a public dinner next Thursday, and by Osgood's advice I accepted it. I would have accepted anyway, and very cheerfully but for the delay of two days--for I was purposing to go to Boston Tuesday and home Wednesday; whereas, now I go to Boston Friday and home Saturday. I have to go by Boston on account of business.

We drove about the steep hills and narrow, crooked streets of this old town during three hours, yesterday, in a sleigh, in a driving snow-storm. The people here don't mind snow; they were all out, plodding around on their affairs--especially the children, who were wallowing around everywhere, like snow images, and having a mighty good time. I wish I could describe the winter costume of the young girls, but I can't. It is grave and simple, but graceful and pretty--the top of it is a brimless fur cap. Maybe it is the costume that makes pretty girls seem so monotonously plenty here. It was a kind of relief to strike a homely face occasionally.

You descend into some of the streets by long, deep stairways; and in the strong moonlight, last night, these were very picturesque. I did wish you were here to see these things. You couldn't by any possibility sleep in these beds, though, or enjoy the food.

Good night, sweetheart, and give my respects to the cubs.

SAML.

It had been hoped that W. D. Howells would join the Canadian excursion, but Howells was not very well that autumn. He wrote that he had been in bed five weeks, "most of the time recovering; so you see how bad I must have been to begin with. But now I am out of any first-class pain; I have a good appetite, and I am as abusive and peremptory as Guiteau." Clemens, returning to Hartford, wrote him a letter that explains itself.

To W. D. Howells, in Boston:

HARTFORD, Dec. 16 '81. MY DEAR HOWELLS,--It was a sharp disappointment--your inability to connect, on the Canadian raid. What a gaudy good time we should have had!

Disappointed, again, when I got back to Boston; for I was promising myself half an hour's look at you, in Belmont; but your note to Osgood showed that that could not be allowed out yet.

The Atlantic arrived an hour ago, and your faultless and delicious Police Report brought that blamed Joe Twichell powerfully before me. There's a man who can tell such things himself (by word of mouth,) and has as sure an eye for detecting a thing that is before his eyes, as any man in the world, perhaps--then why in the nation doesn't he report himself with a pen?

One of those drenching days last week, he slopped down town with his cubs, and visited a poor little beggarly shed where were a dwarf, a fat woman, and a giant of honest eight feet, on exhibition behind tawdry show-canvases, but with nobody to exhibit to. The giant had a broom, and was cleaning up and fixing around, diligently. Joe conceived the idea of getting some talk out of him. Now that never would have occurred to me. So he dropped in under the man's elbow, dogged him patiently around, prodding him with questions and getting irritated snarls in return which would have finished me early--but at last one of Joe's random shafts drove the centre of that giant's sympathies somehow, and fetched him. The fountains of his great deep were broken up, and he rained a flood of personal history that was unspeakably entertaining.

Among other things it turned out that he had been a Turkish (native) colonel, and had fought all through the Crimean war--and so, for the first time, Joe got a picture of the Charge of the Six Hundred that made him see the living spectacle, the flash of flag and tongue-flame, the rolling smoke, and hear the booming of the guns; and for the first time also, he heard the reasons for that wild charge delivered from the mouth of a master, and realized that nobody had "blundered," but that a cold, logical, military brain had perceived this one and sole way to win an already lost battle, and so gave the command and did achieve the victory.

And mind you Joe was able to come up here, days afterwards, and reproduce that giant's picturesque and admirable history. But dern him, he can't write it--which is all wrong, and not as it should be.

And he has gone and raked up the MS autobiography (written in 1848,) of Mrs. Phebe Brown, (author of "I Love to Steal a While Away,") who educated Yung Wing in her family when he was a little boy; and I came near not getting to bed at all, last night, on account of the lurid fascinations of it. Why in the nation it has never got into print, I can't understand.

But, by jings! the postman will be here in a minute; so, congratulations upon your mending health, and gratitude that it is mending; and love to you all. Yrs Ever MARK.

Don't answer--I spare the sick.

XXII.

LETTERS, 1882, MAINLY TO HOWELLS. WASTED FURY. OLD SCENES REVISITED. THE MISSISSIPPI BOOK

A man of Mark Twain's profession and prominence must necessarily be the subject of much newspaper comment. Jest, compliment, criticism --none of these things disturbed him, as a rule. He was pleased that his books should receive favorable notices by men whose opinion he respected, but he was not grieved by adverse expressions. Jests at his expense, if well written, usually amused him; cheap jokes only made him sad; but sarcasms and innuendoes were likely to enrage him, particularly if he believed them prompted by malice. Perhaps among all the letters he ever wrote, there is none more characteristic than this confession of violence and eagerness for reprisal, followed by his acknowledgment of error and a manifest appreciation of his own weakness. It should be said that Mark Twain and Whitelaw Reid were generally very good friends, and perhaps for the moment this fact seemed to magnify the offense.

To W. D. Howells, in Boston:

HARTFORD, Jan. 28 '82. MY DEAR HOWELLS,--Nobody knows better than I, that there are times when swearing cannot meet the emergency. How sharply I feel that, at this moment. Not a single profane word has issued from my lips this mornin --I have not even had the impulse to swear, so wholly ineffectual would swearing have manifestly been, in the circumstances. But I will tell you about it.

About three weeks ago, a sensitive friend, approaching his revelation cautiously, intimated that the N. Y. Tribune was engaged in a kind of crusade against me. This seemed a higher compliment than I deserved; but no matter, it made me very angry. I asked many questions, and gathered, in substance, this: Since Reid's return from Europe, the Tribune had been flinging sneers and brutalities at me with such persistent frequency "as to attract general remark." I was an angered-- which is just as good an expression, I take it, as an hungered. Next, I learned that Osgood, among the rest of the "general," was worrying over these constant and pitiless attacks. Next came the testimony of another friend, that the attacks were not merely "frequent," but "almost daily." Reflect upon that: "Almost daily" insults, for two months on a stretch. What would you have done?

As for me, I did the thing which was the natural thing for me to do, that is, I set about contriving a plan to accomplish one or the other of two things: 1. Force a peace; or 2. Get revenge. When I got my plan finished, it pleased me marvelously. It was in six or seven sections, each section to be used in its turn and by itself; the assault to begin at once with No. 1, and the rest to follow, one after the other, to keep the communication open while I wrote my biography of Reid. I meant to wind up with this latter great work, and then dismiss the subject for good.

Well, ever since then I have worked day and night making notes and collecting and classifying material. I've got collectors at work in England. I went to New York and sat three hours taking evidence while a stenographer set it down. As my labors grew, so also grew my fascination.

Malice and malignity faded out of me--or maybe I drove them out of me, knowing that a malignant book would hurt nobody but the fool who wrote it. I got thoroughly in love with this work; for I saw that I was going to write a book which the very devils and angels themselves would delight to read, and which would draw disapproval from nobody but the hero of it, (and Mrs. Clemens, who was bitter against the whole thing.) One part of my plan was so delicious that I had to try my hand on it right away, just for the luxury of it. I set about it, and sure enough it panned out to admiration. I wrote that chapter most carefully, and I couldn't find a fault with it. (It was not for the biography--no, it belonged to an immediate and deadlier project.)

Well, five days ago, this thought came into my mind(from Mrs. Clemens's): "Wouldn't it be well to make sure that the attacks have been 'almost daily'?--and to also make sure that their number and character will justify me in doing what I am proposing to do?"

I at once set a man to work in New York to seek out and copy every unpleasant reference which had been made to me in the Tribune from Nov. 1st to date. On my own part I began to watch the current numbers, for I had subscribed for the paper.

The result arrived from my New York man this morning. O, what a pitiable wreck of high hopes! The "almost daily" assaults, for two months, consist of--1. Adverse criticism of P. & P. from an enraged idiot in the London Atheneum; 2. Paragraph from some indignant Englishman in the Pall Mall Gazette who pays me the vast compliment of gravely rebuking some imaginary ass who has set me up in the neighborhood of Rabelais; 3. A remark of the Tribune's about the Montreal dinner, touched with an almost invisible satire; 4. A remark of the Tribune's about refusal of Canadian copyright, not complimentary, but not necessarily malicious--and of course adverse criticism which is not malicious is a thing which none but fools irritate themselves about.

There--that is the prodigious bugaboo, in its entirety! Can you conceive of a man's getting himself into a sweat over so diminutive a provocation? I am sure I can't. What the devil can those friends of mine have been thinking about, to spread these 3 or 4 harmless things out into two months of daily sneers and affronts? The whole offense, boiled down, amounts to just this: one uncourteous remark of the Tribune about my book--not me between Nov. 1 and Dec. 20; and a couple of foreign criticisms (of my writings, not me,) between Nov. 1 and Jan. 26! If I can't stand that amount of friction, I certainly need reconstruction. Further boiled down, this vast outpouring of malice amounts to simply this: one jest from the Tribune (one can make nothing more serious than that out of it.) One jest--and that is all; for the foreign criticisms do not count, they being matters of news, and proper for publication in anybody's newspaper.

And to offset that one jest, the Tribune paid me one compliment Dec. 23, by publishing my note declining the New York New England dinner, while merely (in the same breath,) mentioning that similar letters were read from General Sherman and other men whom we all know to be persons of real consequence.

Well, my mountain has brought forth its mouse, and a sufficiently small mouse it is, God knows. And my three weeks' hard work have got to go into the ignominious pigeon-hole. Confound it, I could have earned ten thousand dollars with infinitely less trouble. However, I shouldn't have done it, for I am too lazy, now, in my sere and yellow leaf, to be willing to work for anything but love..... I kind of envy you people who are permitted for your righteousness' sake to dwell in a boarding house; not that I should always want to live in one, but I should like the change occasionally from this housekeeping slavery to that wild independence. A life of don't-care-a-damn in a boarding house is what I have asked for in many a secret prayer. I shall come by and by and require of you what you have offered me there. Yours ever, MARK.

Howells, who had already known something of the gathering storm, replied: "Your letter was an immense relief to me, for although I had an abiding faith that you would get sick of your enterprise, I wasn't easy until I knew that you had given it up."

Joel Chandler Harris appears again in the letters of this period. Twichell, during a trip South about this time, had called on Harris with some sort of proposition or suggestion from Clemens that Harris appear with him in public, and tell, or read, the Remus stories from the platform. But Harris was abnormally diffident. Clemens later pronounced him "the shyest full-grown man" he had ever met, and the word which Twichell brought home evidently did not encourage the platform idea.

To Joel Chandler Harris, in Atlanta:

HARTFORD, Apl. 2, '82. Private.

MY DEAR MR. HARRIS,--Jo Twichell brought me your note and told me of his talk with you. He said you didn't believe you would ever be able to muster a sufficiency of reckless daring to make you comfortable and at ease before an audience. Well, I have thought out a device whereby I believe we can get around that difficulty. I will explain when I see you.

Jo says you want to go to Canada within a month or six weeks--I forget just exactly what he did say; but he intimated the trip could be delayed a while, if necessary. If this is so, suppose you meet Osgood and me in New Orleans early in May--say somewhere between the 1st and 6th?

It will be well worth your while to do this, because the author who goes to Canada unposted, will not know what course to pursue [to secure copyright] when he gets there; he will find himself in a hopeless confusion as to what is the correct thing to do. Now Osgood is the only man in America, who can lay out your course for you and tell you exactly what to do. Therefore, you just come to New Orleans and have a talk with him.

Our idea is to strike across lots and reach St. Louis the 20th of April-- thence we propose to drift southward, stopping at some town a few hours or a night, every day, and making notes.

To escape the interviewers, I shall follow my usual course and use a fictitious name (C. L. Samuel, of New York.) I don't know what Osgood's name will be, but he can't use his own.

If you see your way to meet us in New Orleans, drop me a line, now, and as we approach that city I will telegraph you what day we shall arrive there.

I would go to Atlanta if I could, but shan't be able. We shall go back up the river to St. Paul, and thence by rail X-lots home.

(I am making this letter so dreadfully private and confidential because my movements must be kept secret, else I shan't be able to pick up the kind of book-material I want.)

If you are diffident, I suspect that you ought to let Osgood be your magazine-agent. He makes those people pay three or four times as much as an article is worth, whereas I never had the cheek to make them pay more than double. Yrs Sincerely S. L. CLEMENS.

"My backwardness is an affliction," wrote Harris..... "The ordeal of appearing on the stage would be a terrible one, but my experience is that when a diffident man does become familiar with his surroundings he has more impudence than his neighbors. Extremes meet."

He was sorely tempted, but his courage became as water at the thought of footlights and assembled listeners. Once in New York he appears to have been caught unawares at a Tile Club dinner and made to tell a story, but his agony was such that at the prospect of a similar ordeal in Boston he avoided that city and headed straight for Georgia and safety.

The New Orleans excursion with Osgood, as planned by Clemens, proved a great success. The little party took the steamer Gold Dust from St. Louis down river toward New Orleans. Clemens was quickly recognized, of course, and his assumed name laid aside. The author of "Uncle Remus" made the trip to New Orleans. George W. Cable was there at the time, and we may believe that in the company of Mark Twain and Osgood those Southern authors passed two or three delightful days. Clemens also met his old teacher Bixby in New Orleans, and came back up the river with him, spending most of his time in the pilot-house, as in the old days. It was a glorious trip, and, reaching St. Louis, he continued it northward, stopping off at Hannibal and Quincy.'

To Mrs. Clemens, in Hartford:

QUINCY, ILL. May 17, '82. Livy darling, I am desperately homesick. But I have promised Osgood, and must stick it out; otherwise I would take the train at once and break for home.

I have spent three delightful days in Hannibal, loitering around all day long, examining the old localities and talking with the grey-heads who were boys and girls with me 30 or 40 years ago. It has been a moving time. I spent my nights with John and Helen Garth, three miles from town, in their spacious and beautiful house. They were children with me, and afterwards schoolmates. Now they have a daughter 19 or 20 years old. Spent an hour, yesterday, with A. W. Lamb, who was not married when I saw him last. He married a young lady whom I knew. And now I have been talking with their grown-up sons and daughters. Lieutenant Hickman, the spruce young handsomely-uniformed volunteer of 1846, called on me--a grisly elephantine patriarch of 65 now, his grace all vanished.

That world which I knew in its blossoming youth is old and bowed and melancholy, now; its soft cheeks are leathery and wrinkled, the fire is gone out in its eyes, and the spring from its step. It will be dust and ashes when I come again. I have been clasping hands with the moribund- and usually they said, "It is for the last time."

Now I am under way again, upon this hideous trip to St. Paul, with a heart brimming full of thoughts and images of you and Susie and Bay and the peerless Jean. And so good night, my love.

SAML.

Clemens's trip had been saddened by learning, in New Orleans, the news of the death of Dr. John Brown, of Edinburgh. To Doctor Brown's son, whom he had known as "Jock," he wrote immediately on his return to Hartford.

To Mr. John Brown, in Edinburgh

HARTFORD, June 1, 1882. MY DEAR MR. BROWN,--I was three thousand miles from home, at breakfast in New Orleans, when the damp morning paper revealed the sorrowful news among the cable dispatches. There was no place in America, however remote, or however rich, or poor or high or humble where words of mourning for your father were not uttered that morning, for his works had made him known and loved all over the land. To Mrs. Clemens and me, the loss is personal; and our grief the grief one feels for one who was peculiarly near and dear. Mrs. Clemens has never ceased to express regret that we came away from England the last time without going to see him, and often we have since projected a voyage across the Atlantic for the sole purpose of taking him by the hand and looking into his kind eyes once more before he should be called to his rest.

We both thank you greatly for the Edinburgh papers which you sent. My wife and I join in affectionate remembrances and greetings to yourself and your aunt, and in the sincere tender of our sympathies.

Faithfully yours, S. L. CLEMENS.

Our Susie is still "Megalops." He gave her that name:

Can you spare a photograph of your father? We have none but the one taken in a group with ourselves.

William Dean Howells, at the age of forty-five, reached what many still regard his highest point of achievement in American realism. His novel, The Rise of Silas Lapham, which was running as a Century serial during the summer of 1882, attracted wide attention, and upon its issue in book form took first place among his published novels. Mark Twain, to the end of his life, loved all that Howells wrote. Once, long afterward, he said: "Most authors give us glimpses of a radiant moon, but Howells's moon shines and sails all night long." When the instalments of The Rise of Silas Lapham began to appear, he overflowed in adjectives, the sincerity of which we need not doubt, in view of his quite open criticisms of the author's reading delivery.

To W. D. Howells, in Belmont, Mass.:

MY DEAR HOWELLS,--I am in a state of wild enthusiasm over this July instalment of your story. It's perfectly dazzling--it's masterly-- incomparable. Yet I heard you read it--without losing my balance. Well, the difference between your reading and your writing is-remarkable. I mean, in the effects produced and the impression left behind. Why, the one is to the other as is one of Joe Twichell's yarns repeated by a somnambulist. Goodness gracious, you read me a chapter, and it is a gentle, pearly dawn, with a sprinkle of faint stars in it; but by and by I strike it in print, and shout to myself, "God bless us, how has that pallid former spectacle been turned into these gorgeous sunset splendors!"

Well, I don't care how much you read your truck to me, you can't permanently damage it for me that way. It is always perfectly fresh and dazzling when I come on it in the magazine. Of course I recognize the form of it as being familiar--but that is all. That is, I remember it as pyrotechnic figures which you set up before me, dead and cold, but ready for the match--and now I see them touched off and all ablaze with blinding fires. You can read, if you want to, but you don't read worth a damn. I know you can read, because your readings of Cable and your repeatings of the German doctor's remarks prove that.

That's the best drunk scene--because the truest--that I ever read. There are touches in it that I never saw any writer take note of before. And they are set before the reader with amazing accuracy. How very drunk, and how recently drunk, and how altogether admirably drunk you must have been to enable you to contrive that masterpiece!

Why I didn't notice that that religious interview between Marcia and Mrs. Halleck was so deliciously humorous when you read it to me--but dear me, it's just too lovely for anything. (Wrote Clark to collar it for the "Library.")

Hang it, I know where the mystery is, now; when you are reading, you glide right along, and I don't get a chance to let the things soak home; but when I catch it in the magazine, I give a page 20 or 30 minutes in which to gently and thoroughly filter into me. Your humor is so very subtle, and elusive--(well, often it's just a vanishing breath of perfume which a body isn't certain he smelt till he stops and takes another smell) whereas you can smell other

(Remainder obliterated.)

Among Mark Twain's old schoolmates in Hannibal was little Helen Kercheval, for whom in those early days he had a very tender spot indeed. But she married another schoolmate, John Garth, who in time became a banker, highly respected and a great influence. John and Helen Garth have already been mentioned in the letter of May 17th.

To John Garth, in Hannibal:

HARTFORD, July 3 '82. DEAR JOHN,--Your letter of June i9 arrived just one day after we ought to have been in Elmira, N. Y. for the summer: but at the last moment the baby was seized with scarlet fever. I had to telegraph and countermand the order for special sleeping car; and in fact we all had to fly around in a lively way and undo the patient preparations of weeks-- rehabilitate the dismantled house, unpack the trunks, and so on. A couple of days later, the eldest child was taken down with so fierce a fever that she was soon delirious--not scarlet fever, however. Next, I myself was stretched on the bed with three diseases at once, and all of them fatal. But I never did care for fatal diseases if I could only have privacy and room to express myself concerning them.

We gave early warning, and of course nobody has entered the house in all this time but one or two reckless old bachelors--and they probably wanted to carry the disease to the children of former flames of theirs. The house is still in quarantine and must remain so for a week or two yet-- at which time we are hoping to leave for Elmira. Always your friend S. L. CLEMENS.

By the end of summer Howells was in Europe, and Clemens, in Elmira, was trying to finish his Mississippi book, which was giving him a great deal of trouble. It was usually so with his non-fiction books; his interest in them was not cumulative; he was prone to grow weary of them, while the menace of his publisher's contract was maddening. Howells's letters, meant to be comforting, or at least entertaining, did not always contribute to his peace of mind. The Library of American Humor which they had planned was an added burden. Before sailing, Howells had written: "Do you suppose you can do your share of the reading at Elmira, while you are writing at the Mississippi book?"

In a letter from London, Howells writes of the good times he is having over there with Osgood, Hutton, John Hay, Aldrich, and Alma Tadema, excursioning to Oxford, feasting, especially "at the Mitre Tavern, where they let you choose your dinner from the joints hanging from the rafter, and have passages that you lose yourself in every time you try to go to your room..... Couldn't you and Mrs. Clemens step over for a little while?..... We have seen lots of nice people and have been most pleasantly made of; but I would rather have you smoke in my face, and talk for half a day just for pleasure, than to go to the best house or club in London." The reader will gather that this could not be entirely soothing to a man shackled by a contract and a book that refused to come to an end.

To W. D. Howells, in London:

HARTFORD, CONN. Oct 30, 1882. MY DEAR HOWELLS,--I do not expect to find you, so I shan't spend many words on you to wind up in the perdition of some European dead-letter office. I only just want to say that the closing installments of the story are prodigious. All along I was afraid it would be impossible for you to keep up so splendidly to the end; but you were only, I see now, striking eleven. It is in these last chapters that you struck twelve. Go on and write; you can write good books yet, but you can never match this one. And speaking of the book, I inclose something which has been happening here lately.

We have only just arrived at home, and I have not seen Clark on our matters. I cannot see him or any one else, until I get my book finished. The weather turned cold, and we had to rush home, while I still lacked thirty thousand words. I had been sick and got delayed. I am going to write all day and two thirds of the night, until the thing is done, or break down at it. The spur and burden of the contract are intolerable to me. I can endure the irritation of it no longer. I went to work at nine o'clock yesterday morning, and went to bed an hour after midnight. Result of the day, (mainly stolen from books, tho' credit given,) 9500 words, so I reduced my burden by one third in one day. It was five days work in one. I have nothing more to borrow or steal; the rest must all be written. It is ten days work, and unless something breaks, it will be finished in five. We all send love to you and Mrs. Howells, and all the family. Yours as ever, MARK.

Again, from Villeneuve, on lake Geneva, Howells wrote urging him this time to spend the winter with them in Florence, where they would write their great American Comedy of 'Orme's Motor,' "which is to enrich us beyond the dreams of avarice.... We could have a lot of fun writing it, and you could go home with some of the good old Etruscan malaria in your bones, instead of the wretched pinch-beck Hartford article that you are suffering from now.... it's a great opportunity for you. Besides, nobody over there likes you half as well as I do."

It should be added that 'Orme's Motor' was the provisional title that Clemens and Howells had selected for their comedy, which was to be built, in some measure, at least, around the character, or rather from the peculiarities, of Orion Clemens. The Cable mentioned in Mark Twain's reply is, of course, George W. Cable, who only a little while before had come up from New Orleans to conquer the North with his wonderful tales and readings.

To W. D. Howells, in Switzerland:

HARTFORD, Nov. 4th, 1882. MY DEAR HOWELLS,--Yes, it would be profitable for me to do that, because with your society to help me, I should swiftly finish this now apparently interminable book. But I cannot come, because I am not Boss here, and nothing but dynamite can move Mrs. Clemens away from home in the winter season.

I never had such a fight over a book in my life before. And the foolishest part of the whole business is, that I started Osgood to editing it before I had finished writing it. As a consequence, large areas of it are condemned here and there and yonder, and I have the burden of these unfilled gaps harassing me and the thought of the broken continuity of the work, while I am at the same time trying to build the last quarter of the book. However, at last I have said with sufficient positiveness that I will finish the book at no particular date; that I will not hurry it; that I will not hurry myself; that I will take things easy and comfortably, write when I choose to write, leave it alone when I so prefer. The printers must wait, the artists, the canvassers, and all the rest. I have got everything at a dead standstill, and that is where it ought to be, and that is where it must remain; to follow any other policy would be to make the book worse than it already is. I ought to have finished it before showing to anybody, and then sent it across the ocean to you to be edited, as usual; for you seem to be a great many shades happier than you deserve to be, and if I had thought of this thing earlier, I would have acted upon it and taken the tuck somewhat out of your joyousness.

In the same mail with your letter, arrived the enclosed from Orme the motor man. You will observe that he has an office. I will explain that this is a law office and I think it probably does him as much good to have a law office without anything to do in it, as it would another man to have one with an active business attached. You see he is on the electric light lay now. Going to light the city and allow me to take all the stock if I want to. And he will manage it free of charge. It never would occur to this simple soul how much less costly it would be to me, to hire him on a good salary not to manage it. Do you observe the same old eagerness, the same old hurry, springing from the fear that if he does not move with the utmost swiftness, that colossal opportunity will escape him? Now just fancy this same frantic plunging after vast opportunities, going on week after week with this same man, during fifty entire years, and he has not yet learned, in the slightest degree, that there isn't any occasion to hurry; that his vast opportunity will always wait; and that whether it waits or flies, he certainly will never catch it. This immortal hopefulness, fortified by its immortal and unteachable misjudgment, is the immortal feature of this character, for a play; and we will write that play. We should be fools else. That staccato postscript reads as if some new and mighty business were imminent, for it is slung on the paper telegraphically, all the small words left out. I am afraid something newer and bigger than the electric light is swinging across his orbit. Save this letter for an inspiration. I have got a hundred more.

Cable has been here, creating worshipers on all hands. He is a marvelous talker on a deep subject. I do not see how even Spencer could unwind a thought more smoothly or orderly, and do it in a cleaner, clearer, crisper English. He astounded Twichell with his faculty. You know when it comes down to moral honesty, limpid innocence, and utterly blemishless piety, the Apostles were mere policemen to Cable; so with this in mind you must imagine him at a midnight dinner in Boston the other night, where we gathered around the board of the Summerset Club; Osgood, full, Boyle O'Reilly, full, Fairchild responsively loaded, and Aldrich and myself possessing the floor, and properly fortified. Cable told Mrs. Clemens when he returned here, that he seemed to have been entertaining himself with horses, and had a dreamy idea that he must have gone to Boston in a cattle-car. It was a very large time. He called it an orgy. And no doubt it was, viewed from his standpoint.

I wish I were in Switzerland, and I wish we could go to Florence; but we have to leave these delights to you; there is no helping it. We all join in love to you and all the family. Yours as ever
MARK.

XXIII.

LETTERS, 1883, TO HOWELLS AND OTHERS. A GUEST OF THE MARQUIS OF LORNE. THE HISTORY GAME. A PLAY BY HOWELLS AND MARK TWAIN

Mark Twain, in due season, finished the Mississippi book and placed it in Osgood's hands for publication. It was a sort of partnership arrangement in which Clemens was to furnish the money to make the book, and pay Osgood a percentage for handling it. It was, in fact, the beginning of Mark Twain's adventures as a publisher.

Howells was not as happy in Florence as he had hoped to be. The social life there overwhelmed him. In February he wrote: "Our two months in Florence have been the most ridiculous time that ever even half-witted people passed. We have spent them in chasing round after people for whom we cared nothing, and being chased by them. My story isn't finished yet, and what part of it is done bears the fatal marks of haste and distraction. Of course, I haven't put pen to paper yet on the play. I wring my hands and beat my breast when I think of how these weeks have been wasted; and how I have been forced to waste them by the infernal social circumstances from which I couldn't escape."

Clemens, now free from the burden of his own book, was light of heart and full of ideas and news; also of sympathy and appreciation. Howells's story of this time was "A Woman's Reason." Governor Jewell, of this letter, was Marshall Jewell, Governor of Connecticut from 1871 to 1873. Later, he was Minister to Russia, and in 1874 was United States Postmaster-General.

To W. D. Howells, in Florence:

HARTFORD, March 1st, 1883. MY DEAR HOWELLS,--We got ourselves ground up in that same mill, once, in London, and another time in Paris. It is a kind of foretaste of hell. There is no way to avoid it except by the method which you have now chosen. One must live secretly and cut himself utterly off from the human race, or life in Europe becomes an unbearable burden and work an impossibility. I learned something last night, and maybe it may reconcile me to go to Europe again sometime. I attended one of the astonishingly popular lectures of a man by the name of Stoddard, who exhibits interesting stereopticon pictures and then knocks the interest all out of them with his comments upon them. But all the world go there to look and listen, and are apparently well satisfied. And they ought to be fully satisfied, if the lecturer would only keep still, or die in the first act. But he described how retired tradesmen and farmers in Holland load a lazy scow with the family and the household effects, and then loaf along the waterways of the low countries all the summer long, paying no visits, receiving none, and just lazying a heavenly life out in their own private unpestered society, and doing their literary work, if they have any, wholly uninterrupted. If you had hired such a boat and sent for us we should have a couple of satisfactory books ready for the press now with no marks of interruption, vexatious wearinesses, and other hellishnesses visible upon them anywhere. We shall have to do this another time. We have lost an opportunity for the present. Do you forget that Heaven is packed with a multitude of all nations and that these people are all on the most familiar how-the-hell-are-you footing with Talmage swinging around the circle to all eternity hugging the saints and patriarchs and archangels, and forcing you to do the same unless you choose to make yourself an object of remark if you refrain?

Then why do you try to get to Heaven? Be warned in time.

We have all read your two opening numbers in the Century, and consider them almost beyond praise. I hear no dissent from this verdict. I did not know there was an untouched personage in American life, but I had forgotten the auctioneer. You have photographed him accurately.

I have been an utterly free person for a month or two; and I do not believe I ever so greatly appreciated and enjoyed--and realized the absence of the chains of slavery as I do this time. Usually my first waking thought in the morning is, "I have nothing to do to-day, I belong to nobody, I have ceased from being a slave." Of course the highest pleasure to be got out of freedom, and having nothing to do, is labor. Therefore I labor. But I take my time about it. I work one hour or four as happens to suit my mind, and quit when I please. And so these days are days of entire enjoyment. I told Clark the other day, to jog along comfortable and not get in a sweat. I said I believed you would not be able to enjoy editing that library over there, where you have your own legitimate work to do and be pestered to death by society besides; therefore I thought if he got it ready for you against your return, that that would be best and pleasantest.

You remember Governor Jewell, and the night he told about Russia, down in the library. He was taken with a cold about three weeks ago, and I stepped over one evening, proposing to beguile an idle hour for him with a yarn or two, but was received at the door with whispers, and the information that he was dying. His case had been dangerous during that day only and he died that night, two hours after I left. His taking off was a prodigious surprise, and his death has been most widely and sincerely regretted. Wm. E. Dodge, the father-in-law of one of Jewell's daughters, dropped suddenly dead the day before Jewell died, but Jewell died without knowing that. Jewell's widow went down to New York, to Dodge's house, the day after Jewell's funeral, and was to return here day before yesterday, and she did--in a coffin. She fell dead, of heart disease, while her trunks were being packed for her return home. Florence Strong, one of Jewell's daughters, who lives in Detroit, started East on an urgent telegram, but missed a connection somewhere, and did not arrive here in time to see her father alive. She was his favorite child, and they had always been like lovers together. He always sent her a box of fresh flowers once a week to the day of his death; a custom which he never suspended even when he was in Russia. Mrs. Strong had only just reached her Western home again when she was summoned to Hartford to attend her mother's funeral.

I have had the impulse to write you several times. I shall try to remember better henceforth.

With sincerest regards to all of you, Yours as ever, MARK.

Mark Twain made another trip to Canada in the interest of copyright- this time to protect the Mississippi book. When his journey was announced by the press, the Marquis of Lorne telegraphed an invitation inviting him to be his guest at Rideau Hall, in Ottawa. Clemens accepted, of course, and was handsomely entertained by the daughter of Queen Victoria and her husband, then Governor-General of Canada.

On his return to Hartford he found that Osgood had issued a curious little book, for which Clemens had prepared an introduction. It was an absurd volume, though originally issued with serious intent, its title being The New Guide of the Conversation in Portuguese and English.'--[The New Guide of the Conversation in Portuguese and English, by Pedro Caxolino, with an introduction by Mark Twain. Osgood, Boston, 1883.]--Evidently the "New Guide" was prepared by some simple Portuguese soul with but slight knowledge of English beyond that which could be obtained from a dictionary, and his literal translation of English idioms are often startling, as, for instance, this one, taken at random:

"A little learneds are happies enough for to may to satisfy their fancies on the literature."

Mark Twain thought this quaint book might amuse his royal hostess, and forwarded a copy in what he considered to be the safe and proper form.

To Col. De Winton, in Ottawa, Canada:

HARTFORD, June 4, '83. DEAR COLONEL DE WINTON,--I very much want to send a little book to her Royal Highness--the famous Portuguese phrase book; but I do not know the etiquette of the matter, and I would not wittingly infringe any rule of propriety. It is a book which I perfectly well know will amuse her "some at most" if she has not seen it before, and will still amuse her "some at least," even if she has inspected it a hundred times already. So I will send the book to you, and you who know all about the proper observances will protect me from indiscretion, in case of need, by putting the said book in the fire, and remaining as dumb as I generally was when I was up there. I do not rebind the thing, because that would look as if I thought it worth keeping, whereas it is only worth glancing at and casting aside.

Will you please present my compliments to Mrs. De Winton and Mrs. Mackenzie?--and I beg to make my sincere compliments to you, also, for your infinite kindnesses to me. I did have a delightful time up there, most certainly. Truly yours S. L. CLEMENS.

P. S. Although the introduction dates a year back, the book is only just now issued. A good long delay.

S. L. C.

Howells, writing from Venice, in April, manifested special interest in the play project: "Something that would run like Scheherazade, for a thousand and one nights," so perhaps his book was going better. He proposed that they devote the month of October to the work, and inclosed a letter from Mallory, who owned not only a religious paper, The Churchman, but also the Madison Square Theater, and was anxious for a Howells play. Twenty years before Howells had been Consul to Venice, and he wrote, now: "The idea of my being here is benumbing and silencing. I feel like the Wandering Jew, or the ghost of the Cardiff giant."

He returned to America in July. Clemens sent him word of welcome, with glowing reports of his own undertakings. The story on which he was piling up MS. was The Adventures of Huckleberry Finn, begun seven years before at Quarry Farm. He had no great faith in it then, and though he had taken it up again in 1880, his interest had not lasted to its conclusion. This time, however, he was in the proper spirit, and the story would be finished.

To W. D. Howells, in Boston:

ELMIRA, July 20, '83. MY DEAR HOWELLS,--We are desperately glad you and your gang are home again--may you never travel again, till you go aloft or alow. Charley Clark has gone to the other side for a run--will be back in August. He has been sick, and needed the trip very much.

Mrs. Clemens had a long and wasting spell of sickness last Spring, but she is pulling up, now. The children are booming, and my health is ridiculous, it's so robust, notwithstanding the newspaper misreports.

I haven't piled up MS so in years as I have done since we came here to the farm three weeks and a half ago. Why, it's like old times, to step right into the study, damp from the breakfast table, and sail right in and sail right on, the whole day long, without thought of running short of stuff or words.

I wrote 4000 words to-day and I touch 3000 and upwards pretty often, and don't fall below 1600 any working day. And when I get fagged out, I lie abed a couple of days and read and smoke, and then go it again for 6 or 7 days. I have finished one small book, and am away along in a big one that I half-finished two or three years ago. I expect to complete it in a month or six weeks or two months more. And I shall like it, whether anybody else does or not.

It's a kind of companion to Tom Sawyer. There's a raft episode from it in second or third chapter of life on the Mississippi.....

I'm booming, these days--got health and spirits to waste--got an overplus; and if I were at home, we would write a play. But we must do it anyhow by and by.

We stay here till Sep. 10; then maybe a week at Indian Neck for sea air, then home.

We are powerful glad you are all back; and send love according.

Yrs Ever MARK

To Onion Clemens and family, in Keokuk, Id.:

ELMIRA, July 22, '83. Private

DEAR MA AND ORION AND MOLLIE,--I don't know that I have anything new to report, except that Livy is still gaining, and all the rest of us flourishing. I haven't had such booming working-days for many years. I am piling up manuscript in a really astonishing way. I believe I shall complete, in two months, a book which I have been fooling over for 7 years. This summer it is no more trouble to me to write than it is to lie.

Day before yesterday I felt slightly warned to knock off work for one day. So I did it, and took the open air. Then I struck an idea for the instruction of the children, and went to work and carried it out. It took me all day. I measured off 817 feet of the road-way in our farm grounds, with a foot-rule, and then divided it up among the English reigns, from the Conqueror down to 1883, allowing one foot to the year. I whittled out a basket of little pegs and drove one in the ground at the beginning of each reign, and gave it that King's name--thus:

I measured all the reigns exactly as many feet to the reign as there were years in it. You can look out over the grounds and see the little pegs from the front door--some of them close together, like Richard II, Richard Cromwell, James II, &c; and some prodigiously wide apart, like Henry III, Edward III, George III, &c. It gives the children a realizing sense of the length or brevity of a reign. Shall invent a violent game to go with it.

And in bed, last night, I invented a way to play it indoors--in a far more voluminous way, as to multiplicity of dates and events--on a cribbage board.

Hello, supper's ready. Love to all. Good bye. SAML.

Onion Clemens would naturally get excited over the idea of the game and its commercial possibilities. Not more so than his brother, however, who presently employed him to arrange a quantity of historical data which the game was to teach. For a season, indeed, interest in the game became a sort of midsummer madness which pervaded the two households, at Keokuk and at Quarry Farm. Howells wrote his approval of the idea of "learning history by the running foot," which was a pun, even if unintentional, for in its out-door form it was a game of speed as well as knowledge.

Howells adds that he has noticed that the newspapers are exploiting Mark Twain's new invention of a history game, and we shall presently see how this happened.

Also, in this letter, Howells speaks of an English nobleman to whom he has given a letter of introduction. "He seemed a simple, quiet, gentlemanly man, with a good taste in literature, which he evinced by going about with my books in his pockets, and talking of yours."

To W. D. Howells, in Boston:

MY DEAR HOWELLS,--How odd it seems, to sit down to write a letter with the feeling that you've got time to do it. But I'm done work, for this season, and so have got time. I've done two seasons' work in one, and haven't anything left to do, now, but revise. I've written eight or nine hundred MS pages in such a brief space of time that I mustn't name the number of days; I shouldn't believe it myself, and of course couldn't expect you to. I used to restrict myself to 4 or 5 hours a day and 5 days in the week, but this time I've wrought from breakfast till 5.15 p.m. six days in the week; and once or twice I smouched a Sunday when the boss wasn't looking. Nothing is half so good as literature hooked on Sunday, on the sly.

I wrote you and Twichell on the same night, about the game, and was appalled to get a note from him saying he was going to print part of my letter, and was going to do it before I could get a chance to forbid it. I telegraphed him, but was of course too late.

If you haven't ever tried to invent an indoor historical game, don't. I've got the thing at last so it will work, I guess, but I don't want any more tasks of that kind. When I wrote you, I thought I had it; whereas I was only merely entering upon the initiatory difficulties of it. I might have known it wouldn't be an easy job, or somebody would have invented a decent historical game long ago--a thing which nobody had done. I think I've got it in pretty fair shape--so I have caveated it.

Earl of Onston--is that it? All right, we shall be very glad to receive them and get acquainted with them. And much obliged to you, too. There's plenty of worse people than the nobilities. I went up and spent a week with the Marquis and the Princess Louise, and had as good a time as I want.

I'm powerful glad you are all back again; and we will come up there if our little tribe will give us the necessary furlough; and if we can't get it, you folks must come to us and give us an extension of time. We get home Sept. 11.

Hello, I think I see Waring coming!

Good-by-letter from Clark, which explains for him.

Love to you all from the CLEMENSES.

No--it wasn't Waring. I wonder what the devil has become of that man. He was to spend to-day with us, and the day's most gone, now.

We are enjoying your story with our usual unspeakableness; and I'm right glad you threw in the shipwreck and the mystery--I like it. Mrs. Crane thinks it's the best story you've written yet. We--but we always think the last one is the best. And why shouldn't it be? Practice helps.

P. S. I thought I had sent all our loves to all of you, but Mrs. Clemens says I haven't. Damn it, a body can't think of everything; but a woman thinks you can. I better seal this, now--else there'll be more criticism.

I perceive I haven't got the love in, yet. Well, we do send the love of all the family to all the Howellses. S. L. C.

There had been some delay and postponement in the matter of the play which Howells and

Clemens agreed to write. They did not put in the entire month of October as they had planned, but they did put in a portion of that month, the latter half, working out their old idea. In the end it became a revival of Colonel Sellers, or rather a caricature of that gentle hearted old visionary. Clemens had always complained that the actor Raymond had never brought out the finer shades of Colonel Sellers's character, but Raymond in his worst performance never belied his original as did Howells and Clemens in his dramatic revival. These two, working together, let their imaginations run riot with disastrous results. The reader can judge something of this himself, from The American Claimant the book which Mark Twain would later build from the play.

But at this time they thought it a great triumph. They had "cracked their sides" laughing over its construction, as Howells once said, and they thought the world would do the same over its performance. They decided to offer it to Raymond, but rather haughtily, indifferently, because any number of other actors would be waiting for it.

But this was a miscalculation. Raymond now turned the tables. Though favorable to the idea of a new play, he declared this one did not present his old Sellers at all, but a lunatic. In the end he returned the MS. with a brief note. Attempts had already been made to interest other actors, and would continue for some time.

XXIV

LETTERS, 1884, TO HOWELLS AND OTHERS. CABLE'S GREAT APRIL FOOL. "HUCK FINN" IN PRESS. MARK TWAIN FOR CLEVELAND. CLEMENS AND CABLE

Mark Twain had a lingering attack of the dramatic fever that winter. He made a play of the Prince and Pauper, which Howells pronounced "too thin and slight and not half long enough." He made another of Tom Sawyer, and probably destroyed it, for no trace of the MS. exists to-day. Howells could not join in these ventures, for he was otherwise occupied and had sickness in his household.

To W. D. Howells, in Boston:

Jan. 7, '84. MY DEAR HOWELLS,--"O my goodn's", as Jean says. You have now encountered at last the heaviest calamity that can befall an author. The scarlet fever, once domesticated, is a permanent member of the family. Money may desert you, friends forsake you, enemies grow indifferent to you, but the scarlet fever will be true to you, through thick and thin, till you be all saved or damned, down to the last one. I say these things to cheer you.

The bare suggestion of scarlet fever in the family makes me shudder; I believe I would almost rather have Osgood publish a book for me.

You folks have our most sincere sympathy. Oh, the intrusion of this hideous disease is an unspeakable disaster.

My billiard table is stacked up with books relating to the Sandwich Islands: the walls axe upholstered with scraps of paper penciled with notes drawn from them. I have saturated myself with knowledge of that unimaginably beautiful land and that most strange and fascinating people. And I have begun a story. Its hidden motive will illustrate a but-little considered fact in human nature; that the religious folly you are born in you will die in, no matter what apparently reasonabler religious folly may seem to have taken its place meanwhile, and abolished and obliterated it. I start Bill Ragsdale at 12 years of age, and the heroine at 4, in the midst of the ancient idolatrous system, with its picturesque and amazing customs and superstitions, 3 months before the arrival of the missionaries and the erection of a shallow Christianity upon the ruins of the old paganism. Then these two will become educated Christians, and highly civilized.

And then I will jump 15 years, and do Ragsdale's leper business. When we came to dramatize, we can draw a deal of matter from the story, all ready to our hand. Yrs Ever MARK.

He never finished the Sandwich Islands story which he and Howells were to dramatize later. His head filled up with other projects, such as publishing plans, reading-tours, and the like. The typesetting machine does not appear in the letters of this period, but it was an important factor, nevertheless. It was costing several thousand dollars a month for construction and becoming a heavy drain on Mark Twain's finances. It was necessary to recuperate, and the anxiety for a profitable play, or some other adventure that would bring a quick and generous return, grew out of this need.

Clemens had established Charles L. Webster, his nephew by marriage, in a New York office, as selling agent for the Mississippi book and for his plays. He was also planning to let Webster publish the new book, Huck Finn.

George W. Cable had proven his ability as a reader, and Clemens saw possibilities in a reading combination, which was first planned to include Aldrich, and Howells, and a private car.

But Aldrich and Howells did not warm to the idea, and the car was eliminated from the plan. Cable came to visit Clemens in Hartford, and was taken with the mumps, so that the reading-trip was postponed.

The fortunes of the Sellers play were most uncertain and becoming daily more doubtful. In February, Howells wrote: "If you have got any comfort in regard to our play I wish you would heave it into my bosom."

Cable recovered in time, and out of gratitude planned a great April- fool surprise for his host. He was a systematic man, and did it in his usual thorough way. He sent a "private and confidential" suggestion to a hundred and fifty of Mark Twain's friends and admirers, nearly all distinguished literary men. The suggestion was that each one of them should send a request for Mark Twain's autograph, timing it so that it would arrive on the 1st of April. All seemed to have responded.

Mark Twain's writing-table on April Fool morning was heaped with letters, asking in every ridiculous fashion for his "valuable autograph." The one from Aldrich was a fair sample. He wrote: "I am making a collection of autographs of our distinguished writers, and having read one of your works, Gabriel Convoy, I would like to add your name to the list."

Of course, the joke in this was that Gabriel Convoy was by Bret Harte, who by this time was thoroughly detested by Mark Twain. The first one or two of the letters puzzled the victim; then he comprehended the size and character of the joke and entered into it thoroughly. One of the letters was from Bloodgood H. Cutter, the "Poet Lariat" of Innocents Abroad. Cutter, of course, wrote in "poetry," that is to say, doggerel. Mark Twain's April Fool was a most pleasant one.

Rhymed letter by Bloodgood H. Cutter to Mark Twain:

LITTLE NECK, LONG ISLAND.

LONG ISLAND FARMER, TO HIS FRIEND AND PILGRIM BROTHER, SAMUEL L. CLEMENS, ESQ.

Friends, suggest in each one's behalf To write, and ask your autograph. To refuse that, I will not do, After the long voyage had with you. That was a memorable time You wrote in prose, I wrote in Rhyme To describe the wonders of each place, And the queer customs of each race.

That is in my memory yet For while I live I'll not forget. I often think of that affair And the many that were with us there.

As your friends think it for the best I ask your Autograph with the rest, Hoping you will it to me send 'Twill please and cheer your dear old friend:

Yours truly, BLOODGOOD H. CUTTER.

To W. D. Howells, in Boston:

HARTFORD, Apl 8, '84. MY DEAR HOWELLS, It took my breath away, and I haven't recovered it yet, entirely--I mean the generosity of your proposal to read the proofs of Huck Finn.

Now if you mean it, old man--if you are in earnest--proceed, in God's name, and be by me forever blest. I cannot conceive of a rational man deliberately piling such an atrocious job upon himself; but if there is such a man and you be that man, why then pile it on. It will cost me a pang every time I think of it, but this anguish will be eingebusst to me in the joy and comfort I shall get out of the not having to read the verfluchtete proofs myself. But if you have repented of your augenblichlicher Tobsucht and got back to calm cold reason again, I won't hold you to it unless I find I have got you down in writing somewhere. Herr, I would not read the proof of one of my books for any fair and reasonable sum whatever, if I could get out of it.

The proof-reading on the P & P cost me the last rags of my religion. M.

Howells had written that he would be glad to help out in the reading of the proofs of Huck Finn, which book Webster by this time had in hand. Replying to Clemens's eager and grateful acceptance now, he wrote: "It is all perfectly true about the generosity, unless I am going to read your proofs from one of the shabby motives which I always find at the bottom of my soul if I examine it." A characteristic utterance, though we may be permitted to believe that his shabby motives were fewer and less shabby than those of mankind in general.

The proofs which Howells was reading pleased him mightily. Once, during the summer, he wrote: "if I had written half as good a book as Huck Finn I shouldn't ask anything better than to read the proofs; even as it is, I don't, so send them on; they will always find me somewhere."

This was the summer of the Blaine-Cleveland campaign. Mark Twain, in company with many other leading men, had mugwumped, and was supporting Cleveland. From the next letter we gather something of the aspects of that memorable campaign, which was one of scandal and vituperation. We learn, too, that the young sculptor, Karl Gerhardt, having completed a three years' study in Paris, had returned to America a qualified artist.

To W. D. Howells, in Boston:

ELMIRA, Aug. 21, '84. MY DEAR HOWELLS,--This presidential campaign is too delicious for anything. Isn't human nature the most consummate sham and lie that was ever invented? Isn't man a creature to be ashamed of in pretty much all his aspects? Man, "know thyself "--and then thou wilt despise thyself, to a dead moral certainty. Take three quite good specimens--Hawley, Warner, and Charley Clark. Even I do not loathe Blaine more than they do; yet Hawley is howling for Blaine, Warner and Clark are eating their daily crow in the paper for him, and all three will vote for him. O Stultification, where is thy sting, O slave where is thy hickory!

I suppose you heard how a marble monument for which St. Gaudens was pecuniarily responsible, burned down in Hartford the other day, uninsured--for who in the world would ever think of insuring a marble shaft in a cemetery against a fire?--and left St. Gauden out of pocket $15,000.

It was a bad day for artists. Gerhardt finished my bust that day, and the work was pronounced admirable by all the kin and friends; but in putting it in plaster (or rather taking it out) next day it got ruined. It was four or five weeks hard work gone to the dogs. The news flew, and everybody on the farm flocked to the arbor and grouped themselves about the wreck in a profound and moving silence--the farm-help, the colored servants, the German nurse, the children, everybody--a silence interrupted at wide intervals by absent-minded ejaculations wising from unconscious breasts as the whole size of the disaster gradually worked its way home to the realization of one spirit after another.

Some burst out with one thing, some another; the German nurse put up her hands and said, "Oh, Schade! oh, schrecklich! "But Gerhardt said nothing; or almost that. He couldn't word it, I suppose.

But he went to work, and by dark had everything thoroughly well under way for a fresh start in the morning; and in three days' time had built a new bust which was a trifle better than the old one--and to-morrow we shall put the finishing touches on it, and it will be about as good a one as nearly anybody can make. Yrs Ever MARK.

If you run across anybody who wants a bust, be sure and recommend Gerhardt on my say-so.

But Howells was determinedly for Blaine. "I shall vote for Blaine," he replied. "I do not believe he is guilty of the things they accuse him of, and I know they are not proved against him. As for Cleveland, his private life may be no worse than that of most men, but as an enemy of that contemptible, hypocritical, lop-sided morality which says a woman shall suffer all the shame of unchastity and man none, I want to see him destroyed politically by his past. The men who defend him would take their wives to the White House if he were president, but if he married his concubine--'made her an honest woman' they would not go near him. I can't stand that."

Certainly this was sound logic, in that day, at least. But it left Clemens far from satisfied.

To W. D. Howells, in Boston:

ELMIRA, Sept. 17, '84. MY DEAR HOWELLS,--Somehow I can't seem to rest quiet under the idea of your voting for Blaine. I believe you said something about the country and the party. Certainly allegiance to these is well; but as certainly a man's first duty is to his own conscience and honor--the party or the country come second to that, and never first. I don't ask you to vote at all--I only urge you to not soil yourself by voting for Blaine.

When you wrote before, you were able to say the charges against him were not proven. But you know now that they are proven, and it seems to me that that bars you and all other honest and honorable men (who are independently situated) from voting for him.

It is not necessary to vote for Cleveland; the only necessary thing to do, as I understand it, is that a man shall keep himself clean, (by withholding his vote for an improper man) even though the party and the country go to destruction in consequence. It is not parties that make or save countries or that build them to greatness--it is clean men, clean ordinary citizens, rank and file, the masses. Clean masses are not made by individuals standing back till the rest become clean.

As I said before, I think a man's first duty is to his own honor; not to his country and not to his party. Don't be offended; I mean no offence. I am not so concerned about the rest of the nation, but--well, good-bye. Ys Ever MARK.

There does not appear to be any further discussion of the matter between Howells and Clemens. Their letters for a time contained no suggestion of politics.

Perhaps Mark Twain's own political conscience was not entirely clear in his repudiation of his party; at least we may believe from his next letter that his Cleveland enthusiasm was qualified by a willingness to support a Republican who would command his admiration and honor. The idea of an eleventh-hour nomination was rather startling, whatever its motive.

To Mr. Pierce, in Boston:

HARTFORD, Oct. 22, '84. MY DEAR MR. PIERCE,--You know, as well as I do, that the reason the majority of republicans are going to vote for Blaine is because they feel that they cannot help themselves. Do not you believe that if Mr. Edmunds would consent to run for President, on the Independent ticket--even at this late day--he might be elected?

Well, if he wouldn't consent, but should even strenuously protest and say he wouldn't serve if elected, isn't it still wise and fair to nominate him and vote for him? since his protest would relieve him from all responsibility; and he couldn't surely find fault with people for forcing a compliment upon him. And do not you believe that his name thus compulsorily placed at the head of the Independent column would work absolutely certain defeat to Blain and save the country's honor?

Politicians often carry a victory by springing some disgraceful and rascally mine under the feet of the adversary at the eleventh hour; would it not be wholesome to vary this thing for once and spring as formidable a mine of a better sort under the enemy's works?

If Edmunds's name were put up, I would vote for him in the teeth of all the protesting and blaspheming he could do in a month; and there are lots of others who would do likewise.

If this notion is not a foolish and wicked one, won't you just consult with some chief Independents, and see if they won't call a sudden convention and whoop the thing through? To nominate Edmunds the 1st of November, would be soon enough, wouldn't it?

With kindest regards to you and the Aldriches, Yr Truly S. L. CLEMENS.

Clemens and Cable set out on their reading-tour in November. They were a curiously-assorted pair: Cable was of orthodox religion, exact as to habits, neat, prim, all that Clemens was not. In the beginning Cable undertook to read the Bible aloud to Clemens each evening, but this part of the day's program was presently omitted by request. If they spent Sunday in a town, Cable was up bright and early visiting the various churches and Sunday-schools, while Mark Twain remained at the hotel, in bed, reading or asleep.

XXV

THE GREAT YEAR OF 1885. CLEMENS AND CABLE. PUBLICATION OF "HUCK FINN." THE GRANT MEMOIRS. MARK TWAIN AT FIFTY

The year 1885 was in some respects the most important, certainly the most pleasantly exciting, in

Mark Twain's life. It was the year in which he entered fully into the publishing business and launched one of the most spectacular of all publishing adventures, The Personal Memoirs of General U. S. Grant. Clemens had not intended to do general publishing when he arranged with Webster to become sales- agent for the Mississippi book, and later general agent for Huck Finn's adventures; he had intended only to handle his own books, because he was pretty thoroughly dissatisfied with other publishing arrangements. Even the Library of Humor, which Howells, with Clark, of the Courant, had put together for him, he left with Osgood until that publisher failed, during the spring of 1885. Certainly he never dreamed of undertaking anything of the proportions of the Grant book.

He had always believed that Grant could make a book. More than once, when they had met, he had urged the General to prepare his memoirs for publication. Howells, in his 'My Mark Twain', tells of going with Clemens to see Grant, then a member of the ill-fated firm of Grant and Ward, and how they lunched on beans, bacon and coffee brought in from a near-by restaurant. It was while they were eating this soldier fare that Clemens--very likely abetted by Howells-- especially urged the great commander to prepare his memoirs. But Grant had become a financier, as he believed, and the prospect of literary earnings, however large, did not appeal to him. Furthermore, he was convinced that he was without literary ability and that a book by him would prove a failure.

But then, by and by, came a failure more disastrous than anything he had foreseen--the downfall of his firm through the Napoleonic rascality of Ward. General Grant was utterly ruined; he was left without income and apparently without the means of earning one. It was the period when the great War Series was appeasing in the Century Magazine. General Grant, hard-pressed, was induced by the editors to prepare one or more articles, and, finding that he could write them, became interested in the idea of a book. It is unnecessary to repeat here the story of how the publication of this important work passed into the hands of Mark Twain; that is to say, the firm of Charles L. Webster & Co., the details having been fully given elsewhere.--[See Mark Twain: A Biography, chap. cliv.]--

We will now return for the moment to other matters, as reported in order by the letters. Clemens and Cable had continued their reading-tour into Canada, and in February found themselves in Montreal. Here they were invited by the Toque Bleue Snow-shoe Club to join in one of their weekly excursions across Mt. Royal. They could not go, and the reasons given by Mark Twain are not without interest. The letter is to Mr. George Iles, author of Flame, Electricity, and the Camera, and many other useful works.

To George Iles, far the Toque Blew Snow-shoe Club, Montreal:

DETROIT, February 12, 1885. Midnight, P.S. MY DEAR ILES,--I got your other telegram a while ago, and answered it, explaining that I get only a couple of hours in the middle of the day for social life. I know it doesn't seem rational that a man should have to lie abed all day in order to be rested and equipped for talking an hour at night, and yet in my case and Cable's it is so. Unless I get a great deal of rest, a ghastly dulness settles down upon me on the platform, and turns my performance into work, and hard work, whereas it ought always to be pastime, recreation, solid enjoyment. Usually it is just this latter, but that is because I take my rest faithfully, and prepare myself to do my duty by my audience.

I am the obliged and appreciative servant of my brethren of the Snow-shoe Club, and nothing in the world would delight me more than to come to their house without naming time or terms on my own part--but you see how it is. My cast iron duty is to my audience--it leaves me no liberty and no option.

With kindest regards to the Club, and to you, I am Sincerely yours S. L. CLEMENS.

In the next letter we reach the end of the Clemens-Cable venture and get a characteristic summing up of Mark Twain's general attitude toward the companion of his travels. It must be read only in the clear realization of Mark Twain's attitude toward orthodoxy, and his habit of humor. Cable was as rigidly orthodox as Mark Twain was revolutionary. The two were never anything but the best of friends.

To W. D. Howells, in Boston:

PHILADA. Feb. 27, '85. MY DEAR HOWELLS,--To-night in Baltimore, to-morrow afternoon and night in Washington, and my four-months platform campaign is ended at last. It has been a curious experience. It has taught me that Cable's gifts of mind are greater and higher than I had suspected. But--

That "But" is pointing toward his religion. You will never, never know, never divine, guess, imagine, how loathsome a thing the Christian religion can be made until you come to know and study Cable daily and hourly. Mind you, I like him; he is pleasant company; I rage and swear at him sometimes, but we do not quarrel; we get along mighty happily together; but in him and his person I have learned to hate all religions. He has taught me to abhor and detest the Sabbath-day and hunt up new and troublesome ways to dishonor it.

Nat Goodwin was on the train yesterday. He plays in Washington all the coming week. He is very anxious to get our Sellers play and play it under changed names. I said the only thing I could do would be to write to you. Well, I've done it. Ys Ever MARK.

Clemens and Webster were often at the house of General Grant during these early days of 1885, and it must have been Webster who was present with Clemens on the great occasion described in the following telegram. It was on the last day and hour of President Arthur's administration that the bill was passed which placed Ulysses S. Grant as full General with full pay on the retired list, and it is said that the congressional clock was set back in order that this enactment might become a law before the administration changed. General Grant had by this time developed cancer and was already in feeble health.

Telegram to Mrs. Clemens, in Hartford:

NEW YORK, Mar. 4, 1885. To MRS. S. L. CLEMENS, We were at General Grant's at noon and a telegram arrived that the last act of the expiring congress late this morning retired him with full General's rank and accompanying emoluments. The effect upon him was like raising the dead. We were present when the telegram was put in his hand.

S. L. CLEMENS.

Something has been mentioned before of Mark Twain's investments and the generally unprofitable habit of them. He had a trusting nature, and was usually willing to invest money on any plausible recommendation. He was one of thousands such, and being a person of distinction he now and then received letters of inquiry, complaint, or condolence. A minister wrote him that he had bought some stocks recommended by a Hartford banker and advertised in a religious paper. He added, "After I made that purchase they wrote me that you had just bought a hundred shares and that you were a 'shrewd' man." The writer closed by asking for further information. He received it, as follows:

To the Rev. J----, in Baltimore:

WASHINGTON, Mch. 2,'85. MY DEAR SIR,--I take my earliest opportunity to answer your favor of Feb.

B---- was premature in calling me a "shrewd man." I wasn't one at that time, but am one now-- that is, I am at least too shrewd to ever again invest in anything put on the market by B----. I know nothing whatever about the Bank Note Co., and never did know anything about it. B---- sold me about $4,000 or $5,000 worth of the stock at $110, and I own it yet. He sold me $10,000 worth of another rose-tinted stock about the same time. I have got that yet, also. I judge that a peculiarity of B----'s stocks is that they are of the staying kind. I think you should have asked somebody else whether I was a shrewd man or not for two reasons: the stock was advertised in a religious paper, a circumstance which was very suspicious; and the compliment came to you from a man who was interested to make a purchaser of you. I am afraid you deserve your loss. A financial scheme advertised in any religious paper is a thing which any living person ought to know enough to avoid; and when the factor is added that M. runs that religious paper, a dead person ought to know enough to avoid it. Very Truly Yours S. L. CLEMENS.

The story of Huck Finn was having a wide success. Webster handled it skillfully, and the sales were large. In almost every quarter its welcome was enthusiastic. Here and there, however, could be found an exception; Huck's morals were not always approved of by library reading-committees. The first instance of this kind was reported from Concord; and would seem not to have depressed the author-publisher.

To Chas. L. Webster, in New York:

Mch 18, '85. DEAR CHARLEY,--The Committee of the Public Library of Concord, Mass, have given us a rattling tip-top puff which will go into every paper in the country. They have expelled

Huck from their library as "trash and suitable only for the slums." That will sell 25,000 copies for us sure.

S. L. C.

Perhaps the Concord Free Trade Club had some idea of making amends to Mark Twain for the slight put upon his book by their librarians, for immediately after the Huck Finn incident they notified him of his election to honorary membership.

Those were the days of "authors' readings," and Clemens and Howells not infrequently assisted at these functions, usually given as benefits of one kind or another. From the next letter, written following an entertainment given for the Longfellow memorial, we gather that Mark Twain's opinion of Howells's reading was steadily improving.

To W. D. Howells, in Boston:

HARTFORD, May 5, '85. MY DEAR HOWELLS,--.....Who taught you to read? Observation and thought, I guess. And practice at the Tavern Club?--yes; and that was the best teaching of all:

Well, you sent even your daintiest and most delicate and fleeting points home to that audience-- absolute proof of good reading. But you couldn't read worth a damn a few years ago. I do not say this to flatter. It is true I looked around for you when I was leaving, but you had already gone.

Alas, Osgood has failed at last. It was easy to see that he was on the very verge of it a year ago, and it was also easy to see that he was still on the verge of it a month or two ago; but I continued to hope--but not expect that he would pull through. The Library of Humor is at his dwelling house, and he will hand it to you whenever you want it.

To save it from any possibility of getting mixed up in the failure, perhaps you had better send down and get it. I told him, the other day, that an order of any kind from you would be his sufficient warrant for its delivery to you.

In two days General Grant has dictated 50 pages of foolscap, and thus the Wilderness and Appomattox stand for all time in his own words. This makes the second volume of his book as valuable as the first.

He looks mighty well, these latter days. Yrs Ever MARK.

"I am exceedingly glad," wrote Howells, "that you approve of my reading, for it gives me some hope that I may do something on the platform next winter..... but I would never read within a hundred miles of you, if I could help it. You simply straddled down to the footlights and took that house up in the hollow of your hand and tickled it."

To W. D. Howells, in Boston:

ELMIRA, July 21, 1885. MY DEAR HOWELLS,--You are really my only author; I am restricted to you, I wouldn't give a damn for the rest.

I bored through Middlemarch during the past week, with its labored and tedious analyses of feelings and motives, its paltry and tiresome people, its unexciting and uninteresting story, and its frequent blinding flashes of single-sentence poetry, philosophy, wit, and what not, and nearly died from the overwork. I wouldn't read another of those books for a farm. I did try to read one other-- Daniel Deronda. I dragged through three chapters, losing flesh all the time, and then was honest enough to quit, and confess to myself that I haven't any romance literature appetite, as far as I can see, except for your books.

But what I started to say, was, that I have just read Part II of Indian Summer, and to my mind there isn't a waste line in it, or one that could be improved. I read it yesterday, ending with that opinion; and read it again to-day, ending with the same opinion emphasized. I haven't read Part I yet, because that number must have reached Hartford after we left; but we are going to send down town for a copy, and when it comes I am to read both parts aloud to the family. It is a beautiful story, and makes a body laugh all the time, and cry inside, and feel so old and so forlorn; and gives him gracious glimpses of his lost youth that fill him with a measureless regret, and build up in him a cloudy sense of his having been a prince, once, in some enchanted far-off land, and of being an exile now, and desolate--and Lord, no chance ever to get back there again! That is the thing that hurts. Well, you have done it with marvelous facility and you make all the motives and feelings perfectly clear without analyzing the guts out of them, the way George Eliot does. I can't stand George Eliot and Hawthorne and those people; I see what they are at a hundred years before they get to it and they just tire me to death. And as for "The Bostonians," I would rather be damned to John Bunyan's heaven than read that. Yrs Ever MARK

It is as easy to understand Mark Twain's enjoyment of Indian Summer as his revolt against Daniel Deronda and The Bostonians. He cared little for writing that did not convey its purpose in the simplest and most direct terms. It is interesting to note that in thanking Clemens for his compliment Howells wrote: "What people cannot see is that I analyze as little as possible; they go on talking about the analytical school, which I am supposed to belong to, and I want to thank you for using your eyes..... Did you ever read De Foe's 'Roxana'? If not, then read it, not merely for some of the deepest insights into the lying, suffering, sinning, well-meaning human soul, but for the best and most natural English that a book was ever written in."

General Grant worked steadily on his book, dictating when he could, making brief notes on slips of paper when he could no longer speak. Clemens visited him at Mt. McGregor and brought the dying soldier the comforting news that enough of his books were already sold to provide generously for his family, and that the sales would aggregate at least twice as much by the end of the year.

This was some time in July. On the 23d of that month General Grant died. Immediately there was a newspaper discussion as to the most suitable place for the great chieftain to lie. Mark Twain's contribution to this debate, though in the form of an open letter, seems worthy of preservation here.

To the New York "Sun," on the proper place for Grant's Tomb:

To THE EDITOR OP' THE SUN:--SIR,--The newspaper atmosphere is charged with objections to New York as a place of sepulchre for General Grant, and the objectors are strenuous that Washington is the right place. They offer good reasons--good temporary reasons--for both of these positions.

But it seems to me that temporary reasons are not mete for the occasion. We need to consider posterity rather than our own generation. We should select a grave which will not merely be in the right place now, but will still be in the right place 500 years from now.

How does Washington promise as to that? You have only to hit it in one place to kill it. Some day the west will be numerically strong enough to move the seat of government; her past attempts are a fair warning that when the day comes she will do it. Then the city of Washington will lose its consequence and pass out of the public view and public talk. It is quite within the possibilities that, a century hence, people would wonder and say, "How did your predecessors come to bury their great dead in this deserted place?"

But as long as American civilisation lasts New York will last. I cannot but think she has been well and wisely chosen as the guardian of a grave which is destined to become almost the most conspicuous in the world's history. Twenty centuries from now New York will still be New York, still a vast city, and the most notable object in it will still be the tomb and monument of General Grant.

I observe that the common and strongest objection to New York is that she is not "national ground." Let us give ourselves no uneasiness about that. Wherever General Grant's body lies, that is national ground.

S. L. CLEMENS. ELMIRA, July 27.

The letter that follows is very long, but it seems too important and too interesting to be omitted in any part. General Grant's early indulgence in liquors had long been a matter of wide, though not very definite, knowledge. Every one had heard how Lincoln, on being told that Grant drank, remarked something to the effect that he would like to know what kind of whisky Grant used so that he might get some of it for his other generals. Henry Ward Beecher, selected to deliver a eulogy on the dead soldier, and doubtless wishing neither to ignore the matter nor to make too much of it, naturally turned for information to the publisher of Grant's own memoirs, hoping from an advance copy to obtain light.

To Henry Ward Beecher,.Brooklyn:

ELMIRA, N. Y. Sept. 11, '85. MY DEAR MR. BEECHER,--My nephew Webster is in Europe making contracts for the Memoirs. Before he sailed he came to me with a writing, directed to the printers and binders, to this effect:

"Honor no order for a sight or copy of the Memoirs while I am absent, even though it be signed by Mr. Clemens himself."

I gave my permission. There were weighty reasons why I should not only give my permission, but hold it a matter of honor to not dissolve the order or modify it at any time. So I did all of that-- said the order should stand undisturbed to the end. If a principal could dissolve his promise as innocently as he can dissolve his written order unguarded by his promise, I would send you a copy of the Memoirs instantly. I did not foresee you, or I would have made an exception.

....

My idea gained from army men, is that the drunkenness (and sometimes pretty reckless spreeing, nights,) ceased before he came East to be Lt. General. (Refer especially to Gen. Wm. B. Franklin-- [If you could see Franklin and talk with him--then he would unbosom,]) It was while Grant was still in the West that Mr. Lincoln said he wished he could find out what brand of whisky that fellow used, so he could furnish it to some of the other generals. Franklin saw Grant tumble from his horse drunk, while reviewing troops in New Orleans. The fall gave him a good deal of a hurt. He was then on the point of leaving for the Chattanooga region. I naturally put "that and that together" when I read Gen. O. O. Howards's article in the Christian Union, three or four weeks ago--where he mentions that the new General arrived lame from a recent accident. (See that article.) And why not write Howard?

Franklin spoke positively of the frequent spreeing. In camp--in time of war.

....

Captain Grant was frequently threatened by the Commandant of his Oregon post with a report to the War Department of his conduct unless he modified his intemperance. The report would mean dismissal from the service. At last the report had to be made out; and then, so greatly was the captain beloved, that he was privately informed, and was thus enabled to rush his resignation to Washington ahead of the report. Did the report go, nevertheless? I don't know. If it did, it is in the War Department now, possibly, and seeable. I got all this from a regular army man, but I can't name him to save me.

The only time General Grant ever mentioned liquor to me was about last April or possibly May. He said:

"If I could only build up my strength! The doctors urge whisky and champagne; but I can't take them; I can't abide the taste of any kind of liquor."

Had he made a conquest so complete that even the taste of liquor was become an offense? Or was he so sore over what had been said about his habit that he wanted to persuade others and likewise himself that he hadn't even ever had any taste for it? It sounded like the latter, but that's no evidence.

He told me in the fall of '84 that there was something the matter with his throat, and that at the suggestion of his physicians he had reduced his smoking to one cigar a day. Then he added, in a casual fashion, that he didn't care for that one, and seldom smoked it.

I could understand that feeling. He had set out to conquer not the habit but the inclination--the desire. He had gone at the root, not the trunk. It's the perfect way and the only true way (I speak from experience.) How I do hate those enemies of the human race who go around enslaving God's free people with pledges--to quit drinking instead of to quit wanting to drink.

But Sherman and Van Vliet know everything concerning Grant; and if you tell them how you want to use the facts, both of them will testify. Regular army men have no concealments about each other; and yet they make their awful statements without shade or color or malice with a frankness and a child-like naivety, indeed, which is enchanting-and stupefying. West Point seems to teach them that, among other priceless things not to be got in any other college in this world. If we talked about our guild- mates as I have heard Sherman, Grant, Van Vliet and others talk about theirs--mates with whom they were on the best possible terms--we could never expect them to speak to us again.

....

I am reminded, now, of another matter. The day of the funeral I sat an hour over a single drink and several cigars with Van Vliet and Sherman and Senator Sherman.; and among other things Gen. Sherman said, with impatient scorn:

"The idea of all this nonsense about Grant not being able to stand rude language and indelicate stories! Why Grant was full of humor, and full of the appreciation of it. I have sat with him by the hour listening to Jim Nye's yarns, and I reckon you know the style of Jim Nye's histories, Clemens. It makes me sick--that newspaper nonsense. Grant was no namby- pamby fool, he was a man--all over--rounded and complete."

I wish I had thought of it! I would have said to General Grant: "Put the drunkenness in the Memoirs--and the repentance and reform. Trust the people."

But I will wager there is not a hint in the book. He was sore, there. As much of the book as I have read gives no hint, as far as I recollect.

The sick-room brought out the points of Gen. Grant's character--some of them particularly, to wit:

His patience; his indestructible equability of temper; his exceeding gentleness, kindness, forbearance, lovingness, charity; his loyalty: to friends, to convictions, to promises, half-promises, infinitesimal fractions and shadows of promises; (There was a requirement of him which I considered an atrocity, an injustice, an outrage; I wanted to implore him to repudiate it; Fred Grant said, "Save your labor, I know him; he is in doubt as to whether he made that half-promise or not--and, he will give the thing the benefit of the doubt; he will fulfill that half- promise or kill himself trying;" Fred Grant was right--he did fulfill it;) his aggravatingly trustful nature; his genuineness, simplicity, modesty, diffidence, self-depreciation, poverty in the quality of vanity- and, in no contradiction of this last, his simple pleasure in the flowers and general ruck sent to him by Tom, Dick and Harry from everywhere--a pleasure that suggested a perennial surprise that he should be the object of so much fine attention--he was the most lovable great child in the world; (I mentioned his loyalty: you remember Harrison, the colored body- servant? the whole family hated him, but that did not make any difference, the General always stood at his back, wouldn't allow him to be scolded; always excused his failures and deficiencies with the one unvarying formula, "We are responsible for these things in his race--it is not fair to visit our fault upon them--let him alone;" so they did let him alone, under compulsion, until the great heart that was his shield was taken away; then--well they simply couldn't stand him, and so they were excusable for determining to discharge him--a thing which they mortally hated to do, and by lucky accident were saved from the necessity of doing;) his toughness as a bargainer when doing business for other people or for his country (witness his "terms" at Donelson, Vicksburg, etc.; Fred Grant told me his father wound up an estate for the widow and orphans of a friend in St. Louis--it took several years; at the end every complication had been straightened out, and the property put upon a prosperous basis; great sums had passed through his hands, and when he handed over the papers there were vouchers to show what had been done with every penny) and his trusting, easy, unexacting fashion when doing business for himself (at that same time he was paying out money in driblets to a man who was running his farm for him--and in his first Presidency he paid every one of those driblets again (total, $3,000 F. said,) for he hadn't a scrap of paper to show that he had ever paid them before; in his dealings with me he would not listen to terms which would place my money at risk and leave him protected--the thought plainly gave him pain, and he put it from him, waved it off with his hands, as one does accounts of crushings and mutilations--wouldn't listen, changed the subject;) and his fortitude! He was under, sentence of death last spring; he sat thinking, musing, several days--nobody knows what about; then he pulled himself together and set to work to finish that book, a colossal task for a dying man. Presently his hand gave out; fate seemed to have got him checkmated. Dictation was suggested. No, he never could do that; had never tried it; too old to learn, now. By and by--if he could only do Appomattox-well. So he sent for a stenographer, and dictated 9,000 words at a single sitting!--never pausing, never hesitating for a word, never repeating--and in the written-out copy he made hardly a correction. He dictated again, every two or three days-- the intervals were intervals of exhaustion and slow recuperation-- and at last he was able to tell me that he had written more matter than could be got into the book. I then enlarged the book--had to. Then he lost his voice. He was not quite done yet, however:--there was no end of little plums and spices to be stuck in, here and there; and this work he patiently continued, a few lines a day, with pad and pencil, till far into July, at Mt. McGregor. One day he put his pencil aside, and said he was done--there was nothing more to do. If I had been there I could have foretold the shock that struck the world three days later.

Well, I've written all this, and it doesn't seem to amount to anything. But I do want to help, if I only could. I will enclose some scraps from my Autobiography--scraps about General Grant--they may be of some trifle of use, and they may not--they at least verify known traits of his character. My Autobiography is pretty freely dictated, but my idea is to jack-plane it a little before I die, some day or other; I mean the rude construction and rotten grammar. It is the only dictating I ever did, and it was most troublesome and awkward work. You may return it to Hartford. Sincerely Yours S. L. CLEMENS.

The old long-deferred Library of Humor came up again for discussion, when in the fall of 1885 Howells associated himself with Harper & Brothers. Howells's contract provided that his name was not to appear on any book not published by the Harper firm. He wrote, therefore, offering to sell out his interest in the enterprise for two thousand dollars, in addition to the five hundred which he had already received--an amount considered to be less than he was to have received as joint author and compiler. Mark Twain's answer pretty fully covers the details of this undertaking.

To W. D. Howells, in Boston:

HARTFORD, Oct. 18, 1885. Private.

MY DEAR HOWELLS,--I reckon it would ruin the book that is, make it necessary to pigeon-hole it and leave it unpublished. I couldn't publish it without a very responsible name to support my own on the title page, because it has so much of my own matter in it. I bought Osgood's rights for $3,000 cash, I have paid Clark $800 and owe him $700 more, which must of course be paid whether I publish or not. Yet I fully recognize that I have no sort of moral right to let that ancient and procrastinated contract hamper you in any way, and I most certainly won't. So, it is my decision,--after thinking over and rejecting the idea of trying to buy permission of the Harpers for $2,500 to use your name, (a proposition which they would hate to refuse to a man in a perplexed position, and yet would naturally have to refuse it,) to pigeon-hole the "Library": not destroy it, but merely pigeon-hole it and wait a few years and see what new notion Providence will take concerning it. He will not desert us now, after putting in four licks to our one on this book all this time. It really seems in a sense discourteous not to call it "Providence's Library of Humor."

Now that deal is all settled, the next question is, do you need and must you require that $2,000 now? Since last March, you know, I am carrying a mighty load, solitary and alone--General Grant's book--and must carry it till the first volume is 30 days old (Jan. 1st) before the relief money will begin to flow in. From now till the first of January every dollar is as valuable to me as it could be to a famishing tramp. If you can wait till then--I mean without discomfort, without inconvenience--it will be a large accommodation to me; but I will not allow you to do this favor if it will discommode you. So, speak right out, frankly, and if you need the money I will go out on the highway and get it, using violence, if necessary.

Mind, I am not in financial difficulties, and am not going to be. I am merely a starving beggar standing outside the door of plenty--obstructed by a Yale time-lock which is set for Jan. 1st. I can stand it, and stand it perfectly well; but the days do seem to fool along considerable slower than they used to.

I am mighty glad you are with the Harpers. I have noticed that good men in their employ go there to stay. Yours ever, MARK.

In the next letter we begin to get some idea of the size of Mark Twain's first publishing venture, and a brief summary of results may not be out of place here.

The Grant Life was issued in two volumes. In the early months of the year when the agents' canvass was just beginning, Mark Twain, with what seems now almost clairvoyant vision, prophesied a sale of three hundred thousand sets. The actual sales ran somewhat more than this number. On February 27, 1886, Charles L. Webster & Co. paid to Mrs. Grant the largest single royalty check in the history of book-publishing. The amount of it was two hundred thousand dollars. Subsequent checks increased the aggregate return to considerably more than double this figure. In a memorandum made by Clemens in the midst of the canvass he wrote."

"During 100 consecutive days the sales (i. e., subscriptions) of General Grant's book averaged 3,000 sets (6,000 single volumes) per day: Roughly stated, Mrs. Grant's income during all that time was $5,000 a day."

To W. D. Howells, in Boston:

HOTEL NORMANDIE NEW YORK, Dec. 2, '85. MY DEAR HOWELLS,--I told Webster, this afternoon, to send you that $2,000; but he is in such a rush, these first days of publication, that he may possibly forget it; so I write lest I forget it too. Remind me, if he should forget. When I postponed you lately, I did it because I thought I should be cramped for money until January, but that has turned out to be an error, so I hasten to cut short the postponement.

I judge by the newspapers that you are in Auburndale, but I don't know it officially.

I've got the first volume launched safely; consequently, half of the suspense is over, and I am that much nearer the goal. We've bound and shipped 200,000 books; and by the 10th shall finish and ship the remaining 125,000 of the first edition. I got nervous and came down to help hump-up the binderies; and I mean to stay here pretty much all the time till the first days of March, when the second volume will issue. Shan't have so much trouble, this time, though, if we get to press pretty soon, because we can get more binderies then than are to be had in front of the holidays. One lives and learns. I find it takes 7 binderies four months to bind 325,000 books.

This is a good book to publish. I heard a canvasser say, yesterday, that while delivering eleven books he took 7 new subscriptions. But we shall be in a hell of a fix if that goes on--it will "ball up" the binderies again. Yrs ever MARK.

November 30th that year was Mark Twain's fiftieth birthday, an event noticed by the newspapers generally, and especially observed by many of his friends. Warner, Stockton and many others sent letters; Andrew Lang contributed a fine poem; also Oliver Wendell. Holmes-- the latter by special request of Miss Gilder--for the Critic. These attentions came as a sort of crowning happiness at the end of a golden year. At no time in his life were Mark Twain's fortunes and prospects brighter; he had a beautiful family and a perfect home. Also, he had great prosperity. The reading-tour with Cable had been a fine success. His latest book, The Adventures of Huckleberry Finn, had added largely to his fame and income. The publication of the Grant Memoirs had been a dazzling triumph. Mark Twain had become recognized, not only as America's most distinguished author, but as its most envied publisher. And now, with his fiftieth birthday, had come this laurel from Holmes, last of the Brahmins, to add a touch of glory to all the rest. We feel his exaltation in his note of acknowledgment.

To Dr. Oliver Wendell Holmes, in Boston:

DEAR MR. HOLMES,--I shall never be able to tell you the half of how proud you have made me. If I could you would say you were nearly paid for the trouble you took. And then the family: If I can convey the electrical surprise and gratitude and exaltation of the wife and the children last night, when they happened upon that Critic where I had, with artful artlessness, spread it open and retired out of view to see what would happen--well, it was great and fine and beautiful to see, and made me feel as the victor feels when the shouting hosts march by; and if you also could have seen it you would have said the account was squared. For I have brought them up in your company, as in the company of a warm and friendly and beneficent but far-distant sun; and so, for you to do this thing was for the sun to send down out of the skies the miracle of a special ray and transfigure me before their faces. I knew what that poem would be to them; I knew it would raise me up to remote and shining heights in their eyes, to very fellowship with the chambered Nautilus itself, and that from that fellowship they could never more dissociate me while they should live; and so I made sure to be by when the surprise should come.

Charles Dudley Warner is charmed with the poem for its own felicitous sake; and so indeed am I, but more because it has drawn the sting of my fiftieth year; taken away the pain of it, the grief of it, the somehow shame of it, and made me glad and proud it happened.

With reverence and affection, Sincerely yours, S. L. CLEMENS.

Holmes wrote with his own hand: "Did Miss Gilder tell you I had twenty-three letters spread out for answer when her suggestion came about your anniversary? I stopped my correspondence and made my letters wait until the lines were done."

End of this Project Gutenberg Etext of Letters Vol. 3, by Mark Twain

MARK TWAIN'S LETTERS 1886-1900

ARRANGED WITH COMMENT BY ALBERT BIGELOW PAINE

VOLUME IV.

XXVI

LETTERS, 1886-87. JANE CLEMENS'S ROMANCE. UNMAILED LETTERS, ETC.

When Clemens had been platforming with Cable and returned to Hartford for his Christmas vacation, the Warner and Clemens families had joined in preparing for him a surprise performance of The Prince and the Pauper. The Clemens household was always given to theatricals, and it was about this time that scenery and a stage were prepared--mainly by the sculptor Gerhardt--for these home performances, after which productions of The Prince and the Pauper were given with considerable regularity to audiences consisting of parents and invited friends. The subject is a fascinating one, but it has been dwelt upon elsewhere.--[In Mark Twain: A Biography, chaps. cliff and clx.]--We get a glimpse of one of these occasions as well as of Mark Twain's financial progress in the next brief note.

To W. D. Howells; in Boston:

Jan. 3, '86. MY DEAR HOWELLS,--The date set for the Prince and Pauper play is ten days hence--Jan. 13. I hope you and Pilla can take a train that arrives here during the day; the one that leaves Boston toward the end of the afternoon would be a trifle late; the performance would have already begun when you reached the house.

I'm out of the woods. On the last day of the year I had paid out $182,000 on the Grant book and it was totally free from debt. Yrs ever MARK.

Mark Twain's mother was a woman of sturdy character and with a keen sense of humor and tender sympathies. Her husband, John Marshall Clemens, had been a man of high moral character, honored by all who knew him, respected and apparently loved by his wife. No one would ever have supposed that during all her years of marriage, and almost to her death, she carried a secret romance that would only be told at last in the weary disappointment of old age. It is a curious story, and it came to light in this curious way:

To W. D. Howells, in Boston:

HARTFORD, May 19, '86. MY DEAR HOWELLS,--..... Here's a secret. A most curious and pathetic romance, which has just come to light. Read these things, but don't mention them. Last fall, my old mother--then 82--took a notion to attend a convention of old settlers of the Mississippi Valley in an Iowa town. My brother's wife was astonished; and represented to her the hardships and fatigues of such a trip, and said my mother might possibly not even survive them; and said there could be no possible interest for her in such a meeting and such a crowd. But my mother insisted, and persisted; and finally gained her point. They started; and all the way my mother was young again with excitement, interest, eagerness, anticipation. They reached the town and the hotel. My mother strode with the same eagerness in her eye and her step, to the counter, and said:

"Is Dr. Barrett of St. Louis, here?"

"No. He was here, but he returned to St. Louis this morning."

"Will he come again?"

"No."

My mother turned away, the fire all gone from her, and said, "Let us go home."

They went straight back to Keokuk. My mother sat silent and thinking for many days--a thing which had never happened before. Then one day she said:

"I will tell you a secret. When I was eighteen, a young medical student named Barrett lived in Columbia (Ky.) eighteen miles away; and he used to ride over to see me. This continued for some time. I loved him with my whole heart, and I knew that he felt the same toward me, though no words had been spoken. He was too bashful to speak--he could not do it. Everybody supposed we were engaged--took it for granted we were--but we were not. By and by there was to be a party in a neighboring town, and he wrote my uncle telling him his feelings, and asking him to drive me over in his buggy and let him (Barrett) drive me back, so that he might have that opportunity to propose. My uncle should have done as he was asked, without explaining anything to me; but instead, he read me the letter; and then, of course, I could not go--and did not. He (Barrett) left the country presently, and I, to stop the clacking tongues, and to show him that I did not care, married, in a pet. In all these sixty-four years I have not seen him since. I saw in a paper that he was going to attend that Old Settlers' Convention. Only three hours before we reached that hotel, he had been standing there!"

Since then, her memory is wholly faded out and gone; and now she writes letters to the schoolmates who had been dead forty years, and wonders why they neglect her and do not answer.

Think of her carrying that pathetic burden in her old heart sixty-four years, and no human being ever suspecting it! Yrs ever, MARK.

We do not get the idea from this letter that those two long ago sweethearts quarreled, but Mark Twain once spoke of their having done so, and there may have been a disagreement, assuming that there was a subsequent meeting. It does not matter, now. In speaking of it, Mark Twain once said: "It is as pathetic a romance as any that has crossed the field of my personal experience in a long lifetime."--[When Mark Twain: A Biography was written this letter had not come to light, and the matter was stated there in accordance with Mark Twain's latest memory of it.]

Howells wrote: "After all, how poor and hackneyed all the inventions are compared with the simple and stately facts. Who could have imagined such a heart-break as that? Yet it went along with the fulfillment of everyday duty and made no more noise than a grave under foot. I doubt if fiction will ever get the knack of such things."

Jane Clemens now lived with her son Orion and his wife, in Keokuk, where she was more contented than elsewhere. In these later days her memory had become erratic, her realization of events about her uncertain, but there were times when she was quite her former self, remembering clearly and talking with her old-time gaiety of spirit. Mark Twain frequently sent her playful letters to amuse her, letters full of such boyish gaiety as had amused her long years before. The one that follows is a fair example. It was written after a visit which Clemens and his family had paid to Keokuk.

To Jane Clemens, in Keokuk:

ELMIRA, Aug. 7, '86. DEAR MA,--I heard that Molly and Orion and Pamela had been sick, but I see by your letter that they are much better now, or nearly well. When we visited you a month ago, it seemed to us that your Keokuk weather was pretty hot; Jean and Clara sat up in bed at Mrs. McElroy's and cried about it, and so did I; but I judge by your letter that it has cooled down, now, so that a person is comparatively comfortable, with his skin off. Well it did need cooling; I remember that I burnt a hole in my shirt, there, with some ice cream that fell on it; and Miss Jenkins told me they never used a stove, but cooked their meals on a marble-topped table in the drawing-room, just with the natural heat. If anybody else had told me, I would not have believed it. I was told by the Bishop of Keokuk that he did not allow crying at funerals, because it scalded the furniture. If Miss Jenkins had told me that, I would have believed it. This reminds me that you speak of Dr. Jenkins and his family as if they were strangers to me. Indeed they are not. Don't you suppose I remember gratefully how tender the doctor was with Jean when she hurt her arm, and how quickly he got the pain out of the hurt, whereas I supposed it was going to last at least an hour? No, I don't forget some things as easily as I do others.

Yes, it was pretty hot weather. Now here, when a person is going to die, he is always in a sweat about where he is going to; but in Keokuk of course they don't care, because they are fixed for everything. It has set me reflecting, it has taught me a lesson. By and by, when my health fails, I am going to put all my affairs in order, and bid good-bye to my friends here, and kill all the people I don't like, and go out to Keokuk and prepare for death.

They are all well in this family, and we all send love. Affly Your Son SAM.

The ways of city officials and corporations are often past understanding, and Mark Twain sometimes found it necessary to write picturesque letters of protest. The following to a Hartford lighting company is a fair example of these documents.

To a gas and electric-lighting company, in Hartford:

GENTLEMEN,--There are but two places in our whole street where lights could be of any value, by any accident, and you have measured and appointed your intervals so ingeniously as to leave each of those places in the centre of a couple of hundred yards of solid darkness. When I noticed that you were setting one of your lights in such a way that I could almost see how to get into my gate at night, I suspected that it was a piece of carelessness on the part of the workmen, and would be corrected as soon as you should go around inspecting and find it out. My judgment was right; it is always right, when you axe concerned. For fifteen years, in spite of my prayers and tears, you persistently kept a gas lamp exactly half way between my gates, so that I couldn't find either of them after dark; and then furnished such execrable gas that I had to hang a danger signal on the lamp post to keep teams from running into it, nights. Now I suppose your present idea is, to leave us a little more in the dark.

Don't mind us--out our way; we possess but one vote apiece, and no rights which you are in any way bound to respect. Please take your electric light and go to--but never mind, it is not for me to suggest; you will probably find the way; and any way you can reasonably count on divine assistance if you lose your bearings.

S. L. CLEMENS.

[Etext Editor's Note: Twain wrote another note to Hartford Gas and Electric, which he may not have mailed and which Paine does not include in these volumes: "Gentleman:--Someday you are going to move me almost to the point of irritation with your God-damned chuckle headed fashion of turning off your God-damned gas without giving notice to your God-damned parishioners--and you did it again last night--" D.W.]

Frequently Clemens did not send letters of this sort after they were written. Sometimes he realized the uselessness of such protest, sometimes the mere writing of them had furnished the necessary relief, and he put, the letter away, or into the wastebasket, and wrote something more temperate, or nothing at all. A few such letters here follow.

Clemens was all the time receiving application from people who wished him to recommend one article or another; books, plays, tobacco, and what not. They were generally persistent people, unable to accept a polite or kindly denial. Once he set down some remarks on this particular phase of correspondence. He wrote:

I

No doubt Mr. Edison has been offered a large interest in many and many an electrical project, for the use of his name to float it withal. And no doubt all men who have achieved for their names, in any line of activity whatever, a sure market value, have been familiar with this sort of solicitation. Reputation is a hall-mark: it can remove doubt from pure silver, and it can also make the plated article pass for pure.

And so, people without a hall-mark of their own are always trying to get the loan of somebody else's.

As a rule, that kind of a person sees only one side of the case. He sees that his invention or his painting or his book is--apparently--a trifle better than you yourself can do, therefore why shouldn't you be willing to put your hall-mark on it? You will be giving the purchaser his full money's worth; so who is hurt, and where is the harm? Besides, are you not helping a struggling fellow-craftsman, and is it not your duty to do that?

That side is plenty clear enough to him, but he can't and won't see the other side, to-wit: that you are a rascal if you put your hall-mark upon a thing which you did not produce yourself, howsoever good it may be. How simple that is; and yet there are not two applicants in a hundred who can, be made to see it.

When one receives an application of this sort, his first emotion is an indignant sense of insult; his first deed is the penning of a sharp answer. He blames nobody but that other person. That person is a very base being; he must be; he would degrade himself for money, otherwise it would not occur to him that you would do such a thing. But all the same, that application has done its work, and taken you down in your own estimation. You recognize that everybody hasn't as high an opinion of you as you have of yourself; and in spite of you there ensues an interval during which you are not, in your own estimation as fine a bird as you were before.

However, being old and experienced, you do not mail your sharp letter, but leave it lying a day. That saves you. For by that time you have begun to reflect that you are a person who deals in exaggerations--and exaggerations are lies. You meant yours to be playful, and thought you made them unmistakably so. But you couldn't make them playfulnesses to a man who has no sense of the playful and can see nothing but the serious side of things. You rattle on quite playfully, and with measureless extravagance, about how you wept at the tomb of Adam; and all in good time you find to your astonishment that no end of people took you at your word and believed you. And presently they find out that you were not in earnest. They have been deceived; therefore, (as they argue--and there is a sort of argument in it,) you are a deceiver. If you will deceive in one way, why shouldn't you in another? So they apply for the use of your trade-mark. You are amazed and affronted. You retort that you are not that kind of person. Then they are amazed and affronted; and wonder "since when?"

By this time you have got your bearings. You realize that perhaps there is a little blame on both sides. You are in the right frame, now. So you write a letter void of offense, declining. You mail this one; you pigeon-hole the other.

That is, being old and experienced, you do, but early in your career, you don't: you mail the first one.

II

An enthusiast who had a new system of musical notation, wrote to me and suggested that a magazine article from me, contrasting the absurdities of the old system with the simplicities of his new one, would be sure to make a "rousing hit." He shouted and shouted over the marvels wrought by his system, and quoted the handsome compliments which had been paid it by famous musical people; but he forgot to tell me what his notation was like, or what its simplicities consisted in. So I could not have written the article if I had wanted to--which I didn't; because I hate strangers with axes to grind. I wrote him a courteous note explaining how busy I was--I always explain how busy I am--and casually drooped this remark:

"I judge the X-X notation to be a rational mode of representing music, in place of the prevailing fashion, which was the invention of an idiot."

Next mail he asked permission to print that meaningless remark. I answered, no--courteously, but still, no; explaining that I could not afford to be placed in the attitude of trying to influence people with a mere worthless guess. What a scorcher I got, next mail! Such irony! such sarcasm, such caustic praise of my superhonorable loyalty to the public! And withal, such compassion for my stupidity, too, in not being able to understand my own language. I cannot remember the words of this letter broadside, but there was about a page used up in turning this idea round and round and exposing it in different lights.

Unmailed Answer:

DEAR SIR,--What is the trouble with you? If it is your viscera, you cannot have them taken out and reorganized a moment too soon. I mean, if they are inside. But if you are composed of them, that is another matter. Is it your brain? But it could not be your brain. Possibly it is your skull: you want to look out for that. Some people, when they get an idea, it pries the structure apart. Your system of notation has got in there, and couldn't find room, without a doubt that is what the trouble is. Your skull was not made to put ideas in, it was made to throw potatoes at. Yours Truly.

Mailed Answer:

DEAR SIR,--Come, come--take a walk; you disturb the children. Yours Truly.

There was a day, now happily nearly over, when certain newspapers made a practice of inviting men distinguished in any walk of life to give their time and effort without charge to express themselves on some subject of the day, or perhaps they were asked to send their favorite passages in prose or verse, with the reasons why. Such symposiums were "features" that cost the newspapers only the writing of a number of letters, stationery, and postage. To one such invitation Mark Twain wrote two replies. They follow herewith:

Unmailed Answer:

DEAR SIR,--I have received your proposition--which you have imitated from a pauper London periodical which had previously imitated the idea of this sort of mendicancy from seventh-rate American journalism, where it originated as a variation of the inexpensive "interview."

Why do you buy Associated Press dispatches? To make your paper the more salable, you answer. But why don't you try to beg them? Why do you discriminate? I can sell my stuff; why should I give it to you? Why don't you ask me for a shirt? What is the difference between asking me for the worth of a shirt and asking me for the shirt itself? Perhaps you didn't know you were begging. I would not use that argument--it makes the user a fool. The passage of poetry--or prose, if you will--which has taken deepest root in my thought, and which I oftenest return to and dwell upon with keenest no matter what, is this: That the proper place for journalists who solicit literary charity is on the street corner with their hats in their hands.

Mailed Answer:

DEAR SIR,--Your favor of recent date is received, but I am obliged by press of work to decline.

The manager of a traveling theatrical company wrote that he had taken the liberty of dramatizing Tom Sawyer, and would like also the use of the author's name--the idea being to convey to the public that it was a Mark Twain play. In return for this slight favor the manager sent an invitation for Mark Twain to come and see the play-- to be present on the opening night, as it were, at his (the manager's) expense. He added that if the play should be a go in the cities there might be some "arrangement" of profits. Apparently these inducements did not appeal to Mark Twain. The long unmailed reply is the more interesting, but probably the briefer one that follows it was quite as effective.

Unmailed Answer:

HARTFORD, Sept. 8, '87. DEAR SIR,--And so it has got around to you, at last; and you also have "taken the liberty." You are No. 1365. When 1364 sweeter and better people, including the author, have "tried" to dramatize Tom Sawyer and did not arrive, what sort of show do you suppose you stand? That is a book, dear sir, which cannot be dramatized. One might as well try to dramatize any other hymn. Tom Sawyer is simply a hymn, put into prose form to give it a worldly air.

Why the pale doubt that flitteth dim and nebulous athwart the forecastle of your third sentence? Have no fears. Your piece will be a Go. It will go out the back door on the first night. They've all done it --the 1364. So will 1365. Not one of us ever thought of the simple device of half-soling himself with a stove-lid. Ah, what suffering a little hindsight would have saved us. Treasure this hint.

How kind of you to invite me to the funeral. Go to; I have attended a thousand of them. I have seen Tom Sawyer's remains in all the different kinds of dramatic shrouds there are. You cannot start anything fresh. Are you serious when you propose to pay my expence--if that is the Susquehannian way of spelling it? And can you be aware that I charge a hundred dollars a mile when I travel for pleasure? Do you realize that it is 432 miles to Susquehanna? Would it be handy for you to send me the $43,200 first, so I could be counting it as I come along; because railroading is pretty dreary to a sensitive nature when there's nothing sordid to buck at for Zeitvertreib.

Now as I understand it, dear and magnanimous 1365, you are going to recreate Tom Sawyer dramatically, and then do me the compliment to put me in the bills as father of this shady offspring. Sir, do you know that this kind of a compliment has destroyed people before now? Listen.

Twenty-four years ago, I was strangely handsome. The remains of it are still visible through the rifts of time. I was so handsome that human activities ceased as if spellbound when I came in view, and even inanimate things stopped to look--like locomotives, and district messenger boys and so-on. In San Francisco, in the rainy season I was often mistaken for fair weather. Upon one occasion I was traveling in the Sonora region, and stopped for an hour's nooning, to rest my horse and myself. All the town came out to look. The tribes of Indians gathered to look. A Piute squaw named her baby for me,--a voluntary compliment which pleased me greatly. Other attentions were paid me. Last of all arrived the president and faculty of Sonora University and offered me the post of Professor of Moral Culture and the Dogmatic Humanities; which I accepted gratefully, and entered at once upon my duties. But my name had pleased the Indians, and in the deadly kindness of their hearts they went on naming their babies after me. I tried to stop it, but the Indians could not understand why I should object to so manifest a compliment. The thing grew and grew and spread and spread and became exceedingly embarrassing. The University stood it a couple of years; but then for the sake of the college they felt obliged to call a halt, although I had the sympathy of the whole faculty. The president himself said to me, "I am as sorry as I can be for you, and would still hold out if there were any hope ahead; but you see how it is: there are a hundred and thirty-two of them already, and fourteen precincts to hear from. The circumstance has brought your name into most wide and unfortunate renown. It causes much comment--I believe that that is not an over-statement. Some of this comment is palliative, but some of it --by patrons at a distance, who only know the statistics without the explanation,--is offensive, and in some cases even violent. Nine students have been called home. The trustees of the college have been growing more and more uneasy all these last months--steadily along with the implacable increase in your census--and

I will not conceal from you that more than once they have touched upon the expediency of a change in the Professorship of Moral Culture. The coarsely sarcastic editorial in yesterday's Alta, headed Give the Moral Acrobat a Rest--has brought things to a crisis, and I am charged with the unpleasant duty of receiving your resignation."

I know you only mean me a kindness, dear 1365, but it is a most deadly mistake. Please do not name your Injun for me. Truly Yours.

Mailed Answer:

NEW YORK, Sept. 8. 1887. DEAR SIR,--Necessarily I cannot assent to so strange a proposition. And I think it but fair to warn you that if you put the piece on the stage, you must take the legal consequences. Yours respectfully, S. L. CLEMENS.

Before the days of international copyright no American author's books were pirated more freely by Canadian publishers than those of Mark Twain. It was always a sore point with him that these books, cheaply printed, found their way into the United States, and were sold in competition with his better editions. The law on the subject seemed to be rather hazy, and its various interpretations exasperating. In the next unmailed letter Mark Twain relieves himself to a misguided official. The letter is worth reading today, if for no other reason, to show the absurdity of copyright conditions which prevailed at that time.

Unmailed Letter to H. C. Christiancy, on book Piracy:

HARTFORD, Dec. 18, '87. H. C. CHRISTIANCY, ESQ.

DEAR SIR,--As I understand it, the position of the U. S. Government is this: If a person be captured on the border with counterfeit bonds in his hands--bonds of the N. Y. Central Railway, for instance--the procedure in his case shall be as follows:

1. If the N. Y. C. have not previously filed in the several police offices along the border, proof of ownership of the originals of the bonds, the government officials must collect a duty on the counterfeits, and then let them go ahead and circulate in this country.

2. But if there is proof already on file, then the N. Y. C. may pay the duty and take the counterfeits.

But in no case will the United States consent to go without its share of the swag. It is delicious. The biggest and proudest government on earth turned sneak-thief; collecting pennies on stolen property, and pocketing them with a greasy and libidinous leer; going into partnership with foreign thieves to rob its own children; and when the child escapes the foreigner, descending to the abysmal baseness of hanging on and robbing the infant all alone by itself! Dear sir, this is not any more respectable than for a father to collect toll on the forced prostitution of his own daughter; in fact it is the same thing. Upon these terms, what is a U. S. custom house but a "fence?" That is all it is: a legalized trader in stolen goods.

And this nasty law, this filthy law, this unspeakable law calls itself a "regulation for the protection of owners of copyright!" Can sarcasm go further than that? In what way does it protect them? Inspiration itself could not furnish a rational answer to that question. Whom does it protect, then? Nobody, as far as I can see, but the foreign thief- sometimes--and his fellow-footpad the U. S. government, all the time. What could the Central Company do with the counterfeit bonds after it had bought them of the star spangled banner Master-thief? Sell them at a dollar apiece and fetch down the market for the genuine hundred-dollar bond? What could I do with that 20-cent copy of "Roughing It" which the United States has collared on the border and is waiting to release to me for cash in case I am willing to come down to its moral level and help rob myself? Sell it at ten or fifteen cents--duty added--and destroy the market for the original $3,50 book? Who ever did invent that law? I would like to know the name of that immortal jackass.

Dear sir, I appreciate your courtesy in stretching your authority in the desire to do me a kindness, and I sincerely thank you for it. But I have no use for that book; and if I were even starving for it I would not pay duty on in either to get it or suppress it. No doubt there are ways in which I might consent to go into partnership with thieves and fences, but this is not one of them. This one revolts the remains of my self- respect; turns my stomach. I think I could companion with a highwayman who carried a shot-gun and took many risks; yes, I think I should like that if I were younger; but to go in with a big rich government that robs paupers, and the widows and orphans of paupers and takes no risk--why the thought just gags me.

Oh, no, I shall never pay any duties on pirated books of mine. I am much too respectable for that--yet awhile. But here--one thing that grovels me is this: as far as I can discover--while freely granting that the U. S. copyright laws are far and away the most idiotic that exist anywhere on the face of the earth--they don't authorize the government to admit pirated books into this country, toll or no toll. And so I think that that regulation is the invention of one of those people--as a rule, early stricken of God, intellectually--the departmental interpreters of the laws, in Washington. They can always be depended on to take any reasonably good law and interpret the common sense all out of it. They can be depended on, every time, to defeat a good law, and make it inoperative--yes, and utterly grotesque, too, mere matter for laughter and derision. Take some of the decisions of the Post-office Department, for instance--though I do not mean to suggest that that asylum is any worse than the others for the breeding and nourishing of incredible lunatics--I merely instance it because it happens to be the first to come into my mind. Take that case of a few years ago where the P. M. General suddenly issued an edict requiring you to add the name of the State after Boston, New York, Chicago, &c, in your superscriptions, on pain of having your letter stopped and forwarded to the dead-letter office; yes, and I believe he required the county, too. He made one little concession in favor of New York: you could say "New York City," and stop there; but if you left off the "city," you must add "N. Y." to your "New York." Why, it threw the business of the whole country into chaos and brought commerce almost to a stand-still. Now think of that! When that man goes to--to--well, wherever he is going to--we shan't want the microscopic details of his address. I guess we can find him.

Well, as I was saying, I believe that this whole paltry and ridiculous swindle is a pure creation of one of those cabbages that used to be at the head of one of those Retreats down there--Departments, you know--and that you will find it so, if you will look into it. And moreover--but land, I reckon we are both tired by this time. Truly Yours, MARK TWAIN.

XXVII

MISCELLANEOUS LETTERS OF 1887. LITERARY ARTICLES. PEACEFUL DAYS AT THE FARM. FAVORITE READING. APOLOGY TO MRS. CLEVELAND, ETC.

We have seen in the preceding chapter how unknown aspirants in one field or another were always seeking to benefit by Mark Twain's reputation. Once he remarked, "The symbol of the human race ought to be an ax; every human being has one concealed about him somewhere." He declared when a stranger called on him, or wrote to him, in nine cases out of ten he could distinguish the gleam of the ax almost immediately. The following letter is closely related to those of the foregoing chapter, only that this one was mailed--not once, but many times, in some form adapted to the specific applicant. It does not matter to whom it was originally written, the name would not be recognized.

To Mrs. T. Concerning unearned credentials, etc.

HARTFORD, 1887. MY DEAR MADAM,--It is an idea which many people have had, but it is of no value. I have seen it tried out many and many a time. I have seen a lady lecturer urged and urged upon the public in a lavishly complimentary document signed by Longfellow, Whittier, Holmes and some others of supreme celebrity, but--there was nothing in her and she failed. If there had been any great merit in her she never would have needed those men's help and (at her rather mature age,) would never have consented to ask for it.

There is an unwritten law about human successes, and your sister must bow to that law, she must submit to its requirements. In brief this law is:

1. No occupation without an apprenticeship.

2. No pay to the apprentice.

This law stands right in the way of the subaltern who wants to be a General before he has smelt powder; and it stands (and should stand) in everybody's way who applies for pay or position before he has served his apprenticeship and proved himself. Your sister's course is perfectly plain. Let her enclose this letter to Maj. J. B. Pond, and offer to lecture a year for $10 a week and her expenses, the contract to be annullable by him at any time, after a month's notice, but not annullable by her at all. The second year, he to have her services, if he wants them, at a trifle under the best price offered her by anybody else.

She can learn her trade in those two years, and then be entitled to remuneration--but she can not learn it in any less time than that, unless she is a human miracle.

Try it, and do not be afraid. It is the fair and right thing. If she wins, she will win squarely and righteously, and never have to blush. Truly yours, S. L. CLEMENS.

Howells wrote, in February, offering to get a publisher to take the Library of Humor off Mark Twain's hands. Howells had been paid twenty-six hundred dollars for the work on it, and his conscience hurt him when he reflected that the book might never be used. In this letter he also refers to one of the disastrous inventions in which Clemens had invested--a method of casting brass dies for stamping book-covers and wall-paper. Howells's purpose was to introduce something of the matter into his next story. Mark Twain's reply gives us a light on this particular invention.

HARTFORD, Feb. 15, '87. DEAR HOWELLS,--I was in New York five days ago, and Webster mentioned the Library, and proposed to publish it a year or a year and half hence. I have written him your proposition to-day. (The Library is part of the property of the C. L. W. & Co. firm.)

I don't remember what that technical phrase was, but I think you will find it in any Cyclopedia under the head of "Brass." The thing I best remember is, that the self-styled "inventor" had a very ingenious way of keeping me from seeing him apply his invention: the first appointment was spoiled by his burning down the man's shop in which it was to be done, the night before; the second was spoiled by his burning down his own shop the night before. He unquestionably did both of these things. He really had no invention; the whole project was a blackmailing swindle, and cost me several thousand dollars.

The slip you sent me from the May "Study" has delighted Mrs. Clemens and me to the marrow. To think that thing might be possible to many; but to be brave enough to say it is possible to you only, I certainly believe. The longer I live the clearer I perceive how unmatchable, how unapproachable, a compliment one pays when he says of a man "he has the courage (to utter) his convictions." Haven't you had reviewers talk Alps to you, and then print potato hills?

I haven't as good an opinion of my work as you hold of it, but I've always done what I could to secure and enlarge my good opinion of it. I've always said to myself, "Everybody reads it and that's something--it surely isn't pernicious, or the most acceptable people would get pretty tired of it." And when a critic said by implication that it wasn't high and fine, through the remark "High and fine literature is wine" I retorted (confidentially, to myself,) "yes, high and fine literature is wine, and mine is only water; but everybody likes water."

You didn't tell me to return that proof-slip, so I have pasted it into my private scrap-book. None will see it there. With a thousand thanks. Ys Ever MARK.

Our next letter is an unmailed answer, but it does not belong with the others, having been withheld for reasons of quite a different sort. Jeanette Gilder, then of the Critic, was one of Mark Twain's valued friends. In the comment which he made, when it was shown to him twenty-two years later, he tells us why he thinks this letter was not sent. The name, "Rest-and-be-Thankful," was the official title given to the summer place at Elmira, but it was more often known as "Quarry Farm."

To Jeannette Gilder (not mailed):

HARTFORD, May 14, '87. MY DEAR MISS GILDER,--We shall spend the summer at the same old place-the remote farm called "Rest-and-be-Thankful," on top of the hills three miles from Elmira, N. Y. Your other question is harder to answer. It is my habit to keep four or five books in process of erection all the time, and every summer add a few courses of bricks to two or three of them; but I cannot forecast which of the two or three it is going to be. It takes seven years to complete a book by this method, but still it is a good method: gives the public a rest. I have been accused of "rushing into print" prematurely, moved thereto by greediness for money; but in truth I have never done that. Do you care for trifles of information? (Well, then, "Tom Sawyer" and "The Prince and the Pauper" were each on the stocks two or three years, and "Old Times on the Mississippi" eight.) One of my unfinished books has been on the stocks sixteen years; another seventeen. This latter book could have been finished in a day, at any time during the past five years. But as in the first of these two narratives all the action takes place in Noah's ark, and as in the other the action takes place in heaven, there seemed to be no hurry, and so I have not hurried. Tales of stirring adventure in those localities do not need to be rushed to publication lest they get stale by waiting. In twenty-one years, with all my time at my free disposal I have written and completed only eleven books, whereas with half the labor that a journalist does I could have written sixty in that time. I do not greatly mind being accused of a proclivity for rushing into print, but at the same time I don't believe that the charge is really well founded. Suppose I did write eleven books, have you nothing to be grateful for? Go to---remember the forty-nine which I didn't write. Truly Yours S. L. CLEMENS.

Notes (added twenty-two years later):

Stormfield, April 30, 1909. It seems the letter was not sent. I probably feared she might print it, and I couldn't find a way to say so without running a risk of hurting her. No one would hurt Jeannette Gilder purposely, and no one would want to run the risk of doing it unintentionally. She is my neighbor, six miles away, now, and I must ask her about this ancient letter.

I note with pride and pleasure that I told no untruths in my unsent answer. I still have the habit of keeping unfinished books lying around years and years, waiting. I have four or five novels on hand at present in a half-finished condition, and it is more than three years since I have looked at any of them. I have no intention of finishing them. I could complete all of them in less than a year, if the impulse should come powerfully upon me: Long, long ago money-necessity furnished that impulse once, (" Following the Equator"), but mere desire for money has never furnished it, so far as I remember. Not even money-necessity was able to overcome me on a couple of occasions when perhaps I ought to have allowed it to succeed. While I was a bankrupt and in debt two offers were made me for weekly literary contributions to continue during a year, and they would have made a debtless man of me, but I declined them, with my wife's full approval, for I had known of no instance where a man had pumped himself out once a week and failed to run "emptyings" before the year was finished.

As to that "Noah's Ark" book, I began it in Edinburgh in 1873;--[This is not quite correct. The "Noah's Ark" book was begun in Buffalo in 1870.] I don't know where the manuscript is now. It was a Diary, which professed to be the work of Shem, but wasn't. I began it again several months ago, but only for recreation; I hadn't any intention of carrying it to a finish --or even to the end of the first chapter, in fact.

As to the book whose action "takes place in Heaven." That was a small thing, ("Captain Stormfield's Visit to Heaven.") It lay in my pigeon-holes 40 years, then I took it out and printed it in Harper's Monthly last year. S. L. C.

In the next letter we get a pretty and peaceful picture of "Rest-and-be-Thankful." These were Mark Twain's balmy days. The financial drain of the type-machine was heavy but not yet exhausting, and the prospect of vast returns from it seemed to grow brighter each day. His publishing business, though less profitable, was still prosperous, his family life was ideal. How gratefully, then, he could enter into the peace of that "perfect day."

To Mrs. Orion Clemens, in Keokuk, Ia.:

ON THE HILL NEAR ELMIRA, July 10, '87. DEAR MOLLIE,--This is a superb Sunday for weather--very cloudy, and the thermometer as low as 65. The city in the valley is purple with shade, as seen from up here at the study. The Cranes are reading and loafing in the canvas-curtained summer-house 50 yards away on a higher (the highest) point; the cats are loafing over at "Ellerslie" which is the children's estate and dwellinghouse in their own private grounds (by deed from Susie Crane) a hundred yards from the study, amongst the clover and young oaks and willows. Livy is down at the house, but I shall now go and bring her up to the Cranes to help us occupy the lounges and hammocks--whence a great panorama of distant hill and valley and city is seeable. The children have gone on a lark through the neighboring hills and woods. It is a perfect day indeed. With love to you all. SAM.

Two days after this letter was written we get a hint of what was the beginning of business trouble--that is to say, of the failing health of Charles L. Webster. Webster was ambitious, nervous, and not robust. He had overworked and was paying the penalty. His trouble was neurasthenia, and he was presently obliged to retire altogether from the business. The "Sam and Mary" mentioned were Samuel Moffet and his wife.

To Mrs. Pamela Moffett, in Fredonia, N. Y.

ELMIRA, July 12, '87 MY DEAR SISTER,--I had no idea that Charley's case was so serious. I knew it was bad, and persistent, but I was not aware of the full size of the matter.

I have just been writing to a friend in Hartford' who treated what I imagine was a similar case surgically last fall, and produced a permanent cure. If this is a like case, Charley must go to him.

If relief fails there, he must take the required rest, whether the business can stand it or not.

It is most pleasant to hear such prosperous accounts of Sam and Mary, I do not see how Sam could well be more advantageously fixed. He can grow up with that paper, and achieve a successful life.

It is not all holiday here with Susie and Clara this time. They have to put in some little time every day on their studies. Jean thinks she is studying too, but I don't know what it is unless it is the horses; she spends the day under their heels in the stables--and that is but a continuation of her Hartford system of culture.

With love from us all to you all. Affectionately SAM.

Mark Twain had a few books that he read regularly every year or two. Among these were 'Pepys's Diary', Suetonius's 'Lives of the Twelve Caesars', and Thomas Carlyle's 'French Revolution'. He had a passion for history, biography, and personal memoirs of any sort. In his early life he had cared very little for poetry, but along in the middle eighties he somehow acquired a taste for Browning and became absorbed in it. A Browning club assembled as often as once a week at the Clemens home in Hartford to listen to his readings of the master. He was an impressive reader, and he carefully prepared himself for these occasions, indicating by graduated underscorings, the exact values he wished to give to words and phrases. Those were memorable gatherings, and they must have continued through at least two winters. It is one of the puzzling phases of Mark Twain's character that, notwithstanding his passion for direct and lucid expression, he should have found pleasure in the poems of Robert Browning.

To W. D. Howells, in Boston:

ELMIRA, Aug. 22, '87. MY DEAR HOWELLS,--How stunning are the changes which age makes in a man while he sleeps. When I finished Carlyle's French Revolution in 1871, I was a Girondin; every time I have read it since, I have read it differently being influenced and changed, little by little, by life and environment (and Taine and St. Simon): and now I lay the book down once more, and recognize that I am a Sansculotte!--And not a pale, characterless Sansculotte, but a Marat. Carlyle teaches no such gospel so the change is in me--in my vision of the evidences.

People pretend that the Bible means the same to them at 50 that it did at all former milestones in their journey. I wonder how they can lie so. It comes of practice, no doubt. They would not say that of Dickens's or Scott's books. Nothing remains the same. When a man goes back to look at the house of his childhood, it has always shrunk: there is no instance of such a house being as big as the picture in memory and imagination call for. Shrunk how? Why, to its correct dimensions: the house hasn't altered; this is the first time it has been in focus.

Well, that's loss. To have house and Bible shrink so, under the disillusioning corrected angle, is loss-for a moment. But there are compensations. You tilt the tube skyward and bring planets and comets and corona flames a hundred and fifty thousand miles high into the field. Which I see you have done, and found Tolstoi. I haven't got him in focus yet, but I've got Browning . . . . Ys Ever MARK.

Mention has been made already of Mark Twain's tendency to absentmindedness. He was always forgetting engagements, or getting them wrong. Once he hurried to an afternoon party, and finding the mistress of the house alone, sat down and talked to her comfortably for an hour or two, not remembering his errand at all. It was only when he reached home that he learned that the party had taken place the week before. It was always dangerous for him to make engagements, and he never seemed to profit by sorrowful experience. We, however, may profit now by one of his amusing apologies.

To Mrs. Grover Cleveland, in Washington:

HARTFORD, Nov. 6, 1887. MY DEAR MADAM,--I do not know how it is in the White House, but in this house of ours whenever the minor half of the administration tries to run itself without the help of the major half it gets aground. Last night when I was offered the opportunity to assist you in the throwing open the Warner brothers superb benefaction in Bridgeport to those fortunate women, I naturally appreciated the honor done me, and promptly seized my chance. I had an engagement, but the circumstances washed it out of my mind. If I had only laid the matter before the major half of the administration on the spot, there would have been no blunder; but I never thought of that. So when I did lay it before her, later, I realized once more that it will not do for the literary fraction of a combination to try to manage affairs which properly belong in the office of the business bulk of it. I suppose the President often acts just like that: goes and makes an impossible promise, and you never find it out until it is next to impossible to break it up and set things straight again. Well, that is just our way, exactly-one half of the administration always busy getting the family into trouble, and the other half busy getting it out again. And so we do seem to be all pretty much alike, after all. The fact is, I had forgotten that we were to have a dinner party on that Bridgeport date--I thought it was the next day: which is a good deal of an improvement for me, because I am more used to being behind a day or two than ahead. But that is just the difference between one end of this kind of an administration and the other end of it, as you have noticed, yourself--the other end does not forget these things. Just so with a funeral; if it is the man's funeral, he is most always there, of course- but that is no credit to him, he wouldn't be there if you depended on hint to remember about it; whereas, if on the other hand--but I seem to have got off from my line of argument somehow; never mind about the funeral. Of course I am not meaning to say anything against funerals-- that is, as occasions--mere occasions--for as diversions I don't think they amount to much But as I was saying--if you are not busy I will look back and see what it was I was saying.

I don't seem to find the place; but anyway she was as sorry as ever anybody could be that I could not go to Bridgeport, but there was no help for it. And I, I have been not only sorry but very sincerely ashamed of having made an engagement to go without first making sure that I could keep it, and I do not know how to apologize enough for my heedless breach of good manners. With the sincerest respect, S. L. CLEMENS.

Samuel Clemens was one of the very few authors to copyright a book in England before the enactment of the international copyright law. As early as 1872 he copyrighted 'Roughing It' in England, and piratical publishers there respected his rights. Finally, in 1887, the inland revenue office assessed him with income tax, which he very willingly paid, instructing his London publishers, Chatto & Windus, to pay on the full amount he had received from them. But when the receipt for his taxes came it was nearly a yard square with due postage of considerable amount. Then he wrote:

To Mr. Chatto, of Chatto & Windus, in London:

HARTFORD, Dec. 5, '87. MY DEAR CHATTO,--Look here, I don't mind paying the tax, but don't you let the Inland Revenue Office send me any more receipts for it, for the postage is something perfectly demoralizing. If they feel obliged to print a receipt on a horse-blanket, why don't they hire a ship and send it over at their own expense?

Wasn't it good that they caught me out with an old book instead of a new one? The tax on a new book would bankrupt a body. It was my purpose to go to England next May and stay the rest of the year, but I've found that tax office out just in time. My new book would issue in March, and they would tax the sale in both countries. Come, we must get up a compromise somehow. You go and work in on the good side of those revenue people and get them to take the profits and give me the tax. Then I will come over and we will divide the swag and have a good time.

I wish you to thank Mr. Christmas for me; but we won't resist. The country that allows me copyright has a right to tax me. Sincerely Yours S. L. CLEMENS.

Another English tax assessment came that year, based on the report that it was understood that he was going to become an English resident, and had leased Buckenham Hall, Norwich, for a year. Clemens wrote his publishers: "I will explain that all that about Buckenham Hall was an English newspaper's mistake. I was not in England, and if I had been I wouldn't have been at Buckenham Hall, anyway, but at Buckingham Palace, or I would have endeavored to find out the reason why." Clemens made literature out of this tax experience. He wrote an open letter to Her Majesty Queen Victoria. Such a letter has no place in this collection. It was published in the "Drawer" of Harper's Magazine, December, 1887, and is now included in the uniform edition of his works under the title of, "A Petition to the Queen of England."

From the following letter, written at the end of the year, we gather that the type-setter costs were beginning to make a difference in the Clemens economies.

To Mrs. Moffett, in Fredonia:

HARTFORD, Dec. 18, '87. DEAR PAMELA,--will you take this $15 and buy some candy or some other trifle for yourself and Sam and his wife to remember that we remember you, by?

If we weren't a little crowded this year by the typesetter, I'd send a check large enough to buy a family Bible or some other useful thing like that. However we go on and on, but the type-setter goes on forever--at $3,000 a month; which is much more satisfactory than was the case the first seventeen months, when the bill only averaged $2,000, and promised to take a thousand years. We'll be through, now, in 3 or 4 months, I reckon, and then the strain will let up and we can breathe freely once more, whether success ensues or failure.

Even with a type-setter on hand we ought not to be in the least scrimped- but it would take a long letter to explain why and who is to blame.

All the family send love to all of you and best Christmas wishes for your prosperity. Affectionately, SAM.

XXVIII

LETTERS,1888. A YALE DEGREE. WORK ON "THE YANKEE." ON INTERVIEWING, ETC.

Mark Twain received his first college degree when he was made Master of Arts by Yale, in June, 1888. Editor of the Courant, Charles H. Clarke, was selected to notify him of his new title. Clarke was an old friend to whom Clemens could write familiarly.

To Charles H. Clarke, in Hartford:

ELMIRA, July 2, '88. MY DEAR CHARLES,--Thanks for your thanks, and for your initiation intentions. I shall be ready for you. I feel mighty proud of that degree; in fact, I could squeeze the truth a little closer and say vain of it. And why shouldn't I be?--I am the only literary animal of my particular subspecies who has ever been given a degree by any College in any age of the world, as far as I know. Sincerely Yours S. L. Clemens M. A.

Reply: Charles H. Clarke to S. L Clemens:

MY DEAR FRIEND, You are "the only literary animal of your particular subspecies" in existence and you've no cause for humility in the fact. Yale has done herself at least as much credit as she has done you, and "Don't you forget it." C. H. C.

With the exception of his brief return to the river in 1882. Mark Twain had been twenty-seven years away from pilots and piloting. Nevertheless, he always kept a tender place in his heart for the old times and for old river comrades. Major "Jack" Downing had been a Mississippi pilot of early days, but had long since retired from the river to a comfortable life ashore, in an Ohio town. Clemens had not heard from him for years when a letter came which invited the following answer.

To Major "Jack" Downing, in Middleport Ohio:

ELMIRA, N. Y.[no month] 1888. DEAR MAJOR,--And has it come to this that the dead rise up and speak? For I supposed that you were dead, it has been so long since I heard your name.

And how young you've grown! I was a mere boy when I knew you on the river, where you had been piloting for 35 years, and now you are only a year and a half older than I am! I mean to go to Hot Springs myself and get 30 or 40 years knocked off my age. It's manifestly the place that Ponce de Leon was striking for, but the poor fellow lost the trail.

Possibly I may see you, for I shall be in St. Louis a day or two in November. I propose to go down the river and "note the changes" once more before I make the long crossing, and perhaps you can come there. Will you? I want to see all the boys that are left alive.

And so Grant Marsh, too, is flourishing yet? A mighty good fellow, and smart too. When we were taking that wood flat down to the Chambers, which was aground, I soon saw that I was a perfect lubber at piloting such a thing. I saw that I could never hit the Chambers with it, so I resigned in Marsh's favor, and he accomplished the task to my admiration. We should all have gone to the mischief if I had remained in authority. I always had good judgement, more judgement than talent, in fact.

No; the nom de plume did not originate in that way. Capt. Sellers used the signature, "Mark Twain," himself, when he used to write up the antiquities in the way of river reminiscences for the New Orleans Picayune. He hated me for burlesquing them in an article in the True Delta; so four years later when he died, I robbed the corpse--that is I confiscated the nom de plume. I have published this vital fact 3,000 times now. But no matter, it is good practice; it is about the only fact that I can tell the same way every time. Very glad, indeed, to hear from you Major, and shall be gladder still to see you in November.

Truly yours, S. L. CLEMENS.

He did not make the journey down the river planned for that year. He had always hoped to make another steamboat trip with Bixby, but one thing and another interfered and he did not go again.

Authors were always sending their books to Mark Twain to read, and no busy man was ever more kindly disposed toward such offerings, more generously considerate of the senders. Louis Pendleton was a young unknown writer in 1888, but Clemens took time to read his story carefully, and to write to him about it a letter that cost precious time, thought, and effort. It must have rejoiced the young man's heart to receive a letter like that, from one whom all young authors held supreme.

To Louis Pendleton, in Georgia:

ELMIRA, N. Y., Aug. 4, '88. MY DEAR SIR,--I found your letter an hour ago among some others which had lain forgotten a couple of weeks, and I at once stole time enough to read Ariadne. Stole is the right word, for the summer "Vacation" is the only chance I get for work; so, no minute subtracted from work is borrowed, it is stolen. But this time I do not repent. As a rule, people don't send me books which I can thank them for, and so I say nothing--which looks uncourteous. But I thank you. Ariadne is a beautiful and satisfying story; and true, too--which is the best part of a story; or indeed of any other thing. Even liars have to admit that, if they are intelligent liars; I mean in their private [the word conscientious written but erased] intervals. (I struck that word out because a man's private thought can never be a lie; what he thinks, is to him the truth, always; what he speaks--but these be platitudes.)

If you want me to pick some flaws--very well--but I do it unwillingly. I notice one thing--which one may notice also in my books, and in all books whether written by man or God: trifling carelessness of statement or Expression. If I think that you meant that she took the lizard from the water which she had drawn from the well, it is evidence--it is almost proof--that your words were not as clear as they should have been. True, it is only a trifling thing; but so is mist on a mirror. I would have hung the pail on Ariadne's arm. You did not deceive me when you said that she carried it under her arm, for I knew she didn't; still it was not your right to mar my enjoyment of the graceful picture. If the pail had been a portfolio, I wouldn't be making these remarks. The engraver of a fine picture revises, and revises, and revises--and then revises, and revises, and revises; and then repeats. And always the charm of that picture grows, under his hand. It was good enough before--told its story, and was beautiful. True: and a lovely girl is lovely, with freckles; but she isn't at her level best with them.

This is not hypercriticism; you have had training enough to know that.

So much concerning exactness of statement. In that other not-small matter--selection of the exact single word--you are hard to catch. Still, I should hold that Mrs. Walker considered that there was no occasion for concealment; that "motive" implied a deeper mental search than she expended on the matter; that it doesn't reflect the attitude of her mind with precision. Is this hypercriticism? I shan't dispute it. I only say, that if Mrs. Walker didn't go so far as to have a motive, I had to suggest that when a word is so near the right one that a body can't quite tell whether it is or isn't, it's good politics to strike it out and go for the Thesaurus. That's all. Motive may stand; but you have allowed a snake to scream, and I will not concede that that was the best word.

I do not apologize for saying these things, for they are not said in the speck-hunting spirit, but in the spirit of want-to-help-if-I-can. They would be useful to me if said to me once a month, they may be useful to you, said once.

I save the other stories for my real vacation--which is nine months long, to my sorrow. I thank you again. Truly Yours S. L. CLEMENS.

In the next letter we get a sidelight on the type-setting machine, the Frankenstein monster that was draining their substance and holding out false hopes of relief and golden return. The program here outlined was one that would continue for several years yet, with the end always in sight, but never quite attained.

To Orion Clemens, in Keokuk, Ia.:

Oct. 3, '88. Private

Saturday 29th, by a closely calculated estimate, there were 85 days' work to do on the machine.

We can use 4 men, but not constantly. If they could work constantly it would complete the machine in 21 days, of course. They will all be on hand and under wages, and each will get in all the work there is opportunity for, but by how much they can reduce the 85 days toward the 21 days, nobody can tell.

To-day I pay Pratt & Whitney $10,000. This squares back indebtedness and everything to date. They began about May or April or March 1886--along there somewhere, and have always kept from a dozen to two dozen master-hands on the machine.

That outgo is done; 4 men for a month or two will close up that leak and caulk it. Work on the patents is also kind of drawing toward a conclusion.

Love to you both. All well here.

And give our love to Ma if she can get the idea.

SAM.

Mark Twain that year was working pretty steadily on 'The Yankee at King Arthur's Court', a book which he had begun two years before. He had published nothing since the Huck Finn story, and his company was badly in need of a new book by an author of distinction. Also it was highly desirable to earn money for himself; wherefore he set to work to finish the Yankee story. He had worked pretty steadily that summer in his Elmira study, but on his return to Hartford found a good deal of confusion in the house, so went over to Twichell's, where carpenter work was in progress. He seems to have worked there successfully, though what improvement of conditions he found in that numerous, lively household, over those at home it would be difficult to say.

To Theodore W. Crane, at Quarry Farm, Elmira, N. Y.

Friday, Oct.,5, '88. DEAR THEO,--I am here in Twichell's house at work, with the noise of the children and an army of carpenters to help. Of course they don't help, but neither do they hinder. It's like a boiler-factory for racket, and in nailing a wooden ceiling onto the room under me the hammering tickles my feet amazingly sometimes, and jars my table a good deal; but I never am conscious of the racket at all, and I move my feet into position of relief without knowing when I do it. I began here Monday morning, and have done eighty pages since. I was so tired last night that I thought I would lie abed and rest, to-day; but I couldn't resist. I mean to try to knock off tomorrow, but it's doubtful if I do. I want to finish the day the machine finishes, and a week ago the closest calculations for that indicated Oct. 22--but experience teaches me that their calculations will miss fire, as usual.

The other day the children were projecting a purchase, Livy and I to furnish the money--a dollar and a half. Jean discouraged the idea. She said: "We haven't got any money. Children, if you would think, you would remember the machine isn't done."

It's billiards to-night. I wish you were here. With love to you both S. L. C.

P. S. I got it all wrong. It wasn't the children, it was Marie. She wanted a box of blacking, for the children's shoes. Jean reproved her- and said:

"Why, Marie, you mustn't ask for things now. The machine isn't done."

S. L. C.

The letter that follows is to another of his old pilot friends, one who was also a schoolmate, Will Bowen, of Hannibal. There is today no means of knowing the occasion upon which this letter was written, but it does not matter; it is the letter itself that is of chief value.

To Will Bowen, in Hannibal, Mo.:

HARTFORD, Nov 4, '88. DEAR WILL,--I received your letter yesterday evening, just as I was starting out of town to attend a wedding, and so my mind was privately busy, all the evening, in the midst of the maelstrom of chat and chaff and laughter, with the sort of reflections which create themselves, examine themselves, and continue themselves, unaffected by surroundings -- unaffected, that is understood, by the surroundings, but not uninfluenced by them. Here was the near presence of the two supreme events of life: marriage, which is the beginning of life, and death which is the end of it. I found myself seeking chances to shirk into corners where I might think, undisturbed; and the most I got out of my thought, was this: both marriage and death ought to be welcome: the one promises happiness, doubtless the other assures it. A long procession of people filed through my mind--people whom you and I knew so many years ago--so many centuries ago, it seems like-and these ancient dead marched to the soft marriage music of a band concealed in some remote room of the house; and the contented music and the dreaming shades seemed in right accord with each other, and fitting. Nobody else knew that a procession of the dead was passing though this noisy swarm of the living, but there it was, and to me there was nothing uncanny about it; Rio, they were welcome faces to me. I would have liked to bring up every creature we knew in those days--even the dumb animals--it would be bathing in the fabled Fountain of Youth.

We all feel your deep trouble with you; and we would hope, if we might, but your words deny us that privilege. To die one's self is a thing that must be easy, and of light consequence, but to lose a part of one's self --well, we know how deep that pang goes, we who have suffered that disaster, received that wound which cannot heal. Sincerely your friend S. L. CLEMENS.

His next is of quite a different nature. Evidently the typesetting conditions had alarmed Orion, and he was undertaking some economies with a view of retrenchment. Orion was always reducing economy to science. Once, at an earlier date, he recorded that he had figured his personal living expenses down to sixty cents a week, but inasmuch as he was then, by his own confession, unable to earn the sixty cents, this particular economy was wasted. Orion was a trial, certainly, and the explosion that follows was not without excuse. Furthermore, it was not as bad as it sounds. Mark Twain's rages always had an element of humor in them, a fact which no one more than Orion himself would appreciate. He preserved this letter, quietly noting on the envelope, "Letter from Sam, about ma's nurse."

Letter to Orion Clemens, in Keokuk, Iowa:

NOV. 29, '88. Jesus Christ!--It is perilous to write such a man. You can go crazy on less material than anybody that ever lived. What in hell has produced all these maniacal imaginings? You told me you had hired an attendant for ma. Now hire one instantly, and stop this nonsense of wearing Mollie and yourself out trying to do that nursing yourselves. Hire the attendant, and tell me her cost so that I can instruct Webster & Co. to add it every month to what they already send. Don't fool away any more time about this. And don't write me any more damned rot about "storms," and inability to pay trivial sums of money and--and--hell and damnation! You see I've read only the first page of your letter; I wouldn't read the rest for a million dollars. Yr SAM.

P. S. Don't imagine that I have lost my temper, because I swear. I swear all day, but I do not lose my temper. And don't imagine that I am on my way to the poorhouse, for I am not; or that I am uneasy, for I am not; or that I am uncomfortable or unhappy--for I never am. I don't know what it is to be unhappy or uneasy; and I am not going to try to learn how, at this late day. SAM.

Few men were ever interviewed oftener than Mark Twain, yet he never welcomed interviewers and was seldom satisfied with them. "What I say in an interview loses it character in print," he often remarked, "all its life and personality. The reporter realizes this himself, and tries to improve upon me, but he doesn't help matters any."

Edward W. Bok, before he became editor of the Ladies Home Journal, was conducting a weekly syndicate column under the title of "Bok's Literary Leaves." It usually consisted of news and gossip of writers, comment, etc., literary odds and ends, and occasional interviews with distinguished authors. He went up to Hartford one day to interview Mark Twain. The result seemed satisfactory to Bok, but wishing to be certain that it would be satisfactory to Clemens, he sent him a copy for approval. The interview was not returned; in the place of it came a letter-not altogether disappointing, as the reader may believe.

To Edward W. Bok, in New York:

MY DEAR MR. BOK,--No, no. It is like most interviews, pure twaddle and valueless.

For several quite plain and simple reasons, an "interview" must, as a rule, be an absurdity, and chiefly for this reason--It is an attempt to use a boat on land or a wagon on water, to speak figuratively. Spoken speech is one thing, written speech is quite another. Print is the proper vehicle for the latter, but it isn't for the former. The moment "talk" is put into print you recognize that it is not what it was when you heard it; you perceive that an immense something has disappeared from it. That is its soul. You have nothing but a dead carcass left on your hands. Color, play of feature, the varying modulations of the voice, the laugh, the smile, the informing inflections, everything that gave that body warmth, grace, friendliness and charm and commended it to your affections--or, at least, to your tolerance--is gone and nothing is left but a pallid, stiff and repulsive cadaver.

Such is "talk" almost invariably, as you see it lying in state in an "interview". The interviewer seldom tries to tell one how a thing was said; he merely puts in the naked remark and stops there. When one writes for print his methods are very different. He follows forms which have but little resemblance to conversation, but they make the reader understand what the writer is trying to convey. And when the writer is making a story and finds it necessary to report some of the talk of his characters observe how cautiously and anxiously he goes at that risky and difficult thing. "If he had dared to say that thing in my presence," said Alfred, "taking a mock heroic attitude, and casting an arch glance upon the company, blood would have flowed."

"If he had dared to say that thing in my presence," said Hawkwood, with that in his eye which caused more than one heart in that guilty assemblage to quake, "blood would have flowed."

"If he had dared to say that thing in my presence," said the paltry blusterer, with valor on his tongue and pallor on his lips, "blood would have flowed."

So painfully aware is the novelist that naked talk in print conveys no meaning that he loads, and often overloads, almost every utterance of his characters with explanations and interpretations. It is a loud confession that print is a poor vehicle for "talk"; it is a recognition that uninterpreted talk in print would result in confusion to the reader, not instruction.

Now, in your interview, you have certainly been most accurate; you have set down the sentences I uttered as I said them. But you have not a word of explanation; what my manner was at several points is not indicated. Therefore, no reader can possibly know where I was in earnest and where I was joking; or whether I was joking altogether or in earnest altogether. Such a report of a conversation has no value. It can convey many meanings to the reader, but never the right one. To add interpretations which would convey the right meaning is a something which would require -- what? An art so high and fine and difficult that no possessor of it would ever be allowed to waste it on interviews.

No; spare the reader, and spare me; leave the whole interview out; it is rubbish. I wouldn't talk in my sleep if I couldn't talk better than that.

If you wish to print anything print this letter; it may have some value, for it may explain to a reader here and there why it is that in interviews, as a rule, men seem to talk like anybody but themselves. Very sincerely yours, MARK TWAIN.

XXIX

LETTERS, 1889. THE MACHINE. DEATH OF MR. CRANE. CONCLUSION OF THE YANKEE

In January, 1889, Clemens believed, after his long seven years of waiting, fruition had come in the matter of the type machine. Paige, the inventor, seemed at last to have given it its finishing touches. The mechanical marvel that had cost so much time, mental stress, and a fortune in money, stood complete, responsive to the human will and touch --the latest, and one of the greatest, wonders of the world. To George Standring, a London printer and publisher, Clemens wrote: "The machine is finished!" and added, "This is by far the most marvelous invention ever contrived by man. And it is not a thing of rags and patches; it is made of massive steel, and will last a century."

In his fever of enthusiasm on that day when he had actually seen it in operation, he wrote a number of exuberant letters. They were more or less duplicates, but as the one to his brother is of fuller detail and more intimate than the others, it has been selected for preservation here.

To Orion Clemens, in Keokuk:

HARTFORD, Jan. 5, '89. DEAR ORION,--At 12.20 this afternoon a line of movable types was spaced and justified by machinery, for the first time in the history of the world! And I was there to see. It was done automatically--instantly-- perfectly. This is indeed the first line of movable types that ever was perfectly spaced and perfectly justified on this earth.

This was the last function that remained to be tested--and so by long odds the most amazing and extraordinary invention ever born of the brain of man stands completed and perfect. Livy is down stairs celebrating.

But it's a cunning devil, is that machine!--and knows more than any man that ever lived. You shall see. We made the test in this way. We set up a lot of random letters in a stick--three-fourths of a line; then filled out the line with quads representing 14 spaces, each space to be 35/1000 of an inch thick. Then we threw aside the quads and put the letters into the machine and formed them into 15 two-letter words, leaving the words separated by two-inch vacancies. Then we started up the machine slowly, by hand, and fastened our eyes on the space-selecting pins. The first pin-block projected its third pin as the first word came traveling along the race-way; second block did the same; but the third block projected its second pin!

"Oh, hell! stop the machine--something wrong--it's going to set a 30/1000 space!"

General consternation. "A foreign substance has got into the spacing plates." This from the head mathematician.

"Yes, that is the trouble," assented the foreman.

Paige examined. "No--look in, and you can see that there's nothing of the kind." Further examination. "Now I know what it is--what it must be: one of those plates projects and binds. It's too bad--the first testis a failure." A pause. "Well, boys, no use to cry. Get to work-- take the machine down.--No--Hold on! don't touch a thing! Go right ahead! We are fools, the machine isn't. The machine knows what it's about. There is a speck of dirt on one of those types, and the machine is putting in a thinner space to allow for it!"

That was just it. The machine went right ahead, spaced the line, justified it to a hair, and shoved it into the galley complete and perfect! We took it out and examined it with a glass. You could not tell by your eye that the third space was thinner than the others, but the glass and the calipers showed the difference. Paige had always said that the machine would measure invisible particles of dirt and allow for them, but even he had forgotten that vast fact for the moment.

All the witnesses made written record of the immense historical birth-- the first justification of a line of movable type by machinery--and also set down the hour and the minute. Nobody had drank anything, and yet everybody seemed drunk. Well-dizzy, stupefied, stunned.

All the other wonderful inventions of the human brain sink pretty nearly into commonplace contrasted with this awful mechanical miracle. Telephones, telegraphs, locomotives, cotton gins, sewing machines, Babbage calculators, jacquard looms, perfecting presses, Arkwright's frames-- all mere toys, simplicities! The Paige Compositor marches alone and far in the lead of human inventions.

In two or three weeks we shall work the stiffness out of her joints and have her performing as smoothly and softly as human muscles, and then we shall speak out the big secret and let the world come and gaze.

Return me this letter when you have read it.

SAM.

Judge of the elation which such a letter would produce in Keokuk! Yet it was no greater than that which existed in Hartford--for a time.

Then further delays. Before the machine got "the stiffness out of her joints" that "cunning devil" manifested a tendency to break the types, and Paige, who was never happier than when he was pulling things to pieces and making improvements, had the type-setter apart again and the day of complete triumph was postponed.

There was sadness at the Elmira farm that spring. Theodore Crane, who had long been in poor health, seemed to grow daily worse. In February he had paid a visit to Hartford and saw the machine in operation, but by the end of May his condition was very serious. Remembering his keen sense of humor, Clemens reported to him cheering and amusing incidents.

To Mrs. Theodore Crane. in Elmira, N. Y.:

HARTFORD, May 28, '89. Susie dear, I want you to tell this to Theodore. You know how absent-minded Twichell is, and how desolate his face is when he is in that frame. At such times, he passes the word with a friend on the street and is not aware of the meeting at all. Twice in a week, our Clara had this latter experience with him within the past month. But the second instance was too much for her, and she woke him up, in his tracks, with a reproach. She said:

"Uncle Joe, why do you always look as if you were just going down into the grave, when you meet a person on the street?"--and then went on to reveal to him the funereal spectacle which he presented on such occasions. Well, she has met Twichell three times since then, and would swim the Connecticut to avoid meeting him the fourth. As soon as he sights her, no matter how public the place nor how far off she is, he makes a bound into the air, heaves arms and legs into all sorts of frantic gestures of delight, and so comes prancing, skipping and pirouetting for her like a drunken Indian entering heaven.

With a full invoice of love from us all to you and Theodore.

S. L. C.

The reference in the next to the "closing sentence" in a letter written by Howells to Clemens about this time, refers to a heart-broken utterance of the former concerning his daughter Winnie, who had died some time before. She had been a gentle talented girl, but never of robust health. Her death had followed a long period of gradual decline.

To W. D. Howells, in Boston:

HARTFORD, Judy 13, '89. DEAR HOWELLS,--I came on from Elmira a day or two ago, where I left a house of mourning. Mr. Crane died, after ten months of pain and two whole days of dying, at the farm on the hill, the 3rd inst: A man who had always hoped for a swift death. Mrs. Crane and Mrs. Clemens and the children were in a gloom which brought back to me the days of nineteen years ago, when Mr. Langdon died. It is heart-breaking to see Mrs. Crane. Many a time, in the past ten days, the sight of her has reminded me, with a pang, of the desolation which uttered itself in the closing sentence of your last letter to me. I do see that there is an argument against suicide: the grief of the worshipers left behind; the awful famine in their hearts, these are too costly terms for the release.

I shall be here ten days yet, and all alone: nobody in the house but the servants. Can't Mrs. Howells spare you to me? Can't you come and stay with me? The house is cool and pleasant; your work will not be interrupted; we will keep to ourselves and let the rest of the world do the same; you can have your choice of three bedrooms, and you will find the Children's schoolroom (which was built for my study,) the perfection of a retired and silent den for work. There isn't a fly or a mosquito on the estate. Come--say you will.

With kindest regards to Mrs. Howells, and Pilla and John, Yours Ever MARK.

Howells was more hopeful. He wrote: "I read something in a strange book, The Physical Theory of Another Life, that consoles a little; namely, we see and feel the power of Deity in such fullness that we ought to infer the infinite justice and Goodness which we do not see or feel." And a few days later, he wrote: "I would rather see and talk with you than any other man in the world outside my own blood."

A Connecticut Yankee at King Arthur's Court was brought to an end that year and given to the artist and printer. Dan Beard was selected for the drawings, and was given a free hand, as the next letter shows.

To Fred J. Hall, Manager Charles L. Webster & Co.:

[Charles L. Webster, owing to poor health, had by this time retired from the firm.]

ELMIRA, July 20, '89. DEAR MR. HALL,--Upon reflection--thus: tell Beard to obey his own inspiration, and when he sees a picture in his mind put that picture on paper, be it humorous or be it serious. I want his genius to be wholly unhampered, I shan't have fears as to the result. They will be better pictures than if I mixed in and tried to give him points on his own trade.

Send this note and he'll understand. Yr S. L. C.

Clemens had made a good choice in selecting Beard for the illustrations. He was well qualified for the work, and being of a socialistic turn of mind put his whole soul into it. When the drawings were completed, Clemens wrote: "Hold me under permanent obligations. What luck it was to find you! There are hundreds of artists that could illustrate any other book of mine, but there was only one who could illustrate this one. Yes, it was a fortunate hour that I went netting for lightning bugs and caught a meteor. Live forever!"

Clemens, of course, was anxious for Howells to read The Yankee, and Mrs. Clemens particularly so. Her eyes were giving her trouble that summer, so that she could not read the MS. for herself, and she had grave doubts as to some of its chapters. It may be said here that the book to-day might have been better if Mrs. Clemens had been able to read it. Howells was a peerless critic, but the revolutionary subject-matter of the book so delighted him that he was perhaps somewhat blinded to its literary defects. However, this is premature. Howells did not at once see the story. He had promised to come to Hartford, but wrote that trivial matters had made his visit impossible. From the next letter we get the situation at this time. The "Mr. Church" mentioned was Frederick S. Church, the well-known artist.

To W. D. Howells, in Boston:

ELMIRA, July 24, '89. DEAR HOWELLS,--I, too, was as sorry as I could be; yes, and desperately disappointed. I even did a heroic thing: shipped my book off to New York lest I should forget hospitality and embitter your visit with it. Not that I think you wouldn't like to read it, for I think you would; but not on a holiday that's not the time. I see how you were situated-- another familiarity of Providence and wholly wanton intrusion--and of course we could not help ourselves. Well, just think of it: a while ago, while Providence's attention was absorbed in disordering some time-tables so as to break up a trip of mine to Mr. Church's on the Hudson, that Johnstown dam got loose. I swear I was afraid to pray, for fear I should laugh. Well, I'm not going to despair; we'll manage a meet yet.

I expect to go to Hartford again in August and maybe remain till I have to come back here and fetch the family. And, along there in August, some time, you let on that you are going to Mexico, and I will let on that I am going to Spitzbergen, and then under cover of this clever stratagem we will glide from the trains at Worcester and have a time. I have noticed that Providence is indifferent about Mexico and Spitzbergen. Ys Ever MARK.

Possibly Mark Twain was not particularly anxious that Howells should see his MS., fearing that he might lay a ruthless hand on some of his more violent fulminations and wild fancies. However this may be, further postponement was soon at an end. Mrs. Clemens's eyes troubled her and would not permit her to read, so she requested that the Yankee be passed upon by soberminded critics, such as Howells and Edmund Clarence Stedman. Howells wrote that even if he hadn't wanted to read the book for its own sake, or for the author's sake, he would still want to do it for Mrs. Clemens's. Whereupon the proofs were started in his direction.

To W. D. Howells, in Boston:

ELMIRA, Aug. 24, '89. DEAR HOWELLS,--If you should be moved to speak of my book in the Study, I shall be glad and proud--and the sooner it gets in, the better for the book; though I don't suppose you can get it in earlier than the November number--why, no, you can't get it in till a month later than that. Well, anyway I don't think I'll send out any other press copy--except perhaps to Stedman. I'm not writing for those parties who miscall themselves critics, and I don't care to have them paw the book at all. It's my swan-song, my retirement from literature permanently, and I wish to pass to the cemetery unclodded.

I judge that the proofs have begun to reach you about this time, as I had some (though not revises,) this morning. I'm sure I'm going to be charmed with Beard's pictures. Observe his nice take-off of Middle-Age art-dinner-table scene. Ys sincerely MARK.

Howells's approval of the Yankee came almost in the form of exultant shouts, one after reading each batch of proof. First he wrote: "It's charming, original, wonderful! good in fancy and sound to the core in morals." And again, "It's a mighty great book, and it makes my heart burn with wrath. It seems God did not forget to put a soul into you. He shuts most literary men off with a brain, merely." Then, a few days later: "The book is glorious--simply noble; what masses of virgin truth never touched in print before!" and, finally, "Last night I read your last chapter. As Stedman says of the whole book, it's titanic."

To W. D. Howells, in Boston:

HARTFORD, Sept. 22, '89. DEAR HOWELLS,--It is immensely good of you to grind through that stuff for me; but it gives peace to Mrs. Clemens's soul; and I am as grateful to you as a body can be. I am glad you approve of what I say about the French Revolution. Few people will. It is odd that even to this day Americans still observe that immortal benefaction through English and other monarchical eyes, and have no shred of an opinion about it that they didn't get at second-hand.

Next to the 4th of July and its results, it was the noblest and the holiest thing and the most precious that ever happened in this earth. And its gracious work is not done yet--not anywhere in the remote neighborhood of it.

Don't trouble to send me all the proofs; send me the pages with your corrections on them, and waste-basket the rest. We issue the book Dec. 10; consequently a notice that appears Dec. 20 will be just in good time.

I am waiting to see your Study set a fashion in criticism. When that happens--as please God it must--consider that if you lived three centuries you couldn't do a more valuable work for this country, or a humaner.

As a rule a critic's dissent merely enrages, and so does no good; but by the new art which you use, your dissent must be as welcome as your approval, and as valuable. I do not know what the secret of it is, unless it is your attitude--man courteously reasoning with man and brother, in place of the worn and wearisome critical attitude of all this long time--superior being lecturing a boy.

Well, my book is written--let it go. But if it were only to write over again there wouldn't be so many things left out. They burn in me; and they keep multiplying and multiplying; but now they can't ever be said. And besides, they would require a library--and a pen warmed up in hell. Ys Ever MARK.

The type-setting machine began to loom large in the background. Clemens believed it perfected by this time. Paige had got it together again and it was running steadily--or approximately so -- setting type at a marvelous speed and with perfect accuracy. In time an expert operator would be able to set as high as eight thousand ems per hour, or about ten times as much as a good compositor could set and distribute by hand. Those who saw it were convinced--most of them--that the type-setting problem was solved by this great mechanical miracle. If there were any who doubted, it was because of its marvelously minute accuracy which the others only admired. Such accuracy, it was sometimes whispered, required absolutely perfect adjustment, and what would happen when the great inventor--"the poet in steel," as Clemens once called him--was no longer at hand to supervise and to correct the slightest variation. But no such breath of doubt came to Mark Twain; he believed the machine as reliable as a constellation.

But now there was need of capital to manufacture and market the wonder. Clemens, casting about in his mind, remembered Senator Jones, of Nevada, a man of great wealth, and his old friend, Joe Goodman, of Nevada, in whom Jones had unlimited confidence. He wrote to Goodman, and in this letter we get a pretty full exposition of the whole matter as it stood in the fall of 1889. We note in this communication that Clemens says that he has been at the machine three years and seven months, but this was only the period during which he had spent the regular monthly sum of three thousand dollars. His interest in the invention had begun as far back as 1880.

To Joseph T. Goodman, in Nevada:

Private. HARTFORD, Oct. 7, '89. DEAR JOE,-I had a letter from Aleck Badlam day before yesterday, and in answering him I mentioned a matter which I asked him to consider a secret except to you and John McComb,--[This is Col. McComb, of the Alta- California, who had sent Mark Twain on the Quaker City excursion]--as I am not ready yet to get into the newspapers.

I have come near writing you about this matter several times, but it wasn't ripe, and I waited. It is ripe, now. It is a type-setting machine which I undertook to build for the inventor(for a consideration). I have been at it three years and seven months without losing a day, at a cost of $3,000 a month, and in so private a way that Hartford has known nothing about it. Indeed only a dozen men have known of the matter. I have reported progress from time to time to the proprietors of the N. Y. Sun, Herald, Times, World, Harper Brothers and John F. Trow; also to the proprietors of the Boston Herald and the Boston Globe. Three years ago I asked all these people to squelch their frantic desire to load up their offices with the Mergenthaler (N. Y. Tribune) machine, and wait for mine and then choose between the two. They have waited--with no very gaudy patience--but still they have waited; and I could prove to them to-day that they have not lost anything by it. But I reserve the proof for the present--except in the case of the N. Y. Herald; I sent an invitation there the other day--a courtesy due a paper which ordered $240,000 worth of our machines long ago when it was still in a crude condition. The Herald has ordered its foreman to come up here next Thursday; but that is the only invitation which will go out for some time yet.

The machine was finished several weeks ago, and has been running ever since in the machine shop. It is a magnificent creature of steel, all of Pratt & Whitney's super-best workmanship, and as nicely adjusted and as accurate as a watch. In construction it is as elaborate and complex as that machine which it ranks next to, by every right--Man--and in performance it is as simple and sure.

Anybody can set type on it who can read--and can do it after only 15 minutes' instruction. The operator does not need to leave his seat at the keyboard; for the reason that he is not required to do anything but strike the keys and set type--merely one function; the spacing, justifying, emptying into the galley, and distributing of dead matter is all done by the machine without anybody's help--four functions.

The ease with which a cub can learn is surprising. Day before yesterday I saw our newest cub set, perfectly space and perfectly justify 2,150 ems of solid nonpareil in an hour and distribute the like amount in the same hour--and six hours previously he had never seen the machine or its keyboard. It was a good hour's work for 3-year veterans on the other type-setting machines to do. We have 3 cubs. The dean of the trio is a school youth of 18. Yesterday morning he had been an apprentice on the machine 16 working days (8-hour days); and we speeded him to see what he could do in an hour. In the hour he set 5,900 ems solid nonpareil, and the machine perfectly spaced and justified it, and of course distributed the like amount in the same hour. Considering that a good fair compositor sets 700 and distributes 700 in the one hour, this boy did the work of about 8 x a compositors in that hour. This fact sends all other type-setting machines a thousand miles to the rear, and the best of them will never be heard of again after we publicly exhibit in New York.

We shall put on 3 more cubs. We have one school boy and two compositors, now,--and we think of putting on a type writer, a stenographer, and perhaps a shoemaker, to show that no special gifts or training are required with this machine. We shall train these beginners two or three months--or until some one of them gets up to 7,000 an hour--then we will show up in New York and run the machine 24 hours a day 7 days in the week, for several months--to prove that this is a machine which will never get out of order or cause delay, and can stand anything an anvil can stand. You know there is no other typesetting machine that can run two hours on a stretch without causing trouble and delay with its incurable caprices.

We own the whole field--every inch of it--and nothing can dislodge us.

Now then, above is my preachment, and here follows the reason and purpose of it. I want you to run over here, roost over the machine a week and satisfy yourself, and then go to John P. Jones or to whom you please, and sell me a hundred thousand dollars' worth of this property and take ten per cent in cash or the "property" for your trouble--the latter, if you are wise, because the price I ask is a long way short of the value.

What I call "property" is this. A small part of my ownership consists of a royalty of $500 on every machine marketed under the American patents. My selling-terms are, a permanent royalty of one dollar on every American-marketed machine for a thousand dollars cash to me in hand paid. We shan't market any fewer than 5,000 machines in 15 years--a return of fifteen thousand dollars for one thousand. A royalty is better than stock, in one way--it must be paid, every six months, rain or shine; it is a debt, and must be paid before dividends are declared. By and by, when we become a stock company I shall buy these royalties back for stock if I can get them for anything like reasonable terms.

I have never borrowed a penny to use on the machine, and never sold a penny's worth of the property until the machine was entirely finished and proven by the severest tests to be what she started out to be--perfect, permanent, and occupying the position, as regards all kindred machines, which the City of Paris occupies as regards the canvas-backs of the mercantile marine.

It is my purpose to sell two hundred dollars of my royalties at the above price during the next two months and keep the other $300.

Mrs. Clemens begs Mrs. Goodman to come with you, and asks pardon for not writing the message herself--which would be a pathetically-welcome spectacle to me; for I have been her amanuensis for 8 months, now, since her eyes failed her. Yours as always MARK.

While this letter with its amazing contents is on its way to astonish Joe Goodman, we will consider one of quite a different, but equally characteristic sort. We may assume that Mark Twain's sister Pamela had been visiting him in Hartford and was now making a visit in Keokuk.

To Mrs. Moffett, in Keokuk:

HARTFORD, Oct 9, '89. DEAR PAMELA,--An hour after you left I was suddenly struck with a realizing sense of the utter chuckle-headedness of that notion of mine: to send your trunk after you. Land! it was idiotic. None but a lunatic would, separate himself from his baggage.

Well, I am soulfully glad the baggage fetcher saved me from consummating my insane inspiration. I met him on the street in the afternoon and paid him again. I shall pay him several times more, as opportunity offers.

I declined the invitation to banquet with the visiting South American Congress, in a polite note explaining that I had to go to New York today. I conveyed the note privately to Patrick; he got the envelope soiled, and asked Livy to put on a clean one. That is why I am going to the banquet; also why I have disinvited the boys I thought I was going to punch billiards with, upstairs to-night.

Patrick is one of the injudiciousest people I ever struck. And I am the other. Your Brother SAM.

The Yankee was now ready for publication, and advance sheets were already in the reviewers' hands. Just at this moment the Brazilian monarchy crumbled, and Clemens was moved to write Sylvester Baxter, of the Boston Herald, a letter which is of special interest in its prophecy of the new day, the dawn of which was even nearer than he suspected.

DEAR MR. BAXTER, Another throne has gone down, and I swim in oceans of satisfaction. I wish I might live fifty years longer; I believe I should see the thrones of Europe selling at auction for old iron. I believe I should really see the end of what is surely the grotesquest of all the swindles ever invented by man-monarchy. It is enough to make a graven image laugh, to see apparently rational people, away down here in this wholesome and merciless slaughter-day for shams, still mouthing empty reverence for those moss-backed frauds and scoundrelisms, hereditary kingship and so-called "nobility." It is enough to make the monarchs and nobles themselves laugh--and in private they do; there can be no question about that. I think there is only one funnier thing, and that is the spectacle of these bastard Americans--these Hamersleys and Huntingtons and such--offering cash, encumbered by themselves, for rotten carcases and stolen titles. When our great brethren the disenslaved Brazilians frame their Declaration of Independence, I hope they will insert this missing link: "We hold these truths to be self-evident: that all monarchs are usurpers, and descendants of usurpers; for the reason that no throne was ever set up in this world by the will, freely exercised, of the only body possessing the legitimate right to set it up--the numerical mass of the nation."

You already have the advance sheets of my forthcoming book in your hands. If you will turn to about the five hundredth page, you will find a state paper of my Connecticut Yankee in which he announces the dissolution of King Arthur's monarchy and proclaims the English Republic. Compare it with the state paper which announces the downfall of the Brazilian monarchy and proclaims the Republic of the United States of Brazil, and stand by to defend the Yankee from plagiarism. There is merely a resemblance of ideas, nothing more. The Yankee's proclamation was already in print a week ago. This is merely one of those odd coincidences which are always turning up. Come, protect the Yank from that cheapest and easiest of all charges--plagiarism. Otherwise, you see, he will have to protect himself by charging approximate and indefinite plagiarism upon the official servants of our majestic twin down yonder, and then there might be war, or some similar annoyance.

Have you noticed the rumor that the Portuguese throne is unsteady, and that the Portuguese slaves are getting restive? Also, that the head slave-driver of Europe, Alexander III, has so reduced his usual monthly order for chains that the Russian foundries are running on only half time now? Also that other rumor that English nobility acquired an added stench the other day--and had to ship it to India and the continent because there wasn't any more room for it at home? Things are working. By and by there is going to be an emigration, may be. Of course we shall make no preparation; we never do. In a few years from now we shall have nothing but played-out kings and dukes on the police, and driving the horse-cars, and whitewashing fences, and in fact overcrowding all the avenues of unskilled labor; and then we shall wish, when it is too late, that we had taken common and reasonable precautions and drowned them at Castle Garden.

There followed at this time a number of letters to Goodman, but as there is much of a sameness in them, we need not print them all. Clemens, in fact, kept the mails warm with letters bulging with schemes for capitalization, and promising vast wealth to all concerned. When the letters did not go fast enough he sent telegrams. In one of the letters Goodman is promised "five hundred thousand dollars out of the profits before we get anything ourselves." One thing we gather from these letters is that Paige has taken the machine apart again, never satisfied with its perfection, or perhaps getting a hint that certain of its perfections were not permanent. A letter at the end of November seems worth preserving here.

To Joseph T. Goodman, in California:

HARTFORD, Nov. 29, '89. DEAR JOE, Things are getting into better and more flexible shape every day. Papers are now being drawn which will greatly simplify the raising of capital; I shall be in supreme command; it will not be necessary for the capitalist to arrive at terms with anybody but me. I don't want to dicker with anybody but Jones. I know him; that is to say, I want to dicker with you, and through you with Jones. Try to see if you can't be here by the 15th of January.

The machine was as perfect as a watch when we took her apart the other day; but when she goes together again the 15th of January we expect her to be perfecter than a watch.

Joe, I want you to sell some royalties to the boys out there, if you can, for I want to be financially strong when we go to New York. You know the machine, and you appreciate its future enormous career better than any man I know. At the lowest conceivable estimate (2,000 machines a year,) we shall sell 34,000 in the life of the patent--17 years.

All the family send love to you--and they mean it, or they wouldn't say it. Yours ever MARK.

The Yankee had come from the press, and Howells had praised it in the "Editor's Study" in Harper's Magazine. He had given it his highest commendation, and it seems that his opinion of it did not change with time. "Of all fanciful schemes of fiction it pleases me most," he in one place declared, and again referred to it as "a greatly imagined and symmetrically developed tale."

In more than one letter to Goodman, Clemens had urged him to come East without delay. "Take the train, Joe, and come along," he wrote early in December. And we judge from the following that Joe had decided to come.

To W. D. Howells, in Boston:

HARTFORD, Dec. 23, '89. DEAR HOWELLS,--The magazine came last night, and the Study notice is just great. The satisfaction it affords us could not be more prodigious if the book deserved every word of it; and maybe it does; I hope it does, though of course I can't realize it and believe it. But I am your grateful servant, anyway and always.

I am going to read to the Cadets at West Point Jan. 11. I go from here to New York the 9th, and up to the Point the 11th. Can't you go with me? It's great fun. I'm going to read the passages in the "Yankee" in which the Yankee's West Point cadets figure--and shall covertly work in a lecture on aristocracy to those boys. I am to be the guest of the Superintendent, but if you will go I will shake him and we will go to the hotel. He is a splendid fellow, and I know him well enough to take that liberty.

And won't you give me a day or two's visit toward the end of January? For two reasons: the machine will be at work again by that time, and we want to hear the rest of the dream-story; Mrs. Clemens keeps speaking about it and hankering for it. And we can have Joe Goodman on hand again by that time, and I want you to get to know him thoroughly. It's well worth it. I am going to run up and stay over night with you as soon as I can get a chance.

We are in the full rush of the holidays now, and an awful rush it is, too. You ought to have been here the other day, to make that day perfect and complete. All alone I managed to inflict agonies on Mrs: Clemens, whereas I was expecting nothing but praises. I made a party call the day after the party--and called the lady down from breakfast to receive it. I then left there and called on a new bride, who received me in her dressing-gown; and as things went pretty well, I stayed to luncheon. The error here was, that the appointed reception-hour was 3 in the afternoon, and not at the bride's house but at her aunt's in another part of the town. However, as I meant well, none of these disasters distressed me. Yrs ever MARK.

The Yankee did not find a very hearty welcome in England. English readers did not fancy any burlesque of their Arthurian tales, or American strictures on their institutions. Mark Twain's publishers had feared this, and asked that the story be especially edited for the English edition. Clemens, however, would not listen to any suggestions of the sort.

To Messrs. Chatto & Windus, in London, Eng.:

GENTLEMEN,--Concerning The Yankee, I have already revised the story twice; and it has been read critically by W. D. Howells and Edmund Clarence Stedman, and my wife has caused me to strike out several passages that have been brought to her attention, and to soften others. Furthermore, I have read chapters of the book in public where Englishmen were present and have profited by their suggestions.

Now, mind you, I have taken all this pains because I wanted to say a Yankee mechanic's say against monarchy and its several natural props, and yet make a book which you would be willing to print exactly as it comes to you, without altering a word.

We are spoken of (by Englishmen) as a thin-skinned people. It is you who are thin-skinned. An Englishman may write with the most brutal frankness about any man or institution among us and we republish him without dreaming of altering a line or a word. But England cannot stand that kind of a book written about herself. It is England that is thin- skinned. It causeth me to smile when I read the modifications of my language which have been made in my English editions to fit them for the sensitive English palate.

Now, as I say, I have taken laborious pains to so trim this book of offense that you might not lack the nerve to print it just as it stands. I am going to get the proofs to you just as early as I can. I want you to read it carefully. If you can publish it without altering a single word, go ahead. Otherwise, please hand it to J. R. Osgood in time for him to have it published at my expense.

This is important, for the reason that the book was not written for America; it was written for England. So many Englishmen have done their sincerest best to teach us something for our betterment that it seems to me high time that some of us should substantially recognize the good intent by trying to pry up the English nation to a little higher level of manhood in turn. Very truly yours, S. L. CLEMENS.

The English nation, at least a considerable portion of it, did not wish to be "pried up to a higher level of manhood" by a Connecticut Yankee. The papers pretty generally denounced the book as coarse; in fact, a vulgar travesty. Some of the critics concluded that England, after all, had made a mistake in admiring Mark Twain. Clemens stood this for a time and then seems to have decided that something should be done. One of the foremost of English critics was his friend and admirer; he would state the case to him fully and invite his assistance.

To Andrew Lang, in London:

[First page missing.]

1889 They vote but do not print. The head tells you pretty promptly whether the food is satisfactory or not; and everybody hears, and thinks the whole man has spoken. It is a delusion. Only his taste and his smell have been heard from--important, both, in a way, but these do not build up the man; and preserve his life and fortify it.

The little child is permitted to label its drawings "This is a cow this is a horse," and so on. This protects the child. It saves it from the sorrow and wrong of hearing its cows and its horses criticized as kangaroos and work benches. A man who is white-washing a fence is doing a useful thing, so also is the man who is adorning a rich man's house with costly frescoes; and all of us are sane enough to judge these performances by standards proper to each. Now, then, to be fair, an author ought to be allowed to put upon his book an explanatory line: "This is written for the Head;" "This is written for the Belly and the Members." And the critic ought to hold himself in honor bound to put away from him his ancient habit of judging all books by one standard, and thenceforth follow a fairer course.

The critic assumes, every time, that if a book doesn't meet the cultivated-class standard, it isn't valuable. Let us apply his law all around: for if it is sound in the case of novels, narratives, pictures, and such things, it is certainly sound and applicable to all the steps which lead up to culture and make culture possible. It condemns the spelling book, for a spelling book is of no use to a person of culture; it condemns all school books and all schools which lie between the child's primer and Greek, and between the infant school and the university; it condemns all the rounds of art which lie between the cheap terra cotta groups and the Venus de Medici, and between the chromo and the Transfiguration; it requires Whitcomb Riley to sing no more till he can sing like Shakespeare, and it forbids all amateur music and will grant its sanction to nothing below the "classic."

Is this an extravagant statement? No, it is a mere statement of fact. It is the fact itself that is extravagant and grotesque. And what is the result? This--and it is sufficiently curious: the critic has actually imposed upon the world the superstition that a painting by Raphael is more valuable to the civilizations of the earth than is a chromo; and the august opera than the hurdy-gurdy and the villagers' singing society; and Homer than the little everybody's-poet whose rhymes are in all mouths today and will be in nobody's mouth next generation; and the Latin classics than Kipling's far-reaching bugle-note; and Jonathan Edwards than the Salvation Army; and the Venus de Medici than the plaster-cast peddler; the superstition, in a word, that the vast and awful comet that trails its cold lustre through the remote abysses of space once a century and interests and instructs a cultivated handful of astronomers is worth more to the world than the sun which warms and cheers all the nations every day and makes the crops to grow.

If a critic should start a religion it would not have any object but to convert angels: and they wouldn't need it. The thin top crust of humanity--the cultivated--are worth pacifying, worth pleasing, worth coddling, worth nourishing and preserving with dainties and delicacies, it is true; but to be caterer to that little faction is no very dignified or valuable occupation, it seems to me; it is merely feeding the over- fed, and there must be small satisfaction in that. It is not that little minority who are already saved that are best worth trying to uplift, I should think, but the mighty mass of the uncultivated who are underneath. That mass will never see the Old Masters--that sight is for the few; but the chromo maker can lift them all one step upward toward appreciation of art; they cannot have the opera, but the hurdy-gurdy and the singing class lift them a little way toward that far light; they will never know Homer, but the passing rhymester of their day leaves them higher than he found them; they may never even hear of the Latin classics, but they will strike step with Kipling's drum-beat, and they will march; for all Jonathan Edwards's help they would die in their slums, but the Salvation Army will beguile some of them up to pure air and a cleaner life; they know no sculpture, the Venus is not even a name to them, but they are a grade higher in the scale of civilization by the ministrations of the plaster-cast than they were before it took its place upon then mantel and made it beautiful to their unexacting eyes.

Indeed I have been misjudged, from the very first. I have never tried in even one single instance, to help cultivate the cultivated classes. I was not equipped for it, either by native gifts or training. And I never had any ambition in that direction, but always hunted for bigger game--the masses. I have seldom deliberately tried to instruct them, but have done my best to entertain them. To simply amuse them would have satisfied my dearest ambition at any time; for they could get instruction elsewhere, and I had two chances to help to the teacher's one: for amusement is a good preparation for study and a good healer of fatigue after it. My audience is dumb, it has no voice in print, and so I cannot know whether I have won its approbation or only got its censure.

Yes, you see, I have always catered for the Belly and the Members, but have been served like the others--criticized from the culture-standard --to my sorrow and pain; because, honestly, I never cared what became of the cultured classes; they could go to the theatre and the opera--they had no use for me and the melodeon.

And now at last I arrive at my object and tender my petition, making supplication to this effect: that the critics adopt a rule recognizing the Belly and the Members, and formulate a standard whereby work done for them shall be judged. Help me, Mr. Lang; no voice can reach further than yours in a case of this kind, or carry greater weight of authority.

Lang's reply was an article in the Illustrated London News on "The Art of Mark Twain." Lang had no admiration to express for the Yankee, which he confessed he had not cared to read, but he glorified Huck Finn to the highest. "I can never forget, nor be ungrateful for the exquisite pleasure with which I read Huckleberry Finn for the first time, years ago," he wrote; "I read it again last night, deserting Kenilworth for Huck. I never laid it down till I had finished it."

Lang closed his article by referring to the story of Huck as the "great American novel which had escaped the eyes of those who watched to see this new planet swim into their ken."

LETTERS, 1890, CHIEFLY TO JOS. T. GOODMAN. THE GREAT MACHINE ENTERPRISE

Dr. John Brown's son, whom Mark Twain and his wife had known in 1873 as "Jock," sent copies of Dr. John Brown and His Sister Isabella, by E. T. McLaren. It was a gift appreciated in the Clemens home.

To Mr. John Brown, in Edinburgh, Scotland:

HARTFORD, Feby 11, 1890. DEAR MR. BROWN,--Both copies came, and we are reading and re-reading the one, and lending the other, to old time adorers of "Rab and his Friends." It is an exquisite book; the perfection of literary workmanship. It says in every line, "Don't look at me, look at him"--and one tries to be good and obey; but the charm of the painter is so strong that one can't keep his entire attention on the developing portrait, but must steal side- glimpses of the artist, and try to divine the trick of her felicitous brush. In this book the doctor lives and moves just as he was. He was the most extensive slave-holder of his time, and the kindest; and yet he died without setting one of his bondmen free. We all send our very, very kindest regards. Sincerely yours S. L. CLEMENS.

If Mark Twain had been less interested in the type-setting machine he might possibly have found a profit that winter in the old Sellers play, which he had written with Howells seven years before. The play had eventually been produced at the Lyceum Theatre in New York, with A. P. Burbank in the leading role, and Clemens and Howells as financial backers. But it was a losing investment, nor did it pay any better when Clemens finally sent Burbank with it on the road. Now, however, James A. Herne, a well-known actor and playwright, became interested in the idea, after a discussion of the matter with Howells, and there seemed a probability that with changes made under Herne's advisement the play might be made sensible and successful.

But Mark Twain's greater interest was now all in the type-machine, and certainly he had no money to put into any other venture. His next letter to Goodman is illuminating--the urgency of his need for funds opposed to that conscientiousness which was one of the most positive forces of Mark Twain's body spiritual. The Mr. Arnot of this letter was an Elmira capitalist.

To Jos. T. Goodman, in California:

HARTFORD, March 31, '90. DEAR JOE,--If you were here, I should say, "Get you to Washington and beg Senator Jones to take the chances and put up about ten or "--no, I wouldn't.

The money would burn a hole in my pocket and get away from me if the furnisher of it were proceeding upon merely your judgment and mine and without other evidence. It is too much of a responsibility.

But I am in as close a place to-day as ever I was; $3,000 due for the last month's machine-expenses, and the purse empty. I notified Mr. Arnot a month ago that I should want $5,000 to-day, and his check arrived last night; but I sent it back to him, because when he bought of me on the 9th of December I said that I would not draw upon him for 3 months, and that before that date Senator Jones would have examined the machine and approved, or done the other thing. If Jones should arrive here a week or ten days from now (as he expects to do,) and should not approve, and shouldn't buy any royalties, my deal with Arnot would not be symmetrically square, and then how could I refund? The surest way was to return his check.

I have talked with the madam, and here is the result. I will go down to the factory and notify Paige that I will scrape together $6,000 to meet the March and April expenses, and will retire on the 30th of April and return the assignment to him if in the meantime I have not found financial relief.

It is very rough; for the machine does at last seem perfect, and just a bird to go! I think she's going to be good for 8,000 ems an hour in the hands of a good ordinary man after a solid year's practice. I may be in error, but I most solidly believe it.

There's an improved Mergenthaler in New York; Paige and Davis and I watched it two whole afternoons. With the love of us all, MARK.

Arnot wrote Clemens urging him to accept the check for five thousand dollars in this moment of need. Clemens was probably as sorely tempted to compromise with his conscience as he had ever been in his life, but his resolution field firm.

To M. H. Arnot, in Elmira, N. Y.:

MR. M. H. ARNOT

DEAR SIR,--No--no, I could not think of taking it, with you unsatisfied; and you ought not to be satisfied until you have made personal examination of the machine and had a consensus of testimony of disinterested people, besides. My own perfect knowledge of what is required of such a machine, and my perfect knowledge of the fact that this is the only machine that can meet that requirement, make it difficult for me to realize that a doubt is possible to less well-posted men; and so I would have taken your money without thinking, and thus would have done a great wrong to you and a great one to myself. And now that I go back over the ground, I remember that where I said I could get along 3 months without drawing on you, that delay contemplated a visit from you to the machine in the interval, and your satisfaction with its character and prospects. I had forgotten all that. But I remember it now; and the fact that it was not "so nominated in the bond" does not alter the case or justify me in making my call so prematurely. I do not know that you regarded all that as a part of the bargain--for you were thoroughly and magnanimously unexacting--but I so regarded it, notwithstanding I have so easily managed to forget all about it.

You so gratified me, and did me so much honor in bonding yourself to me in a large sum, upon no evidence but my word and with no protection but my honor, that my pride in that is much stronger than my desire to reap a money advantage from it.

With the sincerest appreciation I am Truly yours S L. CLEMENS.

P. S. I have written a good many words and yet I seem to have failed to say the main thing in exact enough language--which is, that the transaction between us is not complete and binding until you shall have convinced yourself that the machine's character and prospects are satisfactory.

I ought to explain that the grippe delayed us some weeks, and that we have since been waiting for Mr. Jones. When he was ready, we were not; and now we have been ready more than a month, while he has been kept in Washington by the Silver bill. He said the other day that to venture out of the Capitol for a day at this time could easily chance to hurt him if the bill came up for action, meantime, although it couldn't hurt the bill, which would pass anyway. Mrs. Jones said she would send me two or three days' notice, right after the passage of the bill, and that they would follow as soon as I should return word that their coming would not inconvenience us. I suppose I ought to go to New York without waiting for Mr. Jones, but it would not be wise to go there without money.

The bill is still pending.

The Mergenthaler machine, like the Paige, was also at this time in the middle stages of experimental development. It was a slower machine, but it was simpler, less expensive, occupied less room. There was not so much about it to get out of order; it was not so delicate, not so human. These were immense advantages.

But no one at this time could say with certainty which typesetter would reap the harvest of millions. It was only sure that at least one of them would, and the Mergenthaler people were willing to trade stock for stock with the Paige company in order to insure financial success for both, whichever won. Clemens, with a faith that never faltered, declined this offer, a decision that was to cost him millions.

Winter and spring had gone and summer had come, but still there had been no financial conclusion with Jones, Mackay, and the other rich Californians who were to put up the necessary million for the machine's manufacture. Goodman was spending a large part of his time traveling back and forth between California and Washington, trying to keep business going at both ends. Paige spent most of his time working out improvements for the type-setter, delicate attachments which complicated its construction more and more.

To Joe T. Goodman, in Washington:

HARTFORD, June 22, '90. DEAR JOE,--I have been sitting by the machine 2 hours, this afternoon, and my admiration of it towers higher than ever. There is no sort of mistake about it, it is the Big Bonanza. In the 2 hours, the time lost by type-breakage was 3 minutes.

This machine is totally without a rival. Rivalry with it is impossible. Last Friday, Fred Whitmore (it was the 28th day of his apprenticeship on the machine) stacked up 49,700 ems of solid nonpareil in 8 hours, and the type-breaking delay was only 6 minutes for the day.

I claim yet, as I have always claimed, that the machine's market (abroad and here together,) is today worth $150,000,000 without saying anything about the doubling and trebling of this sum that will follow within the life of the patents. Now here is a queer fact: I am one of the wealthiest grandees in America--one of the Vanderbilt gang, in fact--and yet if you asked me to lend you a couple of dollars I should have to ask you to take my note instead.

It makes me cheerful to sit by the machine: come up with Mrs. Goodman and refresh yourself with a draught of the same. Ys ever MARK.

The machine was still breaking the types now and then, and no doubt Paige was itching to take it to pieces, and only restrained by force from doing so. He was never thoroughly happy unless he was taking the machine apart or setting it up again. Finally, he was allowed to go at it--a disasterous permission, for it was just then that Jones decided to steal a day or two from the Silver Bill and watch the type-setter in operation. Paige already had it in parts when this word came from Goodman, and Jones's visit had to be called off. His enthusiasm would seem to have weakened from that day. In July, Goodman wrote that both Mackay and Jones had become somewhat diffident in the matter of huge capitalization. He thought it partly due, at least, to "the fatal delays that have sicklied over the bloom of original enthusiasm." Clemens himself went down to Washington and perhaps warmed Jones with his eloquence; at least, Jones seemed to have agreed to make some effort in the matter a qualified promise, the careful word of a wary politician and capitalist. How many Washington trips were made is not certain, but certainly more than one. Jones would seem to have suggested forms of contracts, but if he came to the point of signing any there is no evidence of it to-day.

Any one who has read Mark Twain's, "A Connecticut Yankee in King Arthur's Court," has a pretty good idea of his opinion of kings in general, and tyrants in particular. Rule by "divine right," however liberal, was distasteful to him; where it meant oppression it stirred him to violence. In his article, "The Czar's Soliloquy," he gave himself loose rein concerning atrocities charged to the master of Russia, and in a letter which he wrote during the summer of 1890, he offered a hint as to remedies. The letter was written by editorial request, but was never mailed. Perhaps it seemed too openly revolutionary at the moment.

Yet scarcely more than a quarter of a century was needed to make it "timely." Clemens and his family were spending some weeks in the Catskills when it was written.

An unpublished letter on the Czar.

ONTEORA, 1890. TO THE EDITOR OF FREE RUSSIA,--I thank you for the compliment of your invitation to say something, but when I ponder the bottom paragraph on your first page, and then study your statement on your third page, of the objects of the several Russian liberation-parties, I do not quite know how to proceed. Let me quote here the paragraph referred to:

"But men's hearts are so made that the sight of one voluntary victim for a noble idea stirs them more deeply than the sight of a crowd submitting to a dire fate they cannot escape. Besides, foreigners could not see so clearly as the Russians how much the Government was responsible for the grinding poverty of the masses; nor could they very well realize the moral wretchedness imposed by that Government upon the whole of educated Russia. But the atrocities committed upon the defenceless prisoners are there in all their baseness, concrete and palpable, admitting of no excuse, no doubt or hesitation, crying out to the heart of humanity against Russian tyranny. And the Tzar's Government, stupidly confident in its apparently unassailable position, instead of taking warning from the first rebukes, seems to mock this humanitarian age by the aggravation of brutalities. Not satisfied with slowly killing its prisoners, and with burying the flower of our young generation in the Siberian desserts, the Government of Alexander III. resolved to break their spirit by deliberately submitting them to a regime of unheard-of brutality and degradation."

When one reads that paragraph in the glare of George Kennan's revelations, and considers how much it means; considers that all earthly figures fail to typify the Czar's government, and that one must descend into hell to find its counterpart, one turns hopefully to your statement of the objects of the several liberation-parties--and is disappointed. Apparently none of them can bear to think of losing the present hell entirely, they merely want the temperature cooled down a little.

I now perceive why all men are the deadly and uncompromising enemies of the rattlesnake: it is merely because the rattlesnake has not speech. Monarchy has speech, and by it has been able to persuade men that it differs somehow from the rattlesnake, has something valuable about it somewhere, something worth preserving, something even good and high and fine, when properly "modified," something entitling it to protection from the club of the first comer who catches it out of its hole. It seems a most strange delusion and not reconcilable with our superstition that man is a reasoning being. If a house is afire, we reason confidently that it is the first comer's plain duty to put the fire out in any way he can-- drown it with water, blow it up with dynamite, use any and all means to stop the spread of the fire and save the rest of the city. What is the Czar of Russia but a house afire in the midst of a city of eighty millions of inhabitants? Yet instead of extinguishing him, together with his nest and system, the liberation-parties are all anxious to merely cool him down a little and keep him.

It seems to me that this is illogical--idiotic, in fact. Suppose you had this granite-hearted, bloody-jawed maniac of Russia loose in your house, chasing the helpless women and little children--your own. What would you do with him, supposing you had a shotgun? Well, he is loose in your house-Russia. And with your shotgun in your hand, you stand trying to think up ways to "modify" him.

Do these liberation-parties think that they can succeed in a project which has been attempted a million times in the history of the world and has never in one single instance been successful--the "modification" of a despotism by other means than bloodshed? They seem to think they can. My privilege to write these sanguinary sentences in soft security was bought for me by rivers of blood poured upon many fields, in many lands, but I possess not one single little paltry right or privilege that come to me as a result of petition, persuasion, agitation for reform, or any kindred method of procedure. When we consider that not even the most responsible English monarch ever yielded back a stolen public right until it was wrenched from them by bloody violence, is it rational to suppose that gentler methods can win privileges in Russia?

Of course I know that the properest way to demolish the Russian throne would be by revolution. But it is not possible to get up a revolution there; so the only thing left to do, apparently, is to keep the throne vacant by dynamite until a day when candidates shall decline with thanks. Then organize the Republic. And on the whole this method has some large advantages; for whereas a revolution destroys some lives which cannot well be spared, the dynamite way doesn't. Consider this: the conspirators against the Czar's life are caught in every rank of life, from the low to the high. And consider: if so many take an active part, where the peril is so dire, is this not evidence that the sympathizers who keep still and do not show their hands, are countless for multitudes? Can you break the hearts of thousands of families with the awful Siberian exodus every year for generations and not eventually cover all Russia from limit to limit with bereaved fathers and mothers and brothers and sisters who secretly hate the perpetrator of this prodigious crime and hunger and thirst for his life? Do you not believe that if your wife or your child or your father was exiled to the mines of Siberia for some trivial utterances wrung from a smarting spirit by the Czar's intolerable tyranny, and you got a chance to kill him and did not do it, that you would always be ashamed to be in your own society the rest of your life? Suppose that that refined and lovely Russian lady who was lately stripped bare before a brutal soldiery and whipped to death by the Czar's hand in the person of the Czar's creature had been your wife, or your daughter or your sister, and to-day the Czar should pass within reach of your hand, how would you feel--and what would you do? Consider, that all over vast Russia, from boundary to boundary, a myriad of eyes filled with tears when that piteous news came, and through those tears that myriad of eyes saw, not that poor lady, but lost darlings of their own whose fate her fate brought back with new access of grief out of a black and bitter past never to be forgotten or forgiven.

If I am a Swinburnian--and clear to the marrow I am--I hold human nature in sufficient honor to believe there are eighty million mute Russians that are of the same stripe, and only one Russian family that isn't.

MARK TWAIN.

Type-setter matters were going badly. Clemens still had faith in Jones, and he had lost no grain of faith in the machine. The money situation, however, was troublesome. With an expensive establishment, and work of one sort or another still to be done on the machine, his income would not reach. Perhaps Goodman had already given up hope, for he does not seem to have returned from California after the next letter was written--a colorless letter-- in which we feel a note of resignation. The last few lines are sufficient.

To Joe T. Goodman, in California:

DEAR JOE,--...... I wish you could get a day off and make those two or three Californians buy those privileges, for I'm going to need money before long.

I don't know where the Senator is; but out on the Coast I reckon.

I guess we've got a perfect machine at last. We never break a type, now, and the new device for enabling the operator to touch the last letters and justify the line simultaneously works, to a charm. With love to you both, MARK

The year closed gloomily enough. The type-setter seemed to be perfected, but capital for its manufacture was not forthcoming. The publishing business of Charles L. Webster & Co. was returning little or no profit. Clemens's mother had died in Keokuk at the end of October, and his wife's mother, in Elmira a month later. Mark Twain, writing a short business letter to his publishing manager, Fred J. Ball, closed it: "Merry Xmas to you!--and I wish to God I could have one myself before I die."

XXXI

LETTERS, 1891, TO HOWELLS, MRS. CLEMENS AND OTHERS. RETURN TO LITERATURE. AMERICAN CLAIMANT. LEAVING HARTFORD. EUROPE. DOWN THE RHINE

Clemens was still not without hope in the machine, at the beginning of the new year (1891) but it was a hope no longer active, and it presently became a moribund. Jones, on about the middle of February, backed out altogether, laying the blame chiefly on Mackay and the others, who, he said, had decided not to invest. Jones "let his victim down easy" with friendly words, but it was the end, for the present, at least, of machine financiering.

It was also the end of Mark Twain's capital. His publishing business was not good. It was already in debt and needing more money. There was just one thing for him to do and he did it at once, not stopping to cry over spilt milk, but with good courage and the old enthusiasm that never failed him, he returned to the trade of authorship. He dug out half- finished articles and stories, finished them and sold them, and within a week after the Jones collapse he was at work on a novel based an the old Sellers idea, which eight years before he and Howells had worked into a play. The brief letter in which he reported this news to Howells bears no marks of depression, though the writer of it was in his fifty-sixth year; he was by no means well, and his financial prospects were anything but golden.

To W. D. Howells, in Boston:

HARTFORD, Feb. 24, '91 DEAR HOWELLS,--Mrs. Clemens has been sick abed for near two weeks, but is up and around the room now, and gaining. I don't know whether she has written Mrs. Howells or not--I only know she was going to--and will yet, if she hasn't. We are promising ourselves a whole world of pleasure in the visit, and you mustn't dream of disappointing us.

Does this item stir an interest in you? Began a novel four days ago, and this moment finished chapter four. Title of the book

"Colonel Mulberry Sellers. American Claimant Of the Great Earldom of Rossmore' in the Peerage of Great Britain."

Ys Ever MARK.

Probably Mark Twain did not return to literary work reluctantly. He had always enjoyed writing and felt now that he was equipped better than ever for authorship, at least so far as material was concerned. There exists a fragmentary copy of a letter to some unknown correspondent, in which he recites his qualifications. It bears evidence of having been written just at this time and is of unusual interest at this point.

Fragment of Letter to -------, 1891:

. . . . I confine myself to life with which I am familiar when pretending to portray life. But I confined myself to the boy-life out on the Mississippi because that had a peculiar charm for me, and not because I was not familiar with other phases of life. I was a soldier two weeks once in the beginning of the war, and was hunted like a rat the whole time. Familiar? My splendid Kipling himself hasn't a more burnt-in, hard-baked, and unforgetable familiarity with that death-on-the-pale- horse-with-hell-following-after, which is a raw soldier's first fortnight in the field--and which, without any doubt, is the most tremendous fortnight and the vividest he is ever going to see.

Yes, and I have shoveled silver tailings in a quartz-mill a couple of weeks, and acquired the last possibilities of culture in that direction. And I've done "pocket-mining" during three months in the one little patch of ground in the whole globe where Nature conceals gold in pockets--or did before we robbed all of those pockets and exhausted, obliterated, annihilated the most curious freak Nature ever indulged in. There are not thirty men left alive who, being told there was a pocket hidden on the broad slope of a mountain, would know how to go and find it, or have even the faintest idea of how to set about it; but I am one of the possible 20 or 30 who possess the secret, and I could go and put my hand on that hidden treasure with a most deadly precision.

And I've been a prospector, and know pay rock from poor when I find it-- just with a touch of the tongue. And I've been a silver miner and know how to dig and shovel and drill and put in a blast. And so I know the mines and the miners interiorly as well as Bret Harte knows them exteriorly.

And I was a newspaper reporter four years in cities, and so saw the inside of many things; and was reporter in a legislature two sessions and the same in Congress one session, and thus learned to know personally three sample bodies of the smallest minds and the selfishest souls and the cowardliest hearts that God makes.

And I was some years a Mississippi pilot, and familiarly knew all the different kinds of steamboatmen--a race apart, and not like other folk.

And I was for some years a traveling "jour" printer, and wandered from city to city--and so I know that sect familiarly.

And I was a lecturer on the public platform a number of seasons and was a responder to toasts at all the different kinds of banquets--and so I know a great many secrets about audiences--secrets not to be got out of books, but only acquirable by experience.

And I watched over one dear project of mine for years, spent a fortune on it, and failed to make it go--and the history of that would make a large book in which a million men would see themselves as in a mirror; and they would testify and say, Verily, this is not imagination; this fellow has been there--and after would cast dust upon their heads, cursing and blaspheming.

And I am a publisher, and did pay to one author's widow (General Grant's) the largest copyright checks this world has seen--aggregating more than L80,000 in the first year.

And I have been an author for 20 years and an ass for 55.

Now then; as the most valuable capital or culture or education usable in the building of novels is personal experience I ought to be well equipped for that trade.

I surely have the equipment, a wide culture, and all of it real, none of it artificial, for I don't know anything about books.

[No signature.]

Clemens for several years had been bothered by rheumatism in his shoulder. The return now to the steady use of the pen aggravated his trouble, and at times he was nearly disabled. The phonograph for commercial dictation had been tried experimentally, and Mark Twain was always ready for any innovation.

To W. D. Howells, in Boston:

HARTFORD, Feb. 28, '91. DEAR HOWELLS,--Won't you drop-in at the Boylston Building (New England Phonograph Co) and talk into a phonograph in an ordinary conversation- voice and see if another person (who didn't hear you do it) can take the words from the thing without difficulty and repeat them to you. If the experiment is satisfactory (also make somebody put in a message which you don't hear, and see if afterward you can get it out without difficulty) won't you then ask them on what terms they will rent me a phonograph for 3 months and furnish me cylinders enough to carry 75,000 words. 175 cylinders, ain't it?

I don't want to erase any of them. My right arm is nearly disabled by rheumatism, but I am bound to write this book (and sell 100,000 copies of it--no, I mean a million--next fall) I feel sure I can dictate the book into a phonograph if I don't have to yell. I write 2,000 words a day; I think I can dictate twice as many.

But mind, if this is going to be too much trouble to you--go ahead and do it, all the same. Ys ever MARK.

Howells, always willing to help, visited the phonograph place, and a few days later reported results. He wrote: "I talked your letter into a fonograf in my usual tone at my usual gait of speech. Then the fonograf man talked his answer in at his wonted swing and swell. Then we took the cylinder to a type-writer in the next room, and she put the hooks into her ears and wrote the whole out. I send you the result. There is a mistake of one word. I think that if you have the cheek to dictate the story into the fonograf, all the rest is perfectly easy. It wouldn't fatigue me to talk for an hour as I did."

Clemens did not find the phonograph entirely satisfactory, at least not for a time, and he appears never to have used it steadily. His early experience with it, however, seems interesting.

To W. D. Howells, in Boston:

HARTFORD, Apl. 4, '91. DEAR HOWELLS,--I'm ashamed. It happened in this way. I was proposing to acknowledge the receipt of the play and the little book per phonograph, so that you could see that the instrument is good enough for mere letter- writing; then I meant to add the fact that you can't write literature with it, because it hasn't any ideas and it hasn't any gift for elaboration, or smartness of talk, or vigor of action, or felicity of expression, but is just matter-of-fact, compressive, unornamental, and as grave and unsmiling as the devil.

I filled four dozen cylinders in two sittings, then found I could have said about as much with the pen and said it a deal better. Then I resigned.

I believe it could teach one to dictate literature to a phonographer--and some time I will experiment in that line.

The little book is charmingly written, and it interested me. But it flies too high for me. Its concretest things are filmy abstractions to me, and when I lay my grip on one of them and open my hand, I feel as embarrassed as I use to feel when I thought I had caught a fly. I'm going to try to mail it back to you to-day--I mean I am going to charge my memory. Charging my memory is one of my chief industries ....

With our loves and our kindest regards distributed among you according to the proprieties. Yrs ever MARK.

P. S.--I'm sending that ancient "Mental Telegraphy" article to Harper's --with a modest postscript. Probably read it to you years ago. S. L. C.

The "little book" mentioned in this letter was by Swedenborg, an author in whom the Boston literary set was always deeply interested. "Mental Telegraphy" appeared in Harper's Magazine, and is now included in the Uniform Edition of Mark Twain's books. It was written in 1878.

Joe Goodman had long since returned to California, it being clear that nothing could be gained by remaining in Washington. On receipt of the news of the type-setter's collapse he sent a consoling word. Perhaps he thought Clemens would rage over the unhappy circumstance, and possibly hold him in some measure to blame. But it was generally the smaller annoyances of life that made Mark Twain rage; the larger catastrophes were likely to stir only his philosophy.

The Library of American Literature, mentioned in the following letter, was a work in many volumes, edited by Edmund Clarence Stedman and Ellen Mackay Hutchinson.

To Joe T. Goodman:

April [?] 1891. DEAR JOE, Well, it's all right, anyway. Diplomacy couldn't have saved it-- diplomacy of mine--at that late day. I hadn't any diplomacy in stock, anyway. In order to meet Jones's requirements I had to surrender the old contract (a contract which made me boss of the situation and gave me the whip-hand of Paige) and allow the new one to be drafted and put in its place. I was running an immense risk, but it was justified by Jones's promises--promises made to me not merely once but every time I tallied with him. When February arrived, I saw signs which were mighty plain reading. Signs which meant that Paige was hoping and praying that Jones would go back on me--which would leave Paige boss, and me robbed and out in the cold. His prayers were answered, and I am out in the cold. If I ever get back my nine-twentieths interest, it will be by law- suit--which will be instituted in the indefinite future, when the time comes.

I am at work again--on a book. Not with a great deal of spirit, but with enough--yes, plenty. And I am pushing my publishing house. It has turned the corner after cleaning $50,000 a year for three consecutive years, and piling every cent of it into one book--Library of American Literature--and from next January onward it will resume dividends. But I've got to earn $50,000 for it between now and then--which I will do if I keep my health. This additional capital is needed for that same book, because its prosperity is growing so great and exacting.

It is dreadful to think of you in ill health--I can't realize it; you are always to me the same that you were in those days when matchless health. and glowing spirits and delight in life were commonplaces with us. Lord save us all from old age and broken health and a hope-tree that has lost the faculty of putting out blossoms.

With love to you both from us all. MARK.

Mark Twain's residence in Hartford was drawing rapidly to a close. Mrs. Clemens was poorly, and his own health was uncertain. They believed that some of the European baths would help them. Furthermore, Mark Twain could no longer afford the luxury of his Hartford home. In Europe life could be simpler and vastly cheaper. He was offered a thousand dollars apiece for six European letters, by the McClure syndicate and W. M. Laffan, of the Sun. This would at least give him a start on the other side. The family began immediately their sad arrangements for departure.

To Fred J. Hall (manager Chas. L. Webster & Co.), N. Y.:

HARTFORD, Apl. 14, '91. DEAR MR. HALL,--Privately--keep it to yourself--as you, are already aware, we are going to Europe in June, for an indefinite stay. We shall sell the horses and shut up the house. We wish to provide a place for our coachman, who has been with us a 21 years, and is sober, active, diligent, and unusually bright and capable. You spoke of hiring a colored man as engineer and helper in the packing room. Patrick would soon learn that trade and be very valuable. We will cease to need him by the middle or end of June. Have you made irrevocable arrangements with the colored man, or would you prefer to have Patrick, if he thinks he would like to try?

I have not said anything to him about it yet.

Yours S. L. C.

It was to be a complete breaking up of their beautiful establishment. Patrick McAleer, George the butler, and others of their household help had been like members of the family. We may guess at the heartbreak of it all, even though the letters remain cheerful.

Howells, strangely enough, seems to have been about the last one to be told of their European plans; in fact, he first got wind of it from the papers, and wrote for information. Likely enough Clemens had not until then had the courage to confess.

To W. D. Howells, in Boston:

HARTFORD, May 20, '91. DEAR HOWELLS,--For her health's sake Mrs. Clemens must try baths somewhere, and this it is that has determined us to go to Europe. The water required seems to be provided at a little obscure and little- visited nook up in the hills back of the Rhine somewhere and you get to it by Rhine traffic-boat and country stage-coach. Come, get "sick or sorry enough" and join us. We shall be a little while at that bath, and the rest of the summer at Annecy (this confidential to you) in Haute Savoie, 22 miles from Geneva. Spend the winters in Berlin. I don't know how long we shall be in Europe--I have a vote, but I don't cast it. I'm going to do whatever the others desire, with leave to change their mind, without prejudice, whenever they want to. Travel has no longer, any charm for me. I have seen all the foreign countries I want to see except heaven and hell, and I have only a vague curiosity as concerns one of those.

I found I couldn't use the play--I had departed too far from its lines when I came to look at it. I thought I might get a great deal of dialogue out of it, but I got only 15 loosely written pages--they saved me half a days work. It was the cursing phonograph. There was abundance of good dialogue, but it couldn't befitted into the new conditions of the story.

Oh, look here--I did to-day what I have several times in past years thought of doing: answered an interviewing proposition from a rich newspaper with the reminder that they had not stated the terms; that my time was all occupied with writing, at good pay, and that as talking was harder work I should not care to venture it unless I knew the pay was going to be proportionately higher. I wish I had thought of this the other day when Charley Stoddard turned a pleasant Englishman loose on me and I couldn't think of any rational excuse. Ys Ever MARK.

Clemens had finished his Sellers book and had disposed of the serial rights to the McClure syndicate. The house in Hartford was closed early in June, and on the 6th the family, with one maid, Katie Leary, sailed on the Gascogne. Two weeks later they had begun a residence abroad which was to last for more than nine years.

It was not easy to get to work in Europe. Clemens's arm remained lame, and any effort at writing brought suffering. The Century Magazine proposed another set of letters, but by the end of July he had barely begun on those promised to McClure and Laffan. In August, however, he was able to send three: one from Aix about the baths there, another from Bayreuth concerning the Wagner festival, and a third from Marienbad, in Bohemia, where they rested for a time. He decided that he would arrange for no more European letters when the six were finished, but would gather material for a book. He would take a courier and a kodak and go tramping again in some fashion that would be interesting to do and to write.

The idea finally matured when he reached Switzerland and settled the family at the Hotel Beau Rivage, Ouchy, Lausanne, facing Lake Leman. He decided to make a floating trip down the Rhone, and he engaged Joseph Very, a courier that had served him on a former European trip, to accompany him. The courier went over to Bourget and bought for five dollars a flat-bottomed boat and engaged its owner as their pilot. It was the morning of September 20, when they began their floating-trip down the beautiful historic river that flows through the loveliest and most romantic region of France. He wrote daily to Mrs. Clemens, and his letters tell the story of that drowsy, happy experience better than the notes made with a view to publication. Clemens had arrived at Lake Bourget on the evening before the morning of their start and slept on the Island of Chatillon, in an old castle of the same name. Lake Bourget connects with the Rhone by a small canal.

Letters and Memoranda to Mrs. Clemens, in Ouchy, Switzerland:

Sept. 20, 1891. Sunday, 11 a.m. On the lake Bourget--just started. The castle of Chatillon high overhead showing above the trees. It was a wonderfully still place to sleep in. Beside us there was nobody in it but a woman, a boy and a dog. A Pope was born in the room I slept in. No, he became a Pope later.

The lake is smooth as glass--a brilliant sun is shining.

Our boat is comfortable and shady with its awning.

11.20 We have crossed the lake and are entering the canal. Shall presently be in the Rhone.

Noon. Nearly down to the Rhone. Passing the village of Chanaz.

3.15 p. m. Sunday. We have been in the Rhone 3 hours. It is unimaginably still and reposeful and cool and soft and breezy. No rowing or work of any kind to do--we merely float with the current-- we glide noiseless and swift--as fast as a London cab-horse rips along--8 miles an hour--the swiftest current I've ever boated in. We have the entire river to ourselves--nowhere a boat of any kind. Good bye Sweetheart S. L. C.

PORT DE GROLEE, Monday, 4.15 p.m. [Sept. 21, 1891] Name of the village which we left five minutes ago.

We went ashore at 5 p. m. yesterday, dear heart, and walked a short mile to St. Geuix, a big village, and took quarters at the principal inn; had a good dinner and afterwards along walk out of town on the banks of the Guiers till 7.30.

Went to bed at 8.30 and continued to make notes and read books and newspapers till midnight. Slept until 8, breakfasted in bed, and lay till noon, because there had been a very heavy rain in the night and the day was still dark and lowering. But at noon the sun broke through and in 15 minutes we were tramping toward the river. Got afloat at 1 p. m. but at 2.40 we had to rush suddenly ashore and take refuge in the above village. Just as we got ourselves and traps safely housed in the inn, the rain let go and came down in great style. We lost an hour and a half there, but we are off again, now, with bright sunshine.

I wrote you yesterday my darling, and shall expect to write you every day.

Good-day, and love to all of you. SAML.

ON THE RHONE BELOW VILLEBOIS, Tuesday noon. Good morning, sweetheart. Night caught us yesterday where we had to take quarters in a peasant's house which was occupied by the family and a lot of cows and calves--also several rabbits.--[His word for fleas.]--The latter had a ball, and I was the ball-room; but they were very friendly and didn't bite.

The peasants were mighty kind and hearty, and flew around and did their best to make us comfortable. This morning I breakfasted on the shore in the open air with two sociable dogs and a cat. Clean cloth, napkin and table furniture, white sugar, a vast hunk of excellent butter, good bread, first class coffee with pure milk, fried fish just caught. Wonderful that so much cleanliness should come out of such a phenomenally dirty house.

An hour ago we saw the Falls of the Rhone, a prodigiously rough and dangerous looking place; shipped a little water but came to no harm. It was one of the most beautiful pieces of piloting and boat-management I ever saw. Our admiral knew his business.

We have had to run ashore for shelter every time it has rained heretofore, but Joseph has been putting in his odd time making a water- proof sun-bonnet for the boat, and now we sail along dry although we had many heavy showers this morning.

With a word of love to you all and particularly you, SAML.

ON THE RHONE, BELOW VIENNA. I salute you, my darling. Your telegram reached me in Lyons last night and was very pleasant news indeed.

I was up and shaved before 8 this morning, but we got delayed and didn't sail from Lyons till 10.30--an hour and a half lost. And we've lost another hour--two of them, I guess--since, by an error. We came in sight of Vienne at 2 o'clock, several miles ahead, on a hill, and I proposed to walk down there and let the boat go ahead of us. So Joseph and I got out and struck through a willow swamp along a dim path, and by and by came out on the steep bank of a slough or inlet or something, and we followed that bank forever and ever trying to get around the head of that slough. Finally I noticed a twig standing up in the water, and by George it had a distinct and even vigorous quiver to it! I don't know when I have felt so much like a donkey. On an island! I wanted to drown somebody, but I hadn't anybody I could spare. However, after another long tramp we found a lonely native, and he had a scow and soon we were on the mainland--yes, and a blamed sight further from Vienne than we were when we started.

Notes--I make millions of them; and so I get no time to write to you. If you've got a pad there, please send it poste-restante to Avignon. I may not need it but I fear I shall.

I'm straining to reach St. Pierre de Boef, but it's going to be a close fit, I reckon.

AFLOAT, Friday, 3 p.m., '91. Livy darling, we sailed from St. Pierre de Boef six hours ago, and are now approaching Tournon, where we shall not stop, but go on and make Valence, a City Of 25,000 people. It's too delicious, floating with the swift current under the awning these superb sunshiny days in deep peace and quietness. Some of these curious old historical towns strangely persuade me, but it is so lovely afloat that I don't stop, but view them from the outside and sail on. We get abundance of grapes and peaches for next to nothing.

Joseph is perfect. He is at his very best--and never was better in his life. I guess he gets discouraged and feels disliked and in the way when he is lying around--but here he is perfection, and brim full of useful alacrities and helps and ingenuities.

When I woke up an hour ago and heard the clock strike 4, I said "I seem to have been asleep an immensely long time; I must have gone to bed mighty early; I wonder what time I did go to bed."

And I got up and lit a candle and looked at my watch to see.

AFLOAT 2 HOURS BELOW BOURG ST. ANDEOL. Monday, 11 a.m., Sept. 28. Livy darling, I didn't write yesterday. We left La Voulte in a driving storm of cold rain--couldn't write in it--and at 1 p. m. when we were not thinking of stopping, we saw a picturesque and mighty ruin on a high hill back of a village, and I was seized with a desire to explore it; so we landed at once and set out with rubbers and umbrella, sending the boat ahead to St. Andeol, and we spent 3 hours clambering about those cloudy heights among those worn and vast and idiotic ruins of a castle built by two crusaders 650 years ago. The work of these asses was full of interest, and we had a good time inspecting, examining and scrutinizing it. All the hills on both sides of the Rhone have peaks and precipices, and each has its gray and wasted pile of mouldy walls and broken towers. The Romans displaced the Gauls, the Visigoths displaced the Romans, the Saracens displaced the Visigoths, the Christians displaced the Saracens, and it was these pious animals who built these strange lairs and cut each other's throats in the name and for the glory of God, and robbed and burned and slew in peace and war; and the pauper and the slave built churches, and the credit of it went to the Bishop who racked the money out of them. These are pathetic shores, and they make one despise the human race.

We came down in an hour by rail, but I couldn't get your telegram till this morning, for it was Sunday and they had shut up the post office to go to the circus. I went, too. It was all one family-- parents and 5 children--performing in the open air to 200 of these enchanted villagers, who contributed coppers when called on. It was a most gay and strange and pathetic show. I got up at 7 this morning to see the poor devils cook their poor breakfast and pack up their sordid fineries.

This is a 9 k-m. current and the wind is with us; we shall make Avignon before 4 o'clock. I saw watermelons and pomegranates for sale at St. Andeol.

With a power of love, Sweetheart, SAML.

HOTEL D'EUROPE, AVIGNON, Monday, 6 p.m., Sept. 28. Well, Livy darling, I have been having a perfect feast of letters for an hour, and I thank you and dear Clam with all my heart. It's like hearing from home after a long absence.

It is early to be in bed, but I'm always abed before 9, on this voyage; and up at 7 or a trifle later, every morning. If I ever take such a trip again, I will have myself called at the first tinge of dawn and get to sea as soon after as possible. The early dawn on the water-nothing can be finer, as I know by old Mississippi experience. I did so long for you and Sue yesterday morning--the most superb sunrise!--the most marvelous sunrise! and I saw it all from the very faintest suspicion of the coming dawn all the way through to the final explosion of glory. But it had interest private to itself and not to be found elsewhere in the world; for between me and it, in the far distant-eastward, was a silhouette mountain-range in which I had discovered, the previous afternoon, a most noble face upturned to the sky, and mighty form out stretched, which I had named Napoleon Dreaming of Universal Empire--and now, this prodigious face, soft, rich, blue, spirituelle, asleep, tranquil, reposeful, lay against that giant conflagration of ruddy and golden splendors all rayed like a wheel with the upstreaming and far-reaching lances of the sun. It made one want to cry for delight, it was so supreme in its unimaginable majesty and beauty.

We had a curious experience today. A little after I had sealed and directed my letter to you, in which I said we should make Avignon before 4, we got lost. We ceased to encounter any village or ruin mentioned in our "particularizes" and detailed Guide of the Rhone--went drifting along by the hour in a wholly unknown land and on an uncharted river! Confound it, we stopped talking and did nothing but stand up in the boat and search the horizons with the glass and wonder what in the devil had happened. And at last, away yonder at 5 o'clock when some east towers and fortresses hove in sight we couldn't recognize them for Avignon--yet we knew by the broken bridge that it was Avignon.

Then we saw what the trouble was--at some time or other we had drifted down the wrong side of an island and followed a sluggish branch of the Rhone not frequented in modern times. We lost an hour and a half by it and missed one of the most picturesque and gigantic and history-sodden masses of castellated medieval ruin that Europe can show.

It was dark by the time we had wandered through the town and got the letters and found the hotel--so I went to bed.

We shall leave here at noon tomorrow and float down to Arles, arriving about dark, and there bid good bye to the boat, the river-trip finished. Between Arles and Nimes (and Avignon again,) we shall be till Saturday morning--then rail it through on that day to Ouchy, reaching the hotel at 11 at night if the train isn't late.

Next day (Sunday) if you like, go to Basel, and Monday to Berlin. But I shall be at your disposal, to do exactly as you desire and prefer.

With no end of love to all of you and twice as much to you, sweetheart, SAML.

I believe my arm is a trifle better than it was when I started.

The mention in the foregoing letter of the Napoleon effigy is the beginning of what proved to be a rather interesting episode. Mark Twain thought a great deal of his discovery, as he called it--the giant figure of Napoleon outlined by the distant mountain range. In his note-book he entered memoranda telling just where it was to be seen, and added a pencil sketch of the huge profile. But then he characteristically forgot all about it, and when he recalled the incident ten years later, he could not remember the name of the village, Beauchastel, from which the great figure could be seen; also, that he had made a record of the place.

But he was by this time more certain than ever that his discovery was a remarkable one, which, if known, would become one of the great natural wonders, such as Niagara Falls. Theodore Stanton was visiting him at the time, and Clemens urged him, on his return to France, to make an excursion to the Rhone and locate the Lost Napoleon, as he now called it. But Clemens remembered the wonder as being somewhere between Arles and Avignon, instead of about a hundred miles above the last-named town. Stanton naturally failed to find it, and it remained for the writer of these notes, motoring up the Rhone one September day, exactly twenty-two years after the first discovery, to re-locate the vast reclining figure of the first consul of France, "dreaming of Universal Empire." The re-discovery was not difficult--with Mark Twain's memoranda as a guide--and it was worth while. Perhaps the Lost Napoleon is not so important a natural wonder as Mark Twain believed, but it is a striking picture, and on a clear day the calm blue face outlined against the sky will long hold the traveler's attention.

To Clara Clemens, in Ouchy, Switzerland:

AFLOAT, 11.20 a.m., Sept. 29, Tuesday. DEAR OLD BEN,--The vast stone masses and huge towers of the ancient papal palace of Avignon are projected above an intervening wooded island a mile up the river behind me--for we are already on our way to Arles. It is a perfectly still morning, with a brilliant sun, and very hot--outside; but I am under cover of the linen hood, and it is cool and shady in here.

Please tell mamma I got her very last letter this morning, and I perceive by it that I do not need to arrive at Ouchy before Saturday midnight. I am glad, because I couldn't do the railroading I am proposing to do during the next two or three days and get there earlier. I could put in the time till Sunday midnight, but shall not venture it without telegraphic instructions from her to Nimes day after tomorrow, Oct. 1, care Hotel Manivet.

The only adventures we have is in drifting into rough seas now and then. They are not dangerous, but they go thro' all the motions of it. Yesterday when we shot the Bridge of the Holy Spirit it was probably in charge of some inexperienced deputy spirit for the day, for we were allowed to go through the wrong arch, which brought us into a tourbillon below which tried to make this old scow stand on its head. Of course I lost my temper and blew it off in a way to be heard above the roar of the tossing waters. I lost it because the admiral had taken that arch in deference to my opinion that it was the best one, while his own judgment told him to take the one nearest the other side of the river. I could have poisoned him I was so mad to think I had hired such a turnip. A boatman in command should obey nobody's orders but his own, and yield to nobody's suggestions.

It was very sweet of you to write me, dear, and I thank you ever so much. With greatest love and kisses, PAPA.

To Mrs. Clemens, in Ouchy, Switzerland:

ARLES, Sept. 30, noon. Livy darling, I hain't got no time to write today, because I am sight seeing industriously and imagining my chapter.

Bade good-bye to the river trip and gave away the boat yesterday evening. We had ten great days in her.

We reached here after dark. We were due about 4.30, counting by distance, but we couldn't calculate on such a lifeless current as we found. I love you, sweetheart. SAML.

It had been a long time since Clemens had written to his old friend Twichell, but the Rhone trip must have reminded him of those days thirteen years earlier, when, comparatively young men, he and Twichell were tramping through the Black Forest and scaling Gemmi Pass. He sent Twichell a reminder of that happy time.

To Rev. Joseph H. Twichell, in Hartford, Conn:

NIMES, Oct. 1, '91. DEAR JOE,--I have been ten days floating down the Rhone on a raft, from Lake Bourget, and a most curious and darling kind of a trip it has been. You ought to have been along--I could have made room for you easily--and you would have found that a pedestrian tour in Europe doesn't begin with a raft-voyage for hilarity and mild adventure, and intimate contact with the unvisited native of the back settlements, and extinction from the world and newspapers, and a conscience in a state of coma, and lazy comfort, and solid happiness. In fact there's nothing that's so lovely.

But it's all over. I gave the raft away yesterday at Arles, and am loafing along back by short stages on the rail to Ouchy-Lausanne where the tribe are staying. Love to you all MARK.

The Clemenses settled in Berlin for the winter, at 7 Kornerstrasse, and later at the Hotel Royal. There had been no permanent improvement in Mark Twain's arm and he found writing difficult. Some of the letters promised to Laffan and McClure were still unfinished.

Young Hall, his publishing manager in America, was working hard to keep the business afloat, and being full of the optimism of his years did not fail to make as good a showing as he could. We may believe his letters were very welcome to Clemens and his wife, who found little enough in the general prospect to comfort them.

To Mr. Hall, in New York:

BERLIN, Nov. 27, '91. DEAR MR. HALL,--That kind of a statement is valuable. It came this morning. This is the first time since the business began that I have had a report that furnished the kind of information I wanted, and was really enlightening and satisfactory. Keep it up. Don't let it fall into desuetude.

Everything looks so fine and handsome with the business, now, that I feel a great let-up from depression. The rewards of your long and patient industry are on their way, and their arrival safe in port, presently, seems assured.

By George, I shall be glad when the ship comes in!

My arm is so much better that I was able to make a speech last night to 250 Americans. But when they threw my portrait on the screen it was a sorrowful reminder, for it was from a negative of 15 years ago, and hadn't a gray hair in it. And now that my arm is better, I have stolen a couple of days and finished up a couple of McClure letters that have been lying a long time.

I shall mail one of them to you next Tuesday--registered. Lookout for it.

I shall register and mail the other one (concerning the "Jungfrau") next Friday look out for it also, and drop me a line to let me know they have arrived.

I shall write the 6th and last letter by and by when I have studied Berlin sufficiently.

Yours in a most cheerful frame of mind, and with my and all the family's Thanksgiving greetings and best wishes, S. L. CLEMENS.

Postscript by Mrs. Clemens written on Mr. Clemens's letter:

DEAR MR. HALL,--This is my birthday and your letter this morning was a happy addition to the little gifts on the breakfast table. I thought of going out and spending money for something unnecessary after it came, but concluded perhaps I better wait a little longer. Sincerely yours O. L. CLEMENS.

"The German Chicago" was the last of the six McClure letters and was finished that winter in Berlin. It is now included in the Uniform Edition of Mark Twain's works, and is one of the best descriptive articles of the German capital ever written. He made no use of the Rhone notes further than to put them together in literary form. They did not seem to him to contain enough substance to warrant publication. A letter to Hall, written toward the end of December, we find rather gloomy in tone, though he is still able to extract comfort and even cheerfulness from one of Mr. Hall's reports.

Memorandum to Fred J. Hall, in New York:

Among the MSS I left with you are a few that have a recent look and are written on rather stiff pale green paper. If you will have those type- writered and keep the originals and send me the copies (one per mail, not two.) I'll see if I can use them.

But tell Howells and other inquirers that my hopes of writing anything are very slender--I seem to be disabled for life.

Drop McClure a line and tell him the same. I can't dare to make an engagement now for even a single letter.

I am glad Howells is on a magazine, but sorry he gave up the Study. I shall have to go on a magazine myself if this L. A. L. continues to hold my nose down to the grind-stone much longer.

I'm going to hold my breath, now, for 30 days--then the annual statement will arrive and I shall know how we feel! Merry Xmas to you from us all.

Sincerely, S. L. C.

P. S. Just finished the above and finished raging at the eternal German tax-gatherer, and so all the jubilant things which I was going to say about the past year's business got knocked out of me. After writing this present letter I was feeling blue about Huck Finn, but I sat down and overhauled your reports from now back to last April and compared them with the splendid Oct.-Nov. business, and went to bed feeling refreshed and fine, for certainly it has been a handsome year. Now rush me along the Annual Report and let's see how we feel! S. L. C.

XXXII

LETTERS, 1892, CHIEFLY TO MR. HALL AND MRS. CRANE. IN BERLIN, MENTONE, BAD-NAUHEIM, FLORENCE

Mark Twain was the notable literary figure in Berlin that winter, the center of every great gathering. He was entertained by the Kaiser, and shown many special attentions by Germans of every rank. His books were as well known in Berlin as in New York, and at court assemblies and embassies he was always a chief center of interest.

He was too popular for his own good; the gaiety of the capital told on him. Finally, one night, after delivering a lecture in a hot room, he contracted a severe cold, driving to a ball at General von Versen's, and a few days later was confined to his bed with pneumonia. It was not a severe attack, but it was long continued. He could write some letters and even work a little, but he was not allowed to leave his bed for many weeks, a condition which he did not find a hardship, for no man ever enjoyed the loose luxury of undress and the comfort of pillows more than Mark Twain. In a memorandum of that time he wrote: "I am having a booming time all to myself."

Meantime, Hall, in America, was sending favorable reports of the publishing business, and this naturally helped to keep up his spirits. He wrote frequently to Hall, of course, but the letters for the most part are purely of a business nature and of little interest to the general reader.

To Fred J. Hall, in New York:

HOTEL ROYAL, BERLIN, Feb. 12. DEAR MR. HALL,--Daly wants to get the stage rights of the "American Claimant." The foundation from which I wrote the story is a play of the same name which has been in A. P. Burbank's hands 5 or 6 years. That play cost me some money (helping Burbank stage it) but has never brought me any. I have written Burbank (Lotos Club) and asked him to give me back his rights in the old play so that I can treat with Daly and utilize this chance to even myself up. Burbank is a lovely fellow, and if he objects I can't urge him. But you run in at the Lotos and see him; and if he relinquishes his claim, then I would like you to conduct the business with Daly; or have Whitford or some other lawyer do it under your supervision if you prefer.

This morning I seem to have rheumatism in my right foot.

I am ordered south by the doctor and shall expect to be well enough to start by the end of this month.

[No signature.]

It is curious, after Clemens and Howells had tried so hard and so long to place their "Sellers" Play, that now, when the story appeared in book form, Augustin Daly should have thought it worth dramatizing. Daly and Clemens were old friends, and it would seem that Daly could hardly have escaped seeing the play when it was going the rounds. But perhaps there is nothing more mysterious in the world than the ways and wants of theatrical managers. The matter came to nothing, of course, but the fact that Daly should have thought a story built from an old discarded play had a play in it seems interesting.

Clemens and his wife were advised to leave the cold of Berlin as soon as he was able to travel. This was not until the first of March, when, taking their old courier, Joseph Very, they left the children in good hands and journeyed to the south of France.

To Susy Clemens, in Berlin:

MENTONE, Mch 22, '92. SUSY DEAR,--I have been delighted to note your easy facility with your pen and proud to note also your literary superiorities of one kind and another--clearness of statement, directness, felicity of expression, photographic ability in setting forth an incident--style--good style--no barnacles on it in the way of unnecessary, retarding words (the Shipman scrapes off the barnacles when he wants his racer to go her best gait and straight to the buoy.) You should write a letter every day, long or short --and so ought I, but I don't.

Mamma says, tell Clara yes, she will have to write a note if the fan comes back mended.

We couldn't go to Nice to-day--had to give it up, on various accounts-- and this was the last chance. I am sorry for Mamma--I wish she could have gone. She got a heavy fall yesterday evening and was pretty stiff and lame this morning, but is working it off trunk packing.

Joseph is gone to Nice to educate himself in Kodaking--and to get the pictures mounted which Mamma thinks she took here; but I noticed she didn't take the plug out, as a rule. When she did, she took nine pictures on top of each other--composites. With lots of love. PAPA.

In the course of their Italian wanderings they reached Florence, where they were so comfortable and well that they decided to engage a villa for the next winter. Through Prof. Willard Fiske, they discovered the Villa Viviani, near Settignano, an old palace beautifully located on the hilltops east of Florence, commanding a wonderful view of the ancient city. Clemens felt that he could work there, and time proved that he was right.

For the summer, however, they returned to Germany, and located at Bad-Nauheim. Clemens presently decided to make a trip to America to give some personal attention to business matters. For one thing, his publishing-house, in spite of prosperity, seemed constantly to be requiring more capital, and then a Chicago company had been persuaded by Paige to undertake the manufacture of the type-setter. It was the beginning of a series of feverish trips which he would make back and forth across the ocean during the next two years.

To Fred J. Hall, in New York:

BAD-NAUHEIM, June 11, '92. Saturday. DEAR MR. HALL,--If this arrives before I do, let it inform you that I am leaving Bremen for New York next Tuesday in the "Havel."

If you can meet me when the ship arrives, you can help me to get away from the reporters; and maybe you can take me to your own or some other lodgings where they can't find me.

But if the hour is too early or too late for you, I shall obscure myself somewhere till I can come to the office.

Yours sincerely S. L. C.

Nothing of importance happened in America. The new Paige company had a factory started in Chicago and expected to manufacture fifty machines as a beginning. They claimed to have capital, or to be able to command it, and as the main control had passed from Clemens's hands, he could do no more than look over the ground and hope for the best. As for the business, about all that he could do was to sign certain notes necessary to provide such additional capital as was needed, and agree with Hall that hereafter they would concentrate their efforts and resist further temptation in the way of new enterprise. Then he returned to Bad-Nauheim and settled down to literature. This was the middle of July, and he must have worked pretty steadily, for he presently had a variety of MSS. ready to offer.

To Fred J. Hall, in New York:

Aug. 10, '92. DEAR MR. HALT,--I have dropped that novel I wrote you about, because I saw a more effective way of using the main episode--to wit: by telling it through the lips of Huck Finn. So I have started Huck Finn and Tom Sawyer (still 15 years old) and their friend the freed slave Jim around the world in a stray balloon, with Huck as narrator, and somewhere after the end of that great voyage he will work in the said episode and then nobody will suspect that a whole book has been written and the globe circumnavigated merely to get that episode in an effective (and at the same time apparently unintentional) way. I have written 12,000 words of this narrative, and find that the humor flows as easily as the adventures and surprises--so I shall go along and make a book of from 50,000 to 100,000 words.

It is a story for boys, of course, and I think will interest any boy between 8 years and 80.

When I was in New York the other day Mrs. Dodge, editor of St. Nicholas, wrote and, offered me $5,000 for (serial right) a story for boys 50,000 words long. I wrote back and declined, for I had other matter in my mind, then.

I conceive that the right way to write a story for boys is to write so that it will not only interest boys but will also strongly interest any man who has ever been a boy. That immensely enlarges the audience.

Now this story doesn't need to be restricted to a Childs magazine--it is proper enough for any magazine, I should think, or for a syndicate. I don't swear it, but I think so.

Proposed title of the story, "New Adventures of Huckleberry Finn."

[No signature.]

The "novel" mentioned in the foregoing was The Extraordinary Twins, a story from which Pudd'nhead Wilson would be evolved later. It was a wildly extravagant farce--just the sort of thing that now and then Mark Twain plunged into with an enthusiasm that had to work itself out and die a natural death, or mellow into something worth while. Tom Sawyer Abroad, as the new Huck story was finally called, was completed and disposed of to St. Nicholas for serial publication.

The Twichells were in Europe that summer, and came to Bad-Nauheim. The next letter records a pleasant incident. The Prince of Wales of that day later became King Edward VII.

To Mr. and Mrs. Orion Clemens, in Keokuk, Iowa.:

Private. BAD-NAUHEIM, Aug. 23, '92. DEAR ORION AND MOLLIE,--("Private" because no newspaper-man or other gossip must get hold of it)

Livy is getting along pretty well, and the doctor thinks another summer here will cure her.

The Twichell's have been here four days and we have had good times with them. Joe and I ran over to Homburg, the great pleasure resort, Saturday, to dine with some friends, and in the morning I went walking in the promenade and met the British Ambassador to the Court of Berlin, and he introduced me to the Prince of Wales, and I found him a most unusually comfortable and unembarrassing Englishman to talk with--quick to see the obscurest point, and equipped with a laugh which is spontaneous and catching. Am invited by a near friend of his to meet him at dinner day after tomorrow, and there could be a good time, but the brass band will smash the talk and spoil everything.

We are expecting to move to Florence ten or twelve days hence, but if this hot weather continues we shall wait for cooler. I take Clara to Berlin for the winter-music, mainly, with German and French added. Thus far, Jean is our only glib French scholar.

We all send love to you all and to Pamela and Sam's family, and Annie.

SAM

Clemens and family left Bad-Nauheim for Italy by way of Switzerland. In September Mrs. Clemens's sister, Mrs. Crane, who had been with them in Europe during the first year, had now returned to America. Mrs. Clemens had improved at the baths, though she had by no means recovered her health. We get a general report of conditions from the letter which Clemens wrote Mrs. Crane from Lucerne, Switzerland, where the party rested for several days. The "Phelps" mentioned in this letter was William Walter Phelps, United States Minister to Germany. The Phelps and Clemens families had been much associated in Berlin. "Mason" was Frank Mason, Consul General at Frankfort, and in later years at Paris. "Charlie and Ida" were Charles and Mrs. Langdon, of Elmira.

To Mrs. Crane, in Elmira, N. Y.:

LUCERNE, Sept. 18, '92. DEAR AUNT SUE,--Imagine how I felt to find that you had actually gone off without filling my traveling ink stand which you gave me! I found it out yesterday. Livy advised me to write you about it.

I have been driving this pen hard. I wrote 280 pages on a yarn called "Tom Sawyer Abroad," then took up the "Twins" again, destroyed the last half of the manuscript and re-wrote it in another form, and am going to continue it and finish it in Florence. "Tom Sawyer" seems rather pale to the family after the extravagances of the Twins, but they came to like it after they got used to it

We remained in Nauheim a little too long. If we had left there four or five days earlier we should have made Florence in 3 days; but by the time we got started Livy had got smitten with what we feared might be erysipelas--greatly swollen neck and face, and unceasing headaches. We lay idle in Frankfort 4 days, doctoring. We started Thursday and made Bale. Hard trip, because it was one of those trains that gets tired every seven minutes and stops to rest three quarters of an hour. It took us 3 1/2 hours to get here, instead of the regulation 2.20. We reached here Friday evening and will leave tomorrow (Tuesday) morning. The rest has made the headaches better. We shall pull through to Milan tomorrow if possible. Next day we shall start at 10 a. m., and try to make Bologna, 5 hours. Next day (Thursday) Florence, D. V. Next year we will walk, for these excursions have got to be made over again. I've got seven trunks, and I undertook to be courier because I meant to express them to Florence direct, but we were a couple of days too late. All continental roads had issued a peremptory order that no baggage should travel a mile except in the company of the owner. (All over Europe people are howling; they are separated from their baggage and can't get it forwarded to them) I have to re-ship my trunks every day. It is very amusing--uncommonly so. There seemed grave doubts about our being able to get these trunks over the Italian frontier, but I've got a very handsome note from the Frankfort Italian Consul General addressed to all Italian Customs Officers, and we shall get through if anybody does.

The Phelpses came to Frankfort and we had some great times--dinner at his hotel, the Masons, supper at our inn--Livy not in it. She was merely allowed a glimpse, no more. Of course, Phelps said she was merely pretending to be ill; was never looking so well and fine.

The children are all right. They paddle around a little, and drive-so do we all. Lucerne seems to be pretty full of tourists. The Fleulen boat went out crowded yesterday morning.

The Paris Herald has created a public interest by inoculating one of its correspondents with cholera. A man said yesterday he wished to God they would inoculate all of them. Yes, the interest is quite general and strong, and much hope is felt.

Livy says, I have said enough bad things, and better send all our loves to you and Charley and Ida and all the children and shut up. Which I do --and shut up. S. L. C.

They reached Florence on the 26th, and four days later we find Clemens writing again to Mrs. Crane, detailing everything at length. Little comment on this letter is required; it fully explains itself. Perhaps a word of description from one of his memoranda will not be out of place. Of the villa he wrote: "It is a plain, square building, like a box, and is painted light green and has green window-shutters. It stands in a commanding position on the artificial terrace of liberal dimensions, which is walled around with masonry. From the walls the vineyards and olive groves of the estate slant away toward the valley.... Roses overflow the retaining walls and the battered and mossy stone urn on the gate- post, in pink and yellow cataracts, exactly as they do on the drop- curtains in the theaters. The house is a very fortress for strength."

The Mrs. Ross in this letter was Janet Ross, daughter of Lady Duff Gordon, remembered to-day for her Egyptian letters. The Ross castle was but a little distance away.

To Mrs. Crane, in Elmira:

VILLA VIVIANI, SETTIGNANO, FLORENCE. Sept. 30, 1892 DEAR SUE,--We have been in the house several days, and certainly it is a beautiful place,--particularly at this moment, when the skies are a deep leaden color, the domes of Florence dim in the drizzling rain, and occasional perpendicular coils of lightning quivering intensely in the black sky about Galileo's Tower. It is a charming panorama, and the most conspicuous towers and domes down in the city look to-day just as they looked when Boccaccio and Dante used to contemplate them from this hillock five and six hundred years ago.

The Mademoiselle is a great help to Livy in the housekeeping, and is a cheery and cheerful presence in the house. The butler is equipped with a little French, and it is this fact that enables the house to go--but it won't go well until the family get some sort of facility with the Italian tongue, for the cook, the woman-of-all-work and the coachman understand only that. It is a stubborn and devilish language to learn, but Jean and the others will master it. Livy's German Nauheim girl is the worst off of anybody, as there is no market for her tongue at all among the help.

With the furniture in and the curtains up the house is very pretty, and not unhomelike. At midnight last night we heard screams up stairs--Susy had set the lofty window curtains afire with a candle. This sounds kind of frightful, whereas when you come to think of it, a burning curtain or pile of furniture hasn't any element of danger about it in this fortress. There isn't any conceivable way to burn this house down, or enable a conflagration on one floor to climb to the next.

Mrs. Ross laid in our wood, wine and servants for us, and they are excellent. She had the house scoured from Cellar to rook the curtains washed and put up, all beds pulled to pieces, beaten, washed and put together again, and beguiled the Marchese into putting a big porcelain stove in the vast central hall. She is a wonderful woman, and we don't quite see how or when we should have gotten under way without her.

Observe our address above--the post delivers letters daily at the house.

Even with the work and fuss of settling the house Livy has improved--and the best is yet to come. There is going to be absolute seclusion here-- a hermit life, in fact. We (the rest of us) shall run over to the Ross's frequently, and they will come here now and then and see Livy--that is all. Mr. Fiske is away--nobody knows where--and the work on his house has been stopped and his servants discharged. Therefore we shall merely go Rossing--as far as society is concerned--shan't circulate in Florence until Livy shall be well enough to take a share in it.

This present house is modern. It is not much more than two centuries old; but parts of it, and also its foundations are of high antiquity. The fine beautiful family portraits--the great carved ones in the large ovals over the doors of the big hall--carry one well back into the past. One of them is dated 1305--he could have known Dante, you see. Another is dated 1343--he could have known Boccaccio and spent his afternoons in Fiesole listening to the Decameron tales. Another is dated 1463-- he could have met Columbus.....

Evening. The storm thundered away until night, and the rain came down in floods. For awhile there was a partial break, which furnished about such a sunset as will be exhibited when the Last Day comes and the universe tumbles together in wreck and ruin. I have never seen anything more spectacular and impressive.

One person is satisfied with the villa, anyway. Jean prefers it to all Europe, save Venice. Jean is eager to get at the Italian tongue again, now, and I see that she has forgotten little or nothing of what she learned of it in Rome and Venice last spring.

I am the head French duffer of the family. Most of the talk goes over my head at the table. I catch only words, not phrases. When Italian comes to be substituted I shall be even worse off than I am now, I suppose.

This reminds me that this evening the German girl said to Livy, "Man hat mir gesagt loss Sie una candella verlaught habe"--unconsciously dropping in a couple of Italian words, you see. So she is going to join the polyglots, too, it appears. They say it is good entertainment to hear her and the butler talk together in their respective tongues, piecing out and patching up with the universal sign-language as they go along. Five languages in use in the house (including the sign-language-hardest-worked of them all) and yet with all this opulence of resource we do seem to have an uncommonly tough time making ourselves understood.

What we lack is a cat. If we only had Germania! That was the most satisfactory all-round cat I have seen yet. Totally ungermanic in the raciness of his character and in the sparkle of his mind and the spontaneity of his movements. We shall not look upon his like again....

S. L. C.

Clemens got well settled down to work presently. He found the situation, the climate, the background, entirely suited to literary production, and in a little while he had accomplished more than at any other time since his arrival in Europe. From letters to Mrs. Crane and to Mr. Hall we learn something of his employments and his satisfaction.

To Mrs. Crane, in Elmira:

VILLA VIVIANI SETTIGNANO, FLORENCE. Oct. 22, '92. DEAR SUE,--We are getting wonted. The open fires have driven away the cold and the doubt, and now a cheery spirit pervades the place. Livy and the Kings and Mademoiselle having been taking their tea a number of times, lately, on the open terrace with the city and the hills and the sunset for company. I stop work, a few minutes, as a rule, when the sun gets down to the hilltops west of Florence, and join the tea-group to wonder and exclaim. There is always some new miracle in the view, a new and exquisite variation in the show, a variation which occurs every 15 minutes between dawn and night. Once early in the morning, a multitude of white villas not before perceived, revealed themselves on the far hills; then we recognized that all those great hills are snowed thick with them, clear to the summit.

The variety of lovely effects, the infinitude of change, is something not to be believed by any who has not seen it. No view that I am acquainted with in the world is at all comparable to this for delicacy, charm, exquisiteness, dainty coloring, and bewildering rapidity of change. It keeps a person drunk with pleasure all the time. Sometimes Florence ceases to be substantial, and becomes just a faint soft dream, with domes and towers of air, and one is persuaded that he might blow it away with a puff of his breath.

Livy is progressing admirably. This is just the place for her.

[Remainder missing.]

To Fred J. Hall, in New York:

Dec. 12, '92. DEAR MR. HALL,--November check received.

I have lent the Californian's Story to Arthur Stedman for his Author Club Book, so your suggestion that my new spring-book bear that name arrives too late, as he probably would not want us to use that story in a book of ours until the Author book had had its run. That is for him to decide-- and I don't want him hampered at all in his decision. I, for my part, prefer the "$1,000,000 Banknote and Other Stories" by Mark Twain as a title, but above my judgment I prefer yours. I mean this--it is not taffy.

I told Arthur to leave out the former squib or paragraph and use only the Californian's Story. Tell him this is because I am going to use that in the book I am now writing.

I finished "Those Extraordinary Twins" night before last makes 60 or 80,000 words--haven't counted.

The last third of it suits me to a dot. I begin, to-day, to entirely recast and re-write the first two-thirds--new plan, with two minor characters, made very prominent, one major character cropped out, and the Twins subordinated to a minor but not insignificant place.

The minor character will now become the chiefest, and I will name the story after him-- "Puddn'head Wilson."

Merry Xmas to you, and great prosperity and felicity!

S. L. CLEMENS.

XXXIII

LETTERS, 1893, TO MR. HALL, MRS. CLEMENS, AND OTHERS. FLORENCE. BUSINESS TROUBLES. "PUDD'NHEAD WILSON." "JOAN OF ARC." AT THE PLAYERS, NEW YORK

The reader may have suspected that young Mr. Hall in New York was having his troubles. He was by this time one-third owner in the business of Charles L. Webster & Co., as well as its general manager. The business had been drained of its capital one way and another-partly by the publication of unprofitable books; partly by the earlier demands of the typesetter, but more than all by the manufacturing cost and agents' commissions demanded by L. A. L.; that is to say, the eleven large volumes constituting the Library of American Literature, which Webster had undertaken to place in a million American homes. There was plenty of sale for it--indeed, that was just the trouble; for it was sold on payments--small monthly payments--while the cost of manufacture and the liberal agents' commissions were cash items, and it would require a considerable period before the dribble of collections would swell into a tide large enough to satisfy the steady outflow of expense. A sale of twenty-five sets a day meant prosperity on paper, but unless capital could be raised from some other source to make and market those books through a period of months, perhaps even years, to come, it meant bankruptcy in reality. It was Hall's job, with Clemens to back him, to keep their ship afloat on these steadily ebbing financial waters. It was also Hall's affair to keep Mark Twain cheerful, to look pleasant himself, and to show how they were steadily getting rich because orders were pouring in, though a cloud that resembled bankruptcy loomed always a little higher upon the horizon. If Hall had not been young and an optimist, he would have been frightened out of his boots early in the game. As it was, he made a brave steady fight, kept as cheerful and stiff an upper lip as possible, always hoping that something would happen--some grand sale of his other books, some unexpected inflow from the type-setter interests--anything that would sustain his ship until the L. A. L. tide should turn and float it into safety.

Clemens had faith in Hall and was fond of him. He never found fault with him; he tried to accept his encouraging reports at their face value. He lent the firm every dollar of his literary earnings not absolutely needed for the family's support; he signed new notes; he allowed Mrs. Clemens to put in such remnants of her patrimony as the type-setter had spared.

The situation in 1893 was about as here outlined. The letters to Hall of that year are frequent and carry along the story. To any who had formed the idea that Mark Twain was irascible, exacting, and faultfinding, they will perhaps be a revelation.

To Fred J. Hall, in New York:

FLORENCE, Jan. 1, '93. DEAR MR. HALL,--Yours of Dec. 19 is to hand, and Mrs. Clemens is deeply distressed, for she thinks I have been blaming you or finding fault with you about something. But most surely that cannot be. I tell her that although I am prone to write hasty and regrettable things to other people, I am not a bit likely to write such things to you. I can't believe I have done anything so ungrateful. If I have, pile coals of fire on my head, for I deserve it!

I wonder if my letter of credit isn't an encumbrance? Do you have to deposit the whole amount it calls for? If that is so, it is an encumbrance, and we must withdraw it and take the money out of soak. I have never made drafts upon it except when compelled, because I thought you deposited nothing against it, and only had to put up money that I drew upon it; that therefore the less I drew the easier it would be for you.

I am dreadfully sorry I didn't know it would be a help to you to let my monthly check pass over a couple of months. I could have stood that by drawing what is left of Mrs. Clemens's letter of credit, and we would have done it cheerfully.

I will write Whitmore to send you the "Century" check for $1,000, and you can collect Mrs.

Dodge's $2,000 (Whitmore has power of attorney which I think will enable him to endorse it over to you in my name.) If you need that $3,000 put it in the business and use it, and send Whitmore the Company's note for a year. If you don't need it, turn it over to Mr. Halsey and let him invest it for me.

I've a mighty poor financial head, and I may be all wrong--but tell me if I am wrong in supposing that in lending my own firm money at 6 per cent I pay 4 of it myself and so really get only a per cent? Now don't laugh if that is stupid.

Of course my friend declined to buy a quarter interest in the L. A. L. for $200,000. I judged he would. I hoped he would offer $100,000, but he didn't. If the cholera breaks out in America, a few months hence, we can't borrow or sell; but if it doesn't we must try hard to raise $100,000. I wish we could do it before there is a cholera scare.

I have been in bed two or three days with a cold, but I got up an hour ago, and I believe I am all right again.

How I wish I had appreciated the need of $100,000 when I was in New York last summer! I would have tried my best to raise it. It would make us able to stand 1,000 sets of L. A. L. per month, but not any more, I guess.

You have done magnificently with the business, and we must raise the money somehow, to enable you to reap the reward of all that labor. Sincerely Yours S. L. CLEMENS.

"Whitmore," in this letter, was F. G. Whitmore, of Hartford, Mark Twain's financial agent. The money due from Mrs. Dodge was a balance on Tom Sawyer Abroad, which had been accepted by St. Nicholas. Mr. Halsey was a down-town broker.

Clemens, who was growing weary of the constant demands of L. A. L., had conceived the idea that it would be well to dispose of a portion of it for enough cash to finance its manufacture.

We don't know who the friend was to whom he offered a quarter interest for the modest sum of two hundred thousand dollars. But in the next letter we discover designs on a certain very canny Scotchman of Skibo.

To Fred J. Hall, in New York:

FLORENCE, Jan. 28, '92. DEAR MR. HALL,--I want to throw out a suggestion and see what you think of it. We have a good start, and solid ground under us; we have a valuable reputation; our business organization is practical, sound and well-devised; our publications are of a respect-worthy character and of a money-breeding species. Now then I think that the association with us of some one of great name and with capital would give our business a prodigious impetus--that phrase is not too strong.

As I look at it, it is not money merely that is needed; if that were all, the firm has friends enough who would take an interest in a paying venture; we need some one who has made his life a success not only from a business standpoint, but with that achievement back of him, has been great enough to make his power felt as a thinker and a literary man. It is a pretty usual thing for publishers to have this sort of partners. Now you see what a power Carnegie is, and how far his voice reaches in the several lines I speak of. Do you know him? You do by correspondence or purely business talks about his books--but personally, I mean? so that it would not be an intrusion for you to speak to him about this desire of mine--for I would like you to put it before him, and if you fail to interest him in it, you will probably get at least some valuable suggestions from him. I'll enclose a note of introduction--you needn't use it if you don't need to. Yours S. L. C.

P. S. Yes, I think I have already acknowledged the Dec. $1,000 and the Jan. $500--and if another $500 was mailed 3 days ago there's no hiatus.

I think I also reminded you that the new letter of credit does not cover the unexpended balance of the old one but falls considerably short of it.

Do your best with Carnegie, and don't wait to consider any of my intermediate suggestions or talks about our raising half of the $200,000 ourselves. I mean, wait for nothing. To make my suggestion available I should have to go over and see Arnot, and I don't want to until I can mention Carnegie's name to him as going in with us.

My book is type-written and ready for print--"Pudd'nhead Wilson-a Tale." (Or, "Those Extraordinary Twins," if preferable.)

It makes 82,500 words--12,000 more than Huck Finn. But I don't know what to do with it. Mrs. Clemens thinks it wouldn't do to go to the Am. Pub. Co. or anywhere outside of our own house; we have no subscription machinery, and a book in the trade is a book thrown away, as far as money-profit goes. I am in a quandary. Give me a lift out of it.

I will mail the book to you and get you to examine it and see if it is good or if it is bad. I think it is good, and I thought the Claimant bad, when I saw it in print; but as for real judgment, I think I am destitute of it.

I am writing a companion to the Prince and Pauper, which is half done and will make 200,000 words; and I have had the idea that if it were gotten up in handsome style, with many illustrations and put at a high enough price maybe the L. A. L. canvassers would take it and run it with that book. Would they? It could be priced anywhere from $4 up to $10, according to how it was gotten up, I suppose.

I don't want it to go into a magazine. S. L. C.

I am having several short things type-"writered." I will send them to you presently. I like the Century and Harper's, but I don't know that I have any business to object to the Cosmopolitan if they pay as good rates. I suppose a man ought to stick to one magazine, but that may be only superstition. What do you think? S. L. C.

"The companion to The Prince and the Pauper," mentioned in this letter, was the story of Joan of Arc, perhaps the most finished of Mark Twain's literary productions. His interest in Joan had been first awakened when, as a printer's apprentice in Hannibal, he had found blowing along the street a stray leaf from some printed story of her life. That fragment of history had pictured Joan in prison, insulted and mistreated by ruffians. It had aroused all the sympathy and indignation in the boy, Sam Clemens; also, it had awakened his interest in history, and, indeed, in all literature.

His love for the character of Joan had grown with the years, until in time he had conceived the idea of writing her story. As far back as the early eighties he had collected material for it, and had begun to make the notes. One thing and another had interfered, and he had found no opportunity for such a story. Now, however, in Florence, in the ancient villa, and in the quiet garden, looking across the vineyards and olive groves to the dream city along the Arno, he felt moved to take up the tale of the shepherd girl of France, the soldier maid, or, as he called her, "The noble child, the most innocent, the most lovely, the most adorable the ages have produced." His surroundings and background would seem to have been perfect, and he must have written with considerable ease to have completed a hundred thousand words in a period of not more than six weeks.

Perhaps Hall did not even go to see Carnegie; at all events nothing seems to have come of the idea. Once, at a later time, Mask Twain himself mentioned the matter to Carnegie, and suggested to him that it was poor financiering to put all of one's eggs into one basket, meaning into iron. But Carnegie answered, "That's a mistake; put all your eggs into one basket and watch that basket."

It was March when Clemens felt that once more his presence was demanded in America. He must see if anything could be realized from the type-setter or L. A. L.

To Fred J. Hall, in New York:

March 13, '93. DEAR MR. HALL,--I am busy getting ready to sail the 22d, in the Kaiser Wilhelm II.

I send herewith 2 magazine articles.

The Story contains 3,800 to 4,000 words.

The "Diary" contains 3,800 words.

Each would make about 4 pages of the Century.

The Diary is a gem, if I do say it myself that shouldn't.

If the Cosmopolitan wishes to pay $600 for either of them or $1,200 for both, gather in the check, and I will use the money in America instead of breaking into your treasury.

If they don't wish to trade for either, send the articles to the Century, without naming a price, and if their check isn't large enough I will call and abuse them when I come.

I signed and mailed the notes yesterday. Yours S. L. C.

Clemens reached New York on the 3d of April and made a trip to Chicago, but accomplished nothing, except to visit the World's Fair and be laid up with a severe cold. The machine situation had not progressed. The financial stringency of 1893 had brought everything to a standstill. The New York bank would advance Webster & Co. no more money. So disturbed were his affairs, so disordered was everything, that sometimes he felt himself as one walking amid unrealities. A fragment of a letter to Mrs. Crane conveys this:

"I dreamed I was born and grew up and was a pilot on the Mississippi and a miner and a journalist in Nevada and a pilgrim in the Quaker City, and had a wife and children and went to live in a villa at Florence--and this dream goes on and on and sometimes seems so real that I almost believe it is real. I wonder if it is? But there is no way to tell, for if one applies tests they would be part of the dream, too, and so would simply aid the deceit. I wish I knew whether it is a dream or real."

He saw Warner, briefly, in America; also Howells, now living in New York, but he had little time for visiting. On May 13th he sailed again for Europe on the Kaiser Wilhelm II. On the night before sailing he sent Howells a good-by word.

To W. D. Howells, in New York City:

MURRAY HILL HOTEL, NEW YORE, May 12, 1893. Midnight. DEAR HOWELLS--I am so sorry I missed you.

I am very glad to have that book for sea entertainment, and I thank you ever so much for it.

I've had a little visit with Warner at last; I was getting afraid I wasn't going to have a chance to see him at all. I forgot to tell you how thoroughly I enjoyed your account of the country printing office, and how true it all was and how intimately recognizable in all its details. But Warner was full of delight over it, and that reminded me, and I am glad, for I wanted to speak of it.

You have given me a book; Annie Trumbull has sent me her book; I bought a couple of books; Mr. Hall gave me a choice German book; Laflan gave me two bottles of whisky and a box of cigars--I go to sea nobly equipped.

Good-bye and all good fortune attend you and yours--and upon you all I leave my benediction. MARK.

Mention has already been made of the Ross home being very near to Viviani, and the association of the Ross and Clemens families. There was a fine vegetable garden on the Ross estate, and it was in the interest of it that the next letter was written to the Secretary of Agriculture.

To Hon. J. Sterling Morton, in Washington, D. C.: Editorial Department Century Magazine, Union Square,

NEW YORK, April 6, 1893. TO THE HON. J. STERLING MORTON,--Dear Sir: Your petitioner, Mark Twain, a poor farmer of Connecticut--indeed, the poorest one there, in the opinion of many-desires a few choice breeds of seed corn (maize), and in return will zealously support the Administration in all ways honorable and otherwise.

To speak by the card, I want these things to hurry to Italy to an English lady. She is a neighbor of mine outside of Florence, and has a great garden and thinks she could raise corn for her table if she had the right ammunition. I myself feel a warm interest in this enterprise, both on patriotic grounds and because I have a key to that garden, which I got made from a wax impression. It is not very good soil, still I think she can grow enough for one table and I am in a position to select the table. If you are willing to aid and abet a countryman (and Gilder thinks you are,) please find the signature and address of your petitioner below.

Respectfully and truly yours. MARK TWAIN,

67 Fifth Avenue, New York.

P. S.--A handful of choice (Southern) watermelon seeds would pleasantly add to that lady's employments and give my table a corresponding lift.

His idea of business values had moderated considerably by the time he had returned to Florence. He was not hopeless yet, but he was clearly a good deal disheartened--anxious for freedom.

To Fred J. Hall, in New York:

FLORENCE May 30, '93 DEAR MR. HALL,--You were to cable me if you sold any machine royalties-- so I judge you have not succeeded.

This has depressed me. I have been looking over the past year's letters and statements and am depressed still more.

I am terribly tired of business. I am by nature and disposition unfitted for it and I want to get out of it. I am standing on the Mount Morris volcano with help from the machine a long way off-- doubtless a long way further off than the Connecticut Co. imagines.

Now here is my idea for getting out.

The firm owes Mrs. Clemens and me--I do not know quite how much, but it is about $170,000 or $175,000, 1 suppose (I make this guess from the documents here, whose technicalities confuse me horribly.)

The firm owes other sums, but there is stock and cash assets to cover the entire indebtedness and $116,679.20 over. Is that it? In addition we have the L. A. L. plates and copyright, worth more than $130,000--is that correct?

That is to say, we have property worth about $250,000 above indebtedness, I suppose--or, by one of your estimates, $300,000? The greater part of the first debts to me is in notes paying 6 percent. The rest (the old $70,000 or whatever it is) pays no interest.

Now then, will Harper or Appleton, or Putnam give me $200,000 for those debts and my two-thirds interest in the firm? (The firm of course taking the Mount Morris and all such obligations off my hands and leaving me clear of all responsibility.)

I don't want much money. I only want first class notes--$200,000 worth of them at 6 per cent, payable monthly;--yearly notes, renewable annually for 3 years, with $5,000 of the principal payable at the beginning and middle of each year. After that, the notes renewable annually and (perhaps) a larger part of the principal payable semi-annually.

Please advise me and suggest alterations and emendations of the above scheme, for I need that sort of help, being ignorant of business and not able to learn a single detail of it.

Such a deal would make it easy for a big firm to pour in a big cash capital and jump L. A. L. up to enormous prosperity. Then your one-third would be a fortune--and I hope to see that day!

I enclose an authority to use with Whitmore in case you have sold any royalties. But if you can't make this deal don't make any. Wait a little and see if you can't make the deal. Do make the deal if you possibly can. And if any presence shall be necessary in order to complete it I will come over, though I hope it can be done without that.

Get me out of business!

And I will be yours forever gratefully, S. L. CLEMENS.

My idea is, that I am offering my 2/3 of L. A. L. and the business for thirty or forty thousand dollars. Is that it?

P. S. S. The new firm could retain my books and reduce them to a 10 percent royalty. S. L. C.

To Rev. Jos. H. Twichell, in Hartford:

VILLA VIVIANI, SETTIGNANO (FLORENCE) June 9, '93. DEAR JOE,--The sea voyage set me up and I reached here May 27 in tolerable condition--nothing left but weakness, cough all gone.

Old Sir Henry Layard was here the other day, visiting our neighbor Janet Ross, daughter of Lady Duff Gordon, and since then I have been reading his account of the adventures of his youth in the far East. In a footnote he has something to say about a sailor which I thought might interest you--viz:

"This same quartermaster was celebrated among the English in Mesopotamia for an entry which he made in his log-book-after a perilous storm; 'The windy and watery elements raged. Tears and prayers was had recourse to, but was of no manner of use. So we hauled up the anchor and got round the point.'"

There--it isn't Ned Wakeman; it was before his day.

With love, MARK.

They closed Villa Viviani in June and near the end of the month arrived in Munich in order that Mrs. Clemens might visit some of the German baths. The next letter is written by her and shows her deep sympathy with Hall in his desperate struggle. There have been few more unselfish and courageous women in history than Mark Twain's wife.

From Mrs. Clemens to Mr. Hall, in New York:

June 27th 1893 MUNICH. DEAR MR. HALL,--Your letter to Mr. Clemens of June 16th has just reached here; as he has gone to Berlin for Clara I am going to send you just a line in answer to it.

Mr. Clemens did not realize what trouble you would be in when his letter should reach you or he would not have sent it just then. I hope you will not worry any more than you can help. Do not let our interests weigh on you too heavily. We both know you will, as you always have, look in every way to the best interests of all.

I think Mr. Clemens is right in feeling that he should get out of business, that he is not fitted for it; it worries him too much.

But he need be in no haste about it, and of course, it would be the very farthest from his desire to imperil, in the slightest degree, your interests in order to save his own.

I am sure that I voice his wish as well as mine when I say that he would simply like you to bear in mind the fact that he greatly desires to be released from his present anxiety and worry, at a time when it shall not endanger your interest or the safety of the business.

I am more sorry than I can express that this letter of Mr. Clemens' should have reached you when you were struggling under such terrible pressure. I hope now that the weight is not quite so heavy. He would not have written you about the money if he had known that it was an inconvenience for you to send it. He thought the book-keeper whose duty it is to forward it had forgotten.

We can draw on Mr. Langdon for money for a few weeks until things are a little easier with you. As Mr. Clemens wrote you we would say "do not send us any more money at present" if we were not afraid to do so. I will say, however, do not trouble yourself if for a few weeks you are not able to send the usual amount.

Mr. Clemens and I have the greatest possible desire, not to increase in any way your burdens, and sincerely wish we might aid you.

I trust my brother may be able, in his talk with you, to throw some helpful light on the situation.

Hoping you will see a change for the better and begin to reap the fruit of your long and hard labor. Believe me Very Cordially yours OLIVIA L. CLEMENS.

Hall, naturally, did not wish to be left alone with the business. He realized that his credit would suffer, both at the bank and with the public, if his distinguished partner should retire. He wrote, therefore, proposing as an alternate that they dispose of the big subscription set that was swamping them. It was a good plan--if it would work--and we find Clemens entering into it heartily.

To Fred J. Hall, in New York:

MUNICH, July 3, '93. DEAR MR. HALL,--You make a suggestion which has once or twice flitted dimly through my mind heretofore to wit, sell L. A. L.

I like that better than the other scheme, for it is no doubt feasible, whereas the other is perhaps not.

The firm is in debt, but L. A. L. is free--and not only free but has large money owing to it. A proposition to sell that by itself to a big house could be made without embarrassment we merely confess that we cannot spare capital from the rest of the business to run it on the huge scale necessary to make it an opulent success.

It will be selling a good thing--for somebody; and it will be getting rid of a load which we are clearly not able to carry. Whoever buys will have a noble good opening--a complete equipment, a well organized business, a capable and experienced manager, and enterprise not experimental but under full sail, and immediately able to pay 50 per cent a year on every dollar the publisher shall actually invest in it--I mean in making and selling the books.

I am miserably sorry to be adding bothers and torments to the over-supply which you already have in these hideous times, but I feel so troubled, myself, considering the dreary fact that we are getting deeper and deeper in debt and the L. A. L. getting to be a heavier and heavier burden all the time, that I must bestir myself and seek a way of relief.

It did not occur to me that in selling out I would injure you--for that I am not going to do. But to sell L. A. L. will not injure you it will put you in better shape. Sincerely Yours S. L. CLEMENS.

To Fred J. Hall, in New York:

July 8, '92. DEAR MR. HALL,--I am sincerely glad you are going to sell L. A. L. I am glad you are shutting off the agents, and I hope the fatal book will be out of our hands before it will be time to put them on again. With nothing but our non-existent capital to work with the book has no value for us, rich a prize as it will be to any competent house that gets it.

I hope you are making an effort to sell before you discharge too many agents, for I suppose the agents are a valuable part of the property.

We have been stopping in Munich for awhile, but we shall make a break for some country resort in a few days now. Sincerely Yours S. L. C.

July 8 P. S. No, I suppose I am wrong in suggesting that you wait a moment before discharging your L. A. L. agents--in fact I didn't mean that. I judge your only hope of salvation is in discharging them all at once, since it is their commissions that threaten to swamp us. It is they who have eaten up the $14,000 I left with you in such a brief time, no doubt.

I feel panicky.

I think the sale might be made with better advantage, however, now, than later when the agents have got out of the purchaser's reach. S. L. C.

P. S. No monthly report for many months.

Those who are old enough to remember the summer of 1893 may recall it as a black financial season. Banks were denying credit, businesses were forced to the wall. It was a poor time to float any costly enterprise. The Chicago company who was trying to build the machines made little progress. The book business everywhere was bad. In a brief note following the foregoing letters Clemens wrote Hall:

"It is now past the middle of July and no cablegram to say the machine is finished. We are afraid you are having miserable days and worried nights, and we sincerely wish we could relieve you, but it is all black with us and we don't know any helpful thing to say or do."

He inclosed some kind of manuscript proposition for John Brisben Walker, of the Cosmopolitan, with the comment: "It is my ingenious scheme to protect the family against the alms-house for one more year--and after that--well, goodness knows! I have never felt so desperate in my life--and good reason, for I haven't got a penny to my name, and Mrs. Clemens hasn't enough laid up with Langdon to keep us two months."

It was like Mark Twain, in the midst of all this turmoil, to project an entirely new enterprise; his busy mind was always visioning success in unusual undertakings, regardless of immediate conditions and the steps necessary to achievement.

To Fred J. Hall, in New York:

July 26, '93. DEAR MR. HALL,--..... I hope the machine will be finished this month; but it took me four years and cost me $100,000 to finish the other machine after it was apparently entirely complete and setting type like a house-afire.

I wonder what they call "finished." After it is absolutely perfect it can't go into a printing-office until it has had a month's wear, running night and day, to get the bearings smooth, I judge.

I may be able to run over about mid-October. Then if I find you relieved of L. A. L. we will start a magazine inexpensive, and of an entirely unique sort. Arthur Stedman and his father editors of it. Arthur could do all the work, merely submitting it to his father for approval.

The first number should pay--and all subsequent ones--25 cents a number. Cost of first number (20,000 copies) $2,000. Give most of them away, sell the rest. Advertising and other expenses-- cost unknown. Send one to all newspapers--it would get a notice--favorable, too.

But we cannot undertake it until L. A. L, is out of the way. With our hands free and some capital to spare, we could make it hum.

Where is the Shelley article? If you have it on hand, keep it and I will presently tell you what to do with it.

Don't forget to tell me. Yours Sincerely S. L. C.

The Shelley article mentioned in this letter was the "Defense of Harriet Sheller," one of the very best of his essays. How he could have written this splendid paper at a time of such distraction passes comprehension. Furthermore, it is clear that he had revised, indeed rewritten, the long story of Pudd'nhead Wilson.

To Fred J. Hall, in New York:

July 30, '93. DEAR MR. HALL,--This time "Pudd'nhead Wilson" is a success! Even Mrs. Clemens, the most difficult of critics, confesses it, and without reserves or qualifications. Formerly she would not consent that it be published either before or after my death. I have pulled the twins apart and made two individuals of them; I have sunk them out of sight, they are mere flitting shadows, now, and of no importance; their story has disappeared from the book. Aunt Betsy Hale has vanished wholly, leaving not a trace behind; aunt Patsy Cooper and her daughter Rowena have almost disappeared--they scarcely walk across the stage. The whole story is centered on the murder and the trial; from the first chapter the movement is straight ahead without divergence or side-play to the murder and the trial; everything that is done or said or that happens is a preparation for those events. Therefore, 3 people stand up high, from beginning to end, and only 3--Pudd'nhead, "Tom" Driscoll, and his nigger mother, Roxana; none of the others are important, or get in the way of the story or require the reader's attention. Consequently, the scenes and episodes which were the strength of the book formerly are stronger than ever, now.

When I began this final reconstruction the story contained 81,500 words, now it contains only 58,000. I have knocked out everything that delayed the march of the story--even the description of a Mississippi steamboat. There's no weather in, and no scenery--the story is stripped for flight!

Now, then what is she worth? The amount of matter is but 3,000 words short of the American Claimant, for which the syndicate paid $12,500. There was nothing new in that story, but the finger-prints in this one is virgin ground--absolutely fresh, and mighty curious and interesting to everybody.

I don't want any more syndicating--nothing short of $20,000, anyway, and that I can't get--but won't you see how much the Cosmopolitan will stand?

Do your best for me, for I do not sleep these nights, for visions of the poor-house.

This in spite of the hopeful tone of yours of 11th to Langdon (just received) for in me hope is very nearly expiring. Everything does look so blue, so dismally blue!

By and by I shall take up the Rhone open-boat voyage again, but not now- we are going to be moving around too much. I have torn up some of it, but still have 15,000 words that Mrs. Clemens approves of, and that I like. I may go at it in Paris again next winter, but not unless I know I can write it to suit me.

Otherwise I shall tackle Adam once more, and do him in a kind of a friendly and respectful way that will commend him to the Sunday schools. I've been thinking out his first life-days to-day and framing his childish and ignorant impressions and opinions for him.

Will ship Pudd'nhead in a few days. When you get it cable

Mark Twain Care Brownship, London Received.

I mean to ship "Pudd'nhead Wilson" to you-say, tomorrow. It'll furnish me hash for awhile I reckon. I am almost sorry it is finished; it was good entertainment to work at it, and kept my mind away from things.

We leave here in about ten days, but the doctors have changed our plans again. I think we shall be in Bohemia or thereabouts till near the end of September, then go to Paris and take a rest. Yours Sincerely S. L. C.

P. S. Mrs. Clemens has come in since, and read your letter and is deeply distressed. She thinks that in some letter of mine I must have reproached you. She says it is wonderful that you have kept the ship afloat in this storm that has seen fleets and fleets go down; that from what she learns of the American business-situation from her home letters you have accomplished a marvel in the circumstances, and that she cannot bear to have a word said to you that shall voice anything but praise and the heartiest appreciation--and not the shadow of a reproach will she allow.

I tell her I didn't reproach you and never thought of such a thing. And I said I would break open my letter and say so.

Mrs. Clemens says I must tell you not to send any money for a month or two--so that you may be afforded what little relief is in our power. All right--I'm willing; (this is honest) but I wish Brer Chatto would send along his little yearly contribution. I dropped him a line about another matter a week ago--asked him to subscribe for the Daily News for me--you see I wanted to remind him in a covert way that it was pay-up time--but doubtless I directed the letter to you or some one else, for I don't hear from him and don't get any Daily News either.

To Fred J. Hall, in New York:

Aug. 6, '93. DEAR MR. HALL,--I am very sorry--it was thoughtless in me. Let the reports go. Send me once a month two items, and two only:

Cash liabilities--(so much) Cash assets--(so much)

I can perceive the condition of the business at a glance, then, and that will be sufficient.

Here we never see a newspaper, but even if we did I could not come anywhere near appreciating or correctly estimating the tempest you have been buffeting your way through--only the man who is in it can do that-- but I have tried not to burden you thoughtlessly or wantonly. I have been wrought and unsettled in mind by apprehensions, and that is a thing that is not helpable when one is in a strange land and sees his resources melt down to a two months' supply and can't see any sure daylight beyond. The bloody machine offered but a doubtful outlook--and will still offer nothing much better for a long time to come; for when Davis's "three weeks" is up there's three months' tinkering to follow I guess. That is unquestionably the boss machine of the world, but is the toughest one on prophets, when it is in an incomplete state, that has ever seen the light. Neither Davis nor any other man can foretell with any considerable approach to certainty when it will be ready to get down to actual work in a printing office.

[No signature.]

Three days after the foregoing letter was written he wrote, briefly:

"Great Scott but it's a long year-for you and me! I never knew the almanac to drag so. At least since I was finishing that other machine.

"I watch for your letters hungrily--just as I used to watch for the cablegram saying the machine's finished; but when 'next week certainly' swelled into 'three weeks sure' I recognized the old familiar tune I used to hear so much. Ward don't know what sick- heartedness is--but he is in a way to find out."

Always the quaint form of his humor, no matter how dark the way. We may picture him walking the floor, planning, scheming, and smoking--always smoking--trying to find a way out. It was not the kind of scheming that many men have done under the circumstances; not scheming to avoid payment of debts, but to pay them.

To Fred J. Hall, in New York:

Aug. 14, '93 DEAR MR. HALL,--I am very glad indeed if you and Mr. Langdon are able to see any daylight ahead. To me none is visible. I strongly advise that every penny that comes in shall be applied to paying off debts. I may be in error about this, but it seems to me that we have no other course open. We can pay a part of the debts owing to outsiders--none to the Clemenses. In very prosperous times we might regard our stock and copyrights as assets sufficient, with the money owing to us, to square up and quit even, but I suppose we may not hope for such luck in the present condition of things.

What I am mainly hoping for, is to save my royalties. If they come into danger I hope you will cable me, so that I can come over and try to save them, for if they go I am a beggar.

I would sail to-day if I had anybody to take charge of my family and help them through the difficult journeys commanded by the doctors. I may be able to sail ten days hence; I hope so, and expect so.

We can never resurrect the L. A. L. I would not spend any more money on that book. You spoke, a while back, of trying to start it up again as a preparation to disposing of it, but we are not in shape to venture that, I think. It would require more borrowing, and we must not do that. Yours Sincerely S. L. C.

Aug. 16. I have thought, and thought, but I don't seem to arrive in any very definite place. Of course you will not have an instant's safety until the bank debts are paid. There is nothing to be thought of but to hand over every penny as fast as it comes in--and that will be slow enough! Or could you secure them by pledging part of our cash assets and--

I am coming over, just as soon as I can get the family moved and settled. S. L. C.

Two weeks following this letter he could endure the suspense no longer, and on August 29th sailed once more for America. In New York, Clemens settled down at the Players Club, where he could live cheaply, and undertook some literary work while he was casting about for ways and means to relieve the financial situation. Nothing promising occurred, until one night at the Murray

Hill Hotel he was introduced by Dr. Clarence C. Rice to Henry H. Rogers, of the Standard Oil group of financiers. Rogers had a keen sense of humor and had always been a great admirer of Mark Twain's work. It was a mirthful evening, and certainly an eventful one in Mark Twain's life. A day or two later Doctor Rice asked the millionaire to interest himself a little in Clemens's business affairs, which he thought a good deal confused. Just what happened is not remembered now, but from the date of the next letter we realize that a discussion of the matter by Clemens and Rogers must have followed pretty promptly.

To Mrs. Clemens, in Europe:

Oct. 18, '93. DEAR, DEAR SWEETHEART,--I don't seem to get even half a chance to write you, these last two days, and yet there's lots to say.

Apparently everything is at last settled as to the giveaway of L. A. L., and the papers will be signed and the transfer made to-morrow morning.

Meantime I have got the best and wisest man in the whole Standard Oil group of mufti-millionaires a good deal interested in looking into the type-setter (this is private, don't mention it.) He has been searching into that thing for three weeks, and yesterday he said to me, "I find the machine to be all you represented it--I have here exhaustive reports from my own experts, and I know every detail of its capacity, its immense value, its construction, cost, history, and all about its inventor's character. I know that the New York Co. and the Chicago Co. are both stupid, and that they are unbusinesslike people, destitute of money and in a hopeless boggle."

Then he told me the scheme he had planned, then said: "If I can arrange with these people on this basis--it will take several weeks to find out-- I will see to it that they get the money they need. Then the thing will move right along and your royalties will cease to be waste paper. I will post you the minute my scheme fails or succeeds. In the meantime, you stop walking the floor. Go off to the country and try to be gay. You may have to go to walking again, but don't begin till I tell you my scheme has failed." And he added: "Keep me posted always as to where you are--for if I need you and can use you--I want to know where to put my hand on you."

If I should even divulge the fact that the Standard Oil is merely talking remotely about going into the type-setter, it would send my royalties up.

With worlds and worlds of love and kisses to you all, SAML.

With so great a burden of care shifted to the broad financial shoulders of H. H. Rogers, Mark Twain's spirits went ballooning, soaring toward the stars. He awoke, too, to some of the social gaieties about him, and found pleasure in the things that in the hour of his gloom had seemed mainly mockery. We find him going to a Sunday evening at Howells's, to John Mackay's, and elsewhere.

To Mrs. Clemens, in Paris:

Dec. 2, '93. LIVY DARLING,--Last night at John Mackay's the dinner consisted of soup, raw oysters, corned beef and cabbage, and something like a custard. I ate without fear or stint, and yet have escaped all suggestion of indigestion. The men present were old gray Pacific-coasters whom I knew when I and they were young and not gray. The talk was of the days when we went gypsying a long time ago--thirty years. Indeed it was a talk of the dead. Mainly that. And of how they looked, and the harum-scarum things they did and said. For there were no cares in that life, no aches and pains, and not time enough in the day (and three-fourths of the night) to work off one's surplus vigor and energy. Of the mid-night highway robbery joke played upon me with revolvers at my head on the windswept and desolate Gold Hill Divide, no witness is left but me, the victim. All the friendly robbers are gone. These old fools last night laughed till they cried over the particulars of that old forgotten crime.

John Mackay has no family here but a pet monkey--a most affectionate and winning little devil. But he makes trouble for the servants, for he is full of curiosity and likes to take everything out of the drawers and examine it minutely; and he puts nothing back. The examinations of yesterday count for nothing to-day--he makes a new examination every day. But he injures nothing.

I went with Laffan to the Racquet Club the other night and played, billiards two hours without starting up any rheumatism. I suppose it was all really taken out of me in Berlin.

Richard Harding Davis spoke yesterday of Clara's impersonations at Mrs. Van Rensselaer's here and said they were a wonderful piece of work.

Livy dear, I do hope you are comfortable, as to quarters and food at the Hotel Brighton. But if you're not don't stay there. Make one more effort--don't give it up. Dear heart, this is from one who loves you-- which is Saml.

It was decided that Rogers and Clemens should make a trip to Chicago to investigate personally the type-setter situation there. Clemens reports the details of the excursion to Mrs. Clemens in a long subdivided letter, most of which has no general interest and is here omitted. The trip, as a whole, would seem to have been satisfactory. The personal portions of the long Christmas letter may properly be preserved.

To Mrs. Clemens, in Paris:

THE PLAYERS, Xmas, 1893. No. 1. Merry Xmas, my darling, and all my darlings! I arrived from Chicago close upon midnight last night, and wrote and sent down my Christmas cablegram before undressing: "Merry Xmas! Promising progress made in Chicago." It would get to the telegraph office toward 8 this morning and reach you at luncheon.

I was vaguely hoping, all the past week, that my Xmas cablegram would be definite, and make you all jump with jubilation; but the thought always intruded itself, "You are not going out there to negotiate with a man, but with a louse. This makes results uncertain."

I was asleep as Christmas struck upon the clock at mid night, and didn't wake again till two hours ago. It is now half past 10 Xmas morning; I have had my coffee and bread, and shan't get out of bed till it is time to dress for Mrs. Laflan's Christmas dinner this evening--where I shall meet Bram Stoker and must make sure about that photo with Irving's autograph. I will get the picture and he will attend to the rest. In order to remember and not forget--well, I will go there with my dress coat wrong side out; it will cause remark and then I shall remember.

No. 2 and 3. I tell you it was interesting! The Chicago campaign, I mean. On the way out Mr. Rogers would plan out the campaign while I walked the floor and smoked and assented. Then he would close it up with a snap and drop it and we would totally change the subject and take up the scenery, etc.

(Here follows the long detailed report of the Chicago conference, of interest only to the parties directly concerned.)

No. 4. We had nice tripe, going and coming. Mr. Rogers had telegraphed the Pennsylvania Railroad for a couple of sections for us in the fast train leaving at 2 p. m. the 22nd. The Vice President telegraphed back that every berth was engaged (which was not true--it goes without saying) but that he was sending his own car for us. It was mighty nice and comfortable. In its parlor it had two sofas, which could become beds at night. It had four comfortably-cushioned cane arm-chairs. It had a very nice bedroom with a wide bed in it; which I said I would take because I believed I was a little wider than Mr. Rogers--which turned out to be true; so I took it. It had a darling back-porch--railed, roofed and roomy; and there we sat, most of the time, and viewed the scenery and talked, for the weather was May weather, and the soft dream-pictures of hill and river and mountain and sky were clear and away beyond anything I have ever seen for exquisiteness and daintiness.

The colored waiter knew his business, and the colored cook was a finished artist. Breakfasts: coffee with real cream; beefsteaks, sausage, bacon, chops, eggs in various ways, potatoes in various--yes, and quite wonderful baked potatoes, and hot as fire. Dinners--all manner of things, including canvas-back duck, apollinaris, claret, champagne, etc.

We sat up chatting till midnight, going and coming; seldom read a line, day or night, though we were well fixed with magazines, etc.; then I finished off with a hot Scotch and we went to bed and slept till 9.30a.m. I honestly tried to pay my share of hotel bills, fees, etc., but I was not allowed-- and I knew the reason why, and respected the motive. I will explain when I see you, and then you will understand.

We were 25 hours going to Chicago; we were there 24 hours; we were 30 hours returning. Brisk work, but all of it enjoyable. We insisted on leaving the car at Philadelphia so that our waiter and cook (to whom Mr. R. gave $10 apiece,) could have their Christmas-eve at home.

Mr. Rogers's carriage was waiting for us in Jersey City and deposited me at the Players. There--

that's all. This letter is to make up for the three letterless days. I love you, dear heart, I love you all. SAML.

XXXIV

LETTERS 1894. A WINTER IN NEW YORK. BUSINESS FAILURE. END OF THE MACHINE

The beginning of the new year found Mark Twain sailing buoyantly on a tide of optimism. He believed that with H. H. Rogers as his financial pilot he could weather safely any storm or stress. He could divert himself, or rest, or work, and consider his business affairs with interest and amusement, instead of with haggard anxiety. He ran over to Hartford to see an amateur play; to Boston to give a charity reading; to Fair Haven to open the library which Mr. Rogers had established there; he attended gay dinners, receptions, and late studio parties, acquiring the name of the "Belle of New York." In the letters that follow we get the echo of some of these things. The Mrs. Rice mentioned in the next brief letter was the wife of Dr. Clarence C. Rice, who had introduced H. H. Rogers to Mark Twain.

To Mrs. Clemens, in Paris:

Jan. 12, '94 Livy darling, I came down from Hartford yesterday with Kipling, and he and Hutton and I had the small smoking compartment to ourselves and found him at last at his ease, and not shy. He was very pleasant company indeed. He is to be in the city a week, and I wish I could invite him to dinner, but it won't do. I should be interrupted by business, of course. The construction of a contract that will suit Paige's lawyer (not Paige) turns out to be very difficult. He is embarrassed by earlier advice to Paige, and hates to retire from it and stultify himself. The negotiations are being conducted, by means of tedious long telegrams and by talks over the long-distance telephone. We keep the wires loaded.

Dear me, dinner is ready. So Mrs. Rice says.

With worlds of love, SAML.

Clemens and Oliver Wendell Holmes had met and become friends soon after the publication of Innocents Abroad, in 1869. Now, twenty-five years later, we find a record of what without doubt was their last meeting. It occurred at the home of Mrs. James T. Field.

To Mrs. Clemens, in Paris:

BOSTON, Jan. 25, '94. Livy darling, I am caught out worse this time than ever before, in the matter of letters. Tuesday morning I was smart enough to finish and mail my long letter to you before breakfast--for I was suspecting that I would not have another spare moment during the day.

It turned out just so.

In a thoughtless moment I agreed to come up here and read for the poor. I did not reflect that it would cost me three days. I could not get released. Yesterday I had myself called at 8 and ran out to Mr. Rogers's house at 9, and talked business until half past 10; then caught 11 o'clock train and arrived here at 6; was shaven and dressed by 7 and ready for dinner here in Mrs. Field's charming house.

Dr. Oliver Wendell Holmes never goes out now (he is in his 84th year,) but he came out this time-said he wanted to "have a time" once more with me.

Mrs. Fields said Aldrich begged to come and went away crying because she wouldn't let him. She allowed only her family (Sarah Orne Jewett and sister) to be present, because much company would overtax Dr. Holmes.

Well, he was just delightful! He did as brilliant and beautiful talking (and listening) as ever he did in his life, I guess. Fields and Jewett said he hadn't been in such splendid form in years. He had ordered his carriage for 9.

The coachman sent in for him at 9; but he said, "Oh, nonsense!--leave glories and grandeurs like these? Tell him to go away and come in an hour!"

At 10 he was called for again, and Mrs. Fields, getting uneasy, rose, but he wouldn't go--and so we rattled ahead the same as ever. Twice more Mrs. Fields rose, but he wouldn't go--and he didn't go till half past 10 --an unwarrantable dissipation for him in these days. He was prodigiously complimentary about some of my books, and is having Pudd'nhead read to him. I told him you and I used the Autocrat as a courting book and marked it all through, and that you keep it in the sacred green box with the love letters, and it pleased him.

Good-bye, my dear darling, it is 15 minutes to dinner and I'm not dressed yet. I have a reception to-night and will be out very late at that place and at Irving's Theatre where I have a complimentary box. I wish you were all here. SAML.

In the next letter we meet James J. Corbett--"Gentleman Jim," as he was sometimes called--the champion pugilist of that day.

The Howells incident so amusingly dramatized will perhaps be more appreciated if the reader remembers that Mark Twain himself had at intervals been a mind-healing enthusiast. Indeed, in spite of his strictures on Mrs. Eddy, his interest in the subject of mind-cure continued to the end of his life.

To Mrs. Clemens, in Paris:

Sunday, 9.30 a. m. Livy dear, when we got out to the house last night, Mrs. Rogers, who is up and around, now, didn't want to go down stairs to dinner, but Mr. R. persuaded her and we had a very good time indeed. By 8 o'clock we were down again and bought a fifteen-dollar box in the Madison Square Garden (Rogers bought it, not I,) then he went and fetched Dr. Rice while I (went) to the Players and picked up two artists--Reid and Simmons--and thus we filled 5 of the 6 seats. There was a vast multitude of people in the brilliant place. Stanford White came along presently and invited me to go to the World-Champion's dressing room, which I was very glad to do. Corbett has a fine face and is modest and diffident, besides being the most perfectly and beautifully constructed human animal in the world. I said:

"You have whipped Mitchell, and maybe you will whip Jackson in June--but you are not done, then. You will have to tackle me."

He answered, so gravely that one might easily have thought him in earnest:

"No--I am not going to meet you in the ring. It is not fair or right to require it. You might chance to knock me out, by no merit of your own, but by a purely accidental blow; and then my reputation would be gone and you would have a double one. You have got fame enough and you ought not to want to take mine away from me."

Corbett was for a long time a clerk in the Nevada Bank in San Francisco.

There were lots of little boxing matches, to entertain the crowd: then at last Corbett appeared in the ring and the 8,000 people present went mad with enthusiasm. My two artists went mad about his form. They said they had never seen anything that came reasonably near equaling its perfection except Greek statues, and they didn't surpass it.

Corbett boxed 3 rounds with the middle-weight Australian champion--oh, beautiful to see!--then the show was over and we struggled out through a perfect wash of humanity. When we reached the street I found I had left my arctics in the box. I had to have them, so Simmons said he would go back and get them, and I didn't dissuade him. I couldn't see how he was going to make his way a single yard into that solid oncoming wave of people--yet he must plow through it full 50 yards. He was back with the shoes in 3 minutes!

How do you reckon he accomplished that miracle? By saying:

"Way, gentlemen, please--coming to fetch Mr. Corbett's overshoes."

The word flew from mouth to mouth, the Red Sea divided, and Simmons walked comfortably through and back, dry shod. Simmons (this was revealed to me under seal of secrecy by Reid) is the hero of "Gwen," and he and Gwen's author were once engaged to marry. This is "fire-escape" Simmons, the inveterate talker, you know: "Exit--in case of Simmons."

I had an engagement at a beautiful dwelling close to the Players for 10.30; I was there by 10.45. Thirty cultivated and very musical ladies and gentlemen present--all of them acquaintances and many of them personal friends of mine. That wonderful Hungarian Band was there (they charge $500 for an evening.) Conversation and Band until midnight; then a bite of supper; then the company was compactly grouped before me and I told about Dr. B. E. Martin and the etchings, and followed it with the Scotch-Irish Christening. My, but the Martin is a darling story! Next, the head tenor from the Opera sang half a dozen great songs that set the company wild, yes, mad with delight, that nobly handsome young Damrosch accompanying on the piano.

Just a little pause--then the Band burst out into an explosion of weird and tremendous dance music, a Hungarian celebrity and his wife took the floor--I followed; I couldn't help it; the others drifted in, one by one, and it was Onteora over again.

By half past 4 I had danced all those people down--and yet was not tired; merely breathless. I was in bed at 5, and asleep in ten minutes. Up at 9 and presently at work on this letter to you. I think I wrote until 2 or half past. Then I walked leisurely out to Mr. Rogers's (it is called 3 miles but it is short of it) arriving at 3.30, but he was out-- to return at 5.30--(and a person was in, whom I don't particularly like) --so I didn't stay, but dropped over and chatted with the Howellses until 6.

First, Howells and I had a chat together. I asked about Mrs. H. He said she was fine, still steadily improving, and nearly back to her old best health. I asked (as if I didn't know):

"What do you attribute this strange miracle to?"

"Mind-cure--simply mind-cure."

"Lord, what a conversion! You were a scoffer three months ago."

"I? I wasn't."

"You were. You made elaborate fun of me in this very room."

"I did not, Clemens."

"It's a lie, Howells, you did."

I detailed to him the conversation of that time--with the stately argument furnished by Boyesen in the fact that a patient had actually been killed by a mind-curist; and Howells's own smart remark that when the mind-curist is done with you, you have to call in a "regular" at last because the former can't procure you a burial permit.

At last he gave in--he said he remembered that talk, but had now been a mind-curist so long it was difficult for him to realize that he had ever been anything else.

Mrs. H. came skipping in, presently, the very person, to a dot, that she used to be, so many years ago.

Mrs. H. said: "People may call it what they like, but it is just hypnotism, and that's all it is--hypnotism pure and simple. Mind-cure! --the idea! Why, this woman that cured me hasn't got any mind. She's a good creature, but she's dull and dumb and illiterate and--"

"Now Eleanor!"

"I know what I'm talking about!--don't I go there twice a week? And Mr. Clemens, if you could only see her wooden and satisfied face when she snubs me for forgetting myself and showing by a thoughtless remark that to me weather is still weather, instead of being just an abstraction and a superstition--oh, it's the funniest thing you ever saw! A-n-d-when she tilts up her nose-well, it's--it's--Well it's that kind of a nose that--"

"Now Eleanor!--the woman is not responsible for her nose--" and so-on and so-on. It didn't seem to me that I had any right to be having this feast and you not there.

She convinced me before she got through, that she and William James are right--hypnotism and mind-cure are the same thing; no difference between them. Very well; the very source, the very center of hypnotism is Paris. Dr. Charcot's pupils and disciples are right there and ready to your hand without fetching poor dear old Susy across the stormy sea. Let Mrs. Mackay (to whom I send my best respects), tell you whom to go to to learn all you need to learn and how to proceed. Do, do it, honey. Don't lose a minute.

.....At 11 o'clock last night Mr. Rogers said:

"I am able to feel physical fatigue--and I feel it now. You never show any, either in your eyes or your movements; do you ever feel any?"

I was able to say that I had forgotten what that feeling was like. Don't you remember how almost impossible it was for me to tire myself at the Villa? Well, it is just so in New York. I go to bed unfatigued at 3, I get up fresh and fine six hours later. I believe I have taken only one daylight nap since I have been here.

When the anchor is down, then I shall say:

"Farewell--a long farewell--to business! I will never touch it again!"

I will live in literature, I will wallow in it, revel in it, I will swim in ink! Joan of Arc--but all this is premature; the anchor is not down yet.

To-morrow (Tuesday) I will add a P. S. if I've any to add; but, whether or no, I must mail this to morrow, for the mail steamer goes next day.

5.30 p. m. Great Scott, this is Tuesday! I must rush this letter into the mail instantly.

Tell that sassy Ben I've got her welcome letter, and I'll write her as soon as I get a daylight chance. I've most time at night, but I'd druther write daytimes. SAML.

The Reid and Simmons mentioned in the foregoing were Robert Reid and Edward Simmons, distinguished painter--the latter a brilliant, fluent, and industrious talker. The title; "Fire-escape Simmons," which Clemens gives him, originated when Oliver Herford, whose quaint wit has so long delighted New-Yorkers, one day pinned up by the back door of the Players the notice: "Exit in case of Simmons." Gwen, a popular novel of that day, was written by Blanche Willis Howard.

"Jamie" Dodge, in the next letter, was the son of Mrs. Mary Mapes Dodge, editor of St. Nicholas.

To Clara Clemens, in Paris:

MR. ROGERS'S OFFICE, Feb. 5, '94. Dear Benny--I was intending to answer your letter to-day, but I am away down town, and will simply whirl together a sentence or two for good- fellowship. I have bought photographs of Coquelin and Jane Hading and will ask them to sign them. I shall meet Coquelin tomorrow night, and if Hading is not present I will send her picture to her by somebody.

I am to breakfast with Madame Nordica in a few days, and meantime I hope to get a good picture of her to sign. She was of the breakfast company yesterday, but the picture of herself which she signed and gave me does not do her majestic beauty justice.

I am too busy to attend to the photo-collecting right, because I have to live up to the name which Jamie Dodge has given me--the "Belle of New York"--and it just keeps me rushing. Yesterday I had engagements to breakfast at noon, dine at 3, and dine again at 7. I got away from the long breakfast at 2 p. m., went and excused myself from the 3 o'clock dinner, then lunched with Mrs. Dodge in 58th street, returned to the Players and dressed, dined out at 9, and was back at Mrs. Dodge's at 10 p. m. where we had magic-lantern views of a superb sort, and a lot of yarns until an hour after midnight, and got to bed at 2 this morning --a good deal of a gain on my recent hours. But I don't get tired; I sleep as sound as a dead person, and always wake up fresh and strong-- usually at exactly 9.

I was at breakfast lately where people of seven separate nationalities sat and the seven languages were going all the time. At my side sat a charming gentleman who was a delightful and active talker, and interesting. He talked glibly to those folks in all those seven languages and still had a language to spare! I wanted to kill him, for very envy.

I greet you with love and kisses. PAPA.

To Mrs. Clemens, in Paris:

Feb.--. Livy dear, last night I played billiards with Mr. Rogers until 11, then went to Robert

Reid's studio and had a most delightful time until 4 this morning. No ladies were invited this time. Among the people present were--

Coquelin; Richard Harding Davis; Harrison, the great out-door painter; Wm. H. Chase, the artist; Bettini, inventor of the new phonograph. Nikola Tesla, the world-wide illustrious electrician; see article about him in Jan. or Feb. Century. John Drew, actor; James Barnes, a marvelous mimic; my, you should see him! Smedley the artist; Zorn the artist; Zogbaum the artist; Reinhart the artist; Metcalf the artist; Ancona, head tenor at the Opera;

Oh, a great lot of others. Everybody there had done something and was in his way famous.

Somebody welcomed Coquelin in a nice little French speech; John Drew did the like for me in English, and then the fun began. Coquelin did some excellent French monologues--one of them an ungrammatical Englishman telling a colorless historiette in French. It nearly killed the fifteen or twenty people who understood it.

I told a yarn, Ancona sang half a dozen songs, Barnes did his darling imitations, Harding Davis sang the hanging of Danny Deever, which was of course good, but he followed it with that most fascinating (for what reason I don't know) of all Kipling's poems, "On the Road to Mandalay," sang it tenderly, and it searched me deeper and charmed me more than the Deever.

Young Gerrit Smith played some ravishing dance music and we all danced about an hour. There couldn't be a pleasanter night than that one was. Some of those people complained of fatigue but I don't seem to know what the sense of fatigue is.

Coquelin talks quite good English now. He said:

"I have a brother who has the fine mind--ah, a charming and delicate fancy, and he knows your writings so well, and loves them--and that is the same with me. It will stir him so when I write and tell him I have seen you!"

Wasn't that nice? We talked a good deal together. He is as winning as his own face. But he wouldn't sign that photograph for Clara. "That? No! She shall have a better one. I will send it to you."

He is much driven, and will forget it, but Reid has promised to get the picture for me, and I will try and keep him reminded.

Oh, dear, my time is all used up and your letters are not answered.

Mama, dear, I don't go everywhere--I decline most things. But there are plenty that I can't well get out of.

I will remember what you say and not make my yarning too common.

I am so glad Susy has gone on that trip and that you are trying the electric. May you both prosper. For you are mighty dear to me and in my thoughts always. SAML.

The affairs of the Webster Publishing Company were by this time getting into a very serious condition indeed. The effects of the panic of the year before could not be overcome. Creditors were pressing their claims and profits were negligible. In the following letter we get a Mark Twain estimate of the great financier who so cheerfully was willing to undertake the solving of Mark Twain's financial problems.

To Mrs. Clemens, in Paris:

THE PLAYERS, Feb. 15, '94. 11.30 p. m. Livy darling, Yesterday I talked all my various matters over with Mr. Rogers and we decided that it would be safe for me to leave here the 7th of March, in the New York. So his private secretary, Miss Harrison, wrote and ordered a berth for me and then I lost no time in cabling you that I should reach Southampton March 14, and Paris the 15th. Land, but it made my pulses leap, to think I was going to see you again!..... One thing at a time. I never fully laid Webster's disastrous condition before Mr. Rogers until to-night after billiards. I did hate to burden his good heart and over-worked head with it, but he took hold with avidity and said it was no burden to work for his friends, but a pleasure. We discussed it from various standpoints, and found it a sufficiently difficult problem to solve; but he thinks that after he has slept upon it and thought it over he will know what to suggest.

You must not think I am ever rude with Mr. Rogers, I am not. He is not common clay, but fine--fine and delicate--and that sort do not call out the coarsenesses that are in my sort. I am never afraid of wounding him; I do not need to watch myself in that matter. The sight of him is peace.

He wants to go to Japan--it is his dream; wants to go with me--which means, the two families--and hear no more about business for awhile, and have a rest. And he needs it. But it is like all the dreams of all busy men--fated to remain dreams.

You perceive that he is a pleasant text for me. It is easy to write about him. When I arrived in September, lord how black the prospect was --how desperate, how incurably desperate! Webster and Co had to have a small sum of money or go under at once. I flew to Hartford--to my friends--but they were not moved, not strongly interested, and I was ashamed that I went. It was from Mr. Rogers, a stranger, that I got the money and was by it saved. And then--while still a stranger--he set himself the task of saving my financial life without putting upon me (in his native delicacy) any sense that I was the recipient of a charity, a benevolence--and he has accomplished that task; accomplished it at a cost of three months of wearing and difficult labor. He gave that time to me--time which could not be bought by any man at a hundred thousand dollars a month--no, nor for three times the money.

Well, in the midst of that great fight, that long and admirable fight, George Warner came to me and said:

"There is a splendid chance open to you. I know a man--a prominent man-- who has written a book that will go like wildfire; a book that arraigns the Standard Oil fiends, and gives them unmitigated hell, individual by individual. It is the very book for you to publish; there is a fortune in it, and I can put you in communication with the author."

I wanted to say:

"The only man I care for in the world; the only man I would give a damn for; the only man who is lavishing his sweat and blood to save me and mine from starvation and shame, is a Standard Oil fiend. If you know me, you know whether I want the book or not."

But I didn't say that. I said I didn't want any book; I wanted to get out of the publishing business and out of all business, and was here for that purpose and would accomplish it if I could.

But there's enough. I shall be asleep by 3, and I don't need much sleep, because I am never drowsy or tired these days. Dear, dear Susy my strength reproaches me when I think of her and you, my darling.

SAML.

But even so able a man as Henry Rogers could not accomplish the impossible. The affairs of the Webster Company were hopeless, the business was not worth saving. By Mr. Rogers's advice an assignment was made April, 18, 1894. After its early spectacular success less than ten years had brought the business to failure. The publication of the Grant memoirs had been its only great achievement.

Clemens would seem to have believed that the business would resume, and for a time Rogers appears to have comforted him in his hope, but we cannot believe that it long survived. Young Hall, who had made such a struggle for its salvation, was eager to go on, but he must presently have seen the futility of any effort in that direction.

Of course the failure of Mark Twain's firm made a great stir in the country, and it is easy to understand that loyal friends would rally in his behalf.

To Mrs. Clemens, in Paris:

April 22, '94. Dear old darling, we all think the creditors are going to allow us to resume business; and if they do we shall pull through and pay the debts. I am prodigiously glad we made an assignment. And also glad that we did not make it sooner. Earlier we should have made a poor showing; but now we shall make a good one.

I meet flocks of people, and they all shake me cordially by the hand and say "I was so sorry to hear of the assignment, but so glad you did it. It was around, this long time, that the concern was tottering, and all your friends were afraid you would delay the assignment too long."

John Mackay called yesterday, and said, "Don't let it disturb you, Sam-- we all have to do it, at one time or another; it's nothing to be ashamed of."

One stranger out in New York State sent me a dollar bill and thought he would like to get up a dollar-subscription for me. And Poultney Bigelow's note came promptly, with his check for $1,000. I had been meeting him every day at the Club and liking him better and better all the time. I couldn't take his money, of course, but I thanked him cordially for his good will.

Now and then a good and dear Joe Twichell or Susy Warner condoles with me and says "Cheer up--don't be downhearted," and some other friend says, "I am glad and surprised to see how cheerful you are and how bravely you stand it"--and none of them suspect what a burden has been lifted from me and how blithe I am inside. Except when I think of you, dear heart--then I am not blithe; for I seem to see you grieving and ashamed, and dreading to look people in the face. For in the thick of the fight there is cheer, but you are far away and cannot hear the drums nor see the wheeling squadrons. You only seem to see rout, retreat, and dishonored colors dragging in the dirt--whereas none of these things exist. There is temporary defeat, but no dishonor--and we will march again. Charley Warner said to-day, "Sho, Livy isn't worrying. So long as she's got you and the children she doesn't care what happens. She knows it isn't her affair." Which didn't convince me.

Good bye my darling, I love you and all of the kids--and you can tell Clara I am not a spitting gray kitten. SAML.

Clemens sailed for Europe as soon as his affairs would permit him to go. He must get settled where he could work comfortably. Type- setter prospects seemed promising, but meantime there was need of funds.

He began writing on the ship, as was his habit, and had completed his article on Fenimore Cooper by the time he reached London. In August we find him writing to Mr. Rogers from Etretat, a little Norman watering-place.

To H. H. Rogers, in New York:

ETRETAT, (NORMANDIE) CHALET DES ABRIS Aug. 25, '94. DEAR MR. ROGERS,--I find the Madam ever so much better in health and strength. The air is superb and soothing and wholesome, and the Chalet is remote from noise and people, and just the place to write in. I shall begin work this afternoon.

Mrs. Clemens is in great spirits on, account of the benefit which she has received from the electrical treatment in Paris and is bound to take it up again and continue it all the winter, and of course I am perfectly willing. She requires me to drop the lecture platform out of my mind and go straight ahead with Joan until the book is finished. If I should have to go home for even a week she means to go with me--won't consent to be separated again--but she hopes I won't need to go.

I tell her all right, "I won't go unless you send, and then I must."

She keeps the accounts; and as she ciphers it we can't get crowded for money for eight months yet. I didn't know that. But I don't know much anyway. Sincerely yours, S. L. CLEMENS.

The reader may remember that Clemens had written the first half of his Joan of Arc book at the Villa Viviani, in Florence, nearly two years before. He had closed the manuscript then with the taking of Orleans, and was by no means sure that he would continue the story beyond that point. Now, however, he was determined to reach the tale's tragic conclusion.

To H. H. Rogers, in New York:

ETRETAT, Sunday, Sept. 9, '94. DEAR MR. ROGERS, I drove the quill too hard, and I broke down--in my head. It has now been three days since I laid up. When I wrote you a week ago I had added 10,000 words or thereabout to Joan. Next day I added 1,500 which was a proper enough day's work though not a full one; but during Tuesday and Wednesday I stacked up an aggregate of 6,000 words--and that was a very large mistake. My head hasn't been worth a cent since.

However, there's a compensation; for in those two days I reached and passed--successfully--a point which I was solicitous about before I ever began the book: viz., the battle of Patay. Because that would naturally be the next to the last chapter of a work consisting of either two books or one. In the one case one goes right along from that point (as I shall do now); in the other he would add a wind-up chapter and make the book consist of Joan's childhood and military career alone.

I shall resume work to-day; and hereafter I will not go at such an intemperate' rate. My head is pretty cobwebby yet.

I am hoping that along about this time I shall hear that the machine is beginning its test in the Herald office. I shall be very glad indeed to know the result of it. I wish I could be there. Sincerely yours S. L. CLEMENS.

Rouen, where Joan met her martyrdom, was only a short distance away, and they halted there en route to Paris, where they had arranged to spend the winter. The health of Susy Clemens was not good, and they lingered in Rouen while Clemens explored the old city and incidentally did some writing of another sort. In a note to Mr. Rogers he said: "To put in my odd time I am writing some articles about Paul Bourget and his Outre-Mer chapters--laughing at them and at some of our oracular owls who find them important. What the hell makes them important, I should like to know!"

He was still at Rouen two weeks later and had received encouraging news from Rogers concerning the type-setter, which had been placed for trial in the office of the Chicago Herald. Clemens wrote: "I can hardly keep from sending a hurrah by cable. I would certainly do it if I wasn't superstitious." His restraint, though wise, was wasted the end was near.

To H. H. Rogers, in New York:

169 RUE DE L'UNIVERSITE, PARIS, Dec. 22; '94. DEAR MR. ROGERS,--I seemed to be entirely expecting your letter, and also prepared and resigned; but Lord, it shows how little we know ourselves and how easily we can deceive ourselves. It hit me like a thunder-clap. It knocked every rag of sense out of my head, and I went flying here and there and yonder, not knowing what I was doing, and only one clearly defined thought standing up visible and substantial out of the crazy storm-drift that my dream of ten years was in desperate peril, and out of the 60,000 or 90,000 projects for its rescue that came floating through my skull, not one would hold still long enough for me to examine it and size it up. Have you ever been like that? Not so much so, I reckon.

There was another clearly defined idea--I must be there and see it die. That is, if it must die; and maybe if I were there we might hatch up some next-to-impossible way to make it take up its bed and take a walk.

So, at the end of four hours I started, still whirling and walked over to the rue Scribe--4 P. M.-- and asked a question or two and was told I should be running a big risk if I took the 9 P. M. train for London and Southampton; "better come right along at 6.52 per Havre special and step aboard the New York all easy and comfortable." Very! and I about two miles from home, with no packing done.

Then it occurred to me that none of these salvation-notions that were whirl-winding through my head could be examined or made available unless at least a month's time could be secured. So I cabled you, and said to myself that I would take the French steamer tomorrow (which will be Sunday).

By bedtime Mrs. Clemens had reasoned me into a fairly rational and contented state of mind; but of course it didn't last long. So I went on thinking--mixing it with a smoke in the dressing room once an hour--until dawn this morning. Result--a sane resolution; no matter what your answer to my cable might be, I would hold still and not sail until I should get an answer to this present letter which I am now writing, or a cable answer from you saying "Come" or "Remain."

I have slept 6 hours, my pond has clarified, and I find the sediment of my 70,000 projects to be of this character:

[Several pages of suggestions for reconstructing the machine follow.]

Don't say I'm wild. For really I'm sane again this morning.

....

I am going right along with Joan, now, and wait untroubled till I hear from you. If you think I can be of the least use, cable me "Come." I can write Joan on board ship and lose no time. Also I could discuss my plan with the publisher for a deluxe Joan, time being an object, for some of the pictures could be made over here cheaply and quickly, but would cost much time and money in America.

....

If the meeting should decide to quit business Jan. 4, I'd like to have Stoker stopped from paying in any more money, if Miss Harrison doesn't mind that disagreeable job. And I'll have to write them, too, of course. With love, S. L. CLEMENS.

The "Stoker" of this letter was Bram Stoker, long associated with Sir Henry Irving. Irving himself had also taken stock in the machine. The address, 169 Rue de l'Universite, whence these letters are written, was the beautiful studio home of the artist Pomroy which they had taken for the winter.

To H. H. Rogers, in New York:

169 RUE DE L'UNIVERSITE, PARIS, Dec. 27, '94. DEAR MR. ROGERS,--Notwithstanding your heart is "old and hard," you make a body choke up. I know you "mean every word you say" and I do take it "in the same spirit in which you tender it." I shall keep your regard while we two live--that I know; for I shall always remember what you have done for me, and that will insure me against ever doing anything that could forfeit it or impair it. I am 59 years old; yet I never had a friend before who put out a hand and tried to pull me ashore when he found me in deep waters.

It is six days or seven days ago that I lived through that despairing day, and then through a night without sleep; then settled down next day into my right mind (or thereabouts,) and wrote you. I put in the rest of that day till 7 P. M. plenty comfortably enough writing a long chapter of my book; then went to a masked ball blacked up as Uncle Remus, taking Clara along; and we had a good time. I have lost no day since and suffered no discomfort to speak of, but drove my troubles out of my mind and had good success in keeping them out--through watchfulness. I have done a good week's work and put the book a good way ahead in the Great Trial, which is the difficult part which requires the most thought and carefulness. I cannot see the end of the Trial yet, but I am on the road. I am creeping surely toward it.

"Why not leave them all to me." My business bothers? I take you by the hand! I jump at the chance!

I ought to be ashamed and I am trying my best to be ashamed--and yet I do jump at the chance in spite of it. I don't want to write Irving and I don't want to write Stoker. It doesn't seem as if I could. But I can suggest something for you to write them; and then if you see that I am unwise, you can write them something quite different. Now this is my idea:

1. To return Stoker's $100 to him and keep his stock.

2. And tell Irving that when luck turns with me I will make good to him what the salvage from the dead Co. fails to pay him of his $500.

P. S. Madam says No, I must face the music. So I enclose my effort to be used if you approve, but not otherwise.

There! Now if you will alter it to suit your judgment and bang away, I shall be eternally obliged.

We shall try to find a tenant for our Hartford house; not an easy matter, for it costs heavily to live in. We can never live in it again; though it would break the family's hearts if they could believe it.

Nothing daunts Mrs. Clemens or makes the world look black to her--which is the reason I haven't drowned myself.

We all send our deepest and warmest greetings to you and all of yours and a Happy New Year! S. L. CLEMENS.

Enclosure:

MY DEAR STOKER,--I am not dating this because it is not to be mailed at present.

When it reaches you it will mean that there is a hitch in my machine- enterprise--a hitch so serious as to make it take to itself the aspect of a dissolved dream. This letter, then, will contain cheque for the $100 which you have paid. And will you tell Irving for me--I can't get up courage enough to talk about this misfortune myself, except to you, whom by good luck I haven't damaged yet that when the wreckage presently floats ashore he will get a good deal of his $500 back; and a dab at a time I will make up to him the rest.

I'm not feeling as fine as I was when I saw you there in your home. Please remember me kindly to Mrs. Stoker. I gave up that London lecture- project entirely. Had to--there's never been a chance since to find the time. Sincerely yours, S. L. CLEMENS.

XXXV

LETTERS, 1895-96, TO H. H. ROGERS AND OTHERS. FINISHING "JOAN OF ARC." THE TRIP AROUND THE WORLD. DEATH OF SUSY CLEMENS

To H. H. Rogers, in New York City:

[No date.] DEAR MR. ROGERS,--Yours of Dec. 21 has arrived, containing the circular to stockholders and I guess the Co. will really quit--there doesn't seem to be any other wise course.

There's one thing which makes it difficult for me to soberly realize that my ten year dream is actually dissolved; and that is, that it reveries my horoscope. The proverb says, "Born lucky, always lucky," and I am very superstitious. As a small boy I was notoriously lucky. It was usual for one or two of our lads (per annum) to get drowned in the Mississippi or in Bear Creek, but I was pulled out in a 2/3 drowned condition 9 times before I learned to swim, and was considered to be a cat in disguise. When the "Pennsylvania" blew up and the telegraph reported my brother as fatally injured (with 60 others) but made no mention of me, my uncle said to my mother "It means that Sam was somewhere else, after being on that boat a year and a half--he was born lucky." Yes, I was somewhere else. I am so superstitious that I have always been afraid to have business dealings with certain relatives and friends of mine because they were unlucky people. All my life I have stumbled upon lucky chances of large size, and whenever they were wasted it was because of my own stupidity and carelessness. And so I have felt entirely certain that that machine would turn up trumps eventually. It disappointed me lots of times, but I couldn't shake off the confidence of a life-time in my luck.

Well, whatever I get out of the wreckage will be due to good luck--the good luck of getting you into the scheme--for, but for that, there wouldn't be any wreckage; it would be total loss.

I wish you had been in at the beginning. Then we should have had the good luck to step promptly ashore.

Miss Harrison has had a dream which promises me a large bank account, and I want her to go ahead and dream it twice more, so as to make the prediction sure to be fulfilled.

I've got a first rate subject for a book. It kept me awake all night, and I began it and completed it in my mind. The minute I finish Joan I will take it up. Love and Happy New Year to you all. Sincerely yours, S. L. CLEMENS.

This was about the end of the machine interests so far as Clemens was concerned. Paige succeeded in getting some new people interested, but nothing important happened, or that in any way affected Mark Twain. Characteristically he put the whole matter behind him and plunged into his work, facing comparative poverty and a burden of debts with a stout heart. The beginning of the new year found him really poorer in purse than he had ever been in his life, but certainly not crushed, or even discouraged--at least, not permanently--and never more industrious or capable.

To H. H. Rogers, in New York City:

169 RUE DE L'UNIVERSITE, PARIS, Jan. 23, '95. DEAR MR. ROGERS,--After I wrote you, two or three days ago I thought I would make a holiday of the rest of the day--the second deliberate holiday since I had the gout. On the first holiday I wrote a tale of about 6,000 words, which was 3 days' work in one; and this time I did 8,000 before midnight. I got nothing out of that first holiday but the recreation of it, for I condemned the work after careful reading and some

revision; but this time I fared better--I finished the Huck Finn tale that lies in your safe, and am satisfied with it.

The Bacheller syndicate (117 Tribune Building) want a story of 5,000 words (lowest limit of their London agent) for $1,000 and offer to plank the check on delivery, and it was partly to meet that demand that I took that other holiday. So as I have no short story that suits me (and can't and shan't make promises), the best I can do is to offer the longer one which I finished on my second holiday--"Tom Sawyer, Detective."

It makes 27 or 28,000 words, and is really written for grown folks, though I expect young folk to read it, too. It transfers to the banks of the Mississippi the incidents of a strange murder which was committed in Sweden in old times.

I'll refer applicants for a sight of the story to you or Miss Harrison.-- [Secretary to Mr. Rogers.] Yours sincerely, S. L. CLEMENS.

To H. H. Rogers, in New York City:

169 RUE DE L'UNIVERSITE, Apr. 29, '95. DEAR MR. ROGERS,--Your felicitous delightful letter of the 15th arrived three days ago, and brought great pleasure into the house.

There is one thing that weighs heavily on Mrs. Clemens and me. That is Brusnahan's money. If he is satisfied to have it invested in the Chicago enterprise, well and good; if not, we would like to have the money paid back to him. I will give him as many months to decide in as he pleases-- let him name 6 or 10 or 12--and we will let the money stay where it is in your hands till the time is up. Will Miss Harrison tell him so? I mean if you approve. I would like him to have a good investment, but would meantime prefer to protect him against loss.

At 6 minutes past 7, yesterday evening, Joan of Arc was burned at the stake.

With the long strain gone, I am in a sort of physical collapse today, but it will be gone tomorrow. I judged that this end of the book would be hard work, and it turned out so. I have never done any work before that cost so much thinking and weighing and measuring and planning and cramming, or so much cautious and painstaking execution. For I wanted the whole Rouen trial in, if it could be got in in such a way that the reader's interest would not flag--in fact I wanted the reader's interest to increase; and so I stuck to it with that determination in view--with the result that I have left nothing out but unimportant repetitions. Although it is mere history--history pure and simple--history stripped naked of flowers, embroideries, colorings, exaggerations, invention--the family agree that I have succeeded. It was a perilous thing to try in a tale, but I never believed it a doubtful one--provided I stuck strictly to business and didn't weaken and give up: or didn't get lazy and skimp the work. The first two-thirds of the book were easy; for I only needed to keep my historical road straight; therefore I used for reference only one French history and one English one--and shoveled in as much fancy work and invention on both sides of the historical road as I pleased. But on this last third I have constantly used five French sources and five English ones and

I think no telling historical nugget in any of them has escaped me.

Possibly the book may not sell, but that is nothing--it was written for love.

There--I'm called to see company. The family seldom require this of me, but they know I am not working today. Yours sincerely, S. L. CLEMENS.

"Brusnahan," of the foregoing letter, was an employee of the New York Herald, superintendent of the press-room--who had invested some of his savings in the type-setter.

In February Clemens returned to New York to look after matters connected with his failure and to close arrangements for a reading- tour around the world. He was nearly sixty years old, and time had not lessened his loathing for the platform. More than once, however, in earlier years, he had turned to it as a debt-payer, and never yet had his burden been so great as now. He concluded arrangements with Major Pond to take him as far as the Pacific Coast, and with R. S. Smythe, of Australia, for the rest of the tour. In April we find him once more back in Paris preparing to bring the family to America, He had returned by way of London, where he had visited Stanley the explorer--an old friend.

To H. H. Rogers, in New York City:

169 RUE DE L'UNIVERSITE, Sunday, Apr.7,'95. DEAR MR. ROGERS,--..... Stanley is magnificently housed in London, in a grand mansion in the midst of the official world, right off Downing Street and Whitehall. He had an extraordinary assemblage of brains and fame there to meet me--thirty or forty (both sexes) at dinner, and more than a hundred came in, after dinner. Kept it up till after midnight. There were cabinet ministers, ambassadors, admirals, generals, canons, Oxford professors, novelists, playwrights, poets, and a number of people equipped with rank and brains. I told some yarns and made some speeches. I promised to call on all those people next time I come to London, and show them the wife and the daughters. If I were younger and very strong I would dearly love to spend a season in London--provided I had no work on hand, or no work more exacting than lecturing. I think I will lecture there a month or two when I return from Australia.

There were many delightful ladies in that company. One was the wife of His Excellency Admiral Bridge, Commander-in Chief of the Australian Station, and she said her husband was able to throw wide all doors to me in that part of the world and would be glad to do it, and would yacht me and my party around, and excursion us in his flag-ship and make us have a great time; and she said she would write him we were coming, and we would find him ready. I have a letter from her this morning enclosing a letter of introduction to the Admiral. I already know the Admiral commanding in the China Seas and have promised to look in on him out there. He sleeps with my books under his pillow. P'raps it is the only way he can sleep.

According to Mrs. Clemens's present plans--subject to modification, of course--we sail in May; stay one day, or two days in New York, spend June, July and August in Elmira and prepare my lectures; then lecture in San Francisco and thereabouts during September and sail for Australia before the middle of October and open the show there about the middle of November. We don't take the girls along; it would be too expensive and they are quite willing to remain behind anyway.

Mrs. C. is feeling so well that she is not going to try the New York doctor till we have gone around the world and robbed it and made the finances a little easier. With a power of love to you all, S. L. CLEMENS.

There would come moments of depression, of course, and a week later he wrote: "I am tired to death all the time:" To a man of less vitality, less vigor of mind and body, it is easy to believe that under such circumstances this condition would have remained permanent. But perhaps, after all, it was his comic outlook on things in general that was his chief life-saver.

To H. H. Rogers, in New York City:

169 RUE DE L'UNIVERSITE, Apr. 29, '95. DEAR MR. ROGERS,--I have been hidden an hour or two, reading proof of Joan and now I think I am a lost child. I can't find anybody on the place. The baggage has all disappeared, including the family. I reckon that in the hurry and bustle of moving to the hotel they forgot me. But it is no matter. It is peacefuller now than I have known it for days and days and days.

In these Joan proofs which I have been reading for the September Harper I find a couple of tip-top platform readings--and I mean to read them on our trip. If the authorship is known by then; and if it isn't, I will reveal it. The fact is, there is more good platform-stuff in Joan than in any previous book of mine, by a long sight.

Yes, every danged member of the tribe has gone to the hotel and left me lost. I wonder how they can be so careless with property. I have got to try to get there by myself now.

All the trunks are going over as luggage; then I've got to find somebody on the dock who will agree to ship 6 of them to the Hartford Customhouse. If it is difficult I will dump them into the river. It is very careless of Mrs. Clemens to trust trunks and things to me. Sincerely yours, S. L. CLEMENS.

By the latter part of May they were at Quarry Farm, and Clemens, laid up there with a carbuncle, was preparing for his long tour. The outlook was not a pleasant one. To Mr. Rogers he wrote: "I sha'n't be able to stand on the platform before we start west. I sha'n't get a single chance to practice my reading; but will have to appear in Cleveland without the essential preparation. Nothing in this world can save it from being a shabby, poor disgusting performance. I've got to stand; I can't do it and talk to a house, and how in the nation am I going to sit? Land of Goshen, it's this night week! Pray for me."

The opening at Cleveland July 15th appears not to have been much of a success, though from another reason, one that doubtless seemed amusing to him later.

To H. H. Rogers, in New York City:

(Forenoon) CLEVELAND, July 16, '95. DEAR MR. ROGERS,--Had a roaring success at the Elmira reformatory Sunday night. But here, last night, I suffered defeat--There were a couple of hundred little boys behind me on the stage, on a lofty tier of benches which made them the most conspicuous objects in the house. And there was nobody to watch them or keep them quiet. Why, with their scufflings and horse-play and noise, it was just a menagerie. Besides, a concert of amateurs had been smuggled into the program (to precede me,) and their families and friends (say ten per cent of the audience) kept encoring them and they always responded. So it was 20 minutes to 9 before I got the platform in front of those 2,600 people who had paid a dollar apiece for a chance to go to hell in this fashion.

I got started magnificently, but inside of half an hour the scuffling boys had the audience's maddened attention and I saw it was a gone case; so I skipped a third of my program and quit. The newspapers are kind, but between you and me it was a defeat. There ain't going to be any more concerts at my lectures. I care nothing for this defeat, because it was not my fault. My first half hour showed that I had the house, and I could have kept it if I hadn't been so handicapped. Yours sincerely, S. L. CLEMENS.

P. S. Had a satisfactory time at Petoskey. Crammed the house and turned away a crowd. We had $548 in the house, which was $300 more than it had ever had in it before. I believe I don't care to have a talk go off better than that one did.

Mark Twain, on this long tour, was accompanied by his wife and his daughter Clara--Susy and Jean Clemens remaining with their aunt at Quarry Farm. The tour was a financial success from the start. By the time they were ready to sail from Vancouver five thousand dollars had been remitted to Mr. Rogers against that day of settlement when the debts of Webster & Co. were to be paid. Perhaps it should be stated here that a legal settlement had been arranged on a basis of fifty cents on the dollar, but neither Clemens nor his wife consented to this as final. They would pay in full.

They sailed from Vancouver August 23, 1895. About the only letter of this time is an amusing note to Rudyard Kipling, written at the moment of departure.

To Rudyard Kipling, in England:

August, 1895. DEAR KIPLING,--It is reported that you are about to visit India. This has moved me to journey to that far country in order that I may unload from my conscience a debt long due to you. Years ago you came from India to Elmira to visit me, as you said at the time. It has always been my purpose to return that visit and that great compliment some day. I shall arrive next January and you must be ready. I shall come riding my ayah with his tusks adorned with silver bells and ribbons and escorted by a troop of native howdahs richly clad and mounted upon a herd of wild bungalows; and you must be on hand with a few bottles of ghee, for I shall be thirsty. Affectionately, S. L. CLEMENS.

Clemens, platforming in Australia, was too busy to write letters. Everywhere he was welcomed by great audiences, and everywhere lavishly entertained. He was beset by other carbuncles, but would seem not to have been seriously delayed by them. A letter to his old friend Twichell carries the story.

To Rev. Jos. H. Twichell, in Hartford:

FRANK MOELLER'S MASONIC HOTEL, NAPIER, NEW ZEALAND, November 29, '95. DEAR JOE,--Your welcome letter of two months and five days ago has just arrived, and finds me in bed with another carbuncle. It is No. 3. Not a serious one this time. I lectured last night without inconvenience, but the doctors thought best to forbid to-night's lecture. My second one kept me in bed a week in Melbourne.

.....We are all glad it is you who is to write the article, it delights us all through.

I think it was a good stroke of luck that knocked me on my back here at Napier, instead of some hotel in the centre of a noisy city. Here we have the smooth and placidly-complaining sea at our door, with nothing between us and it but 20 yards of shingle--and hardly a suggestion of life in that space to mar it or make a noise. Away down here fifty-five degrees south of the Equator this sea seems to murmur in an unfamiliar tongue--a foreign tongue--tongue bred among the ice-fields of the Antarctic--a murmur with a note of melancholy in it proper to the vast unvisited solitudes it has come from. It was very delicious and solacing to wake in the night and find it still pulsing there. I wish you were here--land, but it would be fine!

Livy and Clara enjoy this nomadic life pretty well; certainly better than one could have expected they would. They have tough experiences, in the way of food and beds and frantic little ships, but they put up with the worst that befalls with heroic endurance that resembles contentment.

No doubt I shall be on the platform next Monday. A week later we shall reach Wellington; talk there 3 nights, then sail back to Australia. We sailed for New Zealand October 30.

Day before yesterday was Livy's birthday (under world time), and tomorrow will be mine. I shall be 60--no thanks for it.

I and the others send worlds and worlds of love to all you dear ones.

MARK.

The article mentioned in the foregoing letter was one which Twichell had been engaged by Harper's Magazine to write concerning the home life and characteristics of Mark Twain. By the time the Clemens party had completed their tour of India--a splendid, triumphant tour, too full of work and recreation for letter-writing--and had reached South Africa, the article had appeared, a satisfactory one, if we may judge by Mark Twain's next.

This letter, however, has a special interest in the account it gives of Mark Twain's visit to the Jameson raiders, then imprisoned at Pretoria.

To Rev. Jos. H. Twichell, in Hartford:

PRETORIA, SOUTH AFRICAN REPUBLIC, The Queen's Birthday, '96. (May 24) DEAR OLD JOE,--Harper for May was given to me yesterday in Johannesburg by an American lady who lives there, and I read your article on me while coming up in the train with her and an old friend and fellow-Missourian of mine, Mrs. John Hays Hammond, the handsome and spirited wife of the chief of the 4 Reformers, who lies in prison here under a 15-year sentence, along with 50 minor Reformers who are in for 1 and 5-year terms. Thank you a thousand times Joe, you have praised me away above my deserts, but I am not the man to quarrel with you for that; and as for Livy, she will take your very hardiest statements at par, and be grateful to you to the bottom of her heart. Between you and Punch and Brander Matthews, I am like to have my opinion of myself raised sufficiently high; and I guess the children will be after you, for it is the study of their lives to keep my self-appreciation down somewhere within bounds.

I had a note from Mrs. Rev. Gray (nee Tyler) yesterday, and called on her to-day. She is well.

Yesterday I was allowed to enter the prison with Mrs. Hammond. A Boer guard was at my elbow all the time, but was courteous and polite, only he barred the way in the compound (quadrangle or big open court) and wouldn't let me cross a white mark that was on the ground--the "death- line" one of the prisoners called it. Not in earnest, though, I think. I found that I had met Hammond once when he was a Yale senior and a guest of Gen. Franklin's. I also found that I had known Capt. Mein intimately 32 years ago. One of the English prisoners had heard me lecture in London 23 years ago. After being introduced in turn to all the prisoners, I was allowed to see some of the cells and examine their food, beds, etc. I was told in Johannesburg that Hammond's salary of $150,000 a year is not stopped, and that the salaries of some of the others are still continued. Hammond was looking very well indeed, and I can say the same of all the others. When the trouble first fell upon them it hit some of them very hard; several fell sick (Hammond among them), two or three had to be removed to the hospital, and one of the favorites lost his mind and killed himself, poor fellow, last week. His funeral, with a sorrowing following of 10,000, took the place of the public demonstration the Americans were getting up for me.

These prisoners are strong men, prominent men, and I believe they are all educated men. They are well off; some of them are wealthy. They have a lot of books to read, they play games and smoke, and for awhile they will be able to bear up in their captivity; but not for long, not for very long, I take it. I am told they have times of deadly brooding and depression. I made them a speech--sitting down. It just happened so. I don't prefer that attitude. Still, it has one advantage--it is only a talk, it doesn't take the form of a speech. I have tried it once before on this trip. However, if a body wants to make sure of having "liberty," and feeling at home, he had better stand up, of course. I advised them at considerable length to stay where they were--they would get used to it and like it presently; if they got out they would only get in again somewhere else, by the look of their countenances; and I promised to go and see the President and do what I could to get him to double their jail-terms.

We had a very good sociable time till the permitted time was up and a little over, and we outsiders had to go. I went again to-day, but the Rev. Mr. Gray had just arrived, and the warden, a genial, elderly Boer named Du Plessis--explained that his orders wouldn't allow him to admit saint and sinner at the same time, particularly on a Sunday. Du Plessis --descended from the Huguenot fugitives, you see, of 200 years ago-- but he hasn't any French left in him now--all Dutch.

It gravels me to think what a goose I was to make Livy and Clara remain in Durban; but I wanted to save them the 30-hour railway trip to Johannesburg. And Durban and its climate and opulent foliage were so lovely, and the friends there were so choice and so hearty that I sacrificed myself in their interests, as I thought. It is just the beginning of winter, and although the days are hot, the nights are cool. But it's lovely weather in these regions, too; and the friends are as lovely as the weather, and Johannesburg and Pretoria are brimming with interest. I talk here twice more, then return to Johannesburg next Wednesday for a fifth talk there; then to the Orange Free State capital, then to some town on the way to Port Elizabeth, where the two will join us by sea from Durban; then the gang will go to Kimberley and presently to the Cape--and so, in the course of time, we shall get through and sail for England; and then we will hunt up a quiet village and I will write and Livy edit, for a few months, while Clara and Susy and Jean study music and things in London.

We have had noble good times everywhere and every day, from Cleveland, July 15, to Pretoria, May 24, and never a dull day either on sea or land, notwithstanding the carbuncles and things. Even when I was laid up 10 days at Jeypore in India we had the charmingest times with English friends. All over India the English well, you will never know how good and fine they are till you see them.

Midnight and after! and I must do many things to-day, and lecture tonight.

A world of thanks to you, Joe dear, and a world of love to all of you.

MARK.

Perhaps for readers of a later day a word as to what constituted the Jameson raid would not be out of place here. Dr. Leander Starr Jameson was an English physician, located at Kimberley. President Kruger (Oom Paul), head of the South African Republic, was one of his patients; also, Lobengula, the Matabele chief. From Lobengula concessions were obtained which led to the formation of the South African Company. Jameson gave up his profession and went in for conquest, associating himself with the projects of Cecil Rhodes. In time he became administrator of Rhodesia. By the end of 1894. he was in high feather, and during a visit to England was feted as a sort of romantic conqueror of the olden time. Perhaps this turned his head; at all events at the end of 1895 came the startling news that "Dr. Jim," as he was called, at the head of six hundred men, had ridden into the Transvaal in support of a Rhodes scheme for an uprising at Johannesburg. The raid was a failure. Jameson, and those other knights of adventure, were captured by the forces of "Oom Paul," and some of them barely escaped execution. The Boer president handed them over to the English Government for punishment, and they received varying sentences, but all were eventually released. Jameson, later, became again prominent in South-African politics, but there is no record of any further raids.

....

The Clemens party sailed from South Africa the middle of July, 1896, and on the last day of the month reached England. They had not planned to return to America, but to spend the winter in or near London in some quiet place where Clemens could write the book of his travels.

The two daughters in America, Susy and Jean, were expected to arrive August 12th, but on that day there came, instead, a letter saying that Susy Clemens was not well enough to sail. A cable inquiry was immediately sent, but the reply when it came was not satisfactory, and Mrs. Clemens and Clara sailed for America without further delay. This was on August 15th. Three days later, in the old home at Hartford, Susy Clemens died of cerebral fever. She had been visiting Mrs. Charles Dudley Warner, but by the physician's advice had been removed to the comfort and quiet of her own home, only a few steps away.

Mark Twain, returning from his triumphant tour of the world in the hope that soon, now, he might be free from debt, with his family happily gathered about him, had to face alone this cruel blow. There was no purpose in his going to America; Susy would be buried long before his arrival. He awaited in England the return of his broken family. They lived that winter in a quiet corner of Chelsea, No. 23 Tedworth Square.

To Rev. Joseph H. Twichell, in Hartford, Conn.:

Permanent address: % CHATTO & WINDUS 111 T. MARTIN'S LANE, LONDON, Sept. 27, '96. Through Livy and Katy I have learned, dear old Joe, how loyally you stood poor Susy's friend, and mine, and Livy's: how you came all the way down, twice, from your summer refuge on your merciful errands to bring the peace and comfort of your beloved presence, first to that poor child, and again to the broken heart of her poor desolate mother. It was like you; like your good great heart, like your matchless and unmatchable self. It was no surprise to me to learn that you stayed by Susy long hours, careless of fatigue and heat, it was no surprise to me to learn that you could still the storms that swept her spirit when no other could; for she loved you, revered you, trusted you, and "Uncle Joe" was no empty phrase upon her lips! I am grateful to you, Joe, grateful to the bottom of my heart, which has always been filled with love for you, and respect and admiration; and I would have chosen you out of all the world to take my place at Susy's side and Livy's in those black hours.

Susy was a rare creature; the rarest that has been reared in Hartford in this generation. And Livy knew it, and you knew it, and Charley Warner and George, and Harmony, and the Hillyers and the Dunhams and the Cheneys, and Susy and Lilly, and the Bunces, and Henry Robinson and Dick Burton, and perhaps others. And I also was of the number, but not in the same degree--for she was above my duller comprehension. I merely knew that she was my superior in fineness of mind, in the delicacy and subtlety of her intellect, but to fully measure her I was not competent. I know her better now; for I have read her private writings and sounded the deeps of her mind; and I know better, now, the treasure that was mine than I knew it when I had it. But I have this consolation: that dull as I was, I always knew enough to be proud when she commended me or my work --as proud as if Livy had done it herself--and I took it as the accolade from the hand of genius. I see now--as Livy always saw--that she had greatness in her; and that she herself was dimly conscious of it.

And now she is dead--and I can never tell her.

God bless you Joe--and all of your house. S. L. C.

To Mr. Henry C. Robinson, Hartford, Conn.:

LONDON, Sept. 28, '96. It is as you say, dear old friend, "the pathos of it" yes, it was a piteous thing--as piteous a tragedy as any the year can furnish. When we started westward upon our long trip at half past ten at night, July 14, 1895, at Elmira, Susy stood on the platform in the blaze of the electric light waving her good-byes to us as the train glided away, her mother throwing back kisses and watching her through her tears. One year, one month, and one week later, Clara and her mother having exactly completed the circuit of the globe, drew up at that platform at the same hour of the night, in the same train and the same car--and again Susy had come a journey and was near at hand to meet them. She was waiting in the house she was born in, in her coffin.

All the circumstances of this death were pathetic--my brain is worn to rags rehearsing them. The mere death would have been cruelty enough, without overloading it and emphasizing it with that score of harsh and wanton details. The child was taken away when her mother was within three days of her, and would have given three decades for sight of her.

In my despair and unassuageable misery I upbraid myself for ever parting with her. But there is no use in that. Since it was to happen it would have happened. With love S. L. C.

The life at Tedworth Square that winter was one of almost complete privacy. Of the hundreds of friends which Mark Twain had in London scarcely half a dozen knew his address. He worked steadily on his book of travels, 'Following the Equator', and wrote few letters beyond business communications to Mr. Rogers. In one of these he said, "I am appalled! Here I am trying to load you up with work again after you have been dray-horsing over the same tiresome ground for a year. It's too bad, and I am ashamed of it."

But late in November he sent a letter of a different sort--one that was to have an important bearing on the life of a girl today of unique and world-wide distinction.

To Mrs. H. H. Rogers, in New York City:

For and in behalf of Helen Keller, stone blind and deaf, and formerly dumb.

DEAR MRS. ROGERS,--Experience has convinced me that when one wishes to set a hard-worked man at something which he mightn't prefer to be bothered with, it is best to move upon him behind his wife. If she can't convince him it isn't worth while for other people to try.

Mr. Rogers will remember our visit with that astonishing girl at Lawrence Hutton's house when she was fourteen years old. Last July, in Boston, when she was 16 she underwent the Harvard examination for admission to Radcliffe College. She passed without a single condition. She was allowed the same amount of time that is granted to other applicants, and this was shortened in her case by the fact that the question papers had to be read to her. Yet she scored an average of 90 as against an average of 78 on the part of the other applicants.

It won't do for America to allow this marvelous child to retire from her studies because of poverty. If she can go on with them she will make a fame that will endure in history for centuries. Along her special lines she is the most extraordinary product of all the ages.

There is danger that she must retire from the struggle for a College degree for lack of support for herself and for Miss Sullivan, (the teacher who has been with her from the start--Mr. Rogers will remember her.) Mrs. Hutton writes to ask me to interest rich Englishmen in her case, and I would gladly try, but my secluded life will not permit it. I see nobody. Nobody knows my address. Nothing but the strictest hiding can enable me to write my long book in time.

So I thought of this scheme: Beg you to lay siege to your husband and get him to interest himself and Mess. John D. and William Rockefeller and the other Standard Oil chiefs in Helen's case; get them to subscribe an annual aggregate of six or seven hundred or a thousand dollars--and agree to continue this for three or four years, until she has completed her college course. I'm not trying to limit their generosity--indeed no, they may pile that Standard Oil, Helen Keller College Fund as high as they please, they have my consent.

Mrs. Hutton's idea is to raise a permanent fund the interest upon which shall support Helen and her teacher and put them out of the fear of want. I shan't say a word against it, but she will find it a difficult and disheartening job, and meanwhile what is to become of that miraculous girl?

No, for immediate and sound effectiveness, the thing is for you to plead with Mr. Rogers for this hampered wonder of your sex, and send him clothed with plenary powers to plead with the other chiefs--they have spent mountains of money upon the worthiest benevolences, and I think that the same spirit which moved them to put their hands down through their hearts into their pockets in those cases will answer "Here!" when its name is called in this one. 638

There--I don't need to apologize to you or to H. H. for this appeal that I am making; I know you too well for that.

Good-bye with love to all of you S. L. CLEMENS.

Laurence Hutton is on the staff of Harper's Monthly--close by, and handy when wanted.

The plea was not made in vain. Mr. and Mrs. Rogers interested themselves most liberally in Helen Keller's fortune, and certainly no one can say that any of those who contributed to her success ever had reason for disappointment.

In his letter of grateful acknowledgment, which follows, Clemens also takes occasion to thank Mr. Rogers for his further efforts in the matter of his own difficulties. This particular reference concerns the publishing, complications which by this time had arisen between the American Publishing Company, of Hartford, and the house in Franklin Square.

LONDON, Dec. 22, '96. DEAR MRS. ROGERS,--It is superb! And I am beyond measure grateful to you both. I knew you would be interested in that wonderful girl, and that Mr. Rogers was already interested in her and touched by her; and I was sure that if nobody else helped her you two would; but you have gone far and away beyond the sum I expected--may your lines fall in pleasant places here and Hereafter for it!

The Huttons are as glad and grateful as they can be, and I am glad for their sakes as well as for Helen's.

I want to thank Mr. Rogers for crucifying himself again on the same old cross between Bliss and Harper; and goodness knows I hope he will come to enjoy it above all other dissipations yet, seeing that it has about it the elements of stability and permanency. However, at any time that he says sign, we're going to do it. Ever sincerely Yours S. L. CLEMENS.

XXXVI

LETTERS 1897. LONDON, SWITZERLAND, VIENNA

Mark Twain worked steadily on his book that sad winter and managed to keep the gloom out of his chapters, though it is noticeable that 'Following the Equator' is more serious than his other books of travel. He wrote few letters, and these only to his three closest friends, Howells, Twichell, and Rogers. In the letter to Twichell, which follows, there is mention of two unfinished manuscripts which he expects to resume. One of these was a dream story, enthusiastically begun, but perhaps with insufficient plot to carry it through, for it never reached conclusion. He had already tried it in one or two forms and would begin it again presently. The identity of the other tale is uncertain.

To Rev. J. H. Twichell, in Hartford:

LONDON, Jan. 19, '97. DEAR JOE,--Do I want you to write to me? Indeed I do. I do not want most people to write, but I do want you to do it. The others break my heart, but you will not. You have a something divine in you that is not in other men. You have the touch that heals, not lacerates. And you know the secret places of our hearts. You know our life--the outside of it--as the others do--and the inside of it--which they do not. You have seen our whole voyage. You have seen us go to sea, a cloud of sail--and the flag at the peak; and you see us now, chartless, adrift--derelicts; battered, water-logged, our sails a ruck of rags, our pride gone. For it is gone. And there is nothing in its place. The vanity of life was all we had, and there is no more vanity left in us. We are even ashamed of that we had; ashamed that we trusted the promises of life and builded high--to come to this!

I did know that Susy was part of us; I did not know that she could go away; I did not know that she could go away, and take our lives with her, yet leave our dull bodies behind. And I did not know what she was. To me she was but treasure in the bank; the amount known, the need to look at it daily, handle it, weigh it, count it, realize it, not necessary; and now that I would do it, it is too late; they tell me it is not there, has vanished away in a night, the bank is broken, my fortune is gone, I am a pauper. How am I to comprehend this? How am I to have it? Why am I robbed, and who is benefited?

Ah, well, Susy died at home. She had that privilege. Her dying eyes rested upon nothing that was strange to them, but only upon things which they had known and loved always and which had made her young years glad; and she had you, and Sue, and Katy, and John, and Ellen. This was happy fortune--I am thankful that it was vouchsafed to her. If she had died in another house-well, I think I could not have borne that. To us, our house was not unsentient matter--it had a heart, and a soul, and eyes to see us with; and approvals, and solicitudes, and deep sympathies; it was of us, and we were in its confidence, and lived in its grace and in the peace of its benediction. We never came home from an absence that its face did not light up and speak out its eloquent welcome--and we could not enter it unmoved. And could we now, oh, now, in spirit we should enter it unshod.

I am trying to add to the "assets" which you estimate so generously. No, I am not. The thought is not in my mind. My purpose is other. I am working, but it is for the sake of the work--the "surcease of sorrow" that is found there. I work all the days, and trouble vanishes away when I use that magic. This book will not long stand between it and me, now; but that is no matter, I have many unwritten books to fly to for my preservation; the interval between the finishing of this one and the beginning of the next will not be more than an hour, at most. Continuances, I mean; for two of them are already well along--in fact have reached exactly the same stage in their journey: 19,000 words each. The present one will contain 180,000 words--130,000 are done. I am well protected; but Livy! She has nothing in the world to turn to; nothing but housekeeping, and doing things for the children and me. She does not see people, and cannot; books have lost their interest for her. She sits solitary; and all the day, and all the days, wonders how it all happened, and why. We others were always busy with our affairs, but Susy was her comrade--had to be driven from her loving persecutions--sometimes at 1 in the morning. To Livy the persecutions were welcome. It was heaven to her to be plagued like that. But it is ended now. Livy stands so in need of help; and none among us all could help her like you.

Some day you and I will walk again, Joe, and talk. I hope so. We could have such talks! We are all grateful to you and Harmony--how grateful it is not given to us to say in words. We pay as we can, in love; and in this coin practicing no economy. Good bye, dear old Joe! MARK.

The letters to Mr. Rogers were, for the most part, on matters of business, but in one of them he said: "I am going to write with all my might on this book, and follow it up with others as fast as I can in the hope that within three years I can clear out the stuff that is in me waiting to be written, and that I shall then die in the promptest kind of a way and no fooling around." And in one he wrote: "You are the best friend ever a man had, and the surest."

To W. D. Howells, in New York

LONDON, Feb. 23, '97. DEAR HOWELLS,-I find your generous article in the Weekly, and I want to thank you for its splendid praises, so daringly uttered and so warmly. The words stir the dead heart of me, and throw a glow of color into a life which sometimes seems to have grown wholly wan. I don't mean that I am miserable; no--worse than that--indifferent. Indifferent to nearly everything but work. I like that; I enjoy it, and stick to it. I do it without purpose and without ambition; merely for the love of it.

This mood will pass, some day--there is history for it. But it cannot pass until my wife comes up out of the submergence. She was always so quick to recover herself before, but now there is no rebound, and we are dead people who go through the motions of life. Indeed I am a mud image, and it will puzzle me to know what it is in me that writes, and has comedy-fancies and finds pleasure in phrasing them. It is a law of our nature, of course, or it wouldn't happen; the thing in me forgets the presence of the mud image and goes its own way, wholly unconscious of it and apparently of no kinship with it. I have finished my book, but I go on as if the end were indefinitely away--as indeed it is. There is no hurry--at any rate there is no limit.

Jean's spirits are good; Clara's are rising. They have youth--the only thing that was worth giving to the race.

These are sardonic times. Look at Greece, and that whole shabby muddle. But I am not sorry to be alive and privileged to look on. If I were not a hermit I would go to the House every day and see those people scuffle over it and blether about the brotherhood of the human race. This has been a bitter year for English pride, and I don't like to see England humbled--that is, not too much. We are sprung from her loins, and it hurts me. I am for republics, and she is the only comrade we've got, in that. We can't count France, and there is hardly enough of Switzerland to count. Beneath the governing crust England is sound-hearted--and sincere, too, and nearly straight. But I am appalled to notice that the wide extension of the surface has damaged her manners, and made her rather Americanly uncourteous on the lower levels.

Won't you give our love to the Howellses all and particular? Sincerely yours S. L. CLEMENS.

The travel-book did not finish easily, and more than once when he thought it completed he found it necessary to cut and add and change. The final chapters were not sent to the printer until the middle of May, and in a letter to Mr. Rogers he commented: "A successful book is not made of what is in it, but what is left out of it." Clemens was at the time contemplating a uniform edition of his books, and in one of his letters to Mr. Rogers on the matter he wrote, whimsically, "Now I was proposing to make a thousand sets at a hundred dollars a set, and do the whole canvassing myself..... I would load up every important jail and saloon in America with de luxe editions of my books. But Mrs. Clemens and the children object to this, I do not know why." And, in a moment of depression: "You see the lightning refuses to strike me--there is where the defect is. We have to do our own striking as Barney Barnato did. But nobody ever gets the courage until he goes crazy."

They went to Switzerland for the summer to the village of Weggis, on Lake Lucerne--"The charmingest place we ever lived in," he declared, "for repose, and restfulness, and superb scenery." It was here that he began work on a new story of Tom and Huck, and at least upon one other manuscript. From a brief note to Mr. Rogers we learn something of his employments and economies.

To Henry H. Rogers, in New York:

LUCERNE, August the something or other, 1897. DEAR MR. ROGERS,--I am writing a novel, and am getting along very well with it.

I believe that this place (Weggis, half an hour from Lucerne,) is the loveliest in the world, and the most satisfactory. We have a small house on the hillside all to ourselves, and our meals are served in it from the inn below on the lake shore. Six francs a day per head, house and food included. The scenery is beyond comparison beautiful. We have a row boat and some bicycles, and good roads, and no visitors. Nobody knows we are here. And Sunday in heaven is noisy compared to this quietness. Sincerely yours S. L. C.

To Rev. J. H. Twichell, in Hartford:

LUCERNE, Aug. 22, '97. DEAR JOE,--Livy made a noble find on the Lucerne boat the other day on one of her shopping trips--George Williamson Smith--did I tell you about it? We had a lovely time with him, and such intellectual refreshment as we had not tasted in many a month.

And the other night we had a detachment of the jubilee Singers--6. I had known one of them in London 24 years ago. Three of the 6 were born in slavery, the others were children of slaves. How charming they were--in spirit, manner, language, pronunciation, enunciation, grammar, phrasing, matter, carriage, clothes--in every detail that goes to make the real lady and gentleman, and welcome guest. We went down to the village hotel and bought our tickets and entered the beer-hall, where a crowd of German and Swiss men and women sat grouped at round tables with their beer mugs in front of them--self-contained and unimpressionable looking people, an indifferent and unposted and disheartened audience--and up at the far end of the room sat the Jubilees in a row. The Singers got up and stood--the talking and glass jingling went on. Then rose and swelled out above those common earthly sounds one of those rich chords the secret of whose make only the Jubilees possess, and a spell fell upon that house. It was fine to see the faces light up with the pleased wonder and surprise of it. No one was indifferent any more; and when the singers finished, the camp was theirs. It was a triumph. It reminded me of Launcelot riding in Sir Kay's armor and astonishing complacent Knights who thought they had struck a soft thing. The Jubilees sang a lot of pieces. Arduous and painstaking cultivation has not diminished or artificialized their music, but on the contrary--to my surprise--has mightily reinforced its eloquence and beauty. Away back in the beginning--to my mind--their music made all other vocal music cheap; and that early notion is emphasized now. It is utterly beautiful, to me; and it moves me infinitely more than any other music can. I think that in the Jubilees and their songs America has produced the perfectest flower of the ages; and I wish it were a foreign product, so that she would worship it and lavish money on it and go properly crazy over it.

Now, these countries are different: they would do all that, if it were native. It is true they praise God, but that is merely a formality, and nothing in it; they open out their whole hearts to no foreigner.

The musical critics of the German press praise the Jubilees with great enthusiasm--acquired technique etc, included.

One of the jubilee men is a son of General Joe Johnson, and was educated by him after the war. The party came up to the house and we had a pleasant time.

This is paradise, here--but of course we have got to leave it by and by. The 18th of August--[Anniversary of Susy Clemens's death.]--has come and gone, Joe--and we still seem to live. With love from us all. MARK.

Clemens declared he would as soon spend his life in Weggis "as anywhere else in the geography," but October found them in Vienna for the winter, at the Hotel Metropole. The Austrian capital was just then in a political turmoil, the character of which is hinted in the following:

To Rev. J. H. Twichell, in Hartford:

HOTEL METROPOLE, VIENNA, Oct. 23, '97. DEAR JOE,--We are gradually getting settled down and wonted. Vienna is not a cheap place to live in, but I have made one small arrangement which: has a distinctly economical aspect. The Vice Consul made the contract for me yesterday-to-wit: a barber is to come every morning 8.30 and shave me and keep my hair trimmed for $2.50 a month. I used to pay $1.50 per shave in our house in Hartford.

Does it suggest to you reflections when you reflect that this is the most important event which has happened to me in ten days--unless I count--in my handing a cabman over to the police day before yesterday, with the proper formalities, and promised to appear in court when his case comes up.

If I had time to run around and talk, I would do it; for there is much politics agoing, and it would be interesting if a body could get the hang of it. It is Christian and Jew by the horns--the advantage with the superior man, as usual--the superior man being the Jew every time and in all countries. Land, Joe, what chance would the Christian have in a country where there were 3 Jews to 10 Christians! Oh, not the shade of a shadow of a chance. The difference between the brain of the average Christian and that of the average Jew--certainly in Europe--is about the difference between a tadpole's and an Archbishop's. It's a marvelous, race--by long odds the most marvelous that the world has produced, I suppose.

And there's more politics--the clash between Czech and Austrian. I wish I could understand these quarrels, but of course I can't.

With the abounding love of us all MARK.

In Following the Equator there was used an amusing picture showing Mark Twain on his trip around the world. It was a trick photograph made from a picture of Mark Twain taken in a steamer-chair, cut out and combined with a dilapidated negro-cart drawn by a horse and an ox. In it Clemens appears to be sitting luxuriously in the end of the disreputable cart. His companions are two negroes. To the creator of this ingenious effect Mark Twain sent a characteristic acknowledgment.

To T. S. Frisbie

VIENNA, Oct. 25, '97. MR. T. S. FRISBIE,--Dear Sir: The picture has reached me, and has moved me deeply. That was a steady, sympathetic and honorable team, and although it was not swift, and not showy, it pulled me around the globe successfully, and always attracted its proper share of attention, even in the midst of the most costly and fashionable turnouts. Princes and dukes and other experts were always enthused by the harness and could hardly keep from trying to buy it. The barouche does not look as fine, now, as it did earlier-but that was before the earthquake.

The portraits of myself and uncle and nephew are very good indeed, and your impressionist reproduction of the palace of the Governor General of India is accurate and full of tender feeling.

I consider that this picture is much more than a work of art. How much more, one cannot say with exactness, but I should think two-thirds more.

Very truly yours MARK TWAIN.

Following the Equator was issued by subscription through Mark Twain's old publishers, the Blisses, of Hartford. The sale of it was large, not only on account of the value of the book itself, but also because of the sympathy of the American people with Mark Twain's brave struggle to pay his debts. When the newspapers began to print exaggerated stories of the vast profits that were piling up, Bliss became worried, for he thought it would modify the sympathy. He cabled Clemens for a denial, with the following result:

To Frank E. Bliss, in Hartford:

VIENNA, Nov. 4, 1897. DEAR BLISS,--Your cablegram informing me that a report is in circulation which purports to come from me and which says I have recently made $82,000 and paid all my debts has just reached me, and I have cabled back my regret to you that it is not true. I wrote a letter--a private letter--a short time ago, in which I expressed the belief that I should be out of debt within the next twelvemonth. If you make as much as usual for me out of the book, that belief will crystallize into a fact, and I shall be wholly out of debt. I am encoring you now.

It is out of that moderate letter that the Eighty-Two Thousand-Dollar mare's nest has developed. But why do you worry about the various reports? They do not worry me. They are not unfriendly, and I don't see how they can do any harm. Be patient; you have but a little while to wait; the possible reports are nearly all in. It has been reported that I was seriously ill--it was another man; dying--it was another man; dead --the other man again. It has been reported that I have received a legacy it was another man; that I am out of debt--it was another man; and now comes this $82,000--still another man. It has been reported that I am writing books--for publication; I am not doing anything of the kind. It would surprise (and gratify) me if I should be able to get another book ready for the press within the next three years. You can see, yourself, that there isn't anything more to be reported--invention is exhausted. Therefore, don't worry, Bliss--the long night is breaking. As far as I can see, nothing remains to be reported, except that I have become a foreigner. When you hear it, don't you believe it. And don't take the trouble to deny it. Merely just raise the American flag on our house in Hartford, and let it talk. Truly yours, MARK TWAIN.

P. S. This is not a private letter. I am getting tired of private letters.

To Rev. J. H. Twichell, in Hartford:

VIENNA HOTEL METROPOLE, NOV. 19, '97. DEAR JOE,--Above is our private (and permanent) address for the winter. You needn't send letters by London.

I am very much obliged for Forrest's Austro-Hungarian articles. I have just finished reading the first one: and in it I find that his opinion and Vienna's are the same, upon a point which was puzzling me--the paucity (no, the absence) of Austrian Celebrities. He and Vienna both say the country cannot afford to allow great names to grow up; that the whole safety and prosperity of the Empire depends upon keeping things quiet; can't afford to have geniuses springing up and developing ideas and stirring the public soul. I am assured that every time a man finds himself blooming into fame, they just softly snake him down and relegate him to a wholesome obscurity. It is curious and interesting.

Three days ago the New York World sent and asked a friend of mine (correspondent of a London daily) to get some Christmas greetings from the celebrities of the Empire. She spoke of this. Two or three bright Austrians were present. They said "There are none who are known all over the world! none who have achieved fame; none who can point to their work and say it is known far and wide in the earth: there are no names; Kossuth (known because he had a father) and Lecher, who made the 12 hour speech; two names-nothing more. Every other country in the world, perhaps, has a giant or two whose heads are away up and can be seen, but ours. We've got the material--have always had it--but we have to suppress it; we can't afford to let it develop; our political salvation depends upon tranquillity--always has."

Poor Livy! She is laid up with rheumatism; but she is getting along now. We have a good doctor, and he says she will be out of bed in a couple of days, but must stay in the house a week or ten.

Clara is working faithfully at her music, Jean at her usual studies, and we all send love. MARK.

Mention has already been made of the political excitement in Vienna. The trouble between the Hungarian and German legislative bodies presently became violent. Clemens found himself intensely interested, and was present in one of the galleries when it was cleared by the police. All sorts of stories were circulated as to what happened to him, one of which was cabled to America. A letter to Twichell sets forth what really happened.

To Rev. J. H. Twichell, in Hartford:

HOTEL METROPOLE, VIENNA, Dec. 10, '97. DEAR JOE,--Pond sends me a Cleveland paper with a cablegram from here in it which says that when the police invaded the parliament and expelled the 11 members I waved my handkerchief and shouted 'Hoch die Deutschen!' and got hustled out. Oh dear, what a pity it is that one's adventures never happen! When the Ordner (sergeant-at-arms) came up to our gallery and was hurrying the people out, a friend tried to get leave for me to stay, by saying, "But this gentleman is a foreigner--you don't need to turn him out--he won't do any harm."

"Oh, I know him very well--I recognize him by his pictures; and I should be very glad to let him stay, but I haven't any choice, because of the strictness of the orders."

And so we all went out, and no one was hustled. Below, I ran across the London Times correspondent, and he showed me the way into the first gallery and I lost none of the show. The first gallery had not misbehaved, and was not disturbed.

. . . We cannot persuade Livy to go out in society yet, but all the lovely people come to see her; and Clara and I go to dinner parties, and around here and there, and we all have a most hospitable good time. Jean's woodcarving flourishes, and her other studies.

Good-bye Joe--and we all love all of you. MARK.

Clemens made an article of the Austrian troubles, one of the best things he ever wrote, and certainly one of the clearest elucidations of the Austro-Hungarian confusions. It was published in Harper's Magazine, and is now included in his complete works.

Thus far none of the Webster Company debts had been paid--at least, none of importance. The money had been accumulating in Mr. Rogers's hands, but Clemens was beginning to be depressed by the heavy burden. He wrote asking for relief.

Part of a letter to H. H. Rogers, in New York:

DEAR MR. ROGERS,--I throw up the sponge. I pull down the flag. Let us begin on the debts. I cannot bear the weight any longer. It totally unfits me for work. I have lost three entire months now. In that time I have begun twenty magazine articles and books--and flung every one of them aside in turn. The debts interfered every time, and took the spirit out of any work. And yet I have worked like a bond slave and wasted no time and spared no effort----

Rogers wrote, proposing a plan for beginning immediately upon the debts. Clemens replied enthusiastically, and during the next few weeks wrote every few days, expressing his delight in liquidation.

Extracts from letters to H. H. Rogers, in New York:

. . . We all delighted with your plan. Only don't leave B--out. Apparently that claim has been inherited by some women--daughters, no doubt. We don't want to see them lose any thing. B----- is an ass, and disgruntled, but I don't care for that. I am responsible for the money and must do the best I can to pay it..... I am writing hard--writing for the creditors.

Dec. 29. Land we are glad to see those debts diminishing. For the first time in my life I am getting more pleasure out of paying money out than pulling it in.

Jan. 2. Since we have begun to pay off the debts I have abundant peace of mind again--no sense of burden. Work is become a pleasure again--it is not labor any longer.

March 7. Mrs. Clemens has been reading the creditors' letters over and over again and thanks you deeply for sending them, and says it is the only really happy day she has had since Susy died.

XXXVII

LETTERS, 1898, TO HOWELLS AND TWICHELL. LIFE IN VIENNA. PAYMENT OF THE DEBTS. ASSASSINATION OF THE EMPRESS

The end of January saw the payment of the last of Mark Twain's debts. Once more he stood free before the world--a world that sounded his praises. The latter fact rather amused him. "Honest men must be pretty scarce," he said, "when they make so much fuss over even a defective specimen." When the end was in sight Clemens wrote the news to Howells in a letter as full of sadness as of triumph.

To W. D. Howells, in New York:

HOTEL METROPOLE, VIENNA, Jan. 22, '98. DEAR HOWELLS,--Look at those ghastly figures. I used to write it "Hartford, 1871." There was no Susy then--there is no Susy now. And how much lies between--one long lovely stretch of scented fields, and meadows, and shady woodlands, and suddenly Sahara! You speak of the glorious days of that old time--and they were. It is my quarrel--that traps like that are set. Susy and Winnie given us, in miserable sport, and then taken away.

About the last time I saw you I described to you the culminating disaster in a book I was going to write (and will yet, when the stroke is further away)--a man's dead daughter brought to him when he had been through all other possible misfortunes--and I said it couldn't be done as it ought to be done except by a man who had lived it--it must be written with the blood out of a man's heart. I couldn't know, then, how soon I was to be made competent. I have thought of it many a time since. If you were here I think we could cry down each other's necks, as in your dream. For we are a pair of old derelicts drifting around, now, with some of our passengers gone and the sunniness of the others in eclipse.

I couldn't get along without work now. I bury myself in it up to the ears. Long hours--8 and 9 on a stretch, sometimes. And all the days, Sundays included. It isn't all for print, by any means, for much of it fails to suit me; 50,000 words of it in the past year. It was because of the deadness which invaded me when Susy died. But I have made a change lately--into dramatic work--and I find it absorbingly entertaining. I don't know that I can write a play that will play: but no matter, I'll write half a dozen that won't, anyway. Dear me, I didn't know there was such fun in it. I'll write twenty that won't play. I get into immense spirits as soon as my day is fairly started. Of course a good deal of this friskiness comes of my being in sight of land--on the Webster & Co. debts, I mean. (Private.) We've lived close to the bone and saved every cent we could, and there's no undisputed claim, now, that we can't cash. I have marked this "private" because it is for the friends who are attending to the matter for us in New York to reveal it when they want to and if they want to. There are only two claims which I dispute and which I mean to look into personally before I pay them. But they are small. Both together they amount to only $12,500. I hope you will never get the like of the load saddled onto you that was saddled onto me 3 years ago. And yet there is such a solid pleasure in paying the things that I reckon maybe it is worth while to get into that kind of a hobble, after all. Mrs. Clemens gets millions of delight out of it; and the children have never uttered one complaint about the scrimping, from the beginning.

We all send you and all of you our love. MARK.

Howells wrote: "I wish you could understand how unshaken you are, you old tower, in every way; your foundations are struck so deep that you will catch the sunshine of immortal years, and bask in the same light as Cervantes and Shakespeare."

The Clemens apartments at the Metropole became a sort of social clearing-house of the Viennese art and literary life, much more like an embassy than the home of a mere literary man. Celebrities in every walk of life, persons of social and official rank, writers for the press, assembled there on terms hardly possible in any other home in Vienna. Wherever Mark Twain appeared in public he was a central figure. Now and then he read or spoke to aid some benefit, and these were great gatherings attended by members of the royal family. It was following one such event that the next letter was written.

(Private) To Rev. J. H. Twichell, in Hartford:

HOTEL METROPOLE, VIENNA, Feb. 3, '98. DEAR JOE, There's that letter that I began so long ago--you see how it is: can't get time to finish anything. I pile up lots of work, nevertheless. There may be idle people in the world, but I'm not one of them. I say "Private" up there because I've got an adventure to tell, and you mustn't let a breath of it get out. First I thought I would lay it up along with a thousand others that I've laid up for the same purpose--to talk to you about, but--those others have vanished out of my memory; and that must not happen with this.

The other night I lectured for a Vienna charity; and at the end of it Livy and I were introduced to a princess who is aunt to the heir apparent of the imperial throne--a beautiful lady, with a beautiful spirit, and very cordial in her praises of my books and thanks to me for writing them; and glad to meet me face to face and shake me by the hand--just the kind of princess that adorns a fairy tale and makes it the prettiest tale there is.

Very well, we long ago found that when you are noticed by supremacies, the correct etiquette is to go, within a couple of days, and pay your respects in the quite simple form of writing your name in the Visitors' Book kept in the office of the establishment. That is the end of it, and everything is squared up and ship-shape.

So at noon today Livy and I drove to the Archducal palace, and got by the sentries all right, and asked the grandly-uniformed porter for the book and said we wished to write our names in it. And he called a servant in livery and was sending us up stairs; and said her Royal Highness was out but would soon be in. Of course Livy said "No--no--we only want the book;" but he was firm, and said, "You are Americans?"

"Yes."

"Then you are expected, please go up stairs."

"But indeed we are not expected--please let us have the book and--"

"Her Royal Highness will be back in a very little while--she commanded me to tell you so--and you must wait."

Well, the soldiers were there close by--there was no use trying to resist--so we followed the servant up; but when he tried to beguile us into a drawing-room, Livy drew the line; she wouldn't go in. And she wouldn't stay up there, either. She said the princess might come in at any moment and catch us, and it would be too infernally ridiculous for anything. So we went down stairs again--to my unspeakable regret. For it was too darling a comedy to spoil. I was hoping and praying the princess would come, and catch us up there, and that those other Americans who were expected would arrive, and be taken for impostors by the portier, and shot by the sentinels--and then it would all go into the papers, and be cabled all over the world, and make an immense stir and be perfectly lovely. And by that time the princess would discover that we were not the right ones, and the Minister of War would be ordered out, and the garrison, and they would come for us, and there would be another prodigious time, and that would get cabled too, and--well, Joe, I was in a state of perfect bliss. But happily, oh, so happily, that big portier wouldn't let us out--he was sorry, but he must obey orders--we must go back up stairs and wait. Poor Livy--I couldn't help but enjoy her distress. She said we were in a fix, and how were we going to explain, if the princess should arrive before the rightful Americans came? We went up stairs again--laid off our wraps, and were conducted through one drawing room and into another, and left alone there and the door closed upon us.

Livy was in a state of mind! She said it was too theatrically ridiculous; and that I would never be able to keep my mouth shut; that I would be sure to let it out and it would get into the papers--and she tried to make me promise--"Promise what?" I said--"to be quiet about this? Indeed I won't--it's the best thing that ever happened; I'll tell it, and add to it; and I wish Joe and Howells were here to make it perfect; I can't make all the rightful blunders myself--it takes all three of us to do justice to an opportunity like this. I would just like to see Howells get down to his work and explain, and lie, and work his futile and inventionless subterfuges when that princess comes raging in here and wanting to know." But Livy could not hear fun--it was not a time to be trying to be funny--we were in a most miserable and shameful situation, and if--

Just then the door spread wide and our princess and 4 more, and 3 little princes flowed in! Our princess, and her sister the Archduchess Marie Therese (mother to the imperial Heir and to the young girl Archduchesses present, and aunt to the 3 little princes)--and we shook hands all around and sat down and had a most sociable good time for half an hour--and by and by it turned out that we were the right ones, and had been sent for by a messenger who started too late to catch us at the hotel. We were invited for 2 o'clock, but we beat that arrangement by an hour and a half.

Wasn't it a rattling good comedy situation? Seems a kind of pity we were the right ones. It would have been such nuts to see the right ones come, and get fired out, and we chatting along comfortably and nobody suspecting us for impostors.

We send lots and lots of love. MARK.

The reader who has followed these pages has seen how prone Mark Twain was to fall a victim to the lure of a patent-right--how he wasted several small fortunes on profitless contrivances, and one large one on that insatiable demon of intricacy and despair, the Paige type-setter. It seems incredible that, after that experience and its attending disaster, he should have been tempted again. But scarcely was the ink dry on the receipts from his creditors when he was once more borne into the clouds on the prospect of millions, perhaps even billions, to be made from a marvelous carpet-pattern machine, the invention of Sczezepanik, an Austrian genius. That Clemens appreciated his own tendencies is shown by the parenthetic line with which he opens his letter on the subject to Mr. Rogers. Certainly no man was ever a more perfect prototype of Colonel Sellers than the creator of that lovely, irrepressible visionary.

To Mr. Rogers, in New York:

March 24, '98. DEAR MR. ROGERS,--(I feel like Col. Sellers).

Mr. Kleinberg [agent for Sczezepanik] came according to appointment, at 8.30 last night, and brought his English-speaking Secretary. I asked questions about the auxiliary invention (which I call "No. 2 ") and got as good an idea of it as I could. It is a machine. It automatically punches the holes in the jacquard cards, and does it with mathematical accuracy. It will do for $1 what now costs $3. So it has value, but "No. 2" is the great thing(the designing invention.) It saves $9 out of $10 and the jacquard looms must have it.

Then I arrived at my new project, and said to him in substance, this:

"You are on the point of selling the No. 2 patents to Belgium, Italy, etc. I suggest that you stop those negotiations and put those people off two or three months. They are anxious now, they will not be less anxious then--just the reverse; people always want a thing that is denied them.

"So far as I know, no great world-patent has ever yet been placed in the grip of a single corporation. This is a good time to begin.

"We have to do a good deal of guess-work here, because we cannot get hold of just the statistics we want. Still, we have some good statistics--and I will use those for a test.

"You say that of the 1500 Austrian textile factories, 800 use the jacquard. Then we will guess that of the 4,000 American factories 2,000 use the jacquard and must have our No. 2.

"You say that a middle-sized Austrian factory employs from 20 to 30 designers and pays them from 800 to 3,000 odd florins a year--(a florin is 2 francs). Let us call the average wage 1500 florins ($600).

"Let us apply these figures (the low wages too) to the 2,000 American factories--with this difference, to guard against over-guessing; that instead of allowing for 20 to 30 designers to a middle-sized factory, we allow only an average of 10 to each of the 2,000 factories--a total of 20,000 designers. Wages at $600, a total of $12,000,000. Let us consider that No. 2 will reduce this expense to $2,000,000 a year. The saving is $5,000,000 per each of the $200,000,000 of capital employed in the jacquard business over there.

"Let us consider that in the countries covered by this patent, an aggregate of $1,500,000,000 of capital is employed in factories requiring No. 2.

"The saving (as above) is $75,000,000 a year. The Company holding in its grip all these patents would collar $50,000,000 of that, as its share. Possibly more.

"Competition would be at an end in the Jacquard business, on this planet. Price-cutting would end. Fluctuations in values would cease. The business would be the safest and surest in the world; commercial panics could not seriously affect it; its stock would be as choice an investment as Government bonds. When the patents died the Company would be so powerful that it could still keep the whole business in its hands. Would you like to grant me the privilege of placing the whole jacquard business of the world in the grip of a single Company? And don't you think that the business would grow-grow like a weed?"

"Ach, America--it is the country of the big! Let me get my breath--then we will talk."

So then we talked--talked till pretty late. Would Germany and England join the combination? I said the Company would know how to persuade them.

Then I asked for a Supplementary Option, to cover the world, and we parted.

I am taking all precautions to keep my name out of print in connection with this matter. And we will now keep the invention itself out of print as well as we can. Descriptions of it have been granted to the "Dry Goods Economist" (New York) and to a syndicate of American papers. I have asked Mr. Kleinberg to suppress these, and he feels pretty sure he can do it. With love, S. L. C.

If this splendid enthusiasm had not cooled by the time a reply came from Mr. Rogers, it must have received a sudden chill from the letter which he inclosed--the brief and concise report from a carpet-machine expert, who said: "I do not feel that it would be of any value to us in our mills, and the number of jacquard looms in America is so limited that I am of the opinion that there is no field for a company to develop the invention here. A cursory examination of the pamphlet leads me to place no very high value upon the invention, from a practical standpoint."

With the receipt of this letter carpet-pattern projects would seem to have suddenly ceased to be a factor in Mark Twain's calculations. Such a letter in the early days of the type-machine would have saved him a great sum in money and years of disappointment. But perhaps he would not have heeded it then.

The year 1898 brought the Spanish-American War. Clemens was constitutionally against all wars, but writing to Twichell, whose son had enlisted, we gather that this one was an exception.

To Rev. J. H. Twichell, in Hartford:

KALTENLEUTGEBEN, NEAR VIENNA, June 17, '98. DEAR JOE,--You are living your war-days over again in Dave, and it must be a strong pleasure, mixed with a sauce of apprehension--

enough to make it just schmeck, as the Germans say. Dave will come out with two or three stars on his shoulder-straps if the war holds, and then we shall all be glad it happened.

We started with Bull Run, before. Dewey and Hobson have introduced an improvement on the game this time.

I have never enjoyed a war--even in written history--as I am enjoying this one. For this is the worthiest one that was ever fought, so far as my knowledge goes. It is a worthy thing to fight for one's freedom; it is another sight finer to fight for another man's. And I think this is the first time it has been done.

Oh, never mind Charley Warner, he would interrupt the raising of Lazarus. He would say, the will has been probated, the property distributed, it will be a world of trouble to settle the rows-- better leave well enough alone; don't ever disturb anything, where it's going to break the soft smooth flow of things and wobble our tranquillity.

Company! (Sh! it happens every day--and we came out here to be quiet.)

Love to you all. MARK.

They were spending the summer at Kaltenleutgeben, a pleasant village near Vienna, but apparently not entirely quiet. Many friends came out from Vienna, including a number of visiting Americans. Clemens, however, appears to have had considerable time for writing, as we gather from the next to Howells.

To W. D. Howells, in America:

KALTENLEUTGEBEN, BEI WIEN, Aug. 16, '98. DEAR HOWELLS,--Your letter came yesterday. It then occurred to me that I might have known (per mental telegraph) that it was due; for a couple of weeks ago when the Weekly came containing that handsome reference to me I was powerfully moved to write you; and my letter went on writing itself while I was at work at my other literature during the day. But next day my other literature was still urgent--and so on and so on; so my letter didn't get put into ink at all. But I see now, that you were writing, about that time, therefore a part of my stir could have come across the Atlantic per mental telegraph. In 1876 or '75 I wrote 40,000 words of a story called "Simon Wheeler" wherein the nub was the preventing of an execution through testimony furnished by mental telegraph from the other side of the globe. I had a lot of people scattered about the globe who carried in their pockets something like the old mesmerizer-button, made of different metals, and when they wanted to call up each other and have a talk, they "pressed the button" or did something, I don't remember what, and communication was at once opened. I didn't finish the story, though I re-began it in several new ways, and spent altogether 70,000 words on it, then gave it up and threw it aside.

This much as preliminary to this remark: some day people will be able to call each other up from any part of the world and talk by mental telegraph--and not merely by impression, the impression will be articulated into words. It could be a terrible thing, but it won't be, because in the upper civilizations everything like sentimentality (I was going to say sentiment) will presently get materialized out of people along with the already fading spiritualities; and so when a man is called who doesn't wish to talk he will be like those visitors you mention: "not chosen"--and will be frankly damned and shut off.

Speaking of the ill luck of starting a piece of literary work wrong-and again and again; always aware that there is a way, if you could only think it out, which would make the thing slide effortless from the pen- the one right way, the sole form for you, the other forms being for men whose line those forms are, or who are capabler than yourself: I've had no end of experience in that (and maybe I am the only one--let us hope so.) Last summer I started 16 things wrong--3 books and 13 mag. articles--and could only make 2 little wee things, 1500 words altogether, succeed:--only that out of piles and stacks of diligently-wrought MS., the labor of 6 weeks' unremitting effort. I could make all of those things go if I would take the trouble to re-begin each one half a dozen times on a new plan. But none of them was important enough except one: the story I (in the wrong form) mapped out in Paris three or four years ago and told you about in New York under seal of confidence--no other person knows of it but Mrs. Clemens--the story to be called "Which was the Dream?"

A week ago I examined the MS--10,000 words--and saw that the plan was a totally impossible one-for me; but a new plan suggested itself, and straightway the tale began to slide from the pen with ease and confidence. I think I've struck the right one this time. I have already put 12,000 words of it on paper and Mrs. Clemens is pretty outspokenly satisfied with it-a hard critic to content. I feel sure that all of the first half of the story--and I hope three-fourths--will be comedy; but by the former plan the whole of it (except the first 3 chapters) would have been tragedy and unendurable, almost. I think I can carry the reader a long way before he suspects that I am laying a tragedy-trap. In the present form I could spin 16 books out of it with comfort and joy; but I shall deny myself and restrict it to one. (If you should see a little short story in a magazine in the autumn called "My Platonic Sweetheart" written 3 weeks ago) that is not this one. It may have been a suggester, though.

I expect all these singular privacies to interest you, and you are not to let on that they don't.

We are leaving, this afternoon, for Ischl, to use that as a base for the baggage, and then gad around ten days among the lakes and mountains to rest-up Mrs. Clemens, who is jaded with housekeeping. I hope I can get a chance to work a little in spots--I can't tell. But you do it--therefore why should you think I can't?

[Remainder missing.]

The dream story was never completed. It was the same that he had worked on in London, and perhaps again in Switzerland. It would be tried at other times and in other forms, but it never seemed to accommodate itself to a central idea, so that the good writing in it eventually went to waste. The short story mentioned, "My Platonic Sweetheart," a charming, idyllic tale, was not published during Mark Twain's lifetime. Two years after his death it appeared in Harper's Magazine.

The assassination of the Empress of Austria at Geneva was the startling event of that summer. In a letter to Twichell Clemens presents the tragedy in a few vivid paragraphs. Later he treated it at some length in a magazine article which, very likely because of personal relations with members of the Austrian court, he withheld from print. It has since been included in a volume of essays, What Is Man, etc.

To Rev. J. H. Twichell, in Hartford:

KALTENLEUTGEBEN, Sep. 13, '98. DEAR JOE,--You are mistaken; people don't send us the magazines. No-- Harper, Century and McClure do; an example I should like to recommend to other publishers. And so I thank you very much for sending me Brander's article. When you say "I like Brander Matthews; he impresses me as a man of parts and power," I back you, right up to the hub--I feel the same way--. And when you say he has earned your gratitude for cuffing me for my crimes against the Leather stockings and the Vicar, I ain't making any objection. Dern your gratitude!

His article is as sound as a nut. Brander knows literature, and loves it; he can talk about it and keep his temper; he can state his case so lucidly and so fairly and so forcibly that you have to agree with him, even when you don't agree with him; and he can discover and praise such merits as a book has, even when they are half a dozen diamonds scattered through an acre of mud. And so he has a right to be a critic.

To detail just the opposite of the above invoice is to describe me. I haven't any right to criticise books, and I don't do it except when I hate them. I often want to criticise Jane Austen, but her books madden me so that I can't conceal my frenzy from the reader; and therefore I have to stop every time I begin.

That good and unoffending lady the Empress is killed by a mad-man, and I am living in the midst of world-history again. The Queen's jubilee last year, the invasion of the Reichsrath by the police, and now this murder, which will still be talked of and described and painted a thousand years from now. To have a personal friend of the wearer of the crown burst in at the gate in the deep dusk of the evening and say in a voice broken with tears, "My God the Empress is murdered," and fly toward her home before we can utter a question-why, it brings the giant event home to you, makes you a part of it and personally interested; it is as if your neighbor Antony should come flying and say "Caesar is butchered--the head of the world is fallen!"

Of course there is no talk but of this. The mourning is universal and genuine, the consternation is stupefying. The Austrian Empire is being draped with black. Vienna will be a spectacle to see, by next Saturday, when the funeral cortege marches. We are invited to occupy a room in the sumptuous new hotel (the "Krantz" where we are to live during the Fall and Winter) and view it, and we shall go.

Speaking of Mrs. Leiter, there is a noble dame in Vienna, about whom they retail similar slanders. She said in French--she is weak in French--that she had been spending a Sunday afternoon in a gathering of the "demimonde." Meaning the unknown land, that mercantile land, that mysterious half-world which underlies the aristocracy. But these Malaproperies are always inventions--they don't happen.

Yes, I wish we could have some talks; I'm full to the eye-lids. Had a noble good one with Parker and Dunham--land, but we were grateful for that visit! Yours with all our loves. MARK.

[Inclosed with the foregoing.]

Among the inadequate attempts to account for the assassination we must concede high rank to the German Emperor's. He justly describes it as a "deed unparalleled for ruthlessness," and then adds that it was "ordained from above."

I think this verdict will not be popular "above." A man is either a free agent or he isn't. If a man is a free agent, this prisoner is responsible for what he has done; but if a man is not a free agent, if the deed was ordained from above, there is no rational way of making this prisoner even partially responsible for it, and the German court cannot condemn him without manifestly committing a crime. Logic is logic; and by disregarding its laws even Emperors as capable and acute as William II can be beguiled into making charges which should not be ventured upon except in the shelter of plenty of lightning-rods. MARK.

The end of the year 1898 found Mark Twain once more in easy, even luxurious, circumstances. The hard work and good fortune which had enabled him to pay his debts had, in the course of another year, provided what was comparative affluence: His report to Howells is characteristic and interesting.

To W. D. Howells, in New York:

HOTEL KRANTZ, WIEN, L. NEVER MARKT 6 Dec. 30, '98. DEAR HOWELLS,--I begin with a date--including all the details--though I shall be interrupted presently by a South-African acquaintance who is passing through, and it may be many days before I catch another leisure moment. Note how suddenly a thing can become habit, and how indestructible the habit is, afterward! In your house in Cambridge a hundred years ago, Mrs. Howells said to me, "Here is a bunch of your letters, and the dates are of no value, because you don't put any in-- the years, anyway." That remark diseased me with a habit which has cost me worlds of time and torture and ink, and millions of vain efforts and buckets of tears to break it, and here it is yet--I could easier get rid of a virtue.....

I hope it will interest you (for I have no one else who would much care to know it) that here lately the dread of leaving the children in difficult circumstances has died down and disappeared and I am now having peace from that long, long nightmare, and can sleep as well as anyone.

Every little while, for these three years, now, Mrs. Clemens has come with pencil and paper and figured up the condition of things (she keeps the accounts and the bank-book) and has proven to me that the clouds were lifting, and so has hoisted my spirits temporarily and kept me going till another figuring-up was necessary. Last night she figured up for her own satisfaction, not mine, and found that we own a house and furniture in Hartford; that my English and American copyrights pay an income which represents a value of $200,000; and that we have $107,000 cash in the bank. I have been out and bought a box of 6-cent cigars; I was smoking 4 1/2 centers before.

At the house of an English friend, on Christmas Eve, we saw the Mouse- Trap played and well played. I thought the house would kill itself with laughter. By George they played with life! and it was most devastatingly funny. And it was well they did, for they put us Clemenses in the front seat, and if they played it poorly I would have assaulted them. The head young man and girl were Americans, the other parts were taken by English, Irish and Scotch girls. Then there was a nigger-minstrel show, of the genuine old sort, and I enjoyed that, too, for the nigger-show was always a passion of mine. This one was created and managed by a Quaker doctor from Philada., (23 years old) and he was the middle man. There were 9 others--5 Americans from 5 States and a Scotchman, 2 Englishmen and an Irishman--all post-graduate-medical young fellows, of course-- or, it could be music; but it would be bound to be one or the other.

It's quite true--I don't read you "as much as I ought," nor anywhere near half as much as I want to; still I read you all I get a chance to. I saved up your last story to read when the numbers should be complete, but before that time arrived some other admirer of yours carried off the papers. I will watch admirers of yours when the Silver Wedding journey begins, and that will not happen again. The last chance at a bound book of yours was in London nearly two years ago--the last volume of your short things, by the Harpers. I read the whole book twice through and some of the chapters several times, and the reason that that was as far as I got with it was that I lent it to another admirer of yours and he is admiring it yet. Your admirers have ways of their own; I don't know where they get them.

Yes, our project is to go home next autumn if we find we can afford to live in New York. We've asked a friend to inquire about flats and expenses. But perhaps nothing will come of it. We do afford to live in the finest hotel in Vienna, and have 4 bedrooms, a dining-room, a drawing-room, 3 bath-rooms and 3 Vorzimmers, (and food) but we couldn't get the half of it in New York for the same money ($600 a month).

Susy hovers about us this holiday week, and the shadows fall all about us of

"The days when we went gipsying A long time ago."

Death is so kind, so benignant, to whom he loves; but he goes by us others and will not look our way. We saw the "Master of Palmyra" last night. How Death, with the gentleness and majesty, made the human grand- folk around him seem little and trivial and silly!

With love from all of us to all of you. MARK.

XXXVIII

LETTERS, 1899, TO HOWELLS AND OTHERS. VIENNA. LONDON. A SUMMER IN SWEDEN

The beginning of 1899 found the Clemens family still in Vienna, occupying handsome apartments at the Hotel Krantz. Their rooms, so often thronged with gay and distinguished people, were sometimes called the "Second Embassy." Clemens himself was the central figure of these assemblies. Of all the foreign visitors in the Austrian capital he was the most notable. Everywhere he was surrounded by a crowd of listeners--his sayings and opinions were widely quoted.

A project for world disarmament promulgated by the Czar of Russia would naturally interest Mark Twain, and when William T. Stead, of the Review of Reviews, cabled him for an opinion on the matter, he sent at first a brief word and on the same day followed it with more extended comment. The great war which has since devastated the world gives to this incident an added interest.

To Wm. T. Stead, in London:

No. 1. VIENNA, Jan. 9. DEAR MR. STEAD,-The Czar is ready to disarm: I am ready to disarm. Collect the others, it should not be much of a task now. MARK TWAIN.

To Wm. T. Stead, in London:

No. 2. DEAR MR. STEAD,--Peace by compulsion. That seems a better idea than the other. Peace by persuasion has a pleasant sound, but I think we should not be able to work it. We should have to tame the human race first, and history seems to show that that cannot be done. Can't we reduce the armaments little by little--on a pro rata basis--by concert of the powers? Can't we get four great powers to agree to reduce their strength 10 per cent a year and thrash the others into doing likewise? For, of course, we cannot expect all of the powers to be in their right minds at one time. It has been tried. We are not going to try to get all of them to go into the scheme peaceably, are we? In that case I must withdraw my influence; because, for business reasons, I must preserve the outward signs of sanity. Four is enough if they can be securely harnessed together. They can compel peace, and peace without compulsion would be against nature and not operative. A sliding scale of reduction of 10 per cent a year has a sort of plausible look, and I am willing to try that if three other powers will join. I feel sure that the armaments are now many times greater than necessary for the requirements of either peace or war. Take wartime for instance. Suppose circumstances made it necessary for us to fight another Waterloo, and that it would do what it did before--settle a large question and bring peace. I will guess that 400,000 men were on hand at Waterloo (I have forgotten the figures). In five hours they disabled 50,000 men. It took them that tedious, long time because the firearms delivered only two or three shots a minute. But we would do the work now as it was done at Omdurman, with shower guns, raining 600 balls a minute. Four men to a gun--is that the number? A hundred and fifty shots a minute per man. Thus a modern soldier is 149 Waterloo soldiers in one. Thus, also, we can now retain one man out of each 150 in service, disband the others, and fight our Waterloos just as effectively as we did eighty-five years ago. We should do the same beneficent job with 2,800 men now that we did with 400,000 then. The allies could take 1,400 of the men, and give Napoleon 1,400 and then whip him.

But instead what do we see? In war-time in Germany, Russia and France, taken together we find about 8 million men equipped for the field. Each man represents 149 Waterloo men, in usefulness and killing capacity. Altogether they constitute about 350 million Waterloo men, and there are not quite that many grown males of the human race now on this planet. Thus we have this insane fact--that whereas those three countries could arm 18,000 men with modern weapons and make them the equals of 3 million men of Napoleon's day, and accomplish with them all necessary war work, they waste their money and their prosperity creating forces of their populations in piling together 349,982,000 extra Waterloo equivalents which they would have no sort of use for if they would only stop drinking and sit down and cipher a little.

Perpetual peace we cannot have on any terms, I suppose; but I hope we can gradually reduce the war strength of Europe till we get it down to where it ought to be--20,000 men, properly armed. Then we can have all the peace that is worth while, and when we want a war anybody can afford it.

VIENNA, January 9. P. S.--In the article I sent the figures are wrong--"350 million" ought to be 450 million; "349,982,000" ought to be 449,982,000, and the remark about the sum being a little more than the present number of males on the planet--that is wrong, of course; it represents really one and a half the existing males.

Now and then one of Mark Twain's old comrades still reached out to him across the years. He always welcomed such letters--they came as from a lost land of romance, recalled always with tenderness. He sent light, chaffing replies, but they were never without an undercurrent of affection.

To Major "Jack" Downing, in Middleport, Ohio:

HOTEL KRANTZ, WEIN, I, NEUER MART 6, Feb. 26, 1899. DEAR MAJOR,--No: it was to Bixby that I was apprenticed. He was to teach me the river for a certain specified sum. I have forgotten what it was, but I paid it. I steered a trip for Bart Bowen, of Keokuk, on the A. T. Lacy, and I was partner with Will Bowen on the A. B. Chambers (one trip), and with Sam Bowen a whole summer on a small Memphis packet.

The newspaper report you sent me is incorrect. Bixby is not 67: he is 97. I am 63 myself, and I couldn't talk plain and had just begun to walk when I apprenticed myself to Bixby who was then passing himself off for 57 and successfully too, for he always looked 60 or 70 years younger than he really was. At that time he was piloting the Mississippi on a Potomac commission granted him by George Washington who was a personal friend of his before the Revolution. He has piloted every important river in America, on that commission, he has also used it as a passport in Russia. I have never revealed these facts before. I notice, too, that you are deceiving the people concerning your age. The printed portrait which you have enclosed is not a portrait of you, but a portrait of me when I was 19. I remember very well when it was common for people to mistake Bixby for your grandson. Is it spreading, I wonder--this disposition of pilots to renew their youth by doubtful methods? Beck Jolly and Joe Bryan--they probably go to Sunday school now--but it will not deceive.

Yes, it is as you say. All of the procession but a fraction has passed. It is time for us all to fall in. Sincerely yours, S. L. CLEMENS.

To W. D. Howells, in New York:

HOTEL KRANTZ, WIEN I. NEUER MARKT 6 April 2, '99. DEAR HOWELLS,--I am waiting for the April Harper, which is about due now; waiting, and strongly interested. You are old enough to be a weary man, with paling interests, but you do not show it. You do your work in the same old delicate and delicious and forceful and searching and perfect way. I don't know how you can--but I suspect. I suspect that to you there is still dignity in human life, and that Man is not a joke--a poor joke--the poorest that was ever contrived. Since I wrote my Bible, (last year)--["What Is Man."]--which Mrs. Clemens loathes, and shudders over, and will not listen to the last half nor allow me to print any part of it, Man is not to me the respect-worthy person he was before; and so I have lost my pride in him, and can't write gaily nor praisefully about him any more. And I don't intend to try. I mean to go on writing, for that is my best amusement, but I shan't print much. (for I don't wish to be scalped, any more than another.)

April 5. The Harper has come. I have been in Leipzig with your party, and then went on to Karlsbad and saw Mrs. Marsh's encounter with the swine with the toothpick and the other manners--["Their Silver Wedding Journey."]--At this point Jean carried the magazine away.

Is it imagination, or--Anyway I seem to get furtive and fleeting glimpses which I take to be the weariness and condolence of age; indifference to sights and things once brisk with interest; tasteless stale stuff which used to be champagne; the boredom of travel: the secret sigh behind the public smile, the private What-in-hell-did-I-come-for!

But maybe that is your art. Maybe that is what you intend the reader to detect and think he has made a Columbus-discovery. Then it is well done, perfectly done. I wrote my last travel book--[Following the Equator.]-- in hell; but I let on, the best I could, that it was an excursion through heaven. Some day I will read it, and if its lying cheerfulness fools me, then I shall believe it fooled the reader. How I did loathe that journey around the world!--except the sea-part and India.

Evening. My tail hangs low. I thought I was a financier--and I bragged to you. I am not bragging, now. The stock which I sold at such a fine profit early in January, has never ceased to advance, and is now worth $60,000 more than I sold it for. I feel just as if I had been spending $20,000 a month, and I feel reproached for this showy and unbecoming extravagance.

Last week I was going down with the family to Budapest to lecture, and to make a speech at a banquet. Just as I was leaving here I got a telegram from London asking for the speech for a New York paper. I (this is strictly private) sent it. And then I didn't make that speech, but another of a quite different character--a speech born of something which the introducer said. If that said speech got cabled and printed, you needn't let on that it was never uttered.

That was a darling night, and those Hungarians were lively people. We were there a week and had a great time. At the banquet I heard their chief orator make a most graceful and easy and beautiful and delicious speech--I never heard one that enchanted me more--although I did not understand a word of it, since it was in Hungarian. But the art of it!- it was superlative.

They are wonderful English scholars, these people; my lecture audience-- all Hungarians-- understood me perfectly--to judge by the effects. The English clergyman told me that in his congregation are 150 young English women who earn their living teaching their language; and that there are. others besides these.

For 60 cents a week the telephone reads the morning news to you at home; gives you the stocks and markets at noon; gives you lessons in 3 foreign languages during 3 hours; gives you the afternoon telegrams; and at night the concerts and operas. Of course even the clerks and seamstresses and bootblacks and everybody else are subscribers.

(Correction. Mrs. Clemens says it is 60 cents a month.)

I am renewing my youth. I made 4 speeches at one banquet here last Saturday night. And I've been to a lot of football matches.

Jean has been in here examining the poll for the Immortals ("Literature," March 24,) in the hope, I think, that at last she should find me at the top and you in second place; and if that is her ambition she has suffered disappointment for the third time--and will never fare any better, I hope, for you are where you belong, by every right. She wanted to know who it is that does the voting, but I was not able to tell her. Nor when the election will be completed and decided.

Next Morning. I have been reading the morning paper. I do it every morning--well knowing that I shall find in it the usual depravities and basenesses and hypocrisies and cruelties that make up civilization, and cause me to put in the rest of the day pleading for the damnation of the human race. I cannot seem to get my prayers answered, yet I do not despair.

(Escaped from) 5 o'clock tea. ('sh!) Oh, the American girl in Europe! Often she is creditable, but sometimes she is just shocking. This one, a minute ago--19, fat-face, raspy voice, pert ways, the self-complacency of God; and with it all a silly laugh (embarrassed) which kept breaking out through her chatter all along, whereas there was no call for it, for she said nothing that was funny. "Spose so many 've told y' how they 'njoyed y'r chapt'r on the Germ' tongue it's bringin' coals to Newcastle Kehe! say anything 'bout it Ke-hehe! Spent m' vacation 'n Russia, 'n saw Tolstoi; he said--" It made me shudder.

April 12. Jean has been in here with a copy of Literature, complaining that I am again behind you in the election of the 10 consecrated members; and seems troubled about it and not quite able to understand it. But I have explained to her that you are right there on the ground, inside the pool-booth, keeping game--and that that makes a large difference in these things.

13th. I have been to the Knustausstellung with Mrs. Clemens. The office of art seems to be to grovel in the dirt before Emperors and this and that and the other damned breed of priests. Yrs ever MARK.

Howells and Clemens were corresponding regularly again, though not with the frequency of former years. Perhaps neither of them was bubbling over with things to say; perhaps it was becoming yearly less attractive to pick up a pen and write, and then, of course, there was always the discouragement of distance. Once Howells wrote: "I know this will find you in Austria before I can well turn round, but I must make believe you are in Kennebunkport before I can begin it." And in another letter: "It ought to be as pleasant to sit down and write to you as to sit down and talk to you, but it isn't..... The only reason why I write is that I want another letter from you, and because I have a whole afternoon for the job. I have the whole of every afternoon, for I cannot work later than lunch. I am fagged by that time, and Sunday is the only day that brings unbearable leisure. I hope you will be in New York another winter; then I shall know what to do with these foretastes of eternity."

Clemens usually wrote at considerable length, for he had a good deal to report of his life in the Austrian capital, now drawing to a close.

To W. D. Howells, in New York:

May 12, 1899. DEAR HOWELLS,--7.15 p. m. Tea (for Mr. and Mrs. Tower, who are leaving for Russia) just over; nice people and rather creditable to the human race: Mr. and Mrs. Tower; the new Minister and his wife; the Secretary of Legation; the Naval (and Military) Attach; several English ladies; an Irish lady; a Scotch lady; a particularly nice young Austrian baron who wasn't invited but came and went supposing it was the usual thing and wondered at the unusually large gathering; two other Austrians and several Americans who were also in his fix; the old Baronin Langeman, the only Austrian invited; the rest were Americans. It made just a comfortable crowd in our parlor, with an overflow into Clara's through the folding doors. I don't enjoy teas, and am daily spared them by Mrs. Clemens, but this was a pleasant one. I had only one accident. The old Baronin Langeman is a person I have a strong fondness for, for we violently disagree on some subjects and as violently agree on others-- for instance, she is temperance and I am not: she has religious beliefs and feelings and I have none; (she's a Methodist!) she is a democrat and so am I; she is woman's rights and so am I; she is laborers' rights and approves trades unions and strikes, and that is me. And so on. After she was gone an English lady whom I greatly like, began to talk sharply against her for contributing money, time, labor, and public expression of favor to a strike that is on (for an 11-hour day) in the silk factories of Bohemia--and she caught me unprepared and betrayed me into over-warm argument. I am sorry: for she didn't know anything about the subject, and I did; and one should be gentle with the ignorant, for they are the chosen of God.

(The new Minister is a good man, but out of place. The Sec. of Legation is a good man, but out of place. The Attache is a good man, but out of place. Our government for displacement beats the new White Star ship; and her possible is 17,200 tons.)

May 13, 4 p. m. A beautiful English girl and her handsome English husband came up and spent the evening, and she certainly is a bird. English parents--she was born and reared in Roumania and couldn't talk English till she was 8 or 10. She came up clothed like the sunset, and was a delight to look at. (Roumanian costume.).....

Twenty-four young people have gone out to the Semmering to-day (and to- morrow) and Mrs. Clemens and an English lady and old Leschetitzky and his wife have gone to chaperon them. They gave me a chance to go, but there are no snow mountains that I want to look at. Three hours out, three hours back, and sit up all night watching the young people dance; yelling conversationally and being yelled at, conversationally, by new acquaintances, through the deafening music, about how I like Vienna, and if it's my first visit, and how long we expect to stay, and did I see the foot-washing, and am I writing a book about Vienna, and so on. The terms seemed too severe. Snow mountains are too dear at the price ....

For several years I have been intending to stop writing for print as soon as I could afford it. At last I can afford it, and have put the pot- boiler pen away. What I have been wanting is a chance to write a book without reserves--a book which should take account of no one's feelings, and no one's prejudices, opinions, beliefs, hopes, illusions, delusions; a book which should say my say, right out of my heart, in the plainest language and without a limitation of any sort. I judged that that would be an unimaginable luxury, heaven on earth.

It is under way, now, and it is a luxury! an intellectual drunk: Twice I didn't start it right; and got pretty far in, both times, before I found it out. But I am sure it is started right this time. It is in tale-form. I believe I can make it tell what I think of Man, and how he is constructed, and what a shabby poor ridiculous thing he is, and how mistaken he is in his estimate of his character and powers and qualities and his place among the animals.

So far, I think I am succeeding. I let the madam into the secret day before yesterday, and locked the doors and read to her the opening chapters. She said--

"It is perfectly horrible--and perfectly beautiful!"

"Within the due limits of modesty, that is what I think."

I hope it will take me a year or two to write it, and that it will turn out to be the right vessel to contain all the abuse I am planning to dump into it. Yours ever MARK.

The story mentioned in the foregoing, in which Mark Twain was to give his opinion of man, was The Mysterious Stranger. It was not finished at the time, and its closing chapter was not found until after his death. Six years later (1916) it was published serially in Harper's Magazine, and in book form.

The end of May found the Clemens party in London, where they were received and entertained with all the hospitality they had known in earlier years. Clemens was too busy for letter-writing, but in the midst of things he took time to report to Howells an amusing incident of one of their entertainments.

To W. D. Howells, in America:

LONDON, July 3, '99 DEAR HOWELLS,--..... I've a lot of things to write you, but it's no use-- I can't get time for anything these days. I must break off and write a postscript to Canon Wilberforce before I go to bed. This afternoon he left a luncheon-party half an hour ahead of the rest, and carried off my hat (which has Mark Twain in a big hand written in it.) When the rest of us came out there was but one hat that would go on my head--it fitted exactly, too. So wore it away. It had no name in it, but the Canon was the only man who was absent. I wrote him a note at 8 p.m.; saying that for four hours I had not been able to take anything that did not belong to me, nor stretch a fact beyond the frontiers of truth, and my family were getting alarmed. Could he explain my trouble? And now at 8.30 p.m. comes a note from him to say that all the afternoon he has been exhibiting a wonder-compelling mental vivacity and grace of expression, etc., etc., and have I missed a hat? Our letters have crossed. Yours ever MARK.

News came of the death of Robert Ingersoll. Clemens had been always one of his most ardent admirers, and a warm personal friend. To Ingersoll's niece he sent a word of heartfelt sympathy.

To Miss Eva Farrell, in New York:

30 WELLINGTON COURT, ALBERT GATE. DEAR MISS FARRELL,--Except my daughter's, I have not grieved for any death as I have grieved for his. His was a great and beautiful spirit, he was a man--all man from his crown to his foot soles. My reverence for him was deep and genuine; I prized his affection for me and returned it with usury. Sincerely Yours, S. L. CLEMENS.

Clemens and family decided to spend the summer in Sweden, at Sauna, in order to avail themselves of osteopathic treatment as practised by Heinrick Kellgren. Kellgren's method, known as the "Swedish movements," seemed to Mark Twain a wonderful cure for all ailments, and he heralded the discovery far and wide. He wrote to friends far and near advising them to try Kellgren for anything they might happen to have. Whatever its beginning, any letter was likely to close with some mention of the new panacea.

To Rev. J. H. Twichell, traveling in Europe:

SANNA, Sept. 6, '99. DEAR JOE,--I've no business in here--I ought to be outside. I shall never see another sunset to begin with it this side of heaven. Venice? land, what a poor interest that is! This is the place to be. I have seen about 60 sunsets here; and a good 40 of them were clear and away beyond anything I had ever imagined before for dainty and exquisite and marvellous beauty and infinite change and variety. America? Italy? The tropics? They have no notion of what a sunset ought to be. And this one--this unspeakable wonder! It discounts all the rest. It brings the tears, it is so unutterably beautiful.

If I had time, I would say a word about this curative system here. The people actually do several of the great things the Christian Scientists pretend to do. You wish to advise with a physician about it? Certainly. There is no objection. He knows next to something about his own trade, but that will not embarrass him in framing a verdict about this one. I respect your superstitions--we all have them. It would be quite natural for the cautious Chinaman to ask his native priest to instruct him as to the value of the new religious specialty which the Western missionary is trying to put on the market, before investing in it. (He would get a verdict.) Love to you all! Always Yours MARK.

Howells wrote that he was going on a reading-tour-dreading it, of course-and asking for any advice that Clemens felt qualified to give. Naturally, Clemens gave him the latest he had in stock, without realizing, perhaps, that he was recommending an individual practice which few would be likely to imitate. Nevertheless, what he says is interesting.

To W. D. Howells, in America:

SANNA, SWEDEN, Sept. 26, '99. DEAR HOWELLS,--Get your lecture by heart--it will pay you. I learned a trick in Vienna--by accident--which I wish I had learned years ago. I meant to read from a Tauchnitz, because I knew I hadn't well memorized the pieces; and I came on with the book and read a few sentences, then remembered that the sketch needed a few words of explanatory introduction; and so, lowering the book and now and then unconsciously using it to gesture with, I talked the introduction, and it happened to carry me into the sketch itself, and then I went on, pretending that I was merely talking extraneous matter and would come to the sketch presently. It was a beautiful success. I knew the substance of the sketch and the telling phrases of it; and so, the throwing of the rest of it into informal talk as I went along limbered it up and gave it the snap and go and freshness of an impromptu. I was to read several pieces, and I played the same game with all of them, and always the audience thought I was being reminded of outside things and throwing them in, and was going to hold up the book and begin on the sketch presently--and so I always got through the sketch before they were entirely sure that it had begun. I did the same thing in Budapest and had the same good time over again. It's a new dodge, and the best one that was ever invented. Try it. You'll never lose your audience--not even for a moment. Their attention is fixed, and never wavers. And that is not the case where one reads from book or MS., or where he stands up without a note and frankly exposes the fact, by his confident manner and smooth phrasing, that he is not improvising, but reciting from memory. And in the heat of telling a thing that is memorised in substance only, one flashes out the happiest suddenly-begotten phrases every now and then! Try it. Such a phrase has a life and sparkle about it that twice as good a one could not exhibit if prepared beforehand, and it "fetches" an audience in such an enthusing and inspiring and uplifting way that that lucky phrase breeds another one, sure.

Your September instalment--["Their Silver Wedding journey."]--was delicious--every word of it. You haven't lost any of your splendid art. Callers have arrived. With love MARK.

"Yes," wrote Howells, "if I were a great histrionic artist like you I would get my poor essays by heart, and recite them, but being what I am I should do the thing so lifelessly that I had better recognise their deadness frankly and read them."

From Vienna Clemens had contributed to the Cosmopolitan, then owned by John Brisben Walker, his first article on Christian Science. It was a delicious bit of humor and found such enthusiastic appreciation that Walker was moved to send an additional $200 check in payment for it. This brought prompt acknowledgment.

To John Brisben Walker, in Irvington, N. Y.:

LONDON, Oct. 19, '99 DEAR MR. WALKER,--By gracious but you have a talent for making a man feel proud and good! To say a compliment well is a high art--and few possess it. You know how to do it, and when you confirm its sincerity with a handsome cheque the limit is reached and compliment can no higher go. I like to work for you: when you don't approve an article you say so, recognizing that I am not a child and can stand it; and when you approve an article I don't have to dicker with you as if I raised peanuts and you kept a stand; I know I shall get every penny the article is worth.

You have given me very great pleasure, and I thank you for it. Sincerely Yours S. L. CLEMENS.

On the same day he sent word to Howells of the good luck which now seemed to be coming his way. The Joan of Arc introduction was the same that today appears in his collected works under the title of Saint Joan of Arc.

To W. D. Howells, in New York:

LONDON, Oct. 19, '99. DEAR HOWELLS,--My, it's a lucky day!--of the sort when it never rains but it pours. I was to write an introduction to a nobler book--the English translation of the Official Record (unabridged) of the Trials and Rehabilitation of Joan of Arc, and make a lot of footnotes. I wrote the introduction in Sweden, and here a few days ago I tore loose from a tale I am writing, and took the MS book and went at the grind of note-making --a fearful job for a man not used to it. This morning brought a note from my excellent friend Murray, a rich Englishman who edits the translation, saying, "Never mind the notes--we'll make the translators do them." That was comfort and joy.

The same mail brought a note from Canon Wilberforce, asking me to talk Joan of Arc in his drawing-room to the Dukes and Earls and M. P.'s-- (which would fetch me out of my seclusion and into print, and I couldn't have that,) and so of course I must run down to the Abbey and explain-- and lose an hour. Just then came Murray and said "Leave that to me --I'll go and do the explaining and put the thing off 3 months; you write a note and tell him I am coming."

(Which I did, later.) Wilberforce carried off my hat from a lunch party last summer, and in to-day's note he said he wouldn't steal my new hat this time. In my note I said I couldn't make the drawing-room talk, now --Murray would explain; and added a P. S.: "You mustn't think it is because I am afraid to trust my hat in your reach again, for I assure you upon honor it isn't. I should bring my old one."

I had suggested to Murray a fortnight ago, that he get some big guns to write introductory monographs for the book.

Miss X, Joan's Voices and Prophecies.

The Lord Chief Justice of England, the legal prodigies which she performed before her judges.

Lord Roberts, her military genius.

Kipling, her patriotism.

And so on. When he came this morning he said he had captured Miss X; that Lord Roberts and Kipling were going to take hold and see if they could do monographs worthy of the book. He hadn't run the others to cover yet, but was on their track. Very good news. It is a grand book, and is entitled to the best efforts of the best people. As for me, I took pains with my Introduction, and I admit that it is no slouch of a performance.

Then I came down to Chatto's, and found your all too beautiful letter, and was lifted higher than ever. Next came letters from America properly glorifying my Christian Science article in the Cosmopolitan (and one roundly abusing it,) and a letter from John Brisben Walker enclosing $200 additional pay for the article (he had already paid enough, but I didn't mention that--which wasn't right of me, for this is the second time he has done such a thing, whereas Gilder has done it only once and no one else ever.) I make no prices with Walker and Gilder--I can trust them.

And last of all came a letter from M-. How I do wish that man was in hell. Even-the briefest line from that idiot puts me in a rage.

But on the whole it has been a delightful day, and with M----in hell it would have been perfect. But that will happen, and I can wait.

Ah, if I could look into the inside of people as you do, and put it on paper, and invent things for them to do and say, and tell how they said it, I could writs a fine and readable book now, for I've got a prime subject. I've written 30,000 words of it and satisfied myself that the stuff is there; so I am going to discard that MS and begin all over again and have a good time with it.

Oh, I know how you feel! I've been in hell myself. You are there tonight. By difference in time you are at luncheon, now--and not eating it. Nothing is so lonesome as gadding around platforming. I have declined 45 lectures to-day-England and Scotland. I wanted the money, but not the torture: Good luck to you!--and repentance. With love to all of you MARK.

LETTERS OF 1900, MAINLY TO TWICHELL. THE BOER WAR. BOXER TROUBLES. THE RETURN TO AMERICA

The New Year found Clemens still in London, chiefly interested in osteopathy and characteristically glorifying the practice at the expense of other healing methods.

To Rev. J. H. Twichell, in Hartford:

LONDON, Jan. 8, 1900. DEAR JOE,--Mental Telepathy has scored another. Mental Telegraphy will be greatly respected a century hence.

By the accident of writing my sister and describing to her the remarkable cures made by Kellgren with his hands and without drugs, I brought upon myself a quite stunning surprise; for she wrote to me that she had been taking this very treatment in Buffalo--and that it was an American invention.

Well, it does really turn out that Dr. Still, in the middle of Kansas, in a village, began to experiment in 1874, only five years after Kellgren began the same work obscurely in the village of Gotha, in Germany. Dr. Still seems to be an honest man; therefore I am persuaded that Kellgren moved him to his experiments by Mental Telegraphy across six hours of longitude, without need of a wire. By the time Still began to experiment, Kellgren had completed his development of the principles of his system and established himself in a good practice in London--1874 --and was in good shape to convey his discovery to Kansas, Mental Telegraphically.

Yes, I was greatly surprised to find that my mare's nest was much in arrears: that this new science was well known in America under the name of Osteopathy. Since then, I find that in the past 3 years it has got itself legalized in 14 States in spite of the opposition of the physicians; that it has established 20 Osteopathic schools and colleges; that among its students are 75 allopathic physicians; that there is a school in Boston and another in Philadelphia, that there are about 100 students in the parent college (Dr. Still's at Kirksville, Missouri,) and that there are about 2,000 graduates practicing in America. Dear me, there are not 30 in Europe. Europe is so sunk in superstitions and prejudices that it is an almost impossible thing to get her to do anything but scoff at a new thing--unless it come from abroad; as witness the telegraph, dentistry, &c.

Presently the Osteopath will come over here from America and will soon make himself a power that must be recognized and reckoned with; and then, 25 years from now, England will begin to claim the invention and tell all about its origin, in the Cyclopedia B-----as in the case of the telegraph, applied anaesthetics and the other benefactions which she heaped her abuse upon when her inventors first offered them to her.

I cannot help feeling rather inordinately proud of America for the gay and hearty way in which she takes hold of any new thing that comes along and gives it a first rate trial. Many an ass in America, is getting a deal of benefit out of X-Science's new exploitation of an age-old healing principle--faith, combined with the patient's imagination--let it boom along! I have no objection. Let them call it by what name they choose, so long as it does helpful work among the class which is numerically vastly the largest bulk of the human race, i.e. the fools, the idiots, the pudd'nheads.

We do not guess, we know that 9 in 10 of the species are pudd'nheads. We know it by various evidences; and one of them is, that for ages the race has respected (and almost venerated) the physician's grotesque system--the emptying of miscellaneous and harmful drugs into a person's stomach to remove ailments which in many cases the drugs could not reach at all; in many cases could reach and help, but only at cost of damage to some other part of the man; and in the remainder of the cases the drug either retarded the cure, or the disease was cured by nature in spite of the nostrums. The doctor's insane system has not only been permitted to continue its follies for ages, but has been protected by the State and made a close monopoly--an infamous thing, a crime against a free-man's proper right to choose his own assassin or his own method of defending his body against disease and death.

And yet at the same time, with curious and senile inconsistency, the State has allowed the man to choose his own assassin--in one detail--the patent-medicine detail--making itself the protector of that perilous business, collecting money out of it, and appointing no committee of experts to examine the medicines and forbid them when extra dangerous. Really, when a man can prove that he is not a jackass, I think he is in the way to prove that he is no legitimate member of the race.

I have by me a list of 52 human ailments--common ones--and in this list I count 19 which the physician's art cannot cure. But there isn't one which Osteopathy or Kellgren cannot cure, if the patient comes early.

Fifteen years ago I had a deep reverence for the physician and the surgeon. But 6 months of closely watching the Kellgren business has revolutionized all that, and now I have neither reverence nor respect for the physician's trade, and scarcely any for the surgeon's,--I am convinced that of all quackeries, the physician's is the grotesquest and the silliest. And they know they are shams and humbugs. They have taken the place of those augurs who couldn't look each other in the face without laughing.

See what a powerful hold our ancient superstitions have upon us: two weeks ago, when Livy committed an incredible imprudence and by consequence was promptly stricken down with a heavy triple attack-- influenza, bronchitis, and a lung affected--she recognized the gravity of the situation, and her old superstitions rose: she thought she ought to send for a doctor--Think of it--the last man in the world I should want around at such a time. Of course I did not say no--not that I was indisposed to take the responsibility, for I was not, my notion of a dangerous responsibility being quite the other way--but because it is unsafe to distress a sick person; I only said we knew no good doctor, and it could not be good policy to choose at hazard; so she allowed me to send for

Kellgren. To-day she is up and around--Lured. It is safe to say that persons hit in the same way at the same time are in bed yet, and booked to stay there a good while, and to be in a shackly condition and afraid of their shadows for a couple of years or more to come.

It will be seen by the foregoing that Mark Twain's interest in the Kellgren system was still an ardent one. Indeed, for a time he gave most of his thought to it, and wrote several long appreciations, perhaps with little idea of publication, but merely to get his enthusiasm physically expressed. War, however, presently supplanted medicine--the Boer troubles in South Africa and the Boxer insurrection in China. It was a disturbing, exciting year.

To W. D. Howells, in Boston:

WELLINGTON COURT, KNIGHTSBRIDGE, Jan. 25, 1900. DEAR HOWELLS,--If you got half as much as Pond prophesied, be content and praise God--it has not happened to another. But I am sorry he didn't go with you; for it is marvelous to hear him yarn. He is good company, cheery and hearty, and his mill is never idle. Your doing a lecture tour was heroic. It was the highest order of grit, and you have a right to be proud of yourself. No mount of applause or money or both could save it from being a hell to a man constituted as you are. It is that even to me, who am made of coarser stuff.

I knew the audiences would come forward and shake hands with you--that one infallible sign of sincere approval. In all my life, wherever it failed me I left the hall sick and ashamed, knowing what it meant.

Privately speaking, this is a sordid and criminal war, and in every way shameful and excuseless. Every day I write (in my head) bitter magazine articles about it, but I have to stop with that. For England must not fall; it would mean an inundation of Russian and German political degradations which would envelop the globe and steep it in a sort of Middle-Age night and slavery which would last till Christ comes again. Even wrong--and she is wrong--England must be upheld. He is an enemy of the human race who shall speak against her now. Why was the human race created? Or at least why wasn't something creditable created in place of it. God had his opportunity. He could have made a reputation. But no, He must commit this grotesque folly--a lark which must have cost him a regret or two when He came to think it over and observe effects. For a giddy and unbecoming caprice there has been nothing like it till this war. I talk the war with both sides--always waiting until the other man introduces the topic. Then I say "My head is with the Briton, but my heart and such rags of morals as I have are with the Boer--now we will talk, unembarrassed and without prejudice." And so we discuss, and have no trouble.

Jan. 26. It was my intention to make some disparaging remarks about the human race; and so I kept this letter open for that purpose, and for the purpose of telling my dream, wherein the Trinity were trying to guess a conundrum, but I can do better--for I can snip out of the "Times" various samples and side-lights which bring the race down to date, and expose it as of yesterday. If you will notice, there is seldom a telegram in a paper which fails to show up one or more members and beneficiaries of our Civilization as promenading in his shirt-tail, with the rest of his regalia in the wash.

I love to see the holy ones air their smug pieties and admire them and smirk over them, and at the same moment frankly and publicly show their contempt for the pieties of the Boer--confidently expecting the approval of the country and the pulpit, and getting it.

I notice that God is on both sides in this war; thus history repeats itself. But I am the only person who has noticed this; everybody here thinks He is playing the game for this side, and for this side only.

With great love to you all MARK.

One cannot help wondering what Mark Twain would have thought of human nature had he lived to see the great World War, fought mainly by the Christian nations who for nearly two thousand years had been preaching peace on earth and goodwill toward men. But his opinion of the race could hardly have been worse than it was. And nothing that human beings could do would have surprised him.

To Rev. J. H. Twichell, in Hartford:

LONDON, Jan. 27, 1900. DEAR JOE,--Apparently we are not proposing to set the Filipinos free and give their islands to them; and apparently we are not proposing to hang the priests and confiscate their property. If these things are so, the war out there has no interest for me.

I have just been examining chapter LXX of "Following the Equator," to see if the Boer's old military effectiveness is holding out. It reads curiously as if it had been written about the present war.

I believe that in the next chapter my notion of the Boer was rightly conceived. He is popularly called uncivilized, I do not know why. Happiness, food, shelter, clothing, wholesale labor, modest and rational ambitions, honesty, kindliness, hospitality, love of freedom and limitless courage to fight for it, composure and fortitude in time of disaster, patience in time of hardship and privation, absence of noise and brag in time of victory, contentment with a humble and peaceful life void of insane excitements--if there is a higher and better form of civilization than this, I am not aware of it and do not know where to look for it. I suppose we have the habit of imagining that a lot of artistic, intellectual and other artificialities must be added, or it isn't complete. We and the English have these latter; but as we lack the great bulk of these others, I think the Boer civilization is the best of the two. My idea of our civilization is that it is a shabby poor thing and full of cruelties, vanities, arrogancies, meannesses, and hypocrisies. As for the word, I hate the sound of it, for it conveys a lie; and as for the thing itself, I wish it was in hell, where it belongs.

Provided we could get something better in the place of it. But that is not possible, perhaps. Poor as it is, it is better than real savagery, therefore we must stand by it, extend it, and (in public) praise it. And so we must not utter any hateful word about England in these days, nor fail to hope that she will win in this war, for her defeat and fall would be an irremediable disaster for the mangy human race.... Naturally, then, I am for England; but she is profoundly in the wrong, Joe, and no (instructed) Englishman doubts it. At least that is my belief.

Maybe I managed to make myself misunderstood, as to the Osteopathists. I wanted to know how the men impress you. As to their Art, I know fairly well about that, and should not value Hartford's opinion of it; nor a physician's; nor that of another who proposed to enlighten me out of his ignorance. Opinions based upon theory, superstition and ignorance are not very precious.

Livy and the others are off for the country for a day or two. Love to you all MARK.

The next letter affords a pleasant variation. Without doubt it was written on realizing that good nature and enthusiasm had led him into indiscretion. This was always happening to him, and letters like this are not infrequent, though generally less entertaining.

To Mr. Ann, in London:

WELLINGTON COURT, Feb. 23, '00. DEAR MR. ANN,--Upon sober second thought, it won't do!--I withdraw that letter. Not because I said anything in it which is not true, for I didn't; but because when I allow my name to be used in forwarding a stock-scheme I am assuming a certain degree of responsibility as toward the investor, and I am not willing to do that. I have another objection, a purely selfish one: trading upon my name, whether the enterprise scored a success or a failure would damage me. I can't afford that; even the Archbishop of Canterbury couldn't afford it, and he has more character to spare than I have. (Ah, a happy thought! If he would sign the letter with me that would change the whole complexion of the thing, of course. I do not know him, yet I would sign any commercial scheme that he would sign. As he does not know me, it follows that he would sign anything that I would sign. This is unassailable logic--but really that is all that can be said for it.)

No, I withdraw the letter. This virgin is pure up to date, and is going to remain so. Ys sincerely, S. L. C.

To Rev. J. H. Twichell, in Hartford:

WELLINGTON COURT, KNIGHTSBRIDGE, Mch. 4, '00. DEAR JOE,--Henry Robinson's death is a sharp wound to me, and it goes very deep. I had a strong affection for him, and I think he had for me. Every Friday, three-fourths of the year for 16 years he was of the billiard-party in our house. When we come home, how shall we have billiard-nights again--with no Ned Bunce and no Henry Robinson? I believe I could not endure that. We must find another use for that room. Susy is gone, George is gone, Libby Hamersley, Ned Bunce, Henry Robinson. The friends are passing, one by one; our house, where such warm blood and such dear blood flowed so freely, is become a cemetery. But not in any repellent sense. Our dead are welcome there; their life made it beautiful, their death has hallowed it, we shall have them with us always, and there will be no parting.

It was a moving address you made over Ward Cheney--that fortunate, youth! Like Susy, he got out of life all that was worth the living, and got his great reward before he had crossed the tropic frontier of dreams and entered the Sahara of fact. The deep consciousness of Susy's good fortune is a constant comfort to me.

London is happy-hearted at last. The British victories have swept the clouds away and there are no uncheerful faces. For three months the private dinner parties (we go to no public ones) have been Lodges of Sorrow, and just a little depressing sometimes; but now they are smiley and animated again. Joe, do you know the Irish gentleman and the Irish lady, the Scotch gentleman and the Scotch lady? These are darlings, every one. Night before last it was all Irish--24. One would have to travel far to match their ease and sociability and animation and sparkle and absence of shyness and self-consciousness.

It was American in these fine qualities. This was at Mr. Lecky's. He is Irish, you know. Last night it was Irish again, at Lady Gregory's. Lord Roberts is Irish; and Sir William Butler; and Kitchener, I think; and a disproportion of the other prominent Generals are of Irish and Scotch breed-keeping up the traditions of Wellington, and Sir Colin Campbell of the Mutiny. You will have noticed that in S. A. as in the Mutiny, it is usually the Irish and the Scotch that are placed in the fore-front of the battle. An Irish friend of mine says this is because the Kelts are idealists, and enthusiasts, with age-old heroisms to emulate and keep bright before the world; but that the low-class Englishman is dull and without ideals, fighting bull-doggishly while he has a leader, but losing his head and going to pieces when his leader falls--not so with the Kelt. Sir Wm. Butler said "the Kelt is the spear-head of the British lance." Love to you all. MARK.

The Henry Robinson mentioned in the foregoing letter was Henry C. Robinson, one-time Governor of Connecticut, long a dear and intimate friend of the Clemens household. "Lecky" was W. E. H. Lecky, the Irish historian whose History of European Morals had been, for many years, one of Mark Twain's favorite books:

In July the Clemenses left the small apartment at 30 Wellington Court and established a summer household a little way out of London, at Dollis Hill. To-day the place has been given to the public under the name of Gladstone Park, so called for the reason that in an earlier time Gladstone had frequently visited there. It was a beautiful spot, a place of green grass and spreading oaks. In a letter in which Mrs. Clemens wrote to her sister she said: "It is simply divinely beautiful and peaceful; the great, old trees are beyond everything. I believe nowhere in the world do you find such trees as in England." Clemens wrote to Twichell: "From the house you can see little but spacious stretches of hay-fields and green turf..... Yet the massed, brick blocks of London are reachable in three minutes on a horse. By rail we can be in the heart of London, in Baker Street, in seventeen minutes--by a smart train in five."

Mail, however, would seem to have been less prompt.

To the Editor of the Times, in London:

SIR,--It has often been claimed that the London postal service was swifter than that of New York, and I have always believed that the claim was justified. But a doubt has lately sprung up in my mind. I live eight miles from Printing House Square; the Times leaves that point at 4 o'clock in the morning, by mail, and reaches me at 5 in the afternoon, thus making the trip in thirteen hours.

It is my conviction that in New York we should do it in eleven.

C. DOLLIS HILL, N. W.

To Rev. J. H. Twichell, in Hartford:

DOLLIS HILL HOUSE, KILBURN, N. W. LONDON, Aug. 12, '00. DEAR JOE,--The Sages Prof. Fiske and Brander Matthews were out here to tea a week ago and it was a breath of American air to see them. We furnished them a bright day and comfortable weather--and they used it all up, in their extravagant American way. Since then we have sat by coal fires, evenings.

We shall sail for home sometime in October, but shall winter in New York where we can have an osteopath of good repute to continue the work of putting this family in proper condition.

Livy and I dined with the Chief justice a month ago and he was as well- conditioned as an athlete.

It is all China, now, and my sympathies are with the Chinese. They have been villainously dealt with by the sceptred thieves of Europe, and I hope they will drive all the foreigners out and keep them out for good. I only wish it; of course I don't really expect it.

Why, hang it, it occurs to me that by the time we reach New York you Twichells will be invading Europe and once more we shall miss the connection. This is thoroughly exasperating. Aren't we ever going to meet again? With no end of love from all of us, MARK.

P. S. Aug. 18. DEAR JOE,--It is 7.30 a. m. I have been waking very early, lately. If it occurs once more, it will be habit; then I will submit and adopt it.

This is our day of mourning. It is four years since Susy died; it is five years and a month that I saw her alive for the last time-throwing kisses at us from the railway platform when we started West around the world.

Sometimes it is a century; sometimes it was yesterday. With love MARK.

We discover in the foregoing letter that the long European residence was drawing to an end. More than nine years had passed since the closing of the Hartford house--eventful years that had seen failure, bereavement, battle with debt, and rehabilitated fortunes. All the family were anxious to get home--Mark Twain most anxious of all.

They closed Dollis Hill House near the end of September, and put up for a brief period at a family hotel, an amusing picture of which follows.

To J. Y. M. MacAlister, in London:

Sep. 1900. MY DEAR MACALISTER,--We do really start next Saturday. I meant to sail earlier, but waited to finish some studies of what are called Family Hotels. They are a London specialty, God has not permitted them to exist elsewhere; they are ramshackle clubs which were dwellings at the time of the Heptarchy. Dover and Albemarle Streets are filled with them. The once spacious rooms are split up into coops which afford as much discomfort as can be had anywhere out of jail for any money. All the modern inconveniences are furnished, and some that have been obsolete for a century. The prices are astonishingly high for what you get. The bedrooms are hospitals for incurable furniture. I find it so in this one. They exist upon a tradition; they represent the vanishing home-like inn of fifty years ago, and are mistaken by foreigners for it. Some quite respectable Englishmen still frequent them through inherited habit and arrested development; many Americans also, through ignorance and superstition. The rooms are as interesting as the Tower of London, but older I think. Older and dearer. The lift was a gift of William the Conqueror, some of the beds are prehistoric. They represent geological periods. Mine is the oldest. It is formed in strata of Old Red Sandstone, volcanic tufa, ignis fatuus, and bicarbonate of hornblende, superimposed upon argillaceous shale, and contains the prints of prehistoric man. It is in No. 149. Thousands of scientists come to see it. They consider it holy. They want to blast out the prints but cannot. Dynamite rebounds from it.

Finished studies and sail Saturday in Minnehaha. Yours ever affectionately, MARK TWAIN.

They sailed for New York October 6th, and something more than a week later America gave them a royal welcome. The press, far and wide, sounded Mark Twain's praises once more; dinners and receptions were offered on every hand; editors and lecture agents clamored for him.

The family settled in the Earlington Hotel during a period of house-hunting. They hoped eventually to return to Hartford, but after a brief visit paid by Clemens alone to the old place he wrote:

To Sylvester Baxter, in Boston:

NEW YORK, Oct. 26, 1900. DEAR MR. BAXTER,--It was a great pleasure to me to renew the other days with you, and there was a pathetic pleasure in seeing Hartford and the house again; but I realize that if we ever enter the house again to live, our hearts will break. I am not sure that we shall ever be strong enough to endure that strain. Sincerely yours, S. L. CLEMENS.

Mr. and Mrs. Rogers wished to have them in their neighborhood, but the houses there were not suitable, or were too expensive. Through Mr. Frank Doubleday they eventually found, at 14 West Tenth Street, a large residence handsomely furnished, and this they engaged for the winter. "We were lucky to get this big house furnished," he wrote MacAlister in London. "There was not another one in town procurable that would answer us, but this one is all right--space enough in it for several families, the rooms all old-fashioned, great size."

The little note that follows shows that Mark Twain had not entirely forgotten the days of Tom Sawyer and Huck Finn.

To a Neighbor on West Tenth Street, New York:

Nov. 30. DEAR MADAM,--I know I ought to respect my duty and perform it, but I am weak and faithless where boys are concerned, and I can't help secretly approving pretty bad and noisy ones, though I do object to the kind that ring door-bells. My family try to get me to stop the boys from holding conventions on the front steps, but I basely shirk out of it, because I think the boys enjoy it.

My wife has been complaining to me this evening about the boys on the front steps and under compulsion I have made some promises. But I am very forgetful, now that I am old, and my sense of duty is getting spongy. Very truly yours, S. L. CLEMENS.

End of this Project Gutenberg Etext of Letters Vol. 4, by Mark Twain

MARK TWAIN'S LETTERS 1901-1906

ARRANGED WITH COMMENT BY ALBERT BIGELOW PAINE

VOLUME V.

XL

LETTERS OF 1901, CHIEFLY TO TWICHELL. MARK TWAIN AS A REFORMER. SUMMER AT SARANAC. ASSASSINATION OF PRESIDENT McKINLEY

An editorial in the Louisville Courier-Journal, early in 1901, said: "A remarkable transformation, or rather a development, has taken place in Mark Twain. The genial humorist of the earlier day is now a reformer of the vigorous kind, a sort of knight errant who does not hesitate to break a lance with either Church or State if he thinks them interposing on that broad highway over which he believes not a part but the whole of mankind has the privilege of passing in the onward march of the ages."

Mark Twain had begun "breaking the lance" very soon after his return from Europe. He did not believe that he could reform the world, but at least he need not withhold his protest against those things which stirred his wrath. He began by causing the arrest of a cabman who had not only overcharged but insulted him; he continued by writing openly against the American policy in the Philippines, the missionary propaganda which had resulted in the Chinese uprising and massacre, and against Tammany politics. Not all of his efforts were in the line of reform; he had become a sort of general spokesman which the public flocked to hear, whatever the subject. On the occasion of a Lincoln Birthday service at Carnegie Hall he was chosen to preside, and he was obliged to attend more dinners than were good for his health. His letters of this period were mainly written to his old friend Twichell, in Hartford. Howells, who lived in New York, he saw with considerable frequency.

In the letter which follows the medicine which Twichell was to take was Plasmon, an English proprietary remedy in which Mark Twain had invested--a panacea for all human ills which osteopathy could not reach.

To Rev. Joseph Twichell, in Hartford:

14 W. 10TH ST. Jan. 23, '01. DEAR JOE,--Certainly. I used to take it in my coffee, but it settled to the bottom in the form of mud, and I had to eat it with a spoon; so I dropped the custom and took my 2 teaspoonfuls in cold milk after breakfast. If we were out of milk I shoveled the dry powder into my mouth and washed it down with water. The only essential is to get it down, the method is not important.

No, blame it, I can't go to the Alumni dinner, Joe. It takes two days, and I can't spare the time. Moreover I preside at the Lincoln birthday celebration in Carnegie Hall Feb. 11 and I must not make two speeches so close together. Think of it--two old rebels functioning there--I as President, and Watterson as Orator of the Day! Things have changed somewhat in these 40 years, thank God.

Look here--when you come down you must be our guest--we've got a roomy room for you, and Livy will make trouble if you go elsewhere. Come straight to 14 West 10th.

Jan. 24. Livy says Amen to that; also, can you give us a day or two's notice, so the room will be sure to be vacant?

I'm going to stick close to my desk for a month, now, hoping to write a small book. Ys Ever MARK

The letter which follows is a fair sample of Mark Twain's private violence on a subject which, in public print, he could only treat effectively by preserving his good humor. When he found it necessary to boil over, as he did, now and then, for relief, he always found a willing audience in Twichell. The mention of his "Private Philosophy" refers to 'What Is Man?', privately published in 1906; reissued by his publishers in 1916.

To Rev. J. H. Twichell, in Hartford:

14 W. 10th Jan. 29, '01. DEAR JOE,--I'm not expecting anything but kicks for scoffing, and am expecting a diminution of my bread and butter by it, but if Livy will let me I will have my say. This nation is like all the others that have been spewed upon the earth--ready to shout for any cause that will tickle its vanity or fill its pocket. What a hell of a heaven it will be, when they get all these hypocrites assembled there!

I can't understand it! You are a public guide and teacher, Joe, and are under a heavy responsibility to men, young and old; if you teach your people--as you teach me--to hide their opinions when they believe the flag is being abused and dishonored, lest the utterance do them and a publisher a damage, how do you answer for it to your conscience? You are sorry for me; in the fair way of give and take, I am willing to be a little sorry for you.

However, I seem to be going counter to my own Private Philosophy--which Livy won't allow me to publish--because it would destroy me. But I hope to see it in print before I die. I planned it 15 years ago, and wrote it in '98. I've often tried to read it to Livy, but she won't have it; it makes her melancholy. The truth always has that effect on people. Would have, anyway, if they ever got hold of a rag of it--Which they don't.

You are supposing that I am supposing that I am moved by a Large Patriotism, and that I am distressed because our President has blundered up to his neck in the Philippine mess; and that I am grieved because this great big ignorant nation, which doesn't know even the A B C facts of the Philippine episode, is in disgrace before the sarcastic world--drop that idea! I care nothing for the rest--I am only distressed and troubled because I am befouled by these things. That is all. When I search myself away down deep, I find this out. Whatever a man feels or thinks or does, there is never any but one reason for it--and that is a selfish one.

At great inconvenience, and expense of precious time I went to the chief synagogue the other night and talked in the interest of a charity school of poor Jew girls. I know--to the finest, shades-- the selfish ends that moved me; but no one else suspects. I could give you the details if I had time. You would perceive how true they are.

I've written another article; you better hurry down and help Livy squelch it.

She's out pottering around somewhere, poor housekeeping slave; and Clara is in the hands of the osteopath, getting the bronchitis pulled and hauled out of her. It was a bad attack, and a little disquieting. It came day before yesterday, and she hasn't sat up till this afternoon. She is getting along satisfactorily, now. Lots of love to you all. MARK

Mark Twain's religion had to do chiefly with humanity in its present incarnation, and concerned itself very little with any possible measure of reward or punishment in some supposed court of the hereafter. Nevertheless, psychic investigation always interested him, and he was good-naturedly willing to explore, even hoping, perhaps, to be convinced that individuality continues beyond death. The letter which follows indicates his customary attitude in relation to spiritualistic research. The experiments here mentioned, however, were not satisfactory.

To Mrs. Charles McQuiston:

DOBBS FERRY, N. Y. March 26, 1901. DEAR MRS. McQUISTON,--I have never had an experience which moved me to believe the living can communicate with the dead, but my wife and I have experimented in the matter when opportunity offered and shall continue to do so.

I enclose a letter which came this morning--the second from the same source. Mrs. K----is a Missourian, and lately she discovered, by accident, that she was a remarkable hypnotiser. Her best subject is a Missouri girl, Miss White, who is to come here soon and sustain strictly scientific tests before professors at Columbia University. Mrs. Clemens and I intend to be present. And we shall ask the pair to come to our house to do whatever things they can do. Meantime, if you thought well of it, you might write her and arrange a meeting, telling her it is by my suggestion and that I gave you her address.

Someone has told me that Mrs. Piper is discredited. I cannot be sure, but I think it was Mr. Myers, President of the London Psychical Research Society--we heard of his death yesterday. He was a spiritualist. I am afraid he was a very easily convinced man. We visited two mediums whom he and Andrew Lang considered quite wonderful, but they were quite transparent frauds.

Mrs. Clemens corrects me: One of those women was a fraud, the other not a fraud, but only an innocent, well-meaning, driveling vacancy. Sincerely yours, S. L. CLEMENS.

In Mark Twain's Bermuda chapters entitled Idle Notes of an Idle Excursion he tells of an old sea captain, one Hurricane Jones, who explained biblical miracles in a practical, even if somewhat startling, fashion. In his story of the prophets of Baal, for instance, the old captain declared that the burning water was nothing more nor less than petroleum. Upon reading the "notes," Professor Phelps of Yale wrote that the same method of explaining miracles had been offered by Sir Thomas Browne.

Perhaps it may be added that Captain Hurricane Jones also appears in Roughing It, as Captain Ned Blakely.

To Professor William Lyon Phelps;

YALE UNIVERSITY, NEW YORK, April 24, 1901. MY DEAR SIR,--I was not aware that old Sir Thomas had anticipated that story, and I am much obliged to you for furnishing me the paragraph. t is curious that the same idea should leave entered two heads so unlike as the head of that wise old philosopher and that of Captain Ned Wakeman, a splendidly uncultured old sailor, but in his own opinion a thinker by divine right. He was an old friend of mine of many years' standing; I made two or three voyages with him, and found him a darling in many ways. The petroleum story was not told to me; he told it to Joe Twichell, who ran across him by accident on a sea voyage where I think the two were the only passengers. A delicious pair, and admirably mated, they took to each other at once and became as thick as thieves. Joe was passing under a fictitious name, and old Wakeman didn't suspect that he was a parson; so he gave his profanity full swing, and he was a master of that great art. You probably know Twichell, and will know that that is a kind of refreshment which he is very capable of enjoying. Sincerely yours, S. L. CLEMENS.

For the summer Clemens and his family found a comfortable lodge in the Adirondacks--a log cabin called "The Lair"--on Saranac Lake. Soon after his arrival there he received an invitation to attend the celebration of Missouri's eightieth anniversary. He sent the following letter:

To Edward L. Dimmitt, in St. Louis:

AMONG THE ADIRONDACK LAKES, July 19, 1901. DEAR MR. DIMMITT,--By an error in the plans, things go wrong end first in this world, and much precious time is lost and matters of urgent importance are fatally retarded. Invitations which a brisk young fellow should get, and which would transport him with joy, are delayed and impeded and obstructed until they are fifty years overdue when they reach him.

It has happened again in this case.

When I was a boy in Missouri I was always on the lookout for invitations but they always miscarried and went wandering through the aisles of time; and now they are arriving when I am old and rheumatic and can't travel and must lose my chance.

I have lost a world of delight through this matter of delaying invitations. Fifty years ago I would have gone eagerly across the world to help celebrate anything that might turn up. IT would have made no difference to me what it was, so that I was there and allowed a chance to make a noise.

The whole scheme of things is turned wrong end to. Life should begin with age and its privileges and accumulations, and end with youth and its capacity to splendidly enjoy such advantages. As things are now, when in youth a dollar would bring a hundred pleasures, you can't have it. When you are old, you get it and there is nothing worth buying with it then.

It's an epitome of life. The first half of it consists of the capacity to enjoy without the chance; the last half consists of the chance without the capacity.

I am admonished in many ways that time is pushing me inexorably along. I am approaching the threshold of age; in 1977 I shall be 142. This is no time to be flitting about the earth. I must cease from the activities proper to youth and begin to take on the dignities and gravities and inertia proper to that season of honorable senility which is on its way and imminent as indicated above.

Yours is a great and memorable occasion, and as a son of Missouri I should hold it a high privilege to be there and share your just pride in the state's achievements; but I must deny myself the indulgence, while thanking you earnestly for the prized honor you have done me in asking me to be present. Very truly yours, S. L. CLEMENS.

In the foregoing Mark Twain touches upon one of his favorite fancies: that life should begin with old age and approach strong manhood, golden youth, to end at last with pampered and beloved babyhood. Possibly he contemplated writing a story with this idea as the theme, but He seems never to have done so.

The reader who has followed these letters may remember Yung Wing, who had charge of the Chinese educational mission in Hartford, and how Mark Twain, with Twichell, called on General Grant in behalf of the mission. Yung Wing, now returned to China, had conceived the idea of making an appeal to the Government of the United States for relief of his starving countrymen.

To J. H. Twichell, in Hartford:

AMPERSAND, N. Y., July 28, '01. DEAR JOE,--As you say, it is impracticable--in my case, certainly. For me to assist in an appeal to that Congress of land-thieves and liars would be to bring derision upon it; and for me to assist in an appeal for cash to pass through the hands of those missionaries out there, of any denomination, Catholic or Protestant, wouldn't do at all. They wouldn't handle money which I had soiled, and I wouldn't trust them with it, anyway. They would devote it to the relief of suffering--I know that-- but the sufferers selected would be converts. The missionary-utterances exhibit no humane feeling toward the others, but in place of it a spirit of hate and hostility. And it is natural; the Bible forbids their presence there, their trade is unlawful, why shouldn't their characters be of necessity in harmony with--but never mind, let it go, it irritates me.

Later.... I have been reading Yung Wing's letter again. It may be that he is over-wrought by his sympathies, but it may not be so. There may be other reasons why the missionaries are silent about the Shensi-2-year famine and cannibalism. It may be that there are so few Protestant converts there that the missionaries are able to take care of them. That they are not likely to largely concern themselves about Catholic converts and the others, is quite natural, I think.

That crude way of appealing to this Government for help in a cause which has no money in it, and no politics, rises before me again in all its admirable innocence! Doesn't Yung Wing know us yet? However, he has been absent since '96 or '97. We have gone to hell since then. Kossuth couldn't raise 30 cents in Congress, now, if he were back with his moving Magyar-Tale.

I am on the front porch (lower one--main deck) of our little bijou of a dwelling-house. The lake-edge (Lower Saranac) is so nearly under me that I can't see the shore, but only the water, small-pored with rain- splashes--for there is a heavy down-pour. It is charmingly like sitting snuggled up on a ship's deck with the stretching sea all around--but very much more satisfactory, for at sea a rain-storm is depressing, while here of course the effect engendered is just a deep sense of comfort and contentment. The heavy forest shuts us solidly in on three sides there are no neighbors. There are beautiful little tan-colored impudent squirrels about. They take tea, 5 p. m., (not invited) at the table in the woods where Jean does my typewriting, and one of them has been brave enough to sit upon Jean's knee with his tail curved over his back and munch his food. They come to dinner, 7 p. m., on the front porch (not invited). They all have the one name--Blennerhasset, from Burr's friend --and none of them answers to it except when hungry.

We have been here since June 21st. For a little while we had some warm days--according to the family's estimate; I was hardly discommoded myself. Otherwise the weather has been of the sort you are familiar with in these regions: cool days and cool nights. We have heard of the hot wave every Wednesday, per the weekly paper--we allow no dailies to intrude. Last week through visitors also--the only ones we have had-- Dr. Root and John Howells.

We have the daily lake-swim; and all the tribe, servants included (but not I) do a good deal of boating; sometimes with the guide, sometimes without him--Jean and Clara are competent with the oars. If we live another year, I hope we shall spend its summer in this house.

We have taken the Appleton country seat, overlooking the Hudson, at Riverdale, 25 minutes from the Grand Central Station, for a year, beginning Oct. 1, with option for another year. We are obliged to be close to New York for a year or two.

Aug. 3rd. I go yachting a fortnight up north in a 20-knot boat 225 feet long, with the owner, (Mr. Rogers), Tom Reid, Dr. Rice, Col. A. G. Paine and one or two others. Judge Howland would go, but can't get away from engagements; Professor Sloane would go, but is in the grip of an illness. Come--will you go? If you can manage it, drop a post-card to me c/o H.H. Rogers, 26 Broadway. I shall be in New York a couple of days before we sail--July 31 or Aug. 1, perhaps the latter,--and I think I shall stop at the Hotel Grosvenor, cor. l0th St and 5th ave.

We all send you and the Harmonies lots and gobs of love. MARK

To Rev. J. H. Twichell, in Hartford:

AMPERSAND, N. Y., Aug. 28. DEAR JOE,--Just a word, to scoff at you, with your extravagant suggestion that I read the biography of Phillips Brooks--the very dullest book that has been printed for a century. Joe, ten pages of Mrs. Cheney's masterly biography of her fathers--no, five pages of it--contain more meat, more sense, more literature, more brilliancy, than that whole basketful of drowsy rubbish put together. Why, in that dead atmosphere even Brooks himself is dull--he wearied me; oh how he wearied me!

We had a noble good time in the Yacht, and caught a Chinese missionary and drowned him. Love from us all to you all. MARK.

The assassination of President McKinley occurred September 6, 1901. Such an event would naturally stir Mark Twain to comment on human nature in general. His letter to Twichell is as individual as it is sound in philosophy. At what period of his own life, or under what circumstances, he made the long journey with tragic intent there is no means of knowing now. There is no other mention of it elsewhere in the records that survive him.

To Rev. J. H. Twichell, in Hartford:

AMPERSAND, Tuesday, (Sept. 10, 1901) DEAR JOE,--It is another off day, but tomorrow I shall resume work to a certainty, and bid a long farewell to letter-scribbling.

The news of the President looks decidedly hopeful, and we are all glad, and the household faces are much improved, as to cheerfulness. Oh, the talk in the newspapers! Evidently the Human Race is the same old Human Race. And how unjust, and unreflectingly discriminating, the talkers are. Under the unsettling effects of powerful emotion the talkers are saying wild things, crazy things-- they are out of themselves, and do not know it; they are temporarily insane, yet with one voice they declare the assassin sane--a man who has been entertaining fiery and reason-- debauching maggots in his head for weeks and months. Why, no one is sane, straight along, year in and year out, and we all know it. Our insanities are of varying sorts, and express themselves in varying forms --fortunately harmless forms as a rule--but in whatever form they occur an immense upheaval of feeling can at any time topple us distinctly over the sanity-line for a little while; and then if our form happens to be of the murderous kind we must look out--and so must the spectator.

This ass with the unpronounceable name was probably more insane than usual this week or two back, and may get back upon his bearings by and by, but he was over the sanity-border when he shot the President. It is possible that it has taken him the whole interval since the murder of the King of Italy to get insane enough to attempt the President's life. Without a doubt some thousands of men have been meditating the same act in the same interval, but new and strong interests have intervened and diverted their over-excited minds long enough to give them a chance to settle, and tranquilize, and get back upon a healthy level again. Every extraordinary occurrence unsettles the heads of hundreds of thousands of men for a few moments or hours or days. If there had been ten kings around when Humbert fell they would have been in great peril for a day or more--and from men in whose presence they would have been quite safe after the excess of their excitement had had an interval in which to cool down. I bought a revolver once and travelled twelve hundred miles to kill a man. He was away. He was gone a day. With nothing else to do, I had to stop and think--and did. Within an hour--within half of it-- I was ashamed of myself--and felt unspeakably ridiculous. I do not know what to call it if I was not insane. During a whole week my head was in a turmoil night and day fierce enough and exhausting enough to upset a stronger reason than mine.

All over the world, every day, there are some millions of men in that condition temporarily. And in that time there is always a moment-- perhaps only a single one when they would do murder if their man was at hand. If the opportunity comes a shade too late, the chances are that it has come permanently too late. Opportunity seldom comes exactly at the supreme moment. This saves a million lives a day in the world--for sure.

No Ruler is ever slain but the tremendous details of it are ravenously devoured by a hundred thousand men whose minds dwell, unaware, near the temporary-insanity frontier--and over they go, now! There is a day--two days--three--during which no Ruler would be safe from perhaps the half of them; and there is a single moment wherein he would not be safe from any of them, no doubt.

It may take this present shooting-case six months to breed another ruler-tragedy, but it will breed it. There is at least one mind somewhere which will brood, and wear, and decay itself to the killing-point and produce that tragedy.

Every negro burned at the stake unsettles the excitable brain of another one--I mean the inflaming details of his crime, and the lurid theatricality of his exit do it--and the duplicate crime follows; and that begets a repetition, and that one another one and so on. Every lynching-account unsettles the brains of another set of excitable white men, and lights another pyre--115 lynchings last year, 102 inside of 8 months this year; in ten years this will be habit, on these terms.

Yes, the wild talk you see in the papers! And from men who are sane when not upset by overwhelming excitement. A U. S. Senator-Cullom--wants this Buffalo criminal lynched! It would breed other lynchings--of men who are not dreaming of committing murders, now, and will commit none if Cullom will keep quiet and not provide the exciting cause.

And a District Attorney wants a law which shall punish with death attempts upon a President's life--this, mind you, as a deterrent. It would have no effect--or the opposite one. The lunatic's mind-space is all occupied--as mine was--with the matter in hand; there is no room in it for reflections upon what may happen to him. That comes after the crime.

It is the noise the attempt would make in the world that would breed the subsequent attempts, by unsettling the rickety minds of men who envy the criminal his vast notoriety--his obscure name tongued by stupendous Kings and Emperors--his picture printed everywhere, the trivialest details of his movements, what he eats, what he drinks; how he sleeps, what he says, cabled abroad over the whole globe at cost of fifty thousand dollars a day--and he only a lowly shoemaker yesterday!--like the assassin of the President of France--in debt three francs to his landlady, and insulted by her--and to-day she is proud to be able to say she knew him "as familiarly as you know your own brother," and glad to stand till she drops and pour out columns and pages of her grandeur and her happiness upon the eager interviewer.

Nothing will check the lynchings and ruler-murder but absolute silence-- the absence of pow-pow about them. How are you going to manage that? By gagging every witness and jamming him into a dungeon for life; by abolishing all newspapers; by exterminating all newspaper men; and by extinguishing God's most elegant invention, the Human Race. It is quite simple, quite easy, and I hope you will take a day off and attend to it, Joe. I blow a kiss to you, and am Lovingly Yours, MARK.

When the Adirondack summer ended Clemens settled for the winter in the beautiful Appleton home at Riverdale-on-the-Hudson. It was a place of wide-spreading grass and shade-a house of ample room. They were established in it in time for Mark Twain to take an active interest in the New York elections and assist a ticket for good government to defeat Tammany Hall.

XLI

LETTERS OF 1902. RIVERDALE. YORK HARBOR. ILLNESS OF MRS. CLEMENS

The year 1902 was an eventful one for Mark Twain. In April he received a degree of LL.D. from the University of Missouri and returned to his native State to accept it. This was his last journey to the Mississippi River. During the summer Mrs. Clemens's health broke down and illnesses of one sort or another visited other members of the family. Amid so much stress and anxiety Clemens had little time or inclination for work. He wrote not many letters and mainly somber ones. Once, by way of diversion, he worked out the idea of a curious club--which he formed--its members to be young girls--girls for the most part whom he had never seen. They were elected without their consent from among those who wrote to him without his consent, and it is not likely that any one so chosen declined membership. One selection from his letters to the French member, Miss Helene Picard, of St.-Die, France, will explain the club and present a side of Mask Twain somewhat different from that found in most of his correspondence.

To Miss Picard, in St.-Die, France:

RIVERDALE-ON-THE-HUDSON, February 22, 1902. DEAR MISS HELENE,--If you will let me call you so, considering that my head is white and that I have grownup daughters. Your beautiful letter has given me such deep pleasure! I will make bold to claim you for a friend and lock you up with the rest of my riches; for I am a miser who counts his spoil every day and hoards it secretly and adds to it when he can, and is grateful to see it grow.

Some of that gold comes, like yourself, in a sealed package, and I can't see it and may never have the happiness; but I know its value without that, and by what sum it increases my wealth.

I have a Club, a private Club, which is all my own. I appoint the Members myself, and they can't help themselves, because I don't allow them to vote on their own appointment and I don't allow them to resign! They are all friends whom I have never seen (save one), but who have written friendly letters to me.

By the laws of my Club there can be only one Member in each country, and there can be no male Member but myself. Some day I may admit males, but I don't know--they are capricious and inharmonious, and their ways provoke me a good deal. It is a matter which the Club shall decide.

I have made four appointments in the past three or four months: You as Member for France, a young Highland girl as Member for Scotland, a Mohammedan girl as Member for Bengal, and a dear and bright young niece of mine as Member for the United States--for I do not represent a country myself, but am merely Member at Large for the Human Race.

You must not try to resign, for the laws of the Club do not allow that. You must console yourself by remembering that you are in the best of company; that nobody knows of your membership except myself--that no Member knows another's name, but only her country; that no taxes are levied and no meetings held (but how dearly I should like to attend one!).

One of my Members is a Princess of a royal house, another is the daughter of a village bookseller on the continent of Europe. For the only qualification for Membership is intellect and the spirit of good will; other distinctions, hereditary or acquired, do not count.

May I send you the Constitution and Laws of the Club? I shall be so pleased if I may. It is a document which one of my daughters typewrites for me when I need one for a new Member, and she would give her eyebrows to know what it is all about, but I strangle her curiosity by saying: "There are much cheaper typewriters than you are, my dear, and if you try to pry into the sacred mysteries of this Club one of your prosperities will perish sure."

My favorite? It is "Joan of Arc." My next is "Huckleberry Finn," but the family's next is "The Prince and the Pauper." (Yes, you are right-- I am a moralist in disguise; it gets me into heaps of trouble when I go thrashing around in political questions.)

I wish you every good fortune and happiness and I thank you so much for your letter. Sincerely yours, S. L. CLEMENS.

Early in the year Clemens paid a visit to Twichell in Hartford, and after one of their regular arguments on theology and the moral accountability of the human race, arguments that had been going on between them for more than thirty years--Twichell lent his visitor Freedom of the Will, by Jonathan Edwards, to read on the way home. The next letter was the result.

To Rev. J. H. Twichell, in Hartford:

RIVERDALE-ON-THE-HUDSON. Feb. '02. DEAR JOE,--"After compliments."--[Meaning "What a good time you gave me; what a happiness it was to be under your roof again; etc., etc." See opening sentence of all translations of letters passing between Lord Roberts and Indian princes and rulers.]--From Bridgeport to New York; thence to home; and continuously until near midnight I wallowed and reeked with Jonathan in his insane debauch; rose immediately refreshed and fine at 10 this morning, but with a strange and haunting sense of having been on a three days' tear with a drunken lunatic. It is years since I have known these sensations. All through the book is the glaze of a resplendent intellect gone mad--a marvelous spectacle. No, not all through the book--the drunk does not come on till the last third, where what I take to be Calvinism and its God begins to show up and shine red and hideous in the glow from the fires of hell, their only right and proper adornment. By God I was ashamed to be in such company.

Jonathan seems to hold (as against the Arminian position) that the Man (or his Soul or his Will) never creates an impulse itself, but is moved to action by an impulse back of it. That's sound!

Also, that of two or more things offered it, it infallibly chooses the one which for the moment is most pleasing to ITSELF. Perfectly correct! An immense admission for a man not otherwise sane.

Up to that point he could have written chapters III and IV of my suppressed "Gospel." But there we seem to separate. He seems to concede the indisputable and unshakable dominion of Motive and Necessity (call them what he may, these are exterior forces and not under the man's authority, guidance or even suggestion)--then he suddenly flies the logic track and (to all seeming) makes the man and not these exterior forces responsible to God for the man's thoughts, words and acts. It is frank insanity.

I think that when he concedes the autocratic dominion of Motive and Necessity he grants, a third position of mine--that a man's mind is a mere machine--an automatic machine--which is handled entirely from the outside, the man himself furnishing it absolutely nothing: not an ounce of its fuel, and not so much as a bare suggestion to that exterior engineer as to what the machine shall do, nor how it shall do it nor when.

After that concession, it was time for him to get alarmed and shirk--for he was pointing straight for the only rational and possible next-station on that piece of road the irresponsibility of man to God.

And so he shirked. Shirked, and arrived at this handsome result:

Man is commanded to do so-and-so. It has been ordained from the beginning of time that some men shan't and others can't.

These are to be blamed: let them be damned.

I enjoy the Colonel very much, and shall enjoy the rest of him with an obscene delight. Joe, the whole tribe shout love to you and yours! MARK.

We have not heard of Joe Goodman since the trying days of '90 and '91, when he was seeking to promote the fortunes of the type-setting machine. Goodman, meantime, who had in turn been miner, printer, publisher, and farmer; had been devoting his energies and genius to something entirely new: he had been translating the prehistoric Mayan inscriptions of Yucatan, and with such success that his work was elaborately published by an association of British scientists. In due time a copy of this publication came to Clemens, who was full of admiration of the great achievement.

To J. T. Goodman, in California:

RIVERDALE-ON-THE-HUDSON, June 13, '02. DEAR JOE,--I am lost in reverence and admiration! It is now twenty-four hours that I have been trying to cool down and contemplate with quiet blood this extraordinary spectacle of energy, industry, perseverance, pluck, analytical genius, penetration, this irruption of thunders and fiery splendors from a fair and flowery mountain that nobody had supposed was a sleeping volcano, but I seem to be as excited as ever. Yesterday I read as much as half of the book, not understanding a word but enchanted nevertheless--partly by the wonder of it all, the study, the erudition, the incredible labor, the modesty, the dignity, the majestic exclusiveness of the field and its lofty remoteness from things and contacts sordid and mean and earthy, and partly by the grace and beauty and limpidity of the book's unsurpassable English. Science, always great and worshipful, goes often in hodden grey, but you have clothed her in garments meet for her high degree.

You think you get "poor pay" for your twenty years? No, oh no. You have lived in a paradise of the intellect whose lightest joys were beyond the reach of the longest purse in Christendom, you have had daily and nightly emancipation from the world's slaveries and gross interests, you have received a bigger wage than any man in the land, you have dreamed a splendid dream and had it come true, and to-day you could not afford to trade fortunes with anybody--not even with another scientist, for he must divide his spoil with his guild, whereas essentially the world you have discovered is your own and must remain so.

It is all just magnificent, Joe! And no one is prouder or gladder than Yours always MARK.

At York Harbor, Maine, where they had taken a cottage for the summer--a pretty place, with Howells not far distant, at Kittery Point--Mrs. Clemens's health gave way. This was at a period when telegraphic communication was far from reliable. The old-time Western Union had fallen from grace; its "system" no longer justified the best significance of that word. The new day of reorganization was coming, and it was time for it. Mark Twain's letter concerning the service at York Harbor would hardly be warranted today, but those who remember conditions of that earlier time will agree that it was justified then, and will appreciate its satire.

To the President of The Western Union, in New York:

"THE PINES" YORK HARBOR, MAINE. DEAR SIR,--I desire to make a complaint, and I bring it to you, the head of the company, because by experience I know better than to carry it to a subordinate.

I have been here a month and a half, and by testimony of friends, reinforced by personal experience I now feel qualified to claim as an established fact that the telegraphic service here is the worst in the world except that Boston.

These services are actually slower than was the New York and Hartford service in the days when I last complained to you--which was fifteen or eighteen years ago, when telegraphic time and train time between the mentioned points was exactly the same, to-wit, three hours and a half. Six days ago--it was that raw day which provoked so much comment--my daughter was on her way up from New York, and at noon she telegraphed me from New Haven asking that I meet her with a cloak at Portsmouth. Her telegram reached me four hours and a quarter later--just 15 minutes too late for me to catch my train and meet her.

I judge that the telegram traveled about 200 miles. It is the best telegraphic work I have seen since I have been here, and I am mentioning it in this place not as a complaint but as a compliment.

I think a compliment ought always to precede a complaint, where one is possible, because it softens resentment and insures for the complaint a courteous and gentle reception.

Still, there is a detail or two connected with this matter which ought perhaps to be mentioned. And now, having smoothed the way with the compliment, I will venture them. The head corpse in the York Harbor office sent me that telegram altho (1) he knew it would reach me too late to be of any value; (2) also, that he was going to send it to me by his boy; (3) that the boy would not take the trolley and come the 2 miles in 12 minutes, but would walk; (4) that he would be two hours and a quarter on the road; (5) and that he would collect 25 cents for transportation, for a telegram which the he knew to be worthless before he started it. From these data I infer that the Western Union owes me 75 cents; that is to say, the amount paid for combined wire and land transportation-- a recoup provided for in the printed paragraph which heads the telegraph- blank.

By these humane and Christian stages we now arrive at the complaint proper. We have had a grave case of illness in the family, and a relative was coming some six hundred miles to help in the sick-room during the convalescing period. It was an anxious time, of course, and I wrote and asked to be notified as to the hour of the expected arrival of this relative in Boston or in York Harbor. Being afraid of the telegraph--which I think ought not to be used in times of hurry and emergency--I asked that the desired message be brought to me by some swift method of transportation. By the milkman, if he was coming this way. But there are always people who think they know more than you do, especially young people; so of course the young fellow in charge of this lady used the telegraph. And at Boston, of all places! Except York Harbor.

The result was as usual; let me employ a statelier and exacter term, and say, historical.

The dispatch was handed to the h. c. of the Boston office at 9 this morning. It said, "Shall bring A. S. to you eleven forty-five this morning." The distance traveled by the dispatch is forty or fifty miles, I suppose, as the train-time is five minutes short of two hours, and the trains are so slow that they can't give a W. U. telegram two hours and twenty minutes start and overtake it.

As I have said, the dispatch was handed in at Boston at 9. The expected visitors left Boston at 9.40, and reached my house at 12 noon, beating the telegram 2 solid hours, and 5 minutes over.

The boy brought the telegram. It was bald-headed with age, but still legible. The boy was prostrate with travel and exposure, but still alive, and I went out to condole with him and get his last wishes and send for the ambulance. He was waiting to collect transportation before turning his passing spirit to less serious affairs. I found him strangely intelligent, considering his condition and where he is getting his training. I asked him at what hour the telegram was handed to the h. c. in Boston. He answered brightly, that he didn't know.

I examined the blank, and sure enough the wary Boston h. c. had thoughtfully concealed that statistic. I asked him at what hour it had started from Boston. He answered up as brightly as ever, and said he didn't know.

I examined the blank, and sure enough the Boston h. c. had left that statistic out in the cold, too. In fact it turned out to be an official concealment--no blank was provided for its exposure. And none required by the law, I suppose. "It is a good one-sided idea," I remarked; "They can take your money and ship your telegram next year if they want to--you've no redress. The law ought to extend the privilege to all of us."

The boy looked upon me coldly.

I asked him when the telegram reached York Harbor. He pointed to some figures following the signature at the bottom of the blank--"12.14. "I said it was now 1.45 and asked--

"Do you mean that it reached your morgue an hour and a half ago?"

He nodded assent.

"It was at that time half an hour too late to be of any use to me, if I wanted to go and meet my people--which was the case--for by the wording of the message you can see that they were to arrive at the station at 11.45. Why did, your h. c. send me this useless message? Can't he read? Is he dead?"

"It's the rules."

"No, that does not account for it. Would he have sent it if it had been three years old, I in the meantime deceased, and he aware of it?"

The boy didn't know.

"Because, you know, a rule which required him to forward to the cemetery to-day a dispatch due three years ago, would be as good a rule as one which should require him to forward a telegram to me to-day which he knew had lost all its value an hour or two before he started it. The construction of such a rule would discredit an idiot; in fact an idiot-- I mean a common ordinary Christian idiot, you understand--would be ashamed of it, and for the sake of his reputation wouldn't make it. What do you think?"

He replied with much natural brilliancy that he wasn't paid for thinking.

This gave me a better opinion of the commercial intelligence pervading his morgue than I had had before; it also softened my feelings toward him, and also my tone, which had hitherto been tinged with bitterness.

"Let bygones be bygones," I said, gently, "we are all erring creatures, and mainly idiots, but God made us so and it is dangerous to criticise." Sincerely S. L. CLEMENS.

One day there arrived from Europe a caller with a letter of introduction from Elizabeth, Queen of

Rumania, better known as Carmen Sylva. The visitor was Madam Hartwig, formerly an American girl, returning now, because of reduced fortunes, to find profitable employment in her own land. Her husband, a man of high principle, had declined to take part in an "affair of honor," as recognized by the Continental code; hence his ruin. Elizabeth of Rumania was one of the most loved and respected of European queens and an author of distinction. Mark Twain had known her in Vienna. Her letter to him and his own letter to the public (perhaps a second one, for its date is two years later) follow herewith.

From Carmen Sylva to Mark Twain:

BUCAREST, May 9, 1902. HONORED MASTER,--If I venture to address you on behalf of a poor lady, who is stranded in Bucarest I hope not to be too disagreeable.

Mrs. Hartwig left America at the age of fourteen in order to learn to sing which she has done thoroughly. Her husband had quite a brilliant situation here till he refused to partake 'dans une afaire onereuse', so it seems. They haven't a penny and each of them must try to find a living. She is very nice and pleasant and her school is so good that she most certainly can give excellent singing lessons.

I beg your pardon for being a bore to one I so deeply love and admire, to whom I owe days and days of forgetfulness of self and troubles and the intensest of all joys: Hero-worship! People don't always realize what a happiness that is! God bless you for every beautiful thought you poured into my tired heart and for every smile on a weary way!

CARMEN SYLVA.

From Mark Twain to the Public:

Nov. 16, '04. TO WHOM IT MAY CONCERN,--I desire to recommend Madame Hartwig to my friends and the public as a teacher of singing and as a concert-vocalist. She has lived for fifteen years at the court of Roumania, and she brought with her to America an autograph letter in which her Majesty the Queen of Roumania cordially certified her to me as being an accomplished and gifted singer and teacher of singing, and expressed a warm hope that her professional venture among us would meet with success; through absence in Europe I have had no opportunity to test the validity of the Queen's judgment in the matter, but that judgment is the utterance of an entirely competent authority--the best that occupies a throne, and as good as any that sits elsewhere, as the musical world well knows--and therefore back it without hesitation, and endorse it with confidence.

I will explain that the reason her Majesty tried to do her friend a friendly office through me instead of through someone else was, not that I was particularly the right or best person for the office, but because I was not a stranger. It is true that I am a stranger to some of the monarchs-- mainly through their neglect of their opportunities--but such is not the case in the present instance. The latter fact is a high compliment to me, and perhaps I ought to conceal it. Some people would.

MARK TWAIN.

Mrs. Clemens's improvement was scarcely perceptible. It was not until October that they were able to remove her to Riverdale, and then only in a specially arranged invalid-car. At the end of the long journey she was carried to her room and did not leave it again for many months.

To Rev. J. H. Twichell, in Hartford:

RIVERDALE, N. Y., Oct. 31, '02. DEAR JOE,--It is ten days since Susy [Twichell] wrote that you were laid up with a sprained shoulder, since which time we have had no news about it. I hope that no news is good news, according to the proverb; still, authoritative confirmation of it will be gladly received in this family, if some of you will furnish it. Moreover, I should like to know how and where it happened. In the pulpit, as like as not, otherwise you would not be taking so much pains to conceal it. This is not a malicious suggestion, and not a personally-invented one: you told me yourself, once, that you threw artificial power and impressiveness into places in your sermons where needed, by "banging the bible"--(your own words.) You have reached a time of life when it is not wise to take these risks. You would better jump around. We all have to change our methods as the infirmities of age creep upon us. Jumping around will be impressive now, whereas before you were gray it would have excited remark.

Poor Livy drags along drearily. It must be hard times for that turbulent spirit. It will be a long time before she is on her feet again. It is a most pathetic case. I wish I could transfer it to myself. Between ripping and raging and smoking and reading, I could get a good deal of a holiday out of it.

Clara runs the house smoothly and capably. She is discharging a trial- cook today and hiring another. A power of love to you all! MARK.

Such was the state of Mrs. Clemens's health that visitors were excluded from the sick room, and even Clemens himself was allowed to see her no more than a few moments at a time. These brief, precious visits were the chief interests of his long days. Occasionally he was allowed to send her a few lines, reporting his occupations, and these she was sometimes permitted to answer. Only one of his notes has been preserved, written after a day, now rare, of literary effort. Its signature, the letter Y, stands for "Youth," always her name for him.

To Mrs. Clemens:

DEAR HEART,--I've done another full day's work, and finished before 4. I have been reading and dozing since and would have had a real sleep a few minutes ago but for an incursion to bring me a couple of unimportant letters. I've stuck to the bed all day and am getting back my lost ground. Next time I will be strictly careful and make my visit very short--just a kiss and a rush. Thank you for your dear, dear note; you who are my own and only sweetheart. Sleep well! Y.

XLII

LETTERS OF 1903. TO VARIOUS PERSONS. HARD DAYS AT RIVERDALE. LAST SUMMER AT ELMIRA. THE RETURN TO ITALY

The reader may perhaps recall that H. H. Rogers, some five or six years earlier, had taken charge of the fortunes of Helen Keller, making it possible for her to complete her education. Helen had now written her first book--a wonderful book--'The Story of My Life', and it had been successfully published. For a later generation it may be proper to explain that the Miss Sullivan, later Mrs. Macy, mentioned in the letter which follows, was the noble woman who had devoted her life to the enlightenment of this blind, dumb girl--had made it possible for her to speak and understand, and, indeed, to see with the eyes of luminous imagination.

The case of plagiarism mentioned in this letter is not now remembered, and does not matter, but it furnished a text for Mark Twain, whose remarks on the subject in general are eminently worth while.

To Helen Keller, in Wrentham, Mass.:

RIVERDALE-ON-THE-HUDSON, ST. PATRICK'S DAY, '03. DEAR HELEN,--I must steal half a moment from my work to say how glad I am to have your book, and how highly I value it, both for its own sake and as a remembrances of an affectionate friendship which has subsisted between us for nine years without a break, and without a single act of violence that I can call to mind. I suppose there is nothing like it in heaven; and not likely to be, until we get there and show off. I often think of it with longing, and how they'll say, "There they come--sit down in front!" I am practicing with a tin halo. You do the same. I was at Henry Rogers's last night, and of course we talked of you. He is not at all well; you will not like to hear that; but like you and me, he is just as lovely as ever.

I am charmed with your book-enchanted. You are a wonderful creature, the most wonderful in the world--you and your other half together-- Miss Sullivan, I mean, for it took the pair of you to make a complete and perfect whole. How she stands out in her letters! her brilliancy, penetration, originality, wisdom, character, and the fine literary competencies of her pen--they are all there.

Oh, dear me, how unspeakably funny and owlishly idiotic and grotesque was that "plagiarism" farce! As if there was much of anything in any human utterance, oral or written, except plagiarism! The kernal, the soul--let us go further and say the substance, the bulk, the actual and valuable material of all human utterances--is plagiarism. For substantially all ideas are second-hand, consciously and unconsciously drawn from a million outside sources, and daily used by the garnerer with a pride and satisfaction born of the superstition that he originated them; whereas there is not a rag of originality about them anywhere except the little discoloration they get from his mental and moral calibre and his temperament, and which is revealed in characteristics of phrasing. When a great orator makes a great speech you are listening to ten centuries and ten thousand men--but we call it his speech, and really some exceedingly small portion of it is his. But not enough to signify. It is merely a Waterloo. It is Wellington's battle, in some degree, and we call it his; but there are others that contributed. It takes a thousand men to invent a telegraph, or a steam engine, or a phonograph, or a photograph, or a telephone or any other important thing--and the last man gets the credit and we forget the others. He added his little mite--that is all he did. These object lessons should teach us that ninety-nine parts of all things that proceed from the intellect are plagiarisms, pure and simple; and the lesson ought to make us modest. But nothing can do that.

Then why don't we unwittingly reproduce the phrasing of a story, as well as the story itself? It can hardly happen--to the extent of fifty words except in the case of a child: its memory-tablet is not lumbered with impressions, and the actual language can have graving-room there, and preserve the language a year or two, but a grown person's memory-tablet is a palimpsest, with hardly a bare space upon which to engrave a phrase. It must be a very rare thing that a whole page gets so sharply printed upon a man's mind, by a single reading, that it will stay long enough to turn up some time or other and be mistaken by him for his own. No doubt we are constantly littering our literature with disconnected sentences borrowed from books at some unremembered time and now imagined to be our own, but that is about the most we can do. In 1866 I read Dr. Holmes's poems, in the Sandwich Islands. A year and a half later I stole his dictation, without knowing it, and used it to dedicate my "Innocents Abroad" with. Then years afterwards I was talking with Dr. Holmes about it. He was not an ignorant ass--no, not he: he was not a collection of decayed human turnips, like your "Plagiarism Court;" and so when I said, "I know now where I stole it, but whom did you steal it from," he said, "I don't remember; I only know I stole it from somebody, because I have never originated anything altogether myself, nor met anybody who had."

To think of those solemn donkeys breaking a little child's heart with their ignorant rubbish about plagiarism! I couldn't sleep for blaspheming about it last night. Why, their whole lives, their whole histories, all their learning, all their thoughts, all their opinions were one solid ruck of plagiarism, and they didn't know it and never suspected it. A gang of dull and hoary pirates piously setting themselves the task of disciplining and purifying a kitten that they think they've caught filching a chop! Oh, dam--

But you finish it, dear, I am running short of vocabulary today. Ever lovingly your friend, MARK.

(Edited and modified by Clara Clemens, deputy to her mother, who for more than 7 months has been ill in bed and unable to exercise her official function.)

The burden of the Clemens household had fallen almost entirely upon Clara Clemens. In addition to supervising its customary affairs, she also shouldered the responsibility of an unusual combination of misfortunes, for besides the critical condition of her mother, her sister, Jean Clemens, was down with pneumonia, no word of which must come to Mrs. Clemens. Certainly it was a difficult position. In some account of it, which he set down later, Clemens wrote: "It was fortunate for us all that Clara's reputation for truthfulness was so well established in her mother's mind. It was our daily protection from disaster. The mother never doubted Clara's word. Clara could tell her large improbabilities without exciting any suspicion, whereas if I tried to market even a small and simple one the case would have been different. I was never able to get a reputation like Clara's."

The accumulation of physical ailments in the Clemens home had somewhat modified Mark Twain's notion of medical practice. He was no longer radical; he had become eclectic. It is a good deal of a concession that he makes to Twichell, after those earlier letters from Sweden, in which osteopathy had been heralded as the anodyne for all human ills.

To Rev. J. H. Twichell, in Hartford:

DEAR JOE,--Livy does really make a little progress these past 3 or 4 days, progress which is visible to even the untrained eye. The physicians are doing good work with her, but my notion is, that no art of healing is the best for all ills. I should distribute the ailments around: surgery cases to the surgeons; lupus to the actinic-ray specialist; nervous prostration to the Christian Scientist; most ills to the allopath and the homeopath; (in my own particular case) rheumatism, gout and bronchial attacks to the osteopathist.

Mr. Rogers was to sail southward this morning--and here is this weather! I am sorry. I think it's a question if he gets away tomorrow. Ys Ever MARK.

It was through J. Y. M. MacAlister, to whom the next letter is written, that Mark Twain had become associated with the Plasmon Company, which explains the reference to "shares." He had seen much of MacAlister during the winter at Tedworth Square, and had grown fond of him. It is a characteristic letter, and one of interesting fact.

To J. Y. M. MacAlister, in London:

RIVERDALE, NEW YORK. April, 7, '03. DEAR MACALISTER,--Yours arrived last night, and God knows I was glad to get it, for I was afraid I had blundered into an offence in some way and forfeited your friendship--a kind of blunder I have made so many times in my life that I am always standing in a waiting and morbid dread of its occurrence.

Three days ago I was in condition--during one horribly long night--to sympathetically roast with you in your "hell of troubles." During that night I was back again where I was in the black days when I was buried under a mountain of debt. I called the daughters to me in private council and paralysed them with the announcement, "Our outgo has increased in the past 8 months until our expenses are now 125 per cent. greater than our income."

It was a mistake. When I came down in the morning a gray and aged wreck, and went over the figures again, I found that in some unaccountable way (unaccountable to a business man but not to me) I had multiplied the totals by 2. By God I dropped 75 years on the floor where I stood.

Do you know it affected me as one is affected when he wakes out of a hideous dream and finds that it was only a dream. It was a great comfort and satisfaction to me to call the daughters to a private meeting of the Board again and say, "You need not worry any more; our outgo is only a third more than our income; in a few months your mother will be out of her bed and on her feet again--then we shall drop back to normal and be all right."

Certainly there is a blistering and awful reality about a well-arranged unreality. It is quite within the possibilities that two or three nights like that night of mine could drive a man to suicide. He would refuse to examine the figures; they would revolt him so, and he could go to his death unaware that there was nothing serious about them. I cannot get that night out of my head, it was so vivid, so real, so ghastly. In any other year of these 33 the relief would have been simple: go where you can cut your cloth to fit your income. You can't do that when your wife can't be moved, even from one room to the next.

Clam spells the trained nurse afternoons; I am allowed to see Mrs. Clemens 20 minutes twice a day and write her two letters a day provided I put no news in them. No other person ever sees her except the physician and now and then a nerve-specialist from New York. She saw there was something the matter that morning, but she got no facts out of me. But that is nothing--she hasn't had anything but lies for 8 months. A fact would give her a relapse.

The doctor and a specialist met in conspiracy five days ago, and in their belief she will by and by come out of this as good as new, substantially. They ordered her to Italy for next winter--which seems to indicate that by autumn she will be able to undertake the voyage. So Clara is writing a Florence friend to take a look round among the villas for us in the regions near that city. It seems early to do this, but Joan Bergheim thought it would be wise.

He and his wife lunched with us here yesterday. They have been abroad in Havana 4 months, and they sailed for England this morning.

I am enclosing an order for half of my (your) Founders shares. You are not to refuse them this time, though you have done it twice before. They are yours, not mine, and for your family's sake if not your own you cannot in these cloudy days renounce this property which is so clearly yours and theirs. You have been generous long enough; be just, now to yourself. Mr. Rogers is off yachting for 5 or 6 weeks--I'll get them when he returns. The head of the house joins me in warmest greetings and remembrances to you and Mrs. MacAlister. Ever yours, Mark.

May 8. Great Scott! I never mailed this letter! I addressed it, put "Registered" on it--then left it lying unsealed on the arm of my chair, and rushed up to my bed quaking with a chill. I've never been out of the bed since--oh, bronchitis, rheumatism, two sets of teeth aching, land, I've had a dandy time for 4 weeks. And to-day--great guns, one of the very worst! . . .

I'm devilish sorry, and I do apologise--for although I am not as slow as you are about answering letters, as a rule, I see where I'm standing this time.

Two weeks ago Jean was taken down again--this time with measles, and I haven't been able to go to her and she hasn't been able to come to me.

But Mrs. Clemens is making nice progress, and can stand alone a moment or two at a time.

Now I'll post this. MARK

The two letters that follow, though written only a few days apart, were separated in their arrival by a period of seven years. The second letter was, in some way, mislaid and not mailed; and it was not until after the writer of it was dead that it was found and forwarded.

Mark Twain could never get up much enthusiasm for the writings of Scott. His praise of Quentin Durward is about the only approval he ever accorded to the works of the great romanticist.

To Brander Matthews, in New York:

NEW YORK CITY, May 4, '03. DEAR BRANDER,--I haven't been out of my bed for four weeks, but--well, I have been reading, a good deal, and it occurs to me to ask you to sit down, some time or other when you have 8 or 9 months to spare, and jot me down a certain few literary particulars for my help and elevation. Your time need not be thrown away, for at your further leisure you can make Colombian lectures out of the results and do your students a good turn.

1. Are there in Sir Walter's novels passages done in good English-- English which is neither slovenly or involved?

2. Are there passages whose English is not poor and thin and commonplace, but is of a quality above that?

3. Are there passages which burn with real fire--not punk, fox-fire, make believe?

4. Has he heroes and heroines who are not cads and cadesses?

5. Has he personages whose acts and talk correspond with their characters as described by him?

6. Has he heroes and heroines whom the reader admires, admires, and knows why?

7. Has he funny characters that are funny, and humorous passages that are humorous?

8. Does he ever chain the reader's interest, and make him reluctant to lay the book down?

9. Are there pages where he ceases from posing, ceases from admiring the placid flood and flow of his own dilutions, ceases from being artificial, and is for a time, long or short, recognizably

sincere and in earnest?

10. Did he know how to write English, and didn't do it because he didn't want to?

11. Did he use the right word only when he couldn't think of another one, or did he run so much to wrong because he didn't know the right one when he saw it?

13. Can you read him? and keep your respect for him? Of course a person could in his day--an era of sentimentality and sloppy romantics-- but land! can a body do it today?

Brander, I lie here dying, slowly dying, under the blight of Sir Walter. I have read the first volume of Rob Roy, and as far as chapter XIX of Guy Mannering, and I can no longer hold my head up nor take my nourishment. Lord, it's all so juvenile! so artificial, so shoddy; and such wax figures and skeletons and spectres. Interest? Why, it is impossible to feel an interest in these bloodless shams, these milk-and-water humbugs. And oh, the poverty of the invention! Not poverty in inventing situations, but poverty in furnishing reasons for them. Sir Walter usually gives himself away when he arranges for a situation--elaborates, and elaborates, and elaborates, till if you live to get to it you don't believe in it when it happens.

I can't find the rest of Rob Roy, I can't stand any more Mannering--I do not know just what to do, but I will reflect, and not quit this great study rashly. He was great, in his day, and to his proper audience; and so was God in Jewish times, for that matter, but why should either of them rank high now? And do they?--honest, now, do they? Dam'd if I believe it.

My, I wish I could see you and Leigh Hunt! ` Sincerely Yours S. L. CLEMENS.

To Brander Matthews, in New York:

RIVERDALE, May 8,'03 (Mailed June, 1910). DEAR BRANDER,--I'm still in bed, but the days have lost their dulness since I broke into Sir Walter and lost my temper. I finished Guy Mannering--that curious, curious book, with its mob of squalid shadows jabbering around a single flesh-and-blood being--Dinmont; a book crazily put together out of the very refuse of the romance-artist's stage properties--finished it and took up Quentin Durward, and finished that.

It was like leaving the dead to mingle with the living: it was like withdrawing from the infant class in the College of journalism to sit under the lectures in English literature in Columbia University.

I wonder who wrote Quentin Durward? Yrs ever MARK.

In 1903, preparations were going on for a great world's fair, to be held in St. Louis, and among other features proposed was a World's Literary Convention, with a week to be set apart in honor of Mark Twain, and a special Mark Twain Day in it, on which the National Association would hold grand services in honor of the distinguished Missourian. A letter asking his consent to the plan brought the following reply.

To T. F. Gatts, of Missouri:

NEW YORK, May 30, 1903. DEAR MR. GATTS,--It is indeed a high compliment which you offer me in naming an association after me and in proposing the setting apart of a Mark Twain day at the great St. Louis fair, but such compliments are not proper for the living; they are proper and safe for the dead only. I value the impulse which moves you to tender me these honors. I value it as highly as any one can, and am grateful for it, but I should stand in a sort of terror of the honors themselves. So long as we remain alive we are not safe from doing things which, however righteously and honorably intended, can wreck our repute and extinguish our friendships.

I hope that no society will be named for me while I am still alive, for I might at some time or other do something which would cause its members to regret having done me that honor. After I shall have joined the dead I shall follow the customs of those people and be guilty of no conduct that can wound any friend; but until that time shall come I shall be a doubtful quantity like the rest of our race. Very truly yours, S. L. CLEMENS.

The National Mark Twain Association did not surrender easily. Mr. Gatts wrote a second letter full of urgent appeal. If Mark Twain was tempted, we get no hint of it in his answer.

To T. F. Gatts, of Missouri:

NEW YORK, June 8, 1903. DEAR MR. GATTS,--While I am deeply touched by the desire of my friends of Hannibal to confer these great honors upon me, I must still forbear to accept them. Spontaneous and unpremeditated honors, like those which came to me at Hannibal, Columbia, St. Louis and at the village stations all down the line, are beyond all price and are a treasure for life in the memory, for they are a free gift out of the heart and they come without solicitations; but I am a Missourian and so I shrink from distinctions which have to be arranged beforehand and with my privity, for I then became a party to my own exalting. I am humanly fond of honors that happen but chary of those that come by canvass and intention. With sincere thanks to you and your associates for this high compliment which you have been minded to offer me, I am, Very truly yours, S. L. CLEMENS.

We have seen in the letter to MacAlister that Mark Twain's wife had been ordered to Italy and plans were in progress for an establishment there. By the end of June Mrs. Clemens was able to leave Riverdale, and she made the journey to Quarry Farm, Elmira, where they would remain until October, the month planned for their sailing. The house in Hartford had been sold; and a house which, prior to Mrs. Clemens's breakdown they had bought near Tarrytown (expecting to settle permanently on the Hudson) had been let. They were going to Europe for another indefinite period.

At Quarry Farm Mrs. Clemens continued to improve, and Clemens, once more able to work, occupied the study which Mrs. Crane had built for him thirty years before, and where Tom Sawyer and Huck Finn and the Wandering Prince had been called into being.

To Rev. J. H. Twichell, in Hartford, Conn.:

QUARRY FARM, ELMIRA, N. Y., July 21, '03. DEAR JOE,--That love-letter delighted Livy beyond any like utterance received by her these thirty years and more. I was going to answer it for her right away, and said so; but she reserved the privilege to herself. I judge she is accumulating Hot Stuff--as George Ade would say . . . .

Livy is coming along: eats well, sleeps some, is mostly very gay, not very often depressed; spends all day on the porch, sleeps there a part of the night, makes excursions in carriage and in wheel-chair; and, in the matter of superintending everything and everybody, has resumed business at the old stand.

Did you ever go house-hunting 3,000 miles away? It costs three months of writing and telegraphing to pull off a success. We finished 3 or 4 days ago, and took the Villa Papiniano (dam the name, I have to look at it a minutes after writing it, and then am always in doubt) for a year by cable. Three miles outside of Florence, under Fiesole--a darling location, and apparently a choice house, near Fiske.

There's 7 in our gang. All women but me. It means trunks and things. But thanks be! To-day (this is private) comes a most handsome voluntary document with seals and escutcheons on it from the Italian Ambassador (who is a stranger to me) commanding the Customs people to keep their hands off the Clemens's things. Now wasn't it lovely of him? And wasn't it lovely of me to let Livy take a pencil and edit my answer and knock a good third of it out?

And that's a nice ship--the Irene! new--swift--13,000 tons--rooms up in the sky, open to sun and air--and all that. I was desperately troubled for Livy--about the down-cellar cells in the ancient "Latin."

The cubs are in Riverdale, yet; they come to us the first week in August. With lots and lots of love to you all, MARK.

The arrangement for the Villa Papiniano was not completed, after all, and through a good friend, George Gregory Smith, a resident of Florence, the Villa Quarto, an ancient home of royalty, on the hills west of Florence, was engaged. Smith wrote that it was a very beautiful place with a south-eastern exposure, looking out toward Valombrosa and the Chianti Hills. It had extensive grounds and stables, and the annual rental for it all was two thousand dollars a year. It seemed an ideal place, in prospect, and there was great hope that Mrs. Clemens would find her health once more in the Italian climate which she loved.

Perhaps at this point, when Mark Twain is once more leaving America, we may offer two letters from strangers to him--letters of appreciation--such as he was constantly receiving from those among the thousands to whom he had given happiness. The first is from Samuel Merwin, one day to become a popular novelist, then in the hour of his beginnings.

To Mark Twain, from Samuel Merwin:

PLAINFIELD, N. J. August 4, 1903. DEAR MR. CLEMENS,--For a good many years I have been struggling with the temptation to write you and thank you for the work you have done; and to- day I seem to be yielding.

During the past two years I have been reading through a group of writers who seem to me to represent about the best we have--Sir Thomas Malory, Spenser, Shakespeare, Boswell, Carlyle, Le Sage. In thinking over one and then another, and then all of them together, it was plain to see why they were great men and writers: each brought to his time some new blood, new ideas,--turned a new current into the stream. I suppose there have always been the careful, painstaking writers, the men who are always taken so seriously by their fellow craftsmen. It seems to be the unconventional man who is so rare--I mean the honestly unconventional man, who has to express himself in his own big way because the conventional way isn't big enough, because ne needs room and freedom.

We have a group of the more or less conventional men now--men of dignity and literary position. But in spite of their influence and of all the work they have done, there isn't one of them to whom one can give one's self up without reservation, not one whose ideas seem based on the deep foundation of all true philosophy,--except Mark Twain.

I hope this letter is not an impertinence. I have just been turning about, with my head full of Spenser and Shakespeare and "Gil Blas," looking for something in our own present day literature to which I could surrender myself as to those five gripping old writings. And nothing could I find until I took up "Life on the Mississippi," and "Huckleberry Finn," and, just now, the "Connecticut Yankee." It isn't the first time I have read any of these three, and it's because I know it won't be the last, because these books are the only ones written in my lifetime that claim my unreserved interest and admiration and, above all, my feelings, that I've felt I had to write this letter.

I like to think that "Tom Sawyer" and "Huckleberry Finn" will be looked upon, fifty or a hundred years from now, as the picture of buoyant, dramatic, human American life. I feel, deep in my own heart, pretty sure that they will be. They won't be looked on then as the work of a "humorist" any more than we think of Shakespeare as a humorist now. I don't mean by this to set up a comparison between Mark Twain and Shakespeare: I don't feel competent to do it; and I'm not at all sure that it could be done until Mark Twain's work shall have its fair share of historical perspective. But Shakespeare was a humorist and so, thank Heaven! is Mark Twain. And Shakespeare plunged deep into the deep, sad things of life; and so, in a different way (but in a way that has more than once brought tears to my eyes) has Mark Twain. But after all, it isn't because of any resemblance for anything that was ever before written that Mark Twain's books strike in so deep: it's rather because they've brought something really new into our literature--new, yet old as Adam and Eve and the Apple. And this achievement, the achievement of putting something into literature that was not there before, is, I should think, the most that any writer can ever hope to do. It is the one mark of distinction between the "lonesome" little group of big men and the vast herd of medium and small ones. Anyhow, this much I am sure of--to the young man who hopes, however feebly, to accomplish a little something, someday, as a writer, the one inspiring example of our time is Mark Twain. Very truly yours, SAMUEL MERWIN.

Mark Twain once said he could live a month on a good compliment, and from his reply, we may believe this one to belong in, that class.

To Samuel Merwin, in Plainfield, N. J.:

Aug. 16, '03. DEAR MR. MERWIN,--What you have said has given me deep pleasure--indeed I think no words could be said that could give me more. Very sincerely yours, S. L. CLEMENS.

The next "compliment" is from one who remains unknown, for she failed to sign her name in full. But it is a lovely letter, and loses nothing by the fact that the writer of it was willing to remain in obscurity.

To Mark Twain, from Margaret M----:

PORTLAND, OREGON Aug. 18, 1903. MY DEAR, DEAR MARK TWAIN,--May a little girl write and tell you how dearly she loves and admires your writings? Well, I do and I want to tell you your ownself. Don't think me too impertinent for indeed I don't mean to be that! I have read everything of yours that I could get and parts that touch me I have read over and over again. They seem such dear friends to me, so like real live human beings talking and laughing, working and suffering too! One cannot but feel that it is your own life and experience that you have painted. So do not wonder that you seem a dear friend to me who has never even seen you. I often think of you as such in my own thoughts. I wonder if you will laugh when I tell you I have made a hero of you? For when people seem very sordid and mean and stupid (and it seems as if everybody was) then the thought will come like a little crumb of comfort "well, Mark Twain isn't anyway." And it does really brighten me up.

You see I have gotten an idea that you are a great, bright spirit of kindness and tenderness. One who can twist everybody's-even your own- faults and absurdities into hearty laughs. Even the person mocked must laugh! Oh, Dear! How often you have made me laugh! And yet as often you have struck something infinite away down deep in my heart so that I want to cry while half laughing!

So this all means that I want to thank you and to tell you. "God always love Mark Twain!" is often my wish. I dearly love to read books, and I never tire of reading yours; they always have a charm for me. Good-bye, I am afraid I have not expressed what I feel. But at least I have tried. Sincerely yours. MARGARET M.----

Clemens and family left Elmira October the 5th for New York City. They remained at the Hotel Grosvenor until their sailing date, October 24th. A few days earlier, Mr. Frank Doubleday sent a volume of Kipling's poems and de Blowitz's Memoirs for entertainment on the ship. Mark Twain's acknowledgment follows.

To F. N. Doubleday, in New York:

THE GROSVENOR, October 12, '03. DEAR DOUBLEDAY,--The books came--ever so many thanks. I have been reading "The Bell Buoy" and "The Old Men" over and over again--my custom with Kipling's work-and saving up the rest for other leisurely and luxurious meals. A bell-buoy is a deeply impressive fellow-being. In these many recent trips up and down the Sound in the Kanawha-- [Mr. Rogers's yacht.]--he has talked to me nightly, sometimes in his pathetic and melancholy way, sometimes with his strenuous and urgent note, and I got his meaning--now I have his words! No one but Kipling could do this strong and vivid thing. Some day I hope to hear the poem chanted or sung--with the bell-buoy breaking in, out of the distance.

"The Old Men," delicious, isn't it? And so comically true. I haven't arrived there yet, but I suppose I am on the way.... Yours ever, MARK.

P. S. Your letter has arrived. It makes me proud and glad--what Kipling says. I hope Fate will fetch him to Florence while we are there. I would rather see him than any other man.

We've let the Tarrytown house for a year. Man, you would never have believed a person could let a house in these times. That one's for sale, the Hartford one is sold. When we buy again may we--may I--be damned....

I've dipped into Blowitz and find him quaintly and curiously interesting. I think he tells the straight truth, too. I knew him a little, 23 years ago.

The appreciative word which Kipling had sent Doubleday was: "I love to think of the great and God-like Clemens. He is the biggest man you have on your side of the water by a damn sight, and don't you forget it. Cervantes was a relation of his."

XLIII

LETTERS OF 1904. TO VARIOUS PERSONS. LIFE IN VILLA QUARTO. DEATH OF MRS. CLEMENS. THE RETURN TO AMERICA

Mrs. Clemens stood the voyage to Italy very well and, in due time, the family were installed in the Villa Reale di Quarto, the picturesque old Palace of Cosimo, a spacious, luxurious place, even if not entirely cheerful or always comfortable during the changeable Tuscan winter. Congratulated in a letter from MacAlister in being in the midst of Florentine sunshine, he answered: "Florentine sunshine? Bless you, there isn't any. We have heavy fogs every morning, and rain all day. This house is not merely large, it is vast--therefore I think it must always lack the home feeling."

Neither was their landlady, the American wife of an Italian count, all that could be desired. From a letter to Twichell, however, we learn that Mark Twain's work was progressing well.

To Rev. J. H. Twichell, in Hartford:

VILLA DI QUARTO, FLORENCE, Jan. 7, '04. DEAR JOE,--. . . I have had a handsome success, in one way, here. I left New York under a sort of half promise to furnish to the Harper magazines 30,000 words this year. Magazining is difficult work because every third page represents 2 pages that you have put in the fire; (because you are nearly sure to start wrong twice) and so when you have finished an article and are willing to let it go to print it represents only 10 cents a word instead of 30.

But this time I had the curious (and unprecedented) luck to start right in each case. I turned out 37,000 words in 25 working days; and the reason I think I started right every time is, that not only have I approved and accepted the several articles, but the court of last resort (Livy) has done the same.

On many of the between-days I did some work, but only of an idle and not necessarily necessary sort, since it will not see print until I am dead. I shall continue this (an hour per day) but the rest of the year I expect to put in on a couple of long books (half-completed ones.) No more magazine-work hanging over my head.

This secluded and silent solitude this clean, soft air and this enchanting view of Florence, the great valley and the snow-mountains that frame it are the right conditions for work. They are a persistent inspiration. To-day is very lovely; when the afternoon arrives there will be a new picture every hour till dark, and each of them divine--or progressing from divine to diviner and divinest. On this (second) floor Clara's room commands the finest; she keeps a window ten feet high wide open all the time and frames it in. I go in from time to time, every day and trade sass for a look. The central detail is a distant and stately snow-hump that rises above and behind blackforested hills, and its sloping vast buttresses, velvety and sun-polished with purple shadows between, make the sort of picture we knew that time we walked in Switzerland in the days of our youth.

I wish I could show your letter to Livy--but she must wait a week or so for it. I think I told you she had a prostrating week of tonsilitis a month ago; she has remained very feeble ever since, and confined to the bed of course, but we allow ourselves to believe she will regain the lost ground in another month. Her physician is Professor Grocco--she could not have a better. And she has a very good trained nurse.

Love to all of you from all of us. And to all of our dear Hartford friends. MARK

P. S. 3 days later.

Livy is as remarkable as ever. The day I wrote you--that night, I mean-- she had a bitter attack of gout or rheumatism occupying the whole left arm from shoulder to fingers, accompanied by fever.

The pains racked her 50 or 6o hours; they have departed, now--and already she is planning a trip to Egypt next fall, and a winter's sojourn there! This is life in her yet.

You will be surprised that I was willing to do so much magazine-writing-- a thing I have always been chary about--but I had good reasons. Our expenses have been so prodigious for a year and a half, and are still so prodigious, that Livy was worrying altogether too much about them, and doing a very dangerous amount of lying awake on their account. It was necessary to stop that, and it is now stopped.

Yes, she is remarkable, Joe. Her rheumatic attack set me to cursing and swearing, without limit as to time or energy, but it merely concentrated her patience and her unconquerable fortitude. It is the difference between us. I can't count the different kinds of ailments which have assaulted her in this fiendish year and a half--and I forgive none of them--but here she comes up again as bright and fresh and enterprising as ever, and goes to planning about Egypt, with a hope and a confidence which are to me amazing.

Clara is calling for me--we have to go into town and pay calls.

MARK.

In Florence, that winter, Clemens began dictating to his secretary some autobiographical chapters. This was the work which was "not to see print until I am dead." He found it a pleasant, lazy occupation and wrote his delight in it to Howells in a letter which seems not to have survived. In his reply, Howells wrote: "You do stir me mightily with the hope of dictating and I will try it when I get the chance. But there is the temperamental difference. You are dramatic and unconscious; you count the thing more than yourself; I am cursed with consciousness to the core, and can't say myself out; I am always saying myself in, and setting myself above all that I say, as of more worth. Lately I have felt as if I were rotting with egotism. I don't admire myself; I am sick of myself; but I can't think of anything else. Here I am at it now, when I ought to be rejoicing with you at the blessing you have found .... I'd like, immensely, to read your autobiography. You always rather bewildered me by your veracity, and I fancy you may tell the truth about yourself. But all of it? The black truth which we all know of ourselves in our hearts, or only the whity-brown truth of the pericardium, or the nice, whitened truth of the shirtfront? Even you won't tell the black heart's--truth. The man who could do it would be famed to the last day the sun shone upon."

We gather from Mark Twain's answer that he was not deceiving himself in the matter of his confessions.

To W. D. Howells, in New York:

VILLA DI QUARTO, FLORENCE, March 14, '04. DEAR HOWELLS,--Yes, I set up the safeguards, in the first day's dictating; taking this position: that an autobiography is the truest of all books; for while it inevitably consists mainly of extinctions of the truth, shirkings of the truth, partial revealments of the truth, with hardly an instance of plain straight truth, the remorseless truth is there, between the lines, where the author is raking dust upon it, the result being that the reader knows the author in spite of his wily diligences.

The summer in England! you can't ask better luck than that. Then you will run over to Florence; we shall all be hungry to see you-all. We are hunting for another villa, (this one is plenty large enough but has no room in it) but even if we find it I am afraid it will be months before we can move Mrs. Clemens. Of course it will. But it comforts us to let on that we think otherwise, and these pretensions help to keep hope alive in her. Good-bye, with love, Amen. Yours ever MARK.

News came of the death of Henry M. Stanley, one of Mark Twain's oldest friends. Clemens once said that he had met Stanley in St. Louis where he (Clemens) had delivered a lecture which Stanley had reported. In the following letter he fixes the date of their meeting as early in 1867, which would be immediately after Mark Twain's return from California, and just prior to the Quaker City excursion--a fact which is interesting only because it places the two men together when each was at the very beginning of a great career.

To Lady Stanley, in England:

VILLA DI QUARTO, FIRENZE, May 11, '04. DEAR LADY STANLEY,--I have lost a dear and honored friend--how fast they fall about me now, in my age! The world has lost a tried and proved hero. And you--what have you lost? It is beyond estimate--we who know you, and what he was to you, know that. How far he stretches across my life! I knew him when his work was all before him five years before the great day that he wrote his name far-away up on the blue of the sky for the world to see and applaud and remember; I have known him as friend and intimate ever since. It is 37 years. I have known no other friend and intimate so long, except John Hay--a friendship which dates from the same year and the same half of it, the first half of 1867. I grieve with you and with your family, dear Lady Stanley, it is all I can do; but that I do out of my heart. It would be we, instead of I, if Mrs. Clemens knew, but in all these 20 months that she has lain a prisoner in her bed we have hidden from her all things that could sadden her. Many a friend is gone whom she still asks about and still thinks is living.

In deepest sympathy I beg the privilege of signing myself Your friend, S. L. CLEMENS.

To Rev. J. H. Twichell, in Hartford:

VILLA DI QUARTO, May 11, '04 DEAR JOE,--Yours has this moment arrived--just as I was finishing a note to poor Lady Stanley. I believe the last country-house visit we paid in England was to Stanley's. Lord, how my friends and acquaintances fall about me now, in my gray-headed days! Vereschagin, Mommsen, Dvorak, Lenbach, Jokai--all so recently, and now Stanley. I had known Stanley 37 years. Goodness, who is it I haven't known! As a rule the necrologies find me personally interested--when they treat of old stagers. Generally when a man dies who is worth cabling, it happens that I have run across him somewhere, some time or other.

Oh, say! Down by the Laurentian Library there's a marble image that has been sitting on its pedestal some 450 Years, if my dates are right-- Cosimo I. I've seen the back of it many a time, but not the front; but yesterday I twisted my head around after we had driven by, and the profane exclamation burst from my mouth before I could think: "there's Chauncey Depew!"

I mean to get a photo of it--and use it if it confirms yesterday's conviction. That's a very nice word from the Catholic Magazine and I am glad you sent it. I mean to show it to my priest--we are very fond of him. He is a stealing man, and is also learnedly scientific. He invented the thing which records the seismatic disturbances, for the peoples of the earth. And he's an astronomer and has an observatory of his own.

Ah, many's the cry I have, over reflecting that maybe we could have had Young Harmony for Livy, and didn't have wit enough to think of it.

Speaking of Livy reminds me that your inquiry arrives at a good time (unberufen) It has been weeks (I don't know how many!) since we could have said a hopeful word, but this morning Katy came the minute the day- nurse came on watch and said words of a strange and long-forgotten sound: "Mr. Clemens, Mrs. Clemens is really and truly better!--anybody can see it; she sees it herself; and last night at 9 o'clock she said it."

There--it is heart-warming, it is splendid, it is sublime; let us enjoy it, let us make the most of it today--and bet not a farthing on tomorrow. The tomorrows have nothing for us. Too many times they have breathed the word of promise to our ear and broken it to our hope. We take no tomorrow's word any more.

You've done a wonder, Joe: you've written a letter that can be sent in to Livy--that doesn't often happen, when either a friend or a stranger writes. You did whirl in a P. S. that wouldn't do, but you wrote it on a margin of a page in such a way that I was able to clip off the margin clear across both pages, and now Livy won't perceive that the sheet isn't the same size it used to was. It was about Aldrich's son, and I came near forgetting to remove it. It should have been written on a loose strip and enclosed. That son died on the 5th of March and Aldrich wrote me on the night before that his minutes were numbered. On the 18th Livy asked after that patient, and I was prepared, and able to give her a grateful surprise by telling her "the Aldriches are no longer uneasy about him."

I do wish I could have been present and heard Charley Clark. When he can't light up a dark place nobody can. With lots of love to you all. MARK.

Mrs. Clemens had her bad days and her good days-days when there seemed no ray of light, and others that seemed almost to promise recovery. The foregoing letter to Twichell, and the one which follows, to Richard Watson Gilder, reflect the hope and fear that daily and hourly alternated at Villa Quarto

To Richard Watson Gilder, in New York:

VILLA DI QUARTO, FLORENCE, May 12, '04. DEAR GILDER,--A friend of ours (the Baroness de Nolda) was here this afternoon and wanted a note of introduction to the Century, for she has something to sell to you in case you'll want to make her an offer after seeing a sample of the goods. I said "With pleasure: get the goods ready, send the same to me, I will have Jean typewrite them, then I will mail them to the Century and tonight I will write the note to Mr. Gilder and start it along. Also write me a letter embodying what you have been saying to me about the goods and your proposed plan of arranging and explaining them, and I will forward that to Gilder too."

As to the Baroness. She is a German; 30 years old; was married at 17; is very pretty--indeed I might say very pretty; has a lot of sons (5) running up from seven to 12 years old. Her husband is a Russian. They live half the time in Russia and the other half in Florence, and supply population alternately to the one country and then to the other. Of course it is a family that speaks languages. This occurs at their table--I know it by experience: It is Babel come again. The other day, when no guests were present to keep order, the tribes were all talking at once, and 6 languages were being traded in; at last the littlest boy lost his temper and screamed out at the top of his voice, with angry sobs: "Mais, vraiment, io non capisco gar nichts."

The Baroness is a little afraid of her English, therefore she will write her remarks in French--I said there's a plenty of translators in New York. Examine her samples and drop her a line.

For two entire days, now, we have not been anxious about Mrs. Clemens (unberufen). After 20 months of bed-ridden solitude and bodily misery she all of a sudden ceases to be a pallid shrunken shadow, and looks bright and young and pretty. She remains what she always was, the most wonderful creature of fortitude, patience, endurance and recuperative power that ever was. But ah, dear, it won't last; this fiendish malady will play new treacheries upon her, and I shall go back to my prayers again--unutterable from any pulpit! With love to you and yours, S. L. C.

May 13 10 A.M. I have just paid one of my pair of permitted 2 minutes visits per day to the sick room. And found what I have learned to expect--retrogression, and that pathetic something in the eye which betrays the secret of a waning hope.

The year of the World's Fair had come, and an invitation from Gov. Francis, of Missouri, came to Mark Twain in Florence, personally inviting him to attend the great celebration and carry off first prize. We may believe that Clemens felt little in the spirit of humor, but to such an invitation he must send a cheerful, even if disappointing, answer.

To Gov. Francis, of Missouri:

VILLA DI QUARTO, FIRENZE, May 26, 1904. DEAR GOVERNOR FRANCIS,--It has been a dear wish of mine to exhibit myself at the Great Fair and get a prize, but circumstances beyond my control have interfered, and I must remain in Florence. Although I have never taken prizes anywhere else I used to take them at school in Missouri half a century ago, and I ought to be able to repeat, now, if I could have a chance. I used to get the medal for good spelling, every week, and I could have had the medal for good conduct if there hadn't been so much curruption in Missouri in those days; still, I got it several times by trading medals and giving boot. I am willing to give boot now, if-- however, those days are forever gone by in Missouri, and perhaps it is better so. Nothing ever stops the way it was in this changeable world. Although I cannot be at the Fair, I am going to be represented there anyway, by a portrait, by Professor Gelli. You will find it excellent. Good judges here say it is better than the original. They say it has all the merits of the original and keeps still, besides. It sounds like flattery, but it is just true.

I suppose you will get a prize, because you have created the most prodigious and in all ways most wonderful Fair the planet has ever seen. Very well, you have indeed earned it: and with it the gratitude of the State and the nation. Sincerely yours, MARK TWAIN

It was only a few days after the foregoing was written that death entered Villa Quarto-- unexpectedly at last--for with the first June days Mrs. Clemens had seemed really to improve. It was on Sunday, June 5th, that the end came. Clemens, with his daughter Jean, had returned from a long drive, during which they had visited a Villa with the thought of purchase. On their return they were told that their patient had been better that afternoon than for three months. Yet it was only a few hours later that she left them, so suddenly and quietly that even those near her did not at first realize that she was gone.

To W. D. Howells, in New York.

VILLA DI QUARTO, FLORENCE, June 6, '94. [1904] DEAR HOWELLS,--Last night at 9.20 I entered Mrs. Clemens's room to say the usual goodnight--and she was dead--tho' no one knew it. She had been cheerfully talking, a moment before. She was sitting up in bed--she had not lain down for months--and Katie and the nurse were supporting her. They supposed she had fainted, and they were holding the oxygen pipe to her mouth, expecting to revive her. I bent over her and looked in her face, and I think I spoke--I was surprised and troubled that she did not notice me. Then we understood, and our hearts broke. How poor we are today!

But how thankful I am that her persecutions are ended. I would not call her back if I could.

Today, treasured in her worn old Testament, I found a dear and gentle letter from you, dated Far Rockaway, Sept. 13, 1896, about our poor Susy's death. I am tired and old; I wish I were with Livy.

I send my love-and hers-to you all. S. L. C.

In a letter to Twichell he wrote: "How sweet she was in death; how young, how beautiful, how like her dear, girlish self cf thirty years ago; not a gray hair showing."

The family was now without plans for the future until they remembered the summer home of R. W. Gilder, at Tyringham, Massachusetts, and the possibility of finding lodgment for themselves in that secluded corner of New England. Clemens wrote without delay, as follows:

To R. W. Gilder, in New York:

VILLA DI QUARTO, FLORENCE, June 7, '04. DEAR GILDER FAMILY,--I have been worrying and worrying to know what to do: at last I went to the girls with an idea: to ask the Gilders to get us shelter near their summer home. It was the first time they have not shaken their heads. So to-morrow I will cable to you and shall hope to be in time.

An, hour ago the best heart that ever beat for me and mine went silent out of this house, and I am as one who wanders and has lost his way. She who is gone was our head, she was our hands. We are now trying to make plans--we: we who have never made a plan before, nor ever needed to. If she could speak to us she would make it all simple and easy with a word, and our perplexities would vanish away. If she had known she was near to death she would have told us where to go and what to do: but she was not suspecting, neither were we. (She had been chatting cheerfully a moment before, and in an instant she was gone from us and we did not know it. We were not alarmed, we did not know anything had happened. It was a blessed death--she passed away without knowing it.) She was all our riches and she is gone: she was our breath, she was our life and now we are nothing.

We send you our love--and with it the love of you that was in her heart when she died. S. L. CLEMENS.

Howells wrote his words of sympathy, adding: "The character which now remains a memory was one of the most perfect ever formed on the earth," and again, after having received Clemens's letter: "I cannot speak of your wife's having kept that letter of mine where she did. You know how it must humiliate a man in his unworthiness to have anything of his so consecrated. She hallowed what she touched, far beyond priests."

To W. D. Howells, in New York:

VILLA DI QUARTO, '04. June 12, 6 p. m. DEAR HOWELLS,--We have to sit and hold our hands and wait--in the silence and solitude of this prodigious house; wait until June 25, then we go to Naples and sail in the Prince Oscar the 26th. There is a ship 12 days earlier (but we came in that one.) I see Clara twice a day--morning and evening--greeting--nothing more is allowed. She keeps her bed, and says nothing. She has not cried yet. I wish she could cry. It would break Livy's heart to see Clara. We excuse ourselves from all the friends that call--though of course only intimates come. Intimates--but they are not the old old friends, the friends of the old, old times when we laughed.

Shall we ever laugh again? If I could only see a dog that I knew in the old times! and could put my arms around his neck and tell him all, everything, and ease my heart.

Think-in 3 hours it will be a week!--and soon a month; and by and by a year. How fast our dead fly from us.

She loved you so, and was always as pleased as a child with any notice you took of her.

Soon your wife will be with you, oh fortunate man! And John, whom mine was so fond of. The sight of him was such a delight to her. Lord, the old friends, how dear they are. S. L. C.

To Rev. J. R. Twichell, in Hartford:

VILLA DI QUARTO, FLORENCE, June 18, '04. DEAR JOE,--It is 13 days. I am bewildered and must remain so for a time longer. It was so sudden, so unexpected. Imagine a man worth a hundred millions who finds himself suddenly penniless and fifty million in debt in his old age.

I was richer than any other person in the world, and now I am that pauper without peer. Some day I will tell you about it, not now. MARK.

A tide of condolence flowed in from all parts of the world. It was impossible to answer all. Only a few who had been their closest friends received a written line, but the little printed acknowledgment which was returned was no mere formality. It was a heartfelt, personal word.

They arrived in America in July, and were accompanied by Twichell to Elmira, and on the 14th Mrs. Clemens was laid to rest by the side of Susy and little Langdon. R. W. Gilder had arranged for them to occupy, for the summer, a cottage on his place at Tyringham, in the Berkshire Hills. By November they were at the Grosvenor, in New York, preparing to establish themselves in a house which they had taken on the corner of Ninth Street and Fifth Avenue--Number 21.

To F. N. Doubleday, in New York:

DEAR DOUBLEDAY,--I did not know you were going to England: I would have freighted you with such messages of homage and affection to Kipling. And I would have pressed his hand, through you, for his sympathy with me in my crushing loss, as expressed by him in his letter to Gilder. You know my feeling for Kipling and that it antedates that expression.

I was glad that the boys came here to invite me to the house-warming and I think they understood why a man in the shadow of a calamity like mine could not go.

It has taken three months to repair and renovate our house--corner of 9th and 5th Avenue, but I shall be in it in io or 15 days hence. Much of the furniture went into it today (from Hartford). We have not seen it for 13 years. Katy Leary, our old housekeeper, who has been in our service more than 24 years, cried when she told me about it to-day. She said "I had forgotten it was so beautiful, and it brought Mrs. Clemens right back to me--in that old time when she was so young and lovely."

Jean and my secretary and the servants whom we brought from Italy because Mrs. Clemens liked them so well, are still keeping house in the Berkshire hills--and waiting. Clara (nervously wrecked by her mother's death) is in the hands of a specialist in 69th St., and I shall not be allowed to have any communication with her--even telephone--for a year. I am in this comfortable little hotel, and still in bed--for I dasn't budge till I'm safe from my pet devil, bronchitis.

Isn't it pathetic? One hour and ten minutes before Mrs. Clemens died I was saying to her "To-day, after five months search, I've found the villa that will content you: to-morrow you will examine the plans and give it your consent and I will buy it." Her eyes danced with pleasure, for she longed for a home of her own. And there, on that morrow, she lay white and cold. And unresponsive to my reverent caresses--a new thing to me and a new thing to her; that had not happened before in five and thirty years.

I am coming to see you and Mrs. Doubleday by and bye. She loved and honored Mrs. Doubleday and her work. Always yours, MARK.

It was a presidential year and the air was thick with politics. Mark Twain was no longer actively interested in the political situation; he was only disheartened by the hollowness and pretense of office-seeking, and the methods of office-seekers in general. Grieved that Twichell should still pin his faith to any party when all parties were so obviously venal and time-serving, he wrote in outspoken and rather somber protest.

To Rev. J. H. Twichell, in Hartford:

THE GROSVENOR, Nov. 4, '04. Oh, dear! get out of that sewer--party politics--dear Joe. At least with your mouth. We hail only two men who could make speeches for their parties and preserve their honor and their dignity. One of them is dead. Possibly there were four. I am sorry for John Hay; sorry and ashamed. And yet I know he couldn't help it. He wears the collar, and he had to pay the penalty. Certainly he had no more desire to stand up before a mob of confiding human incapables and debauch them than you had. Certainly he took no more real pleasure in distorting history, concealing facts, propagating immoralities, and appealing to the sordid side of human nature than did you; but he was his party's property, and he had to climb away down and do it.

It is interesting, wonderfully interesting--the miracles which party- politics can do with a man's mental and moral make-up. Look at McKinley, Roosevelt, and yourself: in private life spotless in character; honorable, honest, just, humane, generous; scorning trickeries, treacheries, suppressions of the truth, mistranslations of the meanings of facts, the filching of credit earned by another, the condoning of crime, the glorifying of base acts: in public political life the reverse of all this.

McKinley was a silverite--you concealed it. Roosevelt was a silverite-- you concealed it. Parker was a silverite--you publish it. Along with a shudder and a warning: "He was unsafe then. Is he any safer now?"

Joe, even I could be guilty of such a thing as that--if I were in party- politics; I really believe it.

Mr. Cleveland gave the country the gold standard; by implication you credit the matter to the

Republican party.

By implication you prove the whole annual pension-scoop, concealing the fact that the bulk of the money goes to people who in no way deserve it. You imply that all the batteners upon this bribery-fund are Republicans. An indiscreet confession, since about half of them must have been Democrats before they were bought.

You as good as praise Order 78. It is true you do not shout, and you do not linger, you only whisper and skip--still, what little you do in the matter is complimentary to the crime.

It means, if it means anything, that our outlying properties will all be given up by the Democrats, and our flag hauled down. All of them? Not only the properties stolen by Mr. McKinley and Mr. Roosevelt, but the properties honestly acquired? Joe, did you believe that hardy statement when you made it? Yet you made it, and there it stands in permanent print. Now what moral law would suffer if we should give up the stolen ones? But--

"You know our standard-bearer. He will maintain all that we have gained"--by whatever process. Land, I believe you!

By George, Joe, you are as handy at the game as if you had been in training for it all your life. Your campaign Address is built from the ground up upon the oldest and best models. There isn't a paragraph in it whose facts or morals will wash--not even a sentence, I believe.

But you will soon be out of this. You didn't want to do it--that is sufficiently apparent, thanks be!--but you couldn't well get out of it. In a few days you will be out of it, and then you can fumigate yourself and take up your legitimate work again and resume your clean and wholesome private character once more and be happy--and useful.

I know I ought to hand you some guff, now, as propitiation and apology for these reproaches, but on the whole I believe I won't.

I have inquired, and find that Mitsikuri does not arrive here until to- morrow night. I shall watch out, and telephone again, for I greatly want to see him. Always Yours, MARK.

P. S.--Nov. 4. I wish I could learn to remember that it is unjust and dishonorable to put blame upon the human race for any of its acts. For it did not make itself, it did not make its nature, it is merely a machine, it is moved wholly by outside influences, it has no hand in creating the outside influences nor in choosing which of them it will welcome or reject, its performance is wholly automatic, it has no more mastership nor authority over its mind than it has over its stomach, which receives material from the outside and does as it pleases with it, indifferent to it's proprietor's suggestions, even, let alone his commands; wherefore, whatever the machine does--so called crimes and infamies included--is the personal act of its Maker, and He, solely, is responsible. I wish I could learn to pity the human race instead of censuring it and laughing at it; and I could, if the outside influences of old habit were not so strong upon my machine. It vexes me to catch myself praising the clean private citizen Roosevelt, and blaming the soiled President Roosevelt, when I know that neither praise nor blame is due to him for any thought or word or deed of his, he being merely a helpless and irresponsible coffee-mill ground by the hand of God.

Through a misunderstanding, Clemens, something more than a year earlier, had severed his connection with the Players' Club, of which he had been one of the charter members. Now, upon his return to New York, a number of his friends joined in an invitation to him to return. It was not exactly a letter they sent, but a bit of an old Scotch song--

"To Mark Twain from The Clansmen. Will ye no come back again, Will ye no come back again? Better lo'ed ye canna be. Will ye no come back again?"

Those who signed it were David Monroe, of the North American Review; Robert Reid, the painter, and about thirty others of the Round Table Group, so called because its members were accustomed to lunching at a large round table in a bay window of the Player dining-room. Mark Twain's reply was prompt and heartfelt. He wrote:

To Robt. Reid and the Others:

WELL-BELOVED,--Surely those lovely verses went to Prince Charley's heart, if he had one, and certainly they have gone to mine. I shall be glad and proud to come back again after such a moving and beautiful compliment as this from comrades whom I have loved so long. I hope you can poll the necessary vote; I know you will try, at any rate. It will be many months before I can foregather with you, for this black border is not perfunctory, not a convention; it symbolizes the loss of one whose memory is the only thing I worship.

It is not necessary for me to thank you--and words could not deliver what I feel, anyway. I will put the contents of your envelope in the small casket where I keep the things which have become sacred to me.

S. L. C.

A year later, Mark Twain did "come back again," as an honorary life member, and was given a dinner of welcome by those who had signed the lines urging his return.

XLIV

LETTERS OF 1905. TO TWICHELL, MR. DUNEKA AND OTHERS. POLITICS AND HUMANITY. A SUMMER AT DUBLIN. MARK TWAIN AT 70

In 1884 Mark Twain had abandoned the Republican Party to vote for Cleveland. He believed the party had become corrupt, and to his last day it was hard for him to see anything good in

Republican policies or performance. He was a personal friend of Thedore Roosevelt's but, as we have seen in a former letter, Roosevelt the politician rarely found favor in his eyes. With or without justification, most of the President's political acts invited his caustic sarcasm and unsparing condemnation. Another letter to Twichell of this time affords a fair example.

To Rev. J. H. Twichell, in Hartford:

Feb. 16, '05. DEAR JOE,--I knew I had in me somewhere a definite feeling about the President if I could only find the words to define it with. Here they are, to a hair--from Leonard Jerome: "For twenty years I have loved Roosevelt the man and hated Roosevelt the statesman and politician."

It's mighty good. Every time, in 25 years, that I have met Roosevelt the man, a wave of welcome has streaked through me with the hand-grip; but whenever (as a rule) I meet Roosevelt the statesman and politician, I find him destitute of morals and not respectworthy. It is plain that where his political self and his party self are concerned he has nothing resembling a conscience; that under those inspirations he is naively indifferent to the restraints of duty and even unaware of them; ready to kick the Constitution into the back yard whenever it gets in the way; and whenever he smells a vote, not only willing but eager to buy it, give extravagant rates for it and pay the bill not out of his own pocket or the party's, but out of the nation's, by cold pillage. As per Order 78 and the appropriation of the Indian trust funds.

But Roosevelt is excusable--I recognize it and (ought to) concede it. We are all insane, each in his own way, and with insanity goes irresponsibility. Theodore the man is sane; in fairness we ought to keep in mind that Theodore, as statesman arid politician, is insane and irresponsible.

Do not throw these enlightenments aside, but study them, let them raise you to higher planes and make you better. You taught me in my callow days, let me pay back the debt now in my old age out of a thesaurus with wisdom smelted from the golden ores of experience. Ever yours for sweetness and light MARK.

The next letter to Twichell takes up politics and humanity in general, in a manner complimentary to neither. Mark Twain was never really a pessimist, but he had pessimistic intervals, such as come to most of us in life's later years, and at such times he let himself go without stint concerning "the damned human race," as he called it, usually with a manifest sense of indignation that he should be a member of it. In much of his later writing-- A Mysterious Stranger for example--he said his say with but small restraint, and certainly in his purely intellectual moments he was likely to be a pessimist of the most extreme type, capably damning the race and the inventor of it. Yet, at heart, no man loved his kind more genuinely, or with deeper compassion, than Mark Twain, perhaps for its very weaknesses. It was only that he had intervals --frequent intervals, and rather long ones--when he did not admire it, and was still more doubtful as to the ways of providence.

To Rev. J. H. Twichell, in Hartford:

March 14, '05. DEAR JOE,--I have a Puddn'head maxim:

"When a man is a pessimist before 48 he knows too much; if he is an optimist after it, he knows too little."

It is with contentment, therefore, that I reflect that I am better and wiser than you. Joe, you seem to be dealing in "bulks," now; the "bulk" of the farmers and U. S. Senators are "honest." As regards purchase and sale with money? Who doubts it? Is that the only measure of honesty? Aren't there a dozen kinds of honesty which can't be measured by the money-standard? Treason is treason--and there's more than one form of it; the money-form is but one of them. When a person is disloyal to any confessed duty, he is plainly and simply dishonest, and knows it; knows it, and is privately troubled about it and not proud of himself. Judged by this standard--and who will challenge the validity of it?--there isn't an honest man in Connecticut, nor in the Senate, nor anywhere else. I do not even except myself, this time.

Am I finding fault with you and the rest of the populace? No--I assure you I am not. For I know the human race's limitations, and this makes it my duty--my pleasant duty--to be fair to it. Each person in it is honest in one or several ways, but no member of it is honest in all the ways required by--by what? By his own standard. Outside of that, as I look at it, there is no obligation upon him.

Am I honest? I give you my word of honor (private) I am not. For seven years I have suppressed a book which my conscience tells me I ought to publish. I hold it a duty to publish it. There are other difficult duties which I am equal to, but I am not equal to that one. Yes, even I am dishonest. Not in many ways, but in some. Forty-one, I think it is. We are certainly all honest in one or several ways--every man in the world--though I have reason to think I am the only one whose black-list runs so light. Sometimes I feel lonely enough in this lofty solitude.

Yes, oh, yes, I am not overlooking the "steady progress from age to age of the coming of the kingdom of God and righteousness." "From age to age"--yes, it describes that giddy gait. I (and the rocks) will not live to see it arrive, but that is all right--it will arrive, it surely will. But you ought not to be always ironically apologizing for the Deity. If that thing is going to arrive, it is inferable that He wants it to arrive; and so it is not quite kind of you, and it hurts me, to see you flinging sarcasms at the gait of it. And yet it would not be fair in me not to admit that the sarcasms are deserved. When the Deity wants a thing, and after working at it for "ages and ages" can't show even a shade of progress toward its accomplishment, we--well, we don't laugh, but it is only because we dasn't. The source of "righteousness"--is in the heart? Yes. And engineered and directed by the brain? Yes. Well, history and tradition testify that the heart is just about what it was in the beginning; it has undergone no shade of change. Its good and evil impulses and their consequences are the same today that they were in Old Bible times, in Egyptian times, in Greek times, in Middle Age times, in Twentieth Century times. There has been no change.

Meantime, the brain has undergone no change. It is what it always was. There are a few good brains and a multitude of poor ones. It was so in Old Bible times and in all other times--Greek, Roman, Middle Ages and Twentieth Century. Among the savages--all the savages--the average brain is as competent as the average brain here or elsewhere. I will prove it to you, some time, if you like. And there are great brains among them, too. I will prove that also, if you like.

Well, the 19th century made progress--the first progress after "ages and ages"--colossal progress. In what? Materialities. Prodigious acquisitions were made in things which add to the comfort of many and make life harder for as many more. But the addition to righteousness? Is that discoverable? I think not. The materialities were not invented in the interest of righteousness; that there is more righteousness in the world because of them than there, was before, is hardly demonstrable, I think. In Europe and America, there is a vast change (due to them) in ideals--do you admire it? All Europe and all America, are feverishly scrambling for money. Money is the supreme ideal--all others take tenth place with the great bulk of the nations named. Money-lust has always existed, but not in the history of the world was it ever a craze, a madness, until your time and mine. This lust has rotted these nations; it has made them hard, sordid, ungentle, dishonest, oppressive.

Did England rise against the infamy of the Boer war? No--rose in favor of it. Did America rise against the infamy of the Phillipine war? No-- rose in favor of it. Did Russia rise against the infamy of the present war? No--sat still and said nothing. Has the Kingdom of God advanced in Russia since the beginning of time?

Or in Europe and America, considering the vast backward step of the money-lust? Or anywhere else? If there has been any progress toward righteousness since the early days of Creation--which, in my ineradicable honesty, I am obliged to doubt--I think we must confine it to ten per cent of the populations of Christendom, (but leaving, Russia, Spain and South America entirely out.) This gives us 320,000,000 to draw the ten per cent from. That is to say, 32,000,000 have advanced toward righteousness and the Kingdom of God since the "ages and ages" have been flying along, the Deity sitting up there admiring. Well, you see it leaves 1,200,000,000 out of the race. They stand just where they have always stood; there has been no change.

N. B. No charge for these informations. Do come down soon, Joe. With love, MARK.

St. Clair McKelway, of The Brooklyn Eagle, narrowly escaped injuries in a railway accident, and received the following. Clemens and McKelway were old friends.

To St. Clair McKelway, in Brooklyn:

21 FIFTH AVE. Sunday Morning. April 30, 1905. DEAR McKELWAY, Your innumerable friends are grateful, most grateful.

As I understand the telegrams, the engineer of your train had never seen a locomotive before. Very well, then, I am once more glad that there is an Ever-watchful Providence to foresee possible results and send Ogdens and McIntyres along to save our friends.

The Government's Official report, showing that our railways killed twelve hundred persons last year and injured sixty thousand convinces me that under present conditions one Providence is not enough to properly and efficiently take care of our railroad business. But it is characteristically American--always trying to get along short-handed and save wages.

I am helping your family congratulate themselves, and am your friend as always. S. L. CLEMENS.

Clemens did not spend any more summers at Quarry Farm. All its associations were beautiful and tender, but they could only sadden him. The life there had been as of another world, sunlit, idyllic, now forever vanished. For the summer of 1905 he leased the Copley Green house at Dublin, New Hampshire, where there was a Boston colony of writing and artistic folk, including many of his long-time friends. Among them was Colonel Thomas Wentworth Higginson, who wrote a hearty letter of welcome when he heard the news. Clemens replied in kind.

To Col. Thomas Wentworth Higginson, in Boston:

21 FIFTH AVE. Sunday, March 26, z9o.5. DEAR COL. HIGGINSON,--I early learned that you would be my neighbor in the Summer and I rejoiced, recognizing in you and your family a large asset. I hope for frequent intercourse between the two households. I shall have my youngest daughter with me. The other one will go from the rest-cure in this city to the rest-cure in Norfolk Conn and we shall not see her before autumn. We have not seen her since the middle of October.

Jean (the youngest daughter) went to Dublin and saw the house and came back charmed with it. I know the Thayers of old--manifestly there is no lack of attractions up there. Mrs. Thayer and I were shipmates in a wild excursion perilously near 40 years ago.

You say you "send with this" the story. Then it should be here but it isn't, when I send a thing with another thing, the other thing goes but the thing doesn't, I find it later--still on the premises. Will you look it up now and send it?

Aldrich was here half an hour ago, like a breeze from over the fields, with the fragrance still upon his spirit. I am tired of waiting for that man to get old. Sincerely yours, S. L. C.

Mark Twain was in his seventieth year, old neither in mind nor body, but willing to take life more quietly, to refrain from travel and gay events. A sort of pioneers' reunion was to be held on the Pacific Coast, and a letter from Robert Fulton, of Reno, Nevada, invited Clemens to attend. He did not go, but he sent a letter that we may believe was the next best thing to those who heard it read.

To Robert Fulton, in Reno, Nevada:

IN THE MOUNTAINS, May 24, 1905. DEAR MR. FULTON,--I remember, as if it were yesterday, that when I disembarked from the overland stage in front of the Ormsby in Carson City in August, 1861, I was not expecting to be asked to come again. I was tired, discouraged, white with alkali dust, and did not know anybody; and if you had said then, "Cheer up, desolate stranger, don't be down-hearted--pass on, and come again in 1905," you cannot think how grateful I would have been and how gladly I would have closed the contract. Although I was not expecting to be invited, I was watching out for it, and was hurt and disappointed when you started to ask me and changed it to, "How soon are you going away?"

But you have made it all right, now, the wound is closed. And so I thank you sincerely for the invitation; and with you, all Reno, and if I were a few years younger I would accept it, and promptly. I would go. I would let somebody else do the oration, but, as for me, I would talk-- just talk. I would renew my youth; and talk--and talk--and talk --and have the time of my life! I would march the unforgotten and unforgettable antiques by, and name their names, and give them reverent Hailand-farewell as they passed: Goodman, McCarthy, Gillis, Curry, Baldwin, Winters, Howard, Nye, Stewart; Neely Johnson, Hal Clayton, North, Root,--and my brother, upon whom be peace!--and then the desperadoes, who made life a joy and the "Slaughter-house" a precious possession: Sam Brown, Farmer Pete, Bill Mayfield, Six-fingered Jake, Jack Williams and the rest of the crimson discipleship--and so on and so on. Believe me, I would start a resurrection it would do you more good to look at than the next one will, if you go on the way you are doing now.

Those were the days! those old ones. They will come no more. Youth will come no more. They were so full to the brim with the wine of life; there have been no others like them. It chokes me up to think of them. Would you like me to come out there and cry? It would not beseem my white head.

Good-bye. I drink to you all. Have a good time--and take an old man's blessing. MARK TWAIN.

A few days later he was writing to H. H. Bancroft, of San Francisco, who had invited him for a visit in event of his coming to the Coast. Henry James had just been there for a week and it was hoped that Howells would soon follow.

To H. H. Bancroft, in San Francisco:

UP IN NEW HAMPSHIRE, May 27, 1905. DEAR MR. BANCROFT,--I thank you sincerely for the tempting hospitalities which you offer me, but I have to deny myself, for my wandering days are over, and it is my desire and purpose to sit by the fire the rest of my remnant of life and indulge myself with the pleasure and repose of work --work uninterrupted and unmarred by duties or excursions.

A man who like me, is going to strike 70 on the 30th of next November has no business to be flitting around the way Howells does--that shameless old fictitious butter fly. (But if he comes, don't tell him I said it, for it would hurt him and I wouldn't brush a flake of powder from his wing for anything. I only say it in envy of his indestructible youth, anyway. Howells will be 88 in October.) With thanks again, Sincerely yours, S. L. C.

Clemens found that the air of the New Hampshire hills agreed with him and stimulated him to work. He began an entirely new version of The Mysterious Stranger, of which he already had a bulky and nearly finished manuscript, written in Vienna. He wrote several hundred pages of an extravaganza entitled, Three Thousand Years Among the Microbes, and then, having got his superabundant vitality reduced (it was likely to expend itself in these weird mental exploits), he settled down one day and wrote that really tender and beautiful idyl, Eve's Diary, which he had begun, or at least planned, the previous summer at Tyringham. In a letter to Mr. Frederick A. Duneka, general manager of Harper & Brothers, he tells something of the manner of the story; also his revised opinion of Adam's Diary, written in '93, and originally published as a souvenir of Niagara Falls.

To Frederick A. Duneka, in New York:

DUBLIN, July 16, '05. DEAR MR. DUNEKA,--I wrote Eve's Diary, she using Adam's Diary as her (unwitting and unconscious) text, of course, since to use any other text would have been an imbecility--then I took Adam's Diary and read it. It turned my stomach. It was not literature; yet it had been literature once--before I sold it to be degraded to an advertisement of the Buffalo Fair. I was going to write and ask you to melt the plates and put it out of print.

But this morning I examined it without temper, and saw that if I abolished the advertisement it would be literature again.

So I have done it. I have struck out 700 words and inserted 5 MS pages of new matter (650 words), and now Adam's Diary is dam good--sixty times as good as it ever was before.

I believe it is as good as Eve's Diary now--no, it's not quite that good, I guess, but it is good enough to go in the same cover with Eve's. I'm sure of that.

I hate to have the old Adam go out any more--don't put it on the presses again, let's put the new one in place of it; and next Xmas, let us bind Adam and Eve in one cover. They score points against each other--so, if not bound together, some of the points would not be perceived.....

P. S. Please send another Adam's Diary, so that I can make 2 revised copies. Eve's Diary is Eve's love-Story, but we will not name it that. Yrs ever, MARK.

The peace-making at Portsmouth between Japan and Russia was not satisfactory to Mark Twain, who had fondly hoped there would be no peace until, as he said, "Russian liberty was safe. One more battle would have abolished the waiting chains of millions upon millions of unborn Russians and I wish it could have been fought." He set down an expression of his feelings for the Associated Press, and it invited many letters. Charles Francis Adams wrote, "It attracted my attention because it so exactly expresses the views I have myself all along entertained."

Clemens was invited by Colonel George Harvey to dine with the Russian emissaries, Baron Rosen and Sergius Witte. He declined, but his telegram so pleased Witte that he asked permission to publish it, and announced that he would show it to the Czar.

Telegram. To Col. George Harvey, in New York:

TO COLONEL HARVEY,--I am still a cripple, otherwise I should be more than glad of this opportunity to meet the illustrious magicians who came here equipped with nothing but a pen, and with it have divided the honors of the war with the sword. It is fair to presume that in thirty centuries history will not get done admiring these men who attempted what the world regarded as impossible and achieved it.

Witte would not have cared to show the Czar the telegram in its original form, which follows.

Telegram (unsent). To Col. George Harvey, in New York:

TO COLONEL HARVEY,--I am still a cripple, otherwise I should be more than glad of this opportunity to meet those illustrious magicians who with the pen have annulled, obliterated, and abolished every high achievement of the Japanese sword and turned the tragedy of a tremendous war into a gay and blithesome comedy. If I may, let me in all respect and honor salute them as my fellow-humorists, I taking third place, as becomes one who was not born to modesty, but by diligence and hard work is acquiring it. MARK.

Nor still another unsent form, perhaps more characteristic than either of the foregoing.

Telegram (unsent). To Col. George Harvey, in New York:

DEAR COLONEL,--No, this is a love-feast; when you call a lodge of sorrow send for me. MARK.

To Mrs. Crane, Quarry Farm:

DUBLIN, Sept. 24, '05. Susy dear, I have had a lovely dream. Livy, dressed in black, was sitting up in my bed (here) at my right and looking as young and sweet as she used to do when she was in health. She said: "what is the name of your sweet sister?" I said, "Pamela." "Oh, yes, that is it, I thought it was--" (naming a name which has escaped me) "Won't you write it down for me?" I reached eagerly for a pen and pad--laid my hands upon both--then said to myself, "It is only a dream," and turned back sorrowfully and there she was, still. The conviction flamed through me that our lamented disaster was a dream, and this a reality. I said, "How blessed it is, how blessed it is, it was all a dream, only a dream!" She only smiled and did not ask what dream I meant, which surprised me. She leaned her head against mine and I kept saying, "I was perfectly sure it was a dream, I never would have believed it wasn't."

I think she said several things, but if so they are gone from my memory. I woke and did not know I had been dreaming. She was gone. I wondered how she could go without my knowing it, but I did not spend any thought upon that, I was too busy thinking of how vivid and real was the dream that we had lost her and how unspeakably blessed it was to find that it was not true and that she was still ours and with us. S. L. C.

One day that summer Mark Twain received a letter from the actress, Minnie Maddern Fiske, asking him to write something that would aid her in her crusade against bull-fighting. The idea appealed to him; he replied at once.

To Mrs. Fiske:

DEAR MRS. FISKE,--I shall certainly write the story. But I may not get it to suit me, in which case it will go in the fire. Later I will try again--and yet again--and again. I am used to this. It has taken me twelve years to write a short story--the shortest one I ever wrote, I think.--[Probably "The Death Disk."]--So do not be discouraged; I will stick to this one in the same way. Sincerely yours, S. L. CLEMENS.

He did not delay in his beginning, and a few weeks later was sending word to his publisher about it.

To Frederick A. Duneka, in New York:

Oct. 2, '05. DEAR MR. DUNEKA,--I have just finished a short story which I "greatly admire," and so will you--"A Horse's Tale"--about 15,000 words, at a rough guess. It has good fun in it, and several characters, and is lively. I shall finish revising it in a few days or more, then Jean will type it.

Don't you think you can get it into the Jan. and Feb. numbers and issue it as a dollar booklet just after the middle of Jan. when you issue the Feb. number?

It ought to be ably illustrated.

Why not sell simultaneous rights, for this once, to the Ladies' Home Journal or Collier's, or both, and recoup yourself?--for I would like to get it to classes that can't afford Harper's. Although it doesn't preach, there's a sermon concealed in it. Yr sincerely, MARK.

Five days later he added some rather interesting facts concerning the new story.

To F. A. Duneka, in New York:

Oct. 7, 1906. ['05] DEAR MR. DUNEKA,--..... I've made a poor guess as to number of words. I think there must be 20,000. My usual page of MS. contains about 130 words; but when I am deeply interested in my work and dead to everything else, my hand-writing shrinks and shrinks until there's a great deal more than 130 on a page--oh, yes, a deal more. Well, I discover, this morning, that this tale is written in that small hand.

This strong interest is natural, for the heroine is my daughter, Susy, whom we lost. It was not intentional--it was a good while before I found it out.

So I am sending you her picture to use--and to reproduce with photographic exactness the unsurpassable expression and all. May you find an artist who has lost an idol!

Take as good care of the picture as you can and restore it to me when I come.

I hope you will illustrate this tale considerably. Not humorous pictures. No. When they are good (or bad) one's humor gets no chance to play surprises on the reader. A humorous subject illustrated seriously is all right, but a humorous artist is no fit person for such work. You see, the humorous writer pretends to absolute seriousness (when he knows his trade) then for an artist--to step in and give his calculated gravity all away with a funny picture--oh, my land! It gives me the dry gripes just to think of it. It would be just about up to the average comic artist's intellectual level to make a funny picture of the horse kicking the lungs out of a trader. Hang it, the remark is funny--because the horse is not aware of it but the fact is not humorous, it is tragic and it is no subject for a humorous picture.

Could I be allowed to sit in judgment upon the pictures before they are accepted--at least those in which Cathy may figure?

This is not essential. It is but a suggestion, and it is hereby withdrawn, if it would be troublesome or cause delay.

I hope you will reproduce the cat-pile, full page. And save the photo for me in as good condition as possible. When Susy and Clara were little tots those cats had their profoundest worship, and there is no duplicate of this picture. These cats all had thundering names, or inappropriate ones--furnished by the children with my help. One was named Buffalo Bill.

Are you interested in coincidences?

After discovering, about the middle of the book, that Cathy was Susy Clemens, I put her picture with my MS., to be reproduced. After the book was finished it was discovered that Susy had a dim model of Soldier Boy in her arms; I had forgotten all about that toy.

Then I examined the cat-picture and laid it with the MS. for introduction; but it was not until yesterday that I remembered that one of the cats was named Buffalo Bill. Sincerely yours, MARK.

The reference in this letter to shrinkage of his hand-writing with the increasing intensity of his interest, and the consequent addition of the number of words to the page, recalls another fact, noted by Mr. Duneka, viz.: that because of his terse Anglo-Saxon diction, Mark Twain could put more words on a magazine page than any other writer. It is hardly necessary to add that he got more force into what he put on the page for the same reason.

There was always a run of reporters at Mark Twain's New York home. His opinion was sought for on every matter of public interest, and whatever happened to him in particular was considered good for at least half a column of copy, with his name as a catch-line at the top. When it was learned that he was to spend the summer in New Hampshire, the reporters had all wanted to find out about it. Now that the summer was ending, they began to want to know how he had liked it, what work he had done and what were his plans for another year. As they frequently applied to his publishers for these details it was finally suggested to him that he write a letter furnishing the required information. His reply, handed to Mr. Duneka, who was visiting him at the moment, is full of interest.

Mem. for Mr. Duneka:

DUBLIN, Oct. 9, 1905. .....As to the other matters, here are the details.

Yes, I have tried a number of summer homes, here and in Europe together.

Each of these homes had charms of its own; charms and delights of its own, and some of them-- even in Europe had comforts. Several of them had conveniences, too. They all had a "view."

It is my conviction that there should always be some water in a view-- a lake or a river, but not the ocean, if you are down on its level. I think that when you are down on its level it seldom inflames you with an ecstasy which you could not get out of a sand-flat. It is like being on board ship, over again; indeed it is worse than that, for there's three months of it. On board ship one tires of the aspects in a couple of days, and quits looking. The same vast circle of heaving humps is spread around you all the time, with you in the centre of it and never gaining an inch on the horizon, so far as you can see; for variety, a flight of flying-fish, mornings; a flock of porpoises throwing summersaults afternoons; a remote whale spouting, Sundays; occasional phosphorescent effects, nights; every other day a streak of black smoke trailing along under the horizon; on the one single red letter day, the illustrious iceberg. I have seen that iceberg thirty-four times in thirty-seven voyages; it is always the same shape, it is always the same size, it always throws up the same old flash when the sun strikes it; you may set it on any New York door-step of a June morning and light it up with a mirror-flash; and I will engage to recognize it. It is artificial, and it is provided and anchored out by the steamer companies. I used to like the sea, but I was young then, and could easily get excited over any kind of monotony, and keep it up till the monotonies ran out, if it was a fortnight.

Last January, when we were beginning to inquire about a home for this summer, I remembered that Abbott Thayer had said, three years before, that the New Hampshire highlands was a good place. He was right--it was a good place. Any place that is good for an artist in paint is good for an artist in morals and ink. Brush is here, too; so is Col. T. W. Higginson; so is Raphael Pumpelly; so is Mr. Secretary Hitchcock; so is Henderson; so is Learned; so is Summer; so is Franklin MacVeigh; so is Joseph L. Smith; so is Henry Copley Greene, when I am not occupying his house, which I am doing this season. Paint, literature, science, statesmanship, history, professorship, law, morals,--these are all represented here, yet crime is substantially unknown.

The summer homes of these refugees are sprinkled, a mile apart, among the forest-clad hills, with access to each other by firm smooth country roads which are so embowered in dense foliage that it is always twilight in there, and comfortable. The forests are spider-webbed with these good roads, they go everywhere; but for the help of the guide-boards, the stranger would not arrive anywhere.

The village--Dublin--is bunched together in its own place, but a good telephone service makes its markets handy to all those outliars. I have spelt it that way to be witty. The village executes orders on, the Boston plan--promptness and courtesy.

The summer homes are high-perched, as a rule, and have contenting outlooks. The house we occupy has one. Monadnock, a soaring double hump, rises into the sky at its left elbow--that is to say, it is close at hand. From the base of the long slant of the mountain the valley spreads away to the circling frame of the hills, and beyond the frame the billowy sweep of remote great ranges rises to view and flows, fold upon fold, wave upon wave, soft and blue and unwordly, to the horizon fifty miles away. In these October days Monadnock and the valley and its framing hills make an inspiring picture to look at, for they are sumptuously splashed and mottled and be-torched from sky-line to sky-line with the richest dyes the autumn can furnish; and when they lie flaming in the full drench of the mid-afternoon sun, the sight affects the spectator physically, it stirs his blood like military music.

These summer homes are commodious, well built, and well furnished--facts which sufficiently indicate that the owners built them to live in themselves. They have furnaces and wood fireplaces, and the rest of the comforts and conveniences of a city home, and can be comfortably occupied all the year round.

We cannot have this house next season, but I have secured Mrs. Upton's house which is over in the law and science quarter, two or three miles from here, and about the same distance from the art, literary, and scholastic groups. The science and law quarter has needed improving, this good while.

The nearest railway-station is distant something like an hour's drive; it is three hours from there to Boston, over a branch line. You can go to New York in six hours per branch lines if you change cars every time you think of it, but it is better to go to Boston and stop over and take the trunk line next day, then you do not get lost.

It is claimed that the atmosphere of the New Hampshire highlands is exceptionally bracing and stimulating, and a fine aid to hard and continuous work. It is a just claim, I think. I came in May, and wrought 35 successive days without a break. It is possible that I could not have done it elsewhere. I do not know; I have not had any disposition to try it, before. I think I got the disposition out of the atmosphere, this time. I feel quite sure, in fact, that that is where it came from.

I am ashamed to confess what an intolerable pile of manuscript I ground out in the 35 days, therefore I will keep the number of words to myself. I wrote the first half of a long tale--"The Adventures of a Microbe" and put it away for a finish next summer, and started another long tale--"The Mysterious Stranger;" I wrote the first half of it and put it with the other for a finish next summer. I stopped, then. I was not tired, but I had no books on hand that needed finishing this year except one that was seven years old. After a little I took that one up and finished it. Not for publication, but to have it ready for revision next summer.

Since I stopped work I have had a two months' holiday. The summer has been my working time for 35 years; to have a holiday in it (in America) is new for me. I have not broken it, except to write "Eve's Diary" and "A Horse's Tale"--short things occupying the mill 12 days.

This year our summer is 6 months long and ends with November and the flight home to New York, but next year we hope and expect to stretch it another month and end it the first of December.

[No signature.]

The fact that he was a persistent smoker was widely known, and many friends and admirers of Mark Twain sent him cigars, most of which he could not use, because they were too good. He did not care for Havana cigars, but smoked the fragrant, inexpensive domestic tobacco with plenty of "pep" in it, as we say today. Now and then he had an opportunity to head off some liberal friend, who wrote asking permission to contribute to his cigar collection, as instance the following.

To Rev. L. M. Powers, in Haverhill, Mass.:

Nov. 9, 1905. DEAR MR. POWERS,--I should accept your hospitable offer at once but for the fact I couldn't do it and remain honest. That is to say if I allowed you to send me what you believe to be good cigars it would distinctly mean that I meant to smoke them, whereas I should do nothing of the kind. I know a good cigar better than you do, for I have had 60 years experience.

No, that is not what I mean; I mean I know a bad cigar better than anybody else; I judge by the price only; if it costs above 5 cents I know it to be either foreign or half-foreign, and unsmokeable. By me. I have many boxes of Havana cigars, of all prices from 20 cts apiece up to 1.66 apiece; I bought none of them, they were all presents, they are an accumulation of several years. I have never smoked one of them and never shall, I work them off on the visitor. You shall have a chance when you come.

Pessimists are born not made; optimists are born not made; but no man is born either pessimist wholly or optimist wholly, perhaps; he is pessimistic along certain lines and optimistic along certain others. That is my case. Sincerely yours, S. L. CLEMENS.

In spite of all the fine photographs that were made of him, there recurred constantly among those sent him to be autographed a print of one which, years before, Sarony had made and placed on public sale. It was a good photograph, mechanically and even artistically, but it did not please Mark Twain. Whenever he saw it he recalled Sarony with bitterness and severity. Once he received an inquiry concerning it, and thus feelingly expressed himself.

To Mr. Row (no address):

21 FIFTH AVENUE, NEW YORK, November 14, 1905. DEAR MR. ROW,--That alleged portrait has a private history. Sarony was as much of an enthusiast about wild animals as he was about photography; and when Du Chaillu brought the first Gorilla to this country in 1819 he came to me in a fever of excitement and asked me if my father was of record and authentic. I said he was; then Sarony, without any abatement of his excitement asked if my grandfather also was of record and authentic. I said he was. Then Sarony, with still rising excitement and with joy added to it, said he had found my great grandfather in the person of the gorilla, and had recognized him at once by his resemblance to me. I was deeply hurt but did not reveal this, because I knew Saxony meant no offense for the gorilla had not done him any harm, and he was not a man who would say an unkind thing about a gorilla wantonly. I went with him to inspect the ancestor, and examined him from several points of view, without being able to detect anything more than a passing resemblance. "Wait," said Sarony with confidence, "let me show you." He borrowed my overcoat--and put it on the gorilla. The result was surprising. I saw that the gorilla while not looking distinctly like me was exactly what my great grand father would have looked like if I had had one. Sarong photographed the creature in that overcoat, and spread the picture about the world. It has remained spread about the world ever since. It turns up every week in some newspaper somewhere or other. It is not my favorite, but to my exasperation it is everybody else's. Do you think you could get it suppressed for me? I will pay the limit. Sincerely yours, S. L. CLEMENS.

The year 1905 closed triumphantly for Mark Twain. The great "Seventieth Birthday" dinner planned by Colonel George Harvey is remembered to-day as the most notable festival occasion in New York literary history. Other dinners and ovations followed. At seventy he had returned to the world, more beloved, more honored than ever before.

XLV

LETTERS, 1906, TO VARIOUS PERSONS. THE FAREWELL LECTURE. A SECOND SUMMER IN DUBLIN. BILLIARDS AND COPYRIGHT

MARK TWAIN at "Pier Seventy," as he called it, paused to look backward and to record some memoirs of his long, eventful past. The Autobiography dictations begun in Florence were resumed, and daily he traveled back, recalling long-ago scenes and all-but-forgotten places. He was not without reminders. Now and again there came some message that brought back the old days--the Tom Sawyer and Huck Finn days--or the romance of the river that he never recalled other than with tenderness and a tone of regret that it was gone. An invitation to the golden wedding of two ancient friends moved and saddened him, and his answer to it conveys about all the story of life.

To Mr. and Mrs. Gordon:

21 FIFTH AVENUE, Jan. 24, '06. DEAR GORDONS,--I have just received your golden-

wedding "At Home" and am trying to adjust my focus to it and realize how much it means. It is inconceivable! With a simple sweep it carries me back over a stretch of time measurable only in astronomical terms and geological periods. It brings before me Mrs. Gordon, young, round-limbed, handsome; and with her the Youngbloods and their two babies, and Laura Wright, that unspoiled little maid, that fresh flower of the woods and the prairies. Forty-eight years ago!

Life was a fairy-tale, then, it is a tragedy now. When I was 43 and John Hay 41 he said life was a tragedy after 40, and I disputed it. Three years ago he asked me to testify again: I counted my graves, and there was nothing for me to say.

I am old; I recognize it but I don't realize it. I wonder if a person ever really ceases to feel young--I mean, for a whole day at a time. My love to you both, and to all of us that are left. MARK.

Though he used very little liquor of any kind, it was Mark Twain's custom to keep a bottle of Scotch whiskey with his collection of pipes and cigars and tobacco on a little table by his bed-side. During restless nights he found a small quantity of it conducive to sleep. Andrew Carnegie, learning of this custom, made it his business to supply Scotch of his own special importation. The first case came, direct from Scotland. When it arrived Clemens sent this characteristic acknowledgment.

To Andrew Carnegie, in Scotland:

21 FIFTH AVE. Feb. 10, '06. DEAR ST. ANDREW,--The whisky arrived in due course from over the water; last week one bottle of it was extracted from the wood and inserted into me, on the instalment plan, with this result: that I believe it to be the best, smoothest whisky now on the planet. Thanks, oh, thanks: I have discarded Peruna.

Hoping that you three are well and happy and will be coming back before the winter sets in. I am, Sincerely yours, MARK.

It must have been a small bottle to be consumed by him in a week, or perhaps he had able assistance. The next brief line refers to the manuscript of his article, "Saint Joan of Arc," presented to the museum at Rouen.

To Edward E. Clarke:

21 FIFTH AVE., Feb., 1906. DEAR SIR,--I have found the original manuscript and with great pleasure I transmit it herewith, also a printed copy.

It is a matter of great pride to me to have any word of mine concerning the world's supremest heroine honored by a place in that Museum. Sincerely yours, S. L. CLEMENS.

The series of letters which follows was prepared by Mark Twain and General Fred Grant, mainly with a view of advertising the lecture that Clemens had agreed to deliver for the benefit of the

Robert Fulton Monument Association. It was, in fact, to be Mark Twain's "farewell lecture," and the association had really proposed to pay him a thousand dollars for it. The exchange of these letters, however, was never made outside of Mark Twain's bed-room. Propped against the pillows, pen in hand, with General Grant beside him, they arranged the series with the idea of publication. Later the plan was discarded, so that this pleasant foolery appears here for the first, time.

PRIVATE AND CONFIDENTIAL

(Correspondence)

Telegram

Army Headquarters (date) MARK TWAIN, New York,--Would you consider a proposal to talk at Carnegie Hall for the benefit of the Robert Fulton Monument Association, of which you are a Vice President, for a fee of a thousand dollars? F. D. GRANT, President, Fulton Monument Association.

Telegraphic Answer:

MAJOR-GENERAL F. D. GRANT, Army Headquarters,--I shall be glad to do it, but I must stipulate that you keep the thousand dollars and add it to the Monument fund as my contribution. CLEMENS.

Letters:

DEAR MR. CLEMENS,--You have the thanks of the Association, and the terms shall be as you say. But why give all of it? Why not reserve a portion --why should you do this work wholly without compensation? Truly yours FRED. D. GRANT.

MAJOR GENERAL GRANT, Army Headquarters.

DEAR GENERAL,--Because I stopped talking for pay a good many years ago, and I could not resume the habit now without a great deal of personal discomfort. I love to hear myself talk, because I get so much instruction and moral upheaval out of it, but I lose the bulk of this joy when I charge for it. Let the terms stand.

General, if I have your approval, I wish to use this good occasion to retire permanently from the platform. Truly yours S. L. CLEMENS.

DEAR MR. CLEMENS,--Certainly. But as an old friend, permit me to say, Don't do that. Why should you?--you are not old yet. Yours truly, FRED D. GRANT.

DEAR GENERAL,--I mean the pay-platform; I shan't retire from the gratis- platform until after I am dead and courtesy requires me to keep still and not disturb the others.

What shall I talk about? My idea is this: to instruct the audience about Robert Fulton, and..... Tell me—was that his real name, or was it his nom de plume? However, never mind, it is not important—I can skip it, and the house will think I knew all about it, but forgot. Could you find out for me if he was one of the Signers of the Declaration, and which one? But if it is any trouble, let it alone, I can skip it. Was he out with Paul Jones? Will you ask Horace Porter? And ask him if he brought both of them home. These will be very interesting facts, if they can be established. But never mind, don't trouble Porter, I can establish them anyway. The way I look at it, they are historical gems—gems of the very first water.

Well, that is my idea, as I have said: first, excite the audience with a spoonful of information about Fulton, then quiet down with a barrel of illustration drawn by memory from my books—and if you don't say anything the house will think they never heard of it before, because people don't really read your books, they only say they do, to keep you from feeling bad. Next, excite the house with another spoonful of Fultonian fact, then tranquilize them again with another barrel of illustration. And so on and so on, all through the evening; and if you are discreet and don't tell them the illustrations don't illustrate anything, they won't notice it and I will send them home as well-informed about Robert Fulton as I am myself. Don't be afraid; I know all about audiences, they believe everything you say, except when you are telling the truth. Truly yours, S. L. CLEMENS.

P.S. Mark all the advertisements "Private and Confidential," otherwise the people will not read them. M. T.

DEAR MR. CLEMENS,—How long shall you talk? I ask in order that we may be able to say when carriages may be called. Very Truly yours, HUGH GORDON MILLER, Secretary.

DEAR MR. MILLER,—I cannot say for sure. It is my custom to keep on talking till I get the audience cowed. Sometimes it takes an hour and fifteen minutes, sometimes I can do it in an hour. Sincerely yours, S. L. CLEMENS.

Mem. My charge is 2 boxes free. Not the choicest—sell the choicest, and give me any 6-seat boxes you please. S. L. C.

I want Fred Grant (in uniform) on the stage; also the rest of the officials of the Association; also other distinguished people—all the attractions we can get. Also, a seat for Mr. Albert Bigelow Paine, who may be useful to me if he is near me and on the front. S. L. C.

The seat chosen for the writer of these notes was to be at the front of the stage in order that the lecturer might lean over now and then and pretend to be asking information concerning Fulton. I was not entirely happy in the thought of this showy honor, and breathed more freely when this plan was abandoned and the part assigned to General Grant.

The lecture was given in Carnegie Hall, which had been gayly decorated for the occasion. The house was more than filled, and a great sum of money was realized for the fund.

It was that spring that Gorky and Tchaikowski, the Russian revolutionists, came to America hoping to arouse interest in their cause. The idea of the overthrow of the Russian dynasty was pleasant to Mark Twain. Few things would have given him greater comfort than to have known that a little more than ten years would see the downfall of Russian imperialism. The letter which follows was a reply to an invitation from Tchaikowski, urging him to speak at one of the meetings.

DEAR MR. TCHAIKOWSKI,--I thank you for the honor of the invitation, but I am not able to accept it, because on Thursday evening I shall be presiding at a meeting whose object is to find remunerative work for certain classes of our blind who would gladly support themselves if they had the opportunity.

My sympathies are with the Russian revolution, of course. It goes without saying. I hope it will succeed, and now that I have talked with you I take heart to believe it will. Government by falsified promises; by lies, by treacheries, and by the butcher-knife for the aggrandizement of a single family of drones and its idle and vicious kin has been borne quite long enough in Russia, I should think, and it is to be hoped that the roused nation, now rising in its strength, will presently put an end to it and set up the republic in its place. Some of us, even of the white headed, may live to see the blessed day when Czars and Grand Dukes will be as scarce there as I trust they are in heaven. Most sincerely yours, MARK TWAIN.

There came another summer at Dublin, New Hampshire, this time in the fine Upton residence on the other slope of Monadnock, a place of equally beautiful surroundings, and an even more extended view. Clemens was at this time working steadily on his so-called Autobiography, which was not that, in fact, but a series of remarkable chapters, reminiscent, reflective, commentative, written without any particular sequence as to time or subject-matter. He dictated these chapters to a stenographer, usually in the open air, sitting in a comfortable rocker or pacing up and down the long veranda that faced a vast expanse of wooded slope and lake and distant blue mountains. It became one of the happiest occupations of his later years.

To W. D. Howells, in Maine:

DUBLIN, Sunday, June 17, '06. DEAR HOWELLS,--..... The dictating goes lazily and pleasantly on. With intervals. I find that I have been at it, off and on, nearly two hours a day for 155 days, since Jan. 9. To be exact I've dictated 75 hours in 80 days and loafed 75 days. I've added 60,000 words in the month that I've been here; which indicates that I've dictated during 20 days of that time--40 hours, at an average of 1,500 words an hour. It's a plenty, and I am satisfied.

There's a good deal of "fat" I've dictated, (from Jan. 9) 210,000 words, and the "fat" adds about 50,000 more.

The "fat" is old pigeon-holed things, of the years gone by, which I or editors didn't das't to print. For instance, I am dumping in the little old book which I read to you in Hartford about 30 years ago and which you said "publish--and ask Dean Stanley to furnish an introduction; he'll do it." ("Captain Stormfield's Visit to Heaven.") It reads quite to suit me, without altering a word, now that it isn't to see print until I am dead.

To-morrow I mean to dictate a chapter which will get my heirs and assigns burnt alive if they venture to print it this side of 2006 A.D.--which I judge they won't. There'll be lots of such chapters if I live 3 or 4 years longer. The edition of A.D. 2006 will make a stir when it comes out. I shall be hovering around taking notice, along with other dead pals. You are invited. MARK.

His tendency to estimate the measure of the work he was doing, and had completed, must have clung to him from his old printer days.

The chapter which was to get his heirs and assigns burned alive was on the orthodox God, and there was more than one such chapter. In the next letter he refers to two exquisite poems by Howells, and the writer of these notes recalls his wonderful reading of them aloud. 'In Our Town' was a collection of short stories then recently issued by William Allen White. Howells had recommended them.

To W. D. Howells, in Maine:

21 FIFTH AVE., Tuesday Eve. DEAR HOWELLS,--It is lovely of you to say those beautiful things--I don't know how to thank you enough. But I love you, that I know.

I read "After the Wedding" aloud and we felt all the pain of it and the truth. It was very moving and very beautiful--would have been over- comingly moving, at times, but for the haltings and pauses compelled by the difficulties of MS--these were a protection, in that they furnished me time to brace up my voice, and get a new start. Jean wanted to keep the MS for another reading-aloud, and for "keeps," too, I suspected, but I said it would be safest to write you about it.

I like "In Our Town," particularly that Colonel, of the Lookout Mountain Oration, and very particularly pages 212-16. I wrote and told White so.

After "After the Wedding" I read "The Mother" aloud and sounded its human deeps with your deep-sea lead. I had not read it before, since it was first published.

I have been dictating some fearful things, for 4 successive mornings--for no eye but yours to see until I have been dead a century--if then. But I got them out of my system, where they had been festering for years--and that was the main thing. I feel better, now.

I came down today on business--from house to house in 12 1/2 hours, and expected to arrive dead, but am neither tired nor sleepy. Yours as always MARK.

To William Allen White, in Emporia, Kans.:

DUBLIN, NEW HAMPSHIRE, June 24, 1906. DEAR MR. WHITE,--Howells told me that "In Our Town" was a charming book, and indeed it is. All of it is delightful when read one's self, parts of it can score finely when subjected to the most exacting of tests--the reading aloud. Pages 197 and 216 are of that grade. I have tried them a couple of times on the family, and pages 212 and 216 are qualified to fetch any house of any country, caste or color, endowed with those riches which are denied to no nation on the planet--humor and feeling.

Talk again--the country is listening. Sincerely yours, S. L. CLEMENS.

Witter Bynner, the poet, was one of the editors of McClure's Magazine at this time, but was trying to muster the courage to give up routine work for verse-making and the possibility of poverty. Clemens was fond of Bynner and believed in his work. He did not advise him, however, to break away entirely from a salaried position--at least not immediately; but one day Bynner did so, and reported the step he had taken, with some doubt as to the answer he would receive.

To Witter Bynner, in New York:

DUBLIN, Oct. 5, 1906. DEAR POET,--You have certainly done right for several good reasons; at least, of them, I can name two:

1. With your reputation you can have your freedom and yet earn your living. 2. if you fall short of succeeding to your wish, your reputation will provide you another job. And so in high approval I suppress the scolding and give you the saintly and fatherly pat instead. MARK TWAIN.

On another occasion, when Bynner had written a poem to Clara Clemens, her father pretended great indignation that the first poem written by Bynner to any one in his household should not be to him, and threatened revenge. At dinner shortly after he produced from his pocket a slip of paper on which he had set down what he said was "his only poem." He read the lines that follow:

"Of all sad words of tongue or pen, The saddest are these: It might have been. Ah, say not so! as life grows longer, leaner, thinner, We recognize, O God, it might have Bynner!"

He returned to New York in October and soon after was presented by Mrs. H. H. Rogers with a handsome billiard-table.

He had a passion for the game, but had played comparatively little since the old Hartford days of fifteen years before, when a group of his friends used to assemble on Friday nights in the room at the top of the house for long, strenuous games and much hilarity. Now the old fever all came back; the fascinations of the game superseded even his interest in the daily dictations.

To Mrs. H. H. Rogers, in New York:

21 FIFTH AVENUE, Monday, Nov., 1906. DEAR MRS. ROGERS,--The billiard table is better than the doctors. It is driving out the heartburn in a most promising way. I have a billiardist on the

premises, and I walk not less than ten miles every day with the cue in my hand. And the walking is not the whole of the exercise, nor the most health-giving part of it, I think. Through the multitude of the positions and attitudes it brings into play every muscle in the body and exercises them all.

The games begin right after luncheon, daily, and continue until midnight, with 2 hours' intermission for dinner and music. And so it is 9 hours' exercise per day, and 10 or 12 on Sunday. Yesterday and last night it was 12--and I slept until 8 this morning without waking. The billiard table, as a Sabbath breaker can beat any coal-breaker in Pennsylvania, and give it 30 in, the game. If Mr. Rogers will take to daily billiards he can do without doctors and the massageur, I think.

We are really going to build a house on my farm, an hour and a half from New York. It is decided. It is to be built by contract, and is to come within $25,000. With love and many thanks. S. L. C.

P.S. Clara is in the sanitarium--till January 28 when her western concert tour will begin. She is getting to be a mighty competent singer. You must know Clara better; she is one of the very finest and completest and most satisfactory characters I have ever met. Others knew it before, but I have always been busy with other matters.

The "billiardist on the premises" was the writer of these notes, who, earlier in the year, had become his biographer, and, in the course of time, his daily companion and friend. The farm mentioned was one which he had bought at Redding, Connecticut, where, later, he built the house known as "Stormfield."

Henry Mills Alden, for nearly forty years editor of Harper's Magazine, arrived at his seventieth birthday on November 11th that year, and Harper & Brothers had arranged to give him a great dinner in the offices of Franklin Square, where, for half a century, he had been an active force. Mark Twain, threatened with a cold, and knowing the dinner would be strenuous, did not feel able to attend, so wrote a letter which, if found suitable, could be read at the gathering.

To Mr. Henry Alden:

ALDEN,--dear and ancient friend--it is a solemn moment. You have now reached the age of discretion. You have been a long time arriving. Many years ago you docked me on an article because the subject was too old; later, you docked me on an article because the subject was too new; later still, you docked me on an article because the subject was betwixt and between. Once, when I wrote a Letter to Queen Victoria, you did not put it in the respectable part of the Magazine, but interred it in that potter's field, the Editor's Drawer. As a result, she never answered it. How often we recall, with regret, that Napoleon once shot at a magazine editor and missed him and killed a publisher. But we remember, with charity, that his intentions were good.

You will reform, now, Alden. You will cease from these economies, and you will be discharged. But in your retirement you will carry with you the admiration and earnest good wishes of the oppressed and toiling scribes. This will be better than bread. Let this console you when the bread fails.

You will carry with you another thing, too--the affection of the scribes; for they all love you in spite of your crimes. For you bear a kind heart in your breast, and the sweet and winning spirit that charms away all hostilities and animosities, and makes of your enemy your friend and keeps him so. You have reigned over us thirty-six years, and, please God, you shall reign another thirty-six-- "and peace to Mahmoud on his golden throne!" Always yours MARK

A copyright bill was coming up in Washington and a delegation of authors went down to work for it. Clemens was not the head of the delegation, but he was the most prominent member of it, as well as the most useful. He invited the writer to accompany him, and elsewhere I have told in detail the story of that excursion,--[See Mark Twain; A Biography, chap. ccli,]--which need be but briefly touched upon here.

His work was mainly done aside from that of the delegation. They had him scheduled for a speech, however, which he made without notes and with scarcely any preparation. Meantime he had applied to Speaker Cannon for permission to allow him on the floor of the House, where he could buttonhole the Congressmen. He was not eligible to the floor without having received the thanks of Congress, hence the following letter:

To Hon. Joseph Cannon, House of Representatives:

Dec. 7, 1906. DEAR UNCLE JOSEPH,--Please get me the thanks of the Congress--not next week but right away. It is very necessary. Do accomplish this for your affectionate old friend right away; by persuasion, if you can, by violence if you must, for it is imperatively necessary that I get on the floor for two or three hours and talk to the members, man by man, in behalf of the support, encouragement and protection of one of the nation's most valuable assets and industries--its literature. I have arguments with me, also a barrel, with liquid in it.

Give me a chance. Get me the thanks of Congress. Don't wait for others; there isn't time. I have stayed away and let Congress alone for seventy- one years and I am entitled to thanks. Congress knows it perfectly well and I have long felt hurt that this quite proper and earned expression of gratitude has been merely felt by the House and never publicly uttered. Send me an order on the Sergeant-at-Arms quick. When shall I come? With love and a benediction. MARK TWAIN.

This was mainly a joke. Mark Twain did not expect any "thanks," but he did hope for access to the floor, which once, in an earlier day, had been accorded him. We drove to the Capitol and he delivered his letter to "Uncle Joe" by hand. "Uncle Joe" could not give him the privilege of the floor; the rules had become more stringent. He declared they would hang him if he did such a thing. He added that he had a private room down-stairs, where Mark Twain might establish headquarters, and that he would assign his colored servant, Neal, of long acquaintanceship with many of the members, to pass the word that Mark Twain was receiving.

The result was a great success. All that afternoon members of Congress poured into the Speaker's room and, in an atmosphere blue with tobacco smoke, Mark Twain talked the gospel of copyright to his heart's content.

The bill did not come up for passage that session, but Mark Twain lived to see his afternoon's lobbying bring a return. In 1909, Champ Clark, and those others who had gathered around him that afternoon, passed a measure that added fourteen years to the copyright term.

The next letter refers to a proposed lobby of quite a different sort.

To Helen Keller, in Wrentham, Mass.:

21 FIFTH AVENUE, Dec. 23, '06. DEAR HELEN KELLER,--. . . You say, "As a reformer, you know that ideas must be driven home again and again."

Yes, I know it; and by old experience I know that speeches and documents and public meetings are a pretty poor and lame way of accomplishing it. Last year I proposed a sane way--one which I had practiced with success for a quarter of a century--but I wasn't expecting it to get any attention, and it didn't.

Give me a battalion of 200 winsome young girls and matrons, and let me tell them what to do and how to do it, and I will be responsible for shining results. If I could mass them on the stage in front of the audience and instruct them there, I could make a public meeting take hold of itself and do something really valuable for once. Not that the real instruction would be done there, for it wouldn't; it would be previously done privately, and merely repeated there.

But it isn't going to happen--the good old way will be stuck to: there'll be a public meeting: with music, and prayer, and a wearying report, and a verbal description of the marvels the blind can do, and 17 speeches--then the call upon all present who are still alive, to contribute. This hoary program was invented in the idiot asylum, and will never be changed. Its function is to breed hostility to good causes.

Some day somebody will recruit my 200--my dear beguilesome Knights of the Golden Fleece-- and you will see them make good their ominous name.

Mind, we must meet! not in the grim and ghastly air of the platform, mayhap, but by the friendly fire--here at 21. Affectionately your friend, S. L. CLEMENS.

They did meet somewhat later that winter in the friendly parlors of No. 21, and friends gathered in to meet the marvelous blind girl and to pay tribute to Miss Sullivan (Mrs. Macy) for her almost incredible achievement.

End of this Project Gutenberg Etext of Letters Vol. 5, by Mark Twain

MARK TWAIN'S LETTERS 1907-1910

ARRANGED WITH COMMENT BY ALBERT BIGELOW PAINE

VOLUME VI.

XLVI

LETTERS 1907-08. A DEGREE FROM OXFORD. THE NEW HOME AT REDDING

The author, J. Howard Moore, sent a copy of his book, The Universal Kinship, with a letter in which he said: "Most humorists have no anxiety except to glorify themselves and add substance to their pocket-books by making their readers laugh. You have shown, on many occasions, that your mission is not simply to antidote the melancholy of a world, but includes a real and intelligent concern for the general welfare of your fellowman."

The Universal Kinship was the kind of a book that Mark Twain appreciated, as his acknowledgment clearly shows.

To Mr. J. Howard Moore:

Feb. 2, '07. DEAR MR. MOORE, The book has furnished me several days of deep pleasure and satisfaction; it has compelled my gratitude at the same time, since it saves me the labor of stating my own long-cherished opinions and reflections and resentments by doing it lucidly and fervently and irascibly for me.

There is one thing that always puzzles me: as inheritors of the mentality of our reptile ancestors we have improved the inheritance by a thousand grades; but in the matter of the morals which they left us we have gone backward as many grades. That evolution is strange, and to me unaccountable and unnatural. Necessarily we started equipped with their perfect and blemishless morals; now we are wholly destitute; we have no real, morals, but only artificial ones--morals created and preserved by the forced suppression of natural and hellish instincts. Yet we are dull enough to be vain of them. Certainly we are a sufficiently comical invention, we humans. Sincerely Yours, S. L. CLEMENS.

Mark Twain's own books were always being excommunicated by some librarian, and the matter never failed to invite the attention and amusement of the press, and the indignation of many correspondents. Usually the books were Tom Sawyer and Huck Finn, the morals of which were not regarded as wholly exemplary. But in 1907 a small library, in a very small town, attained a day's national notoriety by putting the ban on Eve's Diary, not so much on account of its text as for the chaste and exquisite illustrations by Lester Ralph. When the reporters came in a troop to learn about it, the author said: "I believe this time the trouble is mainly with the pictures. I did not draw them. I wish I had--they are so beautiful."

Just at this time, Dr. William Lyon Phelps, of Yale, was giving a literary talk to the Teachers' Club, of Hartford, dwelling on the superlative value of Mark Twain's writings for readers old and young. Mrs. F. G. Whitmore, an old Hartford friend, wrote Clemens of the things that Phelps had said, as consolation for Eve's latest banishment. This gave him a chance to add something to what he had said to the reporters.

To Mrs. Whitmore, in Hartford:

Feb. 7, 1907. DEAR MRS. WHITMORE,--But the truth is, that when a Library expels a book of mine and leaves an unexpurgated Bible lying around where unprotected youth and age can get hold of it, the deep unconscious irony of it delights me and doesn't anger me. But even if it angered me such words as those of Professor Phelps would take the sting all out. Nobody attaches weight to the freaks of the Charlton Library, but when a man like Phelps speaks, the world gives attention. Some day I hope to meet him and thank him for his courage for saying those things out in public. Custom is, to think a handsome thing in private but tame it down in the utterance.

I hope you are all well and happy; and thereto I add my love. Sincerely yours, S. L. CLEMENS.

In May, 1907, Mark Twain was invited to England to receive from Oxford the degree of Literary Doctor. It was an honor that came to him as a sort of laurel crown at the end of a great career, and gratified him exceedingly. To Moberly Bell, of the London Times, he expressed his appreciation. Bell had been over in April and Clemens believed him concerned in the matter.

To Moberly Bell, in London:

21 FIFTH AVENUE, May 3, '07 DEAR MR. BELL,--Your hand is in it! and you have my best thanks. Although I wouldn't cross an ocean again for the price of the ship that carried me, I am glad to do it for an Oxford degree. I shall plan to sail for England a shade before the middle of June, so that I can have a few days in London before the 26th. Sincerely, S. L. CLEMENS.

He had taken a house at Tuxedo for the summer, desiring to be near New York City, and in the next letter he writes Mr. Rogers concerning his London plans. We discover, also, in this letter that he has begun work on the Redding home and the cost is to come entirely out of the autobiographical chapters then running in the North American Review. It may be of passing interest to note here that he had the usual house-builder's fortune. He received thirty thousand dollars for the chapters; the house cost him nearly double that amount.

To H. H. Rogers, in New York:

TUXEDO PARK, May 29, '07. DEAR ADMIRAL,--Why hang it, I am not going to see you and Mrs. Rogers at all in England! It is a great disappointment. I leave there a month from now--June 29. No, I shall see you; for by your itinerary you are most likely to come to London June 21st or along there. So that is very good and satisfactory. I have declined all engagements but two-- Whitelaw Reid (dinner) June 21, and the Pilgrims (lunch), June 25. The Oxford ceremony is June 26. I have paid my return passage in the Minne- something, but it is just possible that I may want to stay in England a week or two longer--I can't tell, yet. I do very much want to meet up with the boys for the last time.

I have signed the contract for the building of the house on my Connecticut farm and specified the cost limit, and work has been begun. The cost has to all come out of a year's instalments of Autobiography in the N. A. Review.

Clara, is winning her way to success and distinction with sure and steady strides. By all accounts she is singing like a bird, and is not afraid on the concert stage any more.

Tuxedo is a charming place; I think it hasn't its equal anywhere.

Very best wishes to you both. S. L. C.

The story of Mark Twain's extraordinary reception and triumph in England has been told.--[Mark Twain; A Biography, chaps. cclvi- cclix]--It was, in fact, the crowning glory of his career. Perhaps one of the most satisfactory incidents of his sojourn was a dinner given to him by the staff of Punch, in the historic offices at 10 Bouverie Street where no other foreign visitor had been thus honored--a notable distinction. When the dinner ended, little joy Agnew, daughter of the chief editor, entered and presented to the chief guest the original drawing of a cartoon by Bernard Partridge, which had appeared on the front page of Punch. In this picture the presiding genius of the paper is offering to Mark Twain health, long life, and happiness from "The Punch Bowl."

A short time after his return to America he received a pretty childish letter from little Miss Agnew acknowledging a photograph he had sent her, and giving a list of her pets and occupations. Such a letter always delighted Mark Twain, and his pleasure in this one is reflected in his reply.

To Miss Joy Agnew, in London:

TUXEDO PARK, NEW YORK. Unto you greetings and salutation and worship, you dear, sweet little rightly-named Joy! I can see you now almost as vividly as I saw you that night when you sat flashing and beaming upon those sombre swallow-tails.

"Fair as a star when only one Is shining in the sky."

Oh, you were indeed the only one--there wasn't even the remotest chance of competition with you, dear! Ah, you are a decoration, you little witch!

The idea of your house going to the wanton expense of a flower garden!-- aren't you enough? And what do you want to go and discourage the other flowers for? Is that the right spirit? is it considerate? is it kind? How do you suppose they feel when you come around--looking the way you look? And you so pink and sweet and dainty and lovely and supernatural? Why, it makes them feel embarrassed and artificial, of course; and in my opinion it is just as pathetic as it can be. Now then you want to reform--dear--and do right.

Well certainly you are well off, Joy:

3 bantams; 3 goldfish; 3 doves; 6 canaries; 2 dogs; 1 cat;

All you need, now, to be permanently beyond the reach of want, is one more dog--just one more good, gentle, high principled, affectionate, loyal dog who wouldn't want any nobler service than the golden privilege of lying at your door, nights, and biting everything that came along--and I am that very one, and ready to come at the dropping of a hat.

Do you think you could convey my love and thanks to your "daddy" and Owen Seaman and those other oppressed and down-trodden subjects of yours, you darling small tyrant?

On my knees! These--with the kiss of fealty from your other subject--

MARK TWAIN

Elinor Glyn, author of Three Weeks and other erotic tales, was in America that winter and asked permission to call on Mark Twain. An appointment was made and Clemens discussed with her, for an hour or more, those crucial phases of life which have made living a complex problem since the days of Eve in Eden. Mrs. Glyn had never before heard anything like Mark Twain's wonderful talk, and she was anxious to print their interview. She wrote what she could remember of it and sent it to him for approval. If his conversation had been frank, his refusal was hardly less so.

To Mrs. Elinor Glyn, in New York:

Jan. 22, '08. DEAR MRS. GLYN, It reads pretty poorly--I get the sense of it, but it is a poor literary job; however, it would have to be that because nobody can be reported even approximately, except by a stenographer. Approximations, synopsized speeches, translated poems, artificial flowers and chromos all have a sort of value, but it is small. If you had put upon paper what I really said it would have wrecked your type-machine. I said some fetid, over-vigorous things, but that was because it was a confidential conversation. I said nothing for print. My own report of the same conversation reads like Satan roasting a Sunday school. It, and certain other readable chapters of my autobiography will not be published until all the Clemens family are dead--dead and correspondingly indifferent. They were written to entertain me, not the rest of the world. I am not here to do good--at least not to do it intentionally. You must pardon me for dictating this letter; I am sick a-bed and not feeling as well as I might. Sincerely Yours, S. L. CLEMENS.

Among the cultured men of England Mark Twain had no greater admirer, or warmer friend, than Andrew Lang. They were at one on most literary subjects, and especially so in their admiration of the life and character of Joan of Arc. Both had written of her, and both held her to be something almost more than mortal. When, therefore, Anatole France published his exhaustive biography of the maid of Domremy, a book in which he followed, with exaggerated minuteness and innumerable footnotes, every step of Joan's physical career at the expense of her spiritual life, which he was inclined to cheapen, Lang wrote feelingly, and with some contempt, of the performance, inviting the author of the Personal Recollections to come to the rescue of their heroine. "Compare every one of his statements with the passages he cites from authorities, and make him the laughter of the world" he wrote. "If you are lazy about comparing I can make you a complete set of what the authorities say, and of what this amazing novelist says that they say. When I tell you that he thinks the Epiphany (January 6, Twelfth Night) is December 25th--Christmas Day-you begin to see what an egregious ass he is. Treat him like Dowden, and oblige"--a reference to Mark Twain's defense of Harriet Shelley, in which he had heaped ridicule on Dowden's Life of the Poet--a masterly performance; one of the best that ever came from Mark Twain's pen.

Lang's suggestion would seem to have been a welcome one.

To Andrew Lang, in London:

NEW YORK, April 25, 1908. DEAR MR. LANG,--I haven't seen the book nor any review of it, but only not very-understandable references to it--of a sort which discomforted me, but of course set my interest on fire. I don't want to have to read it in French--I should lose the nice shades, and should do a lot of gross misinterpreting, too. But there'll be a translation soon, nicht wahr? I will wait for it. I note with joy that you say: "If you are lazy about comparing, (which I most certainly am), I can make you a complete set of what the authorities say, and of what this amazing novelist says that they say."

Ah, do it for me! Then I will attempt the article, and (if I succeed in doing it to my satisfaction,) will publish it. It is long since I touched a pen (3 1/2 years), and I was intending to continue this happy holiday to the gallows, but--there are things that could beguile me to break this blessed Sabbath. Yours very sincerely, S. L. CLEMENS.

Certainly it is an interesting fact that an Englishman--one of the race that burned Joan--should feel moved to defend her memory against the top-heavy perversions of a distinguished French author.

But Lang seems never to have sent the notes. The copying would have been a tremendous task, and perhaps he never found the time for it. We may regret to-day that he did not, for Mark Twain's article on the French author's Joan would have been at least unique.

Samuel Clemens could never accustom himself to the loss of his wife. From the time of her death, marriage-which had brought him his greatest joy in life-presented itself to him always with the thought of bereavement, waiting somewhere just behind. The news of an approaching wedding saddened him and there was nearly always a somber tinge in his congratulations, of which the following to a dear friend is an example:

To Father Fitz-Simon, in Washington:

June 5, '08. DEAR FATHER FITZ-SIMON,--Marriage--yes, it is the supreme felicity of life, I concede it. And it is also the supreme tragedy of life. The deeper the love the surer the tragedy. And the more disconsolating when it comes.

And so I congratulate you. Not perfunctorily, not lukewarmly, but with a fervency and fire that no word in the dictionary is strong enough to convey. And in the same breath and with the same depth and sincerity, I grieve for you. Not for both of you and not for the one that shall go first, but for the one that is fated to be left behind. For that one there is no recompense.--For that one no recompense is possible.

There are times--thousands of times--when I can expose the half of my mind, and conceal the other half, but in the matter of the tragedy of marriage I feel too deeply for that, and I have to bleed it all out or shut it all in. And so you must consider what I have been through, and am passing through and be charitable with me.

Make the most of the sunshine! and I hope it will last long--ever so long.

I do not really want to be present; yet for friendship's sake and because I honor you so, I would be there if I could. Most sincerely your friend, S. L. CLEMENS.

The new home at Redding was completed in the spring of 1908, and on the 18th of June, when it was entirely fitted and furnished, Mark Twain entered it for the first time. He had never even seen the place nor carefully examined plans which John Howells had made for his house. He preferred the surprise of it, and the general avoidance of detail. That he was satisfied with the result will be seen in his letters. He named it at first "Innocence at Home"; later changing this title to "Stormfield."

The letter which follows is an acknowledgment of an interesting souvenir from the battle-field of Tewksbury (1471), and some relics of the Cavalier and Roundhead Regiments encamped at Tewksbury in 1643.

To an English admirer:

INNOCENCE AT HOME, REDDING, CONNECTICUT, Aug. 15, '08. DEAR SIR,--I highly prize the pipes, and shall intimate to people that "Raleigh" smoked them, and doubtless he did. After a little practice I shall be able to go further and say he did; they will then be the most interesting features of my library's decorations. The Horse-shoe is attracting a good deal of attention, because I have intimated that the conqueror's horse cast it; it will attract more when I get my hand in and say he cast it, I thank you for the pipes and the shoe; and also for the official guide, which I read through at a single sitting. If a person should say that about a book of mine I should regard it as good evidence of the book's interest. Very truly yours, S. L. CLEMENS.

In his philosophy, What Is Man?, and now and again in his other writings, we find Mark Twain giving small credit to the human mind as an originator of ideas. The most original writer of his time, he took no credit for pure invention and allowed none to others. The mind, he declared, adapted, consciously or unconsciously; it did not create. In a letter which follows he elucidates this doctrine. The reference in it to the "captain" and to the kerosene, as the reader may remember, have to do with Captain "Hurricane" Jones and his theory of the miracles of "Isaac and of the prophets of Baal," as expounded in Some Rambling Notes of an Idle Excursion.

By a trick of memory Clemens gives The Little Duke as his suggestion for The Prince and the Pauper; he should have written The Prince and the Page, by the same author.

To Rev. F. Y. Christ, in New York:

REDDING, CONN., Aug., '08. DEAR SIR,--You say "I often owe my best sermons to a suggestion received in reading or from other exterior sources." Your remark is not quite in accordance with the facts. We must change it to--"I owe all my thoughts, sermons and ideas to suggestions received from sources outside of myself." The simplified English of this proposition is--"No man's brains ever originated an idea." It is an astonishing thing that after all these ages the world goes on thinking the human brain machinery can originate a thought.

It can't. It never has done it. In all cases, little and big, the thought is born of a suggestion; and in all cases the suggestions come to the brain from the outside. The brain never acts except from exterior impulse.

A man can satisfy himself of the truth of this by a single process,--let him examine every idea that occurs to him in an hour; a day; in a week --in a lifetime if he please. He will always find that an outside something suggested the thought, something which he saw with his eyes or heard with his ears or perceived by his touch--not necessarily to-day, nor yesterday, nor last year, nor twenty years ago, but sometime or other. Usually the source of the suggestion is immediately traceable, but sometimes it isn't.

However, if you will examine every thought that occurs to you for the next two days, you will find that in at least nine cases out of ten you can put your finger on the outside suggestion--And that ought to convince you that No. 10 had that source too, although you cannot at present hunt it down and find it.

The idea of writing to me would have had to wait a long time if it waited until your brain originated it. It was born of an outside suggestion-- Sir Thomas and my old Captain.

The hypnotist thinks he has invented a new thing--suggestion. This is very sad. I don't know where my captain got his kerosene idea. (It was forty-one years ago, and he is long ago dead.) But I know that it didn't originate in his head, but it was born from a suggestion from the outside.

Yesterday a guest said, "How did you come to think of writing 'The Prince and the Pauper?'" I didn't. The thought came to me from the outside-- suggested by that pleasant and picturesque little history-book, Charlotte M. Yonge's "Little Duke," I doubt if Mrs. Burnett knows whence came to her the suggestion to write "Little Lord Fauntleroy," but I know; it came to her from reading "The Prince and the Pauper." In all my life I have never originated an idea, and neither has she, nor anybody else.

Man's mind is a clever machine, and can work up materials into ingenious fancies and ideas, but it can't create the material; none but the gods can do that. In Sweden I saw a vast machine receive a block of wood, and turn it into marketable matches in two minutes. It could do everything but make the wood. That is the kind of machine the human mind is. Maybe this is not a large compliment, but it is all I can afford..... Your friend and well-wisher S. L. CLEMENS.

To Mrs. H. H. Rogers, in Fair Hawn, Mass.:

REDDING, CONN, Aug. 12, 1908. DEAR MRS. ROGERS, I believe I am the wellest man on the planet to-day, and good for a trip to Fair Haven (which I discussed with the Captain of the New Bedford boat, who pleasantly accosted me in the Grand Central August 5) but the doctor came up from New York day before yesterday, and gave positive orders that I must not stir from here before frost. It is because I was threatened with a swoon, 10 or 12 days ago, and went to New York a day or two later to attend my nephew's funeral and got horribly exhausted by the heat and came back here and had a bilious collapse. In 24 hours I was as sound as a nut again, but nobody believes it but me.

This is a prodigiously satisfactory place, and I am so glad I don't have to go back to the turmoil and rush of New York. The house stands high and the horizons are wide, yet the seclusion is perfect. The nearest public road is half a mile away, so there is nobody to look in, and I don't have to wear clothes if I don't want to. I have been down stairs in night-gown and slippers a couple of hours, and have been photographed in that costume; but I will dress, now, and behave myself.

That doctor had half an idea that there is something the matter with my brain. . . Doctors do know so little and they do charge so much for it. I wish Henry Rogers would come here, and I wish you would come with him. You can't rest in that crowded place, but you could rest here, for sure! I would learn bridge, and entertain you, and rob you. With love to you both, Ever yours, S. L. C.

In the foregoing letter we get the first intimation of Mark Twain's failing health. The nephew who had died was Samuel E. Moffett, son of Pamela Clemens. Moffett, who was a distinguished journalist--an editorial writer on Collier's Weekly, a man beloved by all who knew him--had been drowned in the surf off the Jersey beach.

To W. D. Howells, Kittery Point, Maine:

Aug. 12, '08. DEAR HOWELLS,--Won't you and Mrs. Howells and Mildred come and give us as many days as you can spare, and examine John's triumph? It is the most satisfactory house I am acquainted with, and the most satisfactorily situated.

But it is no place to work in, because one is outside of it all the time, while the sun and the moon are on duty. Outside of it in the loggia, where the breezes blow and the tall arches divide up the scenery and frame it.

It's a ghastly long distance to come, and I wouldn't travel such a distance to see anything short of a memorial museum, but if you can't come now you can at least come later when you return to New York, for the journey will be only an hour and a half per express-train. Things are gradually and steadily taking shape inside the house, and nature is taking care of the outside in her ingenious and wonderful fashion--and she is competent and asks no help and gets none. I have retired from New York for good, I have retired from labor for good, I have dismissed my stenographer and have entered upon a holiday whose other end is in the cemetery. Yours ever, MARK.

From a gentleman in Buffalo Clemens one day received a letter inclosing an incompleted list of the world's "One Hundred Greatest Men," men who had exerted "the largest visible influence on the life and activities of the race." The writer asked that Mark Twain examine the list and suggest names, adding "would you include Jesus, as the founder of Christianity, in the list?"

To the list of statesmen Clemens added the name of Thomas Paine; to the list of inventors, Edison and Alexander Graham Bell. The question he answered in detail.

To-----------, Buffalo, N. Y.

Private. REDDING, CONN, Aug. 28, '08. DEAR SIR,--By "private," I mean don't print any remarks of mine.

.... I like your list.

The "largest visible influence."

These terms require you to add Jesus. And they doubly and trebly require you to add Satan. From A.D. 350 to A.D. 1850 these gentlemen exercised a vaster influence over a fifth part of the human race than was exercised over that fraction of the race by all other influences combined. Ninety-nine hundredths of this influence proceeded from Satan, the remaining fraction of it from Jesus. During those 1500 years the fear of Satan and Hell made 99 Christians where love of God and Heaven landed one. During those 1500 years, Satan's influence was worth very nearly a hundred times as much to the business as was the influence of all the rest of the Holy Family put together.

You have asked me a question, and I have answered it seriously and sincerely. You have put in

Buddha--a god, with a following, at one time, greater than Jesus ever had: a god with perhaps a little better evidence of his godship than that which is offered for Jesus's. How then, in fairness, can you leave Jesus out? And if you put him in, how can you logically leave Satan out? Thunder is good, thunder is impressive; but it is the lightning that does the work. Very truly yours, S. L. CLEMENS.

The "Children's Theatre" of the next letter was an institution of the New York East Side in which Mark Twain was deeply interested. The children were most, if not all, of Hebrew parentage, and the performances they gave, under the direction of Alice M. Herts, were really remarkable. It seemed a pity that lack of funds should have brought this excellent educational venture to an untimely end.

The following letter was in reply to one inclosing a newspaper clipping reporting a performance of The Prince and the Pauper, given by Chicago school children.

To Mrs. Hookway, in Chicago: Sept., 1908. DEAR MRS. HOOKWAY,--Although I am full of the spirit of work this morning, a rarity with me lately--I must steal a moment or two for a word in person: for I have been reading the eloquent account in the Record- Herald and am pleasurably stirred, to my deepest deeps. The reading brings vividly back to me my pet and pride. The Children's Theatre of the East side, New York. And it supports and re-affirms what I have so often and strenuously said in public that a children's theatre is easily the most valuable adjunct that any educational institution for the young can have, and that no otherwise good school is complete without it.

It is much the most effective teacher of morals and promoter of good conduct that the ingenuity of man has yet devised, for the reason that its lessons are not taught wearily by book and by dreary homily, but by visible and enthusing action; and they go straight to the heart, which is the rightest of right places for them. Book morals often get no further than the intellect, if they even get that far on their spectral and shadowy pilgrimage: but when they travel from a Children's Theatre they do not stop permanently at that halfway house, but go on home.

The children's theatre is the only teacher of morals and conduct and high ideals that never bores the pupil, but always leaves him sorry when the lesson is over. And as for history, no other teacher is for a moment comparable to it: no other can make the dead heroes of the world rise up and shake the dust of the ages from their bones and live and move and breathe and speak and be real to the looker and listener: no other can make the study of the lives and times of the illustrious dead a delight, a splendid interest, a passion; and no other can paint a history-lesson in colors that will stay, and stay, and never fade.

It is my conviction that the children's theatre is one of the very, very great inventions of the twentieth century; and that its vast educational value--now but dimly perceived and but vaguely understood--will presently come to be recognized. By the article which I have been reading I find the same things happening in the Howland School that we have become familiar with in our Children's Theatre (of which I am President, and sufficiently vain of the distinction.) These things among others;

1. The educating history-study does not stop with the little players, but the whole school catches the infection and revels in it.

2. And it doesn't even stop there; the children carry it home and infect the family with it--even the parents and grandparents; and the whole household fall to studying history, and bygone manners and customs and costumes with eager interest. And this interest is carried along to the studying of costumes in old book-plates; and beyond that to the selecting of fabrics and the making of clothes. Hundreds of our children learn, the plays by listening without book, and by making notes; then the listener goes home and plays the piece--all the parts! to the family. And the family are glad and proud; glad to listen to the explanations and analyses, glad to learn, glad to be lifted to planes above their dreary workaday lives. Our children's theatre is educating 7,000 children--and their families. When we put on a play of Shakespeare they fall to studying it diligently; so that they may be qualified to enjoy it to the limit when the piece is staged.

3. Your Howland School children do the construction-work, stage- decorations, etc. That is our way too. Our young folks do everything that is needed by the theatre, with their own hands; scene-designing, scene-painting, gas-fitting, electric work, costume-designing--costume making, everything and all things indeed--and their orchestra and its leader are from their own ranks.

The article which I have been reading, says--speaking of the historical play produced by the pupils of the Howland School--

"The question naturally arises, What has this drama done for those who so enthusiastically took part?--The touching story has made a year out of the Past live for the children as could no chronology or bald statement of historical events; it has cultivated the fancy and given to the imagination strength and purity; work in composition has ceased to be drudgery, for when all other themes fall flat a subject dealing with some aspect of the drama presented never fails to arouse interest and a rapid pushing of pens over paper."

That is entirely true. The interest is not confined to the drama's story, it spreads out all around the period of the story, and gives to all the outlying and unrelated happenings of that period a fascinating interest--an interest which does not fade out with the years, but remains always fresh, always inspiring, always welcome. History-facts dug by the job, with sweat and tears out of a dry and spiritless text-book--but never mind, all who have suffered know what that is. . . I remain, dear madam, Sincerely yours, S. L. CLEMENS.

Mark Twain had a special fondness for cats. As a boy he always owned one and it generally had a seat beside him at the table. There were cats at Quarry Farm and at Hartford, and in the house at Redding there was a gray mother-cat named Tammany, of which he was especially fond. Kittens capering about were his chief delight. In a letter to a Chicago woman he tells how those of Tammany assisted at his favorite game.

To Mrs. Mabel Larkin Patterson, in Chicago:

REDDING, CONNECTICUT, Oct. 2, '08. DEAR MRS. PATTERSON,--The contents of your letter are very pleasant and very welcome, and I thank you for them, sincerely. If I can find a photograph of my "Tammany" and her kittens, I will enclose it in this.

One of them likes to be crammed into a corner-pocket of the billiard table--which he fits as snugly as does a finger in a glove and then he watches the game (and obstructs it) by the hour, and spoils many a shot by putting out his paw and changing the direction of a passing ball. Whenever a ball is in his arms, or so close to him that it cannot be played upon without risk of hurting him, the player is privileged to remove it to anyone of the 3 spots that chances to be vacant.

Ah, no, my lecturing days are over for good and all. Sincerely yours, S. L. CLEMENS.

The letter to Howells which follows was written a short time before the passage of the copyright extension bill, which rendered Mark Twain's new plan, here mentioned, unneeded--at least for the time.

To W. D. Howells, in New York:

Monday, Oct. 26, '08. Oh, I say! Where are you hiding, and why are you hiding? You promised to come here and you didn't keep your word. (This sounds like astonishment--but don't be misled by that.)

Come, fire up again on your fiction-mill and give us another good promise. And this time keep it--for it is your turn to be astonished. Come and stay as long as you possibly can. I invented a new copyright extension scheme last Friday, and sat up all night arranging its details. It will interest you. Yesterday I got it down on paper in as compact a form as I could. Harvey and I have examined the scheme, and to-morrow or next day he will send me a couple of copyright-experts to arrange about getting certain statistics for me.

Authors, publishers and the public have always been damaged by the copyright laws. The proposed amendment will advantage all three--the public most of all. I think Congress will pass it and settle the vexed question permanently.

I shall need your assent and the assent of about a dozen other authors. Also the assent of all the large firms of the 300 publishers. These authors and publishers will furnish said assent I am sure. Not even the pirates will be able to furnish a serious objection, I think.

Come along. This place seemed at its best when all around was summer- green; later it seemed at its best when all around was burning with the autumn splendors; and now once more it seems at its best, with the trees naked and the ground a painter's palette. Yours ever, MARK.

Clemens was a great admirer of the sea stories of W. W. Jacobs and generally kept one or more of this author's volumes in reach of his bed, where most of his reading was done. The acknowledgment that follows was sent when he had finished Salthaven.

To W. W. Jacobs, in England:

REDDING, CONN, Oct. 28, '08. DEAR MR. JACOBS,--It has a delightful look. I will not venture to say how delightful, because the words would sound extravagant, and would thereby lose some of their strength and to that degree misrepresent me. It is my conviction that Dialstone Lane holds the supremacy over all purely humorous books in our language, but I feel about Salthaven as the Cape Cod poet feels about Simon Hanks:

"The Lord knows all things, great and small, With doubt he's not perplexed: 'Tis Him alone that knows it all But Simon Hanks comes next."

The poet was moved by envy and malice and jealousy, but I am not: I place Salthaven close up next to Dialstone because I think it has a fair and honest right to that high position. I have kept the other book moving; I shall begin to hand this one around now.

And many thanks to you for remembering me.

This house is out in the solitudes of the woods and the hills, an hour and a half from New York, and I mean to stay in it winter and summer the rest of my days. I beg you to come and help occupy it a few days the next time you visit the U.S. Sincerely yours, S. L. CLEMENS.

One of the attractions of Stormfield was a beautiful mantel in the billiard room, presented by the Hawaiian Promotion Committee. It had not arrived when the rest of the house was completed, but came in time to be set in place early in the morning of the owner's seventy-third birthday. It was made of a variety of Hawaiian woods, and was the work of a native carver, F. M. Otremba. Clemens was deeply touched by the offering from those "western isles"--the memory of which was always so sweet to him.

To Mr. Wood, in Hawaii:

Nov. 30, '08. DEAR MR. WOOD,--The beautiful mantel was put in its place an hour ago, and its friendly "Aloha" was the first uttered greeting my 73rd birthday received. It is rich in color, rich in quality, and rich in decoration, therefore it exactly harmonizes with the taste for such things which was born in me and which I have seldom been able to indulge to my content. It will be a great pleasure to me, daily renewed, to have under my eye this lovely reminder of the loveliest fleet of islands that lies anchored in any ocean, and I beg to thank the Committee for providing me that pleasure. Sincerely Yours, S. L. CLEMENS.

XLVII

LETTERS, 1909. TO HOWELLS AND OTHERS. LIFE AT STORMFIELD. COPYRIGHT EXTENSION. DEATH OF JEAN CLEMENS

Clemens remained at Stormfield all that winter. New York was sixty miles away and he did not often care to make the journey. He was constantly invited to this or that public gathering, or private party, but such affairs had lost interest for him. He preferred the quiet of his luxurious home with its beautiful outlook, while for entertainment he found the billiard afternoons sufficient. Guests came from the city, now and again, for week-end visits, and if he ever was restless or lonely he did not show it.

Among the invitations that came was one from General O. O. Howard asking him to preside at a meeting to raise an endowment fund for a Lincoln Memorial University at Cumberland Gap, Tennessee. Closing his letter, General Howard said, "Never mind if you did fight on the other side."

To General O. O. Howard:

STORMFIELD, REDDING, CONNECTICUT, Jan, 12, '09. DEAR GENERAL HOWARD,-- You pay me a most gratifying compliment in asking me to preside, and it causes me very real regret that I am obliged to decline, for the object of the meeting appeals strongly to me, since that object is to aid in raising the $500,000 Endowment Fund for Lincoln Memorial University. The Endowment Fund will be the most fitting of all the memorials the country will dedicate to the memory of Lincoln, serving, as it will, to uplift his very own people.

I hope you will meet with complete success, and I am sorry I cannot be there to witness it and help you rejoice. But I am older than people think, and besides I live away out in the country and never stir from home, except at geological intervals, to fill left-over engagements in mesozoic times when I was younger and indiscreeter.

You ought not to say sarcastic things about my "fighting on the other side." General Grant did not act like that. General Grant paid me compliments. He bracketed me with Zenophon--it is there in his Memoirs for anybody to read. He said if all the confederate soldiers had followed my example and adopted my military arts he could never have caught enough of them in a bunch to inconvenience the Rebellion. General Grant was a fair man, and recognized my worth; but you are prejudiced, and you have hurt my feelings. But I have an affection for you, anyway. MARK TWAIN.

One of Mark Twain's friends was Henniker-Heaton, the so-called "Father of Penny Postage" between England and America. When, after long years of effort, he succeeded in getting the rate established, he at once bent his energies in the direction of cheap cable service and a letter from him came one day to Stormfield concerning his new plans. This letter happened to be over-weight, which gave Mark Twain a chance for some amusing exaggerations at his expense.

To Henniker-Heaton, in London:

STORMFIELD, REDDING, CONNECTICUT, Jan. 18, 1909. DEAR HENNIKER-HEATON,--I do hope you will succeed to your heart's desire in your cheap-cablegram campaign, and I feel sure you will. Indeed your cheap-postage victory, achieved in spite of a quarter-century of determined opposition, is good and rational prophecy that you will. Wireless, not being as yet imprisoned in a Chinese wall of private cash and high-placed and formidable influence, will come to your aid and make your new campaign briefer and easier than the other one was.

Now then, after uttering my serious word, am I privileged to be frivolous for a moment? When you shall have achieved cheap telegraphy, are you going to employ it for just your own selfish profit and other people's pecuniary damage, the way you are doing with your cheap postage? You get letter-postage reduced to 2 cents an ounce, then you mail me a 4-ounce letter with a 2-cent stamp on it, and I have to pay the extra freight at this end of the line. I return your envelope for inspection. Look at it. Stamped in one place is a vast "T," and under it the figures "40," and under those figures appears an "L," a sinister and suspicious and mysterious L. In another place, stamped within a circle, in offensively large capitals, you find the words "DUE 8 CENTS." Finally, in the midst of a desert space up nor-noreastard from that circle you find a figure "3" of quite unnecessarily aggressive and insolent magnitude--and done with a blue pencil, so as to be as conspicuous as possible. I inquired about these strange signs and symbols of the postman. He said they were P. O. Department signals for his instruction.

"Instruction for what?"

"To get extra postage."

"Is it so? Explain. Tell me about the large T and the 40.

"It's short for Take 40--or as we postmen say, grab 40"

Go on, please, while I think up some words to swear with."

"Due 8 means, grab 8 more."

"Continue."

"The blue-pencil 3 was an afterthought. There aren't any stamps for afterthoughts; the sums vary, according to inspiration, and they whirl in the one that suggests itself at the last moment. Sometimes they go several times higher than this one. This one only means hog 3 cents more. And so if you've got 51 cents about you, or can borrow it--"

"Tell me: who gets this corruption?"

"Half of it goes to the man in England who ships the letter on short postage, and the other half goes to the P.O.D. to protect cheap postage from inaugurating a deficit."

"------------------"

"I can't blame you; I would say it myself in your place, if these ladies were not present. But you see I'm only obeying orders, I can't help myself."

"Oh, I know it; I'm not blaming you. Finally, what does that L stand for?"

"Get the money, or give him L. It's English, you know."

"Take it and go. It's the last cent I've got in the world--."

After seeing the Oxford pageant file by the grand stand, picture after picture, splendor after splendor, three thousand five hundred strong, the most moving and beautiful and impressive and historically-instructive show conceivable, you are not to think I would miss the London pageant of next year, with its shining host of 15,000 historical English men and women dug from the misty books of all the vanished ages and marching in the light of the sun--all alive, and looking just as they were used to look! Mr. Lascelles spent yesterday here on the farm, and told me all about it. I shall be in the middle of my 75th year then, and interested in pageants for personal and prospective reasons.

I beg you to give my best thanks to the Bath Club for the offer of its hospitalities, but I shall not be able to take advantage of it, because I am to be a guest in a private house during my stay in London. Sincerely yours, S. L. CLEMENS.

It was in 1907 that Clemens had seen the Oxford Pageant--during the week when he had been awarded his doctor's degree. It gave him the greatest delight, and he fully expected to see the next one, planned for 1910.

In the letter to Howells which follows we get another glimpse of Mark Twain's philosophy of man, the irresponsible machine.

To W. D. Howells, in New York:

STORMFIELD, REDDING, CONN., Jan. 18, '09. DEAR HOWELLS,--I have to write a line, lazy as I am, to say how your Poe article delighted me; and to say that I am in agreement with substantially all you say about his literature. To me his prose is unreadable--like Jane Austin's. No, there is a difference. I could read his prose on salary, but not Jane's. Jane is entirely impossible. It seems a great pity that they allowed her to die a natural death.

Another thing: you grant that God and circumstances sinned against Poe, but you also grant that he sinned against himself--a thing which he couldn't do and didn't do.

It is lively up here now. I wish you could come. Yrs ever, MARK

To W. D. Howells, in New York:

STORMFIELD, REDDING, CONNECTICUT, 3 in the morning, Apl. 17, '09. [Written with pencil]. My pen has gone dry and the ink is out of reach. Howells, Did you write me day-before-day before yesterday, or did I dream it? In my mind's eye I most vividly see your hand-write on a square blue envelop in the mailpile. I have hunted the house over, but there is no such letter. Was it an illusion?

I am reading Lowell's letter, and smoking. I woke an hour ago and am reading to keep from wasting the time. On page 305, vol. I. I have just margined a note:

"Young friend! I like that! You ought to see him now."

It seemed startlingly strange to hear a person call you young. It was a brick out of a blue sky, and knocked me groggy for a moment. Ah me, the pathos of it is, that we were young then. And he--why, so was he, but he didn't know it. He didn't even know it 9 years later, when we saw him approaching and you warned me, saying, "Don't say anything about age--he has just turned fifty, and thinks he is old and broods over it."

[Well, Clara did sing! And you wrote her a dear letter.]

Time to go to sleep. Yours ever, MARK.

To Daniel Kiefer:

[No date.] DANL KIEFER ESQ. DEAR SIR,--I should be far from willing to have a political party named after me.

I would not be willing to belong to a party which allowed its members to have political aspirations or to push friends forward for political preferment. Yours very truly, S. L. CLEMENS.

The copyright extension, for which the author had been working so long, was granted by Congress in 1909, largely as the result of that afternoon in Washington when Mark Twain had "received" in "Uncle Joe" Cannon's private room, and preached the gospel of copyright until the daylight faded and the rest of the Capitol grew still. Champ Clark was the last to linger that day and they had talked far into the dusk. Clark was powerful, and had fathered the bill. Now he wrote to know if it was satisfactory.

To Champ Clark, in Washington:

STORMFIELD, REDDING, CONN., June 5, '09. DEAR CHAMP CLARK--Is the new copyright law acceptable to me? Emphatically, yes! Clark, it is the only sane, and clearly defined, and just and righteous copyright law that has ever existed in the United States. Whosoever will compare it with its predecessors will have no trouble in arriving at that decision.

The bill which was before the committee two years ago when I was down there was the most stupefying jumble of conflicting and apparently irreconcilable interests that was ever seen; and we all said "the case is hopeless, absolutely hopeless--out of this chaos nothing can be built." But we were in error; out of that chaotic mass this excellent bill has been instructed; the warring interests have been reconciled, and the result is as comely and substantial a legislative edifice as lifts its domes and towers and protective lightning rods out of the statute book, I think. When I think of that other bill, which even the Deity couldn't understand, and of this one which even I can understand, I take off my hat to the man or men who devised this one. Was it R. U. Johnson? Was it the Author's League? Was it both together? I don't know, but I take off my hat, anyway. Johnson has written a valuable article about the new law--I enclose it.

At last--at last and for the first time in copyright history we are ahead of England! Ahead of her in two ways: by length of time and by fairness to all interests concerned. Does this sound like shouting? Then I must modify it: all we possessed of copyright-justice before the fourth of last March we owed to England's initiative. Truly Yours, S. L. CLEMENS.

Because Mark Twain amused himself with certain aspects of Christian Science, and was critical of Mrs. Eddy, there grew up a wide impression that he jeered at the theory of mental healing; when, as a matter of fact, he was one of its earliest converts, and never lost faith in its power. The letter which follows is an excellent exposition of his attitude toward the institution of Christian Science and the founder of the church in America.

To J. Wylie Smith, Glasgow, Scotland:

"STORMFIELD," August 7, 1909 DEAR SIR,--My view of the matter has not changed. To wit, that Christian Science is valuable; that it has just the same value now that it had when Mrs. Eddy stole it from Quimby; that its healing principle (its most valuable asset) possesses the same force now that it possessed a million years ago before Quimby was born; that Mrs. Eddy. . . organized that force, and is entitled to high credit for that. Then, with a splendid sagacity she hitched it to. . . a religion, the surest of all ways to secure friends for it, and support. In a fine and lofty way--figuratively speaking--it was a tramp stealing a ride on the lightning express. Ah, how did that ignorant village-born peasant woman know the human being so well? She has no more intellect than a tadpole--until it comes to business then she is a marvel! Am I sorry I wrote the book? Most certainly not. You say you have 500 (converts) in Glasgow. Fifty years from now, your posterity will not count them by the hundred, but by the thousand. I feel absolutely sure of this. Very truly yours, S. L. CLEMENS.

Clemens wrote very little for publication that year, but he enjoyed writing for his own amusement, setting down the things that boiled, or bubbled, within him: mainly chapters on the inconsistencies of human deportment, human superstition and human creeds. The "Letters from the Earth" referred to in the following, were supposed to have been written by an immortal visitant from some far realm to a friend, describing the absurdities of mankind. It is true, as he said, that they would not do for publication, though certainly the manuscript contains some of his mgt delicious writing. Miss Wallace, to whom the next letter is written, had known Mark Twain in Bermuda, and, after his death, published a dainty volume entitled Mark Twain in the Happy Island.

"STORMFIELD," REDDING, CONNECTICUT, Nov. 13, '09. DEAR BETSY,--I've been writing "Letters from the Earth," and if you will come here and see us I will--what? Put the MS in your hands, with the places to skip marked? No. I won't trust you quite that far. I'll read messages to you. This book will never be published--in fact it couldn't be, because it would be felony to soil the mails with it, for it has much Holy Scripture in it of the kind that . . . can't properly be read aloud, except from the pulpit and in family worship. Paine enjoys it, but Paine is going to be damned one of these days, I suppose.

The autumn splendors passed you by? What a pity. I wish you had been here. It was beyond words! It was heaven and hell and sunset and rainbows and the aurora all fused into one divine harmony, and you couldn't look at it and keep the tears back. All the hosannahing strong gorgeousnesses have gone back to heaven and hell and the pole, now, but no matter; if you could look out of my bedroom window at this moment, you would choke up; and when you got your voice you would say: This is not real, this is a dream. Such a singing together, and such a whispering together, and such a snuggling together of cosy soft colors, and such kissing and caressing, and such pretty blushing when the sun breaks out and catches those dainty weeds at it-- you remember that weed-garden of mine?--and then--then the far hills sleeping in a dim blue trance--oh, hearing about it is nothing, you should be here to see it.

Good! I wish I could go on the platform and read. And I could, if it could be kept out of the papers. There's a charity-school of 400 young girls in Boston that I would give my ears to talk to, if I had some more; but--oh, well, I can't go, and it's no use to grieve about it.

This morning Jean went to town; also Paine; also the butler; also Katy; also the laundress. The cook and the maid, and the boy and the roustabout and Jean's coachman are left--just enough to make it lonesome, because they are around yet never visible. However, the Harpers are sending Leigh up to play billiards; therefore I shall survive. Affectionately, S. L. CLEMENS.

Early in June that year, Clemens had developed unmistakable symptoms of heart trouble of a very serious nature. It was angina pectoris, and while to all appearances he was as well as ever and usually felt so, he was periodically visited by severe attacks of acute "breast pains" which, as the months passed, increased in frequency and severity. He was alarmed and distressed--not on his own account, but because of his daughter Jean--a handsome girl, who had long been subject to epileptic seizures. In case of his death he feared that Jean would be without permanent anchorage, his other daughter, Clara--following her marriage to Ossip Gabrilowitsch in October-- having taken up residence abroad.

This anxiety was soon ended. On the morning of December 24th, jean Clemens was found dead in her apartment. She was not drowned in her bath, as was reported, but died from heart exhaustion, the result of her malady and the shock of cold water. [Questionable diagnosis! D.W.]

The blow to her father was terrible, but heavy as it was, one may perhaps understand that her passing in that swift, painless way must have afforded him a measure of relief.

To Mrs. Gabrilowitsch, in Europe:

REDDING, CONN., Dec. 29, '09. O, Clara, Clara dear, I am so glad she is out of it and safe-- safe! I am not melancholy; I shall never be melancholy again, I think. You see, I was in such distress when I came to realize that you were gone far away and no one stood between her and danger but me--and I could die at any moment, and then--oh then what would become of her! For she was wilful, you know, and would not have been governable.

You can't imagine what a darling she was, that last two or three days; and how fine, and good, and sweet, and noble-and joyful, thank Heaven!-- and how intellectually brilliant. I had never been acquainted with Jean before. I recognized that.

But I mustn't try to write about her--I can't. I have already poured my heart out with the pen, recording that last day or two.

I will send you that--and you must let no one but Ossip read it.

Good-bye. I love you so! And Ossip. FATHER.

The writing mentioned in the last paragraph was his article 'The Death of Jean,' his last serious writing, and one of the world's most beautiful examples of elegiac prose.--[Harper's Magazine, Dec., 1910,] and later in the volume, 'What Is Man and Other Essays.'

XLVIII

LETTERS OF 1910. LAST TRIP TO BERMUDA. LETTERS TO PAINE. THE LAST LETTER

Mark Twain had returned from a month's trip to Bermuda a few days before Jean died. Now, by his physician's advice, he went back to those balmy islands. He had always loved them, since his first trip there with Twichell thirty-three years earlier, and at "Bay House," the residence of Vice-Consul Allen, where he was always a welcome guest, he could have the attentions and care and comforts of a home. Taking Claude, the butler, as his valet, he sailed January 5th, and presently sent back a letter in which he said, "Again I am leading the ideal life, and am immeasurably content."

By his wish, the present writer and his family were keeping the Stormfield house open for him, in order that he might be able to return to its comforts at any time. He sent frequent letters--one or two by each steamer--but as a rule they did not concern matters of general interest. A little after his arrival, however, he wrote concerning an incident of his former visit--a trivial matter--but one which had annoyed him. I had been with him in Bermuda on the earlier visit, and as I remember it, there had been some slight oversight on his part in the matter of official etiquette--something which doubtless no one had noticed but himself.

To A. B. Paine, in Redding:

BAY HOUSE, Jan. 11, 1910.

DEAR PAINE,--. . . There was a military lecture last night at the Officer's Mess, prospect, and as the lecturer honored me with a special and urgent invitation and said he wanted to lecture to me particularly, I being "the greatest living master of the platform-art," I naturally packed Helen and her mother into the provided carriage and went.

As soon as we landed at the door with the crowd the Governor came to me at once and was very cordial, and apparently as glad to see me as he said he was. So that incident is closed. And pleasantly and entirely satisfactorily. Everything is all right, now, and I am no longer in a clumsy and awkward situation.

I "met up" with that charming Colonel Chapman, and other officers of the regiment, and had a good time.

Commandant Peters of the "Carnegie" will dine here tonight and arrange a private visit for us to his ship, the crowd to be denied access. Sincerely Yours, S. L. C.

"Helen" of this letter was Mr. and Mrs. Allen's young daughter, a favorite companion of his walks and drives. "Loomis" and "Lark," mentioned in the letters which follow, were Edward E. Loomis--his nephew by marriage--named by Mark Twain as one of the trustees of his estate, and Charles T. Lark, Mark Twain's attorney.

To A. B. Paine, in Redding:

HAMILTON, Jan. 21, '10. DEAR PAINE,--Thanks for your letter, and for its contenting news of the situation in that foreign and far-off and vaguely-remembered country where you and Loomis and Lark and other beloved friends are.

I have a letter from Clara this morning. She is solicitous, and wants me well and watchfully taken care of. My, she ought to see Helen and her parents and Claude administer that trust!

Also she says: "I hope to hear from you or Mr. Paine very soon."

I am writing her, and I know you will respond to your part of her prayer. She is pretty desolate now, after Jean's emancipation--the only kindness God ever did that poor unoffending child in all her hard life. Ys ever S. L. C.

Send Clara a copy of Howells's gorgeous letter. I want a copy of my article that he is speaking of.

The "gorgeous letter" was concerning Mark Twain's article, "The Turning-point in My Life" which had just appeared in one of the Harper publications. Howells wrote of it, "While your wonderful words are warm in my mind yet, I want to tell you what you know already: that you never wrote anything greater, finer, than that turning-point paper of yours."

From the early Bermuda letters we may gather that Mark Twain's days were enjoyable enough, and that his malady was not giving him serious trouble, thus far. Near the end of January he wrote: "Life continues here the same as usual. There isn't a flaw in it. Good times, good home, tranquil contentment all day and every day, without a break. I shouldn't know how to go about bettering my situation." He did little in the way of literary work, probably finding neither time nor inclination for it. When he wrote at all it was merely to set down some fanciful drolleries with no thought of publication.

To Prof. William Lyon Phelps, Yale College:

HAMILTON, March 12. DEAR PROFESSOR PHELPS,--I thank you ever so much for the book--[Professor Phelps's Essays on Modern Novelists.]--which I find charming--so charming indeed, that I read it through in a single night, and did not regret the lost night's sleep. I am glad if I deserve what you have said about me: and even if I don't I am proud and well contented, since you think I deserve it.

Yes, I saw Prof. Lounsbury, and had a most pleasant time with him. He ought to have staid longer in this little paradise--partly for his own sake, but mainly for mine.

I knew my poor Jean had written you. I shall not have so dear and sweet a secretary again.

Good health to you, and all good fortune attend you. Sincerely yours, S. L. CLEMENS.

He would appear to have written not many letters besides those to Mrs. Gabrilowitsch and to Stormfield, but when a little girl sent him a report of a dream, inspired by reading The Prince and the Pauper, he took the time and trouble to acknowledge it, realizing, no doubt, that a line from him would give the child happiness.

To Miss Sulamith, in New York:

"BAY HOUSE," BERMUDA, March 21, 1910. DEAR MISS SULAMITH,--I think it is a remarkable dream for a girl of 13 to have dreamed, in fact for a person of any age to have dreamed, because it moves by regular grade and sequence from the beginning to the end, which is not the habit of dreams. I think your report of it is a good piece of work, a clear and effective statement of the vision.

I am glad to know you like the "Prince and the Pauper" so well and I believe with you that the dream is good evidence of that liking. I think I may say, with your sister that I like myself best when I am serious. Sincerely yours, S. L. CLEMENS.

Through February, and most of March, letters and reports from him were about the same. He had begun to plan for his return, and concerning amusements at Stormfield for the entertainment of the neighbors, and for the benefit of the library which he had founded soon after his arrival in Redding. In these letters he seldom mentioned the angina pains that had tortured him earlier. But once, when he sent a small photograph of himself, it seemed to us that his face had become thin and that he had suffered. Certainly his next letter was not reassuring.

To A. B. Paine, in Redding:

DEAR PAINE,--We must look into the magic-lantern business. Maybe the modern lantern is too elaborate and troublesome for back-settlement use, but we can inquire. We must have some kind of a show at "Stormfield" to entertain the countryside with.

We are booked to sail in the "Bermudian" April 23rd, but don't tell anybody, I don't want it known. I may have to go sooner if the pain in my breast doesn't mend its ways pretty considerably. I don't want to die here for this is an unkind place for a person in that condition. I should have to lie in the undertaker's cellar until the ship would remove me and it is dark down there and unpleasant.

The Colliers will meet me on the pier and I may stay with them a week or two before going home. It all depends on the breast pain--I don't want to die there. I am growing more and more particular about the place. With love, S. L. C.

This letter had been written by the hand of his "secretary," Helen Allen: writing had become an effort to him. Yet we did not suspect how rapidly the end was approaching and only grew vaguely alarmed. A week later, however, it became evident that his condition was critical.

DEAR PAINE,--. . . . I have been having a most uncomfortable time for the past 4 days with that breast-pain, which turns out to be an affection of the heart, just as I originally suspected. The news from New York is to the effect that non-bronchial weather has arrived there at last, therefore if I can get my breast trouble in traveling condition I may sail for home a week or two earlier than has heretofore been proposed: Yours as ever S. L. CLEMENS, (per H. S. A.)

In this letter he seems to have forgotten that his trouble had been pronounced an affection of the heart long before he left America, though at first it had been thought that it might be gastritis. The same mail brought a letter from Mr. Allen explaining fully the seriousness of his condition. I sailed immediately for Bermuda, arriving there on the 4th of April. He was not suffering at the moment, though the pains came now with alarming frequency and violence. He was cheerful and brave. He did not complain. He gave no suggestion of a man whose days were nearly ended.

A part of the Stormfield estate had been a farm, which he had given to Jean Clemens, where she had busied herself raising some live stock and poultry. After her death he had wished the place to be sold and the returns devoted to some memorial purpose. The sale had been made during the winter and the price received had been paid in cash. I found him full of interest in all affairs, and anxious to discuss the memorial plan. A day or two later he dictated the following letter-the last he would ever send.

It seemed fitting that this final word from one who had so long given happiness to the whole world should record a special gift to his neighbors.

To Charles T. Lark, in New York:

HAMILTON, BERMUDA. April 6, 1910. DEAR MR. LARK,--I have told Paine that I want the money derived from the sale of the farm, which I had given, but not conveyed, to my daughter Jean, to be used to erect a building for the Mark Twain Library of Redding, the building to be called the Jean L. Clemens Memorial Building.

I wish to place the money $6,000.00 in the hands of three trustees,-- Paine and two others: H. A. Lounsbury and William E. Hazen, all of Redding, these trustees to form a building Committee to decide on the size and plan of the building needed and to arrange for and supervise the work in such a manner that the fund shall amply provide for the building complete, with necessary furnishings, leaving, if possible, a balance remaining, sufficient for such repairs and additional furnishings as may be required for two years from the time of completion.

Will you please draw a document covering these requirements and have it ready by the time I reach New York (April 14th). Very sincerely, S. L. CLEMENS.

We sailed on the 12th of April, reaching New York on the 14th, as he had planned. A day or two later, Mr. and Mrs. Gabrilowitsch, summoned from Italy by cable, arrived. He suffered very little after reaching Stormfield, and his mind was comparatively clear up to the last day. On the afternoon of April 21st he sank into a state of coma, and just at sunset he died. Three days later, at Elmira, New York, he was laid beside Mrs. Clemens and those others who had preceded him.

THE LAST DAY AT STORMFIELD

By BLISS CARMAN.

At Redding, Connecticut, The April sunrise pours Over the hardwood ridges Softening and greening now In the first magic of Spring.

The wild cherry-trees are in bloom, The bloodroot is white underfoot, The serene early light flows on, Touching with glory the world, And flooding the large upper room Where a sick man sleeps. Slowly he opens his eyes, After long weariness, smiles, And stretches arms overhead, While those about him take heart.

With his awakening strength, (Morning and spring in the air, The strong clean scents of earth, The call of the golden shaft, Ringing across the hills) He takes up his heartening book, Opens the volume and reads, A page of old rugged Carlyle, The dour philosopher Who looked askance upon life, Lurid, ironical, grim, Yet sound at the core. But weariness returns; He lays the book aside With his glasses upon the bed, And gladly sleeps. Sleep, Blessed abundant sleep, Is all that he needs.

And when the close of day Reddens upon the hills And washes the room with rose, In the twilight hush The Summoner comes to him Ever so gently, unseen, Touches him on the shoulder; And with the departing sun Our great funning friend is gone.

How he has made us laugh! A whole generation of men Smiled in the joy of his wit. But who knows whether he was not Like those deep jesters of old Who dwelt at the courts of Kings, Arthur's, Pendragon's, Lear's, Plying the wise fool's trade, Making men merry at will, Hiding their deeper thoughts Under a motley array,-- Keen-eyed, serious men, Watching the sorry world, The gaudy pageant of life, With pity and wisdom and love?

Fearless, extravagant, wild, His caustic merciless mirth Was leveled at pompous shams. Doubt not behind that mask There dwelt the soul of a man, Resolute, sorrowing, sage, As sure a champion of good As ever rode forth to fray.

Haply--who knows?--somewhere In Avalon, Isle of Dreams, In vast contentment at last, With every grief done away, While Chaucer and Shakespeare wait, And Moliere hangs on his words, And Cervantes not far off Listens and smiles apart, With that incomparable drawl He is jesting with Dagonet now.

[Copyright, 1910, by Collier's Weekly.]

###

Printed in Poland
by Amazon Fulfillment
Poland Sp. z o.o., Wrocław